Byzantium, Venice and the Medieval Adriatic

The Adriatic has long occupied a liminal position between different cultures, languages and faiths. This book offers the first synthesis of its history between the seventh and the mid-fifteenth century, a period coinciding with the existence of the Byzantine empire which, as heir to the Roman empire, laid claim to the region. The period also saw the rise of Venice and it is important to understand the conditions which would lead to her dominance in the Late Middle Ages. An international team of historians and archaeologists examines trade, administration and cultural exchange between the Adriatic and Byzantium but also within the region itself, and makes more widely known much previously scattered and localised research and the results of archaeological excavations in both Italy and Croatia. Their bold interpretations offer many stimulating ideas for rethinking the entire history of the Mediterranean during the period.

MAGDALENA SKOBLAR was a postdoctoral research fellow at the British School at Athens and the British School at Rome from 2013 to 2015. Specialising in Early Medieval art, she is also the author of *Figural Sculpture in Eleventh-Century Dalmatia and Croatia* (2017).

BRITISH SCHOOL AT ATHENS STUDIES IN GREEK ANTIQUITY

Series editor

John Bennet
Director of the British School at Athens

British School at Athens Studies in Greek Antiquity builds on the School's long-standing engagement with the study of ancient Greece from prehistory to Late Antiquity. This series aims to explore a wide range of topics through a variety of approaches attractive to anyone with interests in the ancient Greek world.

Titles in this Series

Byzantium, Venice and the Medieval Adriatic: Spheres of Maritime Power and Influence, c.700–1453
 Magdalena Skoblar

Human Mobility and Technological Transfer in the Prehistoric Mediterranean
 Evangelia Kiriatzi and Carl Knappett

Byzantium, Venice and the Medieval Adriatic

Spheres of Maritime Power and Influence, c.700–1453

Edited by

MAGDALENA SKOBLAR

CAMBRIDGE
UNIVERSITY PRESS

University Printing House, Cambridge CB2 8BS, United Kingdom

One Liberty Plaza, 20th Floor, New York, NY 10006, USA

477 Williamstown Road, Port Melbourne, VIC 3207, Australia

314–321, 3rd Floor, Plot 3, Splendor Forum, Jasola District Centre, New Delhi – 110025, India

79 Anson Road, #06-04/06, Singapore 079906

Cambridge University Press is part of the University of Cambridge.

It furthers the University's mission by disseminating knowledge in the pursuit of education, learning, and research at the highest international levels of excellence.

www.cambridge.org
Information on this title: www.cambridge.org/9781108840705
DOI: 10.1017/9781108886987

© The British School at Athens 2021

This publication is in copyright. Subject to statutory exception and to the provisions of relevant collective licensing agreements, no reproduction of any part may take place without the written permission of Cambridge University Press.

First published 2021

A catalogue record for this publication is available from the British Library.

Library of Congress Cataloging-in-Publication Data
Names: Skoblar, Magdalena, editor, author. | Herrin, Judith, contributor, writer of foreword. | British School at Athens, sponsoring body. | British School at Rome, sponsoring body.
Title: Byzantium, Venice and the medieval Adriatic : spheres of maritime power and influence, c. 700–1453 / by Magdalena Skoblar, University of Durham, Judith Herrin, King's College London.
Description: First edition. | New York : Cambridge University Press, 2021. | Series: British School at Athens studies in Greek antiquity | The chapters in this volume originated from a three-day conference - The Adriatic as a Threshold to Byzantium - organised at the British School at Rome in January 2015. – Acknowledgements. | Includes bibliographical references and index.
Identifiers: LCCN 2020046710 (print) | LCCN 2020046711 (ebook) | ISBN 9781108840705 (hardback) | ISBN 9781108840705 (paperback) | ISBN 9781108886987 (epub)
Subjects: LCSH: Adriatic Sea Region–History–To 1500. | Adriatic Sea Region–Antiquities. | Byzantine Empire–History. | Byzantine antiquities. | Venice (Italy)–History–697-1508. | Venice (Italy)–Antiquities.
Classification: LCC D971 .B99 2021 (print) | LCC D971 (ebook) | DDC 909/.098224–dc23
LC record available at https://lccn.loc.gov/2020046710
LC ebook record available at https://lccn.loc.gov/2020046711

ISBN 978-1-108-84070-5 Hardback

Cambridge University Press has no responsibility for the persistence or accuracy of URLs for external or third-party internet websites referred to in this publication and does not guarantee that any content on such websites is, or will remain, accurate or appropriate.

Contents

List of Figures and Maps [*page* vii]
List of Tables [xi]
List of Contributors [xii]
Foreword by Judith Herrin [xiv]
Acknowledgements [xix]
Note on Citation, Transliteration, Names, Titles and Dates [xxi]

Introduction [1]
MAGDALENA SKOBLAR

1 The Adriatic Sea 500–1100 [15]
A Corrupted Alterity?
RICHARD HODGES

2 Thinking of Linking [45]
Pottery Connections, Southern Adriatic, Butrint and Beyond
JOANITA VROOM

3 A Winter Sea? [83]
Exchange and Power at the Ebbing of the Adriatic Connection 600–800
FRANCESCO BORRI

4 The Origins of Venice [98]
Between Italy, Byzantium and the Adriatic
STEFANO GASPARRI

5 The Northern Adriatic Area between the Eighth and the Ninth Century [111]
New Landscapes, New Cities
SAURO GELICHI

6 *Provincia Iadrensis* [133]
Heir of Roman Dalmatia or a Stillborn Child of Byzantine Early Medieval Adriatic Policy?
TRPIMIR VEDRIŠ

7 Ravenna and Other Early Rivals of Venice [173]
   Comparative Urban and Economic Development in the Upper
   Adriatic c.751–1050
   THOMAS S. BROWN

8 Byzantine Apulia [188]
   JEAN-MARIE MARTIN

9 From One Coast to Another and Beyond [203]
   Adriatic Connections through the Sigillographic Evidence
   PAGONA PAPADOPOULOU

10 Icons in the Adriatic before the Sack of Constantinople
   in 1204 [245]
   MAGDALENA SKOBLAR

11 The Rise of the Adriatic in the Age of the Crusades [276]
   PETER FRANKOPAN

12 Venice in the Twelfth Century [296]
   Between the Adriatic and the Aegean
   MICHAEL ANGOLD

13 Venice, the Ionian Sea and the Southern Adriatic after the
   Fourth Crusade [316]
   GUILLAUME SAINT-GUILLAIN

14 Sea Power and the Evolution of Venetian Crusading [328]
   CHRISTOPHER WRIGHT

15 Reassessing the Venetian Presence in the Late Medieval
   Eastern Adriatic [351]
   OLIVER JENS SCHMITT

16 'Strangers' in the City? [365]
   The Paradoxes of Communitarianism in Fifteenth-Century Venice
   ÉLISABETH CROUZET-PAVAN

   Conclusion [385]
   CHRIS WICKHAM

   Index [391]

Figures and Maps

Cover Muḥammad ibn Muḥammad al-Idrīsī, *Nuzhat al-muštāq fī iḫtirāq al-āfāq*. Bibliothèque nationale de France, Département des manuscrits, ms. Arabe 2221, fols. 267v–268r, detail of the south Adriatic with Apulia and the Dalmatian coast. Photo © Bibliothèque nationale de France. [*page* 00]

Map 1 The Adriatic with the most important sites mentioned in the volume. Drawn by Cox Cartographic Ltd. [xxiii]

1.1 View of Butrint and the Straits of Corfu. Courtesy of the Butrint Foundation. [19]

1.2 View of the restored western defences (Tower 1). Courtesy of the Butrint Foundation. [21]

1.3 Excavations in Tower 1, 2005. Courtesy of the Butrint Foundation. [22]

1.4 Location of the aristocratic *oikos* on the Vrina Plain in relation to Butrint. Courtesy of the Butrint Foundation. [24]

1.5 Interpretive plan of the aristocratic *oikos* on the Vrina Plain. Courtesy of the Butrint Foundation. [25]

1.6 Five lead seals from the excavations on the Vrina Plain. Courtesy of the Butrint Foundation. [26]

1.7 Map of Butrint in the eleventh century. Courtesy of the Butrint Foundation. [28]

1.8 Tenth- to eleventh-century remains of a post-built structure (dwelling?) in the Triconch Palace excavations. Courtesy of the Butrint Foundation. [29]

1.9 An eleventh-century property wall (part of the enclosure around the Great Basilica) closing off the north end of the Roman bridge at Butrint. Courtesy of the Butrint Foundation. [30]

1.10 View of the eleventh-century stone dwellings on the terrace overlooking the remains of the Roman Forum. Photo: David Hernandez. [31]

1.11 A section of the eleventh-century fortifications of Rogoi, Epiros. Photo: Richard Hodges. [33]

1.12 An interpretative plan of the excavated church of Shën Jan, near Phoinike. Plan: Oliver Gilkes. [38]

2.1 Most important architectural remains at Butrint. Courtesy of the Butrint Foundation. [46]

2.2 Distribution of Medieval pottery finds in Butrint. Graphs by Joanita Vroom. Map courtesy of the Butrint Foundation. [47]

2.3 Western defences in Butrint. Courtesy of the Butrint Foundation. [48]

2.4 Pottery types found in Towers 1 and 2 (WD1 and WD2) of the western defences of Butrint. Graphs by Joanita Vroom. Images courtesy of the Butrint Foundation. [49]

2.5 Possible provenance of pottery finds in Towers 1 and 2 (WD1 and WD2) of the western defences of Butrint. Ground plan courtesy of the Butrint Foundation. [50]

2.6 Reconstruction of Tower 1 in the western defences in Butrint. Courtesy of the Butrint Foundation. Drawing by W.R. Euverman. [51]

2.7 Locations of Early and Middle Byzantine shipwrecks in the eastern Mediterranean. Drawn after Vroom 2016, fig. 1; images after Denker *et al.* 2013a, 204, no. 237. [53]

2.8 Finds of Early Byzantine globular amphorae in Italy and the Adriatic. Drawn by Joanita Vroom; images courtesy of the Butrint Foundation and after Gelichi and Negrelli 2008, figs. 8–9. [54]

2.9 Production zones of various types of 'globular amphorae' in the Mediterranean. Drawn after Vroom 2016. [55]

2.10 Finds of Glazed White Ware I and II in Italy and the Adriatic. Drawn after Vroom 2017, fig. 10.3; image after Peschlow 1977–78, figs. 9, 12. [58]

2.11 Finds of Glazed White Wares in Ephesus. © Austrian Archaeological Institute. Christian Kürtze and Joanita Vroom; image after Ladstätter 2008, pl. 297, K 239. [59]

2.12 Finds of Günsenin 1/Saraçhane 54 amphorae from Ganos in Ephesus. © Austrian Archaeological Institute. Drawn by Christian Kürtze and Joanita Vroom; image after Vroom 2014, 94. [60]

2.13 Finds of Günsenin 1/Saraçhane 54 amphorae from Ganos in Europe. Map drawn by Joanita Vroom; images after Vroom 2014, 94. [61]

2.14 Locations of shipwrecks transporting Günsenin 3/Saraçhane 61 amphorae in the eastern Mediterranean. Map drawn by Joanita Vroom; images after Vroom 2014, 98; Vroom 2016, fig. 4. [62]

List of Figures and Maps ix

2.15 Locations of shipwrecks transporting twelfth- to fourteenth-century glazed table wares in the eastern Mediterranean. Map drawn by Joanita Vroom; images after Papanikola-Bakirtzi 1999, 147, no. 168. [65]

2.16 Distribution of locally made table wares in the Peloponnese and north-western Greece. Graphs by Joanita Vroom; images after Vroom 2014, 84, 90, 124. [66]

2.17 Distribution of imported table wares in the Peloponnese and north-western Greece. Graphs by Joanita Vroom; images after Vroom 2014, 126, 128; Bakourou, Katsara and Kalamara 2003, fig. 5. [67]

2.18 Network analysis of ceramic finds at Peloponnesian sites transported by sea and land. Drawn by J. Preiser-Kapeller after Vroom 2011a. [68]

2.19 Distribution of imported table wares from southern Italy in the Peloponnese and north-western Greece. Maps and graphs by Joanita Vroom; images after Vroom 2014, 126, 128; Vroom 2017, fig. 13.4. [70]

2.20 Ceramic distribution system of Butrint from Early Byzantine to Early Venetian times. Maps drawn by Joanita Vroom. [71]

5.1 Map of the north-east Adriatic with the locations from the text. Elaborated by the Laboratorio Archeologia Medievale, Università Venezia. [112]

5.2 Adria, the Church of Our Lady of the Assumption, frescoes. Photo: Marco Moro. [113]

5.3 San Basilio (Rovigo, Italy), the remains of a Late Antique baptismal font. Photo: Sauro Gelichi. [114]

5.4 *Altinum* (Venice, Italy), aerial photo of the ancient city and interpretation. © Andrea Ninfo. [116]

5.5 The Venetian lagoon in the Roman period. Elaborated by the Laboratorio Archeologia Medievale, Università Venezia. [118]

5.6 Map of the Venetian lagoon and nearby areas. Elaborated by the Laboratorio Archeologia Medievale, Università Venezia. [120]

5.7 The Venetian lagoon. Drawn by Margherita Ferri, Sauro Gelichi and Cecilia Moine after Bondesan and Meneghel 2004, Primon and Mozzi 2014; Gelichi, Ferri and Moine 2017. [122]

5.8 The Venetian lagoon. Possible natural deposits that emerged between the ninth and tenth century and sites of documented places of worship. [124]

5.9 Jesolo (Venice, Italy). The simplified paleo-environmental reconstruction of the site. Drawn by Anita Granzo. [125]

List of Figures and Maps

5.10 Jesolo (Venice, Italy). A zenithal photo of one of the Late Antique *mansio* buildings. Elaborated by the Laboratorio Archeologia Medievale, Università Venezia. [126]

5.11 Jesolo (Venice, Italy). The reconstruction of the settlement of *Equilo* in the late fourth century. Courtesy of Studio InkLink. [127]

5.12 Jesolo (Venice, Italy). Early Medieval cemetery. Drawn by Alessandra Cianciosi. [128]

6.1 East Adriatic coast in the Early Medieval period. Drawn by Trpimir Vedriš. [134]

6.2 Church dedications in Medieval Zadar. Redrawn by Trpimir Vedriš after Klaić and Petricioli 1976. [145]

6.3 Zadar and its hinterland. Drawn by Trpimir Vedriš. [148]

6.4 The ninth-century rotunda of the Holy Trinity (St Donatus) at Zadar. Photo: Pavuša Vežić. [151]

6.5 The ninth-century sarcophagus of St Anastasia in Zadar Cathedral. © Stalna izložba crkvene umjetnosti, Zadar / Permanent Collection of Religious Art, Zadar. Photo: Zoran Alajbeg. [152]

9.1 Map of the seals found in the Adriatic. Drawn by Pagona Papadopoulou and Dimitrios Giovis. [214]

9.2 Map of the seals originating from the Adriatic but found elsewhere. Drawn by Pagona Papadopoulou and Dimitrios Giovis. [225]

10.1 *Hodegetria* of Delterios, 1039–59, Santa Maria di Dionisio, Trani. Photo: Francesco Calò. [248]

10.2 Seal of Niketas, Bishop of Poroi, eleventh century. Seal of Michael, metropolitan of Traïanoupolis and *proedros* of the *protosynkelloi*, eleventh century. © Dumbarton Oaks, Byzantine Collection, Washington, DC. [249]

10.3 Image and schematic drawing of the *Icona vetere*, c.1090, Foggia Cathedral. © Arcidiocesi di Foggia-Bovino. Redrawn by Dalibor Popovič after Belli D'Elia 1989. [258]

10.4 *Madonna greca*, c.1095. Marble, Santa Maria in Porto, Ravenna. © Istituzione Biblioteca Classense. Source: Fondo Mario Mazzotti, CARTOL MAZ A100 00072 0040, inv. POS 439. [260]

10.5 Mosaic of the Virgin *orans* from Ravenna Cathedral, 1112, Museo Arcivescovile, Ravenna. © Arcidiocesi di Ravenna-Cervia. [263]

10.6 Icon of Christ, c.1090, Collegiate Church of St Mary, Rab. © Konzervatorski odjel Rijeka / Conservation Office at Rijeka. Photo: Damir Krizmanić. [265]

Tables

9.1 Byzantine seals found in the Adriatic   [*page* 215]
9.2 Byzantine seals originating from the Adriatic, found outside its limits   [226]

Contributors

MICHAEL ANGOLD
Professor Emeritus at the University of Edinburgh

FRANCESCO BORRI
Researcher in Medieval History at Ca' Foscari University of Venice

THOMAS S. BROWN
Honorary Fellow of the School of History, Classics and Archaeology at the University of Edinburgh

ÉLISABETH CROUZET-PAVAN
Professor of Medieval History at Sorbonne University

PETER FRANKOPAN
Professor of Global History at Oxford University and Stavros Niarchos Foundation Director of the Oxford Centre for Byzantine Research

STEFANO GASPARRI
Former Professor of Medieval History at Ca' Foscari University of Venice

SAURO GELICHI
Professor of Medieval Archaeology at Ca' Foscari University of Venice and Director of the Inter-University Centre for Early Medieval History and Archaeology

JUDITH HERRIN
Professor Emerita in the Department of Classics, King's College London

RICHARD HODGES
President of the American University of Rome

JEAN-MARIE MARTIN
Research Director at the Centre for Near Eastern and Mediterranean Studies of the French National Centre for Scientific Research

PAGONA PAPADOPOULOU
Assistant Professor at the Aristotle University of Thessaloniki

GUILLAUME SAINT-GUILLAIN
Maître de Conférences in Medieval History at the University of Picardy

OLIVER JENS SCHMITT
Professor of South-East European History at the University of Vienna and head of the Department of Balkan Studies at the Austrian Academy of Sciences

MAGDALENA SKOBLAR
Former Adriatic Connections Postdoctoral Research Fellow at the British School at Athens and the British School at Rome

TRPIMIR VEDRIŠ
Senior Lecturer in Medieval History at the Faculty of Humanities and Social Sciences, University of Zagreb

JOANITA VROOM
Professor in Archaeology of Medieval and Early Modern Eurasia at Leiden University

CHRIS WICKHAM
Chichele Professor of Medieval History (emeritus) at the University of Oxford

CHRISTOPHER WRIGHT
Research Associate at Cambridge University (Polonsky Foundation Greek Manuscripts Project)

Foreword

JUDITH HERRIN

Several years ago, when the Directors of the British Schools at Athens and Rome, Dr Cathy Morgan and Dr Christopher Smith, considered ways of strengthening the links between their two institutions, they decided to inaugurate a collaborative venture. The aim was to bring together scholars working in their respective areas of interest to stimulate new research in regions shared by both Greece and Italy, whether in the distant eras BCE or during more recent historical periods. My proposal of a topic focused on the Adriatic seemed to generate considerable potential, both as a threshold for those travelling to Byzantium in the East and as a point of entry to northern Italy and transalpine Europe for those coming to the West. It is a great pleasure to welcome the book that results from this investigation.

Resembling a vast inland fjord, the Adriatic consists of three basins, the northern, central and southern one at the Straits of Otranto that leads into the Ionian Sea and on to the Mediterranean. At its narrowest points, both north and south, it can be comfortably sailed in the summer with a fair wind on a long day, between eleven and twelve hours. As a thoroughfare, most north–south routes hug the Adriatic shores, which present major differences. On the Italian side, the western edge has long sandy beaches that traditionally did not provide much safe mooring, and its small natural harbours were inadequate for larger fleets. Julius Caesar's construction of a much larger port at Classe on the east, matched by another at *Misenum* on the west, provided naval bases for the two Roman fleets attached to the eastern and western basins of the Mediterranean. From Classe, established sea routes linked Ravenna and the Po Valley to Aquileia in the north, to Pula (Pola) in Istria directly opposite and further south to Split (*Salona*). As Bari and Otranto became more active ports in southern Italy they provided comparable links to Durrës (Dyrrachion) and Zadar (Zara) and to the major islands of Corfu (Kerkyra) and Kephalenia and Zakynthos in the Ionian Sea. In Late Antiquity the western coast belonged to the Roman world and was closely related to its hinterland by the Roman road system.

In contrast, the eastern Adriatic is deeply indented and fragmented by numerous islands scattered along its Istrian, Croatian and Dalmatian coastline, with many harbours, hidden pirate bases and small independent communities. The dominant line of the Dinaric Alps that descend to the sea in karst cliffs along several inlets also isolated coastal regions from their hinterland. With much less stable land links to the mainland powers of the interior, inhabitants of the eastern coasts naturally looked seaward for their contacts and mariners and seafaring merchants practised a cabotage or carrying trade under sail between centres rather than using land transport. Yet this geographical setting could be transformed, as when Narses, the Byzantine military commander, in 551 employed local people to build pontoon bridges across the many river indents around the northern head of the Adriatic that normally made it impossible to march an army along this route. As a result, he surprised the Goths when his forces appeared on the coastal road from Aquileia.

While the northern and southern parts of the Adriatic present equally striking differences, a sense of the maritime corridor's unity in linking the provinces of *Venetia* and *Histria* with Epiros and Sicily was very clear to those who made ancient maps such as the *Tabula Peutigeriana* as well as the first portulan maps centuries later. This suggested additional reasons for examining the role of the Adriatic and activity within it from the crucial transitional period of the sixth to eighth centuries and on through the Middle Ages into the fifteenth century. Across this long chronological span, the papers collected in this volume demonstrate how the Adriatic served as such a significant link between West and East.

My own interest in the Adriatic stemmed from an exploration of the role of Ravenna in linking Constantinople to the West, as it did between 540 and 751 when it was ruled by the 'Queen City', capital of the eastern half of the Roman empire. In addition, from 402 Ravenna had served as the *sedes regiae*, the ruling city of the western Roman world and had developed a serious administrative capacity centred on the imperial court, which became in turn the court of the Gothic kings and then of the Byzantine exarchs appointed as governors by Constantinople. With all the trappings of a governmental hub, the city had attracted many ambitious young men and women to find employment and make a career, an advantageous marriage and a fortune. Ravenna was thus distinctly different from ancient Rome, which became a city almost entirely dominated by its bishops, who oversaw its Christian role.

In addition, through its port at Classe, Ravenna was intimately connected with the east Mediterranean. From Constantinople it received a steady stream of career diplomats and military commanders, who also brought news of new artistic fashions, architectural schemes, theological debates and scientific and philosophical developments. From Cyprus it imported portable ovens (*clibani*); from the east Mediterranean amphorae used as acoustic measures in church domes; from Gaza and the Aegean sweet wines – also carried in amphorae – and from Alexandria, its writing material, papyrus, wheat and dates probably stored in baskets of woven palm fronds, as well as Eastern spices, glass, china and silks that entered the Mediterranean world via Egypt. Ravenna was also well connected with the West, importing all manner of ceramic vessels with distinct functions from Carthage, the centre of African Red Slip ware, as well as grain and the famous fish paste, *garum*, which flavoured so many Late Antique dishes from places in the western Mediterranean like Carthagena. The church of Ravenna had profitable estates in Sicily, which provided grain, olive oil and wine and much of this imported grain appears to have been sold on to other distributors in northern Italy.

I was also intrigued by the description of the Adriatic provided by an anonymous cosmographer based in Ravenna around the year 700. Unlike other ancient geographers who wrote a Mediterranean *periplous* (a journey around the entire 'Roman pond') that started at the Pillars of Hercules and worked clockwise around the sea, the anonymous cosmographer began in the city of his birth, *nobelissima* Ravenna, moving down the western coast of the Adriatic, naming all the ports and cities familiar to the Roman world. He proceeded through the Strait of Messina and followed the west coast of Italy around to Gaul and Spain, across to Africa, east to Alexandria and thence to Constantinople, moving anticlockwise. After a complete tour of the Black Sea, his route returned to the Mediterranean to hug the coasts of Greece and finally to enter the Adriatic from the south. In his report on the eastern coast from Durrës (Dyrrachion) to Ravenna, a distance of 16,000 miles, he stated that there were seventy-two cities and listed sixty-nine, many of them well known. He included some inland centres as well as a large number of islands, many with unfamiliar names such as *Nisiris*, *Sarona* and *Malata*, not recorded on ancient maps, others whose names, he said, were not known. In adding to the lists of ports and centres familiar to Late Antique geographers, the anonymous cosmographer provided a base for comparison with later periods when different points became significant and new centres replaced older ones. It is, nonetheless, striking that when Venice gained dominance over the Adriatic, it was precisely along the eastern coastline that it sought to impose its rule, often in the same key places that had been noted by the Ravenna scholar.

The cosmographer's considerable interest in the seventh- and eighth-century Adriatic suggested that a much broader exploration of the sea as a vital link between Istria, Dalmatia, north-eastern Italy and the wider Mediterranean to the south might be a useful collaborative project. My hope that it might lead to new ways of investigating the unity or break-up of the Mediterranean world, theories that had long dominated historical analysis, as well as the much revised Pirenne thesis on the impact of Arab expansion in its trading patterns, is brilliantly summarised in the opening chapter by Richard Hodges. The project also offered an opportunity to involve archaeologists who had been working in Albania, Dalmatia and Croatia together with those from much better-known sites in Italy and the east Mediterranean. This is demonstrated by the work of Richard Hodges and Joanita Vroom from Butrint and case studies by Sauro Gelichi on new settlements in the northern Adriatic, by Trpimir Vedriš on Dalmatia and by Jean-Marie Martin on Apulia. It promised a confrontation of older and more recently elaborated theories of the rise of Venice and its role in the Adriatic, addressed by Stefano Gasparri, Sauro Gelichi, Peter Frankopan and Michael Angold. It also raised the issue of the Byzantine failure to defend Ravenna, which fell decisively under Lombard control in 751 only to be conquered by the Franks, summoned by Pope Stephen II, developments that profoundly altered the formation of western Europe, as well as Constantinople's determination to consolidate imperial loyalty among the inhabitants of the eastern shores of the Adriatic and its success in preserving influence in Apulia. These aspects are addressed by Francesco Borri in his study of the eclipse of Byzantium's imperial presence in the Adriatic, by Tom Brown in the development of Ravenna and other cities post-751 and by Jean-Marie Martin for the development of southern Italy. Here the use of seals, icons and coins by Pagona Papadopoulou, Magdalena Skoblar and Trpimir Vedriš add considerably to our grasp of the material culture of the Adriatic.

Finally, towards the end of the period under consideration, this project addressed aspects of Venetian control over the Adriatic that demonstrated how Venice gradually broke free from its loyalty to Constantinople and the ideal of Christian unity was destroyed by the crusades, a process illuminated by Michael Angold and Peter Frankopan. Given the replacement of the Byzantine imperial capital by the Latin empire established after the Fourth Crusade, this development had to be examined from several different angles. Analysing the evidence for Venetian activity in the eastern Adriatic, Oliver Jens Schmitt corrects the national perspectives that dominated previous research, employing the archive of Korčula, while

Guillaume Saint-Guillain shows how the Venetians recorded their own conquests, though the surviving documents are copies and epitomes of original treaties. Christopher Wright looks at the changes in Venetian participation in the crusading venture and Élisabeth Crouzet-Pavan draws attention to some of the consequences of Venice's ambitions in the migration of Albanians and Dalmatians to the city.

The idea of a conference that would unite the interests of both British Schools of Archaeology has now been realised in the extremely interesting contributions to this volume. I would like to record my special thanks to the Directors of the British Schools of Athens and Rome at the time, to the British Academy for funding the project and to Kirsty Stewart, who took on the major editorial role to bring the project into final form. Above all, I salute Magdalena Skoblar, who developed it into a practical realisation as the conference that took place in Rome in January 2015 and then persuaded the contributors to deliver their work. Without her insistence and dedication, the volume would never have found its printed form in such a fascinating collection of papers.

Acknowledgements

The idea for a volume about the medieval Adriatic was one of the main drivers of the Adriatic Connections programme, which was generously funded by the British Academy from 2013 to 2015. This area was identified as being worthy of research by Judith Herrin and her initiative resulted in a collaborative project that brought together the British School at Athens and the British School at Rome. The two research institutes, led by Catherine Morgan and Christopher Smith (their respective directors during that period), co-hosted my postdoctoral project on the cult of the Virgin Mary in the Early Medieval Adriatic. The chapters in this volume are based on a three-day conference – *The Adriatic as a Threshold to Byzantium* – I organised at the British School at Rome in January 2015. The meeting gathered historians, archaeologists and art historians, both established and emerging, who discussed the nature of the Byzantine presence in the Adriatic. This volume contains most of the papers presented, and over the course of the four years following the conference the contributors have refined their arguments and updated them with new research findings that have emerged since then.

I would like to thank John Bennet, the current director of the British School of Athens, for overseeing the completion of the volume with great patience and Kirsty Stewart without whom the editing process would have stalled. I am thankful for the helpful feedback I received from Liz James while preparing the proposal for this book and I am also thankful to the two anonymous reviewers of the manuscript. I need to mention the superb work of Jean Birrel and Duncan Hardy, who translated two chapters from French into English. I am lucky to have benefitted from the advice of Judith Herrin and Chis Wickham while working on this volume. I feel privileged that they always replied to my queries with kindness and patience. A special thanks goes to the authors of the chapters: I have learnt a lot from their contributions and communicating with them has been a pleasure. Michael Sharp, Hal Churchman and Katie Idle at Cambridge University Press have been extremely helpful – I am grateful to all three. I am indebted to Alessandra Cianciosi, Margherita Ferri and Andrea Ninfo for their help with Sauro Gelichi's illustrations and to Bettina Schwartz and

Christian Kurtze of the Austrian Archaeological Institute at Vienna for providing me with the permits for two of Joanita Vroom's illustrations. Finally, I would like to thank Nikolina Uroda and Ivan Basić for their help with obtaining literature and advice in general. A huge thank you is reserved for Paul Jones for his great patience and support.

Magdalena Skoblar

Note on Citation, Transliteration, Names, Titles and Dates

Throughout the book, I have used a slightly modified author–date referencing system of the *Annual of the British School at Athens* to conform to the prevalent style of the School's publications. For this reason, primary sources are cited in the following manner: John the Deacon, *Istoria Veneticorum* 2.19, where the numbers refer to the relevant book and chapter, or, dependent on the edition, Niketas Choniates, *Historia*, 54–6, where the numbers refer to the pages of the edition used. I have applied minimum capitalisation in the titles of articles and chapters, while maximum capitalisation is used for the titles of books published in English. The titles of non-English publications follow the norms of their respective languages, for example *Archeologia medievale*, *Versus marini*, *Byzance et l'Italie méridionale*.

I have not transliterated the details of publications in Cyrillic and Greek provided in the list of references. For the transliteration of Greek words and phrases in the text, I thought the non-Romanised convention is more appropriate for a volume examining the extent of Byzantine presence in the Adriatic.

With regard to the geographical terminology, it follows the language spoken in the relevant country whenever possible and so there is 'Zadar', 'Dubrovnik' and 'Durrës' either instead of or alongside 'Zara', 'Ragusa' and 'Dyrrachion', that is, 'Durazzo'. Exceptions to this rule are commonly accepted equivalents such as 'Venice' but also mentions of historic regions in the south Adriatic and the Balkans which did not give names to modern-day countries, for example, 'Diokleia' instead of 'Duklja'. For these geographical names and for Greek, that is, Byzantine names, I have followed the transliteration used in the *Oxford Dictionary of Byzantium*, hence the appellative 'Porphyrogennetos' rather than 'Porphyrogenitus.'

Titles such as 'king', 'emperor' and 'bishop' are capitalised when preceding a person's name. Since this volume covers the period in which the inhabitants of Venice had a leader who bore the title of *dux*, I have used the title 'duke' when editing the chapters that mention Venice prior to the eleventh century and the usual 'doge' for the events form the eleventh century onward.

All dates mentioned in the book refer to the Christian Era except for the few which are marked as 'BCE'. With regard to the regnal years of emperors and kings, I have maintained the contributors' choice whether to use them or not; I have done the same for the pontificates of popes and bishops.

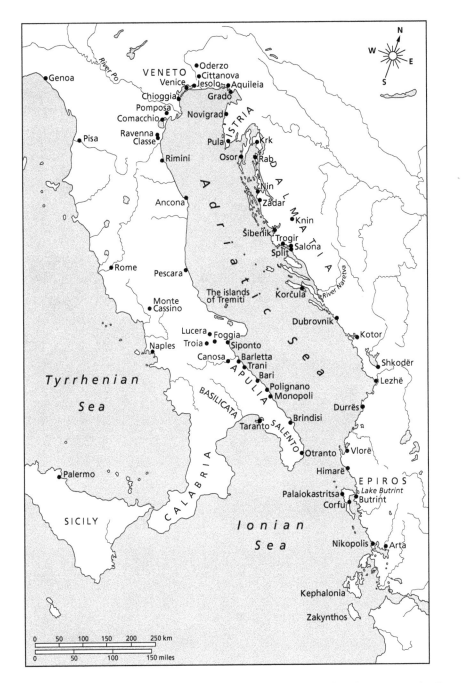

Map 1 The Adriatic with the most important sites mentioned in the volume. Drawn by Cox Cartographic Ltd.

Introduction

MAGDALENA SKOBLAR

A complex, fragmented space in a complex, fragmented time, the Medieval Adriatic is often subsumed into grand historiographic narratives focusing on the great powers that governed it throughout this period. By taking a different perspective, centred on the Adriatic itself, this volume paints a more nuanced picture, which attends to and illuminates the realities of the local communities of this region and their entanglement, first with the Byzantine empire, and then with Venice. Despite being a major channel of communications between East and West in this period, long-standing political fragmentation and linguistic differences have led to a lack of dedicated scholarly attention to this region as a whole. This volume addresses this gap by bringing together the work of an international group of sixteen scholars, from a range of disciplinary backgrounds, to generate powerful new perspectives on the Medieval Adriatic, and makes much material available to a wider audience for the first time, particularly new archaeological evidence and existing scholarship previously only published in Italian or Croatian. This introduction sets up the volume by outlining the broad context for the Adriatic in this period, before underlining the scholarly rationale for this volume in more detail and providing an overview of each chapter.

Positioning the Adriatic

Separated from the rest of the Mediterranean by the length of Italy, the Adriatic resembles an elongated lake, or a sea within a sea; it is only 70 km wide at its southernmost end, the Straits of Otranto, where it becomes the Ionian Sea and laps at the shores of Greece (Map 1). Through Venice, sitting at the top of the sea in the north, the Adriatic is a gateway to the Alps. The settlement that gave the sea its name, Adria near Rovigo, is also found in the north and Ancient Greek writers such as Herodotus and Thucydides referred only to the northern half of the sea as the Adriatic (ὁ Ἀδρίας), while the southern section was called the Ionian Gulf. Conversely, Strabo and Ptolemy called the present-day Ionian Sea the

Adriatic Sea and, in the sixth century, Procopius used the same name for the body of water between Malta and Crete (Rapske 1994; Smith 1878, vol. 1, 28). The long east and west coasts could not be more different, prompting Jacques Le Goff (2001, 7) to call the Adriatic an 'asymmetrical sea'. While the western, Italian side is gently undulating with very few offshore islands, the crenellated eastern shoreline (predominantly in present-day Croatia) features many inlets and island archipelagos with natural anchorages.

As 'not only a sea with two shores, the western and the eastern, but also with two spaces, one northern and another southern' (Sabaté 2016, 11), the Adriatic is a quartered sea, easily given to fragmentation and compartmentalisation. Only the Roman empire managed to claim the whole sea as a unified space and, even then, when Diocletian divided the empire the separation line split it in two down its east–west axis. Following short-lived unifications under Constantine I, Julian the Apostate and Theodosius I, the final division in 395 assigned the Adriatic to the western half of the empire. But this was only the brief endgame of Rome: in the fifth century the western empire collapsed and the Goths made their way into Italy and Dalmatia.

It would take two military campaigns, from 535 to 554, by the Eastern Roman Emperor Justinian I to regain Italy and Dalmatia and bring them under the administration of Constantinople, that is, Byzantium. From this point onwards, what we call the Byzantine empire had a vested interest in the Adriatic. It established an exarchate at Ravenna (584–751), dispatched its own fleet when the Franks advanced too far into the Veneto and Dalmatia (805 and 808), battled against the Normans in Durrës/Dyrrachion (1081) and regained the eastern Adriatic during the reign of Manuel I Komnenos in the second half of the twelfth century. It also fostered the diplomatic practice of bestowing prestigious titles, gifts of luxury objects, money and relics on local rulers and elites in exchange for their support and loyalty. Without this application of what Jonathan Shepard (2018, 4–5) termed Byzantium's 'Soft Power', there would have been no Venice as we know it. This hybrid city, tied to the sea but open to the hinterland, neither western nor eastern, was never Byzantine, and yet has traditionally been perceived as such in the scholarship. Of all the Adriatic cities Byzantium wanted to keep in its sphere of influence, only Venice – a city of no Roman substrate – proved to be a long-term ally, albeit not without challenges.

The loss of the unified Adriatic space of the Roman empire created a vacuum filled by the memory of it, and it is this aspect of Byzantium – Byzantium as the heir of Rome – that proved to be irresistible to the local communities once included in the western half of the empire. Despite this connection, the Latin-speaking men and women of Ravenna, which remained in the hands of Byzantium as the seat of its exarchate until 751, had different mores and concerns to those of faraway Constantinople, which too frequently remains the only yardstick for all things Byzantine.

The same can be said about Venice. In fact, in the early eleventh century, the difference between Venice and Byzantium was so great that when Maria Argyropoula, the Byzantine aristocratic bride of Duke Pietro II Orseolo's son Giovanni, had to leave Constantinople for her new home in the lagoon, she did so with a heavy heart (John the Deacon, *Istoria Veneticorum* 4.71), knowing that she was leaving a society where food was eaten with a fork and regular baths were considered normal. In 1006, not long after she arrived in Venice, Maria, Giovanni and their small son all died of the plague. Maria's ways became the stuff of legends – another indication of a culture difference – and by the second half of the eleventh century St Peter Damian (*Opusculum quinquagesimum*, col. 744), the Ravennate reformer, was using her tragic story as a warning about the 'decadent and sybaritic ways of the east' (Nicol 1999, 46–7); in his interpretation she was a self-indulgent Byzantine princess who was punished for her vanity with an awful death. Her depravity consisted of collecting rainwater for personal hygiene rather than trusting the Venetian water supply, using cutlery and attempting to block out the stench of the canals in her rooms with perfume and incense.

Generating New Perspectives on the Medieval Adriatic

Following the lines of its historical complexity, the areas of the Adriatic and the region as a whole have been fragmented in knowledge, through the compartmentalising processes of different national historiographic narratives. The southern part can be regarded as an offshoot of the Ionian Sea with no focus beyond Apulia and Durrës. The eastern coast can be understood to be interchangeable with the Croatian shoreline and never to include the Albanian portion. The Adriatic as a whole can be understood and portrayed as nothing more than the domain of Venice. The Adriatic as a sea can be interpreted within the framework of the wider Mediterranean and, without specific discussion, subsumed into everything that is argued for the mother sea. In contrast, the work collected in this volume generates a new and different perspective. It draws attention to the complexities of the Adriatic during the period which coincided with the Middle Ages in western Europe and the existence of the Byzantine empire in the East. It challenges grand narratives and broad generalisations. By looking at different topics, periods and areas, it demonstrates that, after the sixth century and the stability of Justinian's reign, the Adriatic entered a long phase of fragmentation during which local elites created their own power bubbles – a situation that lasted into the eleventh century, when Venice began its expansion.

In illuminating the complex histories of different parts of the Adriatic and their relationship with Byzantium, the sixteen chapters collected here fill a gap in the scholarship. Despite being a major channel of communication between the East and West, this region has so far received little attention. There is more than one reason for that. For much of the twentieth century, political restrictions closed the majority of the eastern coast to researchers from western Europe and America. Extensive transnational projects require funding, collaboration and management that go beyond the remit of the national institutions in control of key collections of material. Sharing of information, often in minority languages, was cumbersome, especially before the advent of the digital age. With Croatia's transition from post-Communist nation state to EU member (1991–2013) and the gradual opening up of Albania in the 1990s, followed by its application for EU membership in 2009, barriers facing Western scholars have diminished. A number of important archaeological excavations in the Adriatic also necessitated a re-examination of this region and its relationship with the transalpine world and the East. Excavations by Sauro Gelichi in Comacchio and the Venetian lagoon and by Richard Hodges in Butrint have yielded new finds and findings with which scholarship needs to engage.

This book therefore presents a considerable amount of new material and information that was previously inaccessible to a large English-speaking audience. It also brings together contributions from a group of international scholars whose work on the Adriatic has been produced in different linguistic and political contexts which often did not intersect. The contributors explore a wide range of specific topics, ranging from political, naval and economic history to trade and cultural exchange, in different periods and areas, and through this challenge grand narratives and broad generalisations. Together, they create a picture of the Adriatic as a node between Byzantium, Italy and the West that was thoroughly transformed after the sixth century and the stability of Justinian's reign. The region entered a long phase of fragmented local power until Venetian expansion began in the eleventh century. Cashing in on the fortuitous constellation of events, including the downturn in Byzantine political power after the loss of Anatolia following the defeat at Manzikert in 1071, the loss of Italy to the Normans and the launching of the crusades, Venice began integrating the Adriatic into its own possession – the *Golfo di Venezia*. As early as the twelfth century, the northernmost portion of the sea was known as the gulf of Venice: this is how al-Idrīsī referred to it in the *Book of Roger*. By the end of the fifteenth, the whole Adriatic would be named after the northern city state. Venice's dogged pursuit of what she thought of as rightfully hers resulted in successes such as the renegotiation of a trade deal with Byzantium to include tax exemptions on Corfu and Crete in 1147, the acquisition of Greek territories and Crete after 1204 and the submission of Dalmatia, especially Zadar, which was finally claimed in 1409. What started off as just one of the settlements in a northern Adriatic lagoon had become a powerhouse by the fifteenth century.

The chapters of this book are arranged chronologically in order to provide an overview of these developments and enable readers to navigate easily the diverse range of times, places, topics and disciplinary approaches collected here. Inevitably, Venice looms large because of its historical and historiographic significance and the difficulty in balancing out this focus within this volume indicates a broader asymmetry in the scholarship. Apulia also features prominently (albeit to a lesser degree) and Dalmatia is interwoven into several contributions, as is the city of Ravenna, along with Durrës and Butrint. In fact, the volume opens with a chapter on Butrint (Richard Hodges), which starts with the sixth century before illuminating the Early Medieval dip and the eleventh-century revival of this port. The concluding chapter (Élisabeth Crouzet-Pavan) takes us up to the 1510s with its reassessment of the integration of eastern Adriatic migrants in fifteenth-century Venice.

A number of chapters engage with dominant trends in scholarship, such as the uniformity of the Mediterranean, the Byzantine-ness of Venice and the asymmetric study of the Venetian *Stato da Mar*, which neglects Dalmatia. This zooming in and out of Adriatic subregions and coastal centres helps situate the Adriatic in the wider context of the relationship with the Byzantine empire and, even more broadly, as a part of the Mediterranean. Traits such as ecology, micro-regions and connectivity, identified by Peregrine Horden and Nicholas Purcell in their interpretative model for the Mediterranean as a whole, are also found in the Adriatic. However, this volume demonstrates that their overarching framework does not fit the Adriatic, at least not in the Early Middle Ages.

The Contributions

As Richard Hodges argues in his contribution to this volume, the Early Medieval period was marked by the erosion of unity. He begins the volume by focusing on Butrint from the sixth to the eleventh century, as a case study for the issue of continuity versus discontinuity in the Adriatic and the Mediterranean. Drawing on his archaeological excavations and the research findings of the team associated with the Butrint Foundation project (1994–2010), Hodges gives an overview of this southern Adriatic port in present-day Albania. From its early origins as a marginal place during the Roman empire, Butrint grew in the first half of the sixth century, only to contract, significantly becoming almost a ghost town in the seventh. By the 840s life moved to its outskirts in the Vrina Plain, where an undefended settlement traded goods with Salento and the south-west Balkans. The town itself was renewed only in the second half of the tenth and the early eleventh century, which saw the construction of new fortifications and planned buildings.

By seeing Butrint as a representative example of a wider phenomenon, Hodges questions Horden and Purcell's main argument that the Mediterranean was and remains a unified sea, enabling continuity and connectivity. He disagrees with their assessment of the Early Middle Ages as a one-off 'dip' in their *longue durée* model of continuity, arguing that the unified nature of the Roman Mediterranean was the exception rather than the rule, and that the Adriatic and the Mediterranean were affected by a period of serious discontinuity, beginning in the seventh century. At Butrint, this disconnection lasted until the mid-tenth century. Assessing the Adriatic as a whole, Hodges concludes that it was a unified region only in the first half of the sixth century, and then again in the eleventh.

Joanita Vroom investigates the links between the Adriatic and Byzantium from the perspective of pottery across the seventh to fifteenth centuries. She traces the distribution of imported amphorae and table wares found at Butrint, connecting them to sites in southern Italy, the Adriatic and the Aegean. As indicated by Hodges in his chapter, the contraction of Butrint during the period between the seventh and the ninth century did not mean the end of trade: pottery was still imported from the south and north of Italy, Constantinople and the eastern Mediterranean. Relatively small, modest ships were a common sight in the eastern Aegean and the Adriatic. After the fall of Constantinople in 1204, the trade in Butrint shifted towards the west. Meanwhile, the table wares produced in Salento were exported to the Peloponnese, coinciding with the efforts of the

Angevins to penetrate the eastern Mediterranean via the trade routes of Venetian ships in the Adriatic and the Ionian Sea.

Francesco Borri looks at Byzantine involvement with the Adriatic after the sixth century. Highlighting the turn of the eighth century as a point at which the Byzantine presence in the Adriatic starts to recede and becomes limited to the south, that is, Otranto, but pointing out that this did not halt commercial exchange, Borri investigates what may have been the reason behind Byzantium's failure to maintain control over the majority of the Adriatic. He argues that the empire's inability to punish local communities for not paying taxes resulted in their growing independence. At the same time, the fall of Ravenna meant that its rivals could develop rapidly. These eighth-century developments worried Byzantium but, despite the efforts of Emperor Leo III and his son Constantine V, Byzantine authority could not be re-established in the Adriatic without a military intervention. By the end of the eighth century and the turn of the ninth, the Franks encroached upon the northern Adriatic and although Byzantium did manage to muster a fleet to deal with the threat at this time, it was met with resistance from the local elites.

This northern area is discussed by Stefano Gasparri, who examines the relationship of the nascent duchy of Venice with the Lombard kingdom on the one hand, and Byzantine territories in Italy on the other. He draws attention to the fact that the Venetian lagoon was heavily militarised under the exarchate of Ravenna, which prevented it from forming trade relationships with the Lombards after they captured it. Instead, this opportunity was seized by Comacchio and Venice would have to wait until the ninth century to take the baton of mercantile primacy in the area. With the loss of Ravenna, Byzantium turned to Venice, Istria and Dalmatia and this Romano-Byzantine community in the Adriatic would eventually become Venice's playground. The same area was at the top of the Carolingian list at the turn of the ninth century and it was only after the Treaty of Aachen (812) that things began to settle for Venice. The new duchy remained in the sphere of Byzantium, but Venice's Byzantine character was far from pure and Gasparri contests the historiographical narrative about this, urging us to see Venice for what it was: a hybrid created by a continuing balancing act between Byzantium, the Italian *Terraferma* and the Adriatic.

That the Venetian lagoon was in a state of flux in the Early Medieval period is evident from its settlements, which Sauro Gelichi's contribution elucidates. His archaeological excavations and research in general have shaken up traditional scholarship on the emergence of Venice and continue to challenge the grand historiographical narratives on the city state's origins. In this volume he demonstrates that Early Medieval settlements were cropping up in the northern Adriatic arc and rejects the traditional explanation that this was caused by the mass migration of people from the hinterland in the face of barbarian invasions. Apart from *Altinum*, all the other Roman cities around the lagoon continued to be inhabited. The new settlements, in contrast, were determined by the interests of the emerging aristocracies.

Gelichi interprets these new sites as centres of local power and trade, which aspired to become city-like and refrains from judging them based on whether they succeeded or not. His focus is on the Venetian lagoon and the picture of it that emerges by the eighth century is one of a territory dotted with many sprouting settlements, none of which was dominant. Urban aspirations were fulfilled in those sites that became episcopal seats such as Torcello, Olivolo, Cittanova, Metamauco and *Equilo*, and later on, those that were centres of the political power of a duke, the most famous one being that of Venice (the future doge).

A site on the east Adriatic coast that has been continually inhabited well before Antiquity – Zadar – is discussed in detail by Trpimir Vedriš. A Roman *civitas* that survived what Salona, the Dalmatian metropolis, could not – the raids of the Slavs and the Avars in the seventh century – Zadar became a seat of a Byzantine official by the end of the eighth century, while simultaneously witnessing the settlement of the Croats in its hinterland and the creation of their principality in the ninth. The conflict between the Franks and Byzantium in the upper Adriatic at the turn of the ninth century led to the demarcation between the two empires as stipulated by the aforementioned Treaty of Aachen. Zadar and a handful of other coastal towns, all of them with a Roman past, were all that Byzantium received. After the treaty, at some point before the second half of the ninth century, Dalmatia was elevated to the rank of theme with Zadar as its seat. In arguing this, Vedriš opposes Vivien Prigent's opinion that this theme was located in the southern Adriatic and that, therefore, its governors could not have resided in Zadar. Vedriš points out that, being home to the Latin Church and surrounded by the principality of Croatia in its immediate hinterland, it certainly was not a typical Byzantine theme and, indeed, it did not last long. However, the prestige associated with the imperial administration was readily embraced: Byzantine titles were received, gold coins circulated and letters with lead seals were opened. As was the case at Ravenna, the notion of Roman identity, especially in contrast to the new peoples settled in the hinterland, was embedded in Zadar thanks to the cultural cache of Byzantium as the new Rome.

The local elites bolstered their status by being associated with imperial administration, while nevertheless remaining on the fringes of the Byzantine sphere.

The local component was also a determining factor in the fate of Ravenna after its fall, when it ceased to be a Byzantine stronghold. Tom Brown reassesses the position of post-Byzantine Ravenna by pointing to new research; he gives an overview of the city's transformation into an autonomous organism led by its archbishops, who sought favours from western kings and amassed land holdings. Trade links continued with the eastern Mediterranean, while new mercantile relationships were forged with the towns situated in the Po Valley. Brown emphasises the Late Antique, that is, Roman element of Byzantine Ravenna and states that, even with the rise of local autonomy, the empire remained in the collective consciousness as 'the gold standard' of culture. The rule of the Ravennate archbishops came to an end in the eleventh century with the Investiture Controversy and the growing importance of the neighbouring communes of Bologna and Ferrara.

After the fall of Ravenna in 751, Byzantium only managed to re-establish its rule in the Adriatic by regaining Apulia in the 870s, after a period of Lombard control and the brief existence of the emirate of Bari. Initially, Apulia was attached to the theme of Kephalenia, but at the turn of the tenth century it became the theme of Longobardia. Jean-Marie Martin makes it clear that this did not mean that the empire exercised sovereignty in all of Apulia in the first half of the tenth century, but shows that Byzantium was tempted to obtain loyalty through the concession of high dignities to the local elites rather than create a separate theme. However, the first thing it did was to found new ports on the Adriatic to enable communication with the opposite coast. Around 970, the theme of Longobardia was replaced by the *katepanate* of Italy, corresponding to the same territory, remaining Latin in character and adhering to the Lombard law. The new government set about establishing cities in the interior to populate these areas but managed to impose Byzantine taxation only in the eleventh century. Martin's overview shows that the empire succeeded in integrating Apulia but that it took a very long time and required considerable efforts, something that was not done in the case of Dalmatia. The arrival of the Normans undid what the Byzantines had taken eighty years to achieve and Apulia passed into their hands over the course of two decades.

The next two chapters discuss networks of exchange and trade from the ninth to the eleventh century. Pagona Papadopoulou looks at the sigillographic evidence during this period to identify a communication pattern between the two southern Adriatic coasts, and between both of them and Byzantium. She includes in her examination the Greek coast of the Ionian Sea. Hugely important as primary sources, Byzantine lead seals tell us who communicated with who and in what capacity, but, as Papadopoulou remarks, only when their provenance is known and their inscription is read correctly. Papadopoulou observes an anomaly when it comes to the eastern Adriatic coast that only further archaeological excavations in Albania and Dalmatia might explain better. It lies in the fact that all the seals struck by the officials from this side were found in remote areas and none nearby. Exactly the opposite was the case with Apulia, where the seals of ecclesiastical and military officials tend to be found in the neighbouring areas, although, generally speaking, seals were not used much in Apulia itself.

My own contribution to this volume focuses on the evidence of icons in the Adriatic before 1204. Following the capture of Constantinople by the crusaders in that year, an unprecedented amount of painted panels reached Italy and Dalmatia, where they were readily venerated. I argue in my chapter that the Adriatic was so responsive to this influx because it had already adopted Byzantine icons in the eleventh century. Although only three icons survive from this period (at Ravenna and Trani on the west coast and Rab on the east coast), textual sources record the existence of more icons, both painted and relief, most notably in Apulia. The record of a Marian icon that was carried around Otranto in an expiatory procession at the end of the eleventh century and the mention of two icons exchanged for a portion of a salt pan which the bishop of Siponto obtained from the Tremity Abbey for his church in the 1060s indicate that in Apulia icons did have a liturgical use, albeit not the same as in Byzantine churches.

The six chapters in the second half of this book focus on the Venetian Adriatic, the *Golfo di Venezia*, and showcase the expansion of the city state from the eleventh century to its dominant position in the fifteenth. Peter Frankopan's contribution outlines how Venice came to be a major player in the Adriatic in the second half of the eleventh century and, eventually, to pose a threat to Byzantine interests by the second half of the twelfth. Following the fall of Apulia into Norman hands in 1071 and the crushing defeat the Byzantine army suffered at Manzikert against the Seljuk Turks in the same year, Byzantium was weakened. The Norman leader Robert Guiscard crossed the Adriatic and attacked the empire at Durrës in 1081. Asked to help, the Venetians eventually forced the Normans to retreat to Apulia and unblocked the Adriatic.

Frankopan argues that the trading privileges which Emperor Alexios I Komnenos subsequently gave to the Venetians in 1092 were not a reward for their help against the Norman threat. Not limited to Constantinople alone but including other Byzantine ports, the trade deal gave Venice the opportunity to grow a mercantile network, which is exactly what it did. The emperor also granted Venice authority over the cities along the Dalmatian coast, the same ones that were nominally Byzantine in the ninth century, and in doing so sanctioned the campaigns that the Venetians had been undertaking in Dalmatia since the turn of the millennium.

The involvement with the crusades also spurred Venetian economic growth. The shipping of supplies to the western forces in the Holy Land flowed smoothly down the Adriatic and through the network of ports with commercial concessions courtesy of Byzantium. By the late 1150s, in the eyes of Emperor Manuel I Komnenos, Venice had become too big for its boots and he established a Byzantine base at Ancona in order to lessen the Venetian grip on the Adriatic. His anti-Venetian campaign culminated with the round-up and arrest of the Venetians living in Constantinople in 1171. However, it was too late to harm Venice, which was so strong that it sacked Zadar in 1202 as a prelude to the sacking of Constantinople two years later.

Michael Angold also highlights the arrest of Venetians in 1171 and addresses the question of why Venice did not break away from its relationship with Byzantium in the twelfth century when it had the opportunity to do so. He argues that there were two main reasons for this. The first one was related to self-interest: the privileges guaranteed by Byzantine emperors, beginning with the chrysobull of Alexios I Komnenos, translated into commercial success and political power at home. Faced with trade competitors at Pisa and Genoa, Venice wanted a special relationship with the empire. The second reason for remaining loyal to Byzantium seems to have been ideological. Angold writes that the Venetians were proud of their loyalty to the empire or, as they called it, in their own words, 'Romania'.

As the notion of 'Romania' changed to denote Venetian interests in the territory of Byzantium so did the perception the Venetians had of themselves as *semper defensores Romanie*. The defending of Byzantine interests came to mean the defending of what Venetians thought was best for Byzantium. Emperor Manuel I Komnenos did not appreciate this and wanted to curb growing Venetian self-confidence in general. He negotiated with Pisan merchants, allowed the Genoese to expand their quarter in Constantinople and established a Byzantine presence in Dalmatia and Ancona. After his arrest of the Venetians in the empire, it does seem odd that Venice wanted to remain aligned with Byzantium, but Angold reminds us that the ties between the two ran deep. Peace was re-established in 1187, followed by a new chrysobull of 1198, issued by Emperor Alexios III Angelos, allowing Venetian representatives for the first time to have a degree of legal authority on Byzantine soil.

The next stage in Venice's history, the turning point of the first half of the thirteenth century, is examined by Guillaume Saint-Guillain. In the aftermath of the fall of Constantinople, a document – the *Partitio terrarum imperii Romanie* – was drawn up outlining how the Byzantine territories were to be split between the conquerors. The Venetians were assigned those along the Adriatic and the Ionian Sea. However, this was no guarantee of actual control over these areas and Venice had to implement its assigned rights on a case-by-case basis. The process was arduous and consisted of negotiating pacts with local elites, some of which, for example on the west Peloponnese coast, remained out of reach. The pacts did work in the southern Adriatic and by the second half of the century Martino da Canale could write that 'the Adriatic Sea is part of the duchy of Venice', confident that it rang true. By securing the Straits of Otranto, Venice held the keys to the eastern Mediterranean and Saint-Guillain rightly points out that this access point was the main reason why controlling the entire Adriatic made sense.

The openness of Venice to the east is also integral to Christopher Wright's chapter, centred on Venetian involvement in the crusades. Noting that the route to the Holy Land was nothing new for Venice, given its commercial network of outposts already established in the eastern Mediterranean, he traces the process through which Venice extended its domination from the Adriatic to the Bosphorus by the late fourteenth century. While the Adriatic remained a route that had to be secured in order to reach the final destinations in the east, following the Fourth Crusade in 1204, Venice gained a foothold in the Aegean and started treating it the same way as it did Dalmatia: as a traversing space it needed to control in order to arrive at a destination where it could trade. By benefitting from a set of historical circumstances, such as the change in the demand for its ships to transport crusading armies to the east, which was universal in the thirteenth century but no longer needed in the fourteenth, together with the Ottoman presence in the Balkans and the dwindling naval power of Byzantium, Venice forged its *Stato da Mar*.

The fifteenth-century integration of most of the Adriatic under the aegis of Venice is addressed by Oliver Jens Schmitt from a historiographic perspective. He stresses the importance of studying the Venetian Adriatic as a transnational region and examines the role played by the national historiographies of the countries involved. Focusing mostly on different approaches to Venetian rule over Dalmatia in the fifteenth century among Italian and Croatian scholars, Schmitt outlines how Croatian studies and archives were left out of Italian studies, while Croatian scholarship was engrossed in discussions about the colonial and exploitative nature of Venetian government. Given that the Fascist government utilised Venice's past ruling of Dalmatia to justify its own occupation of the territory, it is not surprising that the topic was a no-go area for Italian post-war scholars and that academics writing in socialist Yugoslavia were tempted to interpret it through the lens of enforced Italianisation. Following the break-up of Yugoslavia, Croatian historians turned to the local archives, but although their findings shed new light on Venetian Dalmatia, until recently they remained unnoticed on the international stage. Schmitt also compares and contrasts the views of Albanian scholars and points out that, unlike Dalmatia, Albania was not seen as belonging to the historical Italian lands, but was viewed as a colony. Their criticism of the Venetian presence as that of a colonial oppressor was more hard-line and developed in a closed society under a severe Communist regime.

The way Schmitt points out the difference between Venetian rule in the Adriatic and the Aegean is particularly useful. The *Stato da Mar* did not encompass only the *Venetokratia* in the Greek world but also included the Adriatic. The Catholic communes along the eastern Adriatic became part of Venice through contracts rather than military might, as was the case in its Orthodox overseas territories.

The volume concludes with Élisabeth Crouzet-Pavan's chapter that illuminates the city of Venice in the fifteenth century as a destination for economic migrants from the east Adriatic with all the challenges that go with such a relocation, including housing, employment and social integration, striking a particularly resonant note for our own times. Crouzet-Pavan re-evaluates the position and contribution of Albanian and Dalmatian settlers in the Venice of that time. Dismissing anachronistic views that lump immigrants together regardless of the length of time they lived in Venice and that interpret their presence as being strictly communitarian rather than being gradually integrated into the host society, she provides a fuller picture of the lives of Albanian and Dalmatian newcomers. Restricted to the run-down areas of Venice to the east of St Mark's Square (Castello) and to the north of the city (Canareggio), the immigrants were mostly employed in shipping and naval roles. For skilled workmen, social mobility became a possibility and Crouzet-Pavan gives examples of Albanian glassmakers and Dalmatian printers. She also emphasises that communities could be integrated as a collective, as demonstrated by the confraternities. These institutions were closed to the members of other nations and tend to be interpreted in the scholarship as fostering isolationism and mutual rivalries. Crouzet-Pavan argues that the fact that painted decorations on the walls of these institutions feature battles in which their members fought for Venice points to their loyalty to, rather than alienation from, Venice.

As indicated by the contributions to this volume, the flexibility of Byzantium towards the Adriatic communities fostered relationships through which a Byzantine presence – political in the case of Apulia, diplomatic in the case of Venice or cultural when it comes to the whole area – was felt on the shores of this sea for eight centuries. By being the purveyor of Roman-ness, Byzantium had no ideological competitors and this knowledge guaranteed its appeal. When Emperor Manuel Komnenos rebuked Doge Vitale II Michiel for attacking Byzantium in 1171, he declared that what prestige the Venetians had, they owed to the Romans. It is the prestige associated with Byzantium that pulled the Adriatic regions, always responsive to the call of the Roman empire, into its orbit, at various times and to varying degrees.

References

John the Deacon. *Istoria Veneticorum*, in Berto, L.A. (ed.), *Giovanni Diacono. Istoria Veneticorum* (Bologna, 1999).

Le Goff, J. 2001. 'Préface', in Cabanes, P. (ed.), *Histoire de l'Adriatique* (Paris).

Nicol, D.M. 1999. *Byzantium and Venice: A Study in Diplomatic and Cultural Relations*, 5th edn. (Cambridge).

Peter Damian. *Opusculum quinquagesimum*, in Migne, J.-P. (ed.), *Patrologia Latina*, vol. 145 (Paris, 1853), 732-51.

Rapske, B.M. 1994. 'Acts, travel and shipwreck', in Gill, W.J. and Gempf, C. (eds.), *The Book of Acts in Its First-Century Setting*, vol. 2, Graeco-Roman Setting (Carlisle), 1-47.

Sabaté, F. 2016. 'The ports of the medieval Adriatic: Open research prospects', *Hortus artium medievalium* 22, 11-23.

Shepard, J. 2018. 'Introduction: Circles overlapping in the upper Adriatic', in Ančić, M., Shepard, J. and Vedriš, T. (eds.), *Imperial Spheres and the Adriatic: Byzantium, the Carolingians and the Treaty of Aachen (812)* (London and New York), 1-22.

Smith, W. (ed.) 1878. *A Dictionary of Greek and Roman Geography*, vol. 1, Abacaenum-Hytanis (London).

1 | The Adriatic Sea 500–1100

A Corrupted Alterity?

RICHARD HODGES

In memoriam Matt Logue

> For those whose interests lie in the 'Pirenne period' and in western Europe, *The Corrupting Sea* brings the added benefit of putting the early Middle Ages in perspective and normalizing them. At least for the post-Pirennians, the removal of Dark Age alterity will seem the most addictive kind of corruption which Horden and Purcell's Mediterranean has to offer.
>
> (Squatriti 2002, 279)

> History is the child of its time.
>
> (Braudel 1980, 6)

In the search for post-nationalist history after the First World War and an appreciation of how the precedents of the Early Medieval Mediterranean set the terms for European and New World development in the Early Modern period, the 28-year-old Fernand Braudel in his seventh year of teaching in a French Algerian *lycée* went to hear the 68-year-old Henri Pirenne lecture (Marino 2011, 391). Pirenne, speaking without notes, so Braudel recalled, gestured continuously, opening and closing his hand as he sparked a vision of a unified Mediterranean, then its ebb and flow, its expansion and closure, its insularity and boundlessness, its complex diversity and yet its unity (Braudel 1972b, 452). Pirenne's lecture presaged his posthumous book, *Mohammed and Charlemagne* (1937). This inspiring encounter in 1931, according to Braudel, with its ideas about closure after the Muslim invasions, became a guiding motif for Braudel's *Mediterranean and the Mediterranean World in the Age of Philip II* (1972a) published eighteen years later. The end of the Roman pond, so it appears, provided the catalyst to a reading of pre-Modern Mediterranean Europe that has eclipsed even Pirenne's enduring thesis.

Thirty years after the death of Braudel, his shadow over Mediterraneanism remains as strong as ever. In large measure, however, as Cyprian Broodbank has shown in his homage to the French master, *The Making of the Middle Sea* (2013), we are the first – the pivotal – generation coming to terms with the astonishing assembling of data about the archaeology and ecology, unavailable when Braudel was describing 'his' Mediterranean in the late 1940s. This is best judged by comparing Grünbart and Stathakopoulos' (2002) clarion call for material studies in Byzantium at the beginning of the new millennium and Decker's (2016) ample illustration of the new evidence. Although by no means as ample in its detail as the written sources, there now exist the means to re-evaluate not only the Mediterranean but also the Adriatic Sea. These new tools compel us to be as bold as Braudel (1972a, 22), who asserted in his *magnum opus* that 'history can do more than study walled gardens!'

Drawing upon my own research at Butrint in southern Albania, I will review 'the Pirenne period' of the lower Adriatic Sea between the sixth and eleventh centuries, essentially arguing that the projected volume two of Peregrine Horden and Nicholas Purcell's ambitious and challenging homage to Braudel, *The Corrupting Sea*, needs to look carefully at the local conditions through the lens of recent (that is, post-2000) archaeological research in order to grasp the trends of the period (Squatriti 2002, 279). This lens will emphasise two patterns: first, that the impact of the *pax romana* is an aberration in a long Adriatic Sea history driven by economic interactions between points at the maritime terminuses of riverine corridors; and second, that the collapse of the Roman Mediterranean in the seventh century was far more profound than most historians have acknowledged and raises questions about the revival of economic interactions by stages between the eighth and eleventh centuries.

Corrupted Sea?

Taking Plato's description of the Mediterranean and seeking to differentiate themselves from Braudel, Horden and Purcell in their *The Corrupting Sea* (2000) defined the Middle Sea as a coherent region based upon four shared characteristics. First, the region has a distinctive regime of risk from Neolithic to modern times, in which bad years are common but outnumbered by good ones. Second, a distinctive logic of production organised around coping with the risk involved a farming strategy of diversification and redistribution. Third, the region shares an extreme topographical fragmentation derived from the tectonic situation. This has led to it being viewed as a constellation of micro-regions. Fourth, the distinctive regime of communications made possible by the geography of landlocked sea with complex coastlines, numerous islands, interlocking coastal lowlands and navigable lagoons and rivers has provided the Mediterranean with what Horden and Purcell called connectivity.

This definition by Horden and Purcell of their Mediterranean has much to commend it. The devil, though, lies in the detail and especially in the chronological conjunctions. The two authors set out their stall with far-reaching implications in two frequently quoted passages from their book and their own re-evaluation of it. First, on towns and ports as nodes serving as points of connection around the Mediterranean:

> Our microecological model answers, then, to the direction that some urban economic historiography has hesitantly taken. It encourages us to conceive towns less as separate and clearly definable entities and more as loci of contact or overlap between different ecologies. Towns are settings in which ecological processes may be intense, and in which the anthropogene effect is at its most pronounced. But they are not – or not simply by definition – more than that. And they should not be presented as conceptually detachable from the remainder of the spectrum of settlement types. (Horden and Purcell 2000, 100-1)

Second, on historical periodisation, that is, chronology as it affects the pre-Modern issues that drew Braudel to this theme, Horden and Purcell concluded in an important reflection on their book:

> And we are interpreted as portraying the Pirenne period as only a depression, as a slight dip, even though we explicitly characterize the period as one that makes audible the 'background noise' of Mediterranean connectivity when the 'strident commercial networks' are silenced. If we use 'depression' and 'abatement' in portraying the period, this should not be taken to mean that we treat such phenomena as mere blips. It means simply that – to change metaphor – our 'degree zero' of Mediterranean exchange is a little higher than that of most other students of the period. (Horden and Purcell 2005, 351-2)

William Harris was not convinced and, indeed, categorically challenged Horden and Purcell on their interpretations:

> Nothing like cultural unity in more general terms was ever reached in the coastlands of the ancient Mediterranean prior to the Roman conquests, that is obvious, but it remains a central and open question of Roman history how much the populations of these territories, and not just their elites, shared social forms, productive technologies, languages, artistic forms, religious practices and beliefs, and many other cultural features. Horden and Purcell claim that such cultural unity as there was lasted into the Middle Ages; be that as it may, the study of cultural unity has to be the study of its formation and disintegration. (Harris 2005, 28)

David Abulafia in his recent book, *The Great Sea*, challenged Horden and Purcell's model of connectivity. He views the Mediterranean through people and their agency. In an earlier book he puts forth his objection to their model cogently:

> Ecological questions certainly cannot be ignored; but to the historian their great importance lies first of all in the living conditions that they imposed on human settlers, and second in the ways the settlers modified the environment (Abulafia 2003, 26).

Broodbank in *The Making of the Middle Sea* takes a different tack. Essentially the history of the Mediterranean in Prehistory, Broodbank's view challenges the unfettered Braudelian love for the Mediterranean as a unified region. He argues for an understanding of the basin before it became a cockpit of monotheistic world religions and the imposed gridiron of national identities and peoples (Broodbank 2013, 51). This reveals, he contends, a tapestry of traditions as opposed to – to cite Jack Davis (2000, 90) – 'a platter of simplistic models of culture history that has passed as common table fare in much popular archaeological prose'. Broodbank calls for an alternative, interactionist, anti-nationalist and more self-aware vision of the Mediterranean past, with its clear analogies to current globalisation and consequent glocalisation. Nuanced in the absence of individuals, as opposed to places, with connectivity taken for granted, it is a clarion call that any history of the Adriatic Sea region between the seventh and eleventh centuries defies at its peril, given the nature of the new archaeological evidence.

The Archaeology of Three Mid-Byzantine Butrints

Butrint, ancient *Buthrotum*, is a typical illustration of a Mediterranean ancient city that declined in Late Antiquity before experiencing a Middle Byzantine revival that endured until the later Middle Ages (Fig. 1.1). Occupying a micro-ecological niche and with access to legendary amounts of fish in Lake Butrint, it appears to fit the stereotype of a Mediterranean coastal location. Buthrotans throughout the millennia, we might surmise, belonged to Abulafia's definition of those who lived with the sea and, while they enjoyed the promise of its connectivity, stamped their mark on their environments. But beyond such generalities, to understand the history of the Adriatic Sea, it is the changing form and scale of this (and other) maritime barometers that matters. New archaeological measures – and by

Fig. 1.1 View of Butrint and the Straits of Corfu.
Courtesy of the Butrint Foundation

analogy, their import for other Adriatic Sea ports and micro-regions – throw new light on the 'platter of simplistic models'.

Originally a Bronze Age site and a small outlying property of the Corinthian colony of Corfu in the seventh century, by the second century BCE Butrint was a thriving settlement based around a cult of Asclepius. It had a brief moment in the political spotlight during the Julio-Claudian epoch when it was designated a colony by Julius Caesar, before it was rededicated by Augustus. Thereafter the town is poorly represented in Roman textual sources. The archaeology shows it was unexceptional until the sixth century, when it again briefly flourished with, amongst its many monuments, a major church, the Great Basilica, and a large baptistery. By the Middle Byzantine period it lay in the region known as *Bagenetia* or *Vagenetia*, a term that can be traced back to the Slavic tribe known as the Baiunetai. The so-called *Partitio terrarum imperii Romaniae*, the document of 1204 describing the division of the Byzantine empire, compiled on the basis of Byzantine tax registers, records the *chartularaton de Bagenetia* (Soustal 2004, 22). More specifically, in the late ninth century (880–4), St Elias the Younger and his companion Daniel were accused of being foreigners (*Hagarenes*) and spies and imprisoned at Butrint (*polis epineios*). Little more is known about Butrint as a town at this time. Arsenios of Corfu (876–953), who apparently visited Epiros to plead with Slav pirates to desist their raids, recorded that Butrint was rich in fish and oysters, with a fertile hinterland. The inventories of bishoprics from the tenth to twelfth centuries identify the bishop of Butrint as a suffragan of the metropolitan bishopric of Naupaktos, the ecclesiastical province that took the name of the old provincial capital of Nikopolis in southern Epiros (Soustal 2004).

The Butrint Foundation project lasted from 1994 to 2010; it confronted the question of the changing nature of a Mediterranean port – in the shadow of Pirenne, Braudel and Horden and Purcell – not through the study of isolated monuments in the context of an established historical narrative, but by documenting and explaining generational changes in the material fabric of the city. Assessing Butrint's environmental context as well as the history of settlement in its hinterland was equally essential to comprehending its history (Bescoby 2013; Bowden and Hodges 2012). The Butrint Foundation programme was able to sample all parts of the ancient city and, therefore, both the presence and absence of relevant material, as well as its precise material character.

The first issue is the nature of continuity at Butrint. The early sixth-century town was a flourishing port with major secular and ecclesiastical monuments within and outside the defences. After 550, though, imported ceramics, especially from Tunisia, dried up and burials began to appear in many places within the city walls, interspersed with dumps of rubbish. The only building belonging to this moment was a small but well-built two-storey building erected in an angle formed by the city wall. This building, dated by a threshold deposit containing a coin of Justin II (565–78), suggests the presence of a type of building that was becoming increasingly common in the western Mediterranean, in which living accommodation was on the upper storey while the ground floor was used for livestock and storage (Bowden and Hodges 2011). This type of structure is a graphic indication of the ways in which lifestyles were changing in the Roman town by the end of the sixth century. By the early seventh century, activity at Butrint had diminished dramatically, with a solitary amphora burial area dating to around 650. In sum, this Adriatic Sea port virtually disappeared within the span of a generation or two following the construction of great monuments like the Great Basilica and Baptistery. No traces of a sack or plague or other cataclysm were found. Instead, the thriving port fell into decline and was largely deserted. Such is the quality of the archaeology that it merits reconsideration of the alleged continuity of other western Byzantine ports.

Butrint as a place, it now appears, was reduced to two (or more) towers in the lower city's landward (western) defences (Kamani 2011; 2013). Vivid remains of the ground and first floor of two towers were found, thanks to a fire that engulfed each around 800. In Tower 1, a wooden internal staircase, the two upper floors and the tiled roof collapsed downwards, crushing the stored contents just inside the ground-floor door (Kamani 2011; 2013) (Fig. 1.2). The contents included a crate of glass comprising sixty-one goblets and cullet – a consignment destined for a glass-maker somewhere. Next to this was a line of smashed amphorae from Otranto and other parts of southern Italy, as well as from the Aegean (possibly Crete) and the Crimea. White Ware jugs from Constantinople and, importantly, local calcite-tempered pots, so-called Avaro-Slavic types including two portable ovens (known as chafing dishes), made up the rest of the assemblage (Vroom 2012). Two cataclysms cannot have been coincidental and suggest that the towers were deliberately fired, presumably in an attack (Fig. 1.3).

Fig. 1.2 View of the restored western defences (Tower 1).
Courtesy of the Butrint Foundation

Fig. 1.3 Excavations in Tower 1, 2005.
Courtesy of the Butrint Foundation

Three key points arise from these contexts, approximately dated by carbon-14 samples. First, the local ceramics are distinctive and have only been found in small numbers elsewhere at Butrint. In other words, at most there was limited occupation of other extant Roman buildings in the old city; the town had been extensively abandoned. Second, the ground-floor contents of Tower 1, especially the consignment of glass and the varied range of imported ceramics, strongly suggest that this was the residence of a key official, probably the *archon*, and the tower or towers represented the first Middle Byzantine *kastron* at Butrint. If this is the case, it sheds a new light on Haldon's seminal definition of a *kastron* as the successor to a Roman city:

> the *kastron*, which retained the name of the ancient *polis*, provided a refuge in case of attack (although in many such cases it may not necessarily have been permanently occupied, still less permanently garrisoned); and that therefore many of the *poleis* of the 7th to 9th centuries survived

as such because their inhabitants, living effectively in distinct villages within the area delineated by the walls, saw themselves as belonging to the *polis* itself, rather than to a village. (Haldon 1999, 15–16)

If Butrint's towers were the new Butrint, its *kastron*, this resembled Theodore Laskaris' description of (thirteenth-century) 'mouseholes' (Whittow 2009, 136). The archaeology brings into focus the variation of settlement forms and, with these, new customs that characterised the Middle Byzantine empire. Third, the limited but varied material culture would indicate directed trade exclusively to the individual(s) in the tower (s) from other Byzantine places. In other words, bulk traffic of long-distance goods was absent at Butrint around 800. This is consistent with other Adriatic Sea central-places at this date, where maritime commercial encounters were limited, compared to either sixth-century Mediterranean bulk commerce (Hodges 2015a), or indeed later eighth-century North Sea commerce (Hodges 2012). However, it challenges the hypothesis that Venice was already a conduit for Mediterranean commerce, particularly for Abbasid silver, and a point of departure for slavers bound for the Levant (McCormick 2007). Any such commercial traffic emanating from Venice would surely have caused Butrint to expand to more than these unprepossessing residences.

Why the occupation was focused in the western defences as opposed to the acropolis remains a mystery. Perhaps these were the most habitable towers, or their occupants wished to have direct over control shipping passing through the Straits of Corfu? We can surmise, though, that Butrint as a place was reduced to little more than this administrative authority, perhaps a bishop and a few other families. The thousands of people in 500 had become a mere hundred or so by 800.

The destruction of the towers broadly coincides with descriptions of other raids and attacks on Byzantine settlements in these western provinces in the earlier ninth century, such as the Slavic attack on Patras in 805, described in the *Chronicle of Monemvasia* (Curta 2004, 535). The significance of these sources, though, is called into question by the next phase in the Butrint settlement sequence (Fig. 1.4). Excavations in the Roman suburb beyond the old city walls on the Vrina Plain brought to light the successor to the tower houses (Greenslade and Hodges 2013). Here, in the ruins of the sixth-century church described above, the aristocratic *oikos* (as termed by Magdalino 1984) of the ninth-century commander was discovered (Fig. 1.5). Post-holes found within the paved narthex of the fifth-century basilica show that its upper floor was reinforced to take a new

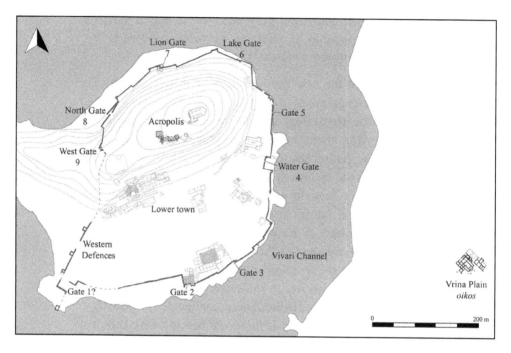

Fig. 1.4 Location of the aristocratic *oikos* on the Vrina Plain in relation to Butrint.
Courtesy of the Butrint Foundation

residence. With the post-holes fire-blasted through the paving stones, the primitive architecture of the house cannot be understated. No less fascinating are the contemporary conditions. Its ground floor, like the areas around the church, was covered in a thick layer of black earth in which forty-eight bronze *folles* spanning c.840–950 and a silver *miliaresion* of Leo VI (866–912) were found, as well as five Byzantine lead seals belonging to the same period (Fig. 1.6). These latter record five imperial officials and clearly suggest that the Vrina Plain site served a significant administrative purpose. A small mausoleum of fifth-century date off the north aisle now housed a single-flue pottery kiln. The church was now reduced to the old apse. Beyond this the nave of the earlier basilica became an inhumation cemetery from the mid-ninth century, graves puncturing the sixth-century mosaic pavement. A grave with a fine copper-alloy openwork ornamental buckle, closely paralleled by a buckle found at Palaiokastritsa on Corfu, dating to the late eighth century (Agallopoulou 1973), accompanied one adult. A secondary cemetery lay beyond the apse of the church. The ceramics, like the prolific coins, appear to distinguish the culture of this household from that found in the tower at Butrint. Amphorae of a

Fig. 1.5 Interpretive plan of the aristocratic *oikos* on the Vrina Plain. Courtesy of the Butrint Foundation

distinctive Otranto Type 1 constitute about 50 per cent of the pottery assemblage (Vroom 2012), while local kitchen wares almost certainly made at the site itself make up the rest.

The rudimentary first-floor dwelling with the associated high-status burials, occupying the Late Antique church, judging from the coins and seals, dates from the mid-ninth to the mid- to later tenth centuries. The coins and seals indicate the administrative role of this household. Several of the coins and seals were of Sicilian origin. The material culture shows significant trade in transport amphorae made at

Fig. 1.6 Five lead seals from the excavations on the Vrina Plain.
Courtesy of the Butrint Foundation

Otranto, presumably containing wine from the Salento region of southern Italy (and possibly Sicily), while the ornamental metal fittings and jewellery show connections to points in the south-west Balkans. Certainly, the material culture distinguishes the household from anything yet found in the large excavations in Butrint, including the towers described above. Within the wall circuit sherds of Otranto, Type 1 amphorae occur in most excavations, but as yet only one possible stone structure of this date has been identified (at the eastern end of the old Roman Forum). In addition, a bishop almost certainly managed the sixth-century Great Basilica, but his associated settlement has left no obvious archaeological traces from this era. In sum, the archaeology points to the existence of an undefended administrative central-place on the Vrina Plain with limited, perhaps periodic commercial activity, focused inside the old city walls. Butrint was growing as a place but was miniscule by comparison with the place between the Republican era and Late Antiquity.

The larger historical picture needs to be emphasised. First, the ninth-century successor settlement to the eighth-century *kastron* in the western defences almost certainly moved to an unfortified location. Like the similar residential unit outside the powerful Antique walls of Aegina (Pennas 2005), Butrint's 'new location' casts doubt upon the historical emphasis on raids in the ninth-century Byzantine texts. Instead, it appears to indicate a rejection of customs and memories directly associated with the walled city. Second, the coins and seals, as well as the imported pottery point to a significantly increased engagement in a trade network encompassing the western Balkans, southern Adriatic Sea and eastern Sicily. This commercial network on this evidence would appear to have started in the 830s or 840s and peaked in the later ninth century. This managed commerce using Byzantine state instruments, following the directed trade of the previous era, indicates new mercantile strategies from the 830s or 840s onwards. Butrint, we may surmise, was in receipt of wine and other material goods in exchange for its fish. On this evidence of an economic upturn, Venice, though not in any way represented in the archaeological finds, was surely now actively engaging with this western Byzantine trade network. Third, this new settlement, like the eighth-century one, made expedient use of pre-existing structures. If any architectural innovation existed, it was confined to the timber structures in the assemblage of buildings. Fourth, by contrast, the residence had a conspicuous wealth of material culture, courtesy of long-distance connections. The scarcity of such materials inside Butrint is striking. Like central-places in northern Europe at this time, it seems likely that the rich material culture was associated with an intense episode of conspicuous consumption of prestige goods, which was restricted to this category of elite site (Hodges 2012). Coins and fine metalwork, in other words, were absent in those households inside Butrint, and contemporary peasant sites have yet to be identified in the surveys of this hinterland, possibly, we may surmise, because of their material poverty.

In sum, for three centuries between the mid-seventh and mid-tenth centuries there was no exact urban continuity at Butrint. In this respect it resembled countless ancient towns in southern and northern Europe. Nevertheless, Butrint remained a central-place in the region of *Vagenetia* with ancient associations, conceivably reinforced by the presence of the Church. The manner of this continuity throws into relief the primitive character of the architecture and, by contrast, the agency of material goods in this economically underdeveloped society.

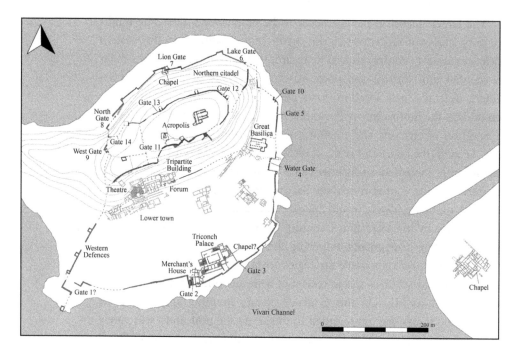

Fig. 1.7 Map of Butrint in the eleventh century.
Courtesy of the Butrint Foundation

Recognisable renewal of the town began in the later tenth century and involved significant, presumably planned investment in the early eleventh century (Hodges 2015b) (Fig. 1.7). Increased silting of the Vivari Channel leading to the Straits of Corfu meant that the waters became shallower and probably less accessible to deep draft boats. Effectively, by the tenth century the central-place on the Vrina Plain was situated in an increasingly marshy and inaccessible location, which may have contributed to its abandonment (Bescoby, Barclay and Andrews 2008). At the same time, with the strong resurgence of Byzantine political and economic power in the western provinces, Butrint and many other Adriatic Sea ports were transformed into powerful fortified settlements.

The numbers of later tenth- and early eleventh-century coins found in the walled town of Butrint have long since indicated that some significant change occurred at this time. The archaeology in the Triconch Palace area indicates two phases of activity. Beginning in the later tenth century, post-built structures were erected above the remains of the Roman buildings (Fig. 1.8). Large quantities of ceramics show a similar picture to that noted on the Vrina Plain (although persisting later in the Triconch area), with globular amphorae from the Salento and a limited number of locally made

Fig. 1.8 Tenth- to eleventh-century remains of a post-built structure (dwelling?) in the Triconch Palace excavations.
Courtesy of the Butrint Foundation

cooking wares. A second phase involved the creation of landfill or terracing across the old Triconch Palace area, raising the level here. The exact date of this second phase cannot be pinpointed except to within the span of the anonymous *folles* of Basil II (976–1025), which were associated with it.

A major initiative of the period spanning these two phases was the construction of new fortifications (described as Medieval 1 type walls). Powerfully built defences now encircled the acropolis, presumably enclosing a *kastron* at its west end, where a later castle was to be constructed. The authority of the new commander at Butrint can be ascertained from his impact upon the lower city. Much of the wall circuit encircling the lower town was refurbished by work-gangs at this date. The new walls made much use of *spolia* taken from collapsed monuments of Hellenistic and earlier Roman date, the stone having been worked into smaller sizes and laid in courses (Hodges 2015b). At the same time or soon after the walls were refurbished, the topography of the lower town was refashioned. Several terraces were now constructed on the slopes. A shallow terrace was made on the mid-slope of the acropolis; a deep terrace was constructed

Fig. 1.9 An eleventh-century property wall (part of the enclosure around the Great Basilica) closing off the north end of the Roman bridge at Butrint.
Courtesy of the Butrint Foundation

at the base of the acropolis slope; and a third terrace was made, raising the level of the ground up to the lower city walls. This earthmoving in the case of the lower two terraces was presumably intended to confront the seasonal rise in the water table. New terracing effectively buried most of the remains of the ancient town. Overlying the middle terrace the remains of a long, poorly constructed, block-built wall were found that must have served as a property boundary, just as a well-preserved wall of this kind now enclosed the Great Basilica (Fig. 1.9). In common with the stone *spolia* in the new fortifications, the blocks used in these property walls were worked and the chippings were found close by. In one surviving section, an anonymous *follis* of late Basil II (976–1025) was found embedded in its fabric. In excavations in the centre of the acropolis, a small enclosure formed of these distinctive blocks was uncovered. In this case, it may have surrounded a simple timber building in the outer area of the hilltop beyond the *kastron*.

In this second period, a short section of gravelled road was discovered leading from the channel gate into the town (Bowden and Hodges 2011). No other evidence of central planning existed. Moreover, the wall overlying, blocking entry to the old Roman road-bridge connecting Butrint to the Vrina Plain (and the preceding central-place), shows that this connection was both symbolically and effectively closed by this time.

Fig. 1.10 View of the eleventh-century stone dwellings on the terrace overlooking the remains of the Roman Forum.
Photo: David Hernandez

Various private dwellings have now been identified: a line of fine masonry buildings with large ground-floor rooms was erected on the mid-slope terrace (Fig. 1.10), whereas modest stone-built and post-built structures were found on the middle and lower terraces. In addition, several small churches were made within existing structures at this time, associated in the area of the Triconch Palace with an inhumation group demonstrated by DNA analysis to belong to the same family (Bowden and Hodges 2011).

This was not a densely occupied town, but it was certainly conceived of as an urban unit with a fortified administrative sector as well as a sector associated with the bishop's church and several private sectors separated by longitudinal property walls and each, in all probability, associated with a small private chapel around which the family were inhumed in simple stone-lined graves.

The material culture reveals patterns well known from the re-establishment of town life in north-west Europe at this time. Once again, coin finds are briefly prominent (as on the Vrina Plain in the mid- to later ninth century), until the urban economy had settled into an established pattern. Late tenth- to eleventh-century coins far outnumber later eleventh- and twelfth-century coins, just as they do at embryonic urban places as diverse as Oslo and York in broadly the same period. The loss of coins was of course connected to their value, which in turn was linked to state minting strategies. The ceramics hint at the underlying objectives behind any economic strategy implemented at Butrint. Immense quantities of Otranto 2 globular amphorae occur in the two phases that defined the making of the new town. The relationship with the Salento peninsula of south-east Italy was undoubtedly central to the new urban economy. The animal bone assemblage contains a surprisingly large amount of cattle remains, as though the Butrint merchants and fishermen were able to procure meat from far beyond the lagoon. The driving force behind the urban revival was almost certainly renewed interest in Butrint's fêted fishing grounds. Fish bones, however, were poorly preserved in most of the excavations, whereas, as has been noted already, mussel processing is a feature of the place. The excavated tenth- and eleventh-century data from the western defences indicates large-scale mussel processing. One possibility is that the rise in mussel processing occurred because these were employed as bait for fish. On the basis of the present evidence, the mussels were de-shelled and preserved for later use, salted or dried either in strong sunlight or over a low smoky fire, either for onsite consumption or for sale in a market which embraced, on ceramic evidence, the southern Adriatic Sea region (Hodges 2015b).

The archaeology raises key historical points about this strategically located port. First, it shows that the refurbished town was conceived and constructed to a plan, probably by gangs of workmen. The task of making the new fortifications, now especially formidable around the acropolis, stands in counterpoint to the earlier undefended settlement on the Vrina Plain. These walls merited careful construction using worked *spolia*, unlike the Early Byzantine and later Medieval walls constructed of rubble. Butrint was not alone in investing in its finely coursed walls. Similar construction of painstakingly reworked *spolia* exists at neighbouring new towns, for example at Rogoi near Arta (Fig. 1.11) to the south and at Himarë on the Albanian coast to the north (Veikou 2012). The same construction technique was employed to refurbish the north-facing side of the old Hellenistic frontier wall of Butrint known as the Dema wall. Like the Hexamilion wall at Isthmia, the renewed frontier 10 km north of Butrint was evidently designed to define the extent of the town's enclave, much as it was in the Ancient Greek era and again in the Venetian period (Hodges 2015b).

Fig. 1.11 A section of the eleventh-century fortifications of Rogoi, Epiros.
Photo: Richard Hodges

The defences clearly connoted a new urban ideology that historically distinguished Butrint from its ruralised circumstances since the mid-seventh century. Part of that ideology undoubtedly involved managing the interior of the settlement but, unlike the Roman colony, there was no obvious civic public space. Instead, there was massive landscaping of the lower city and then its subdivision into properties and sectors. Byzantine Butrint, it may be surmised, was fairly typical in adopting these telltale features of a new urban topography.

This urban process has also been viewed beside the transformation of Butrint's ecological niche and assessed in several systematic and other surveys over the past half century (Hodges *et al.* 2016). Judging from the survey data, the revival of Butrint as a port in the later fifth and sixth centuries was reflected in the short-term reoccupation of earlier Late Republican and Early Imperial points in its immediate hinterland. However, unlike the Julio-Claudian centuriated landscape attached by the road-bridge to the colony, the Late Antique settlement was concentrated in ecological niches, principally the corridor defined by the Pavlass River reaching back from Butrint to the high mountains. Thanks to the excavations at Diaporit and Malathrea, it is clear that certain earlier villas were briefly refurbished (Bowden and Përzhita 2004; Çondi 1984; Giorgi and Bogdani 2012, 252), but with the sudden decline of the port in the later sixth century, the evidence suggests Butrint's hinterland was largely abandoned. Certainly, the intense density of Late Antique sites found in Attic Greece, sometimes exceeding the survey numbers of Early Roman sites, is not found in this part of Epiros (Sanders 2004, 163–8). All the survey data indicates that, even with the substantial renewal of Butrint as a port in the later tenth and eleventh centuries, when a new castle, new city walls and new urban elements were constructed (Hodges 2015b), it was largely disengaged from its surrounding hinterland. The blocking of the Roman road-bridge connecting the town to its hinterland appears to symbolise this detachment. Minimal evidence of Medieval rural settlements was discovered in the surveys, although, of course, post-Classical settlements were probably small communities on hilltops like Mursi and Xarra – thus obfuscated by the later (that is, modern) villages – with small footprints characterised by either post-built or small rubble-built stone structures like those excavated in the Triconch Palace area of Butrint (Bowden and Hodges 2011, 119–44). It seems that Butrint's new occupants, as of the eleventh century, chose instead to employ a less intensive mix of food procurement dependent upon herding into the hills and cultivating gardens within the fortified town and its immediate vicinity.

Mouseholes and Memory

So, approached through the prism of Butrint's new history, was the Adriatic Sea a corrupting or unified or global sea in 500–1100? These data are only a beginning – in effect the discovery of a new chronicle – and there is a need for more analysed assemblages of archaeological and environmental information. This will be found in time.

Presently, the evidence shows that, during the period 500–1100, only for the first half of the sixth century and again in the eleventh century was it a unified region with a commercial reach to much of the Mediterranean and, indirectly, to the northern and Asian worlds. Two examples: just as Raqqa glass (from modern Syria) made it to the upper and lower Adriatic Sea region in the Justinianic period, so it was being marketed to the Tarim Desert and beyond to Edo; likewise, in the eleventh century Byzantine textiles found their way to London, presumably through Venice, just as north German coins found their way to Butrint (Hodges 2012, 118; 2015b). In both periods, towns defined themselves from their hinterlands with fortifications. In Late Antiquity, in the case of Butrint, its riverine corridor occupying the centre of its hinterland was systematically exploited; in the eleventh century, the exploitation of even this corridor was much reduced. In short, urbanism, as Harris contended in his challenge to Horden and Purcell's anthropogene model, played a variable social as well as an economic role. We may picture the sweeping gestures of Pirenne's hand on this point, as Braudel recalled from the lecture in Algiers in 1931.

However, two immediate observations. First, reduced to an issue of commerce, at first sight the Roman era imposed a gridiron on the Mediterranean, a genuine world system. The reach and impact of Rome, in terms of civic investment and centuriation was as profound at Butrint as in most other parts of the Adriatic Sea region. But it proved to be unsustainable, an aberration as opposed to a benchmark around which subsequent levels of investment oscillated.

Second, 'the dip', as Horden and Purcell refer to the changes in the seventh century, is English understatement. Much more acutely accurate is Brent Shaw's (2008) assessment that this marked the end of a Mediterranean world system, a great geopolitical shift. There followed a level of continuity of pre-Bronze Age dimensions focused by memory. Niche occupation, minimising risks and maximising connectivity, certainly survived. The Adriatic Sea communities may have belonged to Jonathan Shepard's (2008) Byzantine Commonwealth, but the scale and volume of this connectivity until the mid-ninth century was largely restricted to prestige goods exchange that played a role in tribal economics. In fact, it is the minimal scale by Levantine, Indian Ocean, Asian or even North Sea measures that is a marvel. However it is defined, the world of the Byzantine and Lombard Adriatic Sea, by Danish or Irish standards, was reduced to what the later chronicler Theodore Laskaris pejoratively called 'mouseholes' (Whittow 2009, 136). This is a metaphor for a polyfocal settlement without any essential civic characteristics (Hodges 2015a). The seventh- to eighth-century tower houses at Butrint were just such mouseholes, collections of residences without any urban matrix other than the memory of place binding them together. Did the same reduction of urban communities to mouseholes occur at Adriatic Sea places like Venice, Ravenna, Durrës, Corfu and Nikopolis? With regard to Ravenna, Enrico Cirelli has argued for a substantial eighth-century urban economy at Ravenna and Classe despite the presence of only one coin from Classe (Cirelli 2015, 110, fig. 7) and pottery that might as well be later seventh as opposed to eighth and later ninth to tenth century in date in the case of a pottery kiln (Cirelli 2015, 117). Chronology, as Braudel pointed out, is critical.

The material agents of change were Byzantine glassware and ceramics in the southern Adriatic region, paralleling, we might speculate, the material agency of the Lombard sculpture and Carolingian-style swords found in Croatia (Steuer 1987). The importance of object-agency, described by Alfred Gell (1998, 231–2) in the context of the Kula exchange system, cannot be understated when it comes to the aforementioned 'mouseholes'. Gell was fascinated by the primary intentionality of things with secondary processes that things possess. As in the Kula ring, a form of cognition existed where internal and outside transactions were fused together. Frankish swords in Baltic and Adriatic Sea contexts, for example, were surely semiotic media of representation that in some way were incentives to local tributary leaders to embark on social upheavals, their possession offering prestige and status of some kind. Mary Helms recently described this powerfully thus:

> succinctly stated, 'materialization' of observation and experience – the combining of the tangible and the material; 'bring[ing] a particular cast of mind out into the world of objects' became richer as social living developed from simple non-sedentary to the several sedentary lifestyles and from contextualization of the spatial or cosmographical axis alone to recognition and intellectual development of the temporal cosmological axis as well. (Helms 2004, 125)

Are not, then, the imported sculpture and swords in Croatia and the Byzantine glassware, both material sets with the first accompanying Italian globular amphorae, respectively indices of the same melding of speculative cosmological and commercial ventures occurring in the upper Adriatic regions? Do they belong in the upper Adriatic to the period following the treaty between the Franks and Venetians in 812, and a little later, in the 840s, in the lower Adriatic region after the Byzantines and Venetians reached an accord?

Certainly, at Butrint the 'mouseholes' were forsaken by the 830s and the 840s. Memory of place evidently mattered, but defence, it seems in the mid-ninth century, did not, as a new Butrint was created in the old suburb where, presumably, the conjunction of increasing trading partnerships could be paired with managing a niche lagoonal landscape. Administrative control and scale capture our attention. In a world of prestige goods exchange, mediated by weak tributary states, the emergence of periodic markets mattered (Hodges 2012). Bulk goods such as globular amphorae with their contents, for example Butrint fish, were now being exchanged as part of a larger Byzantine connectivity – networks – mediated by imperial seals and low value coinage. These networks, we now know, included renewed investment and productivity in Sicily (Molinari 2015; Vaccaro 2017) and Byzantine southern Italy (Noyé 2015). Yet, by any measure, the archaeology of Butrint and other places in this region shows that the central Mediterranean experienced limited economic growth in capacity by Asian, Arabic or even Baltic Sea standards at this time. In sum, the Mediterranean was not in any sense unified, but regionalised around networks, although there was the promise now of regularised economic connectivity. This was the context for the rise of the Islamic interventions in the later ninth century – commerce and conquest – in Sicily and southern Italy. Far from being an episode of wanton destruction by the 'Other', their interventions marked the first post-Classical competition for resources and control of maritime trading systems on the eve of a commercial take-off. By 1100 north African (that is, Islamic) polychrome plates were to be prominent indices of wealth and status in churches along the Tyrrhenian coast, as Byzantine Peloponnesian polychromes were status symbols on the façades of churches with access to the Adriatic seaways (D'Amico 2012).

Long after the burhs of Anglo-Saxon England and the towns of Ireland, Flanders and northern France were taking shape with prominent craft quarters, the Adriatic Sea ports such as Ravenna, Pescara and Otranto, judging from recent archaeological excavations, remained as polyfocal places rather than emerging towns (Hodges 2015a). To this list can surely be added older ports on the Balkan coast like Zadar and Durrës, while new Byzantine centres such as Stari Bar in Montenegro were yet to assume urban shape (Gelichi and Zagarčanin 2013).

The archaeology of renewed town life provides some measure of the next steps (Hodges 2015b). First, in the late tenth century, there was a new focal Butrint, once again within a defined fortified context, marked by the presence of lost (cheap) coinage, presumably to reflate commercial activity connoted by vast amounts of imported pottery. Second, in the 1010s and the 1020s, just as the Baltic towns were imitating those around the North Sea, Butrint was remodelled on an Augustan scale with a new civic centre (the acropolis castle), new defences, new internal landscaping, new urban dwellings and property boundaries and probably allotments. Around it an enclave was defined, while its landscape was effectively forsaken. The historical moment for investment here, as at neighbouring Epirote towns like Himarë and Rogoi (Fig. 1.11) and, conceivably, for Durrës and points further north and south, was renewed and focused Imperial Byzantine intervention in the southern Adriatic Sea (von Falkenhausen 2003). Did the church play any part in shaping this strategy in the tenth century? The archaeology at Butrint has yet to answer this. The excavated church at Shën Jan, located in the countryside between the ancient towns of Butrint and Phoinike, provides a rare (Balkan) measure of the substantial investment around the eleventh century in transforming a small nave church serving a rural constituency into an aisled basilica with appropriate decorated sculpture (Gilkes 2013, 151–3; Muçaj *et al.* 2004, 95) (Fig. 1.12). Did rural

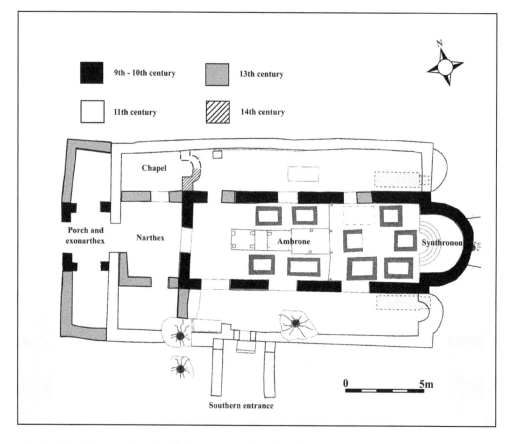

Fig. 1.12 An interpretative plan of the excavated church of Shën Jan, near Phoinike. Plan: Oliver Gilkes

investment in founding and aggrandising existing churches mirror the kind of urban proliferation of small family churches found at Butrint? This might help to explain the discovery, far to the north, of the later tenth-century (sunken) Byzantine vessel off Mljet with its cargo of acoustic wares –amphorae – derived from Aegean potteries (Negrelli 2017) suggesting that imported jars were procured by the church as it re-established itself as a key agent at earlier communities like Shën Jan as well as new ones. In sum, the archaeology as yet offers only a limited measure of this important episode, which was probably as ambitious in aspiration as Augustus's gridiron programming had been. These data provide a tentative step rather than a bound beyond the platter of simplistic models, denounced by Davis (2000).

This discovery begs answers to larger historical issues relating to the revival of regionalised connectivity in the Adriatic Sea region and its part in Mediterranean history. For instance, was this urban revival in the Ionian region in the early eleventh century the context in which bridges along the Via Egnatia were repaired (Amore *et al.* 2001, though see also Curta 2003, 287–8)? This might explain the making at its Adriatic Sea terminus of the dedicatory miniature chapel with wall mosaics inserted into the Trajanic amphitheatre at Durrës, which appears to celebrate investment largely unknown in the region for half a millennium (Bowes and Mitchell 2009). The chapel has been repeatedly attributed to the sixth century as a result of a stylistic analysis of its wall mosaics, but Bowes and Mitchell (2009) show on archaeological grounds that the chapel and mosaics should date to around the end of the first millennium. Were Rome and Constantinople being reconnected, as the impact of Arab trade in the Mediterranean forced Christian communities to prospect new connectivity by pursuing old routes?

But let us not lose sight of Braudel's image of the oscillation of Pirenne's hands. In Augustus' age the centuriation beyond Butrint reached deep into the folds of the mountains. Butrint was at a crossroads that, for several pioneering generations, connected the coastal littoral and the inland with the seaways. So far, the population from the tiny sample of Romans was healthy. Those after the seismic events of the fourth century were malnourished and suffering from degenerative diseases, almost certainly malaria. These diseases typified Butrint's Byzantine communities and surely many others in lagoons along the Adriatic Sea coastlines. The memory of Butrint's mythic Trojan origins may have mattered, but, in common with all these seaborne communities, their health determined the form and scale of their economies and lifeways.

My contention is simple. Adriatic Sea history after 500 has been peddled as one particular story, anchored inevitably around the great city of Venice and its imperial genesis. On this platter it is either corrupted, or unified and global! On the other hand, the measurements of this sea's Prehistoric and Roman antecedence were episodic but ultimately in the Augustan age aspired to form part of a larger unified Mediterranean community, becoming the cockpit of monotheistic religions. After the collapse of the Roman Mediterranean, much as Pirenne believed, there was a reversion to early Prehistoric networks and ultimately, by the eleventh century, aspirations of Iron Age proportion to be unified. In this incipient High Medieval iteration, though, it is the impact of the Indian Ocean, the awakening of the north African littoral and the rise of north-west Europe that triggered Mediterranean Christian leaders to invest. This observation would have surely puzzled Braudel as much as it would have thrilled him, to judge from his reaction to Pirenne's lecture.

I find myself, therefore, in agreement with Broodbank, eager to grasp a more complex, dynamic Mediterranean. This Mediterranean has to be shorn of nationalist manipulation, owing everything to greater chronological measurements – still echoing Braudel's mantra about chronological realities, wherein human ingenuity and creativity managed environmental change and the diseases this involved. The case for more archaeological measures of Adriatic Sea communities and especially their contexts has never been more compelling. We, the pivotal generation, can for the first time see through the beguiling Mediterranean mist of Braudel, past the models of Classical Antiquity, to grasp a Mediterranean, paraphrasing this master, of an ever-shifting kaleidoscope of webs of people and practices changing within and between places.

Acknowledgements

My thanks to the Butrint Foundation in partnership with the Packard Humanities Institute for making the research at Butrint possible. I am hugely indebted to Will Bowden, Kim Bowes, Oliver Gilkes, Simon Greenslade, Inge Lyse Hansen, David Hernandez, Solinda Kamani, Sarah Leppard, the late Matt Logue, John Mitchell, Nevila Molla, Paul Reynolds and Joanita Vroom, who together undertook and helped interpret the Butrint excavations.

References

Abulafia, D. (ed.) 2003. *The Mediterranean in History* (London).
— 2011. *The Great Sea* (Oxford).
Agallopoulou, O. 1973. 'Παλαιοκαστρίτσα', Αρχαιολογικον δελτιον 28, 423–4.
Amore, M.G., Bejko, L., Cerova, Y. and Gjipali, I. 2001. 'The Via Egnatia (Albania) project and the bridge at Topcias', *Journal of Roman Archaeology* 14, 381–9.
Bescoby, D. 2013. 'Landscape and environmental change: New perspectives', in Hansen, I.L., Hodges, R. and Leppard, S. (eds.), *Butrint 4: The Archaeology and Histories of an Ionian Town* (Oxford), 22–30.
Bescoby, D., Barclay, J. and Andrews, J. 2008. 'Saints and sinners: A tephrochronology for Late Antique landscape change in Epirus from the eruptive history of Lipari, Aeolian Islands', *Journal of Archaeological Science* 35, 2574–9.
Bowden, W. and Hodges, R. 2011. *Butrint 3: Excavations at the Triconch Palace* (Oxford).
— 2012. 'An "Ice Age settling on the Roman empire": Post-Roman Butrint between strategy and serendipity', in Christie, N. and Augenti, A. (eds.), *Urbes Extinctae: Archaeologies of Abandoned Classical Sites* (Aldershot), 207–42.
Bowden, W. and Mitchell, M. 2004. 'The Christian topography of Butrint', in Hodges, Bowden and Lako (eds.) 2004, 104–25.
Bowden, W. and Përzhita, L. 2004. 'Archaeology in the landscape of Roman Epirus: Preliminary report on the Diaporit excavations, 2002–3', *Journal of Roman Archaeology* 17, 413–33.
Braudel, F. 1972a. (trans. Reynolds, S.) *The Mediterranean and the Mediterranean World in the Age of Philip II* (London).
— 1972b. 'Personal testimony', *The Journal of Modern History* 44/4, 448–67.
Braudel, F. 1980. (trans. Matthews, S.) *On History* (Chicago).
Broodbank, C. 2013. *The Making of the Middle Sea* (London).
Bowes, K. and Mitchell, J. 2009. 'The main chapel of the Durres amphitheatre: Decoration and chronology', *Mélanges de l'École française de Rome. Antiquité* 121/2 (Rome), 571–97.
Cirelli, E. 2015. 'Material culture in Ravenna and its hinterland between the 8th and 10th century', in West-Harling, V. (ed.), *Three Empires, Three Cities: Identity, Material Culture and Legitimacy in Venice, Ravenna and Rome, 750–1000* (Turnhout), 101–32.
Çondi, Dh. 1984. 'Fortesa – vilë e Malathresë', *Iliria* 2, 131–52.
Curta, F. 2003. 'East central Europe', *Early Medieval Europe* 12/3, 283–91.
— 2004. 'Barbarians in Dark-Age Greece: Slavs or Avars?', in Stepanov, T. and Vachkova, V. (eds.), *Civitas divino-humana. In honorem annorem LX Georgii Bakalov* (Sofia), 513–50.

D'Amico, E. 2012. 'Byzantine finewares in Italy (10th to 14th centuries AD): Social and economic contexts in the Mediterranean world', in Gelichi, S. (ed.), *Atti del IX Congresso internazionale sulla ceramica medievale nel Mediterraneo, Venezia, Scuola grande dei Carmini, Auditorium Santa Margherita, 23–27 novembre 2009* (Florence), 473–9.

Davis, J. 2000. 'Warriors for the fatherland: National consciousness and archaeology in "barbarian" Epirus and "verdant" Ionia, 1912–22', *Journal of Mediterranean Archaeology* 13/1, 76–98.

Decker, M. 2016. *The Byzantine Dark Ages* (London).

Falkenhausen, V. von 2003. 'Between two empires: Southern Italy in the reign of Basil II', in Magdalino, P. (ed.), *Byzantium in the Year 1000* (Leiden), 135–60.

Gelichi, S. and Zagarčanin, M. (eds.) 2013. *Storie di una città: Stari Bar tra Antichità ed epoca moderna attraverso le ricerche archeologiche* (Florence).

Gell, A. 1998. *Art and Agency: An Anthropological Theory* (Oxford).

Gilkes, O. 2013. *Albania: An Archaeological Guide* (London).

Giorgi, E. and Bogdani, J. 2012. *Scavi di Phoinike serie monografica I: Il territorio di Phoinike in Caonia. Archeologia del paesaggio in Albania meridionale* (Bologna).

Greenslade, S. and Hodges, R. 2013. 'The aristocratic *oikos* on the Vrina Plain, Butrint, c. AD 830–1200', *Byzantine and Modern Greek Studies* 37/1, 1–19.

Grünbart, M. and Stathakopoulos, D. 2002. 'Sticks and stones: Byzantine material culture', *Byzantine and Modern Greek Studies* 26, 298–327.

Haldon, J. 1999. 'The idea of the town in the Byzantine empire', in Brogiolo, G.P. and Ward-Perkins, B. (eds.), *The Idea and Ideal of the Town between Late Antiquity and the Early Middle Ages* (Leiden), 25–58.

Harris, W.V. 2005. 'The Mediterranean and ancient history', in Harris, W.V. (ed.), *Rethinking the Mediterranean* (Oxford), 1–44.

Helms, M.W. 2004. 'Tangible materiality and cosmological others in the development of sedentism', in DeMarrais, E., Gosden, C. and Renfrew, C. (eds.), *Rethinking Materiality: The Engagement of Mind with the Material World* (Cambridge), 117–26.

Hodges, R. 2012. *Dark Age Economics: A New Audit* (London).

— 2013. 'Excavating away the "poison": The topographic history of Butrint, ancient *Buthrotum*', in Hansen, I.L., Hodges, R. and Leppard, S. (eds.), *Butrint 4: The Archaeology and Histories of an Ionian Town* (Oxford), 1–21.

— 2015a. 'The idea of the polyfocal "town"? Archaeology and the origins of medieval urbanism in Italy', in Gelichi, S. and Hodges, R. (eds.), *New Directions in European Medieval Archaeology: Spain and Italy Compared. Essays for Riccardo Francovich* (Turnhout), 267–84.

— 2015b. 'A "god-guarded" city? The "new" medieval town of Butrint', *Byzantine and Modern Greek Studies* 39/2, 191–218.

Hodges, R., Bowden, W. and Lako, K. (eds.) 2004. *Byzantine Butrint. Excavations and Surveys 1994–99* (Oxford).

Hodges, R., Carr, E., Sebastiani, A. and Vaccaro, E. 2016. 'Beyond Butrint: The "Mursi" survey, 2008', *Annual of the British School at Athens* 115, 269–97.

Horden, P. and Purcell, N. 2000. *The Corrupting Sea: A Study of Mediterranean History* (Oxford and Malden).

2005. 'Four years of corruption: A response to critics', in Harris, W.V. (ed.), *Rethinking the Mediterranean* (Oxford), 348–76.

Kamani, S. 2011. 'Butrint in the mid-Byzantine period: A new interpretation', *Byzantine and Modern Greek Studies* 35/2, 115–33.

2013. 'The Western Defenses', in Hansen, I.L., Hodges, R. and Leppard, S. (eds.), *Butrint 4: The Archaeology and Histories of an Ionian Town* (Oxford), 245–56.

Magdalino, P. 1984. 'The Byzantine aristocratic *oikos*', in Angold, M. (ed.), *The Byzantine Aristocracy IX to XII Centuries*, BAR International Series 221 (Oxford), 92–111.

Marino, J.A. 2011. 'Mediterranean studies and the remaking of pre-Modern Europe', *Journal of Early Modern History* 15, 385–412.

McCormick, M. 2001. *Origins of the European Economy: Communications and Commerce* AD *300–900* (Cambridge).

2007. 'Where do trading towns come from? Early medieval Venice and the northern *emporia*', in Henning, J. (ed.), *Post-Roman Towns, Trade and Settlement in Europe and Byzantium*, vol. 1, *The Heirs of the Roman West* (Berlin and New York), 41–68.

Molinari, A. 2015. '"Islamization" and the rural world: Sicily and al-Andalus. What kind of archaeology?' in Gelichi, S. and Hodges, R. (eds.), *New Directions in European Medieval Archaeology: Spain and Italy Compared. Essays for Riccardo Francovich* (Turnhout), 187–220.

Muçaj, S., Lako, K., Hobdari, E. and Vitaliotis, Y. 2004. 'Rezultatet e gërmimeve në bazilikën e Shën Janit, Delvinë (2001–2003)', *Candavia* 1, 93–123.

Negrelli, C. 2017. 'Le anfore medievali in Dalmazia: Una prospettiva mediterranea', in Gelichi, S. and Negrelli, C. (eds.), *Adriatico altomedievale (VI–XI secolo): Scambi, porti, produzioni* (Venice), 247–84.

Noyé, G. 2015. 'The still Byzantine Calabria: A case study', in Gelichi, S. and Hodges, R. (eds.), *New Directions in European Medieval Archaeology: Spain and Italy Compared. Essays for Riccardo Francovich* (Turnhout), 221–66.

Pennas, Ch. 2005. *Byzantine Aigina* (Athens).

Sanders, G.D.R. 2004. 'Problems in interpreting rural and urban settlement in southern Greece, AD 365–700', in Christie, N. (ed.), *Landscapes of Change: Rural Evolutions in Late Antiquity and the Early Middle Ages* (Aldershot), 163–94.

Shaw, B.D. 2008. 'After Rome: Transformations of the early Mediterranean world', *New Left Review* 51, 89–114.

Shepard, J. 2008. 'The Byzantine commonwealth 1000–1550', in Angold, M. (ed.), *The Cambridge History of Christianity*, vol. 5, *Eastern Christianity* (Cambridge), 1–52.

Soustal, P. 2004. 'The historical sources for Butrint in the Middle Ages', in Hodges, Bowden and Lako (eds.) 2004, 20–26.

Squatriti, P. 2002. 'Review article: Mohammed, the Early Medieval Mediterranean and Charlemagne', *Early Medieval Europe* 11/3, 263–79.

Steuer, H. 1987. 'Der Handel der Wikingerzeit zwischen Nord- und Westeuropa aufgrund archäologischer Zeugnisse', in Düwel, K. (ed.), *Untersuchungen zu Handel und Verkehr der vor- und frühgeschichtlichen Zeit in Mittel- und Nordeuropa* (Göttingen), 113–97.

Vaccaro, E. 2017. 'Philosofiana in central Italy in the late Roman and Byzantine periods: settlements and economy', in Mitchell, J., Moreland, J. and Leal, B. (eds.), *Encounters, Excavations and Argosies. Essays for Richard Hodges* (Oxford), 300–14.

Veikou, M. 2012. *Byzantine Epirus: A Topography of Transformation. Settlements of the Seventh–Twelfth Centuries in Southern Epirus and Aetoloacarnania, Greece*, The Medieval Mediterranean: Peoples, Economies and Cultures, 400–1500, vol. 95 (Leiden).

Vroom, J. 2012. 'Early Medieval pottery finds from recent excavations at Butrint, Albania', in Gelichi, S. (ed.), *Atti del IX Congresso internazionale sulla ceramica medievale nel Mediterraneo, Venezia, Scuola grande dei Carmini, Auditorium Santa Margherita, 23–27 novembre 2009* (Florence), 289–96.

Whittow, M. 2009. 'Early Medieval Byzantium and the end of the Ancient world', *Journal of Agrarian Change* 9/1, 134–53.

2 | Thinking of Linking

Pottery Connections, Southern Adriatic, Butrint and Beyond

JOANITA VROOM

With my title I do not necessarily mean the very early Beatles song 'Thinking of Linking' which the pre-Fab Four wrote in 1958 but never recorded. They did, however, play this song almost four decades later in 1994 during the reunion of the three surviving members of the band. Just like them, I aim to be thinking of linking here in a *longue durée* perspective. The main question of this study is how to think about the links between the Adriatic region and Byzantium from the perspective of Early Byzantine to Late Medieval ceramic finds. In other words: what can pottery tell us about the connections and relations between the Adriatic and the eastern Mediterranean from the seventh to fifteenth centuries? What does the archaeological record tell us? Are things changing through time and if so, what do these changes signify?

In order to answer these questions, I will discuss some initial results of my research on the distribution of ceramic trading goods found at Butrint in southern Albania in connection to sites in southern Italy, in the Adriatic Sea region and in the Aegean. By ceramic trading goods, I am mainly referring to imported amphorae and table wares. With regard to the pottery chronology, the Early Byzantine period stands for approximately the seventh to ninth centuries, designating everything before that time as Late Roman; the Middle Byzantine period refers roughly to the tenth through to the twelfth and early thirteenth centuries and the Late Byzantine period covers the time from the thirteenth to fifteenth centuries.

Butrint

To come immediately to my case study, I will first examine some features of the Byzantine pottery assemblage from the coastal city of Butrint in south-western Albania. Butrint is a multi-period site, located on a peninsula that is situated directly opposite the island of Corfu, occupying thus a strategic position in a southern Adriatic-Ionian connection. The site is situated 3 km inland from the Straits of Corfu and surrounded by the so-called Vivari Channel which links Lake Butrint to the Ionian Sea. As such, its location is near the narrow Straits of Otranto which is only 72 km wide and permits access from the Mediterranean to the enclosed water zone of the Adriatic Sea (Dorin 2012, 236).

Since 1994, large-scale excavations have been carried out on the peninsula and across from it in the Vrina Plain, on the other side of the Vivari Channel, by a British-Albanian team under the direction of Professor Richard Hodges and the Albanian Institute of Archaeology in Tirana (Bowden and Hodges 2011; 2012; Greenslade 2013; Hodges, Bowden and Lako 2004). Butrint was inhabited in various forms from Archaic times onwards with a peak in the Roman and Byzantine periods (Hansen and Hodges 2007; Hodges 2008; 2015). The most important standing architectural remains on the site, ranging in date from Ancient to post-Medieval times, can be seen on the map in Fig. 2.1.

During the years of excavation, thousands of Medieval and post-Medieval ceramic finds were recorded from various parts of the site. These include finds from the Well of Junia Rufina, the Baptistery, the Triconch Palace, the acropolis, the forum and the western defences

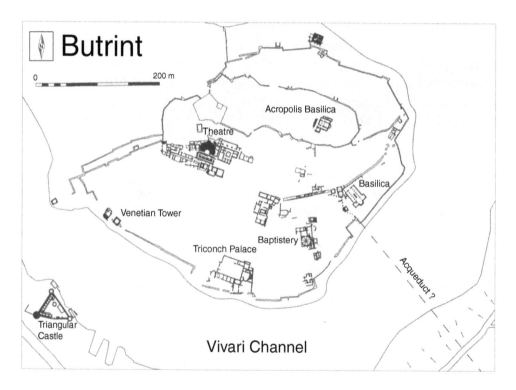

Fig. 2.1 Most important architectural remains at Butrint.
Courtesy of the Butrint Foundation

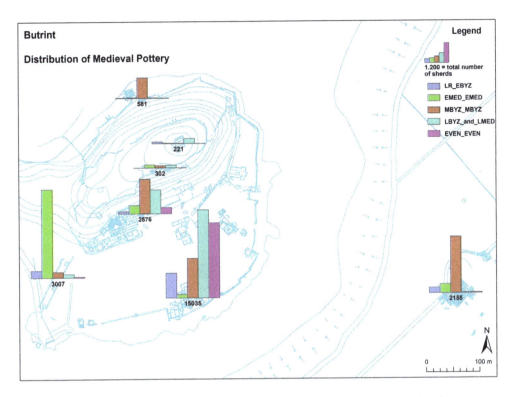

Fig. 2.2 Distribution of Medieval pottery finds in Butrint. LR_EBYZ = Late Roman and Early Byzantine; EMED = Early Medieval; MBYZ = Middle Byzantine; LBYZ_LMED = Late Byzantine and Late Medieval; EVEN = Early Venetian.
Graphs by Joanita Vroom. Map courtesy of the Butrint Foundation

(Hodges and Vroom 2007; Vroom 2004; 2006a; 2008; 2012a; 2012b; 2013a). I aim to study the spatial distribution of the proportions of different wares and different shapes on the site, based on the quantities found, in order to understand ceramic distribution and consumption within a settlement and between periods (Vroom 2013b, figs. 8, 9).

A distribution map in Fig. 2.2 shows the pottery finds per period in Butrint, ranging from Late Roman to Early Venetian times, that is, from the period between the fifth and sixth century to sixteenth. Such maps are not only useful for displaying the location of artefacts but can highlight where on the site pottery with different characteristics in terms of shape, chronology, function and provenance was found.

The first part of this study focuses on the Early Byzantine ceramic finds (c. seventh–ninth centuries) which specifically originate from just one part of Butrint: most of them were recovered at two rectangular towers in the so-called western defences (Fig. 2.3). The two towers (WD1 and WD2) are

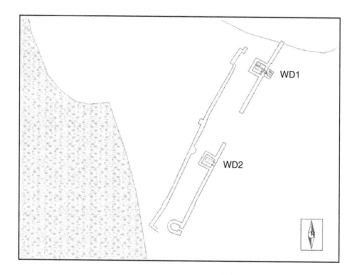

Fig. 2.3 Western defences in Butrint. WD1 and 2 = Towers 1 and 2. Courtesy of the Butrint Foundation

located on the western side of the site as part of the defensive wall that protected the lower part of the town.

Two Amphora Types from Butrint's Western Defences

The western defences comprise of a circuit wall which is 106 m long and can be dated to the late fifth century on the basis of the archaeological finds and their architecture. Somewhere between the seventh or eighth and early ninth centuries a fire (or various fires) seems to have started on the ground floor of both towers, causing the collapse of their upper floors and roofs (Hodges 2008, 64–9; Kamani 2011; 2013). All the material inside the towers was sealed by the collapse material, but the walls of the towers did not entirely collapse.

In Tower 1 we can distinguish, smashed beneath the debris of the burnt rafters and the roof tiles, a large collection of glass (including sixty-nine goblets, window glass and cullet, see Jennings 2010; Jennings and Stark 2013; Vroom 2012b), a metal mechanism for opening a trapdoor and a range of very broken Early Byzantine ceramics. The pottery finds from Tower 2 have now been dated by me to the seventh–eighth centuries and those from Tower 1 to the late eighth and early ninth centuries (Vroom 2012b; Vroom and Kondyli 2015, fig. 7).

The ceramic finds in both towers consist of amphorae, coarse wares, heavy utility vessels (such as large storage jars), plain and painted light

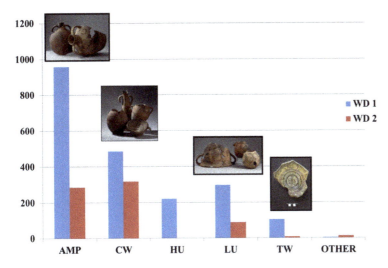

Fig. 2.4 Pottery types found in Towers 1 and 2 (WD1 and WD2) of the western defences of Butrint. AMP = amphorae; CW = coarse ware; HU = heavy utility ware; LU = light utility ware; TW = table ware; OTHER = other pottery types.
Graphs by Joanita Vroom. Images courtesy of the Butrint Foundation

utility vessels and table wares. The graph in Fig. 2.4 demonstrates that amphorae and coarse wares are dominant in both towers and in all four trenches, whereas table wares play hardly any role and are only represented by a few examples (Vroom and Kondyli 2015, figs. 7–9). The amphorae do not have the Butrint fabrics and, therefore, they are not local. The coarse vessels are almost all locally produced, because they are made of the gritty iron-rich fabrics typical of Butrint and fired in low temperatures. The wares of a light utility character include mainly plain and painted wares of calcareous porous fabrics, indicating that they were imports from southern Italy.

It is interesting to look at the provenance of the pottery finds of all periods in both towers. Apart from local products, imported vessels from southern and northern Italy, the eastern Mediterranean and Constantinople are present (Fig. 2.5). It is clear that the majority of pottery in Tower 1 originates from southern Italy, especially from the Salento region in Apulia, followed by locally produced wares. In the interior of Tower 2 the locally manufactured vessels seem to slightly dominate over imports.

I would like to examine in more detail two amphora types from the diverse group of imported amphorae found in Tower 1 of the western defences (Fig. 2.6). This tower yielded an amphora with a painted

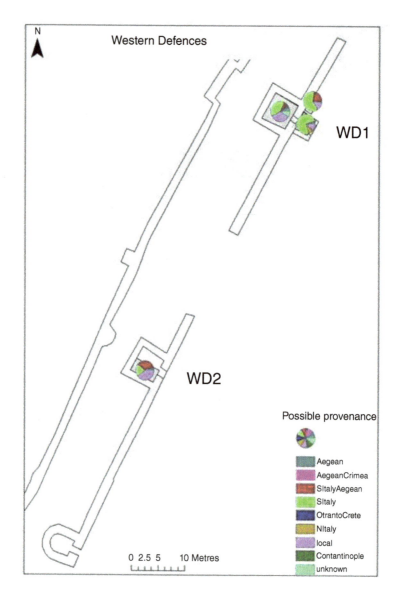

Fig. 2.5 Possible provenance of pottery finds in Towers 1 and 2 (WD1 and WD2) of the western defences of Butrint.
Ground plan courtesy of the Butrint Foundation

decoration of curly dotted stripes in a reddish-brown colour (Vroom 2012a, 374, fig. 18). In addition, we may notice a second amphora type with a short neck and a heavy everted rim, which is a derivative of a Late Roman Amphora 1 (LRA 1 *similis*) and therefore part of the so-called globular amphorae group (Vroom 2012a, 371–2, fig. 17).

Fig. 2.6 Reconstruction of Tower 1 in the western defences in Butrint. Top right: amphora with a painted decoration of curly dotted stripes in reddish brown. Below right: LRA 1 *similis* amphora with a short neck and heavy everted rim.
Courtesy of the Butrint Foundation. Drawing by W.R. Euverman

In an effort to better understand the possible function of Tower 1, an attempt has been made to reconstruct its interior just before the collapse (Fig. 2.6). Focusing on the position of the amphorae in this tower it is clear that these containers were concentrated in the southeast corner of the tower's ground floor. The number and variety of pottery found in the interior of the tower, as well as the predominance of household wares of a utilitarian nature, suggest that the tower was used as a dwelling in which the storage of goods, preparation of food and cooking were all taking place (Vroom and Kondyli 2015, 322–3, fig. 19).

The fabric, shape and painted decoration of the first amphora type from Tower 1 (Fig. 2.6, top right) show many similarities to painted amphorae or storage jars from southern Italy, especially the local products from the Mitello kiln site at Otranto, on the other side of the Adriatic (Imperiale 2004, fig. 3, nos. 3–4, *Tipo Mitello* 2–3; Patterson and Whitehouse 1992, fig. 6.8). Analogous-looking examples were found at other sites along the Adriatic Sea, on the Albanian coast and in the Salento region, for example at Apigliano, as well as in other parts of Italy: Basilicata, Calabria, Campania and the Crypta Balbi site at Rome (Arthur 1997, pl. VI, fig. 5, nos. 10–12; 1999a, 176, fig. 6, no. 4; 1999b, 18, fig. 10, no. 10; Arthur and Imperiale 2015, fig. 22; Paroli 1991, 109, fig. 5, nos. 5–6; Raimondo 2006, fig. 10, no. 8, fig. 12, nos. 5–6). Further south, such amphorae were recovered in eastern Sicily and at the site of Xatt il-Qwabar, Marsa, on the island of Malta (Arcifa 2010, fig. 17a, 17d; Bruno and Cutajar 2002, pl. 1, no. 2, pl. 2, no. 2; 2013, fig. 11).

The second amphora type from Butrint (Fig. 2.6, bottom right) seems to have parallels with similar-looking LRA 1 survivors found in the northern Adriatic Sea region, including Venice (the site of the former cinema San Marco), Torcello, Classe and Comacchio (Calaon, Gelichi and Negrelli 2009, 38, no. 1; Negrelli 2012, figs. 5, 8–9; Toniolo 2007, 102, pl. 5d; 2014, 318). They were also recovered more to the south, at an Early Byzantine shipwreck near Otranto, as well as the site of Tas-Silg on the island of Malta (Auriemma and Quiri 2007, 42–3, fig. 4, nos. 3–4; Bruno 2009, fig. 40, nos. 8–10; Bruno and Cutajar 2002, fig. 4; 2013, fig. 22). In addition, we can recognise comparable examples further to the east, for instance, at shipwrecks recovered at the Yenikapı excavations in Istanbul (the so-called YK 12 shipwreck) and Bozburun in western Turkey (Denker *et al.* 2013a, 204, no. 237; Hocker 1995, 12–14; Vroom 2012a, 371–2).

Evidence from Shipwrecks

An overview of Early to Middle Byzantine shipwrecks found in the eastern Mediterranean is presented in Fig. 2.7. The ninth-century Bozburun shipwreck (Fig. 2.7, no. 4) sunk off the south-west coast of Turkey, near Marmaris, and had contained a cargo of around 1,500–2,000 amphorae of small-sized globular and LRA 1 *similis* types (Hocker 1995; Hocker and Scafuri 1996, 5; Parker 1992, no. 111). The Bozburun containers were mainly carrying wine, although a few had contained olives and grapes (Hocker 1998a, 13–14; 1998b, 6, fig. 5). The amphorae were allocated by the excavators into four major classes (Hocker 1998b, 4–5, fig. 3). The majority of these, especially those known as Bozburun class 1, were not products from the Crimea as was assumed by the excavators, as I will argue below.

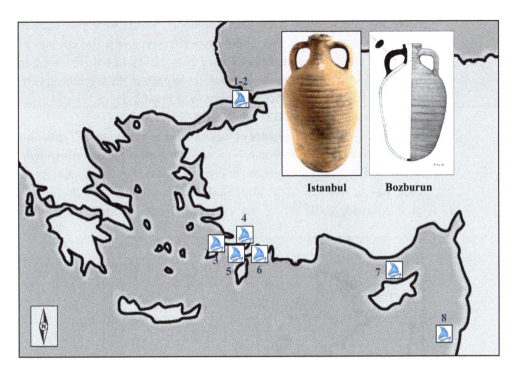

Fig. 2.7 Locations of Early and Middle Byzantine shipwrecks in the eastern Mediterranean: 1. YK 12, Istanbul; 2. YK 1, Istanbul; 3. Yassı Ada; 4. Bozburun; 5. Serçe Limanı; 6. Datça B; 7. Cape Andreas B; 8. Dor. Images: 'Bozburun class I amphora' from YK 12 (left) and from the Bozburun shipwreck (right). Drawn after Vroom 2016, fig. 1; images after Denker *et al.* 2013a, 204, no. 237

The Bozburun class 1 amphora was also recovered from one of the shipwrecks at the Yenikapı excavations in Istanbul (Fig. 2.7, no. 1), where at least thirty-seven buried shipwrecks from the late sixth and the early seventh to the tenth or eleventh centuries were discovered and fully excavated in Constantinople's harbour area (Denker *et al.* 2013a, 204, no. 237; Kocabaş and Özsait-Kosabaş 2013, fig. 3). This LRA 1 *similis* type was not only found in the so-called ninth-century Yenikapı 12 (YK 12) shipwreck in Istanbul, but also looks analogous to amphorae excavated at Cherson and other sites in the Crimea, those found at Sarkel on the left bank of the River Don, as well as those unearthed at Athens, Butrint and the Adriatic region (Romanchuk, Sazanov and Sedikova 1995, pl. 23, nos. 128–9; Sazanov 1997, fig. 2, nos. 23, 25).

In the past ten years, studies seem to extend the time span of certain amphora types of Late Roman times, which were previously dated to the seventh century also into the eighth and ninth centuries (Bonifay 2005; Negrelli 2007, 454–62; Reynolds 2003; Vroom 2007, 287–9; 2011b).

Especially the so-called LRA 2/13 amphorae, which were produced in various parts of the Mediterranean, appear to represent the tail end of the large Late Roman industries (Vroom 2014, 60–1). In Italy the break in imports of amphorae from the East did not happen in the seventh century, as is often supposed, and they continued to be imported until the end of the eighth century (Gelichi 2012, 228; Negrelli 2012, 396–409).

This is shown by the presence of various types of amphorae of Tyrrhenian and Eastern production in Rome, Naples, Sicily, southern and northern Italy, as well as Luni and San Antonino di Perti in Liguria (Fig. 2.8; see also Arcifa 2010, figs. 6, 10c; Ardizzone 2010, fig. 8; Auriemma and Quiri 2007, fig. 7, pl. 4; Murialdo 2001, 287–96, fig. 25.6, pls. 17–19; Vaccaro 2013, fig. 11).

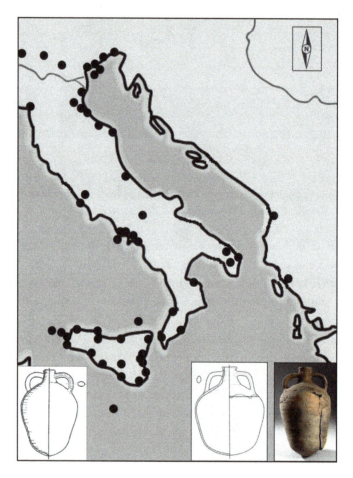

Fig. 2.8 Finds of Early Byzantine globular amphorae in Italy and the Adriatic. Left: Tyrrhenian production. Right: Eastern production. Drawn by Joanita Vroom; images courtesy of the Butrint Foundation and after Gelichi and Negrelli 2008, figs. 8–9

Excavations in the Adriatic Sea region, among which in Venice, Torcello, San Francesco del Deserto, Caorle, Ravenna, Classe, Comacchio, Ancona, the Pescara Valley, Otranto and Butrint, yielded further imports of seventh- to ninth-century amphorae from the Aegean (Augenti and Cirelli 2010, fig. 17; Auriemma and Quiri 2007, fig. 4; Cirelli 2009, fig. 4; Fozzati and Gobbo 2007, 113, fig. 68; Gelichi 2010, 153, 156; Gelichi and Negrelli 2008, figs. 11, 12; Negrelli 2007, figs. 21, 22; 2012, 396–409, figs. 5–10; Toniolo 2007, 98–102, pls. 4a–f, 5a–d; 2014, 318; Siena, Troiano and Verrocchio 1998, 695, fig. 24, nos. 13–14; Vroom 2012a, 370–4; 2012b, figs. 7, 8, 12). In addition, fragments of Early Medieval amphorae from the eastern Mediterranean were recognised at other sites in northern Italy, for example at Verona, Brescia and Milan in the Po Valley area, but also at Grado, Cervia and Rimini in the northern Adriatic arc (Bruno 2007, 162, fig. 16; Gelichi 2012, 228, n. 34, fig. 9.12; Negrelli 2012, 413).

In Fig. 2.9 we can distinguish some main types of these seventh- to ninth-century amphorae in the eastern Mediterranean and their production zones.

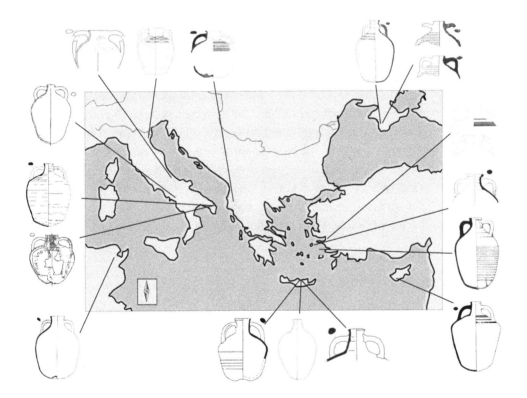

Fig. 2.9 Production zones of various types of 'globular amphorae' in the Mediterranean. Drawn after Vroom 2016, fig. 2

Here we are dealing with a very diverse group of amphorae with different shapes and fabrics, which we group under the term 'globular amphorae'. What these containers share is the fact that they were perfect for medium- and long-distance transport of liquids and were probably used for the distribution and consumption of wine or of oil. Some analysed fragments (Pecci 2009, 40) confirm the presence of wine or tartaric acid and oil – perhaps from olives. Sometimes these transport vessels also contain traces of resins.

Judging from the archaeological material, an intraregional or cabotage movement of small globular amphorae certainly existed among coastal traffic in the eastern Mediterranean during the seventh and eighth centuries (Vroom 2012a, 370–4). These smaller amphorae had less carrying capacity, but facilitated easy handling during short-, medium- and long-distance transport on various means of transfer and during loading and unloading in minor and less sophisticated coastal harbours, such as Butrint or Comacchio, perhaps by smaller-sized merchant ships of around 10–15 m like the ones from the Yenikapı excavations (Özsait-Kocabaş 2013, figs. 1, 10, 11; Pulak 2007, fig. 7; Pulak *et al.* 2013, table 1, figs. 7, 17).

As we have seen, the Early Byzantine amphorae from Butrint (type 2) were distributed to other sites in the Adriatic, for example Comacchio and Venice in the northern Adriatic arc. Furthermore, the type seems to have been imitated by amphorae manufactured at the Mitello kiln site at Otranto, the so-called *Tipo Mitello* 1 amphora (Imperiale 2004, fig. 3, no. 1). The exact provenance of this transport jar found in Butrint, Bozburun and Yenikapı is not yet known (the Crimea now seems dubious), although new evidence hints towards potential workshops of this type on islands in the eastern Aegean – especially on Lipsi, where four amphora kilns were recently excavated, and possibly on Samos (Fig. 2.9; see also Papavassiliou, Sarandini and Papanikolaou 2014, figs. 9a–b; Poulou-Papadimitriou and Nodarou 2007, 758, fig. 6, no. 13).

Glazed White Wares

Together with the amphorae, glazed table wares were also travelling from the East to the West. Apart from imported amphorae, the excavations at Butrint yielded fragments of Glazed White Ware I (Hodges and Vroom 2007, fig. 3.1; Vroom 2012a, fig. 3). The introduction in the Mediterranean of this lead-glazed pottery from Constantinople in the seventh century more clearly marks the ceramic transition from Late Antiquity to Early Byzantine times. Glazed White Ware I is not widely distributed; in fact, it is quite sparse in the western Mediterranean. Until now, it has been found in the Aegean, on Cyprus, in the Crimea and at Carthage in North Africa (Vroom 2014, 62–3; 2012a, fig. 2). Apart from Constantinople, it has mostly been recovered on the western and south-western coasts of Turkey and on a few sites more inland, in central Anatolia (Böhlendorf Arslan 2004, map 3; Hayes 1992, 15–18; Vroom 2006b, 164–5).

In addition, the distribution of Glazed White Ware I in the Adriatic region is very limited. Until now, I have distinguished a few pieces at the excavations in Butrint, among them a base fragment of an open vessel of utilitarian character – probably a mortar – from the Triconch Palace and pieces of a rim and stem from the Vrina Plain excavations (Vroom 2012a, fig. 3; 2013a, fig. 10; 2019a). Furthermore, a rim chafing dish fragment of a type between Glazed White Ware I and II was recovered at the Monastery of Sant'Ilario e Benedetto di Mira near the lagoon of Venice (Gelichi 2013, fig. 10).

The map in Fig. 2.10 shows the distribution of Glazed White Ware II in the southern Adriatic area: Vaccarizza and Cancarro, both located near Troia in the Foggia region, as well as Otranto, Quattro Macine, Previtero in the Salento region and in Butrint in southern Albania (D'Amico 2012, fig. 3; Vroom 2012a, 359–62, figs. 4–6). Glazed White Ware II is another type of lead-glazed pottery in a whitish kaolin fabric produced at Constantinople between the mid-ninth and twelfth centuries and it is more widely distributed than its predecessor (Hayes 1992, 18–29). Until now, Glazed White Ware II has been found on sites in the Aegean, Balkans, Turkey, Crimea, Albania, Italy and even in Sweden (D'Amico 2007, 220–6; Roslund 1997, fig. 16; Vroom 2014, 74–7).

If we look at a different part of the Byzantine world for comparative reasons, for example the coastal city of Ephesus in western Turkey, we can distinguish the distribution of Glazed White Wares in an urban centre, including fragments of both the Glazed White Ware I and II series and varying in date from the seventh to the eleventh centuries (Fig. 2.11). These imported Byzantine wares were concentrated to the southwest of the Ayasoluk Hill and near the harbour in the ancient site of Ephesus (Vroom 2019b). The spread of these imported wares from Constantinople over various parts of the site is more even than was previously expected.

Amphorae from Ganos

The distribution pattern of the Glazed White Wares in Ephesus can be associated with finds of imported amphorae (Fig. 2.12). Various fragments

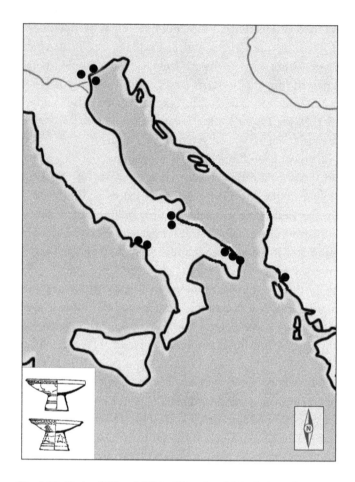

Fig. 2.10 Finds of Glazed White Ware I and II in Italy and the Adriatic.
Drawn after Vroom 2017, fig. 10.3; image after Peschlow 1977–78, figs. 9, 12

of a Middle Byzantine amphora type, the so-called Günsenin 1/Saraçhane 54 amphora from Ganos (modern Gaziköy) in western Turkey, were recovered in Ephesus (Vroom 2014, 94–5). The type was first recognised by the Turkish underwater archaeologist Nergis Günsenin (1989, 269–71, figs. 2–4) who systematically studied Byzantine amphora types in fifty Turkish museums since 1984. John Hayes (1992, 73–5, fig. 24, nos. 1–14) subsequently described the amphora as number 54 in his typology of amphorae for the Saraçhane publication. These small-sized amphorae have two heavy handles, piriform bodies and rounded bases. The pieces have a dull orange fabric (5 YR 7/4) with many voids and a creamy to light yellow orange slip (7.5 YR 8/3) on the exterior surface. They can, in general, be

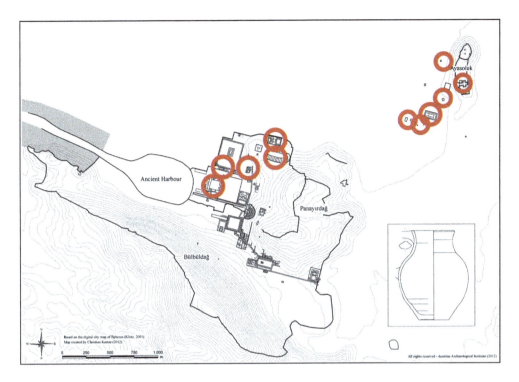

Fig. 2.11 Finds of Glazed White Wares in Ephesus.
© Austrian Archaeological Institute. Drawn by Christian Kürtze and Joanita Vroom; image after Ladstätter 2008, pl. 297, K 239

dated to the tenth-eleventh centuries, but may have circulated until the mid-twelfth century (Vroom 2014, 94–5).

The distribution map (Fig. 2.12) of this wine amphora type in Ephesus shows its appearance in the area south-west of the Ayasoluk Hill, as well as in various parts of the ancient city. Fragments have been recognised at St Mary's Church, the Byzantine Palace, the Stadium and Vedius gymnasium, the Embolos, St Luke's Grave and at the (newly discovered) Medieval harbour near Pamucak (Vroom 2019b).

The Günsenin 1/Saraçhane 54 amphora originated from the northern shore of the Sea of Marmara region, particularly the monastery of Ganos (modern Gaziköy). It was probably manufactured at Ganos as well as at additional production sites on Marmara Island, such as Saraylar and Topağac, since kilns and wasters of this amphora type were found at these places (Günsenin 1999, 19, 21–2; 2002, 127, notes 2 and 132; Günsenin and Hatcher 1997). The Günsenin 1/Saraçhane 54 amphora probably transported wine from Ganos which was an important monastic centre and pilgrimage site, as well as an area of wine production as is confirmed by

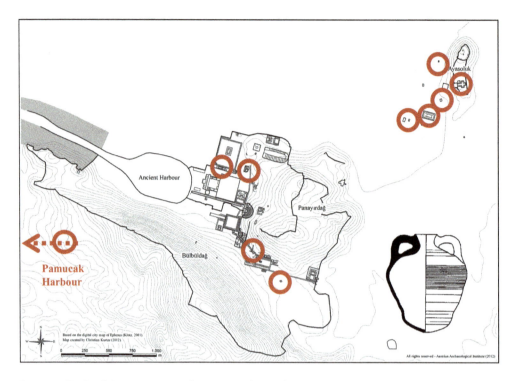

Fig. 2.12 Finds of Günsenin 1/Saraçhane 54 amphorae from Ganos in Ephesus.
© Austrian Archaeological Institute. Drawn by Christian Kürtze and Joanita Vroom; image after Vroom 2014, 94

Ottoman documents (Günsenin 1999, 18; 2009, 145). One of the mid-twelfth-century Prodromic poems remarks that among all the wines consumed in Constantinople, that from Mount Ganos in Thrace is good and is described as 'sweet' (Hesseling and Pernot 1910, 6–62, 3.273–301, 285–313). Byzantine monasteries produced both bulk commodities such as wine but also the ceramic containers (such as amphorae) necessary to transport them.

The amphorae were often incised with Greek graffiti and could be reused, showing that the recycling of Byzantine amphorae was a common practice in those times (van Doorninck 1989, 253–6, figs. 3, 4). Unserviceable Ganos amphorae were recycled and reused as filling material in vaults, as we may notice in the Mangana Palace in Constantinople, in the Church of St Sophia at Ohrid and in the western nave of the Church of St Sophia in Thessaloniki (Bakirtzis 2009, 697–702, figs. 1, 2; Demangel and Mamboury 1939, figs. 197, 198, nos. 4, 199 middle).

Some shipwrecks at the Yenikapı excavations in Istanbul still contained their cargo, often full with amphorae from Ganos, the YK 1 shipwreck in particular, displaying thus regional trade between the capital and the Sea of Marmara (Denker *et al.* 2013b). The role of Constantinople as a large consumer city and a regional and interregional distribution centre of Ganos wine is further shown by the thousands of Günsenin 1/Saraçhane 54 amphorae found at the Yenikapı harbour (Asal 2007, 180–9, figs. 3–6; Pulak 2007, 202–15, fig. 1). The ones from the YK 1 wreck are of the classical Günsenin 1/Saraçhane 54 amphora shape, covered with an exterior beige slip, of the tenth-eleventh century (Fig. 2.7), whereas the others from the YK 12 wreck appear to be ninth-century 'prototypes' with a slightly different body shape (Fig. 2.7), a more pronounced rim and a reddish self-slip cover (Denker *et al.* 2013a, 205–9, nos. 239–244, 246–254; Özsait-Kocabaş 2013, figs. 1, 2).

The map in Fig. 2.13 shows long-distance movements of the Günsenin I/Saraçhane 54 amphora. This popular wine container of the Byzantine empire was widely distributed over the Mediterranean and Europe. Examples have been identified in Egypt, the Near East, Turkey, Greece, Italy, the Balkans, the Black Sea region, Belarus and Armenia (Bjelajac

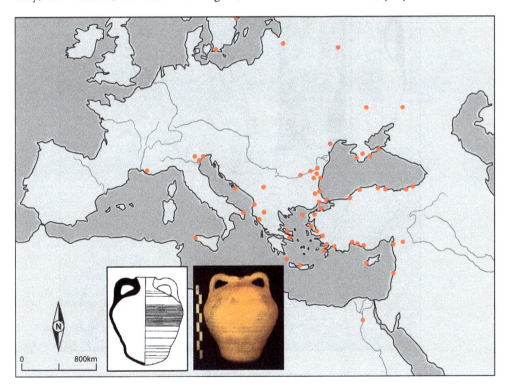

Fig. 2.13 Finds of Günsenin 1/Saraçhane 54 amphorae from Ganos in Europe. Map drawn by Joanita Vroom; images after Vroom 2014, 94

1989, 111–13, fig. 2; Garver 1993, 115–16; Günsenin 2009, 152; Hayes 1992, 75; Vroom 2014, 94–5). Fragments were even recovered as far away as northern Russia (Novgorod) and Sweden (Lund, Sigtuna) (Roslund 1997, figs. 20, 21; Volkov 2006, 146–50, figs. 9.1–3). In the Adriatic Sea region, for instance, this amphora type was found at Otranto, Fusina, Jesolo and near Cape Stoba on the island of Mljet (Arthur 1989, fig. 11; 1992, 207, fig. 7.3, no. 833; Brusić 1976, pl. 1, fig. 2; 2010, fig. 1, nos. 2–3: Toniolo 2007, 101–2, pl. 6a). Furthermore, the excavations in Butrint yielded some pieces of a Günsenin 1/Saraçhane 54 amphora, in particular at the Well of Junia Rufina in the north-eastern part of the fortifications on the peninsula (Vroom 2013a, 238, colour plates 12.2–3).

Günsenin 3 Amphorae

Another significant amphora type of the Middle Byzantine period (Fig. 2.14), which is frequently found as cargo on twelfth- and thirteenth-century

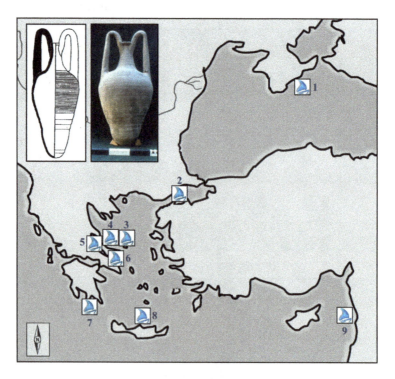

Fig. 2.14 Locations of shipwrecks transporting Günsenin 3/Saraçhane 61 amphorae in the eastern Mediterranean: 1. Novy Svet; 2. Çamaltı Burnu (1); 3. Sporades B; 4. Sporades C; 5. Pagasitikos Gulf; 6. Portolafia; 7. Tainaron; 8. Dhia B=C; 9. Tartus.
Map drawn by Joanita Vroom; images after Vroom 2014, 98; Vroom 2016, fig. 4

shipwrecks in the Mediterranean, has an elongated body shape and two heavy handles rising high above the rim (Günsenin 1989, 271–4, figs. 8–11; Hayes 1992, 76, fig. 26, nos. 10–11, pl. 13c). A characteristic feature is the closely set horizontal grooving which concentrates on the shoulder and covers the upper two-thirds of the vessel wall. The lower third, closer to the bottom, is either smooth or sporadically decorated with single grooves. The height of complete examples varies between 53 and 70 cm. The neck is narrow with an everted thickened rim. The walls are thick, up to 1 cm in section (Sanders 1993, 282, fig. 15).

About 5,000 vessels of this so-called Günsenin 3/Saraçhane 61 amphora were, for example, recovered at a wreck near Tartus (Tortosa) off the Syrian coast (Parker 1992, no. 1136). More examples come from wrecks found near Sudak in the Crimea, in the Sea of Marmara, north of Crete, on the Peloponnese, at the northern Sporades, south of Euboea island, as well as on eight wrecks recovered at the entrance of the Pagasitikos Gulf (Fig. 2.13; see also Günsenin 2001, 118, fig. 9; Parker 1992, no. 361, Dhia B=C, nos. 1110–11, Sporades B and C, no. 1128, Tainaron; Demesticha and Spondylis 2011, 37–8, nos. 1, 3–6, 8, 10–11; Koutsouflakis *et al.* 2012, 53–4, no. 5, fig. 20; Özdaş, Kızıldağ and Okan 2012; Waksman and Teslenko 2010). According to Nergis Günsenin (2001), the shipwreck at Çamaltı Burnu, near Marmaris, which contained a cargo of Günsenin 3 and 4 amphorae, symbolised the last phase of the Byzantine amphora trade.

These amphorae finds from various shipwrecks in the eastern Mediterranean definitely mark the main sea-lanes of ceramic trade from the western Aegean to Constantinople and the Black Sea region as well as to the Levant during the twelfth and thirteenth centuries (Fig. 2.14). The Günsenin 3/Saraçhane 61 amphora has been found throughout the eastern Mediterranean, extending from Italy in the west to Israel in the east, from Cyprus in the south and Novgorod in the north (Garver 1993, 115–16; Günsenin 1989, 271–4, fig. 1; 1990, fig. 16; Sanders 1993, 283). In Greece, the amphorae have been identified at Corinth, Ayios Stephanos, Athens, Chalkis, Marathon, Gytheion and Anthedon (Boeotia) and on the islands of Corfu, Kythera, Antikythera, Kea, Melos, Skyros and Zakynthos (Cherry, Davis and Mantzourani 1991, 354, figs. 18.2, 18.5; Günsenin 1990, 320; Hayes 1992, 76; Johnston, Slane and Vroom 2014, fig. 219e–f; Sanders 1993, 283; Schläger, Blackman and Schäfer 1968, 88, fig. 90; Vroom 2014, 97–9). In the Adriatic region, examples have been recognised at the ports of Hvar and Poreč, as well as at Otranto, Torcello, Venice and its lagoon (Arthur 1989, fig. 12; 1992, 207, fig. 7.3, no. 832; Brusić 2010, fig. 7, nos. 2–3; Toniolo 2007, 103 and pl. 6d). In fact, Günsenin 3/Saraçhane

61 amphorae have been recovered all over the Mediterranean and even up to Russia and Sweden (Vroom 2014, 97–9).

During the Saranda Kolones excavation on Cyprus this type of amphora was found in pre-1222 earthquake destruction layers (Megaw 1972, 322–43, fig. 27; von Wartburg 2001). A date in the later part of the twelfth century and the first quarter of the thirteenth century seems probable. Furthermore, at the excavations in the towns of Lund and Sigtuna in Sweden, several pieces of this amphora type have been found and dated to the twelfth–thirteenth centuries or, more precisely, to the first quarter and the first third of the thirteenth century (Roslund 1997, 273–4, fig. 21.3). This type was perhaps used until amphorae disappeared completely during the fourteenth century and were replaced by wooden barrels.

It has been suggested that the Günsenin 3/Saraçhane 61 amphora was manufactured for the specific purpose of shipping honey or even as a beehive (Cherry, Davis and Mantzourani 1991, 356–7; Hayes 1992, 76). This may have been the case, but amphorae were often multi-functional: they could easily have been used for the transport of all sorts of liquids or goods and were at the same time suitable for every conceivable purpose, including food preparation or storage.

Looking at Günsenin's distribution map (Fig. 2.13), a place of manufacture on the northern coast of Turkey is probable, although Hayes argued for a production centre in Central Greece, such as Boeotia or perhaps Athens (Cherry, Davis and Mantzourani 1991, 354–5; Sanders 1993, 283, n. 49). Its place of manufacture is indeed more plausibly an important harbour in the western Aegean, such as the Boeotian city of Chalkis (Medieval Negroponte), connecting the island of Euboea with the mainland (Vroom 2003, 245–6). Here, evidence of production of Günsenin 3/Saraçhane 61 amphorae has been detected at recent excavations outside the city's fortification walls, among which I observed wasters and firing equipment for amphora production. This also explains the impressive regional spread of this amphora type on various rural sites in the Boeotian hinterland of Chalkis, which was rich in the production of wine, wheat, oil and honey (Vroom 2003, 153–7, figs. 6.7, 6.41).

Distribution of Glazed Table Wares

From the twelfth century onwards ships started to carry glazed table wares as principal cargoes, or as composite cargoes in combination with other goods (Fig. 2.15). The discovery of several shipwrecks with cargoes of Middle Byzantine glazed table wares were of importance, especially the

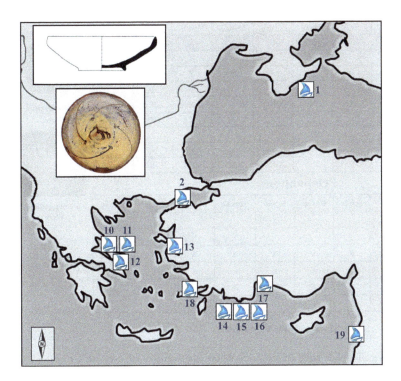

Fig. 2.15 Locations of shipwrecks transporting twelfth- to fourteenth-century glazed table wares in the eastern Mediterranean: 1. Novy Svet; 2. Çamaltı Burnu (1); 10. Skopelos; 11. Pelagonissos; 12. Kavalliani; 13. Izmir; 14. Kastellorizo; 15. Kumluca; 16. Göçük Burnu; 17. Antalya; 18. Tavşan adası; 19. Tyre.
Map drawn by Joanita Vroom; images after Papanikola-Bakirtzi 1999, 147, no. 168

ones recovered near Alonnesos in the northern Sporades and between Kastellorizo and Rhodes in the Dodecanese (Kritzas 1971, 176–85; Papanikola-Bakirtzi 1999, 118–57; Parker 1992, nos. 538, 796). More shipwrecks found in coastal waters near Skopelos, Kavalliani, Izmir, Kumluca and Antalya contained similar late twelfth- and early thirteenth-century glazed table wares, although there is sometimes still limited information about these wrecks and their cargoes (Armstrong 1991; Dimopoulos 2009, 179–81; Döger 2007, 52; Koutsouflakis *et al.* 2012, 58, no. 11, fig. 24; Papanikola-Bakirtzi 1999, 81, notes 119, 84, no. 160; Parker 1992, no. 1099, Skopelos; Stern 2012, vol. 2, table 8.1).

Apart from sea transport, I would like to draw attention to the distribution of these table wares over land. Research carried out on the Peloponnese and on mainland Greece is used as a case study to exemplify the general ceramic trends in this period, as these regions are situated near to the southern Adriatic (Vroom 2011a). Fig. 2.16 shows the distribution of glazed fine wares which were probably locally produced on the

Peloponnese

LOCAL	Meas.	Fi.S.	Inc.S.	Cham.	L.Slip	Mon.G.	Mon.S.	Pol.S.	Zeu.V.
Corinth	X	X	X	X	X	X	X	X	X
Isthmia	X		X		X		X	X	
Argos	X	X	X	X	X	X	X		
Andravida						X			
Berbati-L.			X	X	X		X	X	
Sparta	X	X	X	X	X	X	X	X	X
Mystras		X	X	X	X				
Lakonia		X	X	X	X	X	X	X	X
Kythera		X	X		X	X	X	X	

Incised Sgraffito Ware

Late Slip-painted Ware

North-western Greece

LOCAL	Meas.	Fi.S.	Inc.S.	Cham.	L.Slip	Mon.G.	Mon.S.	Pol.S.	Zeu.V.
Arta		X			X				
Aetolia		X	X			X	X		
Boeotia		X	X	X	X	X	X	X	X
Thebes		X	X	X	X		X	X	X
Athens	X	X	X	X		X	X	X	X
Butrint	X	X	X			X	X		

Fine Sgraffito Ware

Fig. 2.16 Distribution of locally made table wares in the Peloponnese and north-western Greece. Graphs by Joanita Vroom; images after Vroom 2014, 84, 90, 124

Peloponnese and/or in central Greece (Vroom 2014, 80–93; Waksman and von Wartburg 2006). The tables are based on published pottery assemblages from urban sites, such as Corinth, Isthmia and Argos, and from surveys in both areas, for example at Berbati-Limnes near Mycenae, in Lakonia, Aetolia and Boeotia, and include nine types of locally/regionally manufactured table wares dated between the mid-twelfth and mid-fifteenth centuries (Vroom 2011a, tables 1a–b, notes 8–9).

The most common locally produced Byzantine table wares on the Peloponnese are Incised Sgraffito Ware and late Slip-Painted Ware (Fig. 2.16). In north-western Greece, on the other hand, Fine Sgraffito Ware is most common (Fig. 2.16). In general, all wares shown here seem to be fairly well represented and well distributed in both areas. The Peloponnese, Corinth in the north and Sparta in the south have the largest representation of locally made table wares (Fig. 2.16). In Italy, glazed table wares from Byzantine production centres on mainland Greece are mostly recovered in cities along the Adriatic coast, such as Venice, Jesolo, Genoa, Pisa, Naples, Siponto, Trani, Bari, Egnazia, Brindisi and Otranto, but also present as vessels (*bacini*) embedded on façades of Italian churches (Favia 2007, figs. 3–7, 10; Vroom 2014, 80–93).

IMPORT	Ser	The	Zeu	M.G.	PM	RMR	Pai	Met	Rou	Ar.Ma.	Graf	Isl	S.Lu
Corinth	X	X	X	X	X	X	X	X	X	X	X	X	
Isthmia		X	X	X	X	X	X				X		X
Argos	X				X	?		X		X			
Andravida					X								
Berbati-L.										X			
Sparta		X			X	X				X		X	
Mystras			X										
Lakonia										X		X	
Kythera					X								

Peloponnese

Proto-Maiolica

RMR Ware

IMPORT	Ser	The	Zeu	El.In.	PM	RMR	Pai	Met	Rou	Ar.Ma	Graf	Isl	S.Lu
Arta		X			X	X			X				
Aetolia						X	X						
Boeotia		X				X					X		
Thebes			X		X						X		
Athens				X					X		X		
Butrint			X	X	X	X	X	X	X	X	X		X

North-western Greece

Archaic Maiolica

Fig. 2.17 Distribution of imported table wares in the Peloponnese and north-western Greece. Graphs by Joanita Vroom; images after Vroom 2014, 126, 128; Bakourou, Katsara and Kalamara 2003, fig. 5

The maps in Fig. 2.17 tell a different story by showing the distribution of imported table wares in the Peloponnese and north-western Greece. These include three types of imported glazed wares from other production centres in the Byzantine world (such as ceramics from Serres and Thessaloniki), but also five types of imported wares from southern Italy, three from northern Italy, one from the Near East and, finally, one from the Valencia region in Spain (Vroom 2011a, tables 2a–b, notes 8–9).

As can be observed, the imported wares are not evenly distributed in both areas. The largest amounts of imported wares on the Peloponnese can be found in Corinth and Isthmia, with Sparta in the modest third place. The most frequently imported wares in both areas include Proto-Maiolica and the so-called RMR Ware from southern Italy (Vroom 2014, 126–9). This last ware is named after the Italian term *rosso, manganese* and *ramina*, the three colours used in this type of painted pottery (Whitehouse 1980, 82–3).

A network analysis, carried out by Johannes Preiser-Kapeller based on this pottery data, allows us to quantify and map the different densities and geographies of sites within the ceramic distribution on the Peloponnese, showing imports of ceramics along interregional and long-distance trade systems linked to Peloponnesian sites (Fig. 2.18a). It clearly indicates an active distribution system of pottery moving from Italy along the Adriatic

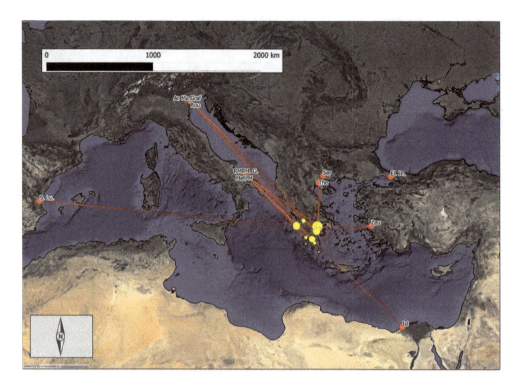

Fig. 2.18 Network analysis of ceramic finds at Peloponnesian sites transported by sea and land: (a) interregional and long-distance trade systems (red dots and lines) linked to Peloponnesian sites (yellow nodes); (b) transport of locally produced table wares (green) and imported table wares (red) over land. Drawn by J. Preiser-Kapeller after Vroom 2011a

Sea to the Peloponnese. Furthermore, we know from excavated contexts at Corinth that the majority of glazed ceramic imports was Italian in origin, and that at least 45 per cent of the Italian imports in thirteenth- and fourteenth-century Corinth came from the Salento region in southern Apulia and in particular from the port town of Brindisi (Sanders 2002, 652, n. 20; Vroom 2011a, 416, figs. 10, 11, table 6).

These imports can perhaps be related to political and commercial relations. In fact, the distribution of table wares from southern Italy to other parts of the Mediterranean often coincides with the political aspirations of the Angevin Dynasty in the east through the mediation of the Venetian fleet along the Adriatic and Ionian coasts (Vroom 2011a, 418–19). This is, for instance, the case in Corinth where large amounts of pottery from Apulia (mostly Proto-Maiolica and RMR Ware) were imported in the late thirteenth century, especially after a marital alliance between the Angevin and Villehardouin dynasties with the marriage of Isabelle de Villehardouin to the son of Charles I, Philip of Anjou, in 1271 (Sanders 2002, 652, n. 20; Vroom 2011a, 416).

The two distribution maps in Fig. 2.19 show the two largest groups of Italian imports, Proto-Maiolica and RMR Ware, to the Peloponnese and north-western Greece. These maps indicate that the Peloponnese was open to western imports from southern Italy from the second half of the thirteenth century onwards. Nevertheless, other parts of Greece received these imports as well, among them Arta and Aetolia under the despotate of Epiros and Venetian-held territories such as Kythera and other Aegean islands.

Until now, Proto-Maiolica, as a high-quality ware with bright painted colours and tin-glazed surface, seems to have been found mostly in urban sites, for example at castles (Chlemoutzi, Tripi and Glarentza) and as *bacini* on the façades of Byzantine churches such as those at Merbaka and Gastouni (Athanasoulis 2003, 63–78; 2005, 44–9; Megaw 1964; 1931–2, 126; Sanders 1989, 189–99; Skartsis 2012, fig. 1; Vroom 2011a, 418, n. 21). Fragments of RMR Ware, as the cheaper variant of Proto-Maiolica with duller painted colours and a lead-glazed surface, have also been found on rural settlements in surveyed areas in north-western Greece, especially in Aetolia and Boeotia (Vroom 2003, 167–9, figs. 6.32, 6.43, W22.1–2; 2011a, table 7).

The network analysis, realised by Preiser-Kapeller based on ceramic data which I collected clearly shows notable differences in the Peloponnese between the transport of locally produced table wares and imported table wares over land (Fig. 2.18b). We see an obvious axis from the north-west to the north-east for the imports and from the north-east to the south-east for the locally made glazed ceramics, indicating overland mechanisms of trade

IMPORT	PM	RMR
Corinth	X	X
Isthmia	X	X
Argos	X	?
Andravida	X	
Berbati-L.		
Sparta	X	X
Mystras		
Lakonia		
Kythera		X
Glarentza	X	
Chlemoutzi	X	

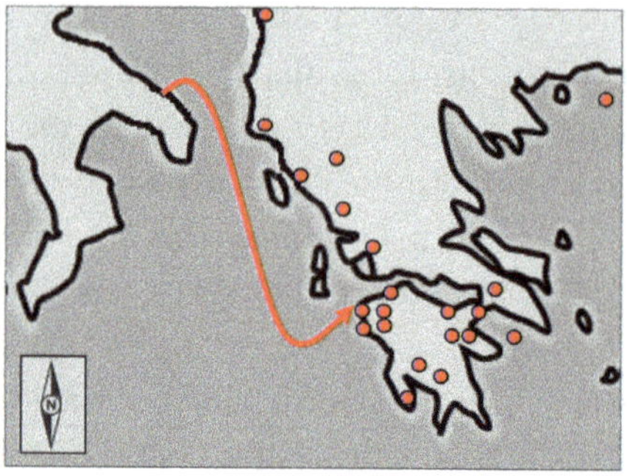

IMPORT	PM	RMR
Arta	X	X
Aetolia		X
Boeotia		X
Thebes	X	
Athens		
Butrint	X	X

PROTO-MAIOLICA

'RMR' WARE

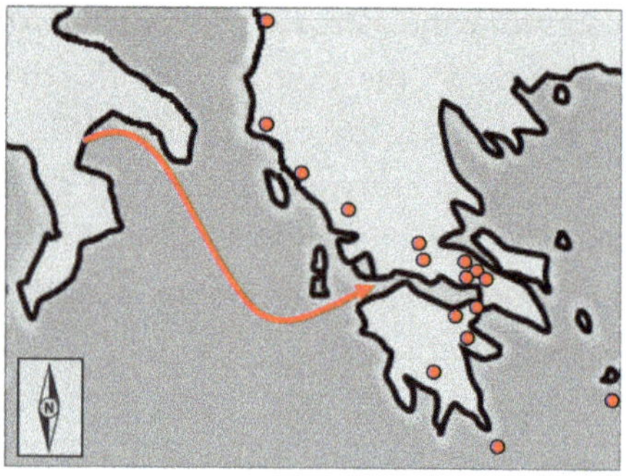

Fig. 2.19 Distribution of imported table wares from southern Italy in the Peloponnese and north-western Greece.
Maps and graphs by Joanita Vroom; images after Vroom 2014, 126, 128; Vroom 2017, fig. 13.4

in this part of the Mediterranean. As we have seen before, this intra-Peloponnesian distribution system over land was connected to broader ceramic transportations by sea (Fig. 2.18a).

Conclusion

Based on the ceramic finds from Butrint we can distinguish some primary distribution patterns of imported wares in this nodal point of the southern Adriatic from Early Byzantine to Late Medieval times and even into the Early Venetian era, ranging from around the seventh to sixteenth centuries. We may notice a continuous growth and expansion of imports in Butrint during the Early Byzantine and Middle Byzantine periods. From Late Antiquity onwards, medium- and long-distance cabotage or tramping voyages on smaller, low-status ships, such as the ones found at the Yenikapı excavations in Istanbul, must have been quite prevalent in the eastern Mediterranean, in particular along the eastern Aegean coast, and in the Adriatic Sea.

Then, in the Late Medieval period (after 1204) we may notice a sudden change of orientation towards the West, as if Butrint was no longer part of the Byzantine world. This change seems to be related to political changes in that period, when Butrint was annexed by Charles I of Anjou who was king of Naples, prince of Achaia and the successor to the kingdom of Sicily in 1270 while a century later, in 1386, it was purchased by the Republic of Venice. It is clear that the end of the Byzantine influence in this part of the Mediterranean took place after 1204, when Greece became divided into several states – and this fragmentation is shown in the archaeology of Butrint.

All in all, we are now able to distinguish during the periods under discussion distinct systems of Byzantine pottery imports, the orientation of which clearly shifts over time as a result of the shifting balance of power in the region. Of course, these networks remained subgroups of the one overarching, umbrella Byzantine trade network. The shifting circles shown in Fig. 2.20 are, of course, a mere schematic visual impression of

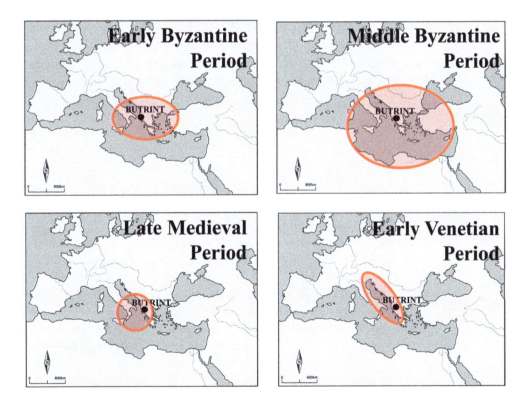

Fig. 2.20 Ceramic distribution system of Butrint from Early Byzantine to Early Venetian times. Maps drawn by Joanita Vroom

trade or commercial networks of ceramics in Byzantine and later times. But they do reflect the spatial provenance of the pottery imports in Butrint known until now. These circles raise tantalising questions and suggest exciting answers. Nevertheless, I would like to emphasise that there are no easy answers in archaeology, and certainly not in our field of research with respect to Byzantine exchange patterns where pottery is often telling its own story.

Acknowledgements

I would like to thank the Butrint Foundation in London, the Albanian Institute of Archaeology in Tirana and especially Professor Richard Hodges, the current director of the American University of Rome, for allowing me to study and publish the finds from Butrint. All colleagues and excavators working at the excavations of Butrint, in particular Simon Greenslade, Sarah Leppard, Pagona Papadopoulou and Paul Reynolds, are much thanked for their co-operation. I am also thankful to Dr Johannes Preiser-Kapeller for the use of Fig. 18a and to Harmen Huigens and Fotini Kondyli for their help with the making of Figs. 10.2, 10.4 and 10.5. Finally, I am much indebted to the Packard Humanities Institute (USA) and the Netherlands Organisation of Scientific Research (NWO) for their financial support of my research on several sites in the Mediterranean, such as Butrint, Athens and Ephesus.

References

Arcifa L. 2010. 'Nuove ipotesi a partire dalla rilettura dei dati archeologici: La Sicilia orientale', in Nef, A. and Prigent, V. (eds.), *La Sicile de Byzance à l'Islam* (Paris), 15–49.

Ardizzone, F. 2010. 'Nuove ipotesi a partire dalla rilettura dei dati archeologici: La Sicilia occidentale', in Nef, A. and Prigent, V. (eds.), *La Sicile de Byzance à l'Islam* (Paris), 51–76.

Armstrong, P. 1991. 'A group of Byzantine bowls from Skopelos', *Oxford Journal of Archaeology* 10/3, 335–47.

Arthur, P. 1989. 'Aspects of Byzantine economy: An evaluation of amphora evidence from Italy', in Déroche, V. and Spieser, J.-M. (eds.), *Recherches sur la céramique byzantine*, Bulletin de correspondance hellénique: Supplément 18 (Athens and Paris), 79–93.

1992. 'Amphorae for bulk transport', in D'Andria, F. and Whitehouse, D. (eds.), *Excavations at Otranto*, vol. 2, *The Finds* (Lecce), 197–217.

1997. 'Un saggio di scavo in prop. Previtero (1995) e la cronologia di ceramiche di età bizantina ad Otranto', *Studi di Antichità* 10, 199–224.

1999a. '*Grubenhauser* nella Puglia bizantina: A proposito di recenti scavi a Supersano (LE)', *Archeologia medievale* 26, 171–7.

1999b. 'Un *chôrion* bizantino?', in Arthur, P. (ed.), *Da Apigliano a Martano: Tre anni di archeologia medioevale (1997–1999)* (Galatina), 14–20.

Arthur, P. and Imperiale, M.L. 2015. 'Le ceramiche di età bizantina (tardo VII–XI secolo)', in Arthur, P., Imperiale, M.L. and Tinelli, M. (eds.), *Apigliano: Un villaggio bizantino e medievale in Terra d'Otranto. I reperti* (Apigliano), 35–46.

Asal, R. 2007. 'İstanbul'un ticareti ve Theodosius Limanı', in Karamani Pekin, A. (ed.), *Gün Işığında. İstanbul'un 8000 yılı. Maramaray, Metro, Sultanahmet kazıları* (Istanbul), 180–9.

Athanasoulis, D. 2003. 'Ἡ αναχρονολόγηση του ναού της Παναγίας της Καθολικής στη Γαστούνη', Δελτίον της Χριστιανικής Αρχαιολογικής Εταιρίας 5, 63–78.

2005. *Glarentza Clarence Γλαρέντζα* (Athens).

Augenti, A. and Cirelli, E. 2010. 'Classe: Un osservatorio privilegiato per il commercio della tarda Antichità', in Menchelli, S., Santoro, S., Pasquinucci, M. and Guiducci, G. (eds.), *LRCW 3: Late Roman Coarse Wares, Cooking Wares and Amphorae in the Mediterranean: Archaeology and Archaeometry. Comparison between Western and Eastern Mediterranean*, BAR International Series 2185, vol. 2 (Oxford), 605–15.

Auriemma, R. and Quiri, E. 2007. 'La circolazione delle anfore in Adriatico tra V e VIII sec. d.C.', in Gelichi, S. and Negrelli, C. (eds.), *La circolazione delle ceramiche nell'Adriatico tra tarda Antichità e Altomedioevo. III Incontro di Studio CER.AM.IS*, Documenti di archeologia 43 (Mantua), 31–64.

Bakirtzis, Ch. 2009. 'Céramiques en comblement des voûtes à Sainte Sophie de Thessalonique', in Zozaya, J., Retuerce, M., Hervás, M.A. and Juan, A. de (eds.), *Actas del VIII Congreso internacional de cerámica medieval en el Mediterráneo, Ciudad Real-Almagro del 27 de febrero al 3 de marzo de 2006*, vol. 2 (Ciudad Real), 697–702.

Bakourou, A., Katsara, E. and Kalamara, P. 2003. 'Argos and Sparta: Pottery of the 12th and 13th centuries', in Bakirtzis, Ch. (ed.), *VIIe Congrès international sur la céramique médiévale en Méditerranée, Thessaloniki, 11–16 Octobre 1999* (Athens), 233–6.

Bjelajac, L. 1989. 'Byzantine amphorae in the Serbian Danubian area in the 11th–12th centuries', in Déroche, V. and Spieser, J.-M. (eds.), *Recherches sur la céramique byzantine, Bulletin de correspondance hellénique: Supplément 18* (Athens and Paris), 109–18.

Böhlendorf Arslan, B. 2004. *Glasierte byzantinische Keramik aus der Türkei* (Istanbul).

Bonifay, M. 2005. 'Observations sur la typologie des amphores africaines de l'Antiquité tardive', in Gurt i Esparraguera, J. Ma., Buxeda i Garrigós, J.

and Cau Ontiveros, M.A. (eds.), *LRCW 1: Late Roman Coarse Wares, Cooking Wares and Amphorae in the Mediterranean. Archaeology and Archaeometry*, BAR International Series 1340 (Oxford), 451-71.

Bowden, W. and Hodges, R. 2011. *Butrint 3: Excavations at the Triconch Palace* (Oxford).

2012. 'An Ice Age settling on the Roman empire': Post-Roman Butrint between strategy and serendipity', in Christie, N. and Augenti, A. (eds.), *Urbes Extinctae: Archaeologies of Abandoned Classical Sites* (Aldershot), 207-42.

Bruno, B. 2007. 'Ceramiche da alcuni contesti tardoantichi e altomedievali di Verona', in Gelichi, S. and Negrelli, C. (eds.), *La circolazione delle ceramiche nell'Adriatico tra tarda Antichità e Altomedioevo. III Incontro di Studio CER.AM.IS*, Documenti di archeologia 43 (Mantua), 157-82.

2009. *Roman and Byzantine Malta: Trade and Economy* (Sta Venera, Malta).

Bruno, B. and Cutajar, N. 2002. 'Archeologia bizantina a Malta: Primi resultati e prospettive di indagine', in Amadasi Guzzo, M.G., Liverani, M. and Matthiae, P. (eds.), *Da Pyrgi a Mozia. Studi sull'archeologia del Mediterraneo in memoria di Antonia Ciasca* (Rome), 109-38.

2013. 'Imported amphorae as indicators of economic activity in Early Medieval Malta', in Michaelides, D., Pergola, P. and Zanini, E. (eds.), *The Insular System of the Early Byzantine Mediterranean. Archaeology and History*, BAR International Series 2523 (Oxford), 15-29.

Brusić, Z. 1976. 'Byzantine amphorae (9th to 12th century) from eastern Adriatic underwater sites', *Archaeologia Iugoslavica* 17, 37-49.

2010. 'Ranosrednjovjekovni nalazi iz hrvatskog podmorja', *Archaeologia Adriatica* 4, 243-55.

Calaon, D., Gelichi, S. and Negrelli, C. 2009. 'Tra VII e VIII secolo: I materiali ceramici da un emporio altomedievale / The ceramic from an Early Medieval emporium: 7th to 8th century', in Gelichi, S. (ed.), *L'isola del vescovo. Gli scavi archeologici intorno alla Cattedrale di Comacchio / The Archaeological Excavations nearby the Comacchio Cathedral* (Florence), 38-9.

Cherry, J.F., Davis, J.L. and Mantzourani, E. (eds.) 1991. *Landscape Archaeology as Long-Term History: Northern Keos in the Cycladic Islands from Earliest Settlement until Modern Times*, Monumenta archaeologica 16 (Los Angeles).

Cipriano, M.T., Paroli, L., Patterson, H., Saguì, L. and Whitehouse, D. 1991. 'La documentazione ceramica dell'Italia centro-meriodionale nell'Altomedioevo: Quadri regionali e contesti campione', in Alves da Silva, L. (ed.), *A cerâmica medieval no Mediterrâneo ocidental, Lisboa, 16-22 de Novembro 1987* (Mértola), 99-122.

Cirelli, E. 2009. 'Anfore globulari a Classe nell "alto Medioevo"', in Volpe, G. (ed.), *Atti del V Congresso nazionale di archeologia medievale* (Florence), 563-8.

D'Amico, E. 2007. 'Glazed white ware in the Italian peninsula: Proposals for a study', in Böhlendorf Arslan, B., Osman Uysal, A., Witte-Orr, J. (eds.),

Çanak: Late Antique and Medieval Pottery and Tiles in Mediterranean Archaeological Contexts, Byzas 7 (Istanbul), 215–38.

2012. 'Byzantine finewares in Italy (10th to 14th centuries AD): Social and economic contexts in the Mediterranean world', in Gelichi, S. (ed.), Atti del IX Congresso internazionale sulla ceramica medievale nel Mediterraneo, Venezia, Scuola grande dei Carmini, Auditorium Santa Margherita, 23–27 novembre 2009 (Florence), 473–9.

Demangel, R. and Mamboury, E. 1939. Le quartier des Manganes et la première région de Constantinople (Paris).

Demesticha, S. and Spondylis, E. 2011. 'Late Roman and Byzantine trade in the Aegean: Evidence from the HIMA Survey Project at Pagasitikos Gulf, Greece', Skyllis 11, 34–40.

Denker, A., Demirkök, F., Kongaz, G., Kiraz, M., Korkmaz Kömürcü, Ö. and Akbaytogan, D. 2013. 'YK 12', in Stories from the Hidden Harbor. Shipwrecks of Yenikapı (Istanbul), 197–209.

Denker, A., Demirkök, F., Kiraz, M. and Akbaytogan, T. 2013. 'YK 1', in Stories from the Hidden Harbor. Shipwrecks of Yenikapı (Istanbul), 210–19.

Dimopoulos, I. 2009. 'Trade of Byzantine red wares, end of the 11th–13th centuries', in Mundell Mango, M. (ed.), Byzantine Trade 4th–12th centuries: The Archaeology of Local, Regional and International Exchange. Society for the Promotion of Byzantine Studies Publications 14 (Aldershot), 179–81.

Döger, L. 2007. 'Halkın imge dünyasında seramik sanatı / The art of ceramics in the imagination of the folk', in Ödekan, A. (ed.), 'Kalanlar': 12. ve 13. yüzyıllarda Türkiye'de Bizans / 'The Remnants': 12th and 13th Centuries Byzantine Objects in Turkey (Istanbul), 48–55.

Doorninck, F.H. van 1989. 'The cargo amphoras on the 7th century Yassi Ada and 11th century Serçe Limanı shipwrecks: Two examples of a reuse of Byzantine amphoras as transport jars', in Déroche, V. and Spieser, J.-M. (eds.), Recherches sur la céramique byzantine, Bulletin de correspondance hellénique: Supplément 18 (Athens and Paris), 247–57.

Dorin, R.W. 2012. 'Adriatic trade networks in the twelfth and thirteenth centuries', in Morrisson, C. (ed.), Trade and Markets in Byzantium (Washington, DC), 235–79.

Favia, P. 2007. 'Rapporti con l'Oriente e mediazioni technologiche e culturali nella produzione ceramica bassomedievale della Puglia centrosettentrionale: Gli influssi bizantini, la presenza saracena e le elaborazioni locali', in Atti del XL Convegno internazionale della ceramica. Italia, medio ed estremo Oriente: Commerci, trasferimenti di tecnologie e influssi decorativi tra basso Medioevo ed età moderna (Albisola), 77–94.

Fozzati, L. and Gobbo, V. 2007. 'Le indagini archeologiche nell'area urbana e nel territorio di Caorle', in Fozzati, L. (ed.), Caorle archeologica tra mare, fiume e terra (Venice), 65–121.

Garver, E.L. 1993. 'Byzantine amphoras of the ninth through thirteenth centuries in the Bodrum Museum of Underwater Archaeology' (MA thesis, Texas A&M University).

Gelichi, S. 2010. 'Venice, Comacchio and the Adriatic emporia between the Lombard and Carolingian ages', in Willemsen, A. and Kik, H. (eds.), *Dorestad in an International Framework: New Research on Centres of Trade and Coinage in Carolingian Times* (Turnhout), 149–57.

—— 2012. 'Local and interregional exchanges in the lower Po Valley, eighth-ninth centuries', in Morrisson, C. (ed.), *Trade and Markets in Byzantium* (Washington, DC), 219–33.

—— 2013. 'Paesaggio e insediamenti nell'arco Adriatico nell'alto Medioevo: Osservazioni su alcuni paradigmi', in Cuscito, G. (ed.), *Le modificazioni del paesaggio nell'Altoadriatico tra pre-protostoria ed Altomedioevo*, Antichità altoadriatiche 76 (Trieste), 163–79.

Gelichi, S. and Negrelli, C. 2008. 'Anfore e commerci nell'alto Adriatico tra VIII e IX secolo', *Mélanges de l'École française de Rome. Moyen Âge 120/2 = Les destinées de l'Illyricum méridional pendant le haut Moyen Âge*, 307–26.

Greenslade, S. 2013. 'The Vrina Plain settlement between the 1st–13th centuries', in Hansen, I.L., Hodges, R. and Leppard, S. (eds.), *Butrint 4: The Archaeology and Histories of an Ionian Town* (Oxford), 123–64.

Günsenin, N. 1989. 'Recherches sur les amphores byzantines dans les musées turcs', in Déroche, V. and Spieser, J.-M. (eds.), *Recherches sur la céramique byzantine, Bulletin de correspondance hellénique: Supplément 18* (Athens and Paris), 267–76.

—— 1990. *Les amphores byzantines (Xe–XIIIe Siècles): Typologie, production, circulation d'après les collections turques* (Paris).

—— 1999. 'From Ganos to Serçe Limanı: Social and economic activities in the Propontis during Medieval times, illuminated by recent archaeological and historical discoveries', *The Institute of Nautical Archaeology Quarterly* 26/3, 18–23.

—— 2001. 'L'épave de Çamaltı Burnu I (Île de Marmara, Proconnèse): Résultats des campagnes 1998–2000', *Anatolia antiqua* 9, 117–33.

—— 2002. 'Medieval trade in the Sea of Marmara: the evidence of shipwrecks', in Macrides, R. (ed.), *Travel in the Byzantine World*, Society for the Promotion of Byzantine Studies Publications 10 (Aldershot), 125–35.

—— 2009. 'Ganos wine and its circulation in the 11th century', in Mundell Mango, M. (ed.), *Byzantine Trade 4th–12th centuries: The Archaeology of Local, Regional and International Exchange*. Society for the Promotion of Byzantine Studies Publications 14 (Aldershot), 145–53.

Günsenin, N. and Hatcher, H. 1997. 'Analyses chimiques comparatives des amphores de Ganos, de l'Île de Marmara et de l'épave de Serçe Limanı (Glass-Wreck)', *Anatolia antiqua* 5, 249–60.

Hansen, I.L. and Hodges, R. 2007. *Roman Butrint: An Assessment* (Oxford).

Hayes, J.W. 1992. *Excavations at Saraçhane in Istanbul*, vol. 2, *The Pottery* (Princeton).

Hesseling, D.C. and Pernot, H. (eds.) 1910. *Poèmes prodromiques en grec vulgaire* (Amsterdam).

Hocker, F.M. 1995. 'A ninth-century shipwreck near Bozburun, Turkey', *The Institute of Nautical Archaeology Quarterly* 22/1, 12–14.

— 1998a. 'The Byzantine shipwreck at Bozburun, Turkey: The 1997 field season', *The Institute of Nautical Archaeology Quarterly* 25/2, 12–17.

— 1998b. 'Bozburun Byzantine shipwreck excavation: The final campaign 1998', *The Institute of Nautical Archaeology Quarterly* 25/4, 3–13.

Hocker, F.M. and Scafuri, M.P. 1996. 'The Bozburun Byzantine shipwreck excavation: 1996 campaign', *The Institute of Nautical Archaeology Quarterly* 23/4, 3–9.

Hodges, R. 2008. *Shkëlqimi dhe rënia e Butrintit bizantin / The Rise and Fall of Byzantine Butrint* (London and Tirana).

— 2015. 'A "god-guarded" city? The "new" medieval town of Butrint', *Byzantine and Modern Greek Studies* 39/2, 191–218.

Hodges, R., Bowden, W. and Lako, K. (eds.) 2004. *Byzantine Butrint. Excavations and Surveys 1994–99* (Oxford).

Hodges, R. and Vroom, J. 2007. 'Late Antique and Early Medieval ceramics from Butrint, Albania', in Gelichi, S. and Negrelli, C. (eds.), *La circolazione delle ceramiche nell'Adriatico tra tarda Antichità e Altomedioevo. III Incontro di Studio CER.AM.IS*, Documenti di archeologia 43 (Mantua), 375–88.

Imperiale, M.L. 2004. 'Otranto, cantiere Mitello: Un centro produttivo nel Mediterraneo bizantino', in Patitucci Uggeri, S. (ed.), *La ceramica altomedievale in Italia* (Florence), 327–42.

Jennings, S. 2010. 'A group of glass ca. 800 AD from Tower 2 on the Western Defences, Butrint, Albania', in Drauschke, J. and Keller, D. (eds.), *Glass in Byzantium: Production, Usage, Analyses. The Fascination of Glass Production*, Römisch-Germanisches Zentralmuseum Tagungen 8 (Mainz), 225–35.

Jennings, S. and Stark, K. 2013. 'Appendix: The glass from Tower 1 in the Western Defences', in Hansen, I.L., Hodges, R. and Leppard, S. (eds.), *Butrint 4: The Archaeology and Histories of an Ionian Town* (Oxford), 257–59.

Johnston, A., Slane, K. and Vroom, J. 2014. '*Kythera* forty years on: The pottery from historical Kastri revisited', *Annual of the British School at Athens* 109, 3–64.

Kamani, S. 2011. 'Butrint in the mid-Byzantine period: A new interpretation', *Byzantine and Modern Greek Studies* 35/2, 115–33.

— 2013. 'The Western Defences', in Hansen, I.L., Hodges, R. and Leppard, S. (eds.), *Butrint 4: The Archaeology and Histories of an Ionian Town* (Oxford), 245–56.

Kocabaş, U. and Özsait-Kocabaş, I. 2013. 'A new milestone in ship archaeology: The Yenikapı shipwrecks project', in *Stories from the Hidden Harbor. Shipwrecks of Yenikapı* (Istanbul), 35–46.

Koutsouflakis, G., Argiris, X., Papadopoulou, Ch. and Sapoundis, J. 2012. 'Υποβρύχια Αναγνωριστική Έρευνα στο Νότιο Ευβοϊκό (2006-2008)', Ενάλια 11, 40-69.

Kritzas, Ch. 1971. 'Το βυζαντινόν ναυάγιον Πελαγοννήσου – Αλοννήσου', Αρχαιολογικά ανάλεκτα εξ Αθηνών 4/2, 176-85.

Ladstätter, S. 2008. 'Funde: Römische, spätantike und byzantinische Keramik', in Steskal, M. and La Torre, M. (eds.), *Das Vediusgymnasium in Ephesos: Archäologie und Baubefund*, Forschungen in Ephesos 14/1 (Vienna), 97-189.

Megaw, A.H.S. 1931-32. 'The chronology of some Middle Byzantine churches', *Annual of the British School at Athens* 32, 90-130.

— 1964. 'Glazed bowls in Byzantine churches', Δελτίον της Χριστιανικήσ Αρχαιολογικήσ Εταιρείας 4, 145-62.

— 1972. 'Supplementary excavations on a castle site at Paphos, Cyprus, 1970-1971', *Dumbarton Oaks Papers* 26, 322-43.

Murialdo, G. 2001. 'Le anfore da transporto', in Mannoni, T. and Murialdo, G. (eds.), *S. Antonino: Un insediamento fortificato nella Liguria bizantina* (Bordighera), 255-96.

Negrelli, C. 2007. 'Produzione, circolazione e consumo tra VI e IX secolo: Dal territorio del Padovetere a Comacchio', in Berti, F., Bollini, M., Gelichi, S. and Ortalli, G. (eds.), *Genti nel delta da Spina a Comacchio: Uomini, territorio e culto dall'Antichità all'alto Medioevo, Catalogo della mostra 16 dicembre-14 ottobre 2006* (Ferrara), 437-69.

— 2012. 'Towards a definition of Early Medieval pottery: Amphorae and other vessels in the northern Adriatic between the 7th and the 8th centuries', in Gelichi, S. and Hodges, R. (eds.), *From One Sea to Another: Trading Places in the European and Mediterranean Early Middle Ages. Proceedings of the International Conference, Comacchio, 27th-29th March 2009* (Turnhout), 393-415.

Özdaş, H., Kızıldağ, N. and Okan, E. 2012. 'Akdeniz kıyıları arkeolojik sualtı araştırmaları 2011 / Underwater archaeological surveys along the Mediterranean coastline 2011', *ANMED: Anadolu Akdenizi Arkeoloji Haberleri / News Bulletin on Archaeology from Mediterranean Anatolia* 10, 119-24.

Özsait-Kocabaş, I. 2013. 'The centuries-long voyage of ship Yenikapı 12', in *Stories from the Hidden Harbor. Shipwrecks of Yenikapı* (Istanbul), 47-55.

Papanikola-Bakirtzi, D. (ed.) 1999. *Byzantine Glazed Ceramics. The Art of Sgraffito* (Athens).

Papavassiliou, E., Sarantidis, K. and Papanikolaou, E. 2014. 'A ceramic workshop of the Early Byzantine period on the island of Lipsi in the Dodecanese (Greece): A preliminary approach', in Poulou-Papadimitriou, N., Nodarou, E. and Kilikoglou, V. (eds.), *LRCW 4: Late Roman Coarse Wares, Cooking Wares and Amphorae in the Mediterranean. Archaeology and Archaeometry*, BAR International Series 2616, vol. 1 (Oxford), 159-68.

Parker, A.J. 1992. *Ancient Shipwrecks of the Mediterranean and the Roman Provinces*, BAR International Series 580 (Oxford).

Paroli, L. 1991. 'Ceramica acroma depurata, dipinta in rosso e invetriata', in Cipriano, M.T. *et al.* 1991, 105–11.

— 1992. 'Ceramiche invetriate da un contesto dell'VIII secolo della Crypta Balbi – Roma', in Paroli, L. (ed.), *La ceramica invetriata tardoantica e altomedievale in Italia* (Florence), 351–77.

Patterson, H. and Whitehouse, D. 1992. 'Medieval domestic pottery', in D'Andria, F. and Whitehouse, D. (eds.), *Excavations at Otranto*, vol. 2, *The Finds* (Lecce), 87–195.

Pecci, A. 2009. 'Anfore e ceramiche depurate: Per contenere che cosa? / Amphorae und unglazed wares: The contents', in Gelichi, S. (ed.), *L'isola del vescovo: Gli scavi archeologici intorno alla cattedrale di Comacchio / The Archaeological Excavations nearby the Comacchio Cathedral* (Florence), 40.

Peschlow, U. 1977–78. 'Byzantinische Keramik aus Istanbul', *Istanbuler Mitteilungen* 27–28, 363–414.

Poulou-Papadimitriou, N. and Nodarou, E. 2007. 'La céramique protobyzantine de Pseira: La production locale et les importations, étude typologique et pétrographique', in Bonifay, M. and Tréglia, J.-C. (eds.), *LRCW 2: Late Roman Coarse Wares, Cooking Wares and Amphorae in the Mediterranean. Archaeology and Archaeometry*, BAR International Series 1662, vol. 2 (Oxford), 755–66.

Pulak, C. 2007. 'Yenikapı Bizans batıkları', in Karamani Pekin, A. (ed.), *Gün Işığında. İstanbul'un 8000 yılı. Maramaray, Metro, Sultanahmet kazıları* (Istanbul), 202–15.

Pulak, C., Ingram, R., Jones, M. and Matthews, S. 2013. 'The shipwrecks of Yenikapı and their contribution to the study of ship construction', in *Stories from the Hidden Harbor. Shipwrecks of Yenikapı* (Istanbul), 22–34.

Raimondo, C. 2006. 'Aspetti di economia e società nella Calabria bizantina: Le produzioni ceramiche del medio Ionio calabrese', in Jacob, A., Martin, J.-M. and Noyé, G. (eds.), *Histoire et culture dans l'Italie byzantine: Acquis et nouvelles recherches*, Collection de l'École française de Rome 363 (Rome), 407–43.

Reynolds, P. 2003. 'Pottery and the economy in 8th century Beirut: An Umayyad assemblage from the Roman imperial baths (BEY 045)', in Bakirtzis, Ch. (ed.), *VIIe Congrès international sur la céramique médiévale en Méditerranée, Thessaloniki, 11–16 Octobre 1999* (Thessaloniki), 725–34.

Romanchuk, A.I., Sazanov, A.V. and Sedikova, L.V. 1995. Амфоры из комплексов византийского Херсона (Ekaterinburg).

Roslund, M. 1997. 'Crumbs from the rich man's table: Byzantine finds in Lund and Sigtuna, c.980–1250', in Andersson, H., Carelli, P. and Ersgård, L. (eds.), *Visions of the Past: Trends and Traditions in Swedish Medieval Archaeology* (Lund and Stockholm), 239–97.

Sanders, G.D.R. 1989. 'Three Peloponnesian churches and their importance for the chronology of the late 13th and early 14th century pottery in the eastern Mediterranean', in Déroche, V. and Spieser, J.-M. (eds.), *Recherches sur la céramique byzantine, Bulletin de correspondance hellénique: Supplément 18* (Athens and Paris), 189–99.

1993. 'Excavations at Sparta: The Roman Stoa, 1988-1991. Preliminary report, part 1: (c) Medieval pottery', *Annual of the British School at Athens* 88, 251–86.

2002. 'Corinth', in Laiou, A.E. (ed.), *The Economic History of Byzantium: From the Seventh through the Fifteenth Century*, vol. 2 (Washington, DC), 647–54.

Sazanov, A. 1997. 'Les amphores de l'antiquité tardive et du moyen âge: Continuité ou rupture? Le cas de la mer Noire', in Démians d'Archimbaud, G. (ed.), *La céramique médiévale en Méditerranée. Actes du VIe Congrès de l'AIECM2, Aix-en-Provence, 13-18 novembre 1995* (Aix-en-Provence), 87–102.

Schläger, H., Blackman, D. and Schäfer, J. 1968. 'Der Hafen von Anthedon mit Beiträgen zur Topographie und Geschichte der Stadt', *Archäologischer Anzeiger* 83, 21–98.

Sebastiani, A., Gooney, D., Mitchell, J., Papadopoulou, P., Reynolds, P., Vaccaro, E. and Vroom, J. 2013. 'The Medieval church and cemetery at the Well of Junia Rufina', in Hodges, R., Hansen, I.L. and Leppard, S. (eds.), *Butrint 4: The Archaeology and Histories of an Ionian Town* (Oxford), 215–44.

Siena, E., Troiano, D. and Verrocchio, V. 1998. 'Ceramiche dalla Val Pescara', in Saguì, L. (ed.), *Ceramica in Italia: VI-VII secolo, Atti del Convegno in onore di John W. Hayes, Roma, 11-13 maggio 1995*, vol. 2 (Florence), 665–704.

Skartsis, S.S. 2012. 'Chlemoutsi: Italian glazed pottery from a crusader castle in the Peloponnese (Greece)', in Gelichi, S. (ed.), *Atti del IX Congresso internazionale sulla ceramica medievale nel Mediterraneo, Venezia, Scuola grande dei Carmini, Auditorium Santa Margherita, 23-27 novembre 2009* (Florence), 140–6.

Stern, E.J. 2012. *Akko I: The 1991-1998 Excavations. The Crusader-Period Pottery*, 2 vols. (Jerusalem).

Toniolo, A. 2007. 'Anfore dall "area lagunare"', in Gelichi, S. and Negrelli, C. (eds.), *La circolazione delle ceramiche nell'Adriatico tra tarda Antichità e Altomedioevo. III Incontro di Studio CER.AM.IS*, Documenti di archeologia 43 (Mantua), 91–106.

2014. 'I materiali / Material / Materials', in Fozzati, L. (ed.), *Torcello scavata: Patrimonio condiviso / Izkopan Torcello: Skupna dediščina / Torcello Excavated: A Shared Heritage*, vol. 1, *Gli scavi 1995-2012 / Izkopavanja 1995-2012 / The Excavation Campaigns 1995-2012* (Venice), 291–318.

Vaccaro, E. 2013. 'Sicily in the eighth and ninth centuries AD: A case of persisting economic complexity', *Al-Masāq* 25/1, 34–69.

Volkov, I.V. 2006. 'Amphorae from Novgorod the Great and comments on the wine trade between Byzantium and Medieval Russia', in Orton, C. (ed.), *The Pottery from Medieval Novgorod and Its Region* (Abingdon and New York), 145-59.

Vroom, J. 2003. *After Antiquity: Ceramics and Society in the Aegean from the 7th to the 20th Century A.C.: A Case Study from Boeotia, Greece* (Leiden).

— 2004. 'The Medieval and post-Medieval fine wares and cooking wares from the Triconch Palace and the Baptistery', in Hodges, R., Bowden, W. and Lako, K. (eds.), *Byzantine Butrint. Excavations and Surveys 1994-99* (Oxford), 278-92.

— 2006a. 'Corfu's right eye: Venetian pottery in Butrint (Albania)', in Guštin, M., Gelichi, S. and Spindler, K. (eds.), *The Heritage of the Serenissima: The Presentation of the Architectural and Archaeological Remains of the Venetian Republic. Proceedings of the International Conference Izola – Venezia, 4.-9.11.2005* (Koper), 229-36.

— 2006b. 'Some Byzantine pottery finds from Kaman-Kalehöyük: A first observation', *Anatolian Archaeological Studies* 15, 163-69.

— 2007. 'Limyra in Lycia: Byzantine/Umayyad pottery finds from excavations in the eastern part of the city', in Lemaître, S. (ed.), *Céramiques antiques en Lycie (VIIe S. a.C.-VIIe S. p.C): Les produits et les marchés*, Études 16 (Bordeaux), 261-92.

— 2008. 'Dishing up history: Early Medieval ceramic finds from the Triconch Palace in Butrint', *Mélanges de l'École française de Rome. Moyen Âge 120/2 = Les destinées de l'Illyricum méridional pendant le haut Moyen Âge*, 291-305.

— 2011a. 'The Morea and its links with Southern Italy after AD 1204: Ceramics and identity', *Archeologia medievale* 38, 409-430.

— 2011b. 'The other Dark Ages: Early Medieval pottery finds in the Aegean as an archaeological challenge', in Attoui, R. (ed.), *When did Antiquity End? Archaeological Case Studies in Three Continents*, BAR International Series 2268 (Oxford), 137-58.

— 2012a. 'From one coast to another: Early Medieval ceramics in the southern Adriatic region', in Gelichi, S. and Hodges, R. (eds.), *From One Sea to Another: Trading Places in the European and Mediterranean Early Middle Ages. Proceedings of the International Conference, Comacchio, 27th-29th March 2009* (Turnhout), 375-413.

— 2012b. 'Early Medieval pottery finds from recent excavations at Butrint, Albania', in Gelichi, S. (ed.), *Atti del IX Congresso internazionale sulla ceramica medievale nel Mediterraneo, Venezia, Scuola grande dei Carmini, Auditorium Santa Margherita, 23-27 novembre 2009* (Florence), 289-96.

— 2013a. 'The Medieval and post-Medieval pottery finds', in Sebastiani *et al.* 2013, 234-40.

2013b. 'Digging for the "Byz": Adventures into Byzantine and Ottoman archaeology in the eastern Mediterranean', *Pharos* 19/2, 79-110.

2014. *Byzantine to Modern Pottery in the Aegean: An Introduction and Field Guide*, 2nd revised edn. (Turnhout).

2016. 'Byzantine sea trade in ceramics: Some case studies in the eastern Mediterranean (ca. seventh–fourteenth centuries)', in Magdalino, P. and Necipoğlu, N. (eds.), *Trade in Byzantium. Papers from the Third International Sevgi Gönül Byzantine Studies Symposium* (Istanbul), 157–77.

2017. 'Ceramics', in Niewöhner, P. (ed.), *The Archaeology of Byzantine Anatolia: From the End of Late Antiquity until the Coming of the Turks* (Oxford), 176–93.

2019a. 'The Medieval and Post-Medieval pottery finds from the Vrina Plain excavations', in Greenslade, S. (ed.), *Butrint 6: Excavations on the Vrina Plain*, vol. 2, *The Finds* (Oxford), 1–14.

2019b. 'Medieval Ephesos as a production and consumption centre', in Ladstätter, S. and Magdalino, P. (eds.), *Ephesos from Late Antiquity until the Late Middle Ages. Proceedings of the International Conference at the Research Center for Anatolian Civilizations, Koç University, Istanbul 30th November-2nd December 2012* (Vienna), 231–56.

Vroom, J. and Kondyli, F. 2015. '"Dark Age" Butrint and Athens: Rewriting the history of two Early Byzantine towns', in Vroom, J. (ed.), *Medieval and Post-Medieval Ceramics in the Eastern Mediterranean – Fact and Fiction* (Turnhout), 317–42.

Waksman, S.Y. and Teslenko, I. 2010. '"Novy Svet Ware": An exceptional cargo of glazed wares from a 13th-century shipwreck near Sudak (Crimea, Ukraine). Morphological typology and laboratory investigations', *The International Journal of Nautical Archaeology* 39/2, 357–75.

Waksman, S.Y. and Wartburg, M.-L. von 2006. '"Fine Sgraffito Ware", "Aegean Ware", and other wares: New evidence for a major production of Byzantine ceramics', Report of the Department of Antiquities, Cyprus, 369–88.

Wartburg, M.-L. von 2001. 'Earthquakes and archaeology: Paphos after 1222', in *Acts of the Third International Congress of Cypriot Studies, 1996* (Nicosia), 127–45.

Whitehouse, D. 1980. 'Proto-Maiolica', *Faenza* 66, 77–83.

3 | A Winter Sea?
Exchange and Power at the Ebbing of the Adriatic Connection 600–800

FRANCESCO BORRI

With the death of Pope Gregory the Great in 604 and the fading of his literary production, most notably his epistolary, dusk falls over the Adriatic. For the following two centuries, until the flourishing of the Frankish narratives on the region, the Adriatic Sea barely appears in the histories, letters and charters of the time, written in both Latin and Greek. With few exceptions, such as a laconic entry in the life of John the Almsgiver (Leontios, *Vita Ioannis* 28), we have no account of travellers crossing the sea, as we have for the later years, neither do we possess any mention of routes, or the number of ships nor do we know much about the identity of the people that travelled and the nature of the things that moved. This long silence covering the seventh century and a large part of the eighth was long believed to be symptomatic of a scarcity of communication, with the year 700 representing the low point of the Adriatic exchange. For decades, historians imagined that in such a waterscape a coastal navigation or cabotage with sporadic exchange of luxuries did not attract the attention of the land-oriented authors mostly writing in Italy, Gaul and Constantinople. They suggested that until the lift in connectivity of the last quarter of the eighth century, the Adriatic was undergoing a long winter, with no sails visible at the horizon of its waters. The 715 Pact of Comacchio, the oldest mention of the Italian trade port we possess, seemed to confirm this image, portraying a small costal settlement, mostly involved in the commerce of salt and fish along the river ways of northern Italy (Hartmann 1904, 123–4).

This reductive image proved to be misleading and did not resist the challenge of the most recent discoveries. Exactly in Comacchio, archaeologists uncovered vast timber structures and a variety of vessels revealing the many wares moving through the harbour (Gasparri 2015; 2017a, 99–112; Gelichi *et al.* 2012). Further excavations and a reappraisal of older findings identified globular amphorae emerging in many eighth-century Italian layers and some Dalmatian ones (Negrelli 2012; Radić Rossi 2006). Moreover, it is to the years around 700 that the construction of the church of Santa Maria Assunta in Torcello has been newly dated (De Min 2003, 602), revealing that at the turn of the eighth century powerful commitments moved skilled workforce across the northern Adriatic, together with large and expensive materials. It has, therefore, become clear that literary sources did not reflect the full commercial importance of the Adriatic exchange. Although the reasons for this silence remain somewhat obscure, the macroscopic discrepancy between the material remains and the written records demands an alternative reading of the literary evidence that we have.

In the two centuries examined here, we can trace the main actor of the Adriatic connection, the empire, losing ground after the great but ephemeral successes of Justinian's age. The spread of barbarian polities in Italy and south-eastern Europe progressively limited the Roman possessions on the Adriatic, reducing the geographical extension of the empire, the presence of soldiers and officers, the incidence of their supply and the collection of taxes. A major change that can be noticed is the disappearance of the army of Illyricum that Agathias of Myrina (*Historiae* 5.13) had stated to amount to 17,500 effectives. This force had an important role in the conquest of Dalmatia during the Gothic Wars but afterward we do not see the army operating on the Adriatic again: it may have broken up under the pressure of the Avar conquerors of the region (Haldon 1999, 71; Pillon 2005). The last masters of soldiers for Illyricum (*magistri militum per Illyricum*) seem to have been in charge in the 580s, when two men called Bonus and Theognis perhaps covered the office (Menander Protector, *Historia* 27, 33, 65; Jones, Martindale and Morris 1992, 241, 1303). On the Italian shores of the Adriatic, Ravenna remained among the most important towns of the empire.

Despite these important setbacks, the empire continued to intervene strongly in the Adriatic. An author such as John of Biclaro (*Chronicon* 576; Augenti and Cirelli 2012), spending his youth in Constantinople, recorded the armies and money that reached Ravenna from Constantinople in the last years of the sixth century, a clue to the strong ties between the northern Adriatic and the eastern Mediterranean. His contemporary Menander Protector (*Historia* 22, 24) recorded similar episodes. It was in Ravenna that a patrician took office apparently since 584 (Cosentino 2008b, 136; Ravegnani 2011, 33). Soldiers were stationed in the Dalmatian cities too, at least at the turn of the sixth century, when Pope Gregory the Great (*Epistolae* 4.46; 5.6; 9.177) mentioned soldiers (*milites*) in Zadar and Salona, the latter being somehow under the chain of command of the *patrician* of Italy. In addition, we know of a *proconsul* of Dalmatia and former *scholasticus* called Marcellinus (Gregory, *Epistolae* 3.22; 4.38; 8.24; 9.158; 9.237; Jones, Martindale and Morris 1992, 812; Margetić 1997).

A further *scholasticus*, Venantius, may have lived in Dalmatia in the same years (*Liber pontificalis*, vol. 1, 330; Jones, Martindale and Morris 1992, 1369). Until the final decade of the seventh century the praetorian prefect for Illyricum was still in charge (Brubaker and Haldon 2011, 671; Gkoutzioukostas 2012–13). Pope Gregory the Great (*Epistolae* 2.23; Jones, Martindale and Morris 1992, 716) addressed a man called Iovinus and, much later, the author of the *Miracula s. Demetrii* (2.128.33; Lilie *et al.* 1999–2002, 10719) recorded an anonymous eparch of Illyricum (τοῦ Ἰλλυρικοῦ). Yet, the reach of these officers to the Adriatic in the West is a matter of opinion due to the scant and obscure evidence covering Dalmatia in the central and final decades of the sixth century. Historians maintained, in turn, that Dalmatia returned to the Illyrian prefecture after the Gothic Wars, became a domain of the exarchs of Ravenna or enjoyed a peculiar status like the one Sicily did. Hybrid solutions were also proposed (Bavant 2004, 312; Borri 2009, 24–9; Ferluga 1978, 81–6). Even the great Austrian historian Ernst Stein, so skilled in the working of institutions, was puzzled by the nature of the evidence, proposing two different solutions during his career (Stein 1925, 355; 1949, 801).

Regardless of their institutional status, the Dalmatian harbours showed some continuity despite the silence of the sources, providing seamen and the necessary infrastructures for sailing the Adriatic well into the seventh century. This can be explained by the fact that the sea was generally sailed along the eastern coast. In the shadows of the Balkans, the jagged nature of the coast, the many islands and the skyline of the Dinaric Alps offered fundamental protection from the winds, the necessary lines of sight in pre-Modern navigation and safe harbours (Horden and Purcell 2000, 133–5). Moreover, Croatia is among the top find-spots for Mediterranean shipwrecks, a clue towards the intensity of exchange (Kingsley 2009, 31). When the authors of the Roman *Liber pontificalis* (vol. 1, 319 and 337) inform us of the new exarchs' arrival in Ravenna, such as in 616 or in 649, they indirectly reveal movement through the Adriatic. Therefore, people moved on the Adriatic, reaching the Po Valley from the Aegean sailing up the Dalmatian coast well into the seventh century.

A richer picture stems from the work of Andreas Agnellus, who wrote his *Liber pontificalis ecclesiae Ravennatis* shortly after the battle of Fontenoy in 841. Agnellus is the author who recorded the highest frequency of exchange between Constantinople and his town, bridging the seventh-century evidence with that of the ninth century. Yet, his history is very late and often difficult to interpret. Many narrative levels overlap, bearing clues of their original contexts. He must have had sources he could rely on: relating the whole story of Ravenna's autocephaly, Agnellus (*Liber pontificalis ecclesiae Ravennatis* 110) narrated that the Archbishop Maurus of Ravenna (c.644–c.671) went to Constantinople several times in order to obtain rights for his church. Apart from the anecdotal account of the recurrent travels of the archbishop, Agnellus (*Liber pontificalis ecclesiae Ravennatis* 115) recorded that the Church of Ravenna obtained exemptions from shore tax, gate tax, sales tax and customs tax (*ripaticum, portaticum, siliquaticum* and *teloneum*), from the emperor (Brown 1979, 20-3). The exemptions were a product of the general favour enjoyed by Ravenna from the empire during these years, but they also inform us about the existence of indirect imposition on the region, mostly linked to navigation and commerce. A few years earlier, Constans II (641–68) imposed ship-money (*nauticatio*), together with other poll and land taxes (*diagrafa seu capita*) on the Tyrrhenian shores in the course of his Sicilian enterprise (*Liber pontificalis*, vol. 1, 344; on this passage see Cosentino 2008a; Zuckerman 2005).

We also have mentions of ships. The exarch must have had a small fleet at his disposal and around 590, the imperial seaborne forces were able to lay siege to Pavia with some dromons (*dromones*, see *Epistolae Austrasicae* 40). In the middle of the seventh century, it must have been shared knowledge that 'service' ships (*naves angariales*) were stationed close to Ravenna (*Origo gentis Langobardorum* 5). A letter issued by Emperor Constantine IV (668–85) in 678 and destined to Pope Donus (676–8) confirms this image. The emperor offered to support the pontiff with the warships, *castellati dromones*, at the disposal of Exarch Theodore (Constantine IV, *Sacra ad Donum*; McCormick 2001, 856; Prigent 2008, 394; Ravegnani 2011, 80). Other harbours in the Adriatic must have hosted fleets too: after the death of Constans II in Syracuse in 668, the armies of Africa and Italy converged on Sicily in order to put down the tyrant Mezezius. A contingent reached Sicily sailing through Istrian waters (*per partes Histriae*) as the anonymous author of the *Liber pontificalis* wrote (vol. 1, 346). Paul the Deacon (*Historia Langobardorum* 6.3), writing at the end of the eighth century, recorded that around 650, Duke Rodoald of Friuli had to reach imperial Istria in order to travel to Ravenna and eventually Pavia by boat.

From the turning of the seventh century stems the decree (*iussio*) that Emperor Justinian II (685–95 and 705–11) sent to Pope Conon (686–7) in 687 (Justinian II, *Sacra ad Cononem*). In order to grant strength to his pronouncements, the emperor enlisted the support of the nine armies stationed in his domain. For the western Mediterranean he recorded

Italy, Africa, Sardinia and Ceuta (*Septem*). The army of Illyricum does not appear, as it was disbanded decades earlier, but its forces may have been transferred to the *Karabisianoi*, an army stationed much further south in the Mediterranean waterscape (Haldon 1999, 314; Treadgold 1998, 73). Constantin Zuckerman (2005, 124; see also Brubaker and Haldon 2011, 729) interpreted the *Karabisianoi* as a western navy raised in the region of Sicily and Hellas, whose authority may have extended to the Adriatic too. As we will see, in few years this force we will be the only imperial presence of the Adriatic.

However, at the end of the seventh century, the emperors still fought to secure the routes between Constantinople and its northernmost Adriatic province and they were rather successful. According to Agnellus (*Liber pontificalis ecclesiae Ravennatis* 111), in the second third of the seventh century Ravenna continued to pay conspicuous land taxes to Constantinople (Brubaker and Haldon 2011, 473; Cosentino 2006, 48; Zuckerman 2005, 102-4). In these decades, challenges to Byzantium's hegemony seem to have been scarce. Before the Frankish efforts in the Adriatic in the first decade of the ninth century (Haywood 1991, 135-83 and the critic Bachrach 2001, 376-8), there are almost no mentions of barbarian contenders in the Adriatic, with the possible exception of a seaborne expedition with a large fleet (*cum multitudine navium*) of certain, perhaps Dalmatian, Slavs allegedly dated to 642 and recorded by Paul the Deacon in *Historia Langobardorum* (4.44).

Around 700 this picture seems to have changed. Literary evidence points to an adjustment in the pattern of imperial intervention in the Adriatic. We saw that by the reign of Justinian II a strong fleet was stationed south of the Adriatic. Also suggestive is the narration of Pope Constantine's (708-15) journey to Constantinople in the year 710 (*Liber pontificalis*, vol. 1, 390; McCormick 2001, 463). Travelling south, in Naples the pope met Exarch John, who was coming from the Imperial City. John had some business to attend to in Rome, but we know that for the remaining fifty years of Byzantine rule in northern Italy, the exarchs did not cruise the Adriatic, sailing the vital south Tyrrhenian triangle of Sicily, Calabria, Naples and Rome instead (Saguì 2002; Wickham 2005, 737; 2012, 505), in order to reach Ravenna travelling north the *Via Amerina*. From now, until the renewed intervention of Byzantium in the upper Adriatic in the last decade of the eighth century and the first of the ninth, there are no clear mentions of Byzantine fleets north of the Straits of Otranto, with the possible exception of Manes' cruise of 732 (Brandes 2005; Lilie *et al.* 1999-2002, 4690; Theophanes, *Chronographia* 410).

Imperial authority seems to have been confined to the south of the Adriatic. Otranto remained almost continuously a Byzantine stronghold, the same as Durrës on the Albanian shore (Brown 1992; von Falkenhausen 2007; Gutteridge 2003). Emperor Leo III (717–41) may have completed the military reorganisation of the southern Adriatic setting with the creation of the army of Kephalenia alongside those of Sicily and Hellas, as suggested by Vivien Prigent (2008, 398–401; for a later dating see Brubaker and Haldon 2011, 359). It is also possible that the first appointment of an *archon* (ἄρχων) – the governor – of Early Medieval *Diokleia* (today Montenegro) should be dated to the same years: the well-known seal of Peter, assigned by Gustav Schlumberger (1884, 433) to the tenth century, has been newly dated to the years immediately after 700 (McGeer, Nesbitt and Oikonomides 2005, 154).

Therefore, it seems that the year 700, instead of marking a watershed in the Adriatic connectivity, represented a turning point in the empire's pattern of intervention. In fact, we realise that the same narratives once quoted to suggest an exchange-breach could instead cautiously confirm the picture of continuity in communication as indicated by archaeological findings. I mentioned above the seaborne traffic which circled around upper Dalmatia, Torcello and Comacchio in 700. It is due to a much-isolated entry in the *Liber pontificalis* (vol. 1, 433), that we know that in the middle of the eighth century Venetian ships were trading on the Tyrrhenian shores. However, the exceptionality of the information has more to do with the wares that the Venetians were trading rather than their presence not far from Rome. The anonymous biographer of Pope Zacharias (741–52) tells us that the Venetians were selling a great number of slaves (*moltitudo mancipiorum*), a cruel detail that must have triggered his attention. A further suggestion comes from the *Cosmography* of Aethicus, according to Michael Herren (2011, lxi) a narrative written shortly after 727 from an author with strong ties to the northern Adriatic, perhaps Istria (Wood 2000). The author displayed an unusual maritime perspective showing knowledge of, and interest in, islands and coasts, nautical terminology and ships, stars and winds together with the seasons of navigations (Herren 2011). It seems to be a text stemming from a literary circle sharing great acquaintance with the Adriatic Sea and navigation.

Now, if the absence of the empire cannot be explained by a general lack of exchange, a different reading becomes necessary. A rising estrangement of the Italian aristocracies from the empire in the aftermath of Justinian II's bloody downfall can be noticed in the written records (Brown 1995). It may have resulted in growing fiscal indiscipline. A few years later, when Emperor Leo III faced imminent military threats across the whole empire, he tried to enforce imperial authority on Italy, but things started to disintegrate. Theophanes narrated (*Chronographia* 398; Lilie *et al.* 1999–2002, 5815) that, new to the throne and having crushed the rebellion of Serge, the emperor sent Patrician Paul to Sicily in order to address the western commanders, *archontas ton dytikon* (ἄρχοντας τῶν δυτικῶν). The identity of these rulers or officers is a matter of opinion. The late Tibor Živković (2008), who had the merit of drawing attention to this rather unnoticed passage, proposed that these mysterious officers could have been the lords of the barbarian Slavs settled in the western Balkans. This interpretation could be corroborated by Emperor Constantine VII Porphyrogennetos' usage of the name *archon* (ἄρχων) in order to describe the rulers of the Adriatic Slavs (*De administrando imperio* 29–30). Yet, this usage in not consistent with the early ninth-century context. Danijel Dzino (2010, 156) proposed that these may have been the leaders of imperial Dalmatia instead. It is difficult to understand with any precision who Theophanes meant, but the rulers of Dalmatia may well have been included in that label, which I believe was generally meant to refer to the aloof western imperial aristocracies of Italy, the islands and the Adriatic.

The orders delivered to Paul may have been among the new emperor's first efforts to re-establish imperial rule in the west. In the *Chronographia* (410), we read that, a few years later, the emperor aimed to impose a renewed fiscal burden on Calabria and Sicily. Notwithstanding Theophanes' witness, Leo III's measure seems to have been much more grandiose. The Roman *Liber pontificalis* (vol. 1, 403) recorded a *census* commanded by the emperor, apparently the first step towards the imposition of a poll tax in Rome. The narrative continues by recording the riots that spread like wildfire in 727 to Ravenna, the Pentapolis and Venice in reaction to the emperor's measures (*Liber pontificalis*, vol. 1, 404). This could confirm that the fiscal burden was intended for the whole of imperial Italy (Brandes 2002, 370; Cosentino 2006, 49). Whether the Dalmatian towns revolted or not, we do know that, beyond the edges of the Adriatic, the army of Hellas also rioted against the emperor (Theophanes, *Chronographia* 404; Brubaker and Haldon 2011, 80).

Constantine V (740–75), a ruler energetically involved in many threatened areas of the empire, succeeded his father to the throne. Many letters of the *Codex Carolinus* reflect the anxiety about alleged imperial interventions. In an epistle dated around 760 (*Codex Carolinus* 20), Pope Paul lamented that 300 warships sailed offshore of Rome together with the

Sicilian fleet (*stolus*). If Constantine V really aimed to show his strength, it is possible that the Roman pontiffs strategically exaggerated the consistence of his display in order to bring the Frankish kings to action. Indeed, we may doubt that Constantine V planned to regain authority on the Adriatic with coercion. The only (very questionable) clue for a planned attack against Italy is also recorded in the *Codex Carolinus* and nowhere else and is linked to the rebellion of the Lombard Duke Hrodgaud of 775–6 (Davis 2015, 136–9). In fact, the threats denounced by the popes never materialised: only after Constantine V's death, an attempt was made in 788. On the other hand, western sources richly witness the emperor's involvement in diplomatic actions to preserve the imperial position in Italy and even regain Ravenna (Herrin 1992). Money must have reached coastal regions, including the famous Dalmatian *solidi* found in funerary contexts (Budak 2018; Šeparović 2008). Considering this persisting imperial interest in the upper Adriatic, the lack of military intervention becomes understandable because of Constantinople's limited resources. Defiant armies possessing the territory, resisting tax collection and controlling secondary impositions must have represented a twofold limitation to the enforcement of imperial authority. A large armed intervention might have re-established the authority of Constantinople in the Adriatic, but men and means were needed in the regions central to the empire's survival such as Anatolia, Crete and Sicily (Haldon 2016).

The absence of the empire may have resulted in the sudden growth of Ravenna's rivals, as suggested by Michael McCormick (2012, 479) and Chris Wickham (2012, 507). As mentioned above, from 715 we have the first literary mention of Comacchio. A few years later, King Liutprand's Lombards signed a pact with the inhabitants of Cittanova, here also recorded for the first time (*Pactum Hlotharii* 26). It is possible that similar central-places arose also on the Dalmatian coast, but until the tenth century literary sources mention only Zadar whose relationship with Constantinople seems to have been as complicated as those of the Italian centres, although much less documented. Eventually, the growing challenge posed by the Adriatic harbours, together with their fiscal opposition to the empire, worsened Byzantium's position on the Adriatic and accelerated its waning from these waters. Therefore, Comacchio and Venice were two centres which contended Ravenna's centrality and were able to challenge the prestigious metropolis because of the empire's withdrawal, with their growth aggravating the empire's position, inhibiting its return to the Adriatic.

The empire's position in the eighth-century northern Adriatic was weak despite the practices of the local aristocrats who borrowed customs and institutional concepts from the empire. From the Pact of Liutprand (Hartmann 1904, 123–4) we know that two counts (*comites*) and a master of soldiers (*magister militum*) spoke for the inhabitants of Comacchio in front of the Lombard king. In one of the oldest textual sources on Venice, there is also a master of soldiers, Marcel (*Pactum Hlotharii* 26; Borri 2005; Gasparri 2011; 2017b). This Roman-ness became pronounced in specific social fields: King Aistulf (*Ahistulphi leges* 4) regulated in his laws commerce with the so-called *Romani* in the aftermath of his conquest of Romagna, while in the *Annales regni Francorum* (a. 817) the inhabitants of the coastal towns were also referred to as Romans. These institutions and names clearly echoed a Roman past and a Byzantine present. Yet, if this tells us something about the identity of these coastal communities, it does not tell us much about their political allegiances (Conant 2012). The title of the 'master of soldiers' recorded at Comacchio seems to be more an expression of local interests rather than of a higher authority, such as that of patrician of Ravenna (Delogu 2012, 460). Soldiers (*milites*) are to be found there in the middle of the ninth century, many decades after the authority of Byzantium disappeared (Gasparri 2015; 2017a, 99–112). The same is true for other places in the Adriatic where Byzantine habits and practices grew independently from the factual presence of the empire, as it was the case in Frankish Rimini where the master of soldiers, Maurice, was an influential local figure (*Liber pontificalis*, vol. 1, 477; Cosentino 2012, 293).

The emperors may have had some success in the Adriatic provinces. Yet, evidence is indirect and we may find clues of it in much later material. After the murder of Exarch Paul, the new exarch, Eutychius, actively operated in Italy until the Lombard conquest of Ravenna in 751 but it seems that he did not have much of a following beyond the town walls (Cosentino 2008b, 239). In the Plea of Rižana (*Placitum Risani* 72), the Istrian captains paid tributes of various nature, perhaps including a poll tax, to the emperor of Constantinople. If we do not believe that this order dated back to the age of Justinian, we could suppose that they originated in the aftermath of Leo III's intervention in the west. Restabilising taxation may have been possible because the basic structure had not been fully broken up (Wickham 2005, 149). From a letter (*Epistolae Langobardicae collectae* 19) written in the very last days of the Lombard kingdom, Patriarch John of Grado lamented that, after the imposition of levies by

King Desiderius, he was forced to serve two masters (*quod numquam auditum est in provincia illa quamque nec potest quispiam duobus servire dominis*). One of them may have been the emperor. Even the levies on trade from which Charlemagne exempted the patriarchs of Grado in 802 may have originated in first decades of the eighth century (*Diplomata Karolinorum* 201). There are further clues pointing to the mixed outcome of this policy. If in the 770s, the popes relied on the dukes of Venice as allies of the Franks aiming to take over Italy (*Epistolae Langobardicae collectae* 19), twenty years later, they complained that the Istrians, joined by the Greeks, opposed the entrance of Charlemagne's army to their province (*Codex Carolinus* 63).

In the end, the ebbing of the imperial presence from the eighth century onwards in the Adriatic was less the reflection of a rupture in communications than the outcome of the rise of new communities which, although adopting imperial style and habits, challenged Byzantium's dominion over this sea. I would suggest that, beginning with the reign of Justinian II, local aristocracies resisted tax collection, aiming to appropriate lands and related wealth which included taxes (Cosentino 2006, 51). Emperor Leo III tried to enforce imperial authority but failed to a great extent and his son Constantine V was not very successful either.

When their successors tried to contain the Frankish conquest during the last decade of the eighth century and the first of the ninth, they quickly realised that the local aristocracies had become untenable. The *Annales regni Francorum* (a. 807–10) recorded the bitter resistance met by the imperial armies originating from Kephalenia and Constantinople to enforce imperial authority in regions that, at least in theory, were still under Constantinople. Their failure seems to have had roots in the eighth-century transformation that I have just described. These were the premises for the Byzantine eclipse in the Adriatic and the rise of Venice and other Adriatic towns.

Acknowledgements

The research for this article was financed thanks to the FWF Project 24823: *The Transformation of Roman Dalmatia*. I would like to thank Katharina Winckler for her help and advice. I would also like to thank Johannis Stouraitis for discussing the issue of who Theophanes' western commanders may have been.

References

Agathias of Myrina. *Historiae*, in Keydell, R. (ed.), *Agathiae Myrinaei Historiarum libri quinque*, Corpus fontium historiae Byzantinae 2 (Berlin, 1967).

Agnellus of Ravenna. *Liber pontificalis ecclesiae Ravennatis*, in Deliyannis, D. (ed.), *Corpus Christianorum continuatio mediaevalis*, vol. 199 (Turnhout, 2006).

Ahistulphi leges, in Bluhme, W. (ed.), *MGH Leges nationum Germanicarum*, vol. 4 (Hanover, 1868), 478-85.

Annales regni Francorum, in Kurze, F. (ed.), *MGH Scriptores rerum Germanicarum*, vol. 6 (Hanover, 1895).

Augenti, A. and Cirelli, E. 2012. 'From suburb to port: The rise (and fall) of Classe as a centre of trade and redistribution', in Keay, S. (ed.), *Rome, Portus and the Mediterranean* (London and Rome), 205-21.

Bachrach, B. 2001. *Early Carolingian Warfare: Prelude to Empire* (Philadelphia).

Bavant, B. 2004. 'L'Illyricum', in Morrisson, C. (ed.), *Le monde byzantine*, vol. 1, *L'Empire romain d'Orient (330-641)* (Paris), 307-51.

Borri, F. 2005. 'Duces e magistri militum nell'Italia esarcale (VI-VIII secolo)', *Reti medievali* 6/2, 19-64.

2009. 'La Dalmazia altomedievale tra discontinuità e racconto storico (secc. VII-VIII)', *Studi veneziani* n.s. 58, 15-51.

Brandes, W. 2002. *Finanzverwaltung in Krisenzeit: Untersuchungen zur byzantinischen Administration im 6.-9. Jahrhundert* (Frankfurt).

2005. 'Pejorative Phantomnamen im 8. Jahrhundert: Ein Beitrag zur Quellenkritik des Theophanes', in Hoffmann, L.M. and Monchizadeh, A. (eds.), *Zwischen Polis, Provinz und Peripherie: Beiträge zur byzantinischen Geschichte und Kultur* (Wiesbaden), 93-125.

Brown, T.S. 1979. 'The Church of Ravenna and the imperial administration in the seventh century', *The English Historical Review* 94, 1-28.

1992. 'Otranto in Medieval history', in Michaelides, D. and Wilkinson, D. (eds.), *Excavations at Otranto*, vol. 1, *The Excavation* (Lecce), 27-39.

1995. 'Justinian II and Ravenna', *Byzantinoslavica* 56, 29-36.

Brubaker, L. and Haldon, J. 2011. *Byzantium in the Iconoclastic Era, c.680-850: A History* (Cambridge).

Budak, N. 2018. 'One more Renaissance? Dalmatia and the revival of European economy', in Ančić, M., Vedriš, T. and Shepard, J. (eds.), *Imperial Spheres and the Adriatic: Byzantium, the Carolingians and the Treaty of Aachen* (New York and London), 174-91.

Codex Carolinus, in Gundlach, W. (ed.), *MGH Epistolae*, vol. 3 (Berlin, 1892), 469-657.

Conant, J. 2012. *Staying Roman: Conquest and Identity in Africa and the Mediterranean, 439-700* (Cambridge).

Constantine IV. *Sacra ad Donum*, in Riedinger, R. (ed.), *Acta conciliorum oecumenicorum II*, vol. 1 (Berlin, 1990), 2-10.

Constantine Porphyrogennetos. *De administrando imperio*, in Moravcsik, G. and Jenkins, R.J.H. (eds.), *Constantine Porphyrogenitus. De administrando imperio* (Washington, DC, 1967).

Cosentino, S. 2006. 'Politica e fiscalità nell'Italia bizantina (secc. VI–VIII)', in Augenti, A. (ed.), *Le città italiane tra la tarda Antichità e l'alto Medioevo. Atti del Convegno, Ravenna, 26–28 febbraio 2004* (Florence), 37–53.

2008a. 'Constans II and the Byzantine navy', *Byzantinische Zeitschrift* 100/2, 577–603.

2008b. *Storia dell'Italia bizantina (VI–XI secolo): Da Giustiniano ai Normanni* (Bologna).

2012. 'Potere e autorità nell'esarcato in età post-bizantina', in Martin, J.-M., Peters-Custot, A. and Prigent, V. (eds.), *L'héritage byzantin en Italie (VIIIe–XIIe siècle)*, vol. 2, *Les cadres juridiques et sociaux et les institutions publiques*, Collection de l'École française de Rome 461 (Rome), 279–95.

Davis, J.R. 2015. *Charlemagne's Practice of Empire* (Cambridge).

De Min, M. 2003. 'Edilizia ecclesiale e domestica altomedievale nel territorio lagunare: Nuovi dati conoscitivi da indagini archeologiche nel cantiere di restauro a Torcello', in Lenzi, F. (ed.), *L'archeologia dell'Adriatico dalla Preistoria al Medioevo, Atti del Convegno internazionale, Ravenna, 7–9 giugno 2001* (Florence), 600–15.

Delogu, P. 2012. 'Questioni di mare e di costa', in Gelichi, S. and Hodges, R. (eds.), *From One Sea to Another: Trading Places in the European and Mediterranean Early Middle Ages. Proceedings of the International Conference, Comacchio, 27th–29th March 2009* (Turnhout), 459–66.

Diplomata Karolinorum, in Dopsch, A., Lechner, J. and Tangl, M. (eds.), *MGH Diplomata*, vol. 1 (Hanover, 1906).

Dzino, D. 2010. *Becoming Slav, Becoming Croat: Identity Transformations in Post-Roman and Early Medieval Dalmatia* (Leiden and Boston).

Epistolae Austrasicae, in Malaspina, E. (ed.), *Il liber epistolarum della cancelleria Austrasica (sec. V–VI)* (Rome, 2001).

Epistolae Langobardicae collectae, in Gundlach, W. (ed.), *MGH Epistolae*, vol. 3 (Berlin, 1892), 691–718.

Falkenhausen, V. von 2007. 'Tra Occidente e Oriente: Otranto in epoca bizantina', in Houben, H. (ed.), *Otranto nel Medioevo tra Bisanzio e l'Occidente* (Galatina), 13–60.

Ferluga, J. 1978. *L'amministrazione bizantina in Dalmazia* (Venice).

Gasparri, S. 2011. 'Anno 713: La leggenda di Paulicio e le origini di Venezia', in Israel, U. (ed.), *Venezia: I giorni della storia* (Rome), 27–45.

2015. 'Un placito carolingio e la storia di Comacchio', in Jégou, L., Joye, S., Lienhard, T. and Schneider, J. (eds.), *Faire lien: Aristocratie, réseaux et échanges compétitifs. Mélanges en l'honneur de Régine Le Jan* (Paris), 179–89.

2017a. *Voci dai secoli oscuri. Un percorso nelle fonti dell'alto Medioevo* (Rome).

2017b, 'The first dukes and the origins of Venice', in Gasparri, S. and Gelichi, S. (eds.), *Venice and Its Neighbors from the 8th to 11th Century: Through Renovation and Continuity* (Leiden and Boston), 5–26.

Gelichi, S., Calaon, D., Grandi, E. and Negrelli, C. 2012. 'The history of a forgotten town: Comacchio and its archaeology', in Gelichi, S. and Hodges, R. (eds.), *From One Sea to Another: Trading Places in the European and Mediterranean Early Middle Ages. Proceedings of the International Conference, Comacchio, 27th–29th March 2009* (Turnhout), 169–205.

Gkoutzioukostas, A. 2012-13. 'The prefect of Illyricum and the prefect of Thessaloniki', Βυζαντιακά 30, 45–80.

Gregory the Great. *Epistolae*, in Ewald, P. and Hartmann, L.M. (eds.), *MGH Epistolae*, vols. 1–2 (Berlin, 1891–9).

Gutteridge, A. 2003. 'Cultural geographies and "the ambition of Latin Europe": The city of Durrës and its fortifications c.400–c.1500', *Archeologia medievale* 30, 19–65.

Haldon, J. 1999. *Warfare, State and Society in the Byzantine World: 565–1204* (London).

2016. *The Empire That Would Not Die: The Paradox of Eastern Roman Survival, 640–740* (Cambridge, Mass.).

Hartmann, L.M. (ed.) 1904. *Zur Wirtschaftsgeschichte Italiens im frühen Mittelalter* (Gotha).

Haywood, J. 1991. *Dark Ages Naval Power: A Reassessment of Frankish and Anglo-Saxon Seafaring Activity* (London and New York).

Herren, M. (ed.) 2011. *The Cosmography of Aethicus Ister: Edition, Translation, and Commentary* (Turnhout).

Herrin, J. 1992. 'Constantinople, Rome and the Franks in the seventh and eighth centuries', in Shepard, J. and Franklin, S. (eds.), *Byzantine Diplomacy, Papers from the Twenty-Fourth Spring Symposium of Byzantine Studies, Cambridge, March 1990,* Society for the Promotion of Byzantine Studies Publications 1 (Aldershot), 91–107.

Horden, P. and Purcell, N. 2000. *The Corrupting Sea: A Study of Mediterranean History* (Oxford and Malden).

John of Biclaro. *Chronicon*, in Campos, J. (ed.), *Juan de Bíclaro, obispo de Gerona; Su vida y su obra. Edición crítica* (Madrid, 1960).

Jones, A.H.M., Martindale, J.R. and Morris, J. (eds.) 1992. *The Prosopography of the Later Roman Empire*, vol. 3, *A.D. 527–641* (Cambridge).

Justinian II. *Sacra ad Cononem*, in Riedinger, R. (ed.), *Acta conciliorum oecumenicorum II*, vol. 2 (Berlin, 1992), 886.

Kingsley, S. 2009. 'Mapping trade by shipwrecks', in Mundell Mango, M. (ed.), *Byzantine Trade 4th–12th centuries: The Archaeology of Local, Regional and International Exchange.* Society for the Promotion of Byzantine Studies Publications 14 (Aldershot), 31–6.

Leontios. *Vita Ioannis*, in Festugière, A.J. and Rydén, L. (eds.), *Léontios de Néapolis: Vie de Syméon le Fou et Vie de Jean de Chypre* (Paris, 1974), 251–681.

Liber pontificalis, in Duchesne, L. (ed.), *Le Liber pontificalis: Texte, introduction et commentaire*, vol. 1 (Paris, 1886).

Lilie, R.-J., Ludwig, C., Pratsch, T., Rochow, I. and Zielke, B. (eds.) 1999-2002. *Prosopographie der mittelbyzantinischen Zeit (641–867)*, 6 vols. (Berlin).

Margetić, L. 1997. 'Marcellinus scolasticus e proconsul Dalmatiae', *Atti. Centro di ricerche storiche Rovigno* 27, 471-81.

McCormick, M. 2001. *Origins of the European Economy: Communication and Commerce AD 300-900* (Cambridge).

— 2012. 'Comparing and connecting: Comacchio and the early medieval trading towns', in Gelichi, S. and Hodges, R. (eds.), *From One Sea to Another: Trading Places in the European and Mediterranean Early Middle Ages. Proceedings of the International Conference, Comacchio, 27th-29th March 2009* (Turnhout), 477-502.

McGeer, E., Nesbitt, J. and Oikonomides, N. (eds.) 2005. *Catalogue of Byzantine Seals at Dumbarton Oaks and in the Fogg Museum of Art*, vol. 5, *The East (Continued), Constantinople and Environs, Unknown Locations, Addenda, Uncertain Readings* (Washington, DC).

Menander Protector. *Historia*, in Blockley, R.C. (ed.), *The History of Menander the Guardsman: Introductory Essay, Text, Translation and Historiographical Notes* (Liverpool, 1985).

Miracula s. Demetrii, in Lemerle, P. (ed.), *Le plus anciens recueils des miracles de saint Démétrius et la pénétration des Slaves dans les Balkans*, 2 vols. (Paris, 1979-81).

Negrelli, C. 2012. 'Towards a definition of Early Medieval pottery: Amphorae and other vessels in the northern Adriatic between the 7th and the 8th centuries', in Gelichi, S. and Hodges, R. (eds.), *From One Sea to Another: Trading Places in the European and Mediterranean Early Middle Ages. Proceedings of the International Conference, Comacchio, 27th-29th March 2009* (Turnhout), 393-415.

Origo gentis Langobardorum, in Waitz, G. (ed.), *MGH Scriptores rerum Langobardicarum et Italicarum* (Hanover, 1878), 1-6.

Pactum Hlotharii I, in Boretius, A. and Krause, V. (eds.), *MGH Capitularia regum Francorum*, vol. 2 (Hanover, 1897).

Paul the Deacon. *Historia Langobardorum*, in Bethmann, L. and Waitz, G. (eds.), *MGH Scriptores rerum Langobardicarum et Italicarum saec. VI-IX* (Hanover, 1878), 12-187.

Pillon, M. 2005. 'Armée et défense de l'Illyricum byzantin de Justinien à Héraclius (527–641): De la réorganisation justinienne à l'émergence des "Armées de Cité"', *Erytheia* 26, 7-85.

Placitum Risani, in Krahwinkler, H. (ed.), *In loco qui dicitur Rizano: Die Versammlung in Rižana/Risano bei Koper/Capodistria im Jahre 804* (Koper, 2004).

Prigent, V. 2008. 'Notes sur l'évolution de l'administration byzantine en Adriatique (VIIIe–IXe siècle)', *Mélanges de l'École française de Rome. Moyen Âge* 120/2 = Les destinées de l'Illyricum méridional pendant le haut Moyen Âge, 393-417.

Radić Rossi, I. (ed.) 2006. *Archeologia subacquea in Croazia: Studi e ricerche* (Venice).

Ravegnani, G. 2011. *Gli esarchi d'Italia* (Rome).
Saguì, L. 2002. 'Roma, i centri privilegiati e la lunga durata della tarda Antichità: Dati archeologici dal deposito di VII secolo nell'esedra della Crypta Balbi', *Archeologia medievale* 29, 7–42.
Schlumberger, G. 1884. *Sigillographie de l'Empire byzantin* (Paris).
Stein, E. 1925. 'Untersuchungen zur spätrömischen Verwaltungsgeschichte', *Rheinisches Museum für Philologie* 74/4, 347–94.
Stein, E. 1949. *Histoire du Bas-Empire*, vol. 2, *De la disparition de l'Empire d'Occident à la mort de Justinien (476–565)* (Paris, Brussels and Amsterdam).
Šeparović, T. 2008. 'Coin finds of Emperor Constantine V Copronymus in southern Croatia', in Wołoszyn, M. (ed.), *Byzantine Coins in Central Europe between the 5th and the 10th Century* (Krakow), 553–60.
Theophanes. *Chronographia*, ed. C. de Boor, 2 vols. (Leipzig, 1883–5).
Treadgold, W. 1998. *Byzantium and Its Army, 284–1081* (Stanford).
Wickham, C. 2005. *Framing the Early Middle Ages: Europe and the Mediterranean, 400–800* (Oxford).
2012. 'Comacchio and the central Mediterranean', in Gelichi, S. and Hodges, R. (eds.), *From One Sea to Another: Trading Places in the European and Mediterranean Early Middle Ages. Proceedings of the International Conference, Comacchio, 27th–29th March 2009* (Turnhout), 503–10.
Wood, I. 2000. 'Aethicus Ister: An exercise in difference', in Pohl, W. and Reimitz, H. (eds.), *Grenze und Differenz im frühen Mittelalter* (Vienna), 197–208.
Zuckerman, C. 2005. 'Learning from the enemy and more: Studies in "dark centuries" Byzantium', *Millennium* 2, 79–136.
Živković, T. 2008. 'The strategos Paul and the archontes of the westerners', Βυζαντινὰ σύμμεικτα 15, 161–76.

4 | The Origins of Venice

Between Italy, Byzantium and the Adriatic

STEFANO GASPARRI

Any study of Venice's earliest history is confronted with two contrasting problems. The first is the extreme scarcity of sources and the second, caused by the city's extraordinary success over the following centuries, is that its history has become enveloped by so many myths. As a result, study of Venice's origins has been profoundly shaped by these circumstances. However, in recent years research has made important advances in two areas: the study of important archaeological finds from across the entire Adriatic area is one. The other results from an increased critical analysis of the early Venetian duchy's relations with both the Lombard (and later Italian) kingdom and Byzantine Italy. It is this second subject in particular which I will discuss here.

The Arrival of the Lombards

The lagoon area in which Venice emerged had been located in the large, Late Roman province of *Venetia et Histria* (Giardina 1997). The first significant break with the Roman past, however, only occurred with the Lombard invasion in 569. Over the following centuries, Venetian tradition remembered these events through the construction of a legend that the peoples of the Po Valley, under the leadership of their bishops, fled to the lagoon to escape the barbarian rampage (Bognetti 1964; Castagnetti 1992, 577–82; Dorigo 1983, 223). Despite being only a legend, Italian historiography has sadly repeated the story uncritically until very recently (Gelichi 2015a). Indeed, historians ignored the fact that the mass flight of an entire population before barbarian invaders has never been attested anywhere else, inside or outside Italy. A similar interpretation, equally unconvincing, has often been put forward for the other side of the Adriatic as well (Borri 2013).

The decisive cause of Venice's rise was rather different. The Lombard conquest of most of Italy, particularly northern Italy, first of all brought an end to the territorial extension of *Venetia et Histria*, leaving the Byzantines in control of a much narrower strip of territory than that of the former province which had reached as far as the river Adda, covering almost half of the Po Valley. Paul the Deacon (*Historia Langobardorum* 2.14) noted this territorial change some two centuries later, at the end of the eighth century, when he wrote that in his own day Venice was no longer a large region but only 'a few islands'. The institutional shape of the former province was also subject to equally profound changes, coming under the total control of the military hierarchy. Rather than any romantic notion of refugees taking flight from the cities of the plain to the remote lagoon, it was these changes brought about by the Lombard invasion and the expansion of the kingdom which they founded, that really did establish the conditions for the birth of Venice (Arnaldi and Pavan 1992).

The institutional changes which took place in the province happened in the context of a wider reorganisation of those lands which remained under Byzantine control. In order to resist pressure from the Lombards, these were amalgamated (probably after 584) into the exarchate, a structure under military command with its capital at Ravenna (Guillou 1980, 235–40; Moorhead 2005, 157–8). Despite the importance of Byzantine Italy and its long history over some two centuries, we know little about its internal organisation to the extent that we do not even know how many exarchs there were nor their precise chronology (Cosentino 1996; Ravegnani 2006, 52–6). Nor, as a consequence, is the position of the province of *Venetia* within the exarchate clear. One thing does seem certain though: throughout its earliest history, the only truly significant structure in *Venetia* was its military.

Given the region's location in a hazardous frontier zone, this is not surprising. Indeed, the areas of *Venetia et Histria* which remained under Byzantine control after the first wave of invasions were several times subject to serious military pressure from the Lombard kings, particularly Agilulf, who took Padua and Monselice at the beginning of the seventh century, and later Rothari and Grimoald (Arnaldi and Pavan 1992, 418–22). The close proximity of the Lombard dukes of Friuli was also a danger, even if they occasionally entered into an alliance with the Byzantine empire. Such alliances, however, barely concealed mutual hostility. Thus, it should not be a surprise that Paul the Deacon (*Historia Langobardorum* 4.38) describes an incident around 625 in Oderzo where, at a meeting which must have been organised to seal an alliance, two Friulian dukes, the brothers Taso and Cacco, were killed in a trap laid by the patrician Gregory.

The traditional assumption is that Gregory was the exarch of Ravenna although it is not necessary to maintain this. He could well have been the local commander of the Byzantine army in *Venetia*. Further evidence for the presence of an important military hierarchy in the lagoon is to be found in a famous epigraph from the basilica of Santa Maria in Torcello, datable to the autumn of 639. Alongside the testimony of the Exarch Isacius, who ordered the construction of the church 'through the merits of him and his army', the inscription reveals that Mauricius, commander of the army stationed in the lagoon (*magister militum provincie Venetiarum*) was responsible for physically realising the building (Pertusi 1962). It is notable that the dedicatory epigraph makes reference not to the people in general, but to the army – further evidence of the strong militarisation of Byzantine society in both the exarchate and the lagoon.

Over the course of the seventh century, the province of *Venetia* experienced locally the impact of broader conflicts which shook all of Byzantine Italy and which, in their turn, were an echo of actions taken in Constantinople (Brown 1995). The Exarch Isacius' activity in the lagoon, which was unprecedented, may have been connected to the upheavals surrounding the promulgation of the *ekthesis* (638). This so-called 'edict of union' with the monophysites, issued by the Emperor Heraclius, also led to a harsh attack on Rome and the papacy, again led by Isacius (Ravegnani 2006, 67). At a moment of internal crisis in Byzantine Italy following the papacy's rejection of the *ekthesis*, the exarch's intervention in Venetian affairs might be explained by the need to maintain tight links between Ravenna and the province which was of considerable strategic importance. Furthermore, 639 (the year of the Torcello inscription) was also the year in which the Lombard King Rothari first occupied Oderzo, thus delivering a heavy blow to the Byzantine presence on the Venetian mainland (*Historia Langobardorum* 4.45). Evidently the Lombard strikes were synchronised with Byzantium's religious and political crisis. As a consequence, Byzantine territory continued to diminish. When in 669 the Lombard King Grimoald took Oderzo permanently, Byzantine Venice rapidly shrank to the lagoon and the lands immediately around it (*Historia Langobardorum* 5.28).

Venice between the Lombard Kingdom and the Exarchate

During this whole period, before the birth of the city itself, Venice remained under Byzantine control, albeit within its territory greatly reduced. However, we have no evidence for direct relations with Byzantium or even with Ravenna before the dramatic events of 727–8 when yet another political and religious crisis in the empire, this time triggered by iconoclasm (Haldon 1977; Schreiner 1988), provoked the armies of Venice and the Pentapolis into revolt against the exarch (*Liber pontificalis*, vol. 1, 404). This confirmed the military role of forces in the lagoon.

Some ten years later the situation changed again. Taking advantage of the resistance of Italy's Roman population to Byzantium's iconoclastic politics, the Lombard King Liutprand occupied Ravenna. In response Exarch Eutychius personally sought refuge in *Venetia* (Gasparri 2011, 38–9). After an appeal from Pope Gregory II, however, the Venetian fleet successfully reconquered the city and restored Eutychius to his office, although he was destined to be Italy's last exarch (*Epistolae Langobardicae collectae* 11; *Historia Langobardorum* 6.54).

Compared to the size of its military, ecclesiastical organisation in Byzantine Venice appears to have been much weaker. This was despite the foundation of the patriarchate of Grado which had separated from that of Aquileia after a schism at the beginning of the seventh century (Azzara 2007). Evidence for the presence of churches in the lagoon itself is practically non-existent until the end of the eighth century (McCormick 2007; Gelichi 2015a). The record of the construction of Santa Maria on Torcello in the mid-seventh century is therefore exceptional. The first diocese to be established near Rialto was on the island of Olivolo in 775. Placed under the jurisdiction of Grado, its foundation has traditionally been attributed to the initiative of Duke Maurizio Galbaio (John the Deacon, *Istoria Veneticorum* 2.19). The lagoon's earliest churches – particularly monasteries – only arose with certainty later, at the beginning of the ninth century. The episcopal church of San Pietro on Olivolo is no earlier than this period, even if there may have been an older church on the island (Gelichi 2015a).

Until 751, the year of the Lombard King Aistulf's conquest of Ravenna, Venice formed an integral part of the exarchate of Ravenna (Gasparri 2012, 100–6). Nevertheless, the first signs of autonomy emerged some twenty years earlier during Liutprand's aforementioned offensive against the exarchate, which profoundly weakened the unity of Byzantine Italy. It was almost certainly in this period that the first independent duke, Orso, emerged. Venice must have already been governed before this time by a duke (*dux*), given that we know that there were dukes in both Rome and Naples. But, since the sources are silent on the matter, we do not know at what point the province became a duchy. Orso's election by a section of the local aristocracy must certainly have been connected to the Italian armies' revolt against Byzantium but the circumstances of his election and that of his successors remain completely obscure (Gasparri 2011, 38–9).

The participation of those officials whom the earliest Venetian chronicle (written around 1000 and attributed to John the Deacon) labels the tribunes (*tribuni*) was certainly at the forefront. These were high-ranking officers of the local army who are also attested by other contemporary sources (Lanfranchi-Strina 1965, no. 2, 17–24), such as the famous will left by the Duke Giustiniano Particiaco (828 or 829) which mentions a lot of land formerly owned by the tribunes. However we do not know how the ducal election took place in this early period. The earliest evidence for an electoral ceremony refers to 887 but since it is found in a description by John the Deacon, who wrote it a hundred years later, the suspicion remains that he was projecting the order of the election in his own day backwards. John (*Istoria Veneticorum* 3.32 and 3.35) describes how the new duke was handed a sword, a sceptre and a seat (*sella*) – the symbols of the power which he had assumed. After this record, we have to wait until 1071 and the description of the election of Duke Domenico Silvo. On this occasion we read that there was a great procession of ships which conducted the new duke to the basilica of San Marco, where he took hold of the sceptre (*baculus*) which had been placed on the altar. Ceremonial roles were dominated by both the nobles (*proceres*) and the members of the army (*exercitus*), who accompanied the duke to the palace where he received the oath of the people (Gasparri 1992, 817–8). Taken together, these two records give us some idea of how the election took place since probably the tenth century and perhaps also as early as the ninth century. The ceremony's solemnity has us understand that the dukes, since their earliest history, were the key authority figures across all of Venetian society.

It should be emphasised again that all of the earliest history of the formation of the Venetian duchy is very unclear, since it depends on later and less trustworthy sources which, at times, have been heavily reworked. One fact is certain: even after the fall of the exarchate and the rise of independent dukes elected by the local community in the lagoon, links with Byzantium remained. While a Frankish intervention could have changed this situation, during the first and most fragile phase of the Carolingian conquest of Italy, Venice's anchorage in the Byzantine world was guaranteed by the papacy. Indeed, since the earliest donation made by King Pippin to the Roman Church, the province of *Venetia et Histria* was included among the territories conceded to the pope (Arnaldi 1987, 127–34). This concession did not have any practical consequences. However, because the pope acted as the direct heir to the exarch – and thus was not only the leading religious but also political authority in Byzantine Italy – the inclusion of the region in the donation indicated the clear desire to maintain Venice within the traditional sphere of Byzantine politics, rather than a strict political dependence on Byzantium whose presence in Italy at this point was extremely weak.

Confrontation with the Carolingians

The Venetian duchy's slow and uncertain assertion of autonomy in the eighth century was periodically interrupted by moments of more direct control by Byzantium. Later Venetian historiography, from John the Deacon (*Istoria Veneticorum* 2.11, 2.14, 2.17) onwards, presented this period as alternating between dukes (*duces*) and masters of soldiers (*magistri militum*). Institutionally this distinction does not seem to make much sense, since in this period the two offices had become substantially identical (Borri 2005, 6; Brown 1988, 135–7). John presents this alternation as a consequence of the local aristocracy's striving for greater autonomy in the face of the excessive power of the dukes. More probably, as the majority of historiography has argued, his explanation represents a distorted memory of periods of Byzantine resurgence, which for a time at the end of the eighth century saw Venice return to the empire's political control (Ortalli 1980, 367–8). On the other hand, it is true that there is no evidence of the Byzantine fleet's presence in the northern Adriatic during the eighth century, that is, the time when the exarchate was steadily weakening before disappearing. But, conversely, in the same period, there are clear traces of significant Byzantine presence in Istria whose connections with Venice were most likely never entirely broken (Borri 2012). One example of this presence will suffice here.

In 804, an important judicial assembly (*placitum*) was held at Risano (modern Rižana) in Istria, presided over by representatives (*missi*) sent by Charlemagne (Manaresi 1955, no. 17, 49–56). The *placitum* represented the first attempt by the Franks to bring order to Istria, the peninsula having been contested for almost all of the eighth century by Byzantium and the Lombard kingdom. The *placitum* reveals that the Franks had only recently taken control of Istria since, with the exception of complaints against Fortunatus, the patriarch of Grado, all the grievances brought by the Istrians during the assembly related to the rule of the Frankish Duke John. The period before him, that of the end of the eighth century, is defined in the text as the time of the Greeks (*tempus Grecorum*) referring to a time of direct Byzantine rule.

The *placitum*, when compared to the earliest Venetian documentary evidence which begins shortly afterwards, allows us to glimpse some of the cultural, social and institutional aspects of Byzantine society in the Adriatic, which, after the fall of the exarchate, revolved around the three centres of Venice, Istria and Dalmatia. This document reveals a social structure supported by a strong ecclesiastical hierarchy, a lay hierarchy which exclusively used Byzantine titles (such as tribune and *hypatos*) and the existence of assemblies in different cities, perhaps a survival of earlier forms of municipal organisation. These assemblies also suggest the likely form of the earliest Venetian assemblies which elected the dukes and – most probably – made essential political decisions (Gasparri 1997). Participants who attended assemblies in Istria held separate positions according to the office or honour which they possessed. The members of these assembles are defined in the *placitum* as *primates*, a term which later reappears in Venetian sources. We also have a description of a kind of course of honour (*cursus honorum*), beginning with the office of tribune and ending with that of *hypatos* (or consul) which was obtained from the emperor by going directly to Constantinople. The same procedure is also attested in Venice where, during the ninth century, several dukes sent members of their family (often themselves potential heirs to ducal office) to Constantinople in order to receive Byzantine honours from the emperor himself (Pertusi 1965; Ravegnani 1992).

Among the many abuses denounced in the text which were committed by the Istrian Duke John, including excessive fiscal levies, seizures, compulsory services (*angarie*) and acts of violence, the Istrians also described how they were forced by the duke to sail to Venice, Ravenna, Dalmatia and 'on the rivers' inland from the sea – 'something which we have never done' (*Ambulamus navigio in Venetias, Ravennam, Dalmatia[m], et per flumina, quod numquam fecimus. Non solum Ioanni hoc facimus, se[d] etiam ad filios et filias seu generum suum*), they claimed. By this they were referring only to obligatory naval service which they had been forced to render; they were certainly not saying that they had never sailed to these places before. On the contrary, their familiarity with and proximity to these sites is attested later in the text of the *placitum* itself. The Istrians state how their 'relatives and neighbours' in Venice and Dalmatia had derided them for their impoverishment as a consequence of John's oppression (*Unde omnes devenimus in paupertatem, et derident nostros parentes et convicini nostri Venetias et Dalmatias, etiam Greci, sub cuius antea fuimus potestate*). Despite the exaggerated rhetoric, the appeal to their closeness and kinship with Venice and Dalmatia does appear to be a forceful and conscious assertion.

The assembly at Rižana (Risano) occurred during the peak of Charlemagne's power, closely following his election as emperor. At this point the Carolingians also exerted a degree of control over Venice although this would come to an end with the Aachen peace treaty which was concluded between the two empires in 812 (Borri 2010). Pressure to bring about a settlement reinforcing links with the eastern empire was not only exerted by repeated operations by the Byzantine fleet, which both in 806–7 and 809–10 arrived in the lower Adriatic and the lagoon. It was also maintained by the fact that, as we have just seen, the duchy was deeply embedded in a dense network of political, social and economic relations which extended across the whole northern Adriatic as well as being linked politically and culturally to Byzantium.

Charlemagne himself understood this when he made a solemn *ordinatio* for the dukes and the people of Venice and Dalmatia at Aachen in 806 (*Annales regni Francorum*, a. 806). On this occasion he summoned Obelerius and Beatus, dukes of *Venetia*, together with ambassadors from the Dalmatians, namely Paul and Donatus, the duke and bishop of Zadar. This did not, of course, mean that Charlemagne found two identical situations in the two provinces. The most glaring difference lay in the fact that the province of *Venetia* did not have a city which could represent it, since the city of Venice did not yet exist. By contrast Dalmatia had a capital at Zadar. Nevertheless, the two provinces were profoundly connected and it must have been for this reason that Charlemagne sought to provide them with a common settlement within the empire, which was worth the price to guarantee the Frankish control of the upper Adriatic. That Charlemagne's project failed and that after 812 Venice was stably reintegrated into the Byzantine sphere of influence, does not diminish the significance of what Charlemagne tried to achieve; it reveals his understanding of the northern Adriatic as a deeply interconnected region, bound together by multiple political, cultural and commercial links (Gelichi 2015b).

Venice and Comacchio

Venice's Adriatic character, therefore, only clearly emerges – at least in the written sources – during the time of Charlemagne. This orientation on the Byzantine Adriatic would later be reaffirmed by Venice's continued interest in Istria. With varying fortunes, Venice defended the peninsula from Slav and Saracen attacks throughout the entire ninth century. In the following century, when Venice's commercial and military supremacy was clear, the Venetian lagoon's continued interest in controlling Istria gave birth to a kind of commercial protectorate on the peninsula as witnessed by three treaties in 932, 933 and 976 (Ortalli 1992, 762–8).

Venice's role in the Adriatic should also be compared with the history of the emporium of Comacchio. The written sources which mention Comacchio in the eighth century are far from scarce and they make visible the importance of this centre. Its importance has been strikingly confirmed by the excavations carried out in Comacchio by Sauro Gelichi (2008) over the last years. As a consequence of the new data which has poured out of Comacchio, its comparison with Venice has by now become mandatory. In both cases these were major centres in the Byzantine Adriatic and, moreover, Comacchio as the emporium probably first accumulated its wealth from the salt trade, exhibited many similar characteristics to those later adopted by Venice. The emporium's activity later widened to become a point of commercial exchange between the Byzantine East and the Lombard kingdom of Italy. However, despite the similarities between the two centres, their fates were very different. As Venetian commerce took off in the ninth and even more in the tenth century, attacks by the Saracens and later by the Venetians themselves confirmed the final decline of Comacchio by the end of the first half of the tenth century, sealing a process which was already evident in the ninth century, as archaeological finds confirm (Gasparri 2015).

Comacchio and Venice were both recent foundations and both developed in importance in tandem with the decline of the exarchate and the centralised political structures of Byzantine Italy (McCormick 2012, 477–80). This is not to say that there were no differences. Comacchio's inhabitants were already active in 715 when a well-known commercial treaty, which most likely committed to writing agreements which had existed earlier, was concluded with the Lombard kingdom (Hartmann 1904, 74). Furthermore, the written sources define Comacchio as either a *castrum* or a *civitas*. In Venice, by contrast, there was no proper urban centre to speak of until the very end of the ninth century when what would later become known as the *civitas Rivoalti* developed on the islands of Rialto. This is more than a century later than Comacchio which may even have acquired a bishop some fifty years earlier than Venice did. It should not surprise us then if Comacchio's commercial role in relation to the Italian hinterland, extending across the Po and the other rivers of the Po Valley, was initially much more powerful than that of Venice. It was only during the ninth century that Venice overtook its southern rivals (Gasparri 1992).

Trying to identify the causes of Venice's supremacy over Comacchio should lead us to reconsider the military dimension, something practically undocumented for Comacchio. While it is true that Comacchio's merchants are referred to as soldiers (*milites*) in the sources, this was a traditional title used for inhabitants of Byzantine Italy; it does not suggest that they were members of the military (*exercitus*) comparable to the Venetian army (*exercitus Veneciarum*). Indeed, in military terms the two centres' roles are reversed: a master of soldiers (*magister militum*) is attested in Venice some seventy years before it is attested in Comacchio, in the Torcello epigraph of 639 and the agreement with the Lombards of 715 respectively. Nevertheless, the existence of the office in Comacchio as well demonstrates that the new community established structures which were by now typical in Byzantine Italy.

It may have been precisely Comacchio's military – and thus political – weakness (we do not know what level of autonomy it had from Ravenna), that favoured its initial penetration into the markets of the Po Valley in the heart of the Lombard kingdom, with the sanction of King Liutprand. In the case of Venice, much more heavily marked by its military character (as is amply demonstrated by its role in the temporary reconquest of Ravenna), developing commercial relations with the mainland was more difficult. It is not by chance that these only began to develop fully after the arrival of the Franks and the end of the direct Byzantine presence in the northern Adriatic. Confronted with the troubles caused by the Slavs and Saracens in the Adriatic, the growth of commercial relations with the kingdom was one of the decisive elements of the Venetian take-off in the ninth century.

In conclusion, Venice's political and cultural links with eastern Byzantium should not be overestimated. During the earliest period of its autonomy – despite its Byzantine origins – the formation of Venetian society, its institutions, political identity and the city itself were profoundly influenced by social and institutional developments on the Italian mainland with which it was intimately connected. Here we will just list two examples. A Venetian *placitum* dated to the tenth century, recording an assembly summoned by the duke, does resemble aspects of the assemblies of Byzantine Istria but it also recalls the judicial assemblies of the cities of the kingdom of Italy in the same period. In another example, note how the symbols of ducal power also have a mixed origin, exhibiting both the influence of the Roman (and thus Byzantine) past as well as that of the barbarian mainland (Gasparri 1997).

It is true that after a period of considerable political uncertainty, Venice once again became integrated into Byzantium's political sphere of influence following the 812 peace of Aachen. It is also true that Venice's domination of the upper Adriatic, which was won at a heavy price and only completed by the year 1000, allowed Venice to maintain active links with Byzantium and to position itself as the chief centre of the 'Roman' (or Byzantine) community in the Adriatic, an area which also included Istria and Dalmatia. But none of this means that Venice was simply an appendage of Byzantium on Italian soil. Simultaneously Byzantine, Adriatic and Italian in character, Venice developed in delicate equilibrium with all these different social components. It is precisely in this fact – and not the alleged purity of its eastern or Byzantine character – that Venice's great distinctiveness is to be found.

References

Annales regni Francorum, in Kurze, F. (ed.), *MGH Scriptores rerum Germanicarum*, vol. 6 (Hanover, 1895).

Arnaldi, G. 1987. 'Le origini del patrimonio di S. Pietro', in Arnaldi, G., Toubert, P., Waley, D., Maire Vigueur, J.-C. and Manselli, R. (eds.), *Storia d'Italia*, vol. 7/2, *Comuni e signorie nell'Italia nordorientale e centrale: Lazio, Umbria, Marche, Lucca* (Turin), 3–151.

Arnaldi, G. and Pavan M. 1992. 'Alle origini dell'identità lagunare', in Cracco Ruggini, L., Pavan, M., Cracco G. and Ortalli, G. (eds.), *Storia di Venezia: Dalle origini alla caduta della Serenissima*, vol. 1, *Origini: Età ducale* (Rome), 409–21.

Azzara, C. 2007. 'Il regno longobardo in Italia e i Tre Capitoli', in Chazelle, C. and Cubitt, C. (eds.), *The Crisis of the Oikoumene: The Three Chapters and the Failed Quest for Unity in the Sixth-Century Mediterranean* (Turnhout), 209–22.

Bognetti, G.P. 1964. 'Natura, politica e religione nelle origini di Venezia', in *Le origini di Venezia* (Florence), 14–28.

Borri, F. 2005. 'Duces e magistri militum nell'Italia esarcale (VI–VIII secolo)', *Reti medievali* 6/2, 19–64.

2010. 'L'Adriatico tra Bizantini, Longobardi e Franchi: Dalla conquista di Ravenna alla pace di Aquisgrana (751–812)', *Bullettino dell'Istituto storico italiano per il Medioevo* 112, 1–56.

2012. 'L'Istria tra Bisanzio e i Franchi', in Martin, J.-M., Peters-Custot, A. and Prigent, V. (eds.), *L'héritage byzantin en Italie (VIIIe–XIIe siècle)*, vol. 2, *Les cadres juridiques et sociaux et les institutions publiques*, Collection de l'École française de Rome 461 (Rome), 297–323.

2013. 'Arrivano i barbari a cavallo! Foundation myths and *origines gentium* in the Adriatic arc', in Pohl, W. and Heydemann, G. (eds.), *Post-Roman Transitions: Christian and Barbarian Identities in the Early Medieval West* (Turnhout) 215–70.

Brown, T.S. 1988. 'The interplay between Roman and Byzantine traditions and local sentiment in the exarchate of Ravenna', in *Bisanzio, Roma e l'Italia nell'alto Medioevo*, Settimane di studio del Centro italiano di studi sull'alto Medioevo 34 (Spoleto), 127–60.

1995. 'Byzantine Italy, c.680–c.876', in McKitterick R. (ed.), *The New Cambridge Medieval History*, vol. 2, c.700–c.900 (Cambridge), 320–48.

Castagnetti, A. 1992. 'Insediamenti e "populi"', in Cracco Ruggini, L., Pavan, M., Cracco, G. and Ortalli, G. (eds.), *Storia di Venezia: Dalle origini alla caduta della Serenissima*, vol. 1, *Origini: Età ducale* (Rome), 577–612.

Cosentino, S. 1996. *Prosopografia dell'Italia bizantina (493–804)*, vol. 1, A–F (Bologna).

Dorigo, W. 1983. *Venezia origini: Fondamenti, ipotesi, metodi*, vol. 1 (Milan).

Epistolae Langobardicae collectae, in Gundlach, W. (ed.), *MGH Epistolae*, vol. 3 (Berlin 1892), 691–718.

Gasparri, S. 1992. 'Venezia fra i secoli VIII e IX: Una riflessione sulle fonti', in Ortalli, G. and Scarabello, G. (eds.), *Studi veneti offerti a Gaetano Cozzi* (Venice), 3–18.

1997. 'Venezia fra l'Italia bizantina e il regno italico: La civitas e l'assemblea', in Gasparri, S., Levi, G. and Moro, P. (eds.), *Venezia: Itinerari per la storia della città* (Bologna), 61–82.

2011. 'Anno 713. La leggenda di Paulicio e le origini di Venezia', in Israel, U. (ed.), *Venezia: I giorni della storia* (Rome), 27–45.

2012. *Italia longobarda: Il regno, i Franchi, il papato* (Rome and Bari).

2015. 'Un placito carolingio e la storia di Comacchio', in Jégou, L., Joye, S., Lienhard, T. and Schneider, J. (eds.), *Faire lien: Aristocratie, réseaux et échanges compétitifs. Mélanges en l'honneur de Régine Le Jan* (Paris), 179–89.

Gelichi, S. 2008. 'The eels of Venice: The long eighth century of the emporia of the northern region along the Adriatic coast', in Gasparri, S. (ed.), *774: Ipotesi su una transizione* (Turnhout), 81–117.

2015a. 'La storia di una nuova città attraverso l'archeologia: Venezia nell'alto Medioevo', in West-Harling, V. (ed.), *Three Empires, Three Cities: Identity, Material Culture and Legitimacy in Venice, Ravenna and Rome, 750–1000* (Turnhout), 51–98.

2015b. 'Venice in the Early Middle Ages: The material structures and society of "civitas aput rivoaltum" between the 9th and 10th centuries', in La Rocca, M.C. and Majocchi, P. (eds.), *Urban Identities in Northern Italy (800–1100 ca.)* (Turnhout), 251–71.

Giardina, A. 1997. *L'Italia romana. Storie di un'identità incompiuta* (Rome and Bari).

Guillou, A. 1980. 'L'Italia bizantina dall'invasione longobarda alla caduta di Ravenna', in Delogu, P., Guillou, A. and Ortalli, P. (eds.), *Storia d'Italia*, vol. 1, *Longobardi e Bizantini* (Turin), 219–338.

Haldon, J.F. 1977. 'Some remarks on the background to the Iconoclast Controversy', *Byzantinoslavica* 38, 161–84.

Hartmann, L.M. (ed.) 1904. *Zur Wirtschaftsgeschichte Italiens im frühen Mittelalter* (Gotha).

John the Deacon. *Istoria Veneticorum*, in Berto, L.A. (ed.), *Giovanni Diacono. Istoria Veneticorum* (Bologna, 1999).

Lanfranchi, L. and Strina, B. (eds.) 1965. *SS Ilario e Benedetto e S. Gregorio*, Fonti per la storia di Venezia, sez. 2, Archivi ecclesiastici – Diocesi Castellana (Venice).

Liber pontificalis, in Duchesne, L. (ed.), *Le Liber pontificalis: Texte, introduction et commentaire*, vol. 1 (Paris, 1886).

Manaresi, C. (ed.) 1955. *I placiti del regnum Italiae*, vol. 1 (Rome).

McCormick, M. 2007. 'Where do trading towns come from? Early medieval Venice and the northern *emporia*', in Henning, J. (ed.), *Post-Roman Towns, Trade and Settlement in Europe and Byzantium*, vol. 1, *The Heirs of the Roman West* (Berlin and New York), 41–68.

2012. 'Comparing and connecting: Comacchio and the early medieval trading towns', in Gelichi, S. and Hodges, R. (eds.), *From One Sea to Another: Trading Places in the European and Mediterranean Early Middle Ages. Proceedings of the International Conference, Comacchio, 27th-29th March 2009* (Turnhout), 477–502.

Moorhead, J. 2005. 'Ostrogothic Italy and the Lombard invasions', in Fouracre, P. (ed.), *The New Cambridge Medieval History*, vol. 1, *c.500–c.700* (Cambridge), 140–61.

Ortalli, G. 1980. 'Venezia dalle origini a Pietro II Orseolo', in Delogu, P., Guillou, A. and Ortalli, P. (eds.), *Storia d'Italia*, vol. 1, *Longobardi e Bizantini* (Turin), 341–438.

1992. 'Il ducato e la "civitas Rivoalti": Tra carolingi, bizantini e sassoni', in Cracco Ruggini, L., Pavan, M., Cracco, G. and Ortalli, G. (eds.), *Storia di Venezia: Dalle origini alla caduta della Serenissima*, vol. 1, *Origini: Età ducale* (Rome), 725–90.

Paul the Deacon. *Historia Langobardorum*, in Bethmann, L. and Waitz, G. (eds.), *MGH Scriptores rerum Langobardicarum et Italicarum saec. VI-IX* (Hanover, 1878), 12–187.

Pertusi, A. 1962. 'L'iscrizione torcellana dei tempi di Eraclio', *Bollettino dell'Istituto di storia della società e dello stato veneziano* 4, 9–38.

1965. 'Quedam regalia insigna: Ricerca sulle insegne del potere ducale a Venezia durante il Medioevo', *Studi veneziani* 7, 3–123.

Ravegnani, G. 1992. 'Dignità bizantine dei dogi di Venezia', in Ortalli, G. and Scarabello, G. (eds.), *Studi veneti offerti a Gaetano Cozzi* (Venice), 19–29.

2006. *Introduzione alla storia bizantina* (Bologna).

Schreiner, P. 1988. 'Der byzantinische Bilderstreit: Kritische Analyse der zeitgenössischen Meinungen und das Urteil der Nachwelt bis heute', in *Bisanzio, Roma e l'Italia nell'alto Medioevo*, Settimane di studio del Centro italiano di studi sull'alto Medioevo 34 (Spoleto), 319–407.

5 | The Northern Adriatic Area between the Eighth and the Ninth Century

New Landscapes, New Cities

SAURO GELICHI

During the Early Middle Ages, the entire northern Adriatic appears to have been affected by a very marked phenomenon: the movement of cities. This was a clearly distinctive sign compared to the rest of the north of the Apennine peninsula, where no new cities were founded despite some ancient cities being abandoned. Instead, in the northern Adriatic, new urban settlements were established or, to be more precise, settlements which aspired to become cities and those which markedly reflected the urban model developed. The other peculiarity is that these centres developed along the coast and in locations such as lagoons or river estuaries, that were used rather infrequently in the ancient world as a site for a city although there are some exceptions, for example Ravenna and *Altinum*.

There are various issues that may lead to providing an explanation for this phenomenon yet, generally, they are summarised as reflecting the need of the local population to defend and protect themselves from their enemies: we seem to be faced with the migration of entire populations originating from the mainland areas towards the safer lagoon areas. Such narratives, unfortunately uncritically referred to in more recent historiography, basically derive from historical-narrative texts of more or less recent origin and writing. These are complex texts that normally tend to simplify complex social, political and economic phenomena. Moreover, these refer to paradigms of an ancient mythographic nature, for example that relating to migrations. Such paradigms are used in order to explain – definitely in retrospect – a new state of affairs: in short, to report historical processes in a well-known, legendary and, as such, reassuring context. Thus, they are functional in order to establish – always in hindsight – new identities of populations, drawing on historic episodes that have more value for the present, in which they are elaborated, than for the past to which they were attributed. The changes in inhabited areas were generally linked to the fear of barbarians, first the Huns and then the Lombards, and explained as creating direct descendants of ancient Roman cities on the mainland, either in decline or abandoned, in the lagoon area: Grado for Aquileia, Cittanova or *Equilo* for Oderzo, Torcello for

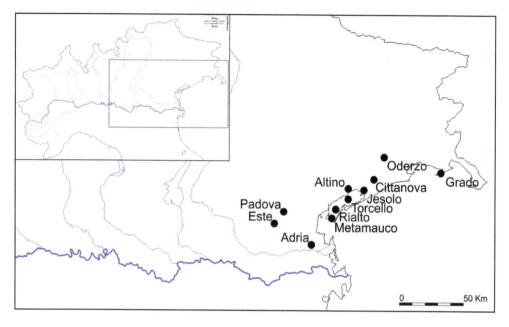

Fig. 5.1 Map of the north-east Adriatic with the locations from the text.
Elaborated by the Laboratorio Archeologia Medievale, Università Venezia

Altinum (Altino) and Metamauco for Padua (Fig. 5.1). In short, the inhabitants of the ancient Roman cities swapped a location on the Lombard mainland or, later on, a location in a Franco-Carolingian area, for another one in the lagoon areas that had remained Byzantine and created new cities as derivations of the Roman world that was left behind.

The reasons for this 'construction' are clear and can be easily identified in the future history, especially that of Venice, that needed to re-create its own past – the moment in which the new city took on a decisive, pre-eminent political and economic role. The text that aided the construction of these narratives is the *Istoria Veneticorum*, written by a certain John the Deacon towards the beginning of the eleventh century. In fact, by examining the narratives focusing on the individual areas in detail and, when possible, integrating them with archaeological data, we realise that these describe a wide variety of situations which have to be borne in mind if one wishes to analyse critically what can be defined as 'traditional explanations'.

New Eras, Different Cities: The Inhabited Areas of the Northern Adriatic during the Early Middle Ages

The archaeology of the northern Adriatic, with a few exceptions, is still far from highlighting suitable stratigraphic sequences in urban contexts and, consequently, appropriate interpretative summaries of a historical nature. The validity of this statement is even more pertinent to the period that followed classical Antiquity. The Venetian lagoon, for example, has seen intense archaeological activity yet, this has been devoid of a specific plan and affected by the aggravating circumstance that the outcomes of such activity remain mainly unpublished (Gelichi 2006; 2010a; 2010b). Some of the important sites situated both in and along the edge of the lagoon have been studied and published more than others, for example Torcello (Calaon, Zendri and Biscontin 2014; Leciejewicz 2000; 2002; Leciejewicz, Tabaczyńska and Tabaczyńsky 1977) or Jesolo, that is, *Equilo* (Gelichi, Cadamuro and Cianciosi 2018) (Fig. 5.1). However, what is truly lacking is an archaeological overview relating to the Rialto archipelago or, in other words, the space that was subsequently occupied by Venice.

We still know very little of the Roman cities situated along the coast or in neighbouring areas belonging to the ancient *Regio X Venetia et Histria*, which were abandoned or presumed to be in decline. Ancient Adria became an episcopal see (Casazza 2001), and a few traces of its Early Medieval past remain, for example the frescoes discovered in 1830 beneath the present-day cathedral (Canova Dal Zio 1986, 81–2) (Fig. 5.2) and the inscription by Bishop

Fig. 5.2 Adria, the Church of Our Lady of the Assumption, frescoes.
Photo: Marco Moro

Bono on the baptismal font from the Basilica of Our Lady of the Assumption or 'della Tomba' (Canova Dal Zio 1986, 81; Gelichi 2013). A recent analysis of archaeological data relating to Late Antiquity and the Early Middle Ages has painted a dismal picture of poverty (Corrò 2016; Mozzi and Negrelli 2013, 56–7) and, despite a reliable paleo-environmental reconstruction, the topography of the inhabited area as well as the places of ecclesiastical power remain hypothetical. Thus, we still have a very limited knowledge of the relationship between the ancient cities and the new towns emerging in the local area, which are partly known from written sources (such as the case of Gavello, see Casazza 2001) and partly from archaeological sources, showing indisputable signs of vitality in the Early Middle Ages.

With regard to the latter, one such site was San Basilio on the Forzello estate (Mozzi and Negrelli 2013, 76–85), where two Early Medieval coins were discovered in the context of a Late Antique church and a baptistery (Fig. 5.3): a Carolingian silver *denarius* bearing the name of Louis the Pious struck by the Venice mint (819–22) and a silver *dirham* of Harun-al Rashid of 798, struck at the Ifriqiya mint. These coins bear witness to the role this location had with regard to communication routes and commerce, especially with reference to the ancient territory of Adria. My observation is based on the information provided next to the objects on display at the National Archaeological Museum in Adria and from the text boards in the

Fig. 5.3 San Basilio (Rovigo, Italy), the remains of a Late Antique baptismal font. Photo: Sauro Gelichi

outdoor archaeological area near which the Church of San Basilio can be seen in its present form as a modest single-nave chapel (Tuzzato 2001).

Very little is known of Este (*Ateste*) after Antiquity until the construction of the castle by the Obertenghi – the problem has been taken up again with the findings about Late Antique churches and fortifications (Brogiolo 2017) while Early Medieval archaeological data is still lacking. In the case of Padua, one of the major cities of the region, the absence of an Early Medieval context is generally explained by the crisis the city underwent following the Lombard conquest. Recent excavations conducted in the episcopal area (Chavarria Arnau 2017) confirm this interpretation. The archaeological sequence documents a radical change that took place around the beginning of the seventh century when a building with fourth-century mosaics, considered pertinent to the first episcopal complex, was destroyed by fire. The area continued to be inhabited (Nicosia *et al.* 2018) but new masonry structures were built only between the tenth and the eleventh centuries: the Romanesque baptistery and the so-called *Chiostro dei canonici*. The juxtaposition of the period of the fire with the destruction of Padua in 601 – according to the story told by Paul the Deacon (*Historia Langobardorum* 4.23) – and the interpretation of the subsequent archaeological findings show that Padua remained a settlement albeit one of a different quality and nature. They also place the episcopal complex in the context of what can be defined a 'traditional' interpretation of the evolution of the city, which highlights that the inhabited area underwent a temporary crisis affecting its civil and ecclesiastical powers. However, the question of why the city of Padua remained an episcopal see during this period and throughout the Early Middle Ages remains unanswered.

The Roman city of *Altinum* has benefitted from greater attention in recent times (Ninfo *et al.* 2009; Tirelli 2011) perhaps because it was abandoned (Fig. 5.4). Nonetheless, the later phases of the city remain little known and the explanations given for the desertion of the city are, once again, too closely associated with the traditional historical narrative. *Altinum* was an episcopal see, but no findings have come to light during the excavations to indicate this status. Some archaeological data dating back to the Early Middle Ages has emerged, for example a number of tombs (Possenti 2011). By contrast, an analysis of numismatic evidence moved the latest archaeological findings forward in time (Asolati 2011). However, when compared to the other aforementioned ancient Roman cities, *Altinum* is the only one to have been completely abandoned during the Early Middle Ages. In the case of Oderzo (*Opitergium*), on closer inspection, the urban archaeological sequences also seem to have ceased to exist after the Byzantine era, the most significant findings from which

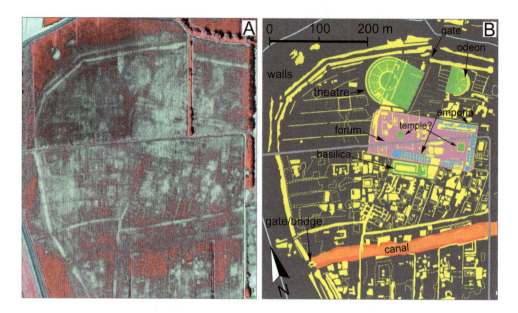

Fig. 5.4 *Altinum* (Venice, Italy), aerial photo of the ancient city and interpretation.
© Andrea Ninfo

are its fortifications (Castagna and Tirelli 1995). More recent excavations that were carried out in the area where the stadium once stood highlighted a settlement phase with wooden buildings dated to the period between the sixth and seventh centuries (Possenti 2004, 150–1).

In sum, with the exception of *Altinum*, none of the ancient Roman cities founded near the Venetian lagoon or slightly further south, disappeared completely. They continued being inhabited and remained significant during the Middle Ages and up to the present day. Therefore, the overall picture that emerges from this appears to agree with 'traditional explanations': but was this really the case?

New Eras, New Cities

Particularly significant for this study is the vocabulary relating to inhabited areas used in the written sources. When it comes to the Venetian lagoon, it is sufficient to consult the aforementioned *Istoria Veneticorum* in order to demonstrate that the same locations are defined in a different way depending on the passage in which they are mentioned. A number of reasons can be given to explain these differences: a different origin of a specific passage from the *Istoria*, different political and social circumstances in which the same place was mentioned (Berto 2001) and, perhaps, a different intention to treat the role played by a specific location according to a hierarchy (Gelichi 2007, 83–4, fig. 5). In any case, such a situation calls for overall reflection and advises caution, especially when it comes to the terms such as *civitas* and *castrum* that, in this period, no longer represented material and institutional entities comparable to those that existed in the ancient world.

Currently, archaeology does not seem to be used in the best possible way to facilitate the understanding of this situation favouring, therefore, interpretations that lean towards what we have defined as 'traditional explanations'. It has to be admitted that the profound changes in the components of 'material culture' make these interpretative options easier. The antinomy of masonry structures versus wooden buildings for housing purposes, or variety and complexity versus poverty and simplification in relation to pottery, helps enhance the perception that the 'new' world represented a negative decline of sorts of the ancient world. The phenomenon of urbanism, a conceptual category and a material entity that underwent changes between the period of Antiquity and the present day, tends to be read and interpreted from this perspective in particular. The impression such perceptions have created is that archaeology as a survey strategy has failed but also that archaeology is unable to fill in the gaps or to correct the distortions in historical narratives. The problem is that the Early Medieval phases of settlements require different archaeological methods and approaches, not only of an instrumental kind but also of a conceptual nature. A useful theoretical concept is that which does not consider the history of cities in a biological sense (birth, growth and death = foundation, life and decline) but views cities as spaces where various lifecycles alternate (Pfunter 2013). Seen from this perspective, it is premature to make generalisations at a moment when it is not possible to compare items of the same nature and of the same qualitative and quantitative value: otherwise we go back to the vicious circle in which a process explains a generalisation that, in turn, explains that process.

An area that is suitable for applying new conceptual and methodological approaches in order to create a different quality of archaeological record and a different type of narrative is precisely the one are currently dealing with here: the establishment of new cities, or better still, of places aspiring to become cities regardless of whether they became one or not. I would like to showcase two examples: Venice as the extremely famous example of a 'successful' site, meaning both the lagoon and the inhabited area of Rialto, and Jesolo (*Equilo*) as an example of an 'unsuccessful' location.

Life Cycles and Settlements: The Cases of the Venetian Lagoon and *Equilo*

During the Roman period, the lagoon was neither mainland nor was it densely (or permanently) inhabited as it has been imagined (Dorigo 2003) (Fig. 5.5). This does not mean that it had never been frequented or exploited, only that no permanent settlement of any sort is known prior to the Late Antique period.

The analysis of the ecosystem of the Venetian lagoon has shown how its environmental conditions changed between the fifth and the sixth centuries

Fig. 5.5 The Venetian lagoon in the Roman period (red dots represent Roman finds). Elaborated by the Laboratorio Archeologia Medievale, Università Venezia

in an interesting coincidence with the initial processes of settlement that we can deem as being permanent, that is, being characterised by buildings with structures partly in masonry, the topographical organisation of space, the preparation of waterfronts, reclamations and backfills (Gelichi 2006). At that time, a worsening of the climate would have caused a strong sea ingression and this too could have contributed to a more intense exploitation in the production of salt. There are good reasons to suspect a development of this kind: the fact that salt is a staple and the fact that it was mentioned by Cassiodorus (*Variae* 12.24) in a famous letter of 537 he sent to the *tribuni maritimorum* of the Venetian areas. We are well aware that the written sources about the exploitation of the publicly owned salt pans date to a much later period (Hocquet 1982). However, there are no impediments to assuming that by the sixth century salt, together with fishing and maritime trade, was one of the major assets of the lagoon economy.

The environmental changes could have affected the development of the settlement in another way. The nearby city of *Altinum* underwent a process of transformation from the late imperial period onward but this did not prevent it from becoming an episcopal see (Calaon 2006). The canals that flowed through the area petered out into marshland and the port functions of *Altinum* were slowly delegated to other locations in the lagoon some of which have been archaeologically surveyed, for example Torcello (Calaon, Zendri and Biscontin 2014; Leciejewicz 2000; 2002; Leciejewicz, Tabaczyńska and Tabaczyńsky 1977), San Lorenzo di Ammiana (Gelichi and Moine 2012) and San Francesco del Deserto (De Min 2000) (Fig. 5.6). Such settlements had to fulfil a commercial and transportation function and constitute a phenomenon that, according to the current state of research, has no parallel in the south part of the lagoon.

From an archaeological point of view, this process is linked to two types of data. The first is the presence of permanent forms of occupation characterised by buildings of a residential nature and of good quality when compared to wooden warehouses and waterfronts (such as those found in San Francesco del Deserto) that bear witness to the constant interest in preserving the inhabitable and usable area. The second set of archaeological data consists of a substantial quantity of imported products, such as pottery and amphoras of Mediterranean origin, which does not correspond to the low density of the lagoon settlements and, above all, to what we could define as its key social factor (Gelichi *et al.* 2017). Instead, the presence of these types of objects, in association with such settlements, can be explained by a new function that the Venetian lagoon took on from this period. The aforementioned letter by Cassiodorus tells us that the lagoon

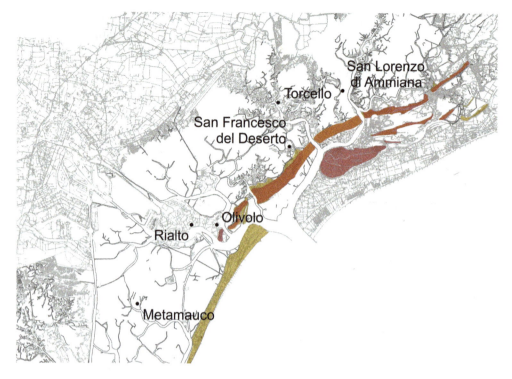

Fig. 5.6 Map of the Venetian lagoon and nearby areas with the locations from the text. Elaborated by the Laboratorio Archeologia Medievale, Università Venezia

played an important role in maritime communications by constituting a transit point in the transport of Istrian oil, wheat and wine to Ravenna, the new capital of the empire and, subsequently, of the Ostrogothic kingdom. In this period, the entire north part of the lagoon seemed anything but in crisis. Moreover, it appeared to slowly replace the functions that had once belonged to the great emporium of *Altinum* to which it was still closely linked as were the aristocrats who must have still depended on its bishop.

The next step must be to acknowledge a process of the selection and concentration of the habitation in the north part of the lagoon. This process is evident in certain settlements that were abandoned or converted into funerary areas, such as San Lorenzo di Ammiana, between the sixth and the seventh centuries. Other settlements evolved, as perhaps did the Ammiana district itself, giving life to real urban agglomerations. Thus, between the sixth and the seventh centuries the progressive loss of the urban functions of the *Altinum* district caused the birth and development of the residential area and later the emporium of Torcello and, in the middle of the lagoon, of Olivolo. Significantly, both cities became episcopal sees: Torcello in the seventh and Olivolo in the eighth century. This was also the period in which the historic, narrative sources bore witness to the first ducal power at Cittanova in the eighth century.

In short, up to the eighth century the Venetian lagoon appeared to be at the centre of a plurifocal process, at least in terms of settlements. This multitude of settlements obtained higher visibility through the political formations that they took on or that were subsequently attributed to them. The places that emerged in such a way fulfilled two criteria: either they were the seat of a bishop (Torcello was the first, followed by Olivolo, Cittanova and Metamauco, and finally *Equilo*) or held a position that took on a political role and meaning which, at a later stage, was ducal. It is very likely that this situation reflected tensions, conflicts and competitions among the members of the aristocracy who were slowly freeing themselves from imperial power. The transfer of the *palatium* – and with it the ducal power – from Cittanova first to Metamauco and then to Rialto, as described in the historic narrative sources can be explained according to this logic and in this context.

Among all the places in the Venetian lagoon, the islands in the Rialto archipelago play an extremely significant role. A recent reconstruction of the paleo-environmental picture (Zezza 2014) gives us a very useful starting point for attempting to provide a general interpretation of the poleogenetic processes of this archipelago (Gelichi, Ferri and Moine 2017). In Roman times, the lagoon was slightly different compared to the period that followed immediately afterwards, a change that does not appear to have had much impact or repercussions on the settlement system. The most interesting fact is that the ancient coastal sandbars coincide more or less with those of today as do the mouths of the port, that is, access points to the lagoon from the sea. The proximity between these access points and the easternmost isles of the Rialto archipelago helps explain the reason for the colonisation of the island of Olivolo which seems to constitute, based on the current state of research, the most ancient and significant settlement of the entire complex. Excavations carried out between the late 1980s and early 1990s (Tuzzato 1991; 1994; Tuzzato et al. 1993) brought to light the ruins of a commercial headquarters that was operational between the fifth and the sixth centuries and perhaps directly linked to Byzantine power, as indicated by three seals and a golden coin discovered in a residential complex (Gelichi 2015a–b). Such a hypothesis corresponds to the position

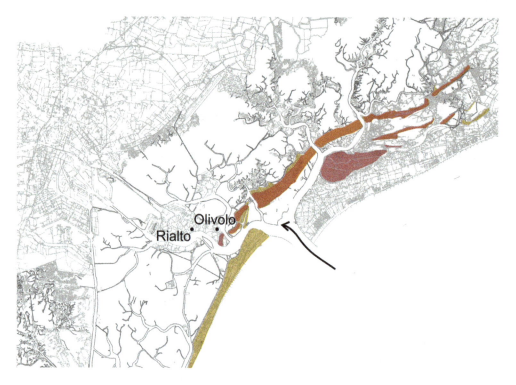

Fig. 5.7 The Venetian lagoon. The coastal sandbanks and access points to the port in the Roman period in relation to Olivolo with the episcopal see and Rialto with the early ninth-century ducal palace and chapel.

Drawn by Margherita Ferri, Sauro Gelichi and Cecilia Moine after Bondesan and Meneghel 2004, Primon and Mozzi 2014; Gelichi, Ferri and Moine 2017

of the site of Olivolo at the far end of the Rialto archipelago and in close proximity to the port inlets, at the same time protected and near the access points into the Adriatic Sea and therefore ideal for stationing a Byzantine fleet (Fig. 5.7). During the eighth century, Olivolo became an episcopal see and this supports the fact that this location had been of particular value for the local community.

Viewed in this context, the decision to transfer the young ducal power – or at least the centre of power – from Olivolo to Rialto which was slightly more inland, makes sense. The decision to move the seat of power fell on the Particiaci family and, once again, it is interesting to note how the venue chosen to host the *palatium*, as well as the entire area surrounding what would later become the Grand Canal, is directly and easily reachable from the south where this family's lands were situated and where, not by chance, the ducal power originated (Corrò, Moine and Primon 2015; Moine, Corrò and Primon 2017). Thus, the choice of Rialto is thoroughly explained not only by its centrality in the lagoon but also by its communications with the outside world. Moreover, it is was here where a fleet, probably first Byzantine and then ducal found a logical raison d'être. The willingness and, I would also add, the necessity to colonise this specific archipelago is also well reflected in the proven reclamation activities. These appear not only as a constant presence in urban archaeological research but can be seen clearly when a map of the land that emerged naturally is placed over the locations of ecclesiastical foundations (Fig. 5.8), that is churches and monasteries (Gelichi, Ferri and Moine 2017, figs. 8–10). Their imperfect matching is a clear indication of the efforts that the nascent Venetian community made in order to occupy as much land as possible, as the main source for this period, the *Istoria Veneticorum*, tells us.

The case of *Equilo* illustrates a number of interesting similarities with Rialto even if the outcomes were completely different (Fig. 5.9). After a phase of occupation during the imperial period, of which we can currently define neither scale nor scope, a *mansio* was founded towards the end of the fourth century (Gelichi, Cadamuro and Cianciosi 2018) (Figs. 5.10–5.11) on one of the isles in the archipelago situated in the coastal lagoon at the mouth of the old Piave. It is likely that here too, this was a place of value for the community. The *mansio* was destroyed by a fire during the fifth century and was not rebuilt. During the sixth century, the area was occupied by a place of worship with mosaic floors and a vast necropolis (Fig. 5.12). This could be linked to an episcopal institution or explained as having to do with the change of ownership of the area, which passed into ecclesiastical hands. The community of *Equilo* must have resided in the surrounding area. This is indicated by the names of the dedicants on the mosaic floor in the sixth-century church, by the necropolis next to it but also by the indirect evidence from Early Medieval sources. In the ninth century, *Equilo* was still an episcopal see; the first definite written evidence of its existence dates to this period. The port of *Equilo* was subsequently referred to as being active during the tenth century: the *Istoria Veneticorum* (4.46) cites the episode of Duke Pietro II Orseolo who made a short stopover with his fleet there in the year 1000 en route to Istria and Dalmatia. Towards the beginning of the twelfth century, the episcopal church was built in a monumental form (Secci 2018, 90–2) and it was only after this period that a crisis, perhaps of paleo-environmental origins or of political and economic nature, provoked the permanent and irreversible abandonment of the inhabited area until even its name was lost in oblivion.

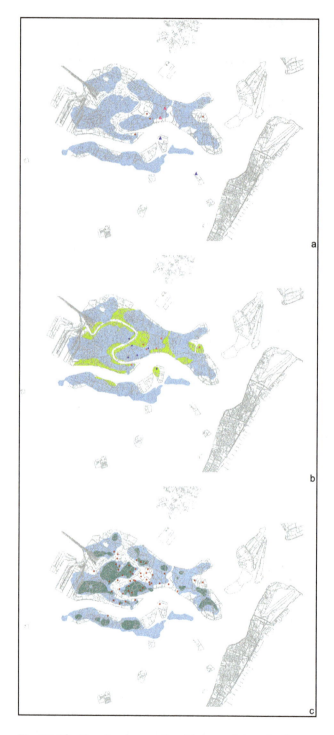

Fig. 5.8 The Venetian lagoon. Possible natural deposits that emerged between the ninth and tenth century and sites of documented places of worship (blue triangle: monastery; pink triangle: convent; red circle: church).

Fig. 5.9 Jesolo (Venice, Italy). The simplified paleo-environmental reconstruction of the site. Drawn by Anita Granzo

Successful and Unsuccessful Locations: A New Narrative about the Cities in the Venetian Lagoon

The outline of the history and settlements in the lagoon that we have just provided points to a number of relatively clear trends. The first significant phenomenon of change that must be noted concerns the shift in communication trends: from sea/land to mainly those of a lagoon/maritime/fluvial nature. This phenomenon produced the development and stabilisation of new settlements in the territory that had previously been poorly or scarcely inhabited, such as those in the Venetian lagoon or neighbouring areas, in other words, in locations where no urban settlement had ever existed.

Fig. 5.10 Jesolo (Venice, Italy). A zenithal photo of one of the Late Antique *mansio* buildings.
Elaborated by the Laboratorio Archeologia Medievale, Università Venezia

The colonisation of inhospitable areas of land led to serious ecological problems, for example, the procurement of water and food and, therefore, it had to be counterbalanced by more favourable things. The traditional reason that is usually cited, indicated by the written sources, is safety. This provides an explanation for the crisis. In reality, the process was not immediate and the success of settlements in the lagoon was uncertain for a long time. It is very likely that the reasons leading to the success of these sites can be found in a concurrent series of factors, predominantly including those of an economic and political nature. Both written and archaeological sources show that the aristocracies gravitating to the Venetian lagoon had maintained significant economic interests in land tenure. Locations such as *Equilo* or Cittanova, both becoming episcopal sees with the latter also gaining ducal rights, document the presence of an elite that moved within economic and political dynamics strongly intertwined with those of the first families that had taken on ducal power.

Fig. 5.11 Jesolo (Venice, Italy). The reconstruction of the settlement of *Equilo* in the late fourth century. Courtesy of Studio InkLink

Is it possible to compare these new centres to cities? The question is as ambiguous and polysemic as the concept of city itself during the centuries under discussion. Perhaps it is more appropriate to say that these centres aspired to become something resembling a city, because it is the ideological model of the ancient city, rather than being one of a material nature, that managed to survive.

Therefore, between the eighth and tenth centuries, settlements still existed in ancient Roman cities on the territory of the *Regio X Venetia et Histria*. Almost all the written sources describe these sites as undergoing situations of crises, some deprived of institutional representation temporarily (Padua) and others permanently (Este). However, with only a few exceptions, these places went back to being cities from the tenth century onwards in a completely different political and economic context. Archaeology has the task of describing this transition or, at least, describing it better than it has done so far.

The lagoons and neighbouring areas appear to be more dynamic. Here, the narratives relating to individual locations, for example Venice, Jesolo, Cittanova and Torcello, are interwoven together to describe images of great

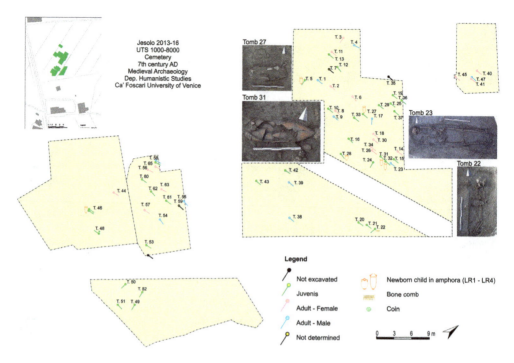

Fig. 5.12 Jesolo (Venice, Italy). Early Medieval cemetery. Drawn by Alessandra Cianciosi

mobility. The emerging aristocracies, generally recognised in the figure of the bishop, act on different territorial fronts and have different economic outlooks. In this way, sites that the sources frequently call cities were created but they did not have anything to do with those of the ancient world, starting from their topographical position. At the same time, these sites were centres of power and spaces of identity but also areas of exchange and trade, as shown by archaeology. In the tenth century, a century of paramount importance, none of these locations had prevailed over any of the others.

Towards the end of the tenth century, chronicler John the Deacon wrote the first great history of Venice and in so doing contributed towards the creation of the first-ever inventory of topical areas of identity, an identity that was, in this case, openly urban or city-like in the historically accepted sense of the term. By writing his history, John the Deacon also ratified the end of a long path: it was not by chance that the other centres in the lagoon and along its edge had already disappeared or would be soon. Those that did not disappear completely survived in a reduced and subordinated way. These new settlements also played a decisive role in the reformulation of the economic scenario in northern Italy: first during the late Byzantine-Lombard period, followed by the Franco-Carolingian era and then during the Ottonian and post-Ottonian dynasties, Venice alone played this decisive role. Finally, these settlements represented the first truly great innovation of post-Antique Italy, precisely because they were the result of 'the no longer and the not yet': they contain traits of the past and at the same time involve – unconsciously of course – the future.

References

Asolati, M. 2011. 'Altino tardoantica: Una prospettiva numismatica', in Tirelli (ed.) 2011, 179.

Berto, L.A., 2001. *Il Vocabolario politico e sociale della "Istoria Veneticorum" di Giovanni Diacono* (Padua).

Bondesan, A. and Meneghel, M. 2004. *Geomorfologia della provincia di Venezia: Note illustrative della carta geomorfologica della provincia di Venezia* (Padua).

Brogiolo, G.P. 2017. 'Este da città a castello degli Obertenghi', in Brogiolo, G.P. (ed.), *Este, l'Adige e i Colli Euganei. Storie di paesaggi* (Mantua), 25–40.

Busana, M.S. 2002. *Architetture rurali nella Venetia romana* (Rome).

Calaon, D. 2006. 'Altino (VE): Strumenti diagnostici (GIS e DTM) per l'analisi delle fasi tardoantiche e altomedievali', in Zaccaria Ruggiu, A. (ed.), *Le missioni archeologiche dell'Università Ca' Foscari di Venezia. V Giornata di studio* (Venice), 143–58.

Calaon, D., Zendri, E. and Biscontin G. (eds.) 2014. *Torcello scavata: Patrimonio condiviso / Izkopan Torcello: Skupna dediščina / Torcello Excavated: A Shared Heritage*, vol. 2, *Lo scavo 2012–2013 / Izkopavanja 2012–2013 / The 2012–2013 Excavation Campaign* (Venice).

Canova Dal Zio, R. 1987. *Le chiese delle Tre Venezie anteriori al Mille* (Padua).

Casazza, L. 2001. *Il territorio di Adria tra VI e X secolo* (Padua).

Castagna, D. and Tirelli, M. 1995. 'Evidenze archeologiche di Oderzo tardoantica ed altomedievale: I risultati preliminari di recenti indagini', in Brogiolo, G.P. (ed.), *Città, castelli, campagne nei territori di frontiera (secoli VI-VII), 5° Seminario sul tardo Antico e l'alto Medioevo in Italia centrosettentrionale, Monte Barro – Galbiate (Lecce) 9–10 giugno 1994* (Mantua), 121–34.

Chavarria Arnau, A. (ed.) 2017. *Ricerche sul centro episcopale di Padova scavi 2011–2012* (Mantua).

Corrò, E. 2016. 'Con un Po di sfondo: Adria e il suo territorio tra la Tardantichità e l'Altomedioevo' (PhD thesis, Università Ca'Foscari Venezia).

Corrò, E., Moine, C. and Primon S. 2015. 'Reazioni uguali e contrarie: Evoluzione paleoambientale e trasformazioni storiche intorno al monastero di Sant'Ilario e Benedetto (Dogaletto di Mira)', *Reti medievali* 16/2, 103–50.

De Min, M. 2000. 'Venezia e il territorio lagunare', in *Ritrovare restaurando. Rinvenimenti e scoperte a Venezia e in laguna* (Cornuda), 15–25.

Dorigo, W. 1983. *Venezia origini: Fondamenti, ipotesi, metodi*, 3 vols. (Milan).

Gelichi, S. 2006. 'Venezia tra archeologia e storia: La costruzione di un'identità urbana', in Augenti, A. (ed.), *Le città italiane tra la tarda Antichità e l'alto Medioevo. Atti del Convegno, Ravenna, 26–28 febbraio 2004* (Florence), 151–83.

— 2007. 'Flourishing places in north-eastern Italy: Towns and *emporia* between late antiquity and the Carolingian age', in Henning, J. (ed.), *Post-Roman Towns, Trade and Settlement in Europe and Byzantium*, vol. 1, *The Heirs of the Roman West* (Berlin and New York), 77–104.

— 2008. 'The eels of Venice: The long eighth century of the emporia of the northern region along the Adriatic coast', in Gasparri, S. (ed.), *774: Ipotesi su una transizione* (Turnhout) 81–117.

— 2010a. 'L'archeologia nella laguna veneziana e la nascita di una nuova città', *Reti medievali* 11/2, 137–67.

— 2010b. 'The future of Venice's past and the archaeology of the north-eastern Adriatic emporia during the Early Middle Ages', in Schryver, J.G. (ed.), *Studies in the Archaeology of the Medieval Mediterranean* (Leiden), 175–210.

— 2013. '*Lupicinus presbyter*: Una breve nota sulle istituzioni ecclesiastiche comacchiesi delle origini', in Barone, G., Esposito, A. and Frova C. (eds.), *Ricerca come incontro: Archeologi, paleografi e storici per Paolo Delogu* (Rome), 41–60.

— 2015a. 'La storia di una nuova città attraverso l'archeologia: Venezia nell'alto Medioevo', in West-Harling, V. (ed.), *Three Empires, Three Cities: Identity, Material Culture and Legitimacy in Venice, Ravenna and Rome, 750–1000* (Turnhout), 51–98.

— 2015b. 'Venice in the Early Middle Ages: The material structures and society of "civitas aput rivoaltum" between the 9th and 10th centuries', in La Rocca, M.C. and Majocchi, P. (eds.), *Urban Identities in Northern Italy (800–1100 ca.)* (Turnhout), 251–71.

Gelichi, S., Cadamuro S. and Cianciosi, A. (eds.) 2018. *In limine: Storie di una comunità ai margini della laguna* (Florence).

Gelichi, S., Ferri, M. and Moine, C. 2017. 'Venezia e la laguna tra IX e X secolo: Strutture materiali, insediamenti, economie', in Gasparri, S. and Gelichi, S. (eds.), *The Age of the Affirmation. Venice, the Adriatic and the Hinterland between the 9th and 10th Centuries* (Turnhout), 79–128.

Gelichi, S. and Moine, C. (eds.) 2012. 'Isole fortunate: La storia della laguna nord di Venezia attraverso lo scavo di San Lorenzo di Ammiana', *Archeologia medievale* 39, 9–56.

Gelichi, S., Negrelli, C., Ferri, M., Cadamuro, S., Cianciosi, A. and Grandi, E. 2017. 'Importare, produrre e consumare nella laguna di Venezia dal IV al XII secolo: Anfore, vetri e ceramiche', in Gelichi, S. and Negrelli, C. (eds.),

Adriatico altomedievale (VI–XI secolo): Scambi, porti, produzioni (Venice), 23–114.

Hocquet, J.-C. 1982. *Le sel et la fortune de Venise*, 2 vols. (Lille).

John the Deacon. *Istoria Veneticorum*, in Berto, L.A. (ed.), *Giovanni Diacono. Istoria Veneticorum* (Bologna, 1999).

Leciejewicz, L. 2000. 'Torcello antica e medievale alla luce delle nuove ricerche archeologiche', in Leciejewicz, L. (ed.), *Torcello: Nuove ricerche archeologiche* (Rome), 87–98.

 2002. 'Italian-Polish researches into the origin of Venice', *Archaeologia polona* 40, 51–71.

Leciejewicz, L., Tabaczyńska, E. and Tabaczyńsky S. (eds.) 1977. *Torcello: Scavi 1961-62* (Rome).

Moine, C., Corrò, E. and Primon, S. 2017. *Paesaggi artificiali a Venezia: Archeologia e geologia nelle terre del monastero di Sant'Ilario tra alto Medioevo ed età moderna* (Florence).

Mozzi, P. and Negrelli, C. (eds.) 2013. 'Paesaggi antichi e potenziale archeologico', in Gelichi, S., Mozzi, P., Panozzo, F., Patassini, D. and Reho, M. (eds.), *Archeologia e paesaggio nell'area costiera veneta: Conoscenza, partecipazione valorizzazione / Arheologija in krajina na obalnem območju Veneta: spoznati, podeliti in ovrednotiti* (Venice), 18–85.

Nicosia, C., Ertani, A., Vianello, A., Nardi, S., Brogiolo, G.P, Chavarria Arnau, A. and Becherini, F. 2018. 'Heart of darkness: An interdisciplinary investigation of the urban anthropic deposits of the Baptistery of Padua (Italy)', *Archaeological and Anthropological Sciences* 11, doi.org/10.1007/s12520-018-0646-2

Ninfo, A., Fontana, A., Mozzi, P. and Ferrarese, F. 2009. 'The map of Altinum, the ancestor of Venice', *Science* 325, 577.

Paul the Deacon. *Historia Langobardorum*, in Bethmann, L. and Waitz, G. (eds.), *MGH Scriptores rerum Langobardicarum et Italicarum saec. VI–IX* (Hanover, 1878), 12–187.

Pfunter, L. 2013. 'Review of N. Christie and A. Augenti (eds.), *Vrbes Extinctae. Archaeologies of Abandoned Classical Towns* (London) 2012', *Rosetta* 14, 88–92.

Possenti, E. 2004. '*La fase altomedievale: Prime considerazioni*', in Ruta Serafini and Tirelli (eds.) 2004, 150–2.

 2011. '*L'età tardo antica e altomedievale (IV secolo d. C.–639 d. C.)*', in Tirelli (ed.) 2011, 172–7.

Primon, S. and Mozzi, P. 2014. 'Torcello e la morfologia della laguna tra l'età romana e il Medioevo', in Calaon, D., Zendri, E. and Biscontin G. (eds.), *Torcello scavata: Patrimonio condiviso / Izkopan Torcello: Skupna dediščina / Torcello Excavated: A Shared Heritage*, vol. 2, *Lo scavo 2012–2013 / Izkopavanja 2012–2013 / The 2012–2013 Excavation Campaign* (Venice), 105–22.

Ruta Serafini, A. and Tirelli, M. (eds.) 2004. 'Dalle origini all'alto Medioevo: Uno spaccato urbano di Oderzo dallo scavo dell'ex stadio', *Quaderni di archeologia del Veneto* 20, 135–52.

Secci, M. 2018. 'Una chiesa fuori scala e l'episcopio di Equilo nel Medioevo / A church out of scale and Equilo's episcopal see in the Middle Ages', in Gelichi, Cadamuro and Cianciosi (eds.) 2008, 90–2.

Tirelli, M. (ed.) 2011. *Altino antica: Dai Veneti a Venezia* (Venice).

Tuzzato, S. 1991. 'Venezia: Gli scavi a San Pietro di Castello (Olivolo). Nota preliminare sulle campagne 1986-1989', *Quaderni di archeologia del Veneto* 7, 92–103.

  1994. 'Le strutture lignee altomedievali a Olivolo (S. Pietro di Castello – Venezia)', in Scarfì, B.M. (ed.), *Studi di archeologia della X Regio in ricordo di Michele Tombolani* (Rome), 479–85.

  2001. 'Risultati degli scavi archeologici a San Basilio', *Il restauro della chiesa di San Basilio, Atti del Convegno di studi, Ariano nel Polesine, 14 dicembre 2000. Quaderni di progetto restauro* 4 (Padua), 9–12.

Tuzzato, S., Favero, V. and Vinals, J. 1993. 'San Pietro di Castello a Venezia. Nota preliminare dopo la campagna 1992', *Quaderni di archeologia del Veneto* 9, 72–80.

Zezza, F. 2004. *Venezia città d'acqua: Le incidenze geologiche su origini, evoluzione e vulnerabilità* (Venice).

6 | *Provincia Iadrensis*
Heir of Roman Dalmatia or a Stillborn Child of Byzantine Early Medieval Adriatic Policy?

TRPIMIR VEDRIŠ

The term *provincia Iadrensis*, the province of Zadar, appears in a single Medieval source, a hagiographic legend narrating the *inventio* of the relics of St Chrysogonus, the patron saint of Zadar (Brunelli 1913, 207–10; Iveković 1931, 48–51). The account tells how this Aquileian martyr found his place of rest in the vicinity of Zadar but admitting, almost as a slip, that he was 'brought to the province of Zadar for the wellbeing of its citizens'. The core of *Translatio beati Grisogoni martiris* was probably composed no earlier than the late ninth century and not long after the late tenth. Setting aside doubts about the precise dating of the legend, Mladen Ančić (2017, 35) proposed that the term *provincia Iadrensis* mirrors the position of Early Medieval Zadar under Byzantine rule. Roman *Iader* (modern Zadar), unlike the Dalmatian metropolis of *Salona*, survived 'the dark' seventh and eighth centuries and re-emerged in the sources in the early ninth century. By then, it had become the capital of a Byzantine *archontia*, soon to be transformed into the theme, of Dalmatia. The origin of the Byzantine administration in the Adriatic was recently reassessed by Vivien Prigent (2008) and Ivan Basić (2020), while the traditional dating of the formation of the theme contested by Tibor Živković (2008). New historiographic paradigms provide a framework for a fresh interpretation of the transformation of the post-Roman Dalmatia (Dzino 2010), the nature of Byzantine rule in the Adriatic (Shepard 2014), the Carolingian impact (Bertelli and Brogiolo 2001; Dzino, Milošević and Vedriš 2018) and the renewal of the church organisation in the region (Basić 2018a). These were supplemented by the finds of new lead seals (Filipčić 2017) and epigraphic material (Basić 2018b; 2018c). It is in the light of these developments that the Byzantine presence in Dalmatia ought to be readdressed.

One of the reasons why the region that lies outside the purview of both Carolingian experts and Byzantinists tends to 'fall out of scholars' scope' has been 'a certain indifference towards what was going on in this double periphery' as well as the lack of knowledge of the languages 'in which much of the literature has been written' (Budak 2018a, 174). While both of these obstacles have played a role, Ančić (2018b, 43–9) pointed out a 'lack of communication with the dominant discourses from which Croatian historians acutely suffer' but also warned of the problem of historiographic 'neo-colonial discourses' in contemporary scholarship. For these reasons, Early Medieval Dalmatia (Fig. 6.1) still receives relatively little attention from scholars outside the region (Budak 2018a, 174; Curta 2013a, 145–6). For example, the annotated survey of the Byzantine sources for the period between 680 and 850 compiled by Brubaker and Haldon (2001) does not mention Dalmatia and the same is true for the chapter on the Iconoclast era in Auzépy (2008). When it comes to the 'Western perspective', Neven Budak (2018a, 184) recently pointed out that the 'otherwise brilliant book by Chris Wickham (2005) mentions Croatia only once in a footnote and makes no reference to Dalmatia whatsoever'. Over the last decades, since the late 1990s, Croatian scholars have been publishing their studies in 'more accessible languages' and this will hopefully foster better engagement with their arguments in the broader academic arena (Majnarić 2018b, 8).

While this chapter inevitably derives from discussion in a 'particular national form', it is not meant to remain 'caged inside its own country-specific preoccupations' (Wickham 2005, 2). On the contrary, hoping to

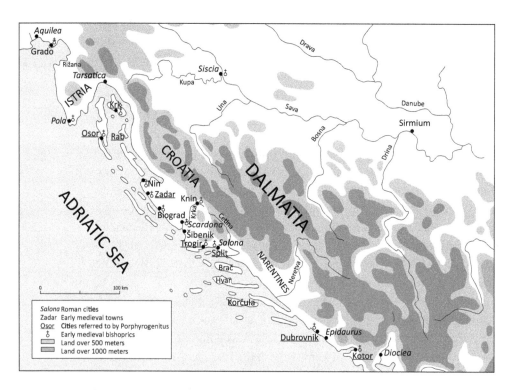

Fig. 6.1 East Adriatic coast in the Early Medieval period.
Drawn by Trpimir Vedriš

avoid the 'cultural solipsism' implied in Wickham's comment, it aims to connect local knowledge to international scholarship and in so doing to avoid an unhealthy monopolisation of perception and interpretation. This historiographic tension can be compared to the situation following the Treaty of Aachen of 812 when Carolingian and Byzantine imperial embassies met to negotiate 'the borders of the Dalmatians, the Romans and the Slavs' (Tremp 1995, 370–1). The 'sheer complexity of delineating them' made Louis the Pious acknowledge 'that this could only be done on the spot, using the expertise of locally based figures' (Shepard 2018, 3). This analogy underlines the importance of including 'local knowledge' in the debate. Rather than downplaying the relevance of the 'broader picture' or neglecting theoretical models, it is necessary to put these interpretative models to the test in a specific historical context. The renewed interest in topics such as the origins of Byzantine administration or the revival of Adriatic economies has provided frameworks for the understanding of local transformations. However, the lack of a 'more grounded' approach renders many inspiring and theoretically innovative studies superficial. By taking a 'bottom-up perspective', this chapter, without denying the need to overcome the borders of national discourses, seeks the missing balance between modern-day academic 'centres and peripheries' in the scholarly dialogue.

Considering all of the above, this case study explores the interaction between international and local factors which contributed to Zadar becoming a capital of a Byzantine province in the late eighth through ninth centuries. This will be done by examining two critical issues closely related to the re-emergence of Byzantine imperial interests in the Adriatic: (1) the local impact of the renovation of the Byzantine administration and (2) the relationship between this development and the position of the Church of Zadar. The issue of relations between Zadar and its immediate surroundings will be approached in the light of (3) the emergence of a new polity in its immediate hinterland and (4) the formation of a new ecclesiastical centre therein.

Setting the Stage

The widely accepted historiographic narrative holds that Zadar preserved its status as the administrative capital of Dalmatia throughout the Early Middle Ages. But what did the Early Medieval author of the *Translatio beati Grisogoni martiris* mean by 'that province'? Did he have in mind the whole of Dalmatia – described by a mid-ninth-century traveller (Lambot 1945, 208) as a very long region (*longissima regio*) or did he think of the immediate hinterland of Zadar and its Roman *ager*? While the former seems unlikely, the argument supporting the latter rests on the fact that during the Middle Ages, unlike the urban district, the bishopric of Zadar retained its territorial shape regardless of the political changes occurring between the ninth and the fifteenth centuries (Ančić 2017, 29). The broader hinterland of Zadar, corresponding to the modern-day area of Ravni Kotari, was interpreted as surviving the collapse of the seventh century and preserving the Late Antique military and church structures up until the late eighth century (Jakšić 1995). The area in question might, therefore, be seen as one of the last enclaves of orderly Romanity in Dalmatia (Dzino 2014). Yet, following the arrival of the Franks at the end of the eighth century it became the cradle of a new 'barbaric' polity – duchy of the Croats. It is thus the 'overlapping of imperial spheres' in the Adriatic at the turn of the ninth century that put Zadar in the diplomatic spotlight of that time.

A Dangerous Sea: The Adriatic in the Late Eighth and Ninth Centuries

The first hypothesis here is that the *provincia Iadrensis* of the *Translatio beati Grisogoni* represents a distant echo of the Late Antique and Byzantine administration in Dalmatia and, as such, resembles the trajectory of another similar *provincia*, that of *Venetia* (or other parts of Italy, for which see Ascheri 2009, 92–101; Tabacco 1989, 136, 176). Despite numerous differences, both originated in Late Antique administrations led by officials bearing the title of duke (*dux*) and both found themselves between two imperial systems – the Byzantine and the Frankish – at the beginning of the ninth century. The parallels surface in the report about the arrival at Charlemagne's court in 805 of 'dukes of Venice and the ambassadors of the Dalmatians, Paul, duke of Zadar, and Donatus, bishop of the same city' when 'the emperor made a provision (*ordinatio*) about the dukes and peoples of both Venice and Dalmatia' (*Annales regni Francorum*, a. 805). During the ensuing conflict, the Byzantine imperial fleet managed to deflect the Frankish forces from Zadar and Venice alike and both cities were 'for the love and because of an alliance made with the emperor of Constantinople, given up to him' (Einhard, *Vita Karoli magni* 15) in 812.

Byzantine rule, however, retreated from Dalmatia during the reign of Michael II (820–9) when the empire could no longer effectively reach the eastern and northern Adriatic. This, in turn, led to the well-explored emancipation of Venice.

As a result of ruptures created by the clash of two imperial centres in the Adriatic, the first half of the ninth century saw the emergence of a series of new political entities in Dalmatia. Among them, the principality of the Croats and other minor 'Slavic' polities (Budak 2008) such as that of the group named Narentines were the most prominent at this point. Their presence made it extremely hard for both the Byzantines and their estranged subjects, the Venetians, to keep the east Adriatic travel routes open and secure. In the early ninth century, according to Amalarius of Metz (c.780–c.850), it was dangerous to travel between Constantinople and Italy not only due to the Saracens but also the Slavs. Referring to his experience in 814 Amalarius (*Versus marini* 60–5) remembered 'running away from the Maurs, fearing the savage Slavs' and avoiding 'the Slavic shores'. The sources for the next decades provide evidence of a growing pressure not only on the east Adriatic routes but also on the coastal cities. The relevant passages of the *Pactum Hlotharii* (I.7) concluded between the king of Italy and the Venetians in 840 note the need for a common effort to keep the inimical Slavic tribes at bay by a 'naval army'.

More precise information on the *generationes Sclavorum* is provided by Venetian chronicler John the Deacon (d. after 1018), who mentioned the baptism of the Narentines in Venice around 830 but reported that the same Slavs captured and killed Venetian merchants in 836 (*Istoria Veneticorum* 2.40 and 46). Ten years later certain Slavs (*Sclavi*) burned *castrum Caprulense* in Istria (*Istoria Veneticorum* 2.51). The Saxon theologian Gottschalk of Orbais (c.800–c.868) witnessed *rex* Trpimir (c.840–64) marching against the 'people of the Greeks and their patrician' (Genke and Gumerlock 2010, 30; Rapanić 2013) which has been interpreted as referring to a local militia or a Byzantine squadron sent to the Adriatic. Around 865 Duke (*dux*) Ursus sailed to confront 'Domagoj, the leader of the Slavs' (*versus Dommagoum Slavorum principem*, see *Istoria Veneticorum* 3.2) and the 'worst tribes of the Slavs and Dalmatians' pillaged Istrian towns in 875 (*Istoria Veneticorum* 3.14). Some of the Slavic leaders were warlords mentioned by name such as Duke Mislav (c.835–9) and the aforementioned Duke Domagoj (864–76). The latter was warned by Pope John VIII for protecting the seafaring bandits (*marini latrunculi*) operating under his name (Stipišić and Šamšalović 1967, 11) as he seems to have been behind the attack on the papal envoys returning from Constantinople in 870. The same raid was described by Anastasius Bibliothecarius and referred to by Popes Hadrian II and John VIII (Borri 2017, 25–6).

At the same time, the naval forces of the *Arentanoi* (according to Byzantine authors) or *Narentani* (of the Venetian sources) gained control of the estuary of the river Neretva and the adjoining archipelago. Temporarily subjugated by the Byzantine forces in the 870s, these ferocious naval warriors – who might have identified themselves as 'Humljani' (Ančić 2011a; 2011b) – proved to be unmanageable due to their crafty use of small naval forces in a closed sea created by the archipelago of the large islands of Korčula, Hvar and Brač. They threatened Venetian shipping so gravely that in 839 Duke Pietro Tradonico had to set sail against them (*Istoria Veneticorum* 2.49). Duke Pietro I Candiano led another expedition which ended in his defeat and death in 887 (*Istoria Veneticorum* 3.32–4). In the face of such persistent threats, Venice 'continued to pay protection money for safe passage of her ships along the Dalmatian coast' and it was not until the year 1000 that Duke Pietro II Orseolo finally 'consolidated Venetian hegemony in the Adriatic' (Pryor and Jeffreys 2006, 68).

At this point it is worth citing the observation that 'piracy comes into existence in given historical circumstances: when trade flourishes enough to sustain it and victims could be looted without certain or excessive punishment' (Borri 2017, 23). This is a useful framework for approaching the competition for the control of sea routes in the ninth-century Adriatic. The development of early Venetian trade and the formation of the infrastructure that supported 'piracy' in Dalmatia are perhaps the most important regional factors for our understanding of the history of the east Adriatic in this period. The Byzantine provinces centred at Venice and Zadar, sealed off by Slavic threats like those posed by the Croats or the *Narentani*, were therefore in a position to develop autonomous political structures. However, this was where their developmental paths diverged. While the Venetian elites situated in the emporium emerged as middlemen between the Frankish world and the eastern Mediterranean (Gelichi 2008), the Zadar elites remained tied up in local affairs. Conditioned by their restricted access to resources their economy developed only around small-scale salt pans, fishing, animal husbandry and olive and wine production on the islands off the coast.

Controlling the Adriatic: Byzantine Administration and the Local Elites

The second hypothesis here is that the Byzantine administration in the Adriatic was more functional than previously held by the historiography. The evidence for this is unfortunately rather scarce. If one discards the interpretation of the imperial command (*keleúsis*) sent by Emperor Leo III through Sicilian *strategos* Paul in 718 to the 'Western *archons*' as being addressed to the Slavic warlords in Dalmatia (Živković 2002, 165–6), the information might indicate the presence of Byzantine officers on the Adriatic coast (Gračanin 2015, 502). Furthermore, the identification of the aforementioned *strategos* Paul with the exarch of Ravenna (Brown 1984, 65) allows the interpretation of a lead seal of Exarch Paul (723–6) found at the site of ancient *Salona* as evidence that Ravenna had authority over Dalmatia (Goldstein 1992; 1998; Nikolajević-Stojković 1961). Whatever the exact nature of this relation was, it ended with the fall of Ravenna in 751. In the following decade the theme of Kephalenia was formed (Prigent 2008, 398–401; Tsatsoulis 2012) 'as the main platform for Byzantine control of the Adriatic' (Ančić 2018a, 29). The restoration of imperial authority is reflected in a little-known inscription bearing the name of Constantine VI (780–97) found at Trogir. Although it represents a rare epigraphic reference to a Byzantine emperor in Dalmatia it confirms that the imperial authority 'was recognized in this Dalmatian town at the end of the eighth century' (Basić 2018c, 87).

Other, indirect, evidence of a Byzantine recovery might be sought in the revival of economic activities in the Adriatic (Budak 2018a; Curta 2010; Hodges 2008; McCormick 2001, 778–9), which may have gone hand in hand with the functioning of imperial administration. The prime evidence of this is a large quantity of eighth-century Byzantine coins found in Dalmatia. The question of commercial trade in Dalmatia remains unsolved given that even when it comes to Venice the 'actual volume is still a matter of debate before the 11th century' (Provesi 2018, 68). It was, however, suggested that the Byzantine gold coins (*solidi*) found in the territory of modern-day Croatia were a gift of the emperor to the members of the local elites (Curta 2010, 270–3). The majority of the coins, mostly *solidi* of Constantine V struck at Syracuse between 760 and 775, but also some coins of Leo III and Leo IV (Budak 2018a, 179–80), were found in the early-ninth-century graves (Delonga 1981). This phenomenon is not easy to interpret. The presence of the *solidi* has been explained as being part of the tribute the Dalmatian towns paid to the Croatian warlords (Šeparović 2003, 132), coins brought from Constantinople by Dalmatian bishops (Milošević 2011, 182) or money 'intended to enforce the defence of the hinterland of the Dalmatian towns' (Budak 2018a, 180–1). These suggestions need to be taken with caution as they divert focus and produce agendas for discussions that are impossible to resolve. What is of real relevance in the context of the reorganisation of Byzantine administration is that a large quantity of coins produced in a single mint reflects a renewed interest from the imperial centre for a remote province in the late eighth century. This dovetails with the indications that Byzantine administrative structures were functioning in Dalmatia.

Finally it has recently been pointed out that the rebellion of Bardanes Tourkos in Anatolia (Treadgold 1988, 131–3) was simultaneously felt in northern Dalmatia. From this perspective, the reference recorded by John the Deacon (*Istoria Veneticorum* 2.23) demonstrates that events in the East had direct 'consequences even for this far-off corner of the empire' (Ančić 2018a, 29). Underlying the fact that this Venetian chronicler did not seem to be 'aware of the fact that rebellion's centre was in Anatolia', Ančić interpreted the events in the upper Adriatic (at *Tarsatica*) as being linked to the formation of the theme of Kephalenia. In this context references to Dalmatia in the treatises *De praedestinatione* and *Responsa de diversis* by Gottschalk of Orbais provide additional food for thought. Departing from 'linguistic peculiarities characteristic of the eastern Adriatic' preserved in these works the usage of Byzantine phraseology in the regional vernacular Latin may be interpreted as a reflection of 'the influence of diplomatic formulas contained in the charters issued by the imperial chancery' (Basić 2018b). This in turn indicates:

> a regular reception of Byzantine administrative documents in Venice, Istria and Dalmatia, as well as regular communication between the people of these areas and Constantinople in relation to ceremonies involving imperial ideology. (Basić 2018b, 196)

Accepting the hypothesis that Byzantine administration in the Adriatic developed from the mid-eighth century onwards and assuming it was functioning efficiently, brings us to the role of Zadar in this administrative system.

At the Imperial Edge: Zadar and the Byzantine Administration

According to Constantine Porphyrogennetos (*De administrando imperio* 29) the 'once populous' Roman province of Dalmatia had been reduced, through wars and bad government, to a handful of cities and islands. His Early Medieval Dalmatian *octapolis* included Osor (*Opsara*), Krk (*Vekla*), Rab (*Arbe*), Zadar (*Diadora*), Trogir (*Tetrangourin*), Split (*Aspalathon*), Dubrovnik (*Raousin*) and Kotor (*Dekatera*). Reference to the 'cities' should be taken with care as all these fortified settlements (*kastra*) fit Jonathan Shepard's (2014, 32–4) definition of 'bunkers' rather than proper urban centres (Fig. 6.1). Some of these 'bunkers', however, started to evolve into 'open cities' when the whole province, neglected by the imperial administration during the early seventh century (Dzino 2014, 137–8), re-emerged in the written sources in the second half of the eighth. Towards the end of that period Dalmatia was administered by a duke (*dux*) or *archon* who most likely resided in Zadar and the province was upgraded to a theme at some point between the Treaty of Aachen of 812 and the second half of the ninth century (Basić 2015b, 450; Oikonomides 1972, 353; Wasilewski 1980).

The establishment of an administrative military-civil unit under the *strategos* has been one of the critical issues in the discussion on the Byzantine presence in Dalmatia. There is no scholarly consensus on the matter; a compromise opinion is that a theme must have been established between two Byzantine naval operations, one in 809 and the other in 867 (Budak 2018c, 164–5). The reference to Duke Paul (*dux Paulus*), if interpreted as representing the entire province at Charlemagne's court in 805, may signal that the process was underway and even more so if one accepts that he was the same person as the aforementioned Paulus, *strategos* of Kephalenia. The view that the Dalmatian theme was organised in the 860s with Zadar as its centre was challenged by the late Tibor Živković (2008, 65, 81) who dated its establishment to the reign of Emperor Leo V (813–20) and Vivien Prigent (2008, 409–13) who disputed that its seat was in Zadar. Disregarding the anachronistic usage of the term in the *De administrando imperio* which reports that this theme existed already in the early seventh century, it does not appear in *De thematibus*, another treaty ascribed to Porphyrogennetos (Pertusi 1952, 41–3). Dalmatian *strategoi*, however, were mentioned in late ninth- and tenth-century imperial administrative lists.

At this point it is opportune to consider Živković's thesis. Finding the earlier arguments for the dating of the *Taktikon Uspensky* to 842–56 'rather tenuous', Živković (2008, 65, 82–3) proposed the *Taktikon* be dated to the reign of Michael I (811–13) instead of the reign of Michael III (842–67). In addition, he called for a revision of earlier assumptions about the emergence of *archontia* which 'necessitates a revision of the dating of the creation of theme of Dalmatia' (Živković 2008, 73). His dating of the *Taktikon Uspensky* has been positively received (Brubaker and

Haldon 2011, 752; Budak 2014, 53; Curta 2010, 267) while argument that the theme of Dalmatia was established by Leo V supports a recent proposal to date the introduction and implementation of the whole 'theme system' to the reign of Nikephoros I (802–11) (Haldon 2016, 246), since his early-ninth-century successors would have continued this project. Therefore, in order to assess Živković's hypotheses, as well as those of Prigent, a brief review of evidence is required.

The *Taktikon Uspensky* mentions an *archon* of Dalmatia (*archon Dalmatias*) and *spatharii* and archons of Dalmatia (*spatharioi kai archontes Dalmatias*, see Oikonomides 1972, 57, 59). The *Kletorologion of Philotheos*, a source composed c.899, refers to a *strategos* of Dalmatia (*strategos Dalmatias*, see Oikonomides 1972, 101, 105, 139) and the same title is found in the *Taktikon Beneševič* (934–44) and the *Escorial Taktikon* (971–5) (Oikonomides 1972, 247, 267). While the position of the *archon* in the *Taktikon Uspensky* might point towards a 'relative frailty of the Byzantine presence in the Adriatic' (Gioanni 2017, 45), these lists obviously do not provide a strong argument for the earlier dating of the theme.

Byzantine lead seals used by local governors, on the other hand, provide a more nunaced picture. Byzantine seals in general attract the attention of the scholars when there is a lack of other sources from a given period (Cheynet and Caseau 2012; Curta 2004; Oikonomides 1983; Prigent 2008, 393). The seals that confirm the existence of Byzantine officials in Dalmatia from the eighth to the eleventh century are eleven in number (Basić 2018b, 188–9). Six are ascribed to the ninth century and of those only two (those of Bryennios and Eustathios) bear the title of *strategos*. The seals of George, Theophylact and two unknown owners reveal their possessors were *archontes* while the seal of Euthymios tells us that he was a duke (*doux*). The earliest seal, dated to 'late eighth-early ninth century' (Nesbitt and Oikonomides 1991, no. 14.2), is that of an anonymous *spatharios* and *archon* of Dalmatia. The seal belonging to the first *spatharios* and *archon* whose name we know (George) is dated to the 'early ninth century' (Nesbitt and Oikonomides 1991, no. 14.1). Another seal bearing the same title is known from the ninth century (Nesbitt and Oikonomides 1991, no. 14.3). The seal of *spatharokandidatos* Euthymios who also held the title of *doux* is dated to the 'ninth-tenth cenutry' (Nesbitt and Oikonomides 1991, no. 14.4) as is the seal of Eustathios, the imperial *protospatharios* and *strategos* of Dalmatia (Nesbitt and Oikonomides 1991, no. 14.5). Finally, the seal of Bryennios, the *spatharios* and *strategos* of Dalmatia is dated to mid-ninth century (Schlumberger 1884, 205–6) but Seibt (1981, 339) and Prigent (2008, 410) doubt the reading of his office as that of a *strategos*. To these officials one should add a seal of Emperor Maurice found in the hinterland of Zadar (Uglešić 2017, 125, 133) and four lead seals recently found at the Kolovare beach in Zadar (Filipčić 2017). Three of these seals have been tentatively dated to the first half of the ninth century: the seal of Leo, the imperial *strategos* of Kephalenia and two seals of Nicholas, a hitherto unidentified imperial *spatharios* and *archon* of Dalmatia. The seal of Leo is particularly interesting as the same *strategos* is known from another lead seal, housed at the National Museum in Athens (Callegher 1994).

The recent discovery of the seals in Zadar seems to add weight to Prigent's views. His first hypothesis is that the Byzantine authority in the Adriatic was renewed through the establishment of the theme of *Kibyrrhaiotai* (Brubaker and Haldon 2011, 729–30) in c.720 and the creation of the theme of Kephalenia in 760s (Prigent 2008, 398–402). The second is the interpretation of the role of the duke (*doux*) of Dyrrachion (modern Durrës) as an example of the development of the administrative role of local elites in the south Adriatic (Prigent 2008, 402–8). The third is his revision of the position of Jadran Ferluga (1953; 1976; 1978) who held that Dalmatian *archontes* were 'independent', that is subjected directly to the emperor (Ferluga 1976, 132). In contrast, Prigent (2008, 409) argued that they were subjected to the *strategos* of Kephalenia (see also Tsatsoulis 2012). According to him, governors of Dalmatia should not be identified with mayors (*priores*) of Zadar and he suggested that these governors originally did not reside in Zadar. Instead, Prigent's (2008, 411–6) Byzantine Dalmatia is a province located in the south Adriatic with the ancient *Diokleia* and *Ragusa* as its seats. The solution to this debate should perhaps be sought in the question of whether or not the governor of a theme need have had a fixed and unequivocally central base – the evidence of which is extremly sparse with hints of some sort of itinerancy (Morris 2020).

The discovery of the seal of *strategos* Leo of Kephalenia strengthens Prigent's first hypothesis. However, the discovery of three seals in Zadar speaks against his argument that Zadar was not the administrative centre of Dalmatia, supporting instead the traditional view that Zadar was a key point in the imperial reappropriation of the eastern Adriatic. Prigent is certainly right that it was not the only one, as it shared that status with Venice in the northern Adriatic and the area of Dubrovnik/Kotor in the south. The imperial gift of relics of St Theodore, St Anastasia and St Tryphon to Venice, Zadar and Kotor at the beginning of the ninth century, followed by the construction of the churches therein

(Osborne 1999, 375–80), confirms the point. As for the question of whether the office of the governor of Dalmatia was held by the members of the local elite or imperial officials, an inquiry into the question of the Greek presence in Dalmatia might help to build a better picture.

The references to 'Greeks' in the Adriatic by western authors are numerous. In a letter sent by Pope Hadrian I to Charlemagne in the 770s, the cruel fate of Bishop Mauritius is blamed on the actions of 'the Greeks who reside in the territory of Istria' (*Epistolae Merowingici et Karolini aevi* 1, 590, no. 63). Besides the 'nefarious Greeks' (*nefandissimi Greci*) of the papal letter, another document from Istria, the Plea (*placitum*) of Rižana (804), provides ample evidence of the Istrians' attachment to the time of the Greeks (*Graecorum tempus*, see Krahwinkler 2004, 79). At the same time, Amalarius, a Frankish traveller in Zadar, referred to those who belonged to the empire of the Greeks (*ad imperium Graecorum pertinent*, see Hanssens 1948, 342) and Gottschalk of Orbais refers to Dalmatians as subjects of the empire of the Greeks (*Graecorum imperio subiecti*) also speaking of the people of the Greeks and their governor (*gens Graecorum et patricius eorum*, see Lambot 1945, 208, 169). In an attempt to interpret these references different answers have been put forward. For example, allowing for the possibility that there were some 'ethnic Greeks settled in Istria', Gračanin (2015, 502–3) concluded that the Greeks of Gottschalk were 'Romans under the Greek rule, citizens of Dalmatian towns'. Charlemagne's letter is, however, quite precise on this issue – the attack on the prelate was committed by the 'Greeks' and 'those Istrians' (*Epistolae Merowingici et Karolini aevi* 1, 590, no. 63). Thus, besides the 'Greek-ruled', Latin-speaking Dalmatians mentioned by Gottschalk, the references to the 'Greeks residing in the region' might indeed denote officials sent from the imperial centre with some form of retinue. The patrician mentioned by Gottschalk could be, thus, interpreted as a Dalmatian *strategos* (Budak 2018c, 166; Margetić 1991) or even more precisely as Bryennios known from the lead seal (Genke and Gumerlock 2010).

Whatever the exact meaning of the term 'Greek' in each particular text, some of these references, as well as the Greek names of the lead seals, do seem to indicate the presence of 'ethnic Greeks' and/or 'cultural Greeks' (whom we would term Byzantines) in Dalmatian offices. It was exactly such a retinue of the centrally appointed official that could mobilise Istrians against Bishop Mauritius or lead local militia in the battle against the Croats. This kind of action, together with what Istrians narrated about the 'good old imperial times' at Rižana in 804, points to the conclusion that the imperial centre could still count on the support of the 'hearts and 'minds' of the local elites (Borri 2008; 2010; 2018) perhaps through the mediation of local officials. One of the expressions of this service (*douleia*) was also the formation of the 'Roman' identity acquired by the population of the Byzantine Adriatic enclaves in this period (Borri 2018). The Venetians, Istrians and Dalmatians readily paid imperial taxes and regularly travelled to Constantinople in order to pay homage to imperial authority and receive titles and dignities, as well as material rewards, in return. This might have been more than enough to make them 'Greeks' in the eyes of the western observers.

Accepting the possibility that Dalmatian provincial governors were residing in Zadar and were sent there directly from Constantinople (Ferluga 1978, 161–2; 183–5), a question of the Greek presence in that city arises. Testimony to Greeks in Zadar can be detected in the local onomastic and toponomastic evidence (Jakić-Cestarić 1972; 1974), hagiotopography (for example, churches dedicated to SS Anastasia, Plato and Thomas, see Fig. 6.2) and hagiography. While local hagiographic legends fit Latin hagiography rather than the Byzantine, traces of the 'Greek times' can be identified on different levels. The *Translatio beati Grisogoni martiris* for

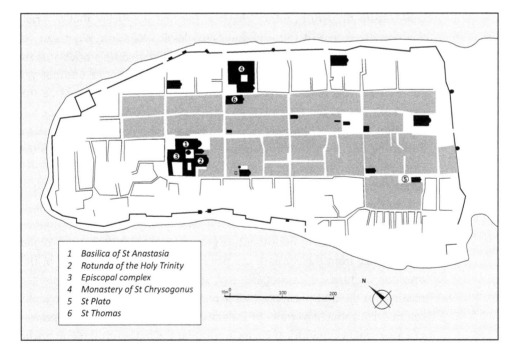

Fig. 6.2 Church dedications in Medieval Zadar.
Redrawn by Trpimir Vedriš after Klaić and Petricioli (1976, 113)

example preserved traces undoubtedly reflecting the 'Greek influences one expects to encounter in Byzantine Dalmatia' (Katičić 1993, 193). Greek names continued to appear in Zadar well into eleventh century and later.

Besides traces of the Greeks in Zadar, the sources of the tenth century also provide evidence of another ethnic group in Zadar. While the scarcity of the material invites caution, it is certain that the process of intermarrying between members of the 'Roman' and Croat 'Slavic' elites of Zadar must have started already in the ninth century (Jakić-Cestarić 1974, 199–214; Nikolić 2003, 151). Local evidence (Budak 2007) confirms that the process of the integration of the Croat elites into the urban society of Zadar was well underway during the tenth century (Jakić-Cestarić 1972; 1974; 1976). The first visible fruit of this process was the appearance of members of the urban elite – no less than a *prior*'s daughter and one of the tribunes – bearing Slavic names (Jakić-Cestarić 1976). References to these earliest known members of the urban elite brings us back to the question of the relation between the local elites in Zadar and the Byzantine administration.

The critical issue in this context is the survival of the offices and titles from Late Antique military organisation in Zadar. Besides that of a duke (*dux*) from the beginning of the ninth century, the earliest reliable evidence comes from the tenth-century charters, the first one being that of *prior* Andrew dated to 918 (Stipišić and Šamšalović 1967, 26). What can be deduced from the charter is that the city was governed by a *prior* at least from c.900. At that moment, however, the position of *prior* was not yet connected to the offices in the Byzantine administration as would be the case from the late tenth century onwards (Ferluga 1978, 218–9). While the donation charter of Andrew does not indicate the relationship between governing the city and administering the province, the charter of Madius from 986 reveals he was the *prior* of the city and the proconsul of Dalmatia (*prior civitatis atque proconsul Dalmatiarum*, Stipišić and Šamšalović 1967, 45). In the tenth and eleventh centuries the position of *prior* – with local authority over the city and its district – was considered more prestigious than the formal title of the Byzantine governor (Nikolić 2003, 125). While the evidence from the eleventh century is more abundant than that of the previous centuries it cannot be used to prove the existence of similar relations in the ninth century. Still it remains the case that after the tenth century, Byzantine governors of Dalmatia were, without exception, *priores* of Zadar which allows for the conclusion that the latter was a requirement for the former (Ferluga 1978, 235).

Furthermore *priores* of Zadar (and other governors of Dalmatia) shared their authority with the tribunes (*tribunes*), another residue of Late Antique military organisation. The Dalmatian *tribunes* are well-documented officials registered for the first time in the four tenth-century charters (Basić 2015a, 186–90). The hypothesis of Margetić (1975) that 'tribunal aristocracy' in Zadar developed from a group of military commanders in charge of the city's urban districts was recently elaborated by Basić (2015a). Analogies with other regions under Byzantine rule such as the exarchate of Ravenna (Brown 1984) or Istria permit assumptions about the existence of these offices in Zadar prior to the tenth century. For example, the Plea (*placitum*) of Rižana reports of *tribuni* still implying military functions (Bileta 2011, 114; Levak 2007, 80). A further point of reference might be sought in the comparison between Istrian and Venetian *tribunes*, whose development followed the same pattern (Gasparri 1992).

To return to the assumptions of Prigent: in the light of the presented evidence, his third hypothesis does not appear wholly convincing. This should however not overshadow his inspiring interpretation of different details concerning the organisation of the Byzantine administration or his conclusion about the two zones of Byzantine influence in the Adriatic (Prigent 2008, 416). Still, the evidence discussed here allows for the assumption that from the Constantinopolitan perspective it was Zadar, rather than the urban nuclei of Upper Dalmatia (such as Dubrovnik, Kotor or *Diokleia*), that was meant to play a leading role in the Byzantine east Adriatic at the beginning of the ninth century. An important point for further exploration is certainly the notion that, as elaborated by Curta (2005; 2011) in relation to the theme of Hellas, a maritime theme, if Dalmatia was one, would have its headquarters situated where the main harbour was located. If compared to the position of Venice 'playing a role of vanguard towards the Western empire and a place of controlled exchange (emporium)', Zadar was to become 'a provincial metropolis and a seat of imperial governor' (Ančić 2017, 34). This observation is supported not only by building activities in Zadar, but also by the fact that 'disobedient and deposed Venetian dukes (*duces*) were sent to Zadar, very likely under the custody of the provincial governor' (Ančić 2017, 34). The presence of the titles of mayor (*prior*) or tribunes (*tribuni*) – although recorded only from the tenth century onwards – point towards the traditional perspective that sees Zadar as the provincial capital.

Between Rome and Constantinople: The Church of Zadar in the Early Ninth Century

The breaking point in the history of Zadar was, at least from the perspective of surviving sources, the moment when the embassy consisting of

Duke Paul and Bishop Donatus reached the court of Charlemagne in Thionville in the winter of 805. Of Paul, whom some authors identified with the homonymous *strategos* of Kephalenia (Gračanin 2015, 506), we shall hear no more. His co-traveller fared much better: Donatus was made a saint in the local tradition and survived in the local cultural memory. The figures of duke (*dux*) and bishop (*episcopus*) are an apt image of the Early Medieval Church (*ecclesia*), a community constituted in the world where ontological distinction between the secular and the sacral has not yet been clearly drawn. That the church made part of the Early Medieval 'republics' undividable comes as no novelty in the Mediterranean where many towns outlived the empire exclusively because they were episcopal sees. These Early Medieval bishoprics, as a rule, claimed continuity with their early Christian past making their memories one of the central arguments in their struggles for supremacy among other emerging ecclesiastical centres. Lacking both martyr tradition and traditional jurisdictional rights, Zadar (Fig. 6.3) could not boast about its grandiose early Christian past comparable to centres like Aquileia or Split (*Salona*), who prided themselves on their (quasi)apostolic traditions (Štih 2017). Even with the position of the

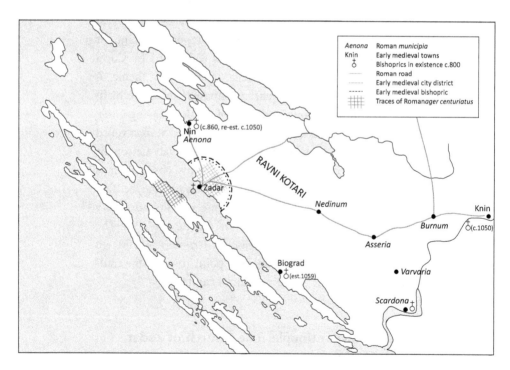

Fig. 6.3 Zadar and its hinterland.
Drawn by Trpimir Vedriš

capital of the province it was no match for Split with its acquired tradition of *Salona* and the support of the Croatian rulers.

The existence of an organised Christian community in Zadar cannot be attested before the first half of the fourth century (Vežić 2005). At that time primacy over the Dalmatian churches was left to the bishop of *Salona*. The bishop of Zadar (*episcopus Iadertinus*) is mentioned for the first time at the Council of Rome in 341 and Felix, the first bishop known by name participated in the Council of Aquileia in 381 (Strika 2004). Interestingly, he also attended the Council of Milan in 390 as the only representative of Dalmatia. The list of the bishops in the fifth century is extremely meagre but by the beginning of the sixth century the bishop of Zadar had consolidated his position as the second prelate in the province (Suić 1981, 330). Soon after the synods of *Salona* in 530 and 533 (Basić 2009; Prozorov 2011; Škegro 2009), evidence of Dalmatian bishops becomes scarce. Information on the bishops between Sabinianus to whom Gregory the Great addressed three letters in 597–8 (Strika 2006, 90) and Donatus (c.805) can hardly be accepted as authentic.

Traditional historiography often took it for granted that some of the ecclesiastical centres on the eastern Adriatic coast survived the Dark Ages without ruptures in their episcopal succession. However, as elaborated by Basić (2018a, 265–7) it was only in the mid-to-late eighth century that a number of bishoprics (re)surfaced in the northern Adriatic. It is still far from certain whether all these bishoprics were restored or founded anew. This restoration corresponds chronologically with the appearance of the Carolingians in northern Italy, the re-emergence of Byzantium in the Adriatic and the reactivation of the papacy under Pope Hadrian (Basić 2018a; Betti 2018). It is thus not easy to discern who gave the crucial impetus to these new ecclesiastical policies. The ancient see of Grado, for example, is a case in point in the development of a new Carolingian ecclesiastical policy in the Adriatic. Grado, like Zadar, lay inside the Byzantine empire yet it was never subjected to the Patriarchate of Constantinople. In 803, two years before the bishop of Zadar reached Thionville, Patriarch Fortunatus of Grado was received by Charlemagne and granted the metropolitan rank as the patriarch of Venice and Istria (*Venetiarum et Istriensium patriarcha*). This 'deliberate act of Frankish sponsorship over a 'Byzantine' metropolitan see' reflects the 'one-sided nature of Frankish interference in the ecclesiastical administration of Byzantium's Adriatic territories' (Basić 2018a, 267). This kind of church policy was made possible by the Carolingian thrust into Pannonia and the establishment of their authority in the area. Whether the process of the re-establishment of the bishoprics took place simultaneously in Dalmatia is a matter of debate (Basić 2018a; Komatina 2018). It stands that the bishop of Zadar was not among the four Dalmatian prelates attending the Council of Nicaea in 787 (Basić 2014; Katičić 1983; Komatina 2018).

Seen in this light, the first decade of the ninth century indeed looks like a new beginning for Zadar. After almost two centuries of silence, the city (re)emerged in the written sources when Bishop Donatus appeared at the imperial court in Thionville after Christmas 805 along with the duke (*dux*) of Zadar, 'representing the Dalmatians' (*Annales regni Francorum*, a. 806). Another local legend, the *Translatio S. Anastasiae* (*Bibliotheca hagiographica Latina*, 402) reports his voyage to Constantinople where he acquired the relics of the Sirmian martyr St Anastasia (Brunelli 1913, 185–8; Farlati 1775, 34–5; Rački 1877, 306–10). The *Translatio* is to be understood in the context of simultaneous imperial donations to other Adriatic centres (Osborne 1999; Preradović 2012; Živković 2007). Following the arrival of the relics, the magnificent rotunda of the Holy Trinity was (re)built (Fig. 6.4) and ample epigraphic evidence confirms that Bishop Donatus furnished other churches (Petricioli 1961, 258–60; Vedriš 2018, 298; Vežić 2002a). In other words, the image of Zadar's 'new beginning' largely depends on the evidence for the activities of this bishop. Local tradition remembered him as travelling between Thionville and Constantinople and interceding between the emperors. He was praised for bringing the relics of the Pannonian martyr Anastasia (Fig. 6.5) and eventually credited with building her a monumental *martyrium*. All this made Bishop Donatus a saint in due time as a result of a long process ending in the rotunda being rededicated to the saintly bishop in the fifteenth century.

Local Late Medieval sources suggest that the citizens of Zadar believed the rotunda to have been built by Bishop Donatus. Archaeological and other evidence suggest it was indeed built sometime between the late eighth and the mid-ninth century. Accepting a hypothesis based on carbon-14 and dendrochronological analysis of the wooden beams found in the first floor of the rotunda (Obelić and Sliepčević 2000, 197–206) as well as other circumstances, allows us to date the second phase of the rotunda's construction to the period between the 750s and 860s (Jarak 1995, 119). The dating comes close to confirming local tradition. In order to summarise a series of complex issues connected to this building one has to rely on the conclusions presented in more detail elsewhere (Ančić 2014, 68–84; Lončar 1999, 235–43; Vežić 2002b), but the assumed connection between the arrival of the relics of St Anastasia and the building of the rotunda raises the question of the original function of this church.

Fig. 6.4 The ninth-century rotunda of the Holy Trinity (St Donatus) at Zadar.
Photo: Pavuša Vežić

Earlier interpretations relied on the local tradition that saw the church being built as 'the oratory of St Donatus'. Taking into consideration its unusual features it was consequently interpreted as the bishop's chapel connected to the episcopal palace (*episcopium*). The second hypothesis was that the rotunda was originally built with the intention that it serve as the

Fig. 6.5 The ninth-century sarcophagus of St Anastasia in Zadar Cathedral.
© Stalna izložba crkvene umjetnosti, Zadar / Permanent Collection of Religious Art, Zadar.
Photo: Zoran Alajbeg

martyrium of St Anastasia (Jakšić 2008, 97; Jeličić-Radonić 1992, 352–3; Vedriš 2012, 64–7; 2018, 297; Vežić 2002b). Finally, arguing that the rebuilding of the church was 'directly related to the Byzantine plans for imperial re-conquest' Ančić concluded that the 'rotunda of the Holy Trinity was intended for a high-ranked representative of the emperor' (Ančić 2014; Dzino and Parry 2014, 3–4). That the project might have been perhaps an even earlier one was proposed by Budak (2018b, 37) pointing to the similarity with the Church of Santa Sofia at Benevento and describing the rotunda as 'incomparable to anything built in Dalmatia after the sixth century and before the eleventh century'. Interpreting the building in the context of Constantine V's 'dispute with Rome over jurisdiction', he interpreted the rotunda as 'a clear sign of the presence of (imperial) power in Zadar, the main Byzantine stronghold in Dalmatia' (Budak 2018b, 37). Understood as the 'display of imperial authority and ideology in the frontier-zone' the (re)construction should be interpreted in relation to the construction of the churches of St Theodore in Venice and

St Tryphon in Kotor (Osborne 1999, 375-80) connected to the restoration of Byzantine authority in the Adriatic.

Whether the church was used as a chapel of the bishop or it was meant to serve as the chapel of the Byzantine official residing in Zadar cannot be decided with certainty. Similarly, different possible ideological layers of this project are not all easy to detect. The choice of a martyr from Illyricum with a strong cult in both Constantinople (Snee 1998) and – often neglected – in Rome (Vedriš 2007, 203–10) gives some clue to the connotations which the gift of Anastasia's relics might have had for the capital of Dalmatia. All these activities, however, should not be taken as evidence of the Byzantine and/or Greek liturgical supremacy or jurisdictional authority of the Constantinopolitan patriarch in Dalmatia as suggested by earlier scholarship (Katičić 1983, 78–9). Nevertheless, the evidence of Bishop Donatus' activities seems to fit well with the new historiographic perspective that the Dalmatian bishops of the late eighth and early ninth century represent a large-scale ecclesiastical restoration (*renovatio*) along the eastern Adriatic coast (Basić 2018a; Vedriš 2018). While the exact position and rank of the bishop of Zadar is far from clear, his ecclesiastical background was undoubtedly in Rome and not Constantinople. This, however, should not cast a shadow on the possibility that in the context of the rupture of 812 the elites of Zadar (both ecclesiastical and secular) sought ways to improve their status and establish Zadar as the regional centre.

In this context, Amalarius' reference to the senior churchman of Zadar as archbishop (*archiepiscopus*) in his letter to Abbot Hilduin remains a puzzle (Vedriš 2018, 291–2, 298). Zadar was not elevated to the rank of an archbishopric and metropolitan see before 1154 (Ančić 2017; Majnarić 2007; Strika 2004). Apart from the curious hint by Amalarius and the even more problematic title of *archipraesul* granted to Donatus by the legend *Translatio S. Anastasiae* (Vedriš 2005, 14–8), there is no evidence that this title was ever bestowed on the bishops of Zadar prior to the mid-twelfth century. As such, mention of an archbishop in Amalarius' letter to Hilduin could perhaps be explained by suggesting that 'the mental image of the city remembered by the learned bishop ... was such that it conformed to the image of a city that is a seat of an archbishop' (Ančić 2014, 77). This speculative interpretation unexpectedly received additional weight with the discovery of the inscription of Archbishop Ursus in Zadar (Basić 2017–18; Vedriš 2018, 299; Vežić 2013, 8–9). Thanks to scrupulous analysis by Basić (2017–18) it is now possible to date the inscription to the early ninth century and to interpret it as the earliest confirmed appearance of the title archbishop (*archiepiscopus*) in Zadar. The interpretation is not without problems. Apart from another, rather dubious, ninth-century epigraphic reference to an archbishop from Krk (Skoblar 2006, 69), this is the sole Early Medieval Dalmatian inscription of an archbishop outside the Church of *Salona*/Split. Ursus himself does not appear in the episcopal lists which makes the inscription the only trace of his existence.

Be that as it may, three references to the archbishop from the early ninth century Zadar, cannot be ignored. In interpreting these one should consider contemporary evidence deriving from Abbot Hilduin of St Denis, actual addressee of Amalarius' letter. Attributing in his *Passio sancti Dionysii* the rank of archbishop (*archiepiscopus*) to the bishop of Athens, Hilduin reflected the fact that in the west the title was sometimes used to be synonymous with that of metropolitan in the east (Komatina 2009, 38). Moreover, following this clue, Komatina has connected the establishment of metropolitan sees in Athens (783–806) and Patras (805–6) with the creation of the theme of the Peloponnese. All the differences notwithstanding, new administrative divisions obviously caused new ecclesiastical organisation 'not based on patterns of old, late Roman principles' (Komatina 2009, 52). While the positions of Dalmatia and the Peloponnese are in many ways not comparable, these observations bring us to the relevance of the Isaurian dynasty's ecclesiastical politics (Turlej 2001, 50–3, 79–85, 139–61) for understanding the position of Zadar at the turn of the ninth century. It is significant that besides the case of Athens, the *Notitia episcopatuum* 3 (c.800) lists Kephalenia (in the form *Kephalia*) as a metropolitan church although it was an ordinary bishopric (Darrouzès 1981; Prigent 2008, 402). In the light of the establishment of the theme of Kephalenia, Prigent (2008, 402) concluded that its administrative position was reflected in the perception of the ecclesiastical rank of the city's bishop adding that this 'metropolis' had an authority over Dalmatian bishoprics. To this one should add an alternative interpretation of *Kephalia* as superimposed to Dalmatia. In his analysis of the mention of the Dalmatian bishops at the Council of Hieria in 754, Basić (2014, 162–8) suggested that these 'Dalmatians' were actually the bishops of 'Ionian Dalmatia', that is, Corfu, Zakynthos, Nikopolis and Dyrrachion.

The issue of the connection between imperial administration and ecclesiastical structures in the context of political reactivation of the eastern empire in Dalmatia has to remain open. While the establishment of *archontia* and subsequently theme certainly cannot be taken as evidence for the jurisdictional authority of the Constantinopolitan patriarch in Dalmatia, the development of Byzantine administration provides a context in which 'an attempt to draw the Dalmatian bishops into the Constantinopolitan orbit is not completely implausible' (Vedriš 2018, 300). Along these lines, all these pieces of evidence – from the relics of St Anastasia and the rotunda of the Holy Trinity, to the inscription of Ursus and Amalarius' hints – may be interpreted as a testimony to a particular moment, irregular and certainly short-lived, in the history of Zadar. Bishops of Zadar might have used the moment when 'superpowers of the day sought to re-affirm their presence in the Adriatic with carrot-and-stick politics' (Vedriš 2018, 300) to promote their cause by claiming the title of archbishop.

The problem with this interpretation derives from the fact that a few decades earlier the Roman Church seemingly promoted the bishop of Split granting him the title of archbishop. According to recent interpretation the Church of Split which strove to present itself as the direct heir to the metropolitan see of *Salona* was in fact re-established only in the second half of the eighth century (Basić 2018a, 268–79). Due to the lack of evidence the issue of the relation between the two ecclesiastical centres at the turn of the ninth century cannot be resolved. Yet, one should bear in mind that the bishop of Zadar did not participate at the council of Nicaea in 787 (Komatina 2018) and the bishop of *Salona*/Split already enjoyed 'a degree of seniority over the three other bishops' – although not yet as their metropolitan (Basić 2018a, 270). Nevertheless, as a result of the transformations of the early ninth century, the bishops of Zadar emerged as strong candidates for the position of the metropolitan of Dalmatia towards the end of the century. The attempts failed as, after the reconstruction of the Dalmatian Church at the synods of 925–8, bishops of Zadar had to remain subject to the metropolitan see of *Salona*/Split. In contrast to other Dalmatian bishoprics that encompassed larger or smaller areas of the Croatian principality, the jurisdiction of the bishop of Zadar remained confined to the narrow strip of territory in the hinterland and the archipelago facing it. In its hinterland it bordered with the territory of two Croatian bishoprics (Fig. 6.3) – that of Nin (established c.860, re-established c.1050) and Biograd (established c.1050).

Dangerous Neighbours? Zadar and Its Hinterland

The territorial onshore reach of the eighth-century Byzantine administration in the eastern Adriatic hinterland seems to have included control of the immediate hinterland of Zadar and *Salona* (Dzino 2014, 138) with possible parallels in Istria and Dyrrachion (Curta 2004, 527; 2006, 103–5; 2013b, 62–5). Unfortunately, owing to the poor state of archaeological research, the boundaries of those administrative units cannot be defined precisely. However, at least one section of the demarcated frontier (*limes*) pertaining to *Salona*/Split is discernible along the river Cetina (Milošević 1995; 2005; 2010; Rapanić 2017). The other, northern segment of the territory centred at Zadar is discernible primarily through the remnants of the churches and fortifications that were in use during the Dark Ages (Jakšić 1993) and were situated along the main communication lines called *Via magna* in later documents (Dzino 2010; Jakšić 2008). The transformation of this space (Fig. 6.3) had been heavily affected by the formation of a new political entity in the Dalmatian hinterland traditionally interpreted as the result of the arrival of the Croats in the seventh century. Yet, a series of unresolved issues concerning the date and nature of this movement means that we have little information prior to the Treaty of Aachen of 812. Over the last two decades new interpretations about the migration of the Croats have challenged this narrative (Ančić 2005; 2018b; Bertelli and Brogiolo 2001; Dzino 2010).

The crux of the new paradigm lies in the friction between the Byzantine empire and that of the Franks but also in the war between the Franks and the Avars; these events sparked small-scale migrations that brought new groups of 'specialists in violence' to the eastern Adriatic hinterland. The newly arrived, ethnically diverse warrior bands mixed with the people already living there and a new polity emerged which by the 820s took the form of a (quasi)vassal dukedom headed by the Duke of the Guduscani (*dux Guduscanorum*) Borna (d. 821) who held the title of duke of Dalmatia and Liburnia (*dux Dalmaciae et Liburniae*) by 819. Material evidence from the period between the 780s to the 840s (Belošević 2007; Petrinec 2009; Sokol 2016) allows for the conclusion that the:

> Carolingians provided not only the "hardware" for the development of this new power structure (in the form of arms and equipment) but also 'software', in the form of organisational schemes for the rule they imposed, as well as the first steps towards Christianisation, led by missionaries mostly from northern Italy. (Ančić 2018a, 30)

The role of Aquileia and its patriarchal see in Dalmatian affairs was formalised in 806 when Charlemagne confirmed the decision of the council gathered on the shores of the Danube (*ad ripas Danubii*) in 796 that the lands south of the river Drava were to be put under the ecclesiastical jurisdiction of the patriarch of Aquileia. As a result, missionaries came to Dalmatia from northern Italy 'bringing in the enduring traditions of the Lombard kingdom' (Ančić 2005, 218). Along with the missionaries their secular counterpart, administrators from Friuli were instrumental in the 'transposition and/or transplantation of the institutions and forms of social conduct from the Frankish world' (Ančić 2005, 214). Although the primary objective of this new power structure was to put pressure on the Byzantine administration, in time it provided a framework for the ascent of one of the groups whose members were called Croats.

The activities of the Croatian warrior elites in the proximity of Zadar seem to have taken a course that was different from the aforementioned naval operations of the *Narentani*. Rather than acts of plundering, the sources record direct interaction between the local Croatian elites and the secular and ecclesiastical institutions at Zadar in the late ninth century. The emergence of the principality of Croatia, partly overlapping with the territory of the late eighth-century Byzantine *archontia*, seems to have been a fruit of the process of transformation and accommodation as much as the migration. While the culture of these elites was traditionally interpreted as a counter to that of urban Roman enclaves two peculiar features should be emphasised. First, there is the existence of a huge corpus of Latin inscriptions found in the territory of the Croatian principality (Delonga 1996; 2001; Mihaljčić and Steindorff 1982; Steindorff 2005). Secondly, it should be stressed that the majority of centres of emerging Croatian polity as a rule emerged in the vicinity of ex-Roman cities – Zadar being one of the cases. In other words, the space sketched as the onshore territory of the Byzantine *archontia*, or at least its northern portion, largely overlaps with the core space of the Croatian principality centred on the area between Nin, Knin and Skradin.

The case of Nin (*Aenona*) is particularly illuminating. This former Roman town (*municipium*) situated 13 km to the north-west of Zadar, was positioned at a strategic point in a protected lagoon, open towards the north Adriatic, at the centre of a densely populated area (Dubolnić-Glavan 2015). The road leading from Nin traversed the cultivated *ager* of Zadar and led to Knin (*Tinium*) and *Salona*. Rich archaeological finds provide evidence that the Christian population at Nin survived the calamities of the seventh and eighth centuries. At the turn of the ninth century, a considerable number of inhumations was done at a large cemetery situated at the site of Ždrijac just outside Nin. More than 340 graves excavated there have been interpreted as belonging to a pagan population traditionally held to be the newly arrived Croats (Belošević 2007), an interpretation questioned recently (Alajbeg 2014). It seems that the two communities mixed during the early ninth century.

To improve our understanding of the relationship between Nin and Zadar, the arrival of the two imperial embassies to Dalmatia in 817

(*Annales regni Francorum*, a. 817) to 'sort out the territorial problems that had arisen from the treaty's implementation' might provide a clue. Namely, 'it is highly probable that these centred on the coastal city of Nin, which had not been handed over to Byzantine administration as the treaty stipulated' (Ančić 2018a, 32–3). The negotiations between the two empires could not yield a solution thus both embassies went to the area – accompanied by the local actors, perhaps Duke Borna and the Byzantine governor from Zadar as suggested by Ančić. His hypothesis raises questions not only of the way the border was to be drawn, but also its exact line.

In all likelihood, the border established between the two empires in 817 followed the ancient demarcation line between the two Roman towns (*municipia*). According to Jakšić (1986, 217–18) the Early Medieval territory of Zadar was the 'petrified territory of the *colonia Iulia Iader* at the time of its foundation'. Thus, understanding the territorial administration of the Roman *municipia* is of crucial importance for understanding the relations between the centres and their territories in the post-Roman period (Suić 1956, 9–12). Zadar's *ager centuriatus* was among the smallest in the eastern Adriatic (Fig. 6.3). Iader bordered four other Roman *municipia*: that of *Aenona* in the west, *Nedinum* (Nadin) in the north and *Asseria* (Podgrađe) and *Varvaria* (Bribir) in the east-south-east. The Roman administrative division of the territory of Late Antique *Iader* (including its *ager extra clusus* as well as *ager publicus*), which developed from the pre-Roman division of land centred on fortified settlements, may be reconstructed with relative certainty (Dubolnić Glavan 2015, 394–400). What is important here is that the reconstruction of its western and northwestern borders based on tenth through eleventh century charters (Jakšić 1986) testifies to the survival of the borders between the Roman districts of *Aenona* (Nin) and *Iader* (Zadar) into the Middle Ages. This observation confirms the notion of the continuity of the territorial administration but also shows to what extent the idea of a 'wild frontier' established as the result of the 'barbaric conquest' may be misleading.

Episcopus Nonensis: Nin as the New Ecclesiastical Centre

Nin became an important centre for the re-Christianisation of Dalmatia in the late eighth century during the Frankish intrusion. Hagiotopography of the region illustrates this through the appearance of imported northern Italian/Frankish saints (Jakšić 2018; Vedriš 2009; 2015). It was, of course, not only the saints who came from on the wings of the Carolingian *Drang nach Osten*. The names of the ninth-century 'missionaries', as they were often referred to, also reflect their north Italian origin. While they were commonly labelled 'Germanic' or 'Frankish' it would be more appropriate to call them Lombard given that their names stand in stark contrast to Croatian dignitaries and court officials whose Slavic names were preserved in ninth-century inscriptions and primary sources (Delonga 1996; 2001; Maraković and Jurković 2007). With all this in mind, it can be said that between the late eighth and the ninth century, the surrounding area of Nin was 'invaded' by the Carolingian missionaries, in fact monks from northern Italy (Vedriš 2015).

The silence of the sources before the end of the eighth century does not allow us to define the relations between the Church of Zadar and its hinterland. However, it is clear that with the division of 812 (perhaps formally in 817, as Ančić suggested) Nin and its surrounding definitely slipped out of the jurisdiction of the bishop in Zadar. The presence of the 'monks and saints' from northern Italy in the area went hand in hand with the activities of their secular counterparts in the guise of Friulian elites. The re-Christianisation of the area occurred alongside the imposition of new institutions and modes of social conduct but also meant reorganisation of the ecclesiastical system along new non-traditional lines. In this, the results of the new Carolingian church politics provide a clear analogy with the process of reshuffling that took place in the areas simultaneously reconquered by the Byzantine empire further to the south. This development as we have seen did not simply imply Lombard conquest under Carolingian guise, but rather the affirmation of the local elites who came to constitute the backbone of the new political entity which by the 830s through 840s started to take the shape of a recognisable Early Medieval *regnum* (Majnarić 2018a).

The ecclesiastical dimension of this coming of age of the Croatian principality became visible in the establishment of the ecclesiastical organisation in Nin around the middle of the ninth century. The bishopric was in all likelihood established during the rule of either Trpimir or his successor Domagoj as can be deduced from the letter of Pope Nicholas I (858–67) to the clergy of Nin. The bishops of Nin soon demonstrated their desire for power by trying to achieve metropolitan status over Dalmatia. The first bishop known by his name, Theodosius (d. before 892) had been ordained in Rome by Pope John VIII in 880 (Stipišić and Šamšalović 1967, 18–19). In 886–7 he 'usurped' the empty see of the bishopric of Split and went to Aquileia to receive episcopal consecration through the hands of Patriarch Walpert (c.875–99). While this act caused shock in Rome and motivated papal condemnation, Pope Stephen V (885–91) was ready to grant Theodosius the *pallium* provided he personally appeared in Rome (Stipišić and Šamšalović 1967, 22). The willingness on the part of the pope to accept Theodosius' usurpation may be interpreted as a result of the desire to unify and consolidate the Dalmatian Church, the majority of which at the time lay under the rule of the Croatian Duke Branimir. Theodosius warned by the pope nevertheless seems to have enjoyed the support of the Spalatines which indicates that the idea of merging the ecclesiastical organisation in Byzantine Dalmatia and Croatia obviously tackled not only the Croatian court but also Dalmatian clergy. The starting positions were different. While Croatian rulers tried to gain control of the coastline and incorporate churches rich in tradition into their realm, the Dalmatian clergy or, rather, bishops of Split were dreaming of re-establishing of the ancient Salonitan jurisdiction over Dalmatia. This included the whole of Croatia described by the Medieval Spalatine chronicler Archdeacon Thomas (*Historia Salonitana* 13) as spreading from the shore of Danube to the Dalmatian sea (*a ripa Danubii usque ad mare Dalmaticum*). Theodosius' refusal to leave the Church of Nin behind certainly did not help to resolve the situation. The project did not succeed. The election of the next bishop of Nin, Adelfreda (892–c.900), may signalise a continuing Aquileian presence in Nin but it proved to be the swansong of northern Italian influence in local ecclesiastical affairs. Both Nin and Zadar definitely lost their race at the church councils in 925 and 928 with the Church of Split finally established as metropolitan see of Dalmatia. Bishop Gregory of Nin (c.900–928) was, as we are informed by the decisions of the second Council of Split, deposed and his bishopric abolished.

The most important factor in this outcome was the effective presence of the Roman Church active in the region since the late eighth century. Letters of popes to Croatian dukes and the clergy of both Nin and Dalmatian cities reflect concern about losing ground in Dalmatia due to the Photian schism. One of the principal aims of the papacy was establishing a bridgehead in Dalmatia and turning it into a bulwark of papal jurisdiction (and Latin Christendom) towards the East. The concerns of the Roman curia for Dalmatia were intensified with the loss of Bulgaria in 869. The advance of the Bulgarian Church with its Byzantine customs (and lurking political influences) corresponded with intense effort by Rome to discipline the local clergy, directing Dalmatia into the safe haven of Roman jurisdiction. One of the outcomes was a concession to Dalmatian clergy in the form of the abolition of the bishopric of Nin. By the mid-tenth century it became obvious that the jurisdiction of the Church of Zadar church would remain more or less confined to Roman *ager publicus*. In this the area of jurisdiction of the bishop of Zadar (*episcopus Iadertinus*) overlapped with the city district administered by the city's *prior* who at the same time held the title of Byzantine *strategos* or *katepano*.

Conclusion: From a Bunker to an Open City

As implied by the arguments presented here, Zadar survived the collapse and recovery of post-Roman Dalmatia, preserving continuity of institutions and control of its territory. In this period, the Late Antique *civitas* was transformed into the Early Medieval *provincia* that developed as a self-sustainable and functional political unit loosely dependent on the imperial administrative system. The question of Zadar's connection to the rest of the province must take into account that Dalmatia, at least from the beginning of the ninth century, seen from different perspectives came to mean different things. In exploring how the interaction between the international and the local factors contributed to Zadar becoming a capital of this 'imaginary Dalmatia', its position in the Byzantine Early Medieval Adriatic should be read primarily in the context of the re-emergence of imperial interest(s) in the late eighth and early ninth century.

The reactivation of the Byzantine empire at sea in the second half of the eighth century resulted in the restoration of the Byzantine administration, originally run from the region of Otranto via Kephalenia and Dyrrachion. Further development led to the connecting of surviving nuclei along the eastern Adriatic coast. These were connected through the system of fortifications situated mostly on the islands (and thus protecting the seaway along the coast) – but also controlling at least two larger onshore territories of the hinterland of Split and Zadar. While Split could claim continuity from ancient *Salona*, Zadar, a former Roman *colonia* without significant early Christian heritage, became prominent primarily because of its strategic position and the preservation of its fully functional and autonomous *civitas* throughout the seventh century. With a spacious hinterland providing fertile soil for a growing population and the control of a large archipelago stretching from the Gulf of Kvarner (Quarnero) to Šibenik, Zadar was a rather obvious choice.

Seen from the Constantinopolitan strategic point of view the territorial arrangements of the Treaty of Aachen for the eastern Adriatic look like a bridgehead against the other, 'barbarian' half of the empire. In this context the Dalmatian *octapolis* was a system of 'bunkers' providing safe naval passage to the point of 'controlled exchange' in the Venetian lagoon, as well as a platform for future negotiations with rulers of the West after they thrust into Illyricum. The pre-eminent among those 'eight bunkers' was obviously Zadar which became a centre of the administrative unit run by *archontes* by the end of the eighth century. The result of the final provision (*ordinatio*) was the border between the empires set in the vicinity of Zadar in 817. Interestingly, the line of division established as the result of the implementation of the Treaty of Aachen followed almost precisely the ancient division between the local Roman *municipia* and ignored the (imagined?) Slavic invasion of previous centuries. The emergence of an armed Carolingian-controlled polity in its rear and the establishment of the new ecclesiastical organisation in Nin hindered the onshore spread of the *provincia*. On the other hand, although administratively and politically divided from its hinterland, Zadar started to attract local rural elites leading to their immigration and integration into the social fabric of Zadar.

At the same time another important process was underway. The merging of local offices with positions in the imperial administration made Zadar the capital of Dalmatia by the tenth century. The question of the exact time of the establishment of the theme of Dalmatia (*thema Dalmatias*) remains open, as does the question of its actual functioning. For most of the period under scrutiny, far from imperial reach, the urban community of Zadar developed in a specific context that might be described as a border society. Latin-speaking and jurisdictionally Roman, this centre of Byzantine administration had to live with centres of Carolingian-supported polity growing up in the nearby hinterland. This narrow strip of land can hardly be imagined as a fully functional imperial theme in the original meaning of the word.

The impact of the renovation of imperial administration in the Adriatic also influenced the position of the Church of Zadar. Two main reasons why Zadar did not achieve the metropolitan position in Dalmatia were its lack of early Christian credentials and the fact that it lay outside the effective control of the Croatian dukes who came to control the major part of ancient Dalmatia. The final failure should not, however, detract from magnifying the short period when circumstances were much more favourable to Zadar than other Dalmatian towns. While remaining under the traditional Roman jurisdiction the bishops of Zadar, it seems, claimed the status of archbishops. While the exact meaning of the fragmentary evidence is unclear, it seems likely that bishops of Zadar tried to achieve an ecclesiastical status that would correspond with their city's administrative position.

Belonging to the empire provided not only ideological arguments but also meant new offices, honours and material gains. The prospects of long-distant trade and the possibility of the arrival of the imperial fleet, if needed, obviously made subjection to the rule of New Rome a desirable option for the citizens of Zadar. The notion of Roman identity *Romanitas* that developed in relation to the new rulers of its hinterland integrated Zadar symbolically within the Adriatic Byzantine *oikoumene*. For the local elites emerging together with these processes, participation in the Byzantine administration was undoubtedly one of the ways to run their own business. They used the imperial reference as a means of enhancing their power in the competition with other regional centres, such as Croatian Nin in its hinterland or Split, the old-new ecclesiastical centre of Dalmatia, which would have failed without the support of the Croatian rulers. It is thus the combination of overlapping imperial circles that made Zadar both a centre of importance on the imperial periphery on the one hand, but also a regional centre on the other. The early ninth century may thus be interpreted as a period offering Zadar prospects of taking the lead in the Adriatic before the stronger ecclesiastical traditions of Split undermined its bishops' ambitions and Venice cast its shadow.

In the context of the dissolution of the Western empire and the alienation of the Eastern, these developments led Zadar into a closer interaction with its hinterland. As a result, a new urban elite emerged in the tenth century. Members of this circle, identified as 'heirs to *prior* Andrew', established control of the ruling and administrative positions as well as the episcopal office in Zadar. The power of this group was further enhanced when its members established marital ties with the aristocracy of the kingdom of Croatia into whose political framework Zadar would be incorporated in the eleventh century. The history of this group connected to the influential abbey of St Chrysogonus at Zadar helps us to understand the composition of the legendary *inventio* of the saint's relics. The elite's own specific consciousness in turn provides clues for the usage of the term 'province of Zadar' in that legend. Imprecise and primarily designed to provide a setting for the urban foundation myth, the notion of *provincia Iadrensis* thus survived as a literary testimony to local *memoria* of the times when Zadar emerged from the mists of the Dark Ages as the centre of the Byzantine Adriatic periphery.

Acknowledgements

I would like to express my gratitude to all those who at various stages read and (extensively) commented and thus helped improve the quality of this paper – most particularly Professor Mladen Ančić, Dr Ivan Basić, Professor Florin Curta, Dr Danijel Dzino, Professor Judith Herrin, Dr Magdalena Skoblar and Professor Jonathan Shepard.

References

Alajbeg, A. 2014. 'O topografskoj kronologiji ranosrednjovjekovnih grobalja s poganskim osobinama pokapanja u sjevernoj Dalmaciji / On the topographical chronology of Early Mediaeval cemeteries with pagan burial characteristics in northern Dalmatia', *Archaeologia Adriatica* 8/1, 141–62.

Amalarius. *Versus marini*, in Dümmler, E. (ed.), *MGH Poetae Latini aevi Carolini*, vol. 1 (Berlin, 1881), 426–8.

Annales regni Francorum, in Kurze, F. (ed.), *MGH Scriptores rerum Germanicarum*, vol. 6 (Hanover, 1895).

Ančić, M. 2005. 'Lombard and Frankish influences in the formation of the Croatian dukedom', in Brogiolo, G. and Delogu, P. (eds.), *L'Adriatico dalla tarda Antichità all'età carolingia. Atti del Convegno di studio, Brescia, 11–13 ottobre 2001* (Brescia), 213–28.

2011a. 'Miho Barada i mit o Neretvanima', *Povijesni prilozi* 41, 17–43.

2011b. 'Ranosrednjovjekovni Neretvani ili Humljani: Tragom zabune koju je prouzročilo djelo De administrando imperio', in Lučić, I. (ed.), *Hum i Hercegovina kroz povijest. Zbornik radova*, vol. 1 (Zagreb), 217–78.

2014. 'Church with incomplete biography: Plans for the consolidation of Byzantine rule on the Adriatic at the beginning of the ninth century', in Dzino and Parry (eds.) 2014, 71–88.

2017. 'Zadarska biskupija u okviru splitske metropolije do 1154', *Ars Adriatica* 7, 29–46.

2018a. 'The Treaty of Aachen: How many empires?', in Ančić, Shepard and Vedriš (eds.) 2018, 25–42.

2018b. 'Migration or transformation: The roots of the Early Medieval Croatian polity', in Dzino, Milošević and Vedriš (eds.) 2018, 43–62.

Ančić, M., Shepard, J. and Vedriš, T. (eds.) 2018. *Imperial Spheres and the Adriatic: Byzantium, the Carolingians and the Treaty of Aachen (812)* (London and New York).

Archdeacon Thomas of Split. *Historia Salonitana*, in Perić, O., Karbić, D., Matijević Sokol, M. and Sweeney, J.R. (eds.), *Thomae archdiaconi Historia Salonitanorum atque Spalatinorum pontificum / Archdeacon Thomas of Split. History of the Bishops of Salona and Split* (Budapest, 2006).

Ascheri, M. 2009. *Medioevo del potere: Le instituzioni laiche ed ecclesiastiche* (Bologna).

Auzépy, M.-F. 2008. 'State of emergency (700–850)', in Shepard, J. (ed.) *The Cambridge History of the Byzantine Empire, c.500–1492* (Cambridge), 251–91.

Basić, I. 2009. 'Pristupna razmatranja uz popise biskupa Zapadnoga Ilirika u aktima crkvenih koncila u Saloni 530. i 533. godine', *Tusculum: Časopis za solinske teme* 2, 59–69.

2014. 'Dalmatinski biskupi na crkvenom saboru u Hijereji 754', in Basić, I. and Rimac, M. (eds.), *Spalatumque dedit ortum: Collected Papers on the Occasion of the 10th Anniversary of the Department of History, Faculty of Humanities and Social Sciences in Split* (Split), 149–95.

2015a. 'Bilješke o problemu konstituiranja tribunata u dalmatinskim pretkomunalnim društvima', in Radić, Ž., Trogrlić, M., Meccarelli, M. and Steindorff, L. (eds.), *Splitski statut iz 1312. godine: Povijest i pravo. Povodom 700. obljetnice* (Split), 173–202.

2015b. 'Sjeverna i srednja Dalmacija u ranome srednjem vijeku', in Nikolić Jakus, Z. (ed.), *Nova zraka u europskom svjetlu: Hrvatske zemlje u ranome srednjem vijeku (o. 550.–o. 1150.)* (Zagreb), 427–62.

2017–18. 'Natpis nadbiskupa Ursa kao izvor za crkvenu povijest ranosrednjovjekovnog Zadra (I. dio)', *Starohrvatska prosvjeta*, 3rd series, 44–5, 153–79.

2018a. 'New evidence for the re-establishment of the Adriatic dioceses in the late eighth century', in Ančić, Shepard and Vedriš (eds.) 2018, 267–81.

2018b. '*Imperium* and *regnum* in Gottschalk's description of Dalmatia', in Dzino, Milošević and Vedriš (eds.) 2018, 170–209.

2018c. 'The sarcophagus with sanction-formula from Trogir (Aspects of the Byzantine diplomatics tradition in early medieval epigraphy of the Adriatic)', *Vjesnik za arheologiju i historiju dalmatinsku* 111, 279–330.

2020. *I vescovi della Dalmazia al concilio di Hieria del 754: Appunti sulla geografia storica dell'Adriatico meridionale bizantino nell'VIII secolo* (Split and Zagreb).

Belošević, J, 2007. *Starohrvatsko groblje na Ždrijacu u Ninu* (Zadar).

Bertelli, C. and Brogiolo, G.-P. (eds.) 2001. *Bizantini, Croati, Carolingi: Alba e tramonto di regni e imperi* (Milan).

Betti, M. 2018. 'Rome and the heritage of ancient Illyricum in the ninth century', in Ančić, Shepard and Vedriš (eds.) 2018, 243–52.

Bibliotheca hagiographica Latina antiquae et mediae aetatis, ed. Société des Bollandistes, vol. 1, *A–I*, Subsidia hagiographica 6 (Brussels, 1899).

Bileta, V. 2011. 'At the crossroads of Late Antiquity and the Early Middle Ages – the rise and fall of the military elite of Byzantine Histria', *Annual of Medieval Studies at Central European University* 17, 100–23.

Borri, F. 2008. 'Neighbors and relatives: The Plea of Rižana as a source for northern Adriatic elites', *Mediterranean Studies* 17, 1–26.

Borri, F. 2010. 'Gli Istriani e i loro parenti: Romani e Slavi alla periferia di Bisanzio', *Jahrbuch der Österreichischen Byzantinistik* 60, 1–25.

Borri, F. 2017. 'Captains and pirates: Ninth-century Dalmatia and its rulers', in Gasparri and Gelichi (eds.) 2017, 9–35.

Borri, F. 2018. 'Dalmatian Romans and their Adriatic friends: Some further remarks', in Pohl, W., Gantner, C., Grifoni, C. and Pollheimer-Mohaupt, M. (eds.), *Transformations of Romanness: Early Medieval Regions and Identities* (Berlin and Boston), 241–52.

Brown, T.S. 1984. *Gentlemen and Officers: Imperial Administration and Aristocratic Power in Byzantine Italy AD 554–800* (London).

Brubaker, L. and Haldon, J.F. 2001. *Byzantium in the Iconoclast Era (c.680–850): The Sources. An Annotated Survey* (Aldershot).

2011. *Byzantium in the Iconoclast Era (c.680–850): A History* (Cambridge).

Brunelli, V. 1913. *Storia della città di Zara dai tempi più remoti sino al MDCCCXV compilata sulle fonti*, vol. 1 (Venice).

Budak, N. 2007. 'Foundations and donations as a link between Croatia and Dalmatia in the Early Middle Ages (9th–11th c.)', *Jahrbücher für Geschichte Osteuropas* 55/4, 483–90.

— 2008. 'Identities in Early Medieval Dalmatia (7th–11th c.)', in Garipzanov, I., Geary, P. and Urbanczyk, P. (eds.), *Franks, Northmen and Slavs: Identities and State Formation in Early Medieval Europe* (Turnhout), 223–41.

— 2014. 'Hrvatska i Bizant u 10. st', *Tabula* 12, 51–63.

— 2018a. 'One more renaissance? Dalmatia and the revival of European economy', in Ančić, Shepard and Vedriš (eds.) 2018, 174–91.

— 2018b. 'Carolingian renaissance or renaissance of the 9th century on the eastern Adriatic?', in Dzino, Milošević and Vedriš (eds.) 2018, 32–9.

— 2018c. *Hrvatska povijest od 550. do 1100* (Zagreb).

Callegher, B. 1994. 'Sigilli bizantini del Museo Bottacin', *Bollettino del Museo civico di Padova* 83, 169–77.

Cheynet, J.-C. and Caseau, B. 2012. 'Sealing practices in the Byzantine Administration', in Regulski, I., Duistermaat K. and Verkinderen P. (eds.), *Seals and Sealing Practices in the Near East: Developments in Administration and Magic from Prehistory to the Islamic Period* (Leuven and Paris).

Constantine Porphyrogennetos. *De administrando imperio*, in Moravcsik, G. and Jenkins, R.J.H. (eds.), *Constantine Porphyrogenitus. De administrando imperio* (Washington, DC, 1967).

Curta, F. 2004. 'L'administration byzantine dans les Balkans pendant la "grande brèche": Le témoignage des sceaux', *Bizantinistica*, 2nd series, 6, 137–90.

— 2005. 'Byzantium in Dark-Age Greece (the numismatic evidence in its Balkan context)', *Byzantine and Modern Greek Studies* 29, 113–46.

— 2006. *Southeastern Europe in the Middle Ages, 500–1250* (Cambridge).

— 2010. 'A note on trade and trade centers in the eastern and northern Adriatic region between the eighth and the ninth century', *Hortus artium medievalium* 16/1, 267–76.

— 2011. *The Edinburgh History of the Greeks, c.500 to 1050: The Early Middle Ages* (Edinburgh).

— 2013a. 'The beginning of the Middle Ages in the Balkans', *Millennium* 10, 145–214.

— 2013b. 'Seventh-century fibulae with bent stem in the Balkans', *Archaeologia Bulgarica* 17, 49–70.

Darrouzès, J. 1981. *Notitiae episcopatuum Ecclesiae Constantinopolitanae: Texte critique, introduction et notes* (Paris).

Delonga, V. 1981. 'Bizantski novac u zbirci Muzeja hrvatskih arheoloških spomenika u Splitu', *Starohrvatska prosvjeta*, 3rd series, 11, 201–28.

— 1996. *The Latin Epigraphic Monuments of Early Medieval Croatia* (Split).

— 2001. 'Il patrimonio epigrafico latino nei territori croati in età carolingia', in Bertelli and Brogiolo (eds.) 2001, 199–229.

Dubolnić-Glavan, M. 2015. '*Civitas Aenona*, primjer romanizacije liburnske općine ' (PhD thesis, University of Zadar).

Dzino, D. 2010. *Becoming Slav, Becoming Croat: Identity Transformations in Post-Roman and Early Medieval Dalmatia* (Leiden and Boston).

2014. 'The rise and fall of the Dalmatian 'big-men': Social structures in Late Antique, post-Roman and Early Medieval Dalmatia (ca. 500–850)', *Studia academica Šumenensia* 1, 127–52.

2018a. 'Post-Roman Dalmatia: Collapse and regeneration of a complex social system', in Ančić, Shepard and Vedriš (eds.) 2018, 155–73.

2018b. 'From Byzantium to the West: "Croats and Carolingians" as a paradigm-change in the research of Early Medieval Dalmatia', in Dzino, Milošević and Vedriš (eds.) 2018, 17–31.

Dzino, D. and Parry, K. (eds.), 2014. *Byzantium, Its Neighbours and Its Cultures* (Brisbane).

Dzino, D., Milošević, A. and Vedriš, T. (eds.), 2018. *Migration, Integration and Connectivity on the Southeastern Frontier of the Carolingian Empire* (Leiden and Boston).

Einhard. *Vita Karoli magni*, in Holder-Egger, O. (ed.), *MGH Scriptores rerum Germanicarum*, vol. 25 (Hanover, 1911).

Epistolae Merowingici et Karolini aevi 1, in Dümmler, E. (ed.), *MGH Epistolae Karolini aevi*, vol. 3 (Berlin, 1892).

Farlati, D. 1775. *Illyricum sacrum*, vol. 5 (Venice).

Ferluga, J. 1953. 'Niže vojno-administrativne jedinice tematskog uređenja', *Zbornik radova Vizantološkog instituta* 2, 61–94.

1976. *Byzantium on the Balkans: Studies on the Byzantine Administration and the Southern Slavs from the 7th to the 12th Centuries* (Amsterdam).

1978. *L'amministrazione bizantina in Dalmazia* (Venice).

Filipčić, D. 2017. 'Bizantske olovne bule s gradske plaže Kolovare u Zadru / Byzantine lead seals from the Kolovare city beach in Zadar', in *Bizantski studiji u Hrvatskoj –Retrospektiva i perspektive / Byzantine Studies in Croatia – Retrospective and Perspectives*, Colloquia mediaevalia Croatica 4, conference brochure (Zagreb), 22–3.

Gasparri, S. 1992. 'Venezia fra i secoli VIII e IX: Una riflessione sulle fonti', in Ortalli, G. and Scarabello, G. (eds.), *Studi veneti offerti a Gaetano Cozzi* (Venice), 3–18.

Gasparri, S. and Gelichi, S. (eds.) 2017. *The Age of Affirmation: Venice, the Adriatic and the Hinterland between the 9th and 10th Centuries* (Turnhout).

Gelichi, S. 2008. 'The eels of Venice: The long eighth century of the emporia of the northern region along the Adriatic coast', in Gasparri, S. (ed.) *774: Ipotesi su una transizione* (Turnhout), 81–117.

Gelichi, S. and Gasparri, S. (eds.) 2018. *Venice and Its Neighbors from the 8th to 11th Century: Through Renovation and Continuity* (Leiden and Boston).

Genke, V. and Gumerlock, F.X. (eds.) 2010. *Gottschalk and a Medieval Predestination Controversy* (Milwaukee).

Gioanni, S. 2017. 'Venise et les missions pontificales vers le *ducatus* et le *regnum* de Dalmatie-Croatiae (IXe–XIe siècle)', in Gasparri and Gelichi (eds.) 2017, 39–58.

Goldstein, I. 1992. *Bizant na Jadranu od Justinijana I. do Bazilija I.* (Zagreb).

— 1998. 'Byzantium on the Adriatic from 550 till 800', *Hortus artium medievalium* 4, 7–14.

Gračanin, H. 2015. 'Bizant na hrvatskom prostoru u ranome srednjem vijeku', in Nikolić Jakus, Z. (ed.), *Nova zraka u europskom svjetlu: Hrvatske zemlje u ranome srednjem vijeku (o. 550.–o. 1150.)* (Zagreb), 495–516.

Haldon, J.F. 2016. 'A context for two "evil deeds": Nikephoros I and the origins of the themata', in Delouis, O., Métivier, S. and Pagès, P. (eds.), *Le saint, le moine et le paysan. Mélanges d'histoire byzantine offerts à Michel Kaplan* (Paris), 245–66.

Hanssens, J.-M. (ed.) 1948. *Amalarii episcopi opera liturgica omnia*, vol. 1 (Rome).

Hodges, R. 2008. 'Aistulf and the Adriatic Sea', *Acta archaeologica* 79, 274–81.

Iveković, Ć.M. 1931. *Crkva i samostan sv. Krševana u Zadru. Hrvatska zadužbina iz X. stoljeća* (Zagreb).

Jakić-Cestarić, V. 1972. 'Etnički odnosi u srednjovjekovnom Zadru prema analizi osobnih imena', *Radovi Instituta Jugoslavenske akademije znanosti i umjetnosti u Zadru* 19, 99–166.

— 1974. 'Ženska osobna imena i hrvatski udio u etnosimbiotskim procesima u Zadru do kraja XII. stoljeća', *Radovi Centra Jugoslavenske akademije znanosti i umjetnosti u Zadru* 21, 291–336.

— 1976. 'Antroponomastička analiza isprave zadarskog priora Andrije s početka X. stoljeća', *Onomastica Iugoslavica* 6, 195–215.

Jakšić, N. 1986. 'Draga Svetog Krševana u Diklu o tisućitoj obljetnici osnutka samostana', *Radovi Filozofskog fakulteta u Zadru* 25/12, 205–28.

— 1993. 'Preživjele starokršćanske crkve u srednjovjekovnoj Ninskoj biskupiji', *Diadora* 15, 127–44.

— 1995. 'La survivance des édifices paléochretiéns dans les terres de la principauté Croate', *Hortus artium medievalium* 1, 36–45.

— 2008. 'Il ruolo delle antiche chiese rurali nella formazione del ducato croato altomedievale', *Hortus artium medievalium* 14, 103–12.

— 2018. 'The installation of the patron saints of Zadar as a result of Carolingian Adriatic politics', in Dzino, Milošević and Vedriš (eds.) 2018, 225–44.

Jarak, M. 1995. 'Je li dokazano ranosrednjovjekovno porijeklo prvotne rotunde sv. Donata?', *Opuscula archaeologica* 19, 117–23.

John the Deacon. *Istoria Veneticorum*, in Berto, L.A. (ed.), *Giovanni Diacono. Istoria Veneticorum* (Bologna, 1999).

Jeličić-Radonić, J. 1992. '*Ta katechoūmena* crkve sv. Trojice (Sv. Donat) u Zadru', *Diadora* 14, 345–55.

Klaić, N. and Petricioli, I. 1976. *Prošlost Zadra*, vol. 2, *Zadar u srednjem vijeku do 1409.* (Zadar).

Katičić, R. 1983. 'Imena dalmatinskih biskupija i njihovih biskupa u aktima ekumenskog koncila u Nikeji godine 787', *Filologija* 11, 75–92.
  1993. *Uz početke hrvatskih početaka* (Split).
Kolega, M. forthcoming. 'Ranosrednjovjekovni horizont grobova na nalazištu Ploče u sklopu župnog kompleksa Crkve sv. Asela u Ninu', in *Hrvatska arheologija i aachenski mir, 812.*
Komatina, P. 2009. 'Osnivanje Patraske i Atinske mitropolije i Sloveni na Peloponezu', *Zbornik radova Vizantološkog instituta* 46, 27–52.
  2018. 'Dalmatian bishops at the Council of Nicaea in 787 and the status of the Dalmatian Church in the eighth and ninth centuries', in Ančić, Shepard and Vedriš (eds.) 2018, 253–60.
Krahwinkler, H. 2004. *In loco qui dicitur Riziano ... Zbor v Rižani pri Kopru leta 804. Die Versammlung in Rižana/Risano bei Koper/Capodistria im Jahre 804* (Kopar).
Lambot, C. 1945. *Œuvres théologiques et grammaticales de Godescalc d'Orbais* (Louvain).
Levak, M. 2007. *Slaveni vojvode Ivana: Kolonizacija Slavena u Istri u početnom razdoblju franačke uprave* (Zagreb).
Lončar, M. 1999. 'On the description of the Churches of St Anastasia and St Donat in Zadar in "De administrando imperio" by Constantine Porphyrogenitus', *Hortus artium medievalium* 5, 235–43.
Majnarić, I. 2007. 'Razmišljanja o historiografskom pristupu problemu uzdizanja Zadra u status nadbiskupije i metropolije 1154', *Croatica Christiana periodica* 31, 101–15.
  2018a. '*Aemulatio imperii* and the south-eastern frontier of the Carolingian world', in Ančić, Shepard and Vedriš (eds.) 2018, 43–56.
  2018b. 'In the shadows of empires: Early Medieval Croatia in the ninth and tenth centuries', *History Compass* 16, 1–11.
Maraković, N. and Jurković, M. 2007. 'Signatures in the stones: The legacy of Early Medieval elites on the territory of modern Croatia', *Hortus artium medievalium* 13, 359–74.
Margetić, L. 1975, 'Tribuni u srednjovjekovnim dalmatinskim gradskim općinama', *Zbornik radova Vizantološkog instituta* 16, 25–53.
  1991. 'Provincijalni arhonti taktikona Uspenskog (s osobitim obzirom na arhonta Dalmacije)', *Zbornik radova Vizantološkog instituta* 29–30, 45–59.
McCormick, M. 2001. *Origins of the European Economy: Communications and Commerce AD 300–900* (Cambridge).
Mihaljčić, R. and Steindorff, L. 1982. *Namentragende Steininschriften in Jugoslawien vom Ende des 7. bis zur Mitte des 13. Jahrhunderts* (Wiesbaden).
Milošević, A. 1995. 'Die spätantike territoriale und kulturelle Kontinuität in der frühmittelalterlichen Cetinagegend', *Hortus artium medievalium* 1, 169–75.
  2005. 'Oggetti preziosi, segni distintivi carolingi della Croazia: I tesori della Croazia altomedievale', in Brogiolo, G. and Delogu, P. (eds.), *L'Adriatico*

dalla tarda Antichità all'età carolingia. Atti del Convegno di studio, Brescia, 11-13 ottobre 2001 (Brescia), 245-70.

2010. 'O ostavštini kasnoantičkih starosjeditelja u ranosrednjovjekovlju Dalmacije', in Dukić, J., Milošević, A. and Rapanić, Ž. (eds.), *Scripta Branimiro Gabričević dicata* (Trilj), 271-303.

2011. *Predromanički zvonici u Dalmaciji i ranosrednjovjekovnoj Hrvatskoj / Campanili preromanici della Dalmazia e della Croazia altomedievale* (Dubrovnik and Split).

Morris, R. 2020. 'Byzantium: 'To have and to hold' – the acquisition and maintenance of elite power', in Holmes, C., Shepard, J., Van Steenbergen, J. and Weiler, B. (eds.), *Political Culture in Three Spheres: The West, Byzantium and Islam, c.700–c.1500: A Framework for Comparison* (Cambridge).

Nesbitt, J. and Oikonomides, N. 1991. *Catalogue of Byzantine Seals at Dumbarton Oaks and in the Fogg Museum of Art*, vol. 1, *Italy, North of the Balkans, North of the Black Sea* (Washington, DC).

Nikolić, Z. 2003. *Rođaci i bližnji: Dalmatinsko gradsko plemstvo u ranom srednjem vijeku* (Zagreb).

Nikolajević-Stojković, I. 1961. 'Solinski pečat egzarha Pavla (723-726)', *Zbornik radova Vizantološkog instituta* 7, 61-6.

Obelić, B. and Sliepčević, A. 2000. 'Correction of the radiocarbon age of wooden beams from St. Donat's Church in Zadar by the dendrochronological method', *Vjesnik Arheološkog muzeja u Zagrebu* 32-3, 197-206.

Oikonomides, N. 1972. *Les listes de préséance byzantines des IXe et Xe siècles* (Paris).

1983. 'The usual lead seal', *Dumbarton Oaks Papers* 37, 147-57.

Osborne, J. 1999. 'Politics, diplomacy and the cult of relics in Venice and the northern Adriatic in the first half of the ninth century', *Early Medieval Europe* 8/3, 369-86.

Pactum Hlotharii I, in Boretius, A. and Krause, V. (eds.), *MGH Capitularia regum Francorum*, vol. 2 (Hanover, 1897).

Pertusi, A. (ed.) 1952. *Constantine VII Porphyrogennetos. De thematibus* (Rome).

Petricioli, I. 1961. 'Ranosrednjovjekovni natpisi iz Zadra', *Diadora* 2, 251-70.

Petrinec, M. 2009. *Gräberfelder aus dem 8. bis 11. Jahrhundert im Gebiet des frühmittelalterlichen Kroatischen Staates* (Split).

Preradović, D. 2012. 'Kultovi svetitelja u vizantijskim gradovima na istočnoj obali Jadrana (VI-IX vek)', *Ниш и Византија* 10, 523-35.

Prigent, V. 2008. 'Notes sur l'évolution de l'administration byzantine en Adriatique (VIIIe-IXe siècle)', *Mélanges de l'École française de Rome. Moyen Âge* 120/2 = *Les destinées de l'Illyricum méridional pendant le haut Moyen Âge*, 393-417.

Provesi, C. 2018. 'Disputes and connections: Venice's affairs in the regnum Italiae', in Gelichi and Gasparri (eds.) 2018, 68-89.

Prozorov, V. 2011. 'Salonitanski crkveni sabori iz šestog stoljeća', *Vjesnik za arheologiju i povijest dalmatinsku* 104, 309-37.

Pryor, J.H. and Jeffreys, E.M. 2006. *The Age of the Dromon: The Byzantine Navy, ca. 500-1204* (Leiden and Boston).
Rački, F. (ed.) 1877. *Documenta historiae Chroaticae periodum antiquam illustrantia* (Zagreb).
Rapanić, Ž. 2013. 'Kralj Tripimir, Venecijanci i Dalmatinci u traktatu teologa Gottschalka iz Orbaisa', *Povijesni prilozi* 44, 22-70.
   2017. *Dalmatinski grad i zaleđe u ranom srednjem vijeku* (Split).
Schlumberger, G. 1884. *Sigillographie de l'Empire byzantin* (Paris).
Seibt, W. 1981. 'Review of J. Ferluga, *L'amministrazione bizantina in Dalmazia* (Venice, 1978)', *Jahrbuch der Österreichischen Byzantinistik* 30, 339.
Shepard, J. 2014. 'Bunkers, open cities and boats in Byzantine diplomacy', in Dzino and Parry (eds.) 2014, 11-44.
   2018. 'Introduction: Circles overlapping in the upper Adriatic', in Ančić, Shepard and Vedriš (eds.) 2018, 1-22.
Skoblar, M. 2006. 'Prilog proučavanju ranosrednjovjekovne skulpture na otoku Krku', *Starohrvatska prosvjeta*, 3rd series, 33, 59-89.
Snee, R. 1998. 'Gregory Nazianzen's Anastasia Church: Arianism, the Goths, and hagiography', *Dumbarton Oaks Papers* 52, 157-86.
Sokol, V. 2016. 'Medieval jewelry and burial assemblages in Croatia: A study of graves and grave goods ca.800 to ca.1450', *East Central and Eastern Europe in the Middle Ages* 36 (Leiden and Boston).
Steindorff, L. 2005. 'Das mittelalterliche epigraphische Erbe Kroatiens', in Lauer, R. (ed.), *Kroatien: Kultur - Sprache - Literatur* (Göttingen), 15-29.
Stipišić, J. and Šamšalović, M. (eds.) 1967. *Codex diplomaticus regni Croatiae, Dalmatiae et Slavoniae*, vol. 1, *Diplomata annorum 743.-1100. continens* (Zagreb).
Strika, Z. 2004. 'Kada i gdje se prvi put spominje zadarski biskup?', *Radovi Zavoda za povijesne znanosti Hrvatske akademije znanosti i umjetnosti u Zadru* 46, 31-64.
   2006. '*Catalogus episcoporum et archiepiscoporum urbis Jadertinae* arhiđakona Valerija Pontea', *Radovi Zavoda za povijesne znanosti Hrvatske akademije znanosti i umjetnosti u Zadru* 48, 81-185.
Suić, M. 1956. 'Ostaci limitacije naših primorskih gradova u ranom srednjem vijeku', *Starohrvatska prosvjeta*, 3rd series, 5, 7-19.
Suić, 1981. *Prošlost Zadra*, vol. 1, *Zadar u starom vijeku* (Zadar).
Šeparović, T. 2003. 'Nove spoznaje o nalazima ranosrednjovjekovnog novca u južnoj Hrvatskoj', *Starohrvatska prosvjeta*, 3rd series, 30, 127-37.
Škegro, A. 2009. 'Akti Salonitanskih metropolitanskih sabora održanih 530. i 533. godine – analiza', *Archaeologia Adriatica* 3, 191-204.
Štih, P. 2017. 'Gradež kot Aquileia nova in Split kot Salona nova? Lokalno zgodovinopisje in oblikovanje krajevne identitete', *Zgodovinski časopis* 71, 350-81.
Tabacco, G. 1989. (trans. Brown Jensen, R.) *The Struggle for Power in Medieval Italy: Structures of Political Rule* (Cambridge).
Treadgold, W. 1988. *The Byzantine Revival, 780-842* (Stanford).

Tremp, E. (ed.) 1995. *Thegan, Die Taten Kaiser Ludwigs (Gesta Hludowici imperatoris); Astronomus, Das Leben Kaiser Ludwigs (Vita Hludowici imperatoris), MGH Scriptores rerum Germanicarum*, vol. 64 (Hanover), 279-555.

Tsatsoulis, C. 2012. 'Some remarks on the date of creation and the role of the maritime theme of Cephalonia (end of the 7th-11th century)', *Studies in Byzantine Sigillography* 11, 153-72.

Turlej, S. 2001. *The Chronicle of Monemvasia* (Krakow).

Uglešić, A. 2017. 'Ranokršćanski nalazi iz okolice Ljupča', in Faričić, J. and Lenkić, J. (eds.), *Župa Ljubač: Zrcalo povijesnih i geografskih mijena u sjeverozapadnom dijelu Ravnih kotara* (Zadar), 112-33.

Vedriš, T. 2005. 'Još jedan franački teolog u Dalmaciji: Amalarije iz Metza i njegovo putovanje u Carigrad 813. godine', *Historijski zbornik* 58, 1-27.

2007. 'Štovanje sv. Anastazije u Sirmiju, Carigradu i Rimu u kasnoj antici i ranome srednjem vijeku', *Diadora* 22, 191-216.

2009. 'Frankish or 'Byzantine' saint? The origins of the cult of St Martin in Dalmatia', in Neocleous, S. (ed.), *Papers from the First and Second Postgraduate Forums in Byzantine Studies: Sailing to Byzantium* (Cambridge), 219-48.

2012. 'Po čemu je u 9. stoljeću rotonda sv. Trojstva u Zadru mogla sličiti crkvi sv. Anastazije u Carigradu?', in Šeparović, T. (ed.), *Zbornik radova znanstvenog skupa "Stjepan Gunjača i hrvatska srednjovjekovna povijesnoarheološka baština" (Split, October 18-21, 2011)* (Split), 63-79.

2015. 'Pokrštavanje i rana kristijanizacija Hrvata', in Nikolić Jakus, Z. (ed.), *Nova zraka u europskom svjetlu: Hrvatske zemlje u ranome srednjem vijeku (o. 550.-o. 1150.)* (Zagreb), 173-200.

2018. 'Amalarius' stay in Zadar reconsidered', in Ančić, Shepard and Vedriš 2018 (eds.) 288-311.

Vežić, P. 2002a. 'Su San Donato, vescovo di Zara', *Hortus artium medievalium* 8, 235-40.

2002b. *Sveti Donat - rotunda Sv. Trojstva u Zadru* (Split).

2005. *Zadar na pragu kršćanstva: Arhitektura ranoga kršćanstva u Zadru i na zadarskome području* (Zadar).

2013. *Episkopalni kompleks u Zadru / Episcopal Complex in Zadar* (Zadar).

Wasilewski, T. 1980. 'Le theme maritime de la Dalmatie byzantine dans les années 805-822 et sa reconstitution par l'empereur Michel III', *Acta Poloniae historica* 31, 35-49.

Wickham, C. 2005. *Framing the Early Middle Ages: Europe and the Mediterranean, 400-800* (Oxford).

Živković, T. 2002. 'The strategos Paul and the archontes of the Westerners', Βυζαντινά σύμμεικτα 15, 161-76.

2007. 'The earliest cults of saints in Ragusa', *Zbornik radova Vizantološkog instituta* 44, 119-27.

2008. 'Uspenskij's Taktikon and the theme of Dalmatia', Βυζαντινά σύμμεικτα 17, 49-85.

7 | Ravenna and Other Early Rivals of Venice

Comparative Urban and Economic Development in the Upper Adriatic c.751–1050

THOMAS S. BROWN

The history of Ravenna, particularly in the period after its loss to the Byzantine empire in 751, has been obscured by misleading historiographical baggage.[*] For a long time, the city and the other territories loyal to the East Roman empire were accorded a degree of attention, which was limited or unsympathetic. The few Byzantine historians who turned their attention westward saw the exarchate as a largely Hellenised province in which eastern officials and troops were dominant – the line taken in the scholarly and groundbreaking work of Charles Diehl (1888) and Ludo Hartmann (1889). Italian scholars, mindful of their country's domination by external powers up to 1860, mostly bought into this view of the imperial territories as 'colonial' possessions occupied by a 'foreign' state and concentrated their attention on the Lombard areas of the peninsula, which were somewhat paradoxically seen as more 'Italian' (Arnaldi 2009; Cosentino 1998).

Only gradually has there been a shift away from this portrayal of Ravenna and the exarchate as an 'alien' entity and proper emphasis placed on the area as a distinct but essentially Roman enclave, which had a dynamic character and development of its own (Brown 1984). Even as late as the 1960s André Guillou (1969) could portray the exarchate as a not untypical regional province of the Byzantine empire. Important elements of the city's distinctive character were its role as the broader zone of the Adriatic and its continued importance in its post-Byzantine phase, even in the face of competing centres such as Venice.

To appreciate this our starting point has to be the sixth century. Ravenna was the capital, first of the Ostrogothic kingdom and later of the Byzantine exarchate, both of which exercised some degree of authority over Dalmatia: Theoderic took over Dalmatia after Odoacer had annexed it c.480 (Moorhead 1992, 9–10) while the authority of the exarch of Italy over Dalmatia appears to have been more sporadic (Guillou 1969, 97). As a

---

[*] Since 2015 when this paper was delivered, a number of important studies on Ravenna, Venice and the northern Adriatic have been published, notably La Rocca and Majocchi 2015; West-Harling 2015 and Gasparri and Gelichi 2017. While this volume was in production, three additional publications appeared: Cosentino 2019; Herrin 2020 and West-Harling 2020.

result, Ravenna had close relations with the opposite eastern shores of the Adriatic in a number of fields. The Church of Ravenna had an extensive patrimony there and famously the mausoleum of Theoderic was built of Istrian stone, including the great 300-ton monolith of its roof. The first and most energetic of Ravenna's archbishops, Maximian, was a deacon of Pula and he commissioned a church there, Santa Maria Formosa, in a Ravennate style (Bovini 1972; Deliyannis 2010a; 2010b, 118, 125; Fasoli 1991, 389; Mazzotti 1956). Clearly connections were close in this early period, but were these ties broken by the disruptive events of the late sixth century onward, such as the Lombard invasions of Italy, the Slav settlement of much of Dalmatia and the abandonment of leading cities such as *Salona* and *Epidaurus* in the first half of the seventh century, or Ravenna's apparent falling out of the Byzantine world after its capture by the Lombards in 751?

For a long time this was the traditional view. Ravenna was seen as a spent force after 751, so that Edward Hutton could write in 1913:

> Ravenna found itself ... little more than a decaying provincial city. [Her] memories ... smoulder in her ruined heart ... Almost nothing ... she became ... a mere body still wrapt in gorgeous raiment stiff with gold, but without a soul ... (Hutton 1913, 211)

It is noteworthy that until recently Hutton's was the only full-length non-art-historical study of Ravenna in English; the publications of Deliyannis (2010b) and Herrin and Nelson (2016) redress this situation. Thanks to the power of the archbishops, who are described as ruling the area 'just like an exarch' (*Iudicavit iste ... totum Pentapolim veluti exarchus*, Deliyannis 2006, 159), Ravenna remained a powerful and rich city, exercising a control over a large swathe of north-east Italy and retaining links further afield. This area of the exarchate and Pentapolis remained distinct in its institutions from the rest of the Lombard, later Frankish then Ottonian, kingdom of Italy, for example in the ranks and titles used, the system of personal names and the organisational and nomenclature of its agrarian estates. For centuries, and indeed up to today, contemporaries termed it *Romania* as opposed to *Longobardia* (Brown 1988; Casadio 2003, 2–3).

What is more Ravenna has preserved a body of evidence which, apart from Lucca, is unparalleled in Early Medieval Italy. For the period up to the 840s we have the remarkably full and opinionated *Liber pontificalis ecclesiae Ravennatis* of the local cleric Agnellus of Ravenna (Deliyannis 2006). Thereafter contemporary historical narratives are lacking, but we can compensate for this by letters, hagiographical works and the acts (*acta*) of local synods and judicial assemblies, that is, *placita* (MacLean 2010). But most importantly we have a lot of documents. The famous early papyri were replaced from c.700 by parchments, mainly preserved in the Archivio Arcivescovile (Benericetti 1999–2002; 2006; 2010; Tjäder 1954–82). There are also remarkable survivals such as a register of 186 transactions commonly known as the *Codex Bavarus*. This was compiled, interestingly in papyrus, in the late tenth century but includes donations, leases and grants involving the church stretching back to c.700 (Rabotti 1985). Altogether Ravenna preserves around 450 documents from the period from 440 to 1002 and the numbers increase rapidly thereafter (Cavarra *et al.* 1991).

Given the common heritage and shared institutions this wealth of documents can perhaps throw light on comparable cities elsewhere in the Adriatic, where the evidence is notoriously scanty. This even applies to Venice, where there is at least a strong historiographical tradition, reflected for the early centuries in the history of John the Deacon (*Istoria Veneticorum*). However, as is well known, these sources project a one-sided and misleading 'myth of Venice' as distinctive and powerful from the start (Brown 1993). The same applies to the short but brilliant life cycle of Comacchio, where the documents are limited but we have first-rate archaeological evidence, thanks especially to the excavations of Sauro Gelichi (Gelichi *et al.* 2012).

As for the cities of Istria they have left us perhaps the most revealing document for the upper Adriatic – the Plea (*placitum*) of Risano (Rižana) of 804 (Borri 2008; Petranović and Margetić 1983–4). However this largely reflects the past rather than the present and Istria can largely be seen after the Aachen treaty of 812 between Charlemagne and the Byzantines as an appendage to Venice, although also claimed by the Patriarch of Aquileia. There is also little that can be said about the towns of southern Dalmatia, such as Dubrovnik and Kotor, partly because the evidence is limited and partly because they are unlikely to have undergone a somewhat distinct development under closer Byzantine authority following the creation of the theme, traditionally dated to the 870s, but probably earlier (Curta 2010; Ferluga 1978; Prigent 2008). It is possibly the towns of northern Dalmatia, Split and especially Zadar, under less direct Byzantine authority, that offer the most illuminating parallels with Ravenna.

After a period of relative neglect fuller attention has been paid to Ravenna after 751 in recent decades (Carile 1991–2; Herrin and Nelson 2016). What has clearly emerged is that for centuries the archbishops succeeded in maintaining a powerful episcopal principality and preserving the traditional 'Romano-Byzantine' society and culture of the exarchate through their skilful courting of the rulers of northern Italy and their amassing of a vast ecclesiastical lordship stretching from Ferrara to northern Umbria (Cosentino 2012; Fasoli 1979). It has also to be admitted that Ravenna did have some characteristics of its own which may not have applied elsewhere. This is particularly true of alluvial and hydrographic changes which would also have occurred northwards along the lagunal area of the north-west Adriatic coast but not further east (Calabrese, Di Cocco and Centineo 2010; Squatriti 1992; Veggiani 1973).

The closest similarities are likely to have been in the sphere of political and institutional development. In the Ravenna area the local landowning elite dominant after 751 had its origins in the military aristocracy of the Byzantine period and remained attached to traditional titles such as duke (*dux*), master of soldiers (*magister militum*), tribune (*tribunus*), and consul. Thus, a trawl of the documents from 751 to 1000 produces thirty-four counts (*comites*), seventy-two dukes (*duces*), sixteen masters of soldiers (*magistri militum*) and a vast number of consuls. This persistence of an entrenched elite from the sixth and seventh centuries is likely to have been the case in other cities, although in cities which retained closer ties with Byzantium, contemporary Byzantine court titles are recorded, such as *spatharios* and *protospatharios* held by the duke of Venice. Ravenna also obtained a great deal of autonomy from the eighth century as a result of the weakness of the imperial control and a series of local revolts and again this appears to have been paralleled elsewhere (Brown 1984).

One particular characteristic of Ravenna was the establishment of a powerful lordship in the hands of the archbishops, based on the generous privileges they received from emperors and kings and their extensive landholdings which they granted out to local lay elite as part of a patronage system (Brown 1979). The pattern was different in Venice where, as is well known, secular powers such as that of its duke exercised remarkable control over the Church from an early stage. It is unlikely, however, that bishops exercised as much power in other cities on the Adriatic although we do find powerful bishops in cities such as Grado and Zadar. Fortunatus and Donatus, bishops of these respective cities, had the kind of close ties with Charlemagne which Ravenna archbishops had with Frankish and Ottonian rulers (Borri 2008, 12; 2010, 43, 46; Vežić 2002, 235–40). Zadar is certainly a case where the example of Ravenna may throw light on its administrative development; the head of the urban administration (*prior*) also held the title of *archon* of Dalmatia (Prigent 2008, 405–6).

If we turn to art and culture, it is clear that the direct Byzantine influence is less present in Ravenna and the other cities of the north Adriatic than in

Rome, where there was a substantial population of Greek monks and other exiles from the East (Ekonomou 2007; Osborne 2011; Sansterre 1983), or in parts of southern Italy and Sicily, where imperial rule was more direct. In Ravenna – and elsewhere in the north – officials and troops sent out from the East in the sixth and seventh centuries evidently integrated into the local population rapidly, as is clear from intermarriage and donations to local churches made in the Ravenna documents (Brown 1984). Indeed, in Ravenna we do not find any important instances of Greek monasticism and knowledge of Greek was very limited, as is likely to have been the case elsewhere. Within the Adriatic area, however, parallels are evident in fields such as art and architecture where the surviving objects suggest regular contacts and influences and a common repertoire of motifs throughout the northern part of the zone. One example is the parallel between the ciborium of Eleucadius now in Sant'Apollinare in Classe and that of Bishop Mauritius at Novigrad (Cittanova) in Istria (Caillet 2009, 19; Galassi 1953, 415–21).

Another area in which parallels are clear is in the veneration of saints. In Ravenna, Venice and elsewhere the veneration of eastern saints, especially military figures such as George and Theodore, seems to have been established in the Early Byzantine period and to have continued strongly thereafter (Brown 1984, 23, 53; Fiori 2008; Orselli 1993).

In the Ravenna area however there appear to have been few additions after 751, perhaps because there was an abundant supply of local, as well as Roman and Milanese, saints – as well as a superabundance of churches. In Istria and Dalmatia we do however have clear examples of 'relic diplomacy' (akin to 'panda diplomacy'?) in the early ninth century – with the translation of relics of St Euphemia to Rovinj, St Tryphon to Kotor and St Anastasia to Zadar – significantly perhaps at a period when Byzantium was striving to maintain its influence over the Adriatic but had to conserve its military resources for struggles against the Arabs and Bulgars (Brown 2020; Vedriš in this volume).

Ravenna also offers evidence of economic expansion, which is reflected both in references to trade, traders (*negotiatores*) and artisans in the documents (Benericetti 1999–2002; 2006; 2010; Vespignani 2001, 67) and the archaeological work of scholars such as Enrico Cirelli (2008). Perhaps this was not as precocious as the take-off in the trade in salt and other commodities along the Po River network which Sauro Gelichi (Gelichi in this volume; Gelichi and Hodges 2012) and other scholars have revealed at Comacchio from the early eighth century, until its sack by the Venetians and the Arabs in the late ninth, but it is still likely that Ravenna participated in the expansion of trade after c.800, which Chris Wickham (2004, 164–74) has characterised as the 'second trade cycle'. Thus, we find a remarkable number of *negotiatores* recorded in the documents (eighty-four for the tenth century alone) and the frequency of references in the documents to Byzantine gold coins (*aurei byzantini* or *infigurati*) must surely reflect a measure of commercial exchange with the Adriatic and eastern Mediterranean (Vespignani 2001, 184–90).

This is not the place to offer a full study of the economy of Early Medieval Ravenna, but there are other clear pointers that it was flourishing after 751. External commerce was accompanied by the export of food and other bulk commodities into the interior, especially by means of the Po and its tributaries.

Wealth is also evident in construction activity in the city and the surrounding area. There was not much new church building from scratch – there was no need with such a rich heritage – apart from one famous example, San Salvatore *ad Calchi*, which is now generally dated to the Carolingian period. But there was restoration of certain churches, for example, the *Basilica Apostolorum* (now San Francesco), the building of new crypts and the erection of numerous impressive campanili. By the late tenth century new churches were built such as San Paolo near the Ottonian palace, associated with Otto I's Queen Adelheid. Nor was this building confined to the city. We also find major projects outside including new monasteries such as San Adalberto at Pereo, north of the city, and Pomposa. There was also the development of a network of baptismal churches in the countryside, known as *pievi*. This system seems to emerge from the eighth century and some imposing examples survive, such as San Giorgio at Argenta and San Michele di Arcangelo near Rimini (Curradi 1984; Torricelli 1989; Vasina 1977, 607–27).

There is also evidence of secular buildings. From the Ottonian period we know of two new palaces, one at Caesarea, just outside the walls and the other at San Severo in Classe. In fact, Ravenna had become a favoured residence of western kings, not just the Ottonians but earlier the Carolingians, presumably because of its imperial associations and this would have given an additional boost to the economy (Brown 2016; Torre, 1963). The city was also the regular site of assemblies and synods. Archaeologists have also found evidence of houses, including elite buildings in brick and stone, often two storey and analogous both to those described in the documents and those found on other sites such as the Fori Imperiali in Rome. Other archaeologists have demonstrated the continued import of goods from the East and the use of wharves within the city well into the eleventh century. The evidence of different kinds for the continued, indeed increased, wealth and importance of Ravenna is therefore, one can conclude, overwhelming.

But what were the forces which helped produce such wealth? Some we have already dealt with – the rich and powerful *curia* of the archbishops, the role of the city as the economic and political centre of a wide area and the presence and favours of successive western kings. Also of course the ninth and tenth centuries are now widely seen as a period of economic resurgence throughout most of Europe. In a recent general book Marios Costambeys and his co-authors (2011, 377) argue that 'the ninth century witnessed gradual transformations in patterns of trade and exchange which ... set the scene for the improved economy conditions of the central Middle Ages'.

However, certain special factors applied in Ravenna and the exarchate. One was the widespread process of clearance and the establishment of new settlements often reclaimed from marshy land or set up in the foothills of the Apennines. The number and importance of these can be traced in the documents and also from the building of *pievi*, partly to serve the pastoral needs of new communities. A central role in such reclamations (*bonifica*) was played by monasteries such as Pomposa (Ferrabino 1963; Rucco 2015; Vasina 1977).

Another factor was the remarkable expansion of trade. It is clear that Ravenna continued to trade throughout the Adriatic zone and with the East. It was joined to new trading centres such as Comacchio, whose emporium was the subject of recent excavations by Gelichi and the focus of an important conference on emporia held in 2009 (Gelichi and Hodges 2012). The continuance of extensive trade with the Adriatic and eastern worlds is demonstrated by the extensive references in the documents to Byzantine gold coins (*aurei byzantini* or *infigurati*) even though the official currency was the Frankish *denarius*. The common view that Venice dominated long-distance maritime trade from an early date needs to be questioned.

Not all this trade was in luxury items imported from the East; there was clearly trade with the inland towns of the Lombard plain, via the waterways of the Po. This could involve the reexport of goods imported from the East but it is probable that it increasingly involved the export of salt, foodstuffs, wine and oil produced on the newly developed estates. This was certainly a role which the Romagna played later gaining it its nickname of 'the breadbasket' of Italy (Larner 1964, 11). Finally, a lot of this economic expansion was part of a 'virtuous cycle' prompted by the wealth and power of local elites, which, as elsewhere in the Carolingian and post-Carolingian world, manifested an increased demand for luxuries and manufactured goods.

How strong were direct links with or influence from Byzantium? At first sight this would appear limited in the case of Ravenna which was after all technically under the authority either of the patrimony of St Peter or the kingdom of Italy, while our other cities were at least nominally under Byzantine suzerainty. In the case of Venice it is well known that the dating of state documents (but not necessarily private or local ones) was done according to Byzantine imperial years, the dukes wore imperial dress and sported Byzantine court titles and Venice lent naval aid to the empire, sometimes in return for generous trading privileges. There is nothing parallel in Ravenna, although Emperor Constantine V does seem keen to recover Ravenna after its loss in 751. This seems to have been a major motive in Constantine's negotiations with the powerful Frankish King Pippin the Short (McCormick 1995, 360, 365) and Patriarch Photius of Constantinople did write a letter to the anti-papal Archbishop of Ravenna, John VIII, in quest of support, datable to 878 or early 879 (Grumel 1936, vol. 1, no. 514, 102–3). Otherwise there are few direct ties to Constantinople, since Ravenna, or especially its archbishops, found it more expedient to proclaim their loyalty to more immediately powerful rulers and potentially benefactors, that is, the emperors and kings who ruled north Italy.

There is clear evidence that Ravenna still to some extent existed within a Byzantine orbit. Topographical echoes of the capital, such as Daphne and Chalke, existed in the city, and Agnellus, writing in the 840s, appears to have regarded travel to and trade with Constantinople as quite normal (Martínez Pizzaro 1995, 14, 88–92). Many of the lavish treasures in the church which he lovingly describes in his work were clearly imported from the East, as is also clear from the similar liturgical objects listed in the Roman *Liber pontificalis*. Such a sense of being part of the Byzantine world is more difficult to discern in the late ninth and tenth centuries. It can be argued however that its continuance is shown by the persistence of Greek personal names and the association with the city of such Greek figures as Nilus of Rossano and the Empress Theophano. Archbishop John IX developed close relations with Byzantium once he was elevated to the papal throne in 914 (Savigni 2007). But more to the point the appeal of Ravenna to the western rulers who visited and patronised the city was partly its 'Byzantine' images and associations – still the 'gold standard' of imperial style and ideology in the eyes of western rulers. It was a 'virtual Constantinople' (Carile 2005).

Another area of comparison which was of concern to all the cities along the coast of the northern Adriatic was the difficulty of maintaining autonomy in the face of often hostile relations with their hinterland. Many of the cities in the East faced continual attacks from the Slavs early on, followed by pressure from more powerful states later, such the kingdoms of Croatia and Hungary, the patriarchate of Aquileia and an aggressively expansionist Venice. Venice itself should be seen as it often is – as either basking in splendidly safe isolation or depending on its subjection to Byzantium. It had to maintain good relations with Frankish and Ottonian rulers by a series of agreements (*pacta*) and diplomatic manoeuvres and an excellent recent paper by Veronica West-Harling (2013) has demonstrated how its aristocratic elite had close links in the spheres of landholding, language and identity with the nearby *Terraferma*.

Often it is difficult to reconstruct how these relations operated. Here, however, Ravenna offers a masterclass in balancing and warding off threatening powers. After the short-lived Lombard occupation, the most serious threat came from papal claims, but these were effectively countered by securing patronage and privileges from a series of Frankish rulers and as a result it maintained its distinctive identity, institutions and traditional elite descended from Romano-Byzantine military landowners. Only from the late ninth century was there some external penetration as Frankish and Alemannic families settled and intermarried – the most prominent being the Guidi family from Tuscany (Canaccini 2009; Curradi 1977). How and why this occurred is mysterious but may be associated with a greater role which the exarchate came to play in the kingdom of Italy and the archbishops' desire to ingratiate themselves with Italian kings and their entourages. This distinct close-knit identity – and the power of the archbishops – finally broke down with the pressures of the investiture contest and the rise of local identities in the newly assertive communes such as Bologna and Ferrara (Vasina 1993; Zimmermann 1993, 107–28).

As we have seen Ravenna also built up lucrative trading links with the previously hostile hinterland of the upper Po Valley. Again, this may offer parallels with other cases of cities in the Adriatic area establishing trading relations with previously hostile neighbours as a result of relatively increased security and greater elite entrepreneurship from around 800. Ravenna remained a key player within the Adriatic zone after 751 and to some extent continued to rival Venice. It was still going to war with Venice over control of sea commerce in the early fourteenth century: in fact, Dante died returning from a diplomatic mission to Venice on this very issue (Petrocchi 2008, 198, 221).

The power of Venetian myth should not blind us to thinking that it was the only player in the Adriatic. Not only did it have rivals but many of them were late in coming under complete Venetian control. As early as c.1000 the dukes could lay claim to the title of duke of Dalmatia (*dux Dalmatiae*) but many cities eluded permanent Venetian control because of assistance from powers opposed to Venice, such as Pisa, Genoa and the kingdom of Hungary (Lane 1973; Nicol 1988). Zadar was only finally captured in the early stages of the notorious Fourth Crusade in 1202 (Gambi 1994; Madden 2007, 133–54) and Ravenna itself only came under Venetian control in 1440.

There are also illuminating social parallels between Ravenna and other cities, most notably a cultural and ideological attachment to Byzantine style which was stronger perhaps than any political and economic links. Byzantine influences were of a voluntary 'pick and mix' variety reflecting a nostalgia and admiration for an empire still seen as 'the gold standard' of rulership and culture, but these borrowings were intended to reinforce local autonomy and identity, rather than submission to Byzantium. In practice the cities were autonomous from an early stage and more of a 'frozen' Late Roman society than an eastern Hellenised one. To characterise this area as 'Byzantine' in the sense used by Diehl is not helpful, while the term 'Roman' is perhaps too ambiguous.

Perhaps, given these enduring links we should speak of a distinctive 'Adriatic' commonality of institutions and culture, which was remarkably persistent. One example is a later, thirteenth-century source. Archdeacon Thomas's *Historia Salonitana* reveals that Split had many features in common with the Italian communes of the central Middle Ages. Thus, the citizens of Split obtained a magistrate (*podestà*) from Ancona to rule their city and of course Ancona was one of the cities of the Italian Adriatic coast which Emperor Manuel I controlled in the twelfth century (Abulafia 1984; Archdeacon Thomas, *Historia Salonitana*). Manuel may also have hoped to also take over Ravenna, where he enjoyed some support (Magdalino 1993, 83, 93).

Thus, the apparent ties to Byzantium that were based on admiration, nostalgia or identity were used as part of strategy of resistance to threatening outside forces. One recalls the term used of the elites of Rome by Pierre Toubert (1973, 697, n. 1): 'le snobisme byzantinisant'. This may apply broadly to the north Adriatic zone. One unifying element was the preservation of a distinct 'Late Roman' society protected at first by a 'Byzantine umbrella'. But as autonomy became entrenched in each area the strongest Byzantine influence remaining, in Ravenna and many other cities of the Adriatic, was the social and cultural cachet which the empire, at least in its image and style, retained.

References

Abulafia, D. 1984. 'Ancona, Byzantium and the Adriatic, 1155–1173', *Papers of the British School at Rome* 52, 195–216.

Agnellus of Ravenna. *Liber pontificalis ecclesiae Ravennatis*, in Deliyannis, D. (ed.), *Corpus Christianorum continuatio mediaevalis*, vol. 199 (Turnhout, 2006).

Archdeacon Thomas of Split. *Historia Salonitana*, in Perić, O., Karbić, D., Matijević Sokol, M. and Sweeney, J.R. (eds.), *Thomae archdiaconi Historia Salonitanorum atque Spalatinorum pontificum / Archdeacon Thomas of Split. History of the Bishops of Salona and Split* (Budapest, 2006).

Arnaldi, G. 2009. (trans. Shugaar, A.) *Italy and Its Invaders* (Cambridge, Mass.).

Benericetti, R. 1999–2002. *Le carte del decimo secolo nell'archivio arcivescovile di Ravenna*, 3 vols. (Ravenna and Imola).

  2006. *Le carte ravennati dei secoli ottavo e nono* (Faenza).

  2010. *Le carte del decimo secolo nell'archivio arcivescovile di Ravenna*, vol. 4, *Archivi minori (Monasteri di S. Andrea Maggiore, S. Vitale e S. Apollinare in Classe)* (Faenza).

Borri, F. 2008. "Neighbors and relatives': The Plea of Rižana as a source for northern Adriatic elites', *Mediterranean Studies* 17, 1–26.

  2010. 'L'Adriatico tra Bizantini, Longobardi e Franchi: Dalla conquista di Ravenna alla pace di Aquisgrana (751–812)', *Bullettino dell'Istituto storico italiano per il Medioevo* 112, 1–56.

Bovini, G. 1972. 'L'opera di Massimiano da Pola a Ravenna', *Aquileia e l'Istria: Lezioni della seconda Settimana di studi aquileiesi, 29 aprile – 5 maggio 1971, Antichità altoadriatiche* 2, 147–65.

Brown, T.S. 1979. 'The Church of Ravenna and the imperial administration in the seventh century', *The English Historical Review* 94, 1–28.

  1984. *Gentlemen and Officers: Imperial Administration and Aristocratic Power in Byzantine Italy* AD *554–800* (London).

  1988. 'The interplay between Roman and Byzantine traditions and local sentiment in the exarchate of Ravenna', in *Bisanzio, Roma e l'Italia nell'alto Medioevo*, Settimane di studio del Centro italiano di studi sull'alto Medioevo 34 (Spoleto), 127–60.

  1993. 'History as myth: Medieval perceptions of Venice's Roman and Byzantine past', in Beaton, R. and Rouché C. (eds.), *The Making of Byzantine History. Studies Dedicated to Donald M. Nicol* (Aldershot), 145–57.

  2016. 'Culture and society in Ottonian Ravenna: Imperial renewal or new beginnings?', in Herrin and Nelson (eds.) 2016, 335–54.

2020. 'The 'political' use of the cult of saints in Early Medieval Ravenna', in DeGregorio, S. and Kershaw, P. (eds.), *Cities, Saints, and Communities in Early Medieval Europe. Essays in Honour of Alan Thacker* (Turnhout).

Caillet, J.-P. 2009. 'L'evergetismo ecclesiastico', in Farioli Campanati, R., Rizzardi, C., Porta, P., Augenti, A. and Baldini Lippolis L. (eds.), *Ideologia e cultura artistica tra Adriatico e Mediterraneo orientale (IV-IX secolo), Atti del Convegno internazionale Bologna-Ravenna, 26-29 Novembre 2007* (Bologna), 13-24.

Calabrese, L., Di Cocco, I. and Centineo, M.C. 2010. 'Hydrographic evolution and palaeogeographic reconstruction of the southwestern Po Plain (Italy) during the last 4,000 years: An example of integration between stratigraphy and archaeology', in *Geology of the Adriatic Area. GeoActa Special Publications* 3, 103-8.

Canaccini, F. 2009. *La lunga storia di una stirpe comitale: I conti Guidi tra Romagna e Toscana* (Florence).

Carile, A. (ed.) 1991-2. *Storia di Ravenna II: Dall'età bizantina all'età ottoniana*, 2 vols. (Venice).

2005. 'Costantinopoli nuova Roma, Ravenna e l'Occidente', in *Ravenna da capitale imperiale a capitale esarcale: Atti del XVII Congresso internazionale di studio sull'alto Medioevo* (Spoleto), 41-61.

Casadio, G. 2003. 'Romania e Romagna', *La Ludla: Bollettino dell'Associazione Istituto Friedrich Schürr per la valorizzazione del patrimonio dialettale romagnolo* 8, 2-3.

Cavarra, B., Gardini, G., Parente, G.B. and Vespignani, G. 1991. 'Gli archivi come fonti della storia di Ravenna', in Carile (ed.) 1991-2, vol. 1, 401-547.

Cirelli, E. 2008. *Ravenna: Archeologia di una città* (Borgo S. Lorenzo).

Cosentino, S. 1998. 'La percezione della storia bizantina nella medievistica italiana tra Ottocento e secondo dopoguerra: Alcune testimonianze', *Studi medievali*, 3rd series, 39, 889-910.

2012. 'Ricchezza ed investimento della chiesa di Ravenna tra la tarda Antichità e l'alto Medioevo', in Gelichi S. and Hodges, R (eds.), *From One Sea to Another: Trading Places in the European and Mediterranean Early Middle Ages. Proceedings of the International Conference, Comacchio, 27th-29th March 2009* (Turnhout), 417-39.

Cosentino, S. (ed.) 2020. *Ravenna and the Traditions of Late Antique and Early Byzantine Craftsmanship: Labour, Culture and Economy*, Millennium Studies 86 (Berlin).

Costambeys, M., Innes, M. and MacLean, S. 2011. *The Carolingian World* (Cambridge).

Curradi, C. 1977. 'I conti Guidi nel secolo X', *Studi romagnoli* 28, 17-64.

1984. *Pievi del territorio riminese nei documenti fino al Mille* (Rimini).

Curta, F. 2010. 'A note on trade and trade centers in the eastern and northern Adriatic region between the eighth and the ninth century', *Hortus artium medievalium* 16/1, 267-76.

Deliyannis, D.M. 2010a. 'The mausoleum of Theoderic and the seven wonders of the world', *Journal of Late Antiquity* 3/2, 365-85.

2010b. *Ravenna in Late Antiquity* (Cambridge).

Diehl, C. 1888. *Études sur l'administration byzantine dans l'exarchat de Ravenne, 568-751* (Paris).

Ekonomou, A.J. 2007. *Byzantine Rome and the Greek Popes: Eastern Influences on Rome and the Papacy from Gregory the Great to Zacharias, AD 590-752* (Lanham).

Fasoli, G. 1979. 'Il dominio territoriale degli arcivescovi di Ravenna fra l'VIII e l'XI secolo', in Mor, C.-G. and Schmidinger, H. (eds.), *I poteri temporali dei vescovi in Italia e in Germania nel Medioevo* (Bologna), 87-140.

1991. 'Il patrimonio della chiesa ravennate', in A. Carile (ed.), *Storia di Ravenna II: Dall'età bizantina all'età ottoniana*, vol. 1 (Venice), 389-400.

Ferluga, J. 1978. *L'amministrazione bizantina in Dalmazia* (Venice).

Ferrabino, A. 1963. *La Bonifica benedettina* (Rome).

Fiori, F. 2008. 'Tracce della presenza bizantina nella toponomastica dei territori dell'esarcato e della Pentapoli fra VII e XIII secolo', in Ravara Montebelli, C. (ed.), *Archeologia e storia di un territorio di confine* (Rome), 85-97.

Galassi, G. 1953. *Roma o Bisanzio*, vol. 2, *Il congedo classico e l'arte nell'alto Medioevo* (Rome).

Gambi, L. (ed.) 1994. *Storia di Ravenna IV: Dalla dominazione veneziana alla conquista francese* (Venice).

Gasparri, S. and Gelichi, S. (eds.) 2017. *The Age of Affirmation: Venice, the Adriatic and the Hinterland between the 9th and 10th Centuries* (Turnhout).

Gelichi, S., Calaon, D., Grandi, E. and Negrelli, C. 2012. 'History of a forgotten town: Comacchio and its archaeology', in Gelichi and Hodges (eds.) 2012, 169-205.

Gelichi, S. and Hodges, R. (eds.) 2012. *From One Sea to Another: Trading Places in the European and Mediterranean Early Middle Ages. Proceedings of the International Conference, Comacchio, 27th-29th March 2009* (Turnhout).

Grumel, V. (ed.) 1936. *Les regestes des actes du patriarcat de Constantinople*, vol. 1, *Les actes des patriarches, fasc. 2, Les regestes de 715 à 1043* (Paris).

Guillou, A. 1969. *Régionalisme et indépendance dans l'Empire byzantin au VIIe siècle: L'exemple de l'Exarchat et de la Pentapole d'Italie* (Rome).

Hartmann, L.M. 1889. *Untersuchungen zur Geschichte der byzantinischen Verwaltung in Italien (540-750)* (Leipzig).

Herrin, J. 2020. *Ravenna. Capital of Empire, Crucible of Europe* (London).

Herrin, J. and Nelson, J. (eds.) 2016. *Ravenna: Its Role in Early Medieval Change and Exchange* (London).

Hutton, E. 1913. *Ravenna: A Study* (London).

John the Deacon. *Istoria Veneticorum*, in Berto, L.A. (ed.), *Giovanni Diacono. Istoria Veneticorum* (Bologna, 1999).

Lane, F.C. 1973. *Venice: A Maritime Republic* (Baltimore).

Larner, J. 1965. *The Lords of Romagna: Romagnol Society and the Origins of the Signorie* (London).

La Rocca, M.C. and Majocchi, P. (eds.) 2015. *Urban Identities in Northern Italy, 800-1100 ca.* (Turnhout).

MacLean, S. 2010. 'Legislation and politics in late Carolingian Italy: The Ravenna constitutions', *Early Medieval Europe* 18/4, 394-416.

Madden, T.F. 2007. *Enrico Dandolo and the Rise of Venice*, 2nd edn. (Baltimore).

Magdalino, P. 1993. *The Empire of Manuel I Komnenos, 1143-1180* (Cambridge).

Martínez Pizzaro, J. 1995. *Writing Ravenna: The Liber pontificalis of Andreas Agnellus* (Ann Arbor).

Mazzotti, M. 1956. 'L'attività edilizia di Massimiano di Pola', *Felix Ravenna*, 3rd series, 20, 5-30.

McCormick, M. 1995. 'Byzantium and the West, 700-900', in McKitterick, R. (ed.), *New Cambridge Medieval History*, vol. 2, *c.700-c.900* (Cambridge), 349-80.

Moorhead, J. 1992. *Theoderic in Italy* (Oxford).

Nicol, D.M. 1988. *Byzantium and Venice: A Study in Diplomatic and Cultural Relations* (Cambridge).

Orselli, A.M. 1993. *Santità militare e culto dei santi militari nell'impero dei Romani (secoli VI-X)* (Bologna).

Osborne, J. 2011. 'Rome and Constantinople in the ninth century' in Bolgia, C., McKitterick, R. and Osborne, J. (eds.), *Rome across Time and Space: Cultural Transmission and the Exchange of Ideas, c.500-1400* (Cambridge), 222-36.

Petranović, A. and Margetić, A. (eds.) 1983-4. 'Plea of Rižana', *Atti. Centro di ricerche storiche Rovigno* 14, 55-75.

Petrocchi, G. 2008. *Vita di Dante*, 5th edn. (Bari).

Prigent, V. 2008. 'Notes sur l'évolution de l'administration byzantine en Adriatique (VIIIe-IXe siècle)', *Mélanges de l'École française de Rome. Moyen Âge* 120/2 = *Les destinées de l'Illyricum méridional pendant le haut Moyen Âge*, 393-417.

Rabotti, G. (ed.) 1985. *Breviarium ecclesiae Ravennatis (Codice Bavaro)* (Rome).

Rucco, A.A. 2015. *Comacchio nell'alto Medioevo: Il paesaggio tra topografia e geoarcheologia* (Florence).

Sansterre, J.-M. 1983. *Les moines grecs et orientaux à Rome aux époques byzantine et carolingienne (milieu du VIe s.-fin du IXe s.)* (Brussels).

Savigni, R. 2007. 'Giovanni IX da Tossignano, arcivescovo di Ravenna (papa Giovanni X) e i suoi rapporti con la corte ducale spoletana', in Tagliaferri, M. (ed.), *Ravenna e Spoleto: I rapporti tra due metropoli, Atti del XXVIII Convegno del Centro studi e ricerche sull'antica provincia ecclesiastica ravennate, Spoleto, 22-24 settembre 2005* (Imola) = *Ravennatensia* 22, 215-46.

Squatriti, P. 1992. 'Marshes and mentalities in Early Medieval Ravenna', *Viator* 23, 1-16.

Tjäder, J.-O. 1954–82. *Die nichtliterarischen lateinischen Papyri Italiens aus der Zeit 445–700*, 3 vols. (Lund).

Toubert, P. 1973. *Les structures du Latium médiéval: Le Latium méridional et la Sabine du IXe siècle à la fin du XIIe siècle*, 2 vols. (Rome).

Torre, A. 1963. 'Ravenna e l'Impero', in *Renovatio imperii, Atti della Giornata internazionale di studi per il millenario, Ravenna 4–5 novembre 1961* (Faenza), 5–13.

Torricelli, M.P. 1989. *Centri plebani e strutture insediative nella Romagna medievale* (Bologna).

Vasina, A. 1977. 'Le pievi dell'area ravennate prima e dopo il Mille', *Le istituzioni ecclesiastiche della "societas christiana" dei secc. XI–XII: Diocesi, pievi, parrocchie, Atti della VI Settimana internazionale di studio, Milano, 1–7 settembre 1974* (Milan), 607–27.

(ed.) 1993. *Storia di Ravenna III: Dal Mille alla fine della signoria polentana* (Venice).

Veggiani, A. 1973. 'Le trasformazioni dell'ambiente naturale del Ravennate negli ultimi millenni', *Studi romagnoli* 24, 3–26.

Vespignani, G. 2001. *La Romània italiana dall'esarcato al patrimonium: Il Codex parisinus (BNP, NAL 2573) testimone della formazione di società locali nel secoli IX e X* (Spoleto).

Vežić P. 2002. 'Su san Donato, vescovo di Zara', *Hortus artium medievalium* 8, 235–40.

West-Harling, V. 2013. 'Venecie due sunt': Venice and its grounding in the Adriatic and north Italian background', in Valenti, M. and Wickham, C. (eds.), *Italy, 888–962: A Turning Point / Italia, 888–962: Una svolta* (Turnhout), 237–64.

(ed.) 2015. *Three Empires, Three Cities: Identity, Material Culture and Legitimacy in Venice, Ravenna and Rome, 750–1000* (Turnhout).

2020. *Rome, Ravenna and Venice, 750–100: Byzantine Heritage, Imperial Present, and the Construction of Civic Identity* (Oxford).

Wickham, C. 2004. 'The Mediterranean around 800: On the brink of the second trade cycle', *Dumbarton Oaks Papers* 58, 161–74.

Zimmermann, H. 1993. 'Nella tradizione di città capitale: Presenza germanica e società locale dall'età sassone a quella sveva', in Vasina (ed.) 1993, 107–28.

8 | Byzantine Apulia

JEAN-MARIE MARTIN

Apulia borders the Adriatic for several hundred kilometres at the very place where it opens into the Ionian Sea and it is for that reason that it became or, rather, returned to being Byzantine between the end of the ninth century and the eleventh century. Indeed, the whole of this region – classical *Apulia et Calabria* which has kept the name of 'Puglia' until today, as well as present-day Basilicata which separates it from Calabria – was part of the Italian territories conquered by the Lombards between the sixth and the seventh century. The north of *Apulia*, except the enclave of Siponto, was conquered at the time of Pope Gregory the Great and the rest during the second half of the seventh century (Martin 1993, 148–54). At that time only the outer south-east of classical *Calabria* with Gallipoli and Otranto, although the latter town was temporarily occupied by the Lombards in the eighth century (von Falkenhausen 1978, 6–10), remained part of the empire. It initially formed part of the duchy of Calabria – hence the transfer of the toponym – along with classical *Bruttium*, before constituting the duchy of Otranto in the second half of the eighth century.

The Establishment of the Theme of Longobardia

It was by evicting the emir of Bari, who had occupied the central area of the region since the 840s, with the help of the Franks that Byzantium conquered Apulia (with the capture of Bari by the Franks in 871 and by the Byzantine empire in 876, see von Falkenhausen 1978, 20–1; Gay 1904, 109) at the very moment when the Arabs were occupying Sicily and being expelled from Calabria.

Apulia was, therefore, a Lombard territory with the exception of its south-eastern extremity which, probably in the ninth century, took in a Greek population fleeing Sicily, as did Calabria (Martin 1985–6; 2014, 39–47). Initially attached to the theme of Kephalenia (Oikonomides 1965; 1976a), Apulia was elevated to the theme of Longobardia in 899–900 (Zuckerman 2014, 207). For the Byzantine authorities, the imperial territory needed to encompass the entirety of the Lombard principalities. The governor of the theme (*strategos*) was installed in Benevento between 891 and 895 (von Falkenhausen 1978, 24, 32). In 899, the Prince of Salerno, Guaimar I, revealed that he had received the dignity of *patrikios* and the government of his principality through a chrysobull – the oldest attested, as communicated to me verbally by Constantin Zuckerman – of the Emperors Leo VI and Alexander (Martin 2000, 622; 2014, 97; Morcaldi, Schiani and De Stephano 1873, no. 111). After the battle of Garigliano in 915, the Princes of Benevento Lantolf I and Atenolf II were respectively named *anthypatos patrikios* and *patrikios*, and the imperial authorities considered making Lantolf *strategos* of the theme of Longobardia in 921 (Martin 2000, 622–4; 2014, 97–9). Here I disagree with Constantin Zuckerman (2014, 212) that he received this duty, which he does not mention in his title. During the first half of the tenth century, therefore, imperial policy aimed to integrate into the empire the southern Lombard principalities but clearly hesitated between simple and direct annexation, that is, the creation of a theme and a protectorate founded on the concession of high dignities to local princes.

This ambiguous policy did not yield convincing results: Zuckerman (2014, 213–15) has shown that, from 920 to 934, no document allows us to affirm that the Byzantines exercised sovereignty in all of Apulia, and this fact seems to be confirmed by local Latin documents. In the end, the solution imposed itself: the theme of Longobardia, reduced to Apulia and Basilicata, coexisted with the Lombard principalities of Benevento, Salerno and, from 981, Capua. However, the theoretical ambiguity was not banished. Concerning the theme of Longobardia, Constantine Porphyrogennetos reveals (*De administrando imperio* 27) that the empire was represented in Italy by two *patrikioi*, that is, *strategoi*: that of Calabria who, in theory, governed Sicily, Calabria, Naples and Amalfi (regions which had not been conquered by the Lombards) and the *strategos* of Longobardia who was supposed to reside in Benevento and govern Pavia and Capua but who in reality resided in Bari and whose real authority encompassed only Apulia and Basilicata.

Notwithstanding the unrealistic pretensions of the empire, this presentation of the situation has the advantage of demonstrating that the two themes which constituted Byzantine Italy, in the period from the ninth to the eleventh century, were very different from one another. Indeed, Calabria, largely populated by Greeks, and Lombard Apulia were separated by vast empty territories in Basilicata and in the north of Calabria. Let us now return to Longobardia. The administration of the region, which was extended as the imperial presence increased, especially in the second half of the tenth century, and the territory developed, had as its sole base a fortified city (*kastron*) which sheltered the agents of the state and the bishop, even if a few documents have been traced to other locations (Martin 2006, 529; 2014, 207).

However, in the tenth century the local administration was of Lombard character. The judge of acts – a position unknown in lands using Roman or Byzantine law – presided over the creation of documents (Martin 1991, 296–8). Above all, general administration was entrusted to local elites who bore the Lombard title of *gastald* (Martin 2006, 530–1; 2014, 207–8): some can be detected from Lucera in the north-west to Massafra near Taranto in the south-east and they even feature in lists of civil servants. A surviving document produced at Lucera in 998, after the creation of the *katepanate* which is discussed below, concerns four *gastalds* who were appointed by Theodore, army commander (*exkoubitos*) of Longobardia, who exercised the functions of an interim *katepano*, 'to wield public power, dispense judgement and govern' (*ad seniorandum, iudicandum et regendum*) and were based in a *palatium* (von Falkenhausen 1973, 397).

Thus, the theme of Longobardia truly merited its name. The Byzantine empire maintained the use of individual Lombard law there, which was reasonably different from classic Byzantine law, notably with regard to the judicial status of women, patrimonial relations between spouses and inheritance (Martin 2002, 97–121). Documents from the Byzantine period explicitly cite the Edict of Rothari and the Novels of Liutprand and Aistulf; a document produced in Capitanata in 1029 even cites a capitulary of Charlemagne (Martin 2006, 548; 2014, 224). This practice endured throughout the entire period of Byzantine domination and continued into the Norman period and beyond.

The *Katepanate* of Italy

Local administration became normalised around the year 1000 during the period of the *katepanate*: in 1003, the *gastalds* of Lucera were replaced by a *tourmarches* who was also an imperial *chartoularios* (Martin 2006, 531; 2014, 208–9) and this reform reached the entire territory. The Apulian *tourmarches* of the eleventh century was the representative of the government of the theme at the level of the city; in particular, he seems to have exercised criminal jurisdiction (Martin 2006, 531–2; 2014, 209–10), while the *iudices* (or *krites*) exercised civil jurisdiction. Overall, the *tourmarchoi* appear to have taken the place of the Lombard *gastalds* while using a title that conformed more closely to the imperial administrative vocabulary. As local notables, these *tourmarchoi* could also exercise an additional function, that of an official on the staff of a *strategos* (*komes tes kortes*), an administrator of an imperial domain (*episkeptites*), a subaltern officer of the army (*komes*) or local judge (Martin 2006, 533–4; 2014, 211). This function evolved: from 1030 onwards in particular, several *tourmarchoi* could be found in the same town, while the new function of the urban theme official *ek prosopou* was appearing (Martin 2006, 534–5; 2014, 211–12). What is clear is that it was only around the year 1000 – over a century after the conquest – that an administration resembling that of the centre of the empire appeared in the towns of the *katepanate*. Moreover, administrative normalisation extended only patchily to the diverse regions of the theme.

The replacement of the *gastalds* with the *tourmarchoi* closely followed the great reform which had transformed the region: the creation of the *katepanate* of Italy in the place of the theme of Longobardia. This occurred in 969 or 970 – according to Jean-Claude Cheynet (2007, 143) the first *katepano* was Michael Abidelas in 970, whereas Vera von Falkenhausen (1978, 85) suggested it was Eugene in 969 – and it is a development that requires close examination. The reform only concerned Longobardia; Calabria continued to be administered by a *strategos* (von Falkenhausen 1978, 104–7). There are only four known cases of concurrent holding of responsibility for the *katepanate* and the theme of Calabria. It should also be noted that the terminological shift from 'Longobardia' to 'Italy' did not mean that the territorial zone in question had expanded, because it still denoted the region with a Lombard population. It probably resulted from the fact that in the Carolingian period the kingdom of the Lombards became the kingdom of Italy. That said, we shall see that the creation of the *katepanate* was accompanied by a significant campaign of territorial organisation and exploitation.

On the institutional and administrative level, the reform initially entailed – logically – the arrival of officers of the imperial regiments (*tagmata*): *scholae* at the end of the tenth century; then *hikanatoi* and *exkoubitoi* from the 980s and the 990s; military officers, such as a *lorikatos* and *protomandator epi ton basilikon armamenton* can also be found (Martin 2006, 537–9; 2014, 214–16; Oikonomides 1976b, 143). The *tagmata* were joined in the eleventh century by troops from central and eastern themes (Opsikion, Thrakesion) and mercenaries, particularly Normans (Martin 2006, 539; 2014, 216). The presence of such troops was considerably less frequent in the tenth century. We know nothing of any thematic army in Longobardia in this era, but we can perceive the existence of military properties in the period of the *katepanate*: the obligatory military service or upkeep of a soldier (*strateia*) is positively attested by three documents made in Conversano in 980, Bari in 1017 and Cannae in 1034 respectively (Coniglio 1975, no. 22; Nitti de Vito 1900, no. 13; 1914, no. 10). In 1032 the *katepano* had to authorise explicitly the alienation of a property subject to the obligation to provide care for the horses and messengers of the imperial post (*strateia* of the *dromos*) (Oikonomides 1996, 287). Finally, army officers (*kometes*) were stationed in vulnerable zones: against the Lombard princes and German emperors in Capitanata and against the Muslims of Sicily in Taranto (Oikonomides 1996, 541–2).

There was a final administrative sector which clearly shows that imperial authority was progressively taking root: the tax system. At the end of the ninth century, the imperial authorities began by continuing the Lombard practice of raising indirect taxes. This is demonstrated by two documentary immunities issued in 892: one for Monte Cassino and the other for San Vincenzo al Volturno (*Chronicon Vulturnense*, no. 80; Leccisotti 1937, no. 2; Trinchera 1865, no. 3). The evolution towards a normal system of taxation was then marked by two exceptions. Firstly, as Nicolas Oikonomides (1996) noted, the *katepano* of Italy enjoyed particular autonomy: he could issue immunities without reference to the central authorities. Furthermore, presumably as in other western themes, the *katepano* did not receive a salary but was remunerated through a special tax (*synetheia*): in 1016 the *katepano* Basil Mesardonites received thirty-six *nomismata* as the *synetheia* from the fortified settlement at Palagiano, near Taranto (*synetheia kastelliou Pelagianou*, Trinchera 1865, no. 16).

The most ancient witness to a 'normal' Byzantine tax system is an official document (*sigillion*, σιγίλλιον) of exemption from 999 (Martin 1993, 697–8; Prologo 1877, no. 8). However, even in the eleventh century, Capitanata (north-west of Apulia) seems to have experienced only indirect taxation of Lombard origin: pasturage fee (*nomistron*, that is, *herbaticum*), market toll (*plateaticum*) and compulsory labour – *angaria* (Martin 2006, 545; 2014, 221). It must be said that the exploitation of this region did not begin until the 1010s and the 1020s.

In the centre of Apulia, a certain number of levies and taxes were designed for the upkeep of the army (*drouggaraton*, *mètaton* and *bandon*, not to mention the *strateia*). The military tax called *kontouron kai kontaraton ekbole* (κοντούρων καὶ κονταράτων ἐκβολή) cited in 1054 in Monopoli (Martin 2006, 543; 2014, 219; Trinchera 1865, no. 42), seems to have been intended for the construction of small ships and the maintenance of the *conterati*, local supplementary infantrymen armed with lances.

The golden age of the *katepanate* was limited to the first half of the eleventh century, which was nevertheless marked by the revolts of Melus (from 1009) which sparked the first Norman invasion of Apulia in 1017 (Gay 1904, 401–11) followed by those of the *conterati* in 1040–1 (Gay 1904, 455; Martin 2006, 540–1; 2014, 217). After the reign of Isaac Komnenos and the government of the Duke Argyros, son of Melus, the imperial authorities sent only small expeditionary forces to Italy to face the Norman invasions, which limited themselves to guarding a few strategic points to defend the Balkans (Cheynet 2007, 160–1). The only important *katepano* by then was Perenos, duke of Dyrrachion (modern Durrës) and Italy (Cheynet 2007, 158). Italy once again became an appendage of a Balkan province and Bari was taken by the Normans in 1071.

It is clear that Longobardia/Italy, the ethnic and judicial character of which had always been preserved, was fairly well integrated within the empire for a few decades despite its originality as the only Latin province in the empire – this was made possible through a policy that was both firm and intelligent. The period in question coincided with the beginning of the demographic and economic recovery which characterised all of the northern shore of the Mediterranean at that time.

The Actions of the Imperial Authorities: The Territory

For this reason, in particular, the Byzantine presence left a durable impression on the region which was badly affected by the Early Medieval crisis: the Tavoliere plain remained practically empty from the sixth to the late eleventh century. Numerous cities, mostly smaller ones such as Ordona, which has been excavated, completely disappeared (Martin 2009, 736–41). In total, only the central coast around Bari and Trani seems to have been well populated. This region had developed already in the ninth century, as did perhaps southern Salento which received an influx of Greek populations. The scale of the work accomplished by the imperial authorities can be measured (Martin 2009, 747): of the episcopal cities attested in the eleventh century in the territory of the *katepanate*, seventeen were of Late Antique origin and twenty-eight were Medieval, that is, Byzantine foundations.

Three systematic campaigns of new city construction have been identified (Martin 2006, 525–8; 2009, 747–51; 2014, 203–6). Already in the aftermath of the conquest it seems that imperial authorities built new ports on the Adriatic coast, in order to facilitate links with the Balkans: Monopoli appeared in 905, Polignano in 916 while Giovinazzo and Molfetta followed a little later.

However, it was during the period of the *katepanate* that this phenomenon really gained traction. Even as the theme was transformed into the *katepanate*, cities multiplied in the still poorly populated interior regions. In 968 the Greek archbishop of Otranto was promoted to the rank of metropolitan and charged with creating new bishoprics in Basilicata where a Greek population then installed itself in the ancient sites of Acerenza and Matera and also in the new towns of Gravina, Tricarico and Tursi. In 983 the new (Latin) metropolitan bishopric of Trani had to establish suffragans in the new sites of Minervino and Montemilone. In 1001–2 the *katepano* Gregory Tarchaneiotes defined the limit between the territories (*diakratesis*) of Acerenza and the new foundation of Tricarico; the document still cites the fortified settlements (*kastellia*) of Pietrapertosa, Tolve and *Kerbanon* (Κερβάνον), the latter being in a ruined state and probably an abortive foundation (Guillou 1970, no. 1; Guillou and Holtzmann 1961). It seems that the mission of the new establishments – fortified settlements both large and small (*kastra* and *kastellia*) – was not only to provide a civil and religious organisation to this region but to populate and exploit it. Indeed, it was at this time that the future province, which Frederick II would call 'Basilicata' two and a half centuries later, was beginning to take form. If the *katepanate* did not manage and, perhaps, did not attempt to integrate the Lombard principalities, it did at least undertake both the administration and the exploitation of the empty zones which separated the *katepanate* from Calabria. The fortified settlement (*castellum*) or town (*civitas*) of *Turri*, between Armento and Guardia Perticara in the province of Potenza, and the fortified settlements (*castella*) of *Appium* and *Acena*, near Bernalda, were also created in what is now Basilicata. Finally, the nearby Roman city of Taranto, abandoned for several decades, was provided with an enclosure in 965–9 (Jacob 1988) while other establishments, such as Palagiano, appeared near the Gulf of Taranto. It is possible that Rapolla, Vaccarizza and Ripalta further to the north in what later became Capitanata also belong to the same generation.

The third and best-known campaign had a different, even opposing, objective: in the 1010s and the 1020s, the *katepano* Basil Boioannes wanted to provide the *katepanate* with a secure and fortified frontier against the principality of Benevento which was allied to the German empire. Thus, Capitanata was created. To the Roman cities of Lucera, Bovino, Ascoli Satriano and other pre-existing Medieval sites cited above were added the new towns of Civitate, Dragonara, Fiorentino, Montecorvino, Biccari,

Tertiveri, Troia, Cisterna, Melfi and perhaps also Monte Serico and Montepeloso (Irsina). In this way, a fortified double line was established with the intention of protecting imperial territory. In fact, it would serve as the expansion zone of the Normans based in Melfi a few decades later.

The new Byzantine cities exhibited common traits (Martin and Noyé 1991). Apart from the port towns of the first campaign, they were foundations situated in the interior of the Byzantine lands, on defensive sites – in Capitanata, these tended to be interfluvial spurs. As such, they had elongated plans and were traversed in their longest dimension by a large central road (*platea*) intersected by perpendicular side roads; they were small in size (a few hundred metres on the longest side); they housed an administration and a bishop but apparently did not carry out specific economic activities (Martin and Noyé 1991, 45–6). These foundations show original features in their manner of occupying the terrain, which is noticeably different from what can be seen in neighbouring regions. The occupation of the countryside was very variable across different zones. Along the central coast and on the first tier of the Murge, demographic development began already in the Lombard period of the ninth century (Martin 1993, 223); the scarcity of water caused by the limestone subsoil forced the population to group itself into very large villages some of which were promoted to cities during the Byzantine period (Martin 2009, 753–4), while others were simply referred to as a village (*locus*, the equivalent of *chorion*). In Basilicata, it seems that the foundation of towns preceded the exploitation of the countryside (Martin 2009, 755). In Capitanata the agricultural development of the plain did not begin before the Norman period.

These fortified towns normally housed the public administration and a bishop, although a few small *kastellia* in Basilicata lacked one. Longobardia/Italy – unlike Sicily and Calabria – was never removed from the authority of the pope but it did see an influx of Greek people in the south of Salento and in Basilicata. Institutionally, only the metropolitan bishopric of Otranto, once attached to Calabria, depended on the patriarch of Constantinople but the sole Greek suffragan to which it definitely gave rise was Tursi. The same is true of the few Greek bishoprics in Salento (Gallipoli, Castro, Lecce) which depended on the Calabrian metropolitan of Santa Severina. In any case, despite the diverging opinions put forward by twentieth-century historians regarding the relations between Greeks and Latins in the Byzantine and Norman periods, one point is clear: it was the language and rite of the local population which determined whether local churches were Greek or Latin. Neither the imperial administration nor that of the Normans that followed sought to impose a particular liturgy against the will of the population: the bishoprics of the new towns of Capitanata, populated by Lombard Latins, were subjected to the Latin metropolitan of Benevento, situated outside of imperial territory, with the agreement of the Byzantine administration (Holtzmann 1960). In Taranto, a majority-Latin town with an important Greek minority, following an ill-fated attempt to impose a Greek bishop at the end of the ninth century, the authorities relinquished the episcopal see to Latins, with a Greek chorbishop ministering to the Greeks (Martin 1990; 2014, 67–74). But all the bishops, Latin and Greek, were obviously subordinate to imperial authority at a time when, in any case, the calls for the freedom of the Church (*libertas Ecclesiae*) were barely beginning in the West. The loyalty of the Latin clergy to the empire is beyond doubt: Archbishop Bisantius of Bari, characterised in 1035 as 'terrible and without fear against all the Greeks' (*terribilis et sine metu contra omnes Graecos, Annales Barenses* 54) evidently because he protected the population against the abuses of Greek administrators, used a Greek seal (*bulla*) (Martin 1993, 569). The (certainly Latin) bishops of Troia and Acerenza were killed in 1041 while fighting in the imperial army (Martin 1993, 625). The beginnings of the reform of the Roman church had only limited effects in this region. Moreover, the pontifical administration of this region was poorly acquainted with its geography.

The recent episcopal sees possessed only limited temporalities. Only the bishop of Oria, a see which replaced Brindisi in the ninth century, had fiscal and judicial immunities confirmed by *katepano* Basil Mesardonites in 1011; his cathedral had peasants (*vaxalli*), probably serfs (*paroikoi*) (De Leo 1940, no. 2), at its disposal.

Society

One of the key distinguishing features of Byzantine Apulia – in relation to the rest of the empire, including Calabria and the West – resided in the almost complete absence of an aristocracy. The local aristocracy, weakly attested in the Lombard ninth century (Martin 1993, 232–4), seems to have disappeared with the episode of the emirate of Bari. Thereafter, only mere notables, to whom were granted the functions of a *gastald* and then a *tourmarches*, can be detected. In the Lombard period the only sizeable landowners attested in Apulia were the abbeys of Campania (Monte Cassino and its dependency of Santa Sofia at Benevento and San Vincenzo al Volturno). In the aftermath of the conquest, the imperial authorities confirmed their possessions: in 892 the *strategos* Symbatikios confirmed Monte Cassino's assets located in imperial territory with a fiscal immunity; the *strategos* George produced a similar document in favour of San Vincenzo (*Chronicon Vulturnense*, no. 80; Martin 1993, 292–301). It was the vicissitudes of the history of the Lombard principalities which forced their abandonment. Following their destruction by Saracen war bands (San Vincenzo al Volturno in 881, Monte Cassino in 883) the two abbeys provisionally ceased administering some of their Apulian possessions (*Chronicon Vulturnense*, no. 76; Leccisotti 1937, no. 10; Trinchera 1865, no. 1). However, it was primarily after their restoration – from the 940s to the late tenth century – that the two abbeys, which now concentrated their power and wealth in fairly compact lordships, abandoned Apulia.

As there were few cathedrals, which were in any case fairly poor, it can be said that large-scale estates, even ecclesiastical ones which are well attested in Calabria, were practically non-existent in Apulia. This situation clearly resulted from the retrograde ambitions of the Macedonian emperors (Lemerle 1979, 88, 112–14). Nevertheless, presumably in order to structure society and provide it with meaningful administration, the authorities set out to create and favour notables capable of taking on public duties. The *strateia*, which only appears in documents in a significant capacity in the eleventh century, has already been mentioned. In 999 the *spatharokandidatos* Christopher Bochomakes received as a donation (*charistiki*) the imperial monastery of San Pietro of Taranto (Trinchera 1865, no. 10). In 1054, Byzantios, a judge in Bari, possessed two small villages one of which was granted to him by the *katepano* (Lefort and Martin 1986). Above all, the authorities distributed dignities which entailed the payment of a salary (*roga*) by the state (Cheynet 1983; Lemerle 1967) and public offices. In the period of the theme, it seems that the authorities liberally distributed the dignities of *protospatharios*, *spatharios* and *spatharokandidatos* in central Apulia; these can even be encountered in secondary agglomerations (Martin 1993, 699). In the period of the *katepanate*, with the normalisation of local administration, local notables were granted local offices: those of *tourmarches*, *topoteretes*, *ek prosopou* or judge (*kritai*). Finally, from 1045 with the arrival of the Normans and until the end of the century, there was a return to the distribution of dignities which were new and significant such as *protosebastos* and *protonobelissimos* (Peters-Custot 2012, 651). In Capitanata which was only beginning to be exploited in the eleventh century, however, there were no officials.

In this way, the Byzantine empire created for itself a network of clients and after the 920s and the 930s there were no further attempts by the

Lombards of Apulia to join the principalities, which were in any case becoming weaker and passing under the influence of the German empire from the middle of the tenth century (Martin 1980; 2014). This did not prevent revolts, but these do not seem to have aimed to extract Apulia from the empire. It is known that Argyros, the son of Melus who directed the large revolt of the beginning of the eleventh century and at one time a rebel himself, was officially and permanently named duke of Italy, Calabria, Sicily and Paphlagonia (*doux Italias, Kalabrias, Sikelias kai Paphlagonias*) in the 1050s (Martin 1993, 704). The reference to Paphlagonia in his title is said to be due to the presence of a *tagma* from that province (Cheynet 2007, 157).

It should not be forgotten that the tenth and eleventh centuries were a period of economic expansion (Arthur 2006). The empire did not impede this expansion but directed it for its own purposes. In particular, it provided Apulia with significant quantities of Constantinopolitan coinage (Martin 1983, 191–7; 2014, 14–18). Whereas Byzantine coins had ceased to circulate in the south of Italy in the eighth and ninth centuries, they returned in force in Apulia with the Byzantine conquest, while Calabria like all of the southern low-lying Tyrrhenian coastal areas used the Muslim *tari* from the beginning of the tenth century to the middle of the eleventh (Martin 1983, 198–202; 2014, 19–22). Apulian charters refer above all to the *solidus* but also the *follis* and, rarely, the *miliaresion*. They make it possible to trace the devaluation of the eleventh century (Morrisson 1976), mentioning the *solidus romanatus* of Romanos III (1028–34), which was of genuine quality, the *stellatus* possibly issued by Constantine IX, the *ducatus* of Constantine X Doukas and, finally, the *michaelatus* of Michael VII (Morrisson 1968), which was worth only half or a third of the value of the *romanatus*. Only Capitanata used the *tari* after the 1030s; we have seen that this region did not contain any officials.

I think that, more than trade with the centre of the empire, it was financial transfers and salaries (*rogai*) which caused the influx of Constantinopolitan coinage in Italy. However, this coinage also served commercial purposes and even small transactions: a hoard of *folleis*, buried at the end of the tenth century at Cannae (Callegher and Morrisson 2008), in the north-western extremity of the well-populated central zone of Apulia, contains 773 *folleis* and half-*folleis*, struck between 820 and 959, worth a total of two and a half *nomismata*. The empire was still transferring very significant salaries (*rogai*) to the Normans at the end of the eleventh century (Bibicou 1959–60). Afterwards, however, the influx halted entirely – at the same moment as that of the Arab *tarin* around the

Tyrrhenian albeit for other reasons. Norman Apulia clearly suffered a severe coinage shortage at the beginning of the twelfth century (Martin 1993, 453–60).

Overall, it is evident that integration into the empire was slow and difficult but successful. In the years between 970 and 1050, the Italy of the *katepano* was an almost normal Byzantine province and more than a mere 'threshold' to the empire, even though its language and rites were Latin and its law Lombard. The lack of an aristocracy and any great estates at the moment of the conquest certainly favoured this integration. The actions of imperial authorities – which did nothing to modify regional identity – profoundly marked the Apulian landscape. They organised the beginnings of an economic expansion which only reached its peak in the twelfth century under Norman domination. Finally, they maintained the organisation of a society that was not greatly differentiated, contenting themselves with favouring the emergence of a class of notables. The Norman seigniory which succeeded the imperial authorities at the end of the eleventh century would have to conform itself to these conditions by developing the jurisdictional component of its lordship (Martin 1993, 301–24), whereas in Calabria it acquired an essentially landed base.

Translated by Duncan Hardy

References

Annales Barenses, in Pertz, G.H. (ed.), *Annales Barenses and Lupus protospatharius Annales*, *MGH Scriptores*, vol. 5 (Hanover, 1844), 51–6.

Arthur, P. 2006. 'Economic expansion in Byzantine Apulia', in Jacob, A., Martin, J.-M. and Noyé, G. (eds.), *Histoire et culture dans l'Italie byzantine: Acquis et nouvelles recherches*, Collection de l'École française de Rome 363 (Rome), 389–405.

Bibicou, H. 1959–60. 'Une page d'histoire diplomatique de Byzance au XIe siècle: Michel VII Doukas, Robert Guiscard et la pension des dignitaires', *Byzantion* 29–30, 43–75.

Callegher, B. and Morrisson, C. 2008. '*Miliareni de follibus*: La trouvaille de folles byzantins de Cannes (milieu du Xe siècle)', in Cuozzo, E., Déroche, V., Peters-Custot, A., and Prigent, V. (eds.), *Puer Apuliae: Mélanges offerts à Jean-Marie Martin*, vol. 1 (Paris), 105–22.

Cheynet, J.-C. 1983. 'Dévaluation des dignités et dévaluation monétaire dans la seconde moitié du XIe siècle', *Byzantion* 53/2, 453–77.

2007. 'La place des catépans d'Italie dans la hiérarchie militaire et sociale de Byzance', Νέα Ῥώμη 4 = Ἀμπελοκήπιον: *Studi di amici e colleghi in onore di Vera von Falkenhausen*, 143–61.

Chronicon Vulturnense, in Federici, V. (ed.), *Chronicon Vulturnense del monaco Giovanni*, vol. 1, Fonti per la storia d'Italia 58 (Rome, 1925).

Coniglio, G. (ed.) 1975. *Codice diplomatico pugliese*, vol. 20, *Le pergamene di Conversano*, vol. 1, *901–1265* (Bari).

Constantine Porphyrogennetos. *De administrando imperio*, in Moravcsik, G. and Jenkins, R.J.H. (eds.), *Constantine Porphyrogenitus. De administrando imperio* (Washington, DC, 1967).

De Leo, A. (ed.) 1940. *Codice diplomatico brindisino*, vol. 1, *492–1299* (Trani).

Falkenhausen, V. von 1973. 'Zur byzantinischen Verwaltung Luceras am Ende des 10. Jahrhunderts', *Quellen und Forschungen aus italienischen Archiven und Bibliotheken* 53, 395–406.

— 1978. *La dominazione bizantina nell'Italia meridionale dal IX all'XI secolo* (Bari).

Gay, J. 1904. *L'Italie méridionale et l'Empire byzantin depuis l'avènement de Basile Ier jusqu'à la prise de Bari par les Normands (867–1071)* (Paris).

Guillou, A. 1970. *Studies on Byzantine Italy* (London).

Guillou, A. and Holtzmann, W. 1961. 'Zwei Katepansurkunden aus Tricarico', *Quellen und Forschungen aus italienischen Archiven und Bibliotheken* 41, 1–28.

Holtzmann, W. 1960. 'Der Katepan Boioannes und die kirchliche Organisation der Capitanata', *Nachrichten der Akademie der Wissenschaften in Göttingen, Philologisch-Historische Klasse* 2, 19–39.

Jacob, A. 1988. 'La reconstruction de Tarente par les Byzantins aux IXe et Xe siècles. À propos de deux inscriptions perdues', *Quellen und Forschungen aus italienischen Archiven und Bibliotheken* 68, 1–17.

Leccisotti, T. (ed.) 1937. *Le colonie cassinesi in Capitanata*, vol. 1, *Lesina (sec. VIII–XI)* (Montecassino).

Lefort, J. and Martin, J.-M. 1986. 'Le sigillion du catépan d'Italie Eustathe Palatinos pour le juge Byzantios (décembre 1045)', *Mélanges de l'École française de Rome. Moyen Âge, Temps modernes* 98/2, 525–42.

Lemerle, P. 1967. '"Roga" et rente d'état aux Xe–XIe siècles', *Revue des études byzantines* 25, 77–100.

— 1979. *The Agrarian History of Byzantium from the Origins to the Twelfth Century: The Sources and Problems* (Galway).

Martin, J.-M. 1980. 'Éléments préféodaux dans les principautés de Bénévent et de Capoue (fin du VIIIe siècle – début du XIe siècle): Modalités de privatisation du pouvoir', in *Structures féodales et féodalisme dans l'Occident méditerranéen (Xe–XIIIe siècles): Bilan et perspectives de recherches, Actes du Colloque de Rome, 10–13 octobre 1978*, Collection de l'École française de Rome 44 (Rome), 553–86.

— 1983. 'Economia naturale ed economia monetaria nell'Italia meridionale longobarda e bizantina (secoli VI-XI)', in Romano, R. and Tucci, U. (eds.), *Storia* d'Italia, Annali 6: Economia naturale, economia monetaria (Turin), 179–219.

1985-6. 'Une origine calabraise pour la Grecìa salentine ?', Rivista di studi bizantini e neoellenici 22-3, 51–63.

1990. 'Κίνναμος ἐπίσκοπος – Cennamus episcopus: Aux avant-postes de l'hellénisme sud-italien vers l'an Mil', Rivista di studi bizantini e neoellenici 27, 89–99.

1991. 'Le juge et l'acte notarié en Italie méridionale du VIIIe au Xe siècle', in Vitolo, G. and Mottola, F. (eds.), Scrittura e produzione documentaria nel Mezzogiorno longobardo, Atti del Convegno internazionale di studio, Badia di Cava, 3-5 ottobre 1990 (Badia di Cava), 287–99.

1993. La Pouille du VIe au XIIe siècle, Collection de l'École française de Rome 179 (Rome).

2000. 'L'Occident chrétien dans le Livre des Cérémonies, II, 48', Travaux et mémoires 13, 617–46.

2002. 'Le droit lombard en Italie méridionale (IXe–XIIIe siècle): Interprétations locales et expansion', in Bougard, F., Feller, L. and Le Jan, R. (eds.), Dots et douaires dans le haut Moyen Age, Collection de l'École française de Rome 295 (Rome), 97–121.

2006. 'Les thèmes italiens: Territoire, population, administration', in Jacob, A., Martin, J.-M. and Noyé, G. (eds.), Histoire et culture dans l'Italie byzantine: Acquis et nouvelles recherches, Collection de l'École française de Rome 363 (Rome), 517–58.

2009. 'L'Italie méridionale', in Città e campagna nei secoli altomedievali, vol. 2, Settimane di studio del Centro italiano di studi sull'alto Medioevo 56 (Spoleto), 733–74.

2014. Byzance et l'Italie méridionale (Paris).

Martin, J.-M. and Noyé, G. 1991. 'Les villes de l'Italie byzantine (IXe–XIe siècles)', in Kravari, V., Lefort, J. and Morrisson C. (eds.), Hommes et richesses dans l'Empire byzantin, vol. 2, VIIIe–XVe siècles (Paris), 27–62.

Morcaldi, M., Schiani, M. and De Stephano, S. (eds.) 1873. Codex diplomaticus Cavensis, vol. 1 (Naples, repr. Badia di Cava 1981).

Morrisson, C. 1968. 'Le Michaèlaton et les noms de monnaies à la fin du XIe siècle', Travaux et mémoires 3, 369–74.

1976. 'La dévaluation de la monnaie byzantine au XIe siècle: Essai d'interprétation', Travaux et mémoires 6, 3–47.

Nitti de Vito, F. (ed.) 1900. Codice diplomatico barese, vol. 4, Le pergamene di S. Nicola di Bari 1: Periodo greco (939-1071) (Bari, repr. 1964).

(ed.) 1914. Codice diplomatico barese, vol. 8, Le pergamene di Barletta. Archivio capitolare (897-1285) (Bari).

Oikonomides, N. 1965. 'Constantin VII Porphyrogénète et les thèmes de Céphalonie et de Longobardie', Revue des études byzantines 23, 118–23.

1976a. *Documents et études sur les institutions de Byzance (VIIe–XVe siècle)* (London).

1976b. 'L'évolution de l'organisation administrative de l'Empire byzantin au XIe siècle (1025–1118)', *Travaux et mémoires* 6, 125–52.

1996. *Fiscalité et exemption fiscale à Byzance (IXe–XIe s.)* (Athens).

Peters-Custot, A. 2012. 'Titulatures byzantines en Pouille et en Calabre', in Martin, J.-M., Peters-Custot, A. and Prigent, V. (eds.), *L'héritage byzantin en Italie (VIIIe–XIIe Siècle)*, vol. 2, *Les cadres juridiques et sociaux et les institutions publiques*, Collection de l'École française de Rome 461 (Rome), 643–58.

Prologo, A. (ed.) 1877. *Le carte che si conservano nell'Archivio del Capitolo metropolitano della città di Trani dal IX secolo fino all'anno 1266* (Barletta).

Trinchera, F. (ed.) 1865. *Syllabus Graecarum membranarum* (Naples).

1978. *La dominazione bizantina nell'Italia meridionale dal IX all'XI secolo* (Bari).

Zuckerman, C. 2014. 'Squabbling *protospatharioi* and other administrative issues from the first half of the tenth century', *Revue des études byzantines* 72, 193–233.

9 | From One Coast to Another and Beyond
Adriatic Connections through the Sigillographic Evidence

PAGONA PAPADOPOULOU

In memory of Vasso Penna

In 2005 the seal of John, *patrikios*, imperial *protospatharios* and *strategos* of Sicily (Table 9.1, no. 25), dated in the first half of the tenth century, was found during excavations in the wider Butrint area undertaken by the Butrint Foundation, the Albanian Archaeological Institute and the University of East Anglia, under the direction of Richard Hodges. Butrint, commonly referred to in Byzantine sources as *Bouthrotos*, is situated in present-day south-west Albania, 3 km inland from the Straits of Corfu, at the south end of Lake Butrint. The site consists of two main parts divided by the Vivari Channel that connects Lake Butrint to the Straits of Corfu. The north-western shore is occupied by the castle and the walled town with remains ranging from the Bronze Age to the Ottoman period (Hansen, Hodges and Leppard 2013; Hodges, Bowden and Lako 2004). On the south-eastern shore lies the Vrina Plain, where recent excavations have unearthed successive occupations dating from the Roman to the Byzantine period (Greenslade 2013). It is in this latter area, in a ninth-century construction occupying the narthex of a fifth-century basilica, that the seal in question was found. The same layer yielded another four lead seals dated between the late ninth and the tenth century, as well as fifty-two coins – fifty-one copper *folleis* covering the period from c.820 to c.1030–42 and a silver *miliaresion* of Leo VI (886–912) (Greenslade and Hodges 2013; Papadopoulou 2012; 2019a; 2019b). Due to these, but also to other finds, it has been suggested that this building be identified as the manor house (*oikos*) of the local *archon* (Greenslade and Hodges 2013). A more recent view, considering the particularities of the ceramic evidence along with other significant finds, suggests viewing it as the seat of a low-ranking Byzantine official, a centre for the supply of the army or even a customs house (Vroom 2018, 290–4). Be that as it may, the five seals found there are of special importance since, to the best of my knowledge, they constitute the only sigillographic evidence from this area.

Given the date of John's seal, the owner must have had his seat in Calabria where the *strategoi* of Sicily resided in the aftermath of the fall of Taormina in 902. Due to this change, the narrative sources refer to them henceforth as *strategoi* of Calabria, but on seals they continue to style themselves *strategoi* of Sicily (Nesbitt and Oikonomides 1991, 19). The Byzantine historian John Skylitzes (*Synopsis historiarum*, 263) mentions a *patrikios* and *strategos* of Calabria in 921–2 named John Mouzalon or Byzalon (von Falkenhausen 1978, 102–3, no. 68). Could we identify him as the owner of the Butrint seal? The existing evidence does not allow us to answer the question positively. Both the State Hermitage Museum (Stepanova 1998, no. 9) and the Dumbarton Oaks collections (Nesbitt and Oikonomides 1991, 28, no. 5.17) have copies of a tenth-century seal with the same name, titles and function as the Butrint seal. In these cases, however, the obverse is decorated by a frontal peacock with outspread tail, whereas the Butrint seal bears an ornamented patriarchal cross. Given the general reluctance of Byzantine officials to change the iconography of their seals, especially when this was not imposed by a change in their titulature (Oikonomides 1983), it is highly unlikely that the two types of seals belonged to the same John. Moreover, the commonness of the owner's name renders any attempt of identification precarious. In any case, for the purposes of the present study the importance of this seal lies in the fact that it provides clear evidence of correspondence between southern Italy and Butrint (*Bouthrotos*).

In 2013, preliminary excavations under the direction of Christian Napolitano in the Montalbano Park, at the feet of Frederick II's castle in Oria (Apulia, Italy), uncovered a seal belonging to an imperial *spatharokandidatos* and *strategos* of Dyrrachion (modern Durrës), that can also be dated to the tenth century (Table 9.1, no. 7). The seal remains unpublished but proves, if proof were needed, that correspondence also circulated the other way, that is, from the Illyrian coast to southern Italy.

Having these two tenth-century seals as a starting point, this study will investigate the connections between the two rims of the Byzantine Adriatic but also those they had with the rest of the empire on the basis of the sigillographic evidence. Since lead seals were more often than not attached to documents of an administrative nature, they offer invaluable evidence about the administrative network of communications.

Taking into consideration the history of the area of interest and its administrative evolution, the geographic scope of the present study extends to both rims of the Adriatic Sea: the whole western coast, of the Italian peninsula, on the one hand and the Balkan, eastern rim of the Adriatic, along with the coast of the Ionian Sea on the other hand. The latter is regarded in the broader sense, that is, including the coasts between the Peloponnese and mainland Greece as far as Naupaktos, the capital of the theme of Nikopolis (Stavrakos 2007), to the north and Patras to the south. However, it excludes Sicily which, along with other particularities, is characterised by a long period of Arab dominion (Prigent 2011, 209; 2012, 607–8). For the sake of brevity, I refer to these areas as the two rims of the Adriatic Sea.

Regarding the chronological frame, it is also imposed by the historical evolution of the region and by the seals themselves. Since earlier seals tend to omit the place in which their owner was active, only a few of them are included, mainly of an ecclesiastical nature. Thus, the bulk of the material considered here covers the ninth through eleventh centuries. For southern Italy the end of Byzantine rule in the eleventh century marks the end for the use of seals of the type considered here. Some later examples from the other rim of the Adriatic and the Ionian Sea are included, although a sharp decline in the use of lead seals in general has been observed for the whole Byzantine empire from the twelfth century onwards (Prigent 2011, 208, n. 6; 2012, 610, n. 30). This century offers the chronological limit of the present study.

Methodological Remarks

As has already been noted by Jean-Claude Cheynet and Cécile Morrisson (1990, 105–6; repr. Cheynet 2008, 85–6) in their seminal study on the findspots and the circulation of Byzantine seals, the corpus of seals that can be of value for the type of research undertaken here is extremely restricted. It includes a very small percentage of the surviving seals, which in turn represent only a small portion of the total seals issued during the Byzantine era. Unfortunately, the vast majority of lead seals are kept in public or private collections without any indication as to their provenance. Thus, any study on the circulation of seals needs to rely mainly on the following two types of evidence.

Seals Hanging from the Original Documents

The richest collection of documents preserving the seals that authenticated them can be found in the monasteries of Mount Athos; they do not comprise, however, seals related to the Adriatic (Cheynet and Morrisson 1990, 107–8, 119–20; repr. Cheynet 2008, 86–7, 96). Nonetheless, other collections include examples regarding the area under consideration: the archives of Monte Cassino in Lazio and the archives of Bari, which are divided between the Basilica of San Nicola at Bari, the Cathedral at Bari and the archive of Badia di Cava in Campania. The latter conserves the documents of the Monastery of Santa Trinità at Bari, which, in the second half of the eleventh century, passed under the jurisdiction of the Badia di Cava (von Falkenhausen 1986, 196). Unfortunately, no relevant archives survive from the eastern rim of the Adriatic.

Seals of Known Provenance

This type of evidence includes seals in public or private collections formed locally – such as the Palermo or the Reggio Calabria collections; seals in collections, whose provenance has been noted, as for example in some of the holdings of the Numismatic Museum in Athens (Avramea, Galani-Krikou and Touratsoglou 1990, 236–7); and finally, seals found accidentally (stray finds) or during archaeological excavations.

Scholarly interest in seals of known provenance intensified after the organisation of the Second International Colloquium of Byzantine Sigillography in Athens in 1988, where a particular session was devoted to 'the dispersion of the seals'. The papers devoted to this subject were published in 1990 in the second volume of the journal *Studies in Byzantine Sigillography*. The number of specimens falling into this category is extremely limited. It is indicative that, leaving aside the seals kept in the Athos archives, in 1990 Cheynet and Morrisson were able to trace only 393 examples with known provenance among around 70,000 surviving seals. Since then, care is being taken in recording the provenance of seals when it is known; nevertheless, their proportion remains extremely low when compared to those of unknown provenance. Moreover, with a few exceptions (Bulgakova 2010; Koltsida-Makre 2011) very few synthetical works examining the circulation of seals in a given geographical area – let alone in the whole empire – have been produced, probably as a result of the dispersion of relevant publications.

An invaluable research tool in that respect is offered by the lists of published seals, often with corrections of erroneous readings and datings, that are included in the volumes of the *Studies in Byzantine Sigillography*. They currently cover the period until 2006 and have proved to be a helpful source of bibliographical guidance for the present study and especially for the preparation of the two tables that accompany it, as far as the period between 1990 and 2006 is concerned. Later publications have been consulted and integrated, but it should be stressed that the provided lists do not pretend to be exhaustive. Nevertheless, they offer a representative picture.

Limitations

Even among seals falling within these two restricted group – seals hanging from the original document and seals of known provenance – other limitations are also imposed. If contact between areas were to be assessed, as in the case of the present study, then only seals mentioning a function with a known or specified place of exercise can be considered. This means that anonymous seals or seals mentioning only the name and the title(s) and function(s) of the owner, had to be excluded.

A characteristic example is the seal of Kallonas, imperial *protospatharios* and *epi ton oikeiakon* (βασιλικὸς πρωτοσπαθάριος καὶ ἐπὶ τῶν οἰκειακῶν) which was found in Butrint (Papadopoulou 2012, 135–6, no. 1). Unlike the eleventh-century *epi ton oikeiakon* Michael, whose seal (Table 9.1, no. 2) informs us that he was also *katepano* of Italy and consequently had his seat in Bari, we cannot be certain of Kallonas' place of residence. The title *epi ton oikeiakon* presents a radical change in its content between 873–4 and the 1030s, with the successive phases of the evolution being still unclear to scholars. The early *epi ton oikeiakon* – known also as *oikeiakoi* or *tou Lausiakou* (οἰκειακοὶ τοῦ Λαυσιακοῦ) – were high dignitaries in the personal service of the emperor, residing mainly in Constantinople, with the exception of those who held an administrative position in the provinces. As noted by Nicolas Oikonomides (1994, 482, 486–9) on the basis of the inscription of the church of Skripou in Boetia (873–4), the founder – 'Leo, the famous imperial *protospatharios* and *epi ton oikeiakon*' – was a man of high status: he bore a very important honorary title, belonged to the elite of the *protospatharioi* of the *Lausiakos* (who were superior to other groups of *protospatharioi* as they formed part of the immediate entourage of the emperor), frequented the palace and was in personal contact with the emperor from whose hands he received each year his stipend (*roga*).

In the 1030s, the *epi ton oikeiakon* ceased to be a title and became a function, related to the homonymous *sekreton* of the *logothesion tou genikou*, with financial duties relevant to state land (*oikeiaka*) (Cheynet, Gökyıldırım and Bulgurlu 2012, 982; Oikonomides 1976, 136–7). The origins of the *sekreton* of the *oikeiakon* are to be sought earlier and certainly before 972–3 when it is first mentioned in the sources as a special treasury controlled by the *logothetes tou genikou* (λογοθέτης τοῦ γενικοῦ, Oikonomides 1976, 136–7; 2002, 992). In the *Kletorologion of Philotheos*, however, dated in 899, there is no mention of the *epi ton oikeiakon* under the *logothetes tou genikou*. It has thus been suggested that in the late ninth century the *epi ton oikeiakon* might have still had responsibilities related to the imperial domains, although it seems rather unlikely that all the *epi ton oikeiakon* attested on ninth- and tenth-century seals were attached to the imperial court, as the *oikeiakoi tou Lausiakou* (Wassiliou and Seibt 2004, 59, no. 31).

An example from the archives of Mount Athos confirms the precarity of any hypothesis regarding the place of residence of the *epi ton oikeiakon*. A document in the Protaton Monastery, dated to August 943, still bears the seal of Zoetos, imperial *protospatharios* and *epi ton oikeiakon* (Karakatsanis 1997, 509, 13.3; Oikonomides 1985, 71–2, no. 67; Papachrysanthou 1975, 197–202, no. 6). Although on his seal Zoetos shares the same titles as Kallonas, we know that he was also judge of the theme of Thessaloniki – thus residing in the homonymous city – since it was in this capacity that he signed the document from which his seal still hangs: Zoetos, imperial *protospatharios* and *epi ton oikeiakon* and judge of the theme (Ζωήτου βασιλικοῦ πρωτοσπαθαρίου καὶ ἐπὶ τῶν οἰκιακῶν καὶ κριτοῦ τοῦ θέματος, Papachrysanthou 1975, 201, line l. 3). About half a century separates the seal of Kallonas from that of Zoetos; nevertheless, both seals belong to a period that seems to mark a turning point regarding the status of the *epi ton oikeiakon* and subsequently their place of residence.

Similar problems could arise also in the case of seals on which the owner's jurisdiction area is mentioned. They can be due to the fact that the geographical term used on the seal is too general or its exact location remains unknown. In the first category fall the seals of the *kommerkiarioi* of the West. The term 'of the West' (τῆς Δύσεως) is attested in the tenth century with regard to the command of the army (*domestikoi* of the Schools of the West, *exkoubitoi* of the West) and, along with the corresponding term 'of the East' (τῆς Ἀνατολῆς), it alludes to a division of the empire in two parts: to the west and the east of Constantinople respectively (Nesbitt and Oikonomides 1991, 1). In the case of the *kommerkiarioi*, the identification of the West is more complicated. The term appears on seals dated to the ninth and tenth centuries, a period during which *kommerkiarioi* were fiscal officials, charged to collect the *kommerkion*, a 10 per cent tax proportionate to the estimated value (*ad valorem*) of the merchandise imported to or exported from Byzantine territory. Their area of jurisdiction was usually defined by the name of a city or a theme and in that respect the term 'of the West' represents an anomaly (Nesbitt and Oikonomides 1991, 12–4, nos. 1.23–9; Oikonomides 1986, 48).

It has been suggested that the *kommerkiarioi* of the West were in charge of the whole Balkan peninsula (Antoniades-Bibicou 1963, 198), a view that cannot be accepted, since for the same period *kommerkiarioi* for cities and themes of this particular area are also attested (Nesbitt and Oikonomides 1991, 12, no. 1.23). Currently, the prevalent view is to identify 'the West' with the empire's westernmost Balkan frontier and/or with the islands to its west. Nevertheless, no consent has been reached among scholars regarding the exact area(s) of jurisdiction of the *kommerkiarioi* of the West. There have been suggested: the Adriatic Sea and the Ionian Sea (Gerolymatou 2008, 214); the Peloponnese, Epiros and possibly Crete, that is, areas that are not attested on *kommerkiarioi* seals in the tenth century (Dunn 1993, 16); Corfu, where the luggage of Liutprand of Cremona had been searched in the 970s (Nesbitt and Oikonomides 1991, 12) and the theme of Kephalenia (Nesbitt and Oikonomides 1994, 1, 36–7, no. 8.30). Another view is that the headquarters of the *kommerkiarios* of the West were transferred according to the reigning political and military circumstances (Gerolymatou 2008, 214–5).

Vasso Penna, who studied in depth the problem of the *kommerkiarioi* of the West most recently, concluded that their seat must have been on the island of Kephalenia, a gateway to the west (Penna 2012, 150–1). Indeed, such a view is supported by two seals belonging to the imperial *vestitor* Joseph. On his first seal, from the second half of the ninth century, Joseph is styled imperial *vestitor* and *kommerkiarios* of Thessaloniki and Kephalenia (Nesbitt and Oikonomides 1994, 36, no. 8.30 with corrections; Zacos and Nesbitt 1984, 467, no. 1075). On his second seal, from the late ninth or early tenth century, he is imperial *vestitor*, *abydikos* and *kommerkiarios* of Thessaloniki, of the West and of the theme of Hellas (Nesbitt and Oikonomides 1994, 35–6, no. 8.30). The substitution of Kephalenia with the term 'West' is indicative (Penna 2012, 150). The complete absence of seals of *kommerkiarioi* of Kephalenia for the tenth century also corroborates this view (Tsatsoulis 2012, 167, Table 9.1).

Following, along with the majority of scholars, the identification of the West with the Ionian islands and perhaps the coast to the east as well, I decided to include in the present study three seals of known provenance belonging to *kommerkiarioi* of the West. They are all dated to the tenth century. Two of them were found in the Peloponnese (the Argos region and Corinth, Table 9.2, nos. 18 and 14 respectively), and one was purchased in the Bulgarian city of Rousse, on the southern bank of the Danube (Table 9.2, no. 24). On the basis of the latter seal, Ivan Jordanov argued that the *kommerkiarios* of the West served the Byzantine-Bulgarian trade relations after 917, when Develtos ceased to function as a *kommerkion* (Jordanov 2009, 425, no. 1205; Penna 2012, 149, n. 34). Although this view cannot be accepted, due to the meagreness of the existing evidence (one seal), one has to admit that the seals' provenances are confusing. There are no finds from the area identified as 'the West', while two finds come from the Eastern Peloponnese and one from the Balkan frontier. This is despite the fact that seals of *kommerkiarioi* tend to be found in the place of their issue (Cheynet and Morrisson 1990, 111–12; repr. Cheynet 2008, 90). Thus, it cannot be excluded that in the future new evidence will change our perception of the term 'West' in this context.

As already mentioned, seals referring to the place of exercise of the owner's function can also be problematic when it is not possible to establish a link between the Medieval and the modern place name. A relevant example regards the area under study and is thus worth noting. In 1994, John Nesbitt and Oikonomides published three parallel specimens, of unknown provenance, of the seal of George, *spatharokandidatos* and *tourmarches* of Spartari (τουρμάρχ(η)ς Σπάρταρου) dated to the tenth-eleventh centuries (Nesbitt and Oikonomides 1994, 19–21, nos. 7.1, a–c). The *tourma* led by George remains unattested in the written sources, as does the geographical name Spartari or Spartaro. The editors of the seals tentatively identified the seat of Georges' *tourma* with the village Spartari (modern Trikoryphon) in Thesprotia, Epiros. Its location on the route leading from the Ionian Sea to the interior could justify the creation of a *tourma* there (Nesbitt and Oikonomides 1994, 19). In 2006, another seal mentioning the *tourma* of Spartari was unearthed during salvage excavations in the city of Sparta. Its owner was John, imperial *protospatharios* and *tourmarches* of Spartaron (τουρμάρχις Σπαρτάρον), and it can be dated in the mid-to-late tenth century (Stavrakos 2010, 134–6). The similarity between Spartari or Spartaron and Sparta, the find-spot of John's seal, led Christos Stavrakos (2010, 135–6) to reconsider the previous identification and to suggest the area of Sparta in Lakedaimonia as the possible location of the *tourma* of Spartaron, as he reconstructed its name. Due to this new identification of the place name, the Sparta find is not included in the present study.

Moreover, even in cases where the place in which the function was exercised is known and can be identified with certainty, one cannot be certain of the place from which a document was sent. We usually assume that correspondence was managed from the capital of an administrative unit, such as theme, *katepanate* and so on. It is a logical assumption and, in most cases, a convenient convention. Nevertheless, when one tries to map contacts between neighbouring regions, as in the case of the two rims of the Adriatic Sea, it can become problematic. This is especially true in the case of officials combining different administrative areas under their jurisdiction, for example in the case of Leo, *kommerkiarios* of Hellas, the Peloponnese and Kephalenia, whose seal was found in Corinth (Table 9.2, no. 12).

Another case in point is the seal of Michael Maurex, *vestarches* and *katepano* of Dyrrachion (Table 9.2, no. 23), which was found in Dorystolon, present-day Silistra, in Bulgaria. Several seals of this person survive that help us reconstruct his course of honour (*cursus honorum*), while mentions of other commanders of Dyrrachion allow us to establish the period during which he was *katepano* of this city, namely from 1065 to 1068 (Seibt 1978, 168–71, no. 58). Although theoretically based in Dyrrachion, according to Latin sources, Mambrita or Mabrica, as they call him, spent most of his time in southern Italy: in 1066 he fought with the imperial fleet in Bari, in 1067 he achieved a victory against the Normans, menaced Bari and Taranto and reconquered Castellaneta (Seibt 1978, 169–70, no. 58). Did he send the document on which the Silistra seal initially hung from the Italian or the Illyrian rim of the Adriatic? We are not in a position to answer this question, but the reasons for which his seal was found in Bulgaria are clearer. His correspondence in the Lower Danube region can be connected to the presence in that area and, more particularly in Dristra, of the *katepano* of Paristrion, as well as of other military commanders, such as Basil Apokapes and the future emperor Nikephoros Botaneiates, who were dispatched there along with their troops in 1064–5 in order to defend the imperial territories against the Guzes (Jordanov 2003, 74, no. 25.2).

Another possibility that should always be borne in mind is that the reading of a seal and, consequently, its association to a given place could be erroneous. Thus, Theophylaktos, *episkeptites* of Longobardia in the second third of the eleventh century, whose seal was found in Sparta (Avramea, Galani-Krikou and Touratsoglou 1990, 256, no. 72[η]), can no longer be included among the officials active in the Adriatic, since the reading of a new specimen showed that the area of his jurisdiction was actually Longinias in Cilicia (Wassiliou and Seibt 2004, 149, no. 137). A more radical correction has been proposed in the case of a seal found in Lykotrichi near Ioannina in Epiros (Table 9.1, no. 27). In the first instance Vitalien Laurent (1975, 317–9, no. 6) attributed the seal to the *exkoubitos* of Longobardia Peter Pardos but Werner Seibt (2007) offered a completely different reading of the seal, identifying its owner as Peter Pardos (or Pleures or Pleuses), *protospatharios* and *kourator* of Bitola and Egibaton. Thus, not only the place of exercise of Peter Pardos' function was transferred from Italy in the area of the Great Prespa and Ohrid lakes, but the nature of his function also changed – from military to financial.

The number and nature of seals struck in a specific area can be affected by local customs regarding the use of seals. In the case of Byzantine Italy, its geographic position at the limits of the empire, along with a turbulent history characterised by frequent changes of overlords, led to divergences regarding the use of seals (Prigent 2011). For the areas of southern Italy that are being considered in the present study, a relative rarity of seals which is in stark contrast to practices observed in other areas of the empire, has been noted for the Middle Byzantine period. The phenomenon is particularly intense in Apulia where even high officials, such as the *katepano*, seem to make restricted use of seals, if we are to judge from the small number of surviving specimens (Cheynet 2007, 146; Prigent 2012, 608). Calabria in the ninth and tenth centuries presents a more regular use of seals, but a decline is observed during the eleventh century, a period that, for the rest of the empire, corresponds to the apogee of the use of seals. It has been suggested that we may connect these phenomena with particular documentary practices prevailing in these areas. On the one hand, it seems that seals were used almost exclusively by state officials and then only for official documents (*sigillia* or *hypomnemata*) issued by them. On the other hand, in the case of other types of southern Italian documents, for the confirmation (*corroboratio*) the presence of a notary and witnesses was preferred over sealing (Prigent 2012, 608–9). As a result of these particularities in the use of seals, the great majority of seals originating from Middle Byzantine Italy belong to military dignitaries of high rank and ecclesiastical officials.

Finally, it should be underlined that the number of seals for a given area depends on the intensity of archaeological research undertaken there. By the term archaeological research, I am not referring only to archaeological excavations or surveys, but also to the formation of collections with a local focus – either public or private. The Italian rim of the Adriatic has a long tradition in that respect, especially with regard to collections formed locally (Guzzetta 1999, 214). A different picture emerges for the Balkan rim. Not only has the existence of such collections not been recorded, but archaeologically revealed sigillographic finds are also scarce. This is especially true in the case of the coast within the borders of present-day Albania, an area that includes the port city of Dyrrachion (modern Durrës). This was an important administrative centre and military base, the capital of the homonymous theme, that was responsible for the defence of the Adriatic coast (Frankopan 2002, 67–8; Nesbitt and Oikonomides 1991, 40). Moreover, Dyrrachion along with Avlona (modern Vlorë) represented the western ends of the two branches of the Via Egnatia, a fact that augmented their significance as commercial centres (Ducellier 1981, 76). The relative abundance of seals from Dyrrachion in collections formed outside Albania – as an example I mention that the Dumbarton Oaks and the Fogg Museum of Art collections hold nineteen specimens originating from the city (Nesbitt and Oikonomides 1991, 40–6) – is an indication that the complete absence of finds from within the theme of Dyrrachion and the overall rarity of sigillographic finds from present-day Albania should be attributed to the lack of research and publications in this field.

Despite the aforementioned constraints, sixty-three seals will be considered in the present study, representing a significant increase in comparison to the twenty-two seals known to Cheynet and Morrisson (1990) almost thirty years ago. They belong to ecclesiastical officials, members of the central and provincial administration – civil and military – and fall into two categories. The first one includes seals found in the Adriatic, that originated both from within and outside this area. They indicate contact between the two rims of the Adriatic Sea. The second one comprises seals struck in the Adriatic which were found outside its limits; they can be used as an indicator of contact between the Adriatic and the rest of the empire.

Within the Adriatic

Thirty seals have been located at the two rims of the Adriatic (Fig. 9.1, Table 9.1). Five among them are still hanging from the documents they authenticated. Two seals belonging to *katepano* of Italy are conserved on documents kept in the archives of the basilica of San Nicola at Bari. The earliest of the two is dated in November 1032 and mentions Michael, *protospatharios, epi tou chrysotriklinou, koitonites*, judge of the Hippodrome and of the Velum, *epi ton oikeiakon* and *katepano* of Italy (πρωτοσπαθάριος, ἐπὶ τοῦ Χρυσοτρικλίνου, κοιτωνίτης, κριτὴς ἐπὶ τοῦ Ἱπποδρόμου καὶ τοῦ βήλου, ἐπὶ τῶν οἰκειακῶν καὶ κατεπάνω Ἰταλίας, Table 9.1, no. 2). The other one (Table 9.1, no. 3) hangs from a document (*sigillion*) dated in December 1045 and belongs to Eustathios Palatinos, *protospatharios* and *katepano* of Italy from 1045 to 1046 (Cheynet 2007, 156–7; von Falkenhausen 1978, 97, 204). The document was issued soon after Palatinos' arrival in Italy in favour of a local judge, Byzantios from Bari, who is being rewarded for his services to the empire by the concession of two villages in Apulia along with their main fiscal revenues and judicial privileges (Lefort and Martin 1986).

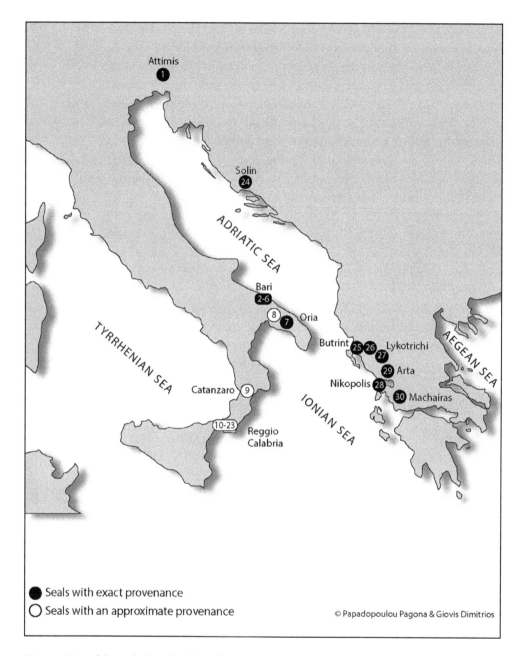

Fig. 9.1 Map of the seals found in the Adriatic.
Drawn by Pagona Papadopoulou and Dimitrios Giovis

The seals of two eleventh-century archbishops of Bari are also to be found still hanging from the documents they sealed. The earliest among them belongs to Byzantios (1025–35) and serves to authenticate a document in Latin dated in February 1031, kept at the archives of the Cathedral

Table 9.1 *Byzantine seals found in the Adriatic*

	Name, title(s), function(s)	Area(s) of jurisdiction	Date	Find-spot	Bibliography
			Italy		
			Gold bulla		
1	Alexios Komnenos, *despotes* (= Emperor Alexios I Komnenos, 1081–1118)	Byzantine empire (Constantinople)	1081–1118	Attimis, Friuli – Venezia Giulia (E)	Buora and Nesbitt 2010
			Lead seals		
2	*Michael, *protospatharios, epi tou chrysotriklinou, koitonites*, judge of the Hippodrome and of the Velum, *epi ton oikeiakon* and *katepano* of Italy	Italy	1032	Bari (A)	Oikonomides 1986, 82, no. 81
3	*Eustathios Palatinos, *protospatharios* and *katepano* of Italy	Italy	1045	Bari (A)	Oikonomides 1986, 88, no. 89
4	*Byzantios, archbishop of Bari	Bari	1031	Bari (A)	Laurent 1963, 730–1, no 923
5	*Nicholas, archbishop of Bari (in Latin)	Bari	1038	Bari (A)	Laurent 1963, 731–2, no. 924
6	*Nicholas, archbishop of Bari and of the holy seat of the Church of Canosa (in Latin)	Bari	1047	Bari (A)	Laurent 1963, 732–3, no. 925
7	P. or B., *spatharokandidatos* and *strategos* of Dyrrachion	Dyrrachion	10th c.	Oria, Apulia (E)	Unpublished

Table 9.1 (cont.)

	Name, title(s), function(s)	Area(s) of jurisdiction	Date	Find-spot	Bibliography
8	Seal of the *noumera* of Dyrrachion	Dyrrachion	c.720–60	Apulia (P?)	Seibt and Zarnitz 1997, 98–9, no. 2.3.8 (erroneous reading); Prigent 2008, 402–8
9	Christopher, bishop of Lesina (in Latin)	Lesina (Apulia)	9th–10th c.	Catanzaro (M)	Laurent 1963, 734–5, no. 927
10	Christopher, bishop of Calabria (in Latin)	Calabria	6th–7th c.	Reggio Calabria (M)	Laurent 1963, 710, no. 903
11	Isidor (?), bishop of Calabria (in Latin)	Calabria	7th c.	Reggio Calabria (M)	Laurent 1963, 711, no. 904
12	N., archbishop of Calabria	Calabria	7th–8th c.	Reggio Calabria (M)	Laurent 1963, 712–3, no. 906
13	John, *spatharios* and *doux* of Calabria	Calabria	750–850	Reggio Calabria (M)	Guzzetta 1999, 218–19; 223, no. 3
14	John, *spatharios* and *doux* of Calabria	Calabria	750–850	Reggio Calabria (M)	Guzzetta 1999, 218–19; 223, no. 4
15	Eirenaios (?), *spatharios* and *doux* of Calabria	Calabria	750–850	Reggio Calabria (M))	Guzzetta 1999, 218–19; 223, no. 5
16	Constantine, *spatharios*, *dioiketes* and *rektor* of Calabria	Calabria	750–850	Reggio Calabria (M)	Guzzetta 1999, 219–22; 223, no. 6
17	N., archbishop of Calabria	Calabria	First half of 9th c.	Reggio Calabria (M)	Laurent 1963, 713, no. 907
18	John, bishop of Rhoussianon	Rhoussianon (=Rossano)	Second half of 9th c.	Reggio Calabria (M)	Laurent 1963, 720, no. 914
19	Theodoulos, *spatharokandidatos* and *katepano* of Laousion	Laousion (=Ragusa/Dubrovnik)	Second third of 9th c.	Reggio Calabria (M)	Prigent 2008, 414–17

20	Judge of Calabria	Calabria	End of 10th–11th c.	Reggio Calabria (M)	Unpublished; Prigent 2012, 609, note 21
21	Georgilas, *protospatharios*, *hypatos* and *strategos* of Calabria	Calabria	11th c.	Reggio Calabria (M)	Guzzetta 1999, 222–3, no. 7 (erroneous reading); Prigent 2012, 609, note 21
22	*Strategos* of Calabria	Calabria	11th c.	Reggio Calabria (M)	Unpublished; Prigent 2012, 609, note 21
23	Nikephoros, *ek prosopou* of Rhegion	Rhegion	Second half of 11th c.	Reggio Calabria (M)	Prigent 2003, 24–5
			Croatia		
24	Paul, exarch of Italy	Italy	8th c. (723–6)	Solin (SF?)	Nikolajević-Stojković 1961
			Albania		
25	John, *patrikios*, *protospatharios* and *strategos* of Sicily	Calabria	First half of 10th c.	Butrint (E)	Papadopoulou 2012, 137–40, no. 3
26	Constantine, *protospatharios* and *strategos* of Dyrrachion	Dyrrachion	Early 10th c.	Butrint (E)	Papadopoulou 2012, 140, no. 4
			Greece		
27	Peter Pardos (or Pleures or Pleuses), *protospatharios* and *kourator* of Bitola and Egibaton	Bitola and Egibaton	Beginning of the 11th c.	Lykotrichi, Ioannina (SF?)	Laurent 1975, 317–9, no. 6 (with erroneous reading and dating); Seibt 2007 (without mention of Laurent's publication)
28	Niketas, metropolitan of Athens	Athens	10th c.	Nikopolis (SF)	Avramea, Galani-Krikou and Touratsoglou 1990, 248, no. 58; see Laurent 1963, 442, no. 591

Table 9.1 (cont.)

Name, title(s), function(s)	Area(s) of jurisdiction	Date	Find-spot	Bibliography
Overstruck seal				
29a First strike: John Branas	Arta (?)	Between 4 and 24 May 1203	Arta (E)	Koltsida-Makre 1990, 58–61 no. III; Wassiliou-Seibt 2016
29b Second strike: Leo Sgouros, *sebastohypertatos*	Nauplia, Argos and Corinth			
30 John, *protospatharios* and judge of Kephalenia	Kephalenia	11th c.	Machairas, Akarnania (E)	Veikou 2012, 249–50, 547–8

* Seals preceded by an asterisk are still hanging from the documents they sealed.

For the provenance of the seals the following abbreviations have been used: (A) Archive; (C) Collection; (D) Donation; (E) Excavation; (M) Museum; (P) Purchase; (SF) Stray find.

at Bari (Table 9.1, no. 4). Based on his name, older scholarship considered Byzantios to be a Greek (Laurent 1963, 731). The name, however, is absent from the rest of the empire but appears to be typical for Medieval Apulia. Thus, Byzantios must have been of local origin, a fact that is in accordance with the testimony of the *Annales Barenses* referring to his vehement albeit not continuous, as revealed by other sources, opposition against the Byzantines (von Falkenhausen 1986, 215–16). Despite these facts, Byzantios is the only archbishop of Bari who inscribed his seal in Greek: Βισάντηος ἀρχη(ε)πίσκοπ[ος δ]οῦλο[ς] Χ(ριστο)ῦ (Byzantios, archbishop, servant of Christ, Laurent 1963, 731). After his death, he was succeeded by the *protospatharios* Romualdo (January-April 1035). The latter's questionable loyalty towards the emperor led to his swift deposition and exile as soon as news of his election reached Constantinople (von Falkenhausen 1986, 216).

He was replaced by Nicholas (1035–62) whose close collaboration with the Byzantines is well attested in the sources. Although theoretically the archbishopric of Bari did not fall under the authority of the patriarchate of Constantinople, but that of the pope, and the election of its archbishop was made by the city's clergy and people, its political importance led the imperial government to interfere in the election of local prelates (von Falkenhausen 1986, 216). Nicholas' seal in Latin (*Nicolaus archiep(iscopus) Bareos*) authenticated a document dated to August 1038 (Table 9.1, no. 5). It is interesting to note that, despite the adoption of a Latin inscription, he did not use the traditional titulature of the prelates of Bari, that is, archbishop of Canosa (*archiepiscopus sancti sedis Canusinae ecclesiae*) but imitated the Byzantine form: 'archbishop of the castle of Bari' (ἀρχιεπίσκοπος κάστρου Βάρεως) even with regard to the use of a Greek genitive in the city's name. A composite form, however, combining the two traditions, is attested later on his seal authenticating a document issued in April 1047, currently kept at the archive of Badia di Cava: Nicholas, archbishop of Bari and Canosa (*Nik[o]laus archiep(iscopus) Bareo[s] sancte sedis Canusinae eccles(iae)*, Table 9.1, no. 6; von Falkenhausen 1986, 214).

If, now, we consider the seals found at the two rims of the Adriatic as a whole, we conclude that most of them belong to archbishops and bishops (ten specimens), the vast majority of which have their sees in Italy (nine seals). Ecclesiastical officials from the eastern rim of the Adriatic are absent from the list but the seal of Niketas, metropolitan of Athens, was found in Nikopolis (Table 9.1, no. 28). Among these ecclesiastical seals can be found the earliest examples comprised in this study, dating from the sixth and seventh centuries, a fact due to the early occurrence of the owner's seat on this type of sigillographic material. These are also the only seals in Latin. It is, however, indicative of the gradual Hellenisation of Calabria that, already in the seventh and eighth centuries, the seal of the archbishop of Calabria is in Greek (Laurent 1963, 712, no. 906). As we have seen, Apulia and, more specifically, Bari present a different picture in that respect, revealing the persistence of a Latin/Lombard tradition even under Byzantine rule (von Falkenhausen 1986, 195).

Another seventeen seals belong to the provincial administration, with a clear predominance of military officials – mainly *katepano* of Italy, *strategoi* and *doukes* of Calabria and *strategoi* of Dyrrachion, whose seals turn up on both sides of the Adriatic (Oria and Butrint). Seals of military officials represent 82 per cent of the seals belonging to the provincial administration and 47 per cent of all seals found in the Adriatic. It is a phenomenon easily explicable by the fact that we are dealing with a frontier zone of the empire and by the particularities in the use of seals in Byzantine Italy, described above.

Only three seals cannot be ascribed to the aforementioned categories. They are all of particular interest, since they are, for different reasons, of an exceptional nature. The first seal was discovered in Attimis, near Udine in northern Italy (Table 9.1, no. 1). It is characterised by two particularities: this is an imperial seal and, unlike the rest of the seals discussed here, it is not made of lead but of gold. It belongs to Emperor Alexios I Komnenos (1081–1118). Gold seals were an imperial prerogative and their use was reserved to the sealing of diplomatic correspondence addressed to foreign rulers and of important domestic documents involving grants of estates and privileges, called *chrysoboulloi logoi/chrysoboulla sigillia* (χρυσόβουλλοι λόγοι / χρυσόβουλλα σιγίλλια) (Grierson 1966, 239–40). They are extremely rare, with the majority of them being kept in the archives of the Mount Athos monasteries and in the Vatican (Grierson 1966, 241). Naturally, they are of extreme rarity as excavation finds, a fact that accrues the importance of the seal from Attimis. Another gold seal of Alexios I Komnenos was found during excavations at Hagios Georgios *sto Vouno* on the island of Kythera, Greece. A contemporary ecclesiastical seal, indicating the existence of an ecclesiastical (monastic?) community, was also revealed on the same site. It is, thus, possible that the gold seal of Kythera was addressed to the community in order to arrange issues of land ownership (Penna 2013, 429–30, 452).

The interpretation of the Italian gold seal, found outside the limits of the Byzantine empire, is more difficult. Its editors present the circumstances of its discovery and the history of the area it came from, but do not discuss how it might have ended up there. Should one assume that it sealed a document of diplomatic nature? Constantine VII Porphyrogennetos (913–59) (*De cerimoniis* 2.48) informs us that the weight of gold seals used on diplomatic documents varied according to the importance of the recipient. Thus, the caliph of Bagdad and the sultan of Egypt were entitled to seals with a weight equal to four gold coins (*tetrasoldiai*), the khan of the Khazars and the patriarchs of Alexandria, Antioch and Jerusalem to seals of three gold coins (*trisoldiai*), most other rulers (kings of Georgia, dukes of Venice, sovereigns of France and Germany and so on) to seals of only two gold coins (*disoldiai*) and the pope to a seal of one gold coin (*monosoldia*). The Italian gold seal, with a weight of 8.45 g, falls within this system and corresponds to a seal of two gold coins. Another, unprovenanced *disoldia* (8.38 g) of Alexios I Komnenos is kept at the Dumbarton Oaks collection (Grierson 1966, 251). It should be stressed, however, that the debased nature of the gold and their manufacture with the use of two separate gold leaves connected by a metal solder must have affected their weight (Grierson 1966, 245). On the contrary, the gold seal found in Kythera weighs only 2.16 g and corresponds to half a gold coin (*solidus*). Gold seals of this weight are absent from Constantine VII's account, but his list is anyway lacunary. Written sources testify to the existence of heavier seals, of twelve gold coins, whereas a seal of five gold coins (*pentasoldia*) of the Emperor Constantine IX Monomachos (1042–55) is preserved in the Musée d'Art et d'Histoire in Geneva (Campagnolo-Pothitou 2016; Campagnolo-Pothitou and Cheynet 2016, 23, no. 8). It is therefore probable that Constantine VII also omitted seals of a weight inferior to one gold coin (*solidus*).

Bearing in mind the absence of lightweight seals from Constantine VII's list of gold seals intended for diplomatic use, the low weight of the Kythera gold seal, and the fact that this was certainly appended to a domestic document, one wonders whether lighter seals were intended for domestic use (*chrysoboulloi logoi*, *chrysoboulla sigillia*), whereas heavier seals for diplomatic purposes. If this were the case, then we could be certain that the Italian seal reached Attimis through diplomatic correspondence, despite the fact that historical sources are silent regarding any connection between this castle and Constantinople. Of course, the available material is extremely limited to support or discard this hypothesis. Four gold seals of Alexios I Komnenos are kept in the archives of the Monastery of Lavra on Mount Athos (Lemerle *et al.* 1970, 10). They initially sealed documents of a domestic nature and could thus have provided the necessary confirmation. Unfortunately, their weights are not known, despite the fact that some of them are detached from any document. Until the weight of these seals becomes known, the suggested dichotomy between gold seals has to remain a hypothesis.

The second seal does not belong to a person, but to a group. I am referring to the seal of the *noumera* of Dyrrachion, reportedly originating from Apulia (Table 9.1, no. 8). On the basis of epigraphic criteria, the seal can be dated with certainty in the period 720–60; it originates, thus, from the period of maximal withdrawal of the Byzantine authority in the Adriatic (Prigent 2008, 402–3). The engraving is of mediocre quality, probably of a *boulloterion* produced locally. Moreover, the first letters of the first line of the reverse, which are crucial for the identification of the owner, are missing.

In the initial edition, this missing part was filled by an abbreviation of the word *doux* and the seal was attributed to the duke (*doux*) of the urban militia of Dyrrachion: [+*do*]*u*(*ki*) *meron tou Durrachiou* ([+δο]υ(κὶ) μερῶν τοῦ Δυρραχίου, Prigent 2008, 403; Seibt and Zarnitz 1997, 98, no. 2.3.8). However, the proposed reading is problematic. The brutal abbreviation of the military title as δου(κὶ), as well as the complete absence of a personal name, are both extremely unusual. For this reason, a different reading has been proposed: [+*no*]*umeron tou Durrachiou* ([+νο]υμέρων τοῦ Δυρραχίου). The *noumera* would normally be the regiments stationed in the city; in this particular case, it has been suggested that the term be interpreted as a civil body composed by the elite of the city, which made use of the ancient military titulature for reasons of prestige. It would thus reflect a change in the social structure of the city (Prigent 2008, 404–8). Be that as it may, the seal offers important evidence regarding the contact between the two rims of Adriatic in a relatively obscure historical period.

The third seal is an overstruck seal (Table 9.1, nos. 29a–b), a feature that, along with the well-known identity of one of its owners, accrues its importance. It was unearthed in Arta, during excavations undertaken in the courtyard of the old cathedral (Koltsida-Makre 1990, 58; Triantafyllides 1977, 167). As revealed by the older strike (Table 9.1, no. 29a), its first owner was a certain John Branas, *sebastos*. Another contemporary metrical seal of a *sebastos* John Branas is also known (Wassiliou-Seibt 2011, 137, no. 215). Despite the similarity in name and titulature, the two seals differ with regard to their inscription but also with regard to their iconography: on the metrical seal is depicted St Theodore, on the overstruck seal the Archangel Michael. As has already been mentioned, Byzantine officials were extremely reluctant to change their seals. Changes in the epigraphy were usually related to a change in the owner's function(s) or title(s).

Changes in the iconography did occur but the relevant cases are scarce. It seems thus that we are dealing with the seals of two different persons (Wassiliou-Seibt 2016, 332). We know that after the fall of Dyrrachion, a *strategos* named John Branas was taken to Sicily as a prisoner (Eustathios of Thessaloniki, *The Capture of Thessaloniki* 53; Niketas Choniates, *Historia* 317). After that incident, he vanishes from the sources but it cannot be excluded that he survived and returned to Byzantium. In any case, there is not enough evidence to support the identification of the *strategos* with the owner of the metrical or the overstruck seal.

John Branas' seal was overstruck by a well-known historical figure, Leo Sgouros, the magnate of Nauplia (Table 9.1, no. 29b). Leo declared himself independent around 1201 and captured Argos and Corinth. Taking advantage of the Fourth Crusade, he moved northwards and reached Thessaly where he married Eudokia, the daughter of Emperor Alexios III (1195–1203), and received the title of *despotes* (Brand 1991; Savvides 1988, 289–90). Since his seal considered here bears the title of *sebastohypertatos*, it should be dated from before that period, namely before 1204 (Koltsida-Makre 1990, 60; Wassiliou-Seibt 2016, 332–3).

Based on the seal's find-spot in Arta and the chronological indication offered by Sgouros' title, Alexandra Wassiliou-Seibt formulated an interesting hypothesis regarding the overstruck seal, that connects it with the events of May 1203, when the fleet of the Fourth Crusade spent three weeks in Corfu. According to the hypothesis, John Branas was the commander of Arta who, alerted by the approaching crusader army, felt the urge to inform the most powerful magnate of southern Greece. Thus, Leo Sgouros received a letter from John Branas bearing his seal. In order to acknowledge the reception of Branas' document, Leo overstruck the seal that was hanging from it with his own *boulloterion* and the object was sent along with Sgouros' reply back to Arta. If this hypothesis is correct, then the overstruck seal is the testimony of the urgent correspondence between Branas and Sgouros caused by the crusader threat and can be dated between 4 and 24 May, that is, during the time period spent by the crusader fleet in Corfu (Wassiliou-Seibt 2016).

If we consider the regions from which these seals originated, we conclude that twenty-six (approximately 87 per cent) are of local origin and only three (around 10 per cent) originate from outside the Adriatic – Alexios Komnenos' imperial gold seal (Table 9.1, no. 1), the seal of the metropolitan of Athens (Table 9.1, no. 28) and the seal of the *kourator* of Bitola and Egibalon (Table 9.1, no. 27). In one case, that of the overstruck seal of John Branas (Table 1, nos. 29a–b), we cannot be certain as to where it originated and it is thus omitted from the calculations. In their overview of the circulation of seals in the Byzantine empire, Cheynet and Morrisson (1990, 116; repr. Cheynet 2008, 93) expressed the 'principle of territoriality', namely that seals tend to be found preponderantly within the region in which they were issued. They established that around 80 per cent of provenanced seals are found in the area from which they originated, around 10 per cent from neighbouring areas and perhaps another 10 per cent from beyond. This rule is confirmed in the sigillographic material from the Adriatic, as it has been presented until now. Given the geographical particularities of the area in question, in which a sea divides the area into two, it would be interesting to apply this method also to each of the Adriatic rims.

In the case of the western rim of the Adriatic, that is, the Byzantine provinces of southern Italy, the territoriality principle is confirmed once more, with a sharp preponderance of seals that originated locally. Out of twenty-three seals found there, only three seals came from the other side of the Adriatic – namely two seals originating from Dyrrachion (Table 9.1, nos. 7–8) and one from Dubrovnik (Ragusa, Table 9.1, no. 19) – which represent around 14 per cent of the total of seals found in the western rim. It is remarkable that there is a complete absence of seals originating from beyond the Adriatic but also from Sicily despite the fact that this island is located in the immediate vicinity of the areas in question, has an important sigillographic tradition (Prigent 2012, 607) and seals seem to have circulated the other way, that is, from southern Italy to Sicily (Table 9.2).

A somewhat different picture is offered by the eastern, Balkan rim, where the principle of territoriality is not as pronounced as elsewhere. Only 28.5 per cent of the seals found here originated from the eastern rim, another 28.5 per cent from the western rim and 43 per cent from areas outside the Adriatic. The fact that this area yielded the only three seals which originated from outside the Adriatic (Table 9.1, nos. 27–29) indicates its closer ties to the rest of the empire. Despite the interest of these remarks, one should consider the limited number of the sample on which they are based (only seven seals) and the aforementioned lack of publications of sigillographic finds from significant military and administrative centres of this area, such as Dyrrachion. If, however, this picture is, even to a certain point, accurate, then the eastern rim of the Adriatic presents itself as an exception to the general rule regarding the circulation of Byzantine seals. This is undoubtedly related to the special importance of this area as the western frontier of the empire and the link between the centre and the provinces of Byzantine Italy.

The Adriatic and the Empire

The second group of seals to be commented upon comprises thirty-three specimens. They originated from the Adriatic, that is, the jurisdiction of their owners lied within this area – but were found outside the Adriatic (Fig. 9.2, Table 9.2): ten of them belong to ecclesiastical officials, fourteen to military dignitaries, six to financial officials and three to *archontes*.

With regard to ecclesiastical seals, the great majority (seven specimens) originated from Italy, while most specimens were found either in continental Italy – Milan and Naples – or in Sicily (six specimens). In this case too, they include the earliest examples of the list, dated in the seventh century, and are the only ones to bear inscriptions in Latin. They represent

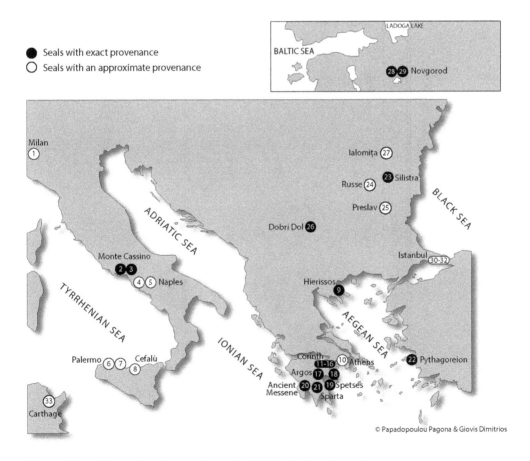

Fig. 9.2 Map of the seals originating from the Adriatic but found elsewhere. Drawn by Pagona Papadopoulou and Dimitrios Giovis

Table 9.2 Byzantine seals originating from the Adriatic, found outside its limits

	Name, title(s), function(s)	Area(s) of jurisdiction	Date	Find spot	Bibliography
			Italy		
1	Leo, archbishop of Calabria	Calabria	9th c.	Milan (C)	Laurent 1963, 714–15, no. 909
2	*Michael, *anthypatos, patrikios* and *katepano* of Italy	Italy	975	Monte Cassino (A)	Oikonomides 1986, 74, no. 70
3	*Gregory Tarchaneiotes, *protospatharios* and *katepano* of Italy	Italy	1000	Monte Cassino (A)	Oikonomides 1986, 76–7, no. 73
4	Romanos, bishop of Taranto (or Trani?) (Greek and Latin)	Taranto (or Trani, Apulia?)	7th c.	Naples (M)	Laurent 1963, 733–4, no. 926; see Nesbitt and Oikonomides 1991, 38–9, no. 11.1
5	Valerius, servant of saint Apollinaris (= bishop of Ravenna) (Latin)	Ravenna	789–810	Naples (M)	Prigent 2011, 214, n. 28 and 221, n. 63
6	John, archbishop of Calabria	Calabria	9th c.	Palermo (M)	Laurent 1963, 715–6, no. 910
7	George, metropolitan of Patras	Patras	First half of 9th c.	Palermo (M)	Laurent 1963, 472, no. 627
8	Nikephoros, bishop of Rhoussianon	Rhoussianon (=Rossano)	10th c.	Cefalù (M)	Laurent 1963, 721, no. 915

Greece

9	Alexios Komnenos, *sebastos* and *doux* of Dyrrachion	Dyrrachion	Beginning of 12th c.	Hierissos, Chalkidike (E)	Tsanana and Eugenikos 2018
10	Leo, *protospatharios* and *strategos* of Kephalenia	Kephalenia	—	Athens (–)	Avramea, Galani-Krikou and Touratsoglou 1990, 241, no. 8
11	Theophylaktos, *archon* of Dalmatia	Dalmatia	9th c.	Corinth (E)	Davidson 1952, 319, no. 2697; Cheynet and Morrisson 1990, 104
12	Leo, *kommerkiarios* of Hellas, the Peloponnese and Kephalenia	Hellas, Peloponnesos and Kephalenia	9th c.	Corinth (E)	Davidson 1952, 319, no. 2706 (incomplete reading); see Nesbitt and Oikonomides 1994, 3, no 1.5
13	Leo, *archon* of Patras	Patras	10th c.	Corinth (E)	Davidson 1952, 319, no. 2705; Cheynet and Morrisson 1990, 127/104
14	N., *kommerkiarios* of the West	West	10th c.	Corinth (E)	Davidson 1952, 319, no. 2715; Dunn 1993, 16–17
15	Stephen, metropolitan of Santa Severina	Santa Severina, Calabria	10th c.	Corinth (E)	Davidson 1952, 321–2, no. 2737; Laurent 1963, 717–18, no. 912
16	Michael, metropolitan of Dyrrachion	Dyrrachion	12th c.	Corinth (E)	Davidson 1952, 327, no. 2817; Laurent 1963, 562, no. 737
17	Andrew (?), *protospatharios* and *strategos* of Kephalenia and Nikopolis	Kephalenia and Nikopolis	925–50	Argos (E)	Yannopoulos 1984 (erroneous reading); Seibt and Seibt 1987, 333–4, no. 6
18	Eustratios, *spatharios* and *kommerkiarios* of the West	West	Last quarter of 10th c.	Argos region (Adheres range) (SF)	Penna 2012, 143–4

Table 9.2 (cont.)

	Name, title(s), function(s)	Area(s) of jurisdiction	Date	Find spot	Bibliography
19	Nicholas (?), *magistros* and *katepano* of Italy	Italy	11th c.	Spetses (SF)	Avramea 1996, 23, no. 18; Cheynet 2007, 145–6, note 9
20	Thomas, *tourmarches* of Kephalenia	Kephalenia	Second half of 9th c.	Ancient Messene (E)	Penna 2012, 151–2
21	Constantine, metropolitan of Patras	Patras	—	Sparta (E)	Avramea, Galani-Krikou and Touratsoglou 1990, 253, no. 67
22	Theodore, *spatharios* and *strategos* of Dyrrachion	Dyrrachion	Early 9th c.	Pythagoreion, Samos (E)	Gerousi 2012, 120–1, no. 1
			Bulgaria		
23	Michael Maurex, *vestarches* and *katepano* of Dyrrachion	Dyrrachion	1065–8	Silistra (SF?)	Jordanov 2003, 74, no. 25.2
24	Pankrates, *kandidatos* and *kommerkiarios* of the West	West	10th c.	Rousse, Silistra region (P)	Jordanov 2009, 424–5, no. 1205
25	Niketas Pegonites, *patrikios* and *strategos* of Dyrrachion	Dyrrachion	Beginning of the 11th c. (1018)	Preslav (M)	Jordanov 2003, 74, no. 25.1
26	Stephen Serblias, *protospatharios* and *kommerkiarios* of Longobardia	Longobardia	11th c.	Dobri Dol, Plovdiv region (SF)	Jordanov 2003, 110–12, no. 45.1; Jordanov 2006, 368–71, no. 645

27	Theodore, *archon* of Vagenetia	Vagenetia	**Romania** Ialomița (–) 8th c.	Bănescu 1938, 116–17 (*non vidi*); Cheynet and Morrisson 1990, 104
28	Theophylaktos, *protospatharios* and *strategos* of Nikopolis	Nikopolis	**Russia** Rjurikovo Gorodišče, Novgorod (SF) End of 10th–beginning of 11th c.	Bulgakova 2010, 74–5, no. 1.2.14 (a)
29	Theophylaktos, *protospatharios* and *strategos* of Nikopolis	Nikopolis	Sofijskaja storona, Novgorod (E) End of 10th–beginning of 11th c.	Bulgakova 2010, 76–7, no. 1.2.14 (b)
30	John, *protospatharios* and *strategos* of Nikopolis	Nikopolis	**Turkey** Istanbul (P) Second half of 9th c.	Cheynet, Gökyıldırım and Bulgurlu 2012, 314–15, no. 3.76
31	N., *anthypatos*, *patrikios*, and *strategos* of Nikopolis	Nikopolis	Istanbul (P) 10th–11th c.	Cheynet, Gökyıldırım and Bulgurlu 2012, 315, no. 3.77
32	N. Kyparissiotes (?), *spatharios*, …, and grand *kourator* (?) of Italy	Italy	Istanbul (D) First half of 11th c.	Cheynet, Gökyıldırım and Bulgurlu 2012, 300, no. 3.61

Table 9.2 (cont.)

Name, title(s), function(s)	Area(s) of jurisdiction	Date	Find spot	Bibliography
Tunisia				
33 Romanos, bishop of Taranto (or Trani?) (Greek and Latin)	Taranto (or Trani, Apulia?)	7th c.	Carthage (M)	Laurent 1963, 733–4, no. 926; see Nesbitt and Oikonomides 1991, 38–9, no. 11.1

* Seals preceded by an asterisk are still hanging from the documents they sealed.
For the provenance of the seals the following abbreviations have been used: (A) Archive; (C) Collection; (D) Donation; (E) Excavation; (M) Museum; (P) Purchase; (SF) Stray find.

30.3 per cent of the total, a percentage close to the one observed in the case of ecclesiastical seals found in the Adriatic (33.3 per cent). The high percentages noted in both cases are perhaps relevant to Vivien Prigent's (2008, 221) conclusion that in Italy the use of lead seals was more regular among the high clergy than among other social groups.

Military officials, with 42.4 per cent, are the best represented group for the reasons already evoked. In this case, military officials from Italy are not as prevalent as they were among seals found within the Adriatic. Only three seals of *katepano* of Italy are included in this group. Two of them still hang from their original documents and are kept in the archive of the Monastery of Monte Cassino in Italy. The first one belongs to Michael, *anthypatos*, *patrikios* and *katepano* of Italy (Table 9.2, no. 2) and seals a document (*hypomnema*) issued in May 975 confirming certain possessions of the Monastery of San Pietro in Taranto (Trinchera 1865, xxviii, 5–6, no. 7, plate 1). The owner of the second seal is Gregory Tarchaneiotes, imperial *protospatharios* and *katepano* of Italy from 998–9 to 1006 (Table 9.2, no. 3; Cheynet 2007, 150–1; von Falkenhausen 1978, 88–9; Leontiades 1998, 35–7, no. 1) who signed and sealed a document confirming some possessions of the Monastery of Monte Cassino in February 1000 (Leontiades 1998, 36; Trinchera 1865, xxviii, 10–12, no. 12, plate 8, no. 1). It is perhaps worth mentioning that this particular seal represents the earliest securely dated example, on which the formal order according to which information was to be engraved on the reverse of a seal (given name – title(s) – function(s) – surname) is attested in full. It represents the adoption by provincial administrators of a trend observed earlier, in the second half of the tenth century, on the seals of members of powerful families of the empire, namely the inclusion of the owner's family name as an indicator of his social position and alliances (Stephenson 1994, 189, 199–202). The third seal was the only one found outside Italy, and more specifically on the island of Spetses in Greece (Table 9.2, no. 19).

Unlike military officials from the Italian rim, represented exclusively by eleventh-century *katepano* whose seals were found mainly in Italy, military dignitaries of Dyrrachion have a prominent presence in the sigillographic material characterised by a wider distribution in space and time. The earliest among their seals is the early ninth-century seal of a *strategos* of Dyrrachion found in Samos (Table 9.2, no. 22), another two eleventh-century seals turned up in Bulgaria (Preslav and Silistra, Table 9.2, nos. 25 and 23 respectively) and an early twelfth-century seal was found in Hierissos, Chalkidiki (Table 9.2, no. 9), on the border with Mount Athos.

This latter seal is of particular interest, since it belongs to a well-known historical personality, the duke (*doux*) of Dyrrachion, Alexios Komnenos (Table 9.2, no. 9). It is known also from another specimen kept in the collection of the Fogg Museum of Art (Nesbitt and Oikonomides 1991, 40–1, no. 12.1). The *sebastos* Alexios Komnenos, nephew of the Emperor Alexios I Komnenos, was appointed *doux* of Dyrrachion in spring 1106. Anna Komnene (*Alexias* 13.3) praises his bravery and successful defence of Dyrrachion against Bohemond's assaults, which ended with a peace treaty in September 1108. It is not known whether Alexios continued to be *doux* of Dyrrachion after that date (Varzos 1984, vol. 1, no. 25, 147–52). Alexios Komnenos is also mentioned in a *chrysoboullos logos* issued by Alexios I Komnenos in August 1106. It informs us that he had been ordered by the emperor to determine the boundaries of the property for the Monastery of the Virgin Eleousa in Stroumitza. The land was then donated to the monastery by the emperor (Petit 1900, 28–9). It has been suggested that it was Alexios Komnenos' connection to the monastery that underlay the iconographic choice of his seal whose obverse is decorated with the rare representation of the Presentation of the Virgin in the Temple. In support of this hypothesis is the fact that the Monastery of the Virgin Eleousa celebrated its patronal feast on 21 November, the feast day of the Presentation of the Virgin in the Temple (Cotsonis 2009, 61, 68). The assignment regarding the property of the monastery was given to Alexios while he was serving as *doux* of Dyrrachion. One thus wonders whether his seal found in Hierissos, a town in close proximity to Mount Athos, might also have been related to a similar case. If Alexios were responsible for an arrangement – most probably involving land property – between the monks and the inhabitants of Hierissos, then his decision, authenticated by his seal, would have been issued for both parties and a copy of the document would have been conserved by the community of Hierissos. It is perhaps significant that the same building where the seal in question was found yielded another two earlier seals (Tsanana and Eugenikos 2018, 375), indicating the existence of a small archive. All this, however, remains speculative, since the archives of the Athonite monasteries do not include any relevant documents.

Besides Dyrrachion, two other administrative areas have a relatively strong presence among military seals: the theme of Nikopolis which was not represented among seals found in the Adriatic and the theme of Kephalenia that was represented by a single seal belonging to an eleventh-century judge (Table 9.1, no. 30). The two themes were at some point led by the same *strategos*, as revealed by a lead seal found in Argos

(Table 9.2, no. 17). The joint command of the two themes has been linked to the Bulgarian menace that was prominent in the second quarter of the tenth century from which the seal dates (Seibt and Seibt 1987, 345).

The theme of Nikopolis is represented by another four seals, two of which were located in Istanbul (Table 9.2, nos. 30–31) and two in Novgorod (Table 9.2, nos. 28–29). The latter belong to the same person, Theophylaktos, *protospatharios* and *strategos* of Nikopolis, a fact that is even more peculiar since they were found in different parts of Novgorod. A plausible explanation for the discovery of the seals in this remote area can be found in the fact that the Rus participated in the wars conducted by Basil II (976–1025) against the Bulgarians (986–1018) (Bulgakova 2004, 74–8, no. 1.2.14), which affected particularly the theme of Nikopolis in the second half of the tenth century (Soustal and Koder 1981, 55).

As for the theme of Kephalenia, it is represented by three seals – including the one from Argos (Table 9.2, nos. 10, 17, 20). A recent study (Tsatsoulis 2012) has questioned the eminence of the theme's military and naval forces as defenders of the western front of the empire. Nevertheless, it kept diachronically its role as a naval station on the way to Italy and its *strategos* always participated in expeditions to Italy, since Kephalenia was one of the westernmost themes of the empire. As expected, the importance of its services to the imperial fleet increased with the loss of the Byzantine strongholds in Sicily under Michael II (820–9) and Theophilos (829–42) (Tsatsoulis 2012). To these developments in Sicily and more specifically to events that took place before and after the fall of Syracuse to the Arabs (878), can perhaps be connected the only military seal in our list from the theme of Kephalenia that does not belong to a *strategos*. I am referring to the seal of Thomas, *tourmarches* of Kephalenia that can be dated to the second half of the ninth century (Table 9.2, no. 20). The seal, found in ancient Messene, is the only surviving seal of a *tourmarches* of this theme. It testifies to the close ties between this theme and the Peloponnese, also evidenced by the Argos seal mentioned previously (Penna 2012, 151–2).

The ties between Kephalenia and the Peloponnese, predominantly with regard to issues of financial administration, are revealed by the existence of the ninth-century seal of Leo, *kommerkiarios* of Hellas, the Peloponnese and Kephalenia (Table 9.2, no. 12). The seal was found in Corinth, but we cannot be certain in which of the themes that fell under Leo's jurisdiction it was issued. It belongs to another distinctive group among the seals of the Adriatic found in other areas of the empire, namely lead seals of financial officials (18.2 per cent). Half the seals in this group belong to *kommerkiarioi* of the West (Table 9.2, nos. 14, 18, 24) and have already been discussed.

Another interesting *kommerkiarios* seal is that of Stephen Serblias, imperial *protospartharios* and *kommerkiarios* of Longobardia, dated to the eleventh century (Table 9.2, no. 26). Its interest lies less in the function of its owner and more in its find-spot, Dobri Dol, a village near Plovdiv (Byzantine Philippopolis) in southern Bulgaria. Seals from the Adriatic found in Bulgaria normally belong to military officials who must have corresponded with their colleagues stationed there. Stephen Serblias, however, along with the *kommerkiarios* of the West, Pankrates (Table 9.2, no. 24), present exceptions to this rule. The Serblias family is well attested by the sources and the sigillographic evidence. Besides Stephen, another eleven members are known all of whom belonged to the civil administration (Cheynet 2010, 178–9, n. 133; Jordanov 2006, 369–70). None of them had any connection to, or presence in, the area of Philippopolis where Stephen Serblias' seal was discovered. Given this fact and the absence of any other information on Stephen in the written sources, we could perhaps envisage that his seal reached this area through private and not official correspondence.

The recent publication of the seals kept in the Archaeological Museum in Istanbul includes another seal of a financial official active in the Adriatic, N. Kyparissiotes, imperial *spatharios* and *megas kourator* of Italy (Table 9.2, no. 32). The seal was a gift to the museum from the Russian Archaeological Institute of Constantinople and its provenance from Istanbul, or at least Turkey, cannot be doubted. It can be dated to the first half of the eleventh century and its particular interest lies in the function exercised by its owner. Unfortunately, the first function of Kyparissiotes is illegible – perhaps *mystographos*? As for the second function, although brutally abbreviated – *m(e)g(alo) k(ouratori) Ital[i(as)]* (μ(ε)γ(άλῳ) κ(ουράτορι) Ἰταλ[ί(ας)]) – it can be reconstructed with a degree of certainty as grand *kourator* (Cheynet, Gökyıldırım and Bulgurlu 2012, 300, no. 3.61). The *kouratores*, along with the *episkeptitai*, were financial officials responsible for the management of the estates of public status (Cheynet 2010, 164). Besides the seal in question, no mention of any of these officials was known for Italy: the area of jurisdiction of *episkeptites* Theophylaktos whose seal was found in Sparta was not Longobardia but Longinias in Cilicia, as we now know thanks to the correction of the erroneous initial reading of the seal (Cheynet 2002, 111; repr. 2008, 266; Wassiliou and Seibt 2004, 149, no. 137).

The seal from Istanbul reveals that, after the partial reconquest of the Italian provinces, Byzantine emperors were keen to maintain certain estates under their direct control. To this end, men like Kyparissiotes were appointed as *kouratores* or *episkeptitai*. This practice is well attested from the tenth century onwards in the newly reconquered areas of the East – Melitene, Tarsus, Seleucia, Antioch and Cyprus (Cheynet 2002, 92, 116–7; repr. 2008, 244, 271; 2010, 175–6; Cheynet, Gökyıldırım and Bulgurlu 2012, 300). Kyparissiotes' family is of Constantinopolitan origin since their name possibly derives from the neighbourhood of Kyparission in which a church dedicated to Saint George was located – the same saint is depicted on the obverse of the seal in question (Cheynet, Gökyıldırım and Bulgurlu 2012, 300, no. 3.61). Although the evidence is restricted, Kyparissiotes seems to meet the standard social profile of financial officials involved in the management of imperial property, as has been sketched by Cheynet (2010, 176–82). He is of Constantinopolitan origin, coming from a family that, at least in the eleventh century, is active in the civil administration (Vranouse 1980, nos. 49, 345, 349) and, if the reading of his first function as *mystographos* is correct, he combines judicial duties along with his financial ones.

A final note should be made regarding the three seals belonging to *archontes* of Vagenetia, that is the area opposite Corfu (Table 9.2, no. 27), Dalmatia (Table 9.2, no. 11) and Patras (Table 9.2, no. 13). They date to the eighth, ninth and tenth centuries respectively and represent 9.1 per cent of the seals originating from the Adriatic but found outside its limits. The exact meaning of the word *archon* and its possible change through these centuries escapes us. Many of them seem to be linked to specific cities, mainly ports – as in the case of the *archontes* of Dyrrachion and Cherson – while others are connected to an administrative circumscription – Dalmatia, Chaldia and Crete. In a recent article, Prigent (2008, 410) argued that the former correspond to a civil body composed by elite citizens, while the latter are officials in imperial service who exercised their duties along with a *strategos*. It is unclear whether this model could also be applied in the case of Vagenetia for which there is no mention of a *strategos*. Given the seal's early date, before the establishment of a military governor on the neighbouring island of Corfu, it is perhaps possible to consider its owner as a local chieftain in the service of the Byzantine emperor during a period of instability (Curta 2006, 102–3). On the contrary, for the seal of the *archon* of the port city of Patras, it is its late date (the tenth century) that raises questions as to whether Prigent's model, regarding the identity of *archontes* in the eighth and ninth centuries, could be applied as well.

If, now, we consider the distribution of seals among the two rims of the Adriatic Sea, we conclude that twelve (around 36 per cent) of the seals found outside its limits originated from the western rim and twenty-one (around 64 per cent) from the eastern rim. The principle of territoriality is confirmed in this case, as well, with a preponderance of seals found in areas in the vicinity of the Adriatic, although regional differences can be observed in that respect. For the western rim, seven seals were found in mainland Italy (Milan, Monte Cassino, Naples) and Sicily (Palermo, Cefalù), three in Carthage, Corinth and Spetses, and only two in areas farther afield (Dobri Dol and Constantinople). In the case of the eastern rim, the large geographic area it covers renders more difficult similar calculations, but some observations can be made: three seals originated from Patras, two seals were found within the Peloponnese (Corinth and Sparta) and one seal in Palermo, thus confirming the principle of territoriality. In the case of the seals of the Ionian coast (including the themes of Kephalenia and Nikopolis, Vagenetia and the West), out of twelve seals, six were found in the Peloponnese (Corinth, Argos and ancient Messene) and in Athens and another six in remote areas (Rousse in Bulgaria, Ialomița in Romania, Istanbul in Turkey and Novgorod in Russia). An even more pronounced divergence from the principle of territoriality is evident in the case of the Adriatic coast proper (Dalmatia and theme of Dyrrachion), since none of the six seals originating from there was found in neighbouring areas. All find-spots (Corinth, Hierissos, Preslav, Silistra and Samos) are at a distance that exceeds 400 km from Dyrrachion. In this case too, the eastern rim departs from the norm, a fact that should also be attributed to its importance as the western frontier of the empire.

The study of the sigillographic material from the Adriatic Sea revealed some general trends that are worth summarising. First of all, several examples of seals found in or originating from the Adriatic demonstrate the methodological difficulties encountered by scholars with regard to the study of the circulation of seals. These difficulties are connected to internal characteristics of the sigillographic material, such as the reading and interpretation of inscriptions or the identification of a seal's owner and his exact function(s) and area(s) of jurisdiction. But they can also be related to external factors, such as patterns for the use of seals prevalent in a specific region and time period and the availability or absence of provenanced sigillographic finds from a given geographic area. In the particular case of the Adriatic Sea, the former is relevant to the western rim where the practice of sealing seems to be less widespread than in the rest of the empire, with state and ecclesiastical officials being those who utilised it and even then only in certain types of documents, while the latter concerns the eastern rim and the paucity of published material observed in some of its parts.

As expected, the majority of seals considered in the present study belong to members of the provincial administration, save for a few exceptions. The most notable among them is the gold seal of the Emperor Alexios I Komnenos found near Udine (Table 9.1, no. 1). Military officials and members of the high clergy are the two groups best represented among the studied material (twenty-eight and twenty seals respectively). Financial officials form the third most numerous group, with seven seals. The specificities in the use of seals in Byzantine southern Italy should account for the high numbers of seals in the case of ecclesiastical officials. It is indicative that 80 per cent of seals in this category originate from Italian archbishoprics and bishoprics. The same reason could be proposed also for the military dignitaries, at least for those active in Byzantine Italy. The decisive factor, however, for the preponderant presence of military officials in the sigillographic material from the Adriatic, is the role of this area as the western front of the empire. Its geographic position on the limits of the empire is probably the reason for the significant presence of seals of financial officials as well, since most of them (70 per cent) belong to *kommerkiarioi*.

With regard to the provenance of seals, finds generally tend to confirm the principle of territoriality, as defined by Cheynet and Morrisson. In the case of specimens found within the Adriatic, the preponderance of seals originating locally is clear. Their percentage (87 per cent) is very close to the one observed from the study of the whole Byzantine empire (80 per cent). When the two rims of the Adriatic are considered separately, though, divergences are noted for the eastern rim in which 43 per cent of the local finds originated from outside the Adriatic.

In the case of seals that originated from the Adriatic but were found outside its limits, there is a tendency for seals issued in the Italian Adriatic rim to be found in neighbouring areas, a trend that conforms to the principle of territoriality. On the contrary, the eastern rim presents again an exception to the rule since among seals originating from the coasts of the Ionian Sea, 50 per cent of the total was found in remote areas while in the case of the Dalmatian and Albanian coasts, the percentage reaches 100 per cent. Undoubtedly, this phenomenon is to a certain extent due to the significance of these areas as military zones where an important administrative and military centre – Dyrrachion – was located. In that respect, it is telling that all seals originating from the Albanian coast were issued by officials of this city. One wonders, though, whether the exceptional picture presented by the Balkan rim of the Adriatic, both in the case of seals found within the Adriatic and of seals of the Adriatic found outside its boundaries, could also be due to the restricted available evidence from the most important part of it, that is the Albanian coast.

This question, along with other ones posed in the present study, will remain unanswered until more sigillographic material of known provenance becomes available. It is hoped that the analysis of the circulation of seals from the Adriatic Sea has proven the value of this type of material for the study of a particular geographic area and its contact with the rest of the empire as evidenced by the remnants of administrative correspondence.

Note

After the completion of this study and, unfortunately, too late to be considered properly, four lead seals from Croatia were brought to my attention. Two seals of the imperial *spatharios* and *archon* of Dalmatia Nikolaos and a seal of Leo, *strategos* of Kephalenia, were unearthed in 2016 at the Kolovare beach in Zadar. They all date from the ninth century. Since the beach was formed by filling up the ruins of the city after 1944, the original provenance of the seals lies somewhere in the Zadar peninsula (Filipčić 2017). A fourth lead seal, belonging to the Emperor Maurice (582–602), was recovered at Ljubač near Nin, that is, the Medieval *Castrum Liube* (Dzino 2017–18, 91–2; Uglešić 2017, 125, 133). With the addition of these seals, the number of seals with a known provenance that are related to the Adriatic attains a total of sixty-seven specimens.

Acknowledgements

I am grateful to Richard Hodges, director of the Butrint excavations, for entrusting me with the study and publication of the sigillographic material from this site. I am also indebted to Christian Napolitano and Patricia Caprino for sharing with me the find from Oria. Vivien Prigent and Nikolaos Siomkos contributed significantly to the preparation of this study. May they find here the expression of my gratitude. I am particularly thankful to Ioanna Koltsida-Makre, Dimitris Minasidis, Bruno Callegher, Joanita Vroom, Aikaterini Amprazogoula, Dimitra Sikalidou and Christos Tsatsoulis for their invaluable assistance. Finally, special thanks are addressed to Dimitris Giovis who designed the two maps (Figs. 9.1, 9.2) that accompany this study.

References

Anna Komnene. *Alexias*, in Reinsch, D. and Kambylis, A. (eds.), *Annae Comnenae Alexias*. Corpus fontium historiae Byzantinae – Series Berolinensis 40 (Berlin, 2001).

Antoniades-Bibicou, H. 1963. *Recherches sur les douanes à Byzance: L'"octava', le 'kommerkion' et les commerciaires*, Cahiers des Annales 20 (Paris).

Avramea, A. 1996. 'Ἀνέκδοτα μολυβδόβουλλα ἀπό τα νησιά του Ἀργολικού κόλπου', Βυζαντινά σύμμεικτα 10, 11–25.

Avramea, A., Galani-Krikou, M. and Touratsoglou, Y. 1990. 'Μολυβδόβουλλα με γνωστή προέλευση από τις συλλογές του Νομισματικού Μουσείου Αθηνών', *Studies in Byzantine Sigillography* 2, 235–72.

Bănescu, N. 1938. 'O colecție de sigilii bizantine inedite', *Academia Română. Memoriile secţiei de ştiinţe istorice*, 3rd series, 20, 115–26.

Brand, C.M. 1991. 'Sgouros, Leo', in Kazhdan, A.P. (ed.), *The Oxford Dictionary of Byzantium*, vol. 3 (New York and Oxford), 1886.

Bulgakova, V. 2004. *Byzantinische Bleisiegel in Osteuropa: Die Funde auf dem Territorium Altrußlands*, Mainzer Veröffentlichungen zur Byzantinistik 6 (Wiesbaden).

Buora, M. and Nesbitt, J. 2010. 'A new gold seal of Alexios I Komnenos from the upper castle at Attimis (Udine, Italy)', *Travaux et mémoires* 16 = *Mélanges Cécile Morrisson*, 117–22.

Campagnolo-Pothitou, M. 2016. 'La bulle de 5 *solidi* (*pentasoldia*) de Constantin IX Monomaque (1042–1055)', *Studies in Byzantine Sigillography* 12, 71–82.

Campagnolo-Pothitou, M. and Cheynet, J.-C. 2016. *Sceaux de la Collection George Zacos au Musée d'art et d'Histoire de Genève*, Collections byzantines du Musée d'Art et d'Histoire – Genève 5 (Geneva and Milan).

Cheynet, J.-C. 2002. 'Episkeptitai et autres gestionnaires des biens publics (d'après les sceaux de l'IFEB)', *Studies in Byzantine Sigillography* 7, 87–117 (repr. in Cheynet 2008, 237–72).

— 2007. 'La place des catépans d'Italie dans la hiérarchie militaire et sociale de Byzance', Νέα Ῥώμη 4 = *Ἀμπελοκήπιον: Studi di amici e colleghi in onore di Vera von Falkenhausen*, 143–61.

— 2008. *La société byzantine. L'apport des sceaux*, vol. 1, Bilans de recherche 3/1 (Paris).

— 2010. 'Les gestionnaires des biens impériaux: Étude sociale (Xe–XIIe siècles)', *Travaux et mémoires* 16 = *Mélanges Cécile Morrisson*, 163–204.

Cheynet, J.-C. and Morrisson, C. 1990. 'Lieux de trouvaille et circulation des sceaux', *Studies in Byzantine Sigillography* 2, 105–36 (repr. in Cheynet 2008, 85–112).

Cheynet, J.-C., Gökyıldırım, T. and Bulgurlu, V. 2012. *Les sceaux byzantins du Musée archéologique d'Istanbul* (Istanbul).

Cotsonis, J. 2009. 'Narrative scenes on Byzantine lead seals (sixth–twelfth centuries): Frequency, iconography, and clientele', *Gesta* 48/1, 55–86.

Curta, F. 2006. *Southeastern Europe in the Middle Ages, 500–1250* (Cambridge).

Davidson, G.R. 1952. *Corinth. Results of Excavations Conducted by the American School of Classical Studies at Athens*, vol. 12, *The Minor Objects* (Princeton, NJ).

Ducellier, A. 1981. *La façade maritime de l'Albanie au Moyen Âge: Durazzo et Valona du XIe au XVe siècle*, Documents et recherches sur l'économie des pays byzantines, islamiques et slaves et leurs relations commerciales au Moyen Âge 13 (Thessaloniki).

Dunn, A. 1993. 'The *kommerkiarios*, the *apotheke*, the *dromos*, the *vardarios*, and the West', *Byzantine and Modern Greek Studies* 17/1, 3–24.

Dzino, D. 2017–18. 'Starokršćanski bazilikalni kompleks i grobovi u tumulima u Ljupču: Odgonetanje „mračnog" doba Dalmacije / Early Christian basilical complex and graves in tumuli in Ljubač: Deciphering 'Dark Ages' of Dalmatia', *Starohrvatska prosvjeta*, 3rd series, 44–5, 89–113.

Falkenhausen, V. von 1978. *La dominazione bizantina nell'Italia meridionale dal IX all'XI secolo* (Bari).

1986. 'Bari bizantina: Profilo di un capoluogo di provincia (secoli IX–XI)', in Rossetti, G. (ed.), *Spazio, società, potere nell'Italia dei comuni* (Pisa and Naples), 195–227.

Filipčić, D. 2017. 'Bizantske olovne bule s gradske plaže Kolovare u Zadru / Byzantine lead seals from the Kolovare city beach in Zadar', in *Bizantski studiji u Hrvatskoj – Retrospektiva i perspektive / Byzantine Studies in Croatia – Retrospective and Perspectives*, Colloquia mediaevalia Croatica 4, conference brochure (Zagreb), 22–3.

Frankopan, P. 2002. 'The imperial governors of Dyrrakhion in the reign of Alexios I Komnenos', *Byzantine and Modern Greek Studies* 26/1, 65–103.

Gerolymatou, M. 2008. Αγορές, έμποροι και εμπόριο στο Βυζάντιο (9ος–12ος αι.), National Hellenic Research Foundation, Institute of Byzantine Research Monographs 9 (Athens).

Gerousi, E. 2012. 'Two 9th-century lead seals from the area of the Byzantine quarter at Pythagoreio, Samos', *Studies in Byzantine Sigillography* 11, 117–24.

Greenslade, S. 2013. 'The Vrina Plain settlement between the 1st–13th centuries', in Hansen, Hodges and Leppard (eds.) 2013, 123–64.

Greenslade, S. and Hodges, R. 2013. 'The aristocratic *oikos* on the Vrina Plain, Butrint, c. AD 830–1200', *Byzantine and Modern Greek Studies* 37/1, 1–19.

Grierson, P. 1966. 'Byzantine gold bullae, with a catalogue of those at Dumbarton Oaks', *Dumbarton Oaks Papers* 20, 239–53.

Guzzetta, G. 1999. 'Dalla "*eparchia* delle Saline" al ducato e al *thema* di Calabria: Testimonianze monetali e diplomatiche', in Leanza, S. (ed.), *Calabria cristiana: Società, religione, cultura nel territorio della diocesi di Oppido*

Mamertina-Palmi, vol. 1, *Dalle origini al Medio Evo, Atti del Convegno di studi, Palmi-Cittanova 21–25 novembre 1994* (Soveria Mannelli), 211–24.

Hansen, I.L., Hodges, R. and Leppard, S. (eds.) 2013. *Butrint 4: The Archaeology and Histories of an Ionian Town* (Oxford).

Hodges, R., Bowden W. and Lako K. (eds.) 2004. *Byzantine Butrint: Excavations and Surveys 1994–99* (Oxford).

John Skylitzes. *Ioannes Scylitzae Synopsis historiarum*, in Thurn, I. (ed.), Corpus fontium historiae Byzantinae – Series Berolinensis 5 (Berlin and New York, 1973).

Jordanov, I. 2003. *Corpus of Byzantine Seals from Bulgaria*, vol. 1, *Byzantine Seals with Geographical Names* (Sofia).

2006. *Corpus of Byzantine Seals from Bulgaria*, vol. 2, *Byzantine Seals with Family Names* (Sofia).

2009. *Corpus of Byzantine Seals from Bulgaria*, vol. 3 (Sofia).

Karakatsanis, A.A. (ed.) 1997. *Treasures of Mount Athos*, 2nd edn. (Thessaloniki).

Koltsida-Makre, I. 1990. 'Overstruck lead seals: An approach to the problem with three examples', *Studies in Byzantine Sigillography* 2, 55–60.

2011. 'Μολυβδόβουλλα από ανασκαφές και γενικότερα γνωστής προέλευσης στον ελλαδικό χώρο', in Stavrakos, Ch. and Papadopoulou, B. (eds.), Ἠπειρόνδε. *Proceedings of the 10th International Symposium of Byzantine Sigillography (Ioannina, 1.–3. October 2009)* (Wiesbaden), 237–55.

Laurent V. 1963. *Le corpus des sceaux de l'Empire byzantin* (Paris).

1975. 'Contributions à la prosopographie du thème de Longobardie. En feuilletant le bullaire', *Bizantino-Sicula II. Miscelanea di scritti in memoriam di Giuseppe Rossi Taibbi* (Palermo), 307–19.

Lefort, J. and Martin, J.-M. 1986. 'Le sigillion du catépan d'Italie Eustathe Palatinos pour le juge Byzantios (décembre 1045)', *Mélanges de l'École française de Rome. Moyen Âge, Temps modernes* 98/2, 525–42.

Lemerle, P., Guillou, A., Svoronos, N. and Papachrysanthou, D. (eds.) 1970. *Actes de Lavra I: Des origines à 1204*, Archives de l'Athos V (Paris).

Leontiades, I.G. 1998. *Die Tarchaneiotai: Eine prosopographisch–sigillographische Studie*, Byzantine Texts and Studies 27 (Thessaloniki).

Melville Jones, J. (ed.) 2017, *Eustathios of Thessaloniki. The Capture of Thessaloniki: Introduction, Translation and Commentary*, Byzantina Australiensia 8 (Canberra 1987; repr. Leiden and Boston 2017).

Nesbitt, J. and Oikonomides, N. 1991. *Catalogue of Byzantine Seals at Dumbarton Oaks and in the Fogg Museum of Art*, vol. 1, *Italy, North of the Balkans, North of the Black Sea* (Washington, DC).

1994. *Catalogue of Byzantine Seals at Dumbarton Oaks and in the Fogg Museum of Art*, vol. 2, *South of the Balkans, the Islands, South of Asia Minor* (Washington, DC).

Niketas Choniates. *Historia*, in Dieten, J.A. van (ed.), *Nicetae Choniatae Historia*. Corpus fontium historiae Byzantinae – Series Berolinensis 11, vol. 1 (Berlin and New York, 1975).

Nikolajević-Stojković, I. 1961. 'Solinski pečat egzarha Pavla (723-726)', *Zbornik radova Vizantološkog instituta* 7, 61-6.

Oikonomides, N. 1976. 'L'évolution de l'organisation administrative de l'Empire byzantin au XIe siècle (1025-1118)', *Travaux et mémoires* 6, 125-52.

—— 1983. 'The usual lead seal', *Dumbarton Oaks Papers* 37, 147-57.

—— 1985. *A Collection of Dated Byzantine Lead Seals* (Washington, DC).

—— 1986. 'Silk trade and production in Byzantium from the sixth to the ninth century: The seals of kommerkiarioi', *Dumbarton Oaks Papers* 40, 33-53.

—— 1994. 'Pour une nouvelle lecture des inscriptions de Skripou en Béotie', *Travaux et mémoires* 12, 479-93, pls. I-IV.

—— 2002. 'The role of the Byzantine state in the economy', in Laiou, A.E. (ed.), *The Economic History of Byzantium: From the Seventh through the Fifteenth Century*, vol. 3 (Washington, DC), 973-1058.

Papachrysanthou, D. (ed.) 1975. *Actes du Prôtaton*, Archives de l'Athos VII (Paris).

Papadopoulou, P. 2012. 'Five lead seals from Byzantine Butrint (Albania)', *Studies in Byzantine Sigillography* 10, 133-42.

—— 2019a. 'Byzantine and early modern coins (9th-17th centuries)', in Greenslade, S. (ed.), *Butrint 6: Excavations of the Vrina Plain*, vol. 2, *The Finds* (Oxford), 41-54.

—— 2019b. 'Lead seals', in Greenslade, S. (ed.), *Butrint 6: Excavations of the Vrina Plain*, vol. 2, *The Finds* (Oxford), 55-8.

Penna, V. 2012. 'Two rare Byzantine lead seals: A contribution to iconographic and administrative matters', *Studies in Byzantine Sigillography* 11, 143-52.

—— 2013. 'Η μαρτυρία των νομισμάτων και των σφραγίδων', in Sakellarakis, Y. (ed.), Κύθηρα. Το μινωικό ιερό κορυφής στον Άγιο Γεώργιο στο Βουνό, vol. 3, Τα Ευρήματα, Βιβλιοθήκη της εν Αθήναις Αρχαιολογικής Εταιρείας 282 (Athens), 419-62.

Petit, L. 1900. 'Le monastère de Notre Dame de Pitié en Macédoine', Известия Русского археологического института в Константинополе 6, 1-153.

Prigent, V. 2003. '*Ek prosôpou* et *stratèges*, notes sur les subordonnés du catépan d'Italie', *Archivio storico per la Calabria e la Lucania* 70, 5-26.

—— 2008. 'Notes sur l'évolution de l'administration byzantine en Adriatique (VIIIe-IXe siècle)', *Mélanges de l'École française de Rome. Moyen Âge* 120/2 = *Les destinées de l'Illyricum méridional pendant le haut Moyen Âge*, 393-417.

—— 2011. 'L'usage du sceau de plomb dans les régions italiennes de tradition byzantine au haut Moyen Âge', in Martin, J.-M., Peters-Custot, A. and Prigent, V. (eds.), *L'héritage byzantin en Italie (VIIIe - XIIe siècle)*, vol. 1, *La fabrique documentaire*, Collection de l'École française de Rome 449 (Rome), 207-40.

—— 2012. 'Notes sur la tradition sigillographique byzantine dans le royaume normand de Sicile', in Martin, J.-M., Peters-Custot, A. and Prigent, V. (eds.), *L'héritage byzantin en Italie (VIIIe-XIIe siècle)*, vol. 2, *Les cadres juridiques et sociaux et les institutions publiques*, Collection de l'École française de Rome 461 (Rome), 605–41.

Savvides, A.G.C., 1988. 'A note on the death of Leo Sgurus in AD 1208', *Byzantine and Modern Greek Studies* 12/1, 289–95.

Seibt, N. and Seibt, W. 1987. 'Die sphragistischen Quellen zum byzantinischen Thema Nikopolis', in Chrysos, E. (ed.), *Nicopolis I. Proceedings of the First International Symposium on Nicopolis (23–29 September 1984)* (Preveza), 327–47, 559–61.

Seibt, W. 1978. *Die byzantinische Bleisiegel in Österreich*, Part 1, *Kaiserhof, Veröffentlichungen der Kommission für Byzantinistik* 2.1 (Vienna).

―― 2007. "Ένα μυστηριώδες μολυβδόβουλλο των αρχών του 11ου αιώνα στα Ιωάννινα', in Zachos, K.L. (ed.), *Nicopolis B. Proceedings of the Second International Nicopolis Symposium (11–15 September 2002)*, 2 vols. (Preveza), 583–6 in vol. 1; 393 in vol. 2.

Seibt, W. and Zarnitz, M.-L. 1997. *Das Byzantinische Bleisiegel als Kunstwerk. Katalog zur Ausstellung* (Vienna).

Soustal, P. and Koder, J. 1981. *Tabula Imperii Byzantini*, vol. 3, *Nikopolis und Kephallenia*, Österreichische Akademie der Wissenschaften, Philosophisch-Historische Klasse Denkschriften 150 (Vienna).

Stavrakos Ch. 2007. 'Ἡ πόλη της Ναυπάκτου ως πρωτεύουσα του θέματος Νικοπόλεως. Νέα δεδομένα για το ρόλο της στην ευρύτερη περιοχή των παραλίων και των νησιών του Ιονίου (9ος–10ος αι. μ.Χ.)', in Zachos, K.L. (ed.), *Nicopolis B. Proceedings of the Second International Nicopolis Symposium (11–15 September 2002)*, 2 vols. (Preveza), 571–9 in vol. 1; 391 in vol. 2.

―― 2010. 'Byzantine lead seals and other minor objects from Mystras: New historical evidence for the region of Byzantine Lakedaimon', *Byzantinische Zeitschrift* 103/1, 129–43.

Stepanova, E.V. 1998. 'Печати Сицилии VIII-XI вв. из собрания Эрмитажа', Античная древность и средние века 29, 290–9, 335–6.

Stephenson, P. 1994. 'A development in nomenclature on the seals of the Byzantine provincial aristocracy in the late tenth century', *Revue des études byzantines* 52, 187–211.

Triantafyllides, D.D. 1977. 'Βυζαντινά, μεσαιωνικά και νεώτερα μνημεία Ηπείρου', Αρχαιολογικον Δελτιον 32, Chronika B1, 157–80.

Trinchera, F. (ed.) 1865. *Syllabus Graecarum membranarum* (Naples).

Tsanana, Ai. and Eugenikos, P. 2018. 'Νέα στοιχεία από την μεσαιωνική Ιερισσό. Η ανασκαφική έρευνα κατά το 2013', Το Αρχαιολογικό Έργο στη Μακεδονία και τη Θράκη 27, 2013 (Thessaloniki), 371–9.

Tsatsoulis, C. 2012. 'Some remarks on the date of creation and the role of the maritime theme of Cephalonia (end of 7th–11th century)', *Studies in Byzantine Sigillography* 11, 153–72.

Uglešić, A. 2017. 'Ranokršćanski nalazi iz okolice Ljupča', in Faričić, J. and Lenkić, J. (eds.), *Župa Ljubač - zrcalo povijesnih i geografskih mijena u sjeverozapadnom dijelu Ravnih kotara* (Zadar), 112–33.

Varzos, K. 1984. Η γενεαλογία των Κομνηνών, 2 vols., Byzantine Texts and Studies 20 (Thessaloniki).

Veikou, M. 2012. *Byzantine Epirus: A Topography of Transformation. Settlements of the Seventh–Twelfth Centuries in Southern Epirus and Aetoloacarnania, Greece*, The Medieval Mediterranean: Peoples, Economies and Cultures, 400–1500, vol. 95 (Leiden).

Vranousi, E. 1980. Βυζαντινά έγγραφα της Μονής Πάτμου. Α' – Αυτοκρατορικά (Athens).

Vroom, J. 2018. 'On the edge: Butrint on the western frontier of the Byzantine empire', in Düring, T.D. and Stek, B.S. (eds.), *The Archaeology of Imperial Landscapes: A Comparative Study of Empires in the Ancient Near East and Mediterranean World* (Cambridge), 272–98.

Wassiliou, A.-K. and Seibt, W. 2004. *Die byzantinischen Bleisiegel in Österreich*, Part 2, *Zentral- und Provinzialverwaltung*, Veröffentlichungen der Kommission für Byzantinistik 2.2 (Vienna)

Wassiliou-Seibt, A.-K. 2011. *Corpus der byzantinischen Siegel mit metrischen Legenden I: Einleitung, Siegellegenden von Alpha bis inclusive My*, Wiener byzantinische Studien vol. 28/1 (Vienna).

2016. 'Das doppelt geprägte Siegel von Leo Sgouros and Ioannes Branas', in Stavrakos, Ch. (ed.), *Inscriptions in the Byzantine and Post-Byzantine History and History of Art. Proceedings of the International Symposium 'Inscriptions: Their Contribution to the Byzantine and Post-Byzantine History and History of Art' (Ioannina, June 26–27, 2015)* (Wiesbaden), 329–39.

Yannopoulos, P.A. 1984. 'Un sceau byzantin du stratège de Céphalonie trouvé à Argos', *Bulletin de correspondance hellénique* 108/1, 615–18.

Zacos, G. and Nesbitt, J. 1984. *Byzantine Lead Seals*, vol. 2 (Bern).

10 | Icons in the Adriatic before the Sack of Constantinople in 1204

MAGDALENA SKOBLAR

'Before 1200, nothing', wrote Pina Belli D'Elia (1988, 20) referring to Medieval painted icons in Apulia. The same situation was mirrored across the Adriatic in Dalmatia where the earliest preserved painted icons also date from the thirteenth century (Demori Staničić 2017). In fact, apart from Rome, the whole of the Latin West seems to have embraced icons simultaneously and overnight as soon as they started coming in great numbers from Constantinople following its capture by the crusaders in 1204. Rome was the exception because the pre-iconoclastic icons that were discovered there in the 1950s 'certify that Rome in late antiquity and the Early Middle Ages must be considered a Byzantine province as regards the venerations of icons' (Belting 1996, 25). Considering that in the West 'icons had neither a liturgical use nor a fixed position within the churches' (Belting 1996, 353), what was it that made Byzantine painted icons appropriated so readily there?

In this chapter I will argue that the Adriatic was so responsive to the wave of thirteenth-century painted icons because it had embraced Byzantine icons, both relief and painted, already in the eleventh century. The difference in the artistic medium was no barrier. Materials and techniques used to make icons ranged from ivory and mosaic to metal, enamel and marble. It was the divine spirit (*pneuma*) that sanctified matter and released grace (*charis*) that made them icons (Pentcheva 2010).

Bissera Pentcheva even argued that by the ninth century relief icons supplanted painted icons as a result of the iconoclastic controversy. According to her (Pentcheva 2010, 83–7), a relief icon represented an imprint of the Divine's visible characteristics on matter. She went on to posit that under the Komnenian dynasty, at the end of the eleventh century, the aesthetic climate changed from the understanding of the icon as an imprint (*typos*) to that of it being a painting (*graphe*), with which painted images were back in vogue (Pentcheva 2010, 208). Charles Barber (2011, 372) objected to her interpretation of the word *typos*, calling it too narrow, and disagreed about the Komnenian return to the pre-iconoclastic theology. In addition, Pentcheva's argument that between the ninth and the eleventh century relief icons were held in higher regard than painted icons was criticised by Robin Cormack (2015, 602) who stated that the use of a more expensive material does not mean that it was more 'effective in its visual impact of the faithful viewer'. Leaving the issue of which artistic medium was more prestigious to one side, Pentcheva's research has expanded the scope of art-historical scholarship which tends to focus predominantly on painted icons.

When Belli D'Elia stated that prior to 1200 there were no icons in Apulia, she made it clear she was referring to the painted ones. William Wixom (1997, 437) did the same when summarising the situation in the whole of the Latin West: he identified only two preserved twelfth-century painted icons that were imported from Byzantium, neither of which reached the West before the mid-thirteenth century, his examples being a *hagiosoritissa* Virgin at Freising and the icon at Spoleto Cathedral. Wixom's overview, therefore, agrees with Belli D'Elia's diagnosis. Hans Belting (1996, 330), on the other hand, acknowledged that imported icons reached the West 'at all times' and observed that the pre-thirteenth-century material is either unrecognisable because of later modifications or just echoed in artworks executed in different media. He too meant painted icons and specified that the painting of 'devotional images emerged in Italy in the thirteenth century with the violence of an explosion, expanding in wider and wider circles' (Belting 1996, 349).

This leaves us with the dreaded question of what an icon is. All answers start by noting that the Greek word *eikon* simply means 'image'. In his book *Icons*, Cormack (2007, 7–8) defined the icon as 'an image used for Christian purposes, a portrait icon of a saint, for example, providing a focus for the veneration and reverence' but clarified that he would use the word throughout the book to 'refer to the paintings on wood panels made for public use in the rituals and decoration of the Byzantine and Orthodox church and for private devotions at home'. In *Likeness and Presence*, Belting (1996, 47) argued that the definition of 'icon' varied from period to period but that, on the whole, it was 'a movable, autonomous image of any material, whether cloth or stone or metal'. The issue is the use of the term 'icon' in art-historical historiography rather than the history of the term itself. Any discussion of what an icon is and whether or not the sixth-century mosaic of the Virgin in the apse of Eufrasius' basilica at Poreč or that in the Durrës amphitheatre chapel depicting *Maria Regina* – dated by most scholars (Andaloro 1986, 107; Osborne 2003, 140) to the sixth or seventh century and by Kim Bowes and John Mitchell (2009, 588–94) to the ninth to eleventh century – constituted icons, would fill a book and goes beyond the scope of this study. Instead, I am focusing on non-architectural images since my aim is to address a problem created by art-historical literature, namely that of the studies on icons focusing on painted panels and their research findings being perceived as indicative of all icons.

Regardless of the aforementioned critical responses of two giants of icon studies, Pentcheva's work on relief icons breathed new life into the well-known fact that the Byzantine icon was a spiritual agent and not just a likeness in matter. With this in mind, it is worth asking if the thirteenth-century boom in painted icons in Italy and Dalmatia had precursors in any medium. Reinhold Lange (1964) and Charles Davis (2006) both provide two examples of relief icons from the Adriatic dated to the eleventh century. The first is the marble *Hodegetria* at Trani, depicting the Mother of God holding the Child and pointing at him and the second is the marble Virgin *orans*, the so-called *Madonna greca*, from Ravenna depicting the Virgin alone with her arms upraised in prayer. The material at Venice outnumbers that from all other Adriatic sites but because the Venetians looted Constantinople during the crusade of 1204 and brought icons in all media as booty, it is impossible to disentangle what was already there and what arrived with the crusaders. As Mara Mason (2012) argued in her article on the icon of the Virgin of the Girdle from Constantinople, the interpretative model that holds only the cherry-picked pieces were brought over and then copied by Venetian artists ought to be challenged in favour of a thorough reassessment of the material itself. According to her, many artworks that the scholarship holds to be Venetian copies are in fact imports from Constantinople. Arne Effenberger (2006, 25) suggested Venice was a channel through which the Ravenna icon was imported from Byzantium following Alexios I Komnenos trade deal with the Venetians in the late eleventh century and I (2012, 179) ascribed the existence of an icon of Christ at Rab in Dalmatia, the only extant icon from the Croatian side of the Adriatic from the period before the thirteenth century, to the Venetian control of the island of Rab in the 1090s.

These three eleventh-century extant icons were not isolated cases in the Adriatic. Primary sources provide evidence about the existence of painted and relief icons on both coasts albeit the Italian side outweighs the opposite one. I will begin with the Trani icon, as it is the earliest preserved icon in the Adriatic, before moving onto the others listed under headers which, when it has been possible to determine, relate to how they were obtained as this sheds light on dissemination channels and hotspots through which the Adriatic connections were flowing.

A Local *Hodegetria* from Trani

A small marble icon depicting the Virgin and Child is today located in the crypt of the Church of Santa Maria di Dionisio at Trani (Fig. 10.1). The posture of the Virgin, pointing at the Christ Child whilst holding him, makes it a *hodegetria* – a title meaning 'she who shows the way'. What makes this icon unusual is the fact that it is an inverted version. The Child is on the right hand of the Mother and the scholarship knows it as a *hodegetria dexiokratousa*. This rare iconographic type did not garner much attention apart from being mentioned as a version of the standard image

Fig. 10.1 *Hodegetria* of Delterios, 1039–1059. Marble, 39 × 35 cm, Santa Maria di Dionisio, Trani.
Photo: Francesco Calò. © Arcidiocesi di Trani-Barletta-Bisceglie. Source: Belli D'Elia 1987, 71

Fig. 10.2 Top: seal of Niketas, Bishop of Poroi, eleventh century. Lead, 1.7 cm in diameter. Bottom: seal of Michael, metropolitan of Traïanoupolis and *proedros* of the *protosynkelloi*, eleventh century. Lead, 2.2 cm in diameter. Byzantine Collection, Dumbarton Oaks, Washington, DC.
Photo credit: © Dumbarton Oaks, Byzantine Collection, Washington, DC

and André Grabar (1968) was the first to give it some attention in his article about the sixth-century *dexiokratousa* at Santa Francesca Romana in Rome. According to him, the key to the understanding of the source model for the inverted *hodegetria* lay in the seals produced during the Macedonian and Komnenian dynasties, which copied an *acheiropoietos* image of the Virgin recorded as being miraculously imprinted on a wall or a column of a church at Lydda in Palestine. The imprint of the Virgin, therefore, would have been a mirror image and it is this image that was removed and brought to Constantinople where the seals copied it. I argued elsewhere (2014, 194) that an eleventh-century lead seal may well have been the sculptor's source for the Trani icon since these small objects feature the *hodegetria dexiokratousa* type in bust form (Fig. 10.2), characterised by the Child positioned higher up the Virgin's chest as at Trani. The proportions of the Virgin and the position of the Child, both of which are perceived as clumsy in the scholarship on the icon, may have been affected by a process of transferring the image from a smaller to a larger scale. My reasoning was that a small-scale object the production of which involved a negative would explain how the mirror image came to be used: the *boulloterion* die in Byzantine seals would have had the standard *hodegetria* which, once imprinted, became the *dexiokratousa* and this end result was what was copied.

The icon is framed by a border with a Greek inscription K(YPI)E BΩIΘH TON ΔOYΛO(N) COY ΔEΛTEPHON TO(Y)PMAPXH which can be translated as 'Lord help your servant Delterios the *tourmarches*' (Guillou 1996, 192–3). The donor mentioned in the invocation, *tourmarches* Delterios, was a local man who worked for the Byzantine administration in Apulia as a judge and tax collector (von Falkenhausen 1984; Skoblar 2014). Mentioned twice in the sources – as Delecterius in 1039 and Dilecterius in 1059 – he lived through the 1042 Norman siege of Trani inflicted by Argyros, who eventually struck a deal with Byzantine representatives and withdrew. Delterios also witnessed the episcopate of Archbishop John II who held the title of *synkellos* and took part in a diplomatic mission on behalf of Argyros, now a Byzantine ally, to the court at Constantinople in 1053 (*Anonymi Barensis chronicon*, 152). The same John II was the recipient of the letter written by Bishop Leo of Ohrid, but orchestrated by Michael I Keroularios, which triggered the religious schism of 1054. His Byzantine ties made him undesirable in the eyes of Pope Nicholas II who deposed him at the Council of Melfi of 1059, at the same time allying the papacy with the Norman leaders (Cosentino 2008, 324; Gay 1904, 547; Loud 2007, 137; Vinaccia 1981, 311).

During this turbulent time, Delterios aligned himself with Byzantine models. As a local man he commissioned an icon, in the 1040s or the 1050s, and had it inscribed in Greek with an invocation typical of Byzantine officials. His choice of a *hodegetria*, which depicts the Virgin pointing to the Christ Child, the Logos Incarnate, as the road to salvation also indicates knowledge of contemporary Constantinopolitan trends. There, the cult of the *Hodegetria* icon, said to have been painted by St Luke, took off by the third quarter of the eleventh century and included the Tuesday procession in which it was carried to a different church each week and placed at the altar during the celebration of mass (Pentcheva 2014, 122, 129, 135). While it is not very likely that Delterios' icon would have been carried in a procession around Trani – as a marble icon it was stationary – the city of Bari has been highlighted by Aleksei Lidov (2004, 301) as an early host to a Tuesday veneration which would have come together with a *hodegetria* from Constantinople in the eleventh century.

An Imported *Hodegetria* at Bari?

According to secondary art-historical literature, Bari Cathedral owned a *hodegetria* icon imported from Constantinople at some point before 1034, that is, the year in which Archbishop Bisantius tore down the old church and started building a new one (Belli D'Elia 1988, 21). However, the source recording the beginning of this building campaign (*Anonymi Barensis chronicon*, 149) does not mention the icon. The assumption about its existence is based on the fact that an earlier document, of 1028, referred to the old cathedral as being dedicated to the Virgin Mary (Nitto de Rossi and Nitti de Vito 1897, 25) which is a shaky ground for the assumption about the icon, since Marian dedications were frequent among early Christian cathedrals on both sides of the Adriatic. Furthermore, in the eleventh century, the original dedication of the cathedral was adapted to include St Sabinus, a local saint from nearby Canosa, whose relics were rediscovered in 1091 by Archbishop Elias (Belli D'Elia 1987, 99). This implies that the cathedral could not compete with the newly arrived relics of St Nicholas of Myra to Bari and that it needed to attract the faithful with something that would rival them. If it had possessed a *hodegetria* icon and a Tuesday procession, it could have competed with the new shrine in town. In fact, even Belli D'Elia (1995, 15) subsequently stated that no Medieval sources confirm the existence of a Marian icon in the cathedral, while Nicola Bux (1995, 135) found no mention of the procession or other forms of icon veneration in the tenth- and eleventh-century liturgical materials from Bari.

Regardless of the above, Belli D'Elia (1995, 20) pointed out that the appearance of the *hodegetria* image on the late eleventh-century seals of the archbishops of Bari could indicate the presence of such an icon at Bari after all. The first episcopal seal with a *hodegetria*, dated to 1083, is that of Ursus, an ally of Robert Guiscard whose taking over of Bari marks the end of the Byzantine control of Apulia (Cioffari 1995, 119, fig. 16). Ursus' successor, the aforementioned Archbishop Elias who built the basilica of St Nicholas, used the same image on his seal despite a degree of rivalry between the two when it came to deciding where the relics of St Nicholas would rest (Cioffari 1995, 120–2, fig. 17). Archbishop Ursus, as expected, wanted them to be housed in the cathedral, while the sailors who brought them and a portion of the citizens of Bari, wanted a new church to be built in the saint's honour. Ursus had to give in after a fight broke out between his supporters and the people, after which Elias was chosen to supervise the construction of the new shrine.

Considering all the above, the evidence for a Marian icon at Bari is inconclusive. Such an icon could have been brought from Constantinople at some point before 1078, the year in which Ursus became archbishop as he was the first to use it on an episcopal seal. However, it also needs to be borne in mind that a *hodegetria* image was imprinted on many other eleventh-century seals and that in the twelfth century two archbishops of Bari chose the Virgin *orans* for their seals. The images on the episcopal seals at Bari, therefore, may not have been determined by the existence of a specific icon in the cathedral. The only piece of information relating to an image of the Virgin, either a fresco or a painted panel, in Bari Cathedral is an inscription of 1233 which records the consecration of an altar to the Assumption of the Virgin 'next to an icon of her' (*iuxta iconam ipsius*) in the south apse (Gelao 1995, 29).

There is evidence, however, that two sites in the vicinity of Bari possessed icons in the eleventh century which would indirectly support Belli D'Elia's hypothesis that one could have been at Bari Cathedral. In 1024, an icon is recorded at Polignano (Coniglio 1975, 80; Martin 1994, 225) while a church of San Prisco *in loco Sao*, today a small town of Triggiano around 11 km from Bari, had two icons which were provided with covers, as can be deduced from the mention of the linen cloths in 1067 (*sex vestiture lineis de cruces et due de yconas*, Martin 1994, 226; Nitto de Rossi and Nitti de Vito 1897, 45). The fact that the icons at San Prisco in Sao were covered with cloths speaks of their liturgical use. Both in Byzantium and Rome, icons were protected by a cover applied directly or suspended from a rod above them (Pentcheva 2014, 159). The *Liber pontificalis* (vol. 2, 10, 79, 96; Davis 2007, 192; 1995, 62, 91) records the donations of icon veils by three ninth-century popes: Leo III, Gregory IV and Sergius II.

If an icon really was imported from Constantinople before the end of the eleventh century, this may have occurred before 1071 when the city fell into Norman hands. We know that Archbishop Nicholas (1035–62) travelled to Constantinople in 1042 and that Empress Theodora donated an old court of the *katepano* of Bari and buildings around it to him in 1055 (Ménager 1981, 143). This donation was mentioned by Robert Guiscard, the Norman duke of Apulia, in a document of 1084 recording the donation of the same property, which also mentions that Archbishop Nicholas had the prestigious Byzantine title of *protosynkellos*.

As far as the Tuesday veneration of the Bari icon is concerned, given that the source cited by Lidov is a nineteenth-century edition of an eighteenth-century forgery purporting to contain a late ninth-century account of the translation of the *Hodegetria* from Constantinople in 733 (Garruba 1834,

75; Musca 1992, 163-4; Pinto 1995, 69-70), it does not constitute a reliable source of information for an alleged contemporary custom. The omission of such a procession from the tenth- and eleventh-century liturgical manuscripts also discredits the source cited by Lidov (Bux 1995, 134-5). In fact, the first time a *hodegetria* icon is mentioned in the sources is in the late sixteenth century when the confraternity of Santa Maria di Costantinopoli set up an altar for it in the cathedral crypt, while the existing icon of that name also dates from the same century (Gelao 1995, 27-30). The legend about the Tuesday rite may have sprung up around the time the cathedral started to be perceived as being dedicated to the Madonna di Costantinopoli.

A Processional Icon at Otranto

The lack of evidence about the Tuesday procession in eleventh-century Bari, does not mean that none existed in other Apulian towns. It was at its southern end, Salento, that St Nicholas the Pilgrim, soon to become the patron saint of Trani, saw a Marian icon being carried from one church to another through Otranto, accompanied by the singing of psalms and hymns for the forgiveness of sins in the early 1090s (Belli D'Elia 1988, 22). The icon in question must have been portable which makes it unlikely that it had been made of stone. The episode is recorded in St Nicholas' *Vita* (3.19) which also provides a fascinating insight into the engagement of the public with this holy image.

While taking part in the procession, Nicholas embraced an old man whose appearance struck him as that of a non-Christian and exclaimed that the same creator made them both. The crowd, recognising the man as a local Jew and angered by Nicholas' gesture, placed the icon of the Virgin before him and ordered him to adore it. When he refused, the citizens started beating him but despite this, he would not budge and, instead, lifted his eyes towards the heaven and shouted, 'Glory to you Lady, glory to you, mistress and queen of the world for it was through your name worthy of all glory and through your glory that my soul was glorified today' (*Vita S. Nicolai in Graecia* 3.19). Unfortunately, the *Vita* does not tell us whether the Virgin Mary was depicted alone or with the Christ Child, nor does it tell us which day of the week the procession took place. Nevertheless, two facts can be gleaned from this account: by the late eleventh century it was considered normal in Otranto to adore an icon and the purpose of the procession was expiatory.

The latter point deserves more attention since the role of the icon was to act as an intercessor in the forgiveness of sins. In general, processions with Marian icons started to develop in the second half of the tenth century in Constantinople with the *hodegetria* procession on Tuesdays (Pentcheva 2014, 130). Although the Constantinopolitan *Hodegetria* was perceived as an intercessor, the icon that bore that name – *signon tes presbeias* (σίγνον της πρεσβείας) – which was carried in an expiatory procession was the *Blachernitissa* icon. The latter image may have been the one depicting the Virgin *orans* with the Christ Child in the hovering medallion, that is, one of the several icons possessed by the Blachernai monastery, and its participation in the procession occurred after the triumph of Orthodoxy over iconoclasm (Pentcheva 2014, 145–6). The procession took place on Fridays and can be traced back to the sixth century (van Esbroeck 1988). The ceremony was referred to as a *presbeia*, meaning intercession, and its route started at the Blachernai shrine and ended at the Chalkoprateia Church (Ševčenko 1991, 51). The practice at Otranto seems to have echoed the Constantinopolitan model which by the late eleventh century reached the southernmost part of the Adriatic.

The Icon Exchange at Tremiti

By the 1060s the desirability of icons in Apulia is attested at Siponto, an old episcopal see some 100 km up the coast from Bari, towards the Monte Gargano peninsula. Re-established in 1022 after being suppressed and merged with the diocese of Benevento for almost 350 years, the bishopric of Siponto had a fully functioning pre-existing basilica which was equipped with new liturgical furnishings by 1049 when it hosted a church synod (Evans and Wixom 1997, 450; Serricchio 1986, 87). It was Archbishop Gerardus (before 1064–80), also spelled Geraldus, who acquired two icons from the abbot of the Benedictine monastery of Tremiti situated on the other side of Monte Gargano. He obtained both in the same way, by receiving them together with a precious fabric in exchange for a third of a salt pan.

The first transaction occurred in 1064 when the abbot of Tremiti was Ursus. The deed states that Gerardus ceded his portion of the salt pan in exchange for a good *scaramagna* and an icon for the use in the aforementioned church (*in cambio una scaramagna bona et una ycona pro utilitat(e) predicte ecclesie*, Petrucci 1960, 229). The *skaramangion* was a long tunic made of silk embroidered with gold thread which was adopted as part of Byzantine imperial dress in the mid-ninth century and worn on feast days

(Parani 2003, 61, n. 38). In a liturgical context, however, the term *skaramangion* denoted a type of fabric rather than a specific garment, from which vestments and textile furnishings were made. For example, an inventory included in a Byzantine monastic *typikon* of 1077 mentions a 'cloth for the holy table made of skaramangion' (Ball 2005, 44). The icon is not described in any detail, but the record clearly states that together with the *skaramangion* it was intended for the cathedral rather than for the archbishop's private use.

The second transaction took place four years later, in 1068, when Tremiti had a new abbot called Adam. Alongside another *skaramangion* embroidered with silk thread and worth 20 gold coins (*solidi*) – Gerardus received a gilt relief icon worth 30 gold coins (*solidi*) featuring an image of the Virgin (*una cona superaurata ubi sculpta est ymago Sante Dei genitricis Marie*, Belli D'Elia 1988, 21, n. 12; Petrucci 1960, 237). The two records are sometimes mixed up in the scholarship and only occasionally both get mentioned (Belli D'Elia 1988, 21; Guillou and Burgarella 1988, 186).

The fact that Gerardus could obtain icons from Tremiti Abbey on two separate occasions indicates that either the monks were in the habit of importing them from Byzantium or that they had their own artistic production going on, as Belli D'Elia (1988, 21) thought. Furthermore, the repeated transaction meant that Tremiti could dispose of two valuable icons which, in turn, implies that, unless this was a business initiative, the abbey had enough icons for its own religious needs.

The historical context of this revelatory exchange is particularly illuminating for the study of how icons were disseminated in the south Adriatic. By 1060, Tremiti had a close connection with Monte Cassino and even hosted a prolonged visit by its future abbot Desiderius who was a close friend of Guisenolf, the abbot of Tremiti from 1048 to 1054. Desiderius became abbot of Monte Cassino in 1059 and in 1066 embarked on a rebuilding of the abbey church sparing no expense when it came to decorating it. He had mosaic makers brought from Constantinople to carry out the work and asked them to train a number of his monks in their craft (Leo of Ostia, *Chronica monasterii Cassinensis* 3.27). Furthermore, he sent one of his monks to Constantinople with 36 pounds of gold and a letter of introduction to Emperor Romanos IV (1068–71) in order to procure liturgical furnishings, such as an antependium and a chancel screen, made of precious metals (Leo of Ostia, *Chronica monasterii Cassinensis* 3.33; Bloch 1986, 66). Leo of Ostia (*Chronica monasterii Cassinensis* 3.32) tells us that Romanos placed the relevant facilities at the disposal of Desiderius' emissaries through imperial privilege and that, among other things made of precious metals such as screens, beams and candlesticks, there were ten square icons 'made of solid silver and gilded in Constantinople' each weighing 12 or 14 pounds (Bloch 1986, 66). The monk sent by Desiderius also obtained five round icons 'painted by Greek artists in colors and figures' while a gilt-silver bilateral icon, also round, was sent to Desiderius as a gift from a local nobleman (Leo of Ostia, *Chronica monasterii Cassinensis* 3.32; Bloch 1986, 66). In addition, Leo (*Chronica monasterii Cassinensis* 3.32; Bloch 1986, 66) recorded icons made by Desiderius' own artists: three square icons made of silver had to match the ten Byzantine ones and were made 'in a similar style' whereas the aforementioned bilateral gilt icon served as a model for a counterpart he commissioned for it. While the gold antependium was definitely made in Constantinople, Bloch (1986, 69) expressed an opinion that the five round painted icons were prepared in Constantinople but finished at Monte Cassino by those Byzantine artists Desiderius had brought over.

Whether the round icons were painted by the artists in Constantinople or by the Byzantine artists who came to Monte Cassino, according to Leo of Ostia, they were attached to the chancel screen separating the sanctuary from the nave. His detailed description of the screen prompted two reconstruction proposals. One was put forward by Kenneth J. Conant and Henry M. Willard (Holt 1957, fig. 1) while the other was done by Jennifer Sheppard (1982, 241–2, figs. 2, 3). Conant and Willard placed the thirteen icons in a row on the chancel screen architrave from which hung five icons, each corresponding to a chancel screen bay, two on each side of the central opening into the sanctuary. In Sheppard's restoration (1982, 238) the weight of the thirteen icons and accompanying lamps is not carried by the same architrave from which the five icons hang but a bronze beam above it. Both reconstructions follow Leo of Ostia's description and position the icons at the front of the chancel screen where they were visible to the faithful. Sheppard (1982, 237) placed the lamps next to the thirteen icons and suggested that this number implied that Desiderius opted for the Byzantine model of the images of the twelve feasts and a Deesis. While the positioning of the icons and their proximity to the lamps bring to mind the comparisons with the Byzantine *iconostasis*, they were placed too high up on the chancel screen and obviously not intended for touching and kissing so that, in this case, one cannot speak of a Byzantine-style veneration (*proskynesis*).

Desiderius had his eye on Tremiti and throughout the 1060s attempted to gain control over it, succeeding only in 1071 when Pope Alexander II allowed him to appoint an abbot of his choosing. The presence of

Byzantine artists and the monks trained by them at Monte Cassino together with the personal links between Desiderius and Tremiti supports the view that the monastic community at Tremiti had access to both painted and relief icons that could be exchanged for the salt pans owned by Siponto Cathedral during the time when their possessions on the mainland were threatened by the Normans.

There is another important angle to the role of Monte Cassino in this case and that is Gerardus's background. Before being elected as archbishop of Siponto in 1063 or 1064, Gerardus was a monk at Monte Cassino (Bloch 1986, 118; Kehr and Holtzmann 1986, 236, n. 14; Loud 2007, 183) under Desiderius and it is likely that he would have been aware of the abbot's plans to bring the artists and artworks from Byzantium. Desiderius' building campaign lasted from 1066 until 1071 when the new abbey church was consecrated – a service which Gerardus attended – while the arrival of the antependium, the chancel screen and its icons would have occurred between 1068 and 1071: Leo of Ostia stated that Emperor Romanos IV helped Desiderius' emissaries find suitable craftsmen and these are the years between which he ruled (Bloch 1986, 67). The icon that Gerardus obtained in 1066 predates the presence of Byzantine imports at Monte Cassino but, nonetheless, belongs to the sphere of Desiderius's influence.

The *Icona Vetere* at Foggia

The *Icona vetere* at Foggia Cathedral, also known in the literature by its modern name of Madonna dei Sette Veli, is entangled in the myth of the origin of Foggia. Seventeenth- and eighteenth-century accounts narrate how it was found wrapped in veils in a marshy pond with three burning lights in 1062 or 1073 (Bianco 2000, 28). Here it is worth mentioning that the place name 'Foggia', sometimes also recorded as *Fogia* or *Fovea* means a pit or marsh. Together with Robert Guiscard's presence in the city in 1080 and the existence of a crypt under the cathedral, these sources cemented the belief that Guiscard built the crypt to house the icon in the second half of the eleventh century. However, there is no evidence for this and the *terminus ante quem* remains the late twelfth century when the new cathedral was dedicated to the icon (Belli D'Elia 1989–1990, 94, n. 1). The Church of *Sancta Maria de Fovea* was mentioned for the first time in a document of 1089 when Guiscard's son, Duke Roger Borsa of Apulia, donated it to the Church of St Nicholas at Bari (Calò Mariani 1997, 13; Nitti de Vito 1903, 28–9).

Fig. 10.3 Right: *Icona vetere*, c.1090. Egg tempera on panel, 152 × 80 cm, Foggia Cathedral. Left: schematic drawing of the icon.
© Arcidiocesi di Foggia-Bovino. Redrawn by Dalibor Popovič after Belli D'Elia 1989–1990, 91, fig. 2

A late eleventh- or a twelfth-century date is indicated by the art-historical analysis of the icon (Fig. 10.3) itself depicting the seated Virgin with the Child (Belli D'Elia 1989–1990, 91; Bianco 2000, 28; Calò Mariani 1997, 74). Although the painted panel was damaged by water at some point before the seventeenth century, when it was covered with a silver mount and hidden behind veils and a textile cover which is how it appears today, Belli D'Elia (1989–1990, 92) found parallels for it in local eleventh- and twelfth-century manuscripts and frescoes. She argued that the Virgin's costume and the absence of a *maphorium* belong to the iconography of *Maria Regina* or *Mater Ecclesia* and as such point to Rome and the Early Christian tradition rather than Byzantium (Belli D'Elia 1989–1990, 92).

The Icon That Came from the Sea to Ravenna

Some Adriatic communities distilled the fascination of their icons' origin in Byzantium into legends that tell of their miraculous arrival by the sea. This was not a phenomenon limited to the Adriatic: Byzantine sources based on *The Letter of the Three Patriarchs*, dated to the mid-ninth century, narrate how in the eighth century Patriarch Germanos of Constantinople cast two icons, one of the Virgin and the other of Christ, into the sea to spare them from being destroyed by iconoclasts and that they made it to Rome in one day (Dobschütz 1903, 174; Walter 1997, lxii). Pope Gregory II saw the icon of Christ standing on the Tiber 'like a column of fire' and took it to St Peter's basilica (Angelidi 2015, 47–8; Munitiz 1997, 48). The second icon was a copy of the Lydda image of the Virgin and after the end of iconoclasm it was returned to Constantinople and placed in the Chalkoprateia Church whereupon it came to be known as *Maria Romaia* (Belting 1996, 63, 190; Pentcheva 2014, 122–3, 229, n. 45).

Back in the Adriatic, a very Constantinopolitan-looking icon (Fig. 10.4), mentioned for the first time in 1613 (Maruli 1613, vol. 1, 20), was believed to have travelled over the sea to Ravenna. Located today in the new Church of Santa Maria in Porto, built between the sixteenth and the eighteenth century, this wonderfully preserved relief icon of the Virgin *orans*, made of Parian marble, has been dated to the late eleventh century by Clementina Rizzardi (2001, 44–7). The Ravenna icon belongs to the group of Byzantine relief icons from the period between the eleventh and the thirteenth century all of which depict the standing Virgin with her hands raised in prayer in various states of preservation, housed in the museums at Istanbul, Thessaloniki and Berlin (Effenberger 2006, 9–36; Rizzardi 2001, 45–6). Among them, the so-called Mangana icon, at the Archaeological Museum at Istanbul, is the earliest. It has been dated to the mid-eleventh century and can be linked to Emperor Constantine IX Monomachos' monastery of St George which was adjacent to the Mangana Palace (Effenberger 2006, 16; Lange 1964, 43–4). The hole drilled in the Virgin's right palm originally enabled water to flow through it as was the case with other fountain icons that followed the model of the tenth-century stone icon of the Virgin with

Fig. 10.4 *Madonna greca*, c.1095. Marble, 116 × 60 cm, Santa Maria in Porto, Ravenna.
© Istituzione Biblioteca Classense. Source: Fondo Mario Mazzotti, CARTOL MAZ A100 00072 0040, inv. POS 439

pierced hands from the Blachernai monastery mentioned by Constantine Porphyrogennetos (*De cerimoniis* 2.12). The icons from Thessaloniki and Berlin have been dated by Arne Effenberger (2006, 9, 22) to the thirteenth century which makes the *Madonna greca* from Ravenna the chronologically closest parallel to the Mangana prototype.

The cult of the *Madonna greca* is believed to have developed at the turn of the twelfth century near the old Church of Santa Maria in Porto, no longer extant, which stood outside the city walls near the port of Classe (Tosti 2003, 56). According to a local legend, first recorded in the seventeenth century (Fabri 1664, 279; 1675, 361), but fleshed out by the nineteenth (Sulfrini, 1887), the icon appeared at dawn on 8 April 1100, that year's *domenica in albis* (first Sunday after Easter), floating on a wave flanked by two angels (Mazzotti 1991, 35). The miraculous arrival of icons by the sea meant that they were foreign to the places they arrived at (Belting 1996, 330–48; Weinryb 2011, 322). Occasionally, other objects washed ashore, for example a sarcophagus with the relics of St Euphemia arrived in this manner at Rovinj in Istria in the early ninth century (Križman 2000, 74). Effenberger (2006, 25) suggested the Ravenna icon may have been imported from Byzantium via Venice in the late eleventh century, following Alexios I Komnenos' trade deal with the Venetians. Regardless of how the icon came to Ravenna, when it did appear 'bearing no inscriptions and following Byzantine traditions of making, it could not have been regarded as anything but a working miraculous or cult image' (Weinryb 2011, 329).

The arrival of the Ravenna icon was linked in the local imagination to Pietro degli Onesti, a cleric and nobleman who, according to the aforementioned legend, had built the Church of St Mary on the Adriatic shore as a fulfilment of a vow he had made to the Virgin during a storm while returning home on a ship from the Holy Land in 1096 (Mazzotti 1991, 34; Rizzardi 2001, 44). One year after the church was completed and a community of canons established next to it, while Pietro and the canons were celebrating matins, a bright light coming from the direction of the sea captured their attention. Having rushed outside, they saw the icon hovering upon the surface of the sea in the company of two angels whose faces were shining brightly. When the canons attempted to take the icon ashore, they could not hold on to it and Pietro was the only one who able to receive it and transport it to the church (Mazzotti 1991, 35–6).

Leaving the stuff of legends aside, the old Church of Santa Maria in Porto (the addition of *fuori* in the scholarship was added to distinguish it from the new church within the city walls to which the religious community relocated) was recorded for the first time in two documents of 1103 with which several local landowners, one of whom was Onesto, son of a certain Petrus de Onesto, transferred their rights to the church to four men listed as its *instauratores* (Fantuzzi 1802, 260, 96; Mazzotti 1991, 28, 30). The term has been understood as 'restorers' by some and 'founders' by others and even Mario Mazzotti, who researched the history of the church extensively, argued in one place that the church was renovated (1991, 32, 46) and in another that it was built anew (1991, 69). Judging from the primary sources, before 1103, the church had had more than one owner all of whom renounced their rights for the benefit of the four *instauratores* who, according to Mazzotti (1991, 46), were laymen and not clerics. Another source from the same year, recording a donation of a salt pan to the church, mentioned that the recipient of the donation was *prior Petrus* (Fantuzzi 1802, 260). Until 1118, this Petrus cropped up in all the land donations for Santa Maria in Porto as the community's leader and was referred to in the sources variably as *clericus, prior, rector* and *praepositus*. Given that by 1120 the new *prior* was Ioannes, it is safe to assume that Petrus was no longer alive which is why he can be identified with *Petrus peccans* who died in 1119 and who was buried in a Late Antique sarcophagus in the church and honoured in a metric epigraph, restored in 1721 (Mazzotti 1991, 67) which says the following:

> Hic situs est Petrus Peccans cognomine dictus
> Cui dedit hanc aulam meritorum condere Christus
> Anno milleno conteno debita soluit
> In decimoque nono defunctus corpore dormit
> Quarto kal. aprilis

> Peter, by name the Sinner, here lies still
> Who built our house for merit, by God's will
> In the year 1119 he paid his debt
> And March the 27th, lay down and slept
> (de Montfaucon 1725, 70)

The scholarship holds that this Petrus *clericus* was none other than the Pietro degli Onesti from the legend of the *Madonna greca*, who built the church as a vow to the Virgin and who was allowed to pick up the icon from the sea. However, there is no evidence that Petrus *clericus*, the *prior* of a community of canons at Porto mentioned in the epitaph, was from the Onesti family. The legend seems to have jumbled together the lineage of St Romuald, a member of that noble family who founded the Camaldolese order, with that of the original co-owner of the church, Onesto, son of Petrus de Onesto. To make matters worse, a certain

Fig. 10.5 Mosaic of the Virgin *orans* from Ravenna Cathedral, 1112. Stone and glass tesserae, 185 × 100 cm, Museo Arcivescovile, Ravenna.
© Arcidiocesi di Ravenna-Cervia

Pietro *peccator* was mentioned as being in the Church of Our Lady on the Adriatic shore in Dante's *Paradise* (21.122). There, we find Peter Damian, another famous Ravennate saint, in the seventh heaven of the blessed souls and he tells us that: 'I was, in that place, Peter Damian, / and Peter the Sinner, in the Abbey of / Our Lady on the Adriatic shore' (Dante 2000, 523). What can be garnered from a re-examination of sources about Santa Maria in Porto and the *Madonna greca* is that the icon was used by a newly established collegiate community centred around a church of St Mary that was either remodelled or recently constructed at the turn of the twelfth century.

Several years later, in 1112, Ravenna Cathedral was decorated with a new mosaic in the main apse which was demolished together with the rest of the old cathedral between 1734 and 1741 (Carile 2016, 81; Rizzardi 2001, 45) but of which some fragments, such as a figure of the Virgin *orans* (Fig. 10.5), still remain. Maria Cristina Carile (2016, 82) noted that in the mosaic, the Virgin is framed by drawn curtains and explained this unusual detail as referring to a veil or curtain that would have protected the marble icon at Porto when not in use. According to her, the apse mosaic promoted the new icon and guaranteed its place in the local visual culture which saw the Virgin *orans* become 'part of the civic identity' (Carile 2016, 82).

The connection between the image of the Virgin with arms raised in prayer and her role as intercessor was promoted by post-iconoclast emperors. In the ninth century Michael III had it depicted in the apse of the Pharos Chapel in the imperial palace at Constantinople (Jenkins and Mango 1956, 125; Mango 1958, 177–90) and Leo VI used it on his gold coins (Pentcheva 2014, 30, fig. 22). Thus, in Byzantium the Virgin *orans* came to be understood as the protector of the imperial house and the military and this iconographic type also seems to have featured in the *Chrysotriklinos* and the Blachernai Church (Pentcheva 2014, 28). The power of her intercession had a wide appeal and in the twelfth century a figure of the Virgin *orans* was chosen to be the only image filling the golden expanse of the conch in the apse of San Donato on the island of Murano in the Venetian lagoon.

The Problem of Dalmatia

I have mentioned above a relief icon of Christ at Rab (Fig. 10.6) dated to the late eleventh century (Skoblar 2012). This is the only icon from the territory of Dalmatia that we know of from the period prior to the thirteenth century. When I say Dalmatia, I am referring to a group of coastal cities and islands

Fig. 10.6 Icon of Christ, c.1090. Marble, 110.5 × 91.5 cm, Collegiate Church of St Mary, Rab. © Konzervatorski odjel Rijeka / Conservation Office at Rijeka. Photo: Damir Krizmanić

that were understood as Dalmatia in the eleventh century. South to north, they are: Kotor, Dubrovnik, Split, Trogir, Zadar and the islands of Rab, Cres and Krk. Considering that these communes used to acknowledge Byzantine control and that the Aachen Treaty of 812 assigned them to the Byzantine sphere of influence, it is surprising that icons do not crop up more. What is even more surprising is that the only other piece of evidence about the existence of icons in the wider area relates to the kingdom of Croatia situated in the hinterland of Zadar and Split.

In the 1040s, a high Croatian dignitary, a *banus* whose name began with an S, donated a church he had built and furnished with his wife Mary to the

Abbey of St Chrysogonus at Zadar (Stipišić and Šamšalović 1967, 76). Among the liturgical books and vestments listed in the donation document were as many as five icons, one of which was made of silver. In addition, although only the first letter of his name remains, the document recorded that *banus* S was an imperial *protospatharios* (Stipišić and Šamšalović 1967, 75). His Croatian title makes him one of the highest-ranking officials in the country, appointed by the king himself. The king in question was Stephen I (1030–58) and, as we learn from a document with which his son and heir Petar Krešimir IV confirmed a land donation to the Abbey of St Chrysogonus, Stephen I appointed three *banus* during his lifetime, one of whom was Stephen Prasca who has been identified as the *protospatharios* who donated the church with icons (Budak 1985, 259).

Although we cannot know if the five icons donated by *banus* Stephen to the Abbey of St Chrysogonus at Zadar were imported from Byzantium or not, they do indicate a knowledge of Byzantine visual culture. Moreover, upon considering the context of other liturgical objects listed in the donation document, it is clear that the icons were a part of the equipment needed for the service such as the chasubles, maniples, stoles, belts, chalices, crosses, candlesticks, psalters, missals and hymn books, as well as basins and hand towels. The icons are listed after the mention of a silver tube and before the three donated crosses, one of which was silver, while one icon was differentiated as also being made of silver (*iconas quinque, unam de argento*, Stipišić and Šamšalović 1967, 76). This means that the other four were probably painted. While it is not known which saints or scenes were depicted in the icons, it is conceivable that they might have been related to the church's titular saints. The church is recorded as having been dedicated to St Nicholas and five other saints – SS Peter, Stephen the Pope, Demetrius, Chrysogonus and Mary – alongside All Saints (*omnium sanctorum Christi*) and it would be plausible to assume, as Trpimir Vedriš suggested verbally to me, that the Virgin was honoured in a silver icon while the four painted icons could have portrayed four of the five remaining titular saints.

The church could not have been too far from Zadar since it must have accessible to the Abbey of St Chrysogonus in that town. The same abbey received a plot of land at Diklo, a suburb of present-day Zadar, from a Croatian king in the tenth century which was confirmed by Petar Krešimir IV in 1066–7 (Stipišić and Šamšalović 1967, 105–6). We do not know what happened to the Church of St Nicholas or how it was used once the Benedictines took possession of it. Even when Abbot Peter explained how he obtained the aforementioned land at Diklo and a church on the island of Pašman, he did not mention this church (Stipišić and Šamšalović

1967, 106-9). The fact that the images are referred to as 'icons' points to the awareness of Byzantine customs albeit in the context of a Latin church, exactly as was the case in contemporary Apulia (Martin 1993, 654). As a recipient of the honorific title of *protospatharios*, Stephen would have been able to procure icons through his connections with Byzantium.

Stephen was not the only Croatian dignitary who was given a Byzantine title. That Byzantium made a diplomatic effort to have good relations with the Croatian kingdom is evident from the example of *spatharokandidatos* Leo whose lead seal, bearing the legend *Leonti vasiliko spatharokandidato kai ... Chrovatias* (Λέοντι βασιλικῷ σπαθαροκανδιδάτῳ καὶ ... Χροβατίας, that is, Leo imperial *spatharokandidatos* and ... of Croatia), has been preserved in the collection at Dumbarton Oaks and dated to the period between 950 and 1050 (Nesbitt and Oikonomides 1991, 48-9, no. 16.1). As for the missing second title, Nesbitt and Oikonomides suggested that *archon* was the likeliest option. The bestowing of titles on Croatian dignitaries indicates a policy of goodwill from Byzantium at a time it needed allies against the Norman threat in Apulia with access to the Adriatic ports.

More Byzantine honorific titles were bestowed on the leaders of Zadar. The title of *protospatharios* was held by Gregory, a nobleman of Zadar and the town's de facto mayor, called *prior* in contemporary sources, who visited Constantinople on three occasions in the 1030s (Skoblar 2017, 34; Wassiliewsky and Jernstedt 1965, 77-8). Thirty years later, another *prior*, Leo was an imperial *protospatharios* and the *katepano* of Dalmatia as recorded in two land-related documents of 1067 and 1069 respectively (*protospatharius ac totius Dalmaciae* [*catepanus*], Stipišić and Šamšalović 1967, 107, 114). In 1075, a certain *spatharokandidatos* John from Zadar features among the representatives of Dalmatian towns who, in a fascinating document demonstrating the complexities of the eleventh-century Adriatic, promised Duke Domenico Silvo not to allow the Normans to come to Dalmatia (Stipišić and Šamšalović 1967, 138). In such a context which must have included diplomatic gifts, as is known from Gregory's example, and trade in general, it does appear odd that, apart from Rab, there is no evidence of icons of any type.

The contacts and communication networks were certainly there. The aforementioned Archbishop Gerardus of Siponto, who obtained two icons from the Tremiti Abbey, acted as a papal legate on two different missions to Dalmatia in 1074. First, in April, Pope Gregory VII sent him to Dubrovnik whose citizens captured and incarcerated Archbishop Vitalis while in November he presided over a church council at Split which settled regional disputes and re-established the suppressed bishopric of Nin in the territory of Croatia (Archdeacon Thomas, *Historia Salonitana* 16; Stipišić and Šamšalović 1967, 134, 136–7). Apart from Gerardus' visits, the links with Apulia are corroborated by the sources at Dubrovnik and Split. The Abbey of Lokrum, just off Dubrovnik, was founded in 1023 by two local clerics one of whom was Peter, a Benedictine monk who came from Tremiti (Petrucci 1960, 29; Stipišić and Šamšalović 1967, 63) while at Split, a monk called John donated a church he had built and dedicated to St Sylvester the Pope on the island of Biševo to the same abbey in 1050 (Petrucci 1960, 134–5; Stipišić and Šamšalović 1967, 78). With these links in mind, it is worth asking why no icons found their way from Tremiti to these two Dalmatian centres, despite *banus* Stephen of Croatia having procured five for a church he gave away.

Conclusion

Before spelling out any conclusions, I need to briefly address the elephant in the room that is Rome. I mentioned at the beginning of this chapter that Rome is the exception when it comes to the lack of preserved pre-thirteenth-century icons in Italy. That is so because in that city one finds still extant pre-iconoclastic Byzantine icons, for example the *Hodegetria dexiokratousa* icon from Santa Francesca Romana or the Madonna della Clemenza in Santa Maria in Trastevere. The cult of icons in Rome has been explained as having to do with a strong Greek presence from early on, which culminated with a series of Greek popes in the seventh century.

The contact with Byzantium, as expected, was a key ingredient when it came to the exposure to icons. Even when no longer extant, icons are well documented in eleventh-century Apulia, which was in Byzantine hands until 1071 when it succumbed to the Normans. The sources tell us that both painted and relief icons made out of stone and metal existed in Apulia. They were primarily imported but some may have been produced locally such as those from Trani and Tremiti Abbey.

All the sources and icons examined here relate to the Latin churches, which means that the context of their cult resides with the western liturgy even though the political administration was Byzantine. Several examples speak of a public and even liturgical use. The covering of icons, as seen in the diocese of Bari at San Prisco in Sao and argued by Carile for the *Madonna greca* at Ravenna, makes it clear that there was a time when they were exposed and a time when they were hidden from view as in Rome and Byzantium. If we understand the phrase 'liturgical use', as Nancy Patterson

Ševčenko (1991, 46) did in a self-confessed narrow meaning, to denote 'what takes place in a regularly repeated and definable office, celebrated in common by a church of monastic congregation, normally under the leadership of professionals – members of the clergy or monks', it is not possible to equate the Byzantine practice with what we learn about the Adriatic in the sources. However, the uncovering and covering of icons and the storage of the textile covers within a church could not have been done by any member of the congregation who happened to have attended a service there. Someone must have been in charge and that someone would have been a priest or a monk.

The icons were predominantly Marian with only two clearly discernible iconographic types: the *hodegetria* (Trani and Foggia) and the *orans* (Ravenna). The sources recording the Marian icon at Tremiti and that at Otranto do not mention the Child, but neither do they specify that the Virgin was alone. The icons of specified saints from Tremiti, San Prisco in Sao and a church near Zadar in Dalmatia, eight all together, while not providing any clues as to their visual qualities, inform us that icons were obtained and listed in the sources as liturgical equipment together with cloths and vessels. The sources also do not fail to mention when they were made of precious metals, for example at Tremiti and in the aforementioned single example from Dalmatia. Except for the preserved icons at Trani and Ravenna, it is difficult to pinpoint other stone icons. The processional icon from Otranto was almost certainly painted, and the same can be said for the icon at Foggia and the alleged one at Bari.

The presence of subsequent legends explaining the arrival of Byzantine icons to the Adriatic cities of Ravenna, Foggia and Bari speaks of their prestige. While at Ravenna and Foggia they miraculously came ashore accompanied by luminescence, the eighteenth-century narrative at Bari links the cathedral icon to pious monks who fled Constantinople during iconoclasm and interprets it as none other than the *Hodegetria*, believed to have been painted by St Luke, which disappeared after the Fall of Constantinople in 1453 and, therefore, could not have been at Bari since the eighth century. The Tuesday procession mentioned in the same legend should not be taken seriously. As demonstrated by Bux, none of the liturgical manuscripts dated to the tenth and eleventh centuries refer to it.

Fortunately, the *Vita* of St Nicholas the Pilgrim gives us a glimpse of a procession with a Marian icon at Otranto at the end of the eleventh century. The cult image was carried from church to church in an act of contrition complete with sung hymns and psalms. This public procession invoked the Virgin's intercessory powers through which the forgiveness of sins can be obtained from God. When the citizens of Otranto forced the icon on St Nicholas the Pilgrim, it was so that by adoring it, he might be forgiven for embracing a Jew. Nicholas, despite being a Greek from Steiri in Boeotia, virtually next door to the monastery of Hosios Loukas and its dazzling apse mosaic of the Theotokos, refused to adore the icon and, instead, directed his praise to the Virgin towards the heaven.

To go back to Belting's statement that icons did not have a liturgical use in the West and the questions highlighted in the introduction to this chapter, the material and textual evidence from the eleventh-century Adriatic reveals that icons were used in cathedrals, abbeys, smaller churches and processions. The earliest record is that of an icon at Polignano in 1024 and after that, two spikes can be detected in the Adriatic: around the mid-eleventh century (Trani, Zadar, Tremiti, Foggia and San Prisco in Sao/Triggiano) and at its very end (Ravenna, Rab and Otranto). By the time Byzantine painted icons started to be imported on a large scale after the capture of Constantinople in 1204, that is, due to theft rather than trade or gift-giving, the Adriatic had already been conditioned to desire them. As expected, the longer an Adriatic area had been Byzantine, the stronger the presence of icons and so Apulia takes the lead followed by Ravenna and Dalmatia. It was not just painterly qualities that enabled the icon boom in the thirteenth century but the fact that what was already known, venerated and prestigious, became more available.

Acknowledgements

I would like to thank those who helped me obtain the illustrations for this chapter either by directing me to the right person or providing me with the images: Floriana Amicucci and Gabriele Pezzi of the Biblioteca Classense in Ravenna; Gioia Bertelli; Maria Cristina Carile; Gerardo Cioffari of the Archivio della Basilica di San Nicola in Bari; Morana Čaušević Bully; Marina Carolina Nardella of the Soprintendenza archeologia, belle arti e paesaggio per le province di Barletta-Andria-Trani e Foggia; Gianluca Piccolo and Don Lorenzo Rossini of the Arcidiocesi Ravenna-Cervia; Dalibor Popovič and Nikolina Uroda of the Museum of Croatian Archaeological Monuments; Dubravka Preradović; Ashley Schwartz at Dumbarton Oaks; Gordana Sobota Matejčić at the Conservation Office at Rijeka.

References

Andaloro, M. 1986. 'I mosaici parietali di Durazzo e dell'origine costantinopolitana del tema iconografico di Maria Regina', in Feld, O. and Peschlow, U. (eds.), *Studien zur spätantiken und byzantinischen Kunst: Friedrich Wilhelm Deichmann gewidmet*, vol. 3 (Bonn), 103–12.

Angelidi, C. 2015. 'Icons in a bottle: Maria Romaia and other stories', in Efthymiadis, S., Messis C., Odorico, P. and Polémis, I. (eds.), *Pour une poétique de Byzance: Hommage à Vassilis Katsaros*, Dossiers byzantines 16 (Paris), 47–56.

Anonymi Barensis chronicon, in Muratori, L.A. (ed.), *Rerum Italicarum scriptores*, vol. 5 (Milan, 1724), 145–56.

Archdeacon Thomas of Split. *Historia Salonitana*, in Perić, O., Karbić, D., Matijević Sokol, M. and Sweeney, J.R. (eds.), *Thomae archdiaconi Historia Salonitanorum atque Spalatinorum pontificum / Archdeacon Thomas of Split. History of the Bishops of Salona and Split* (Budapest, 2006).

Bacci, M. 2005. 'The legacy of the Hodegetria: Holy icons and legends between east and west', in Vassilaki, M. (ed.), *Images of the Mother of God: Perceptions of Theotokos in Byzantium* (Farnham), 321–36.

Ball, J.L. 2005. *Byzantine Dress: Representations of Secular Dress in Eighth- to Twelfth-Century Painting* (New York).

Barber, C. 2011. 'Review of *The Painter Angelos and Icon-Painting in Venetian Crete* by Maria Vassilaki; *The Hand of Angelos: An Icon Painter in Venetian Crete* by Maria Vassilaki; *Space, Time, and Presence in the Icon: Seeing the World with the Eyes of God* by Clemena Antonova; *The Sensual Icon: Space, Ritual, and the Senses in Byzantium* by Bissera V. Pentcheva', *The Art Bulletin* 93/3, 370–4.

Belli D'Elia, P. 1987. *Alle sorgenti del romanico: Puglia XI secolo*, 2nd edn. (Bari).

  1988. 'Fra tradizione e rinnovamento: Le icone dall'XI al XIV secolo', in Belli D'Elia, P. (ed.), *Icone di Puglia e Basilicata dal Medioevo al Settecento* (Milan), 19–30.

  1989-90. 'Contributo al recupero di una immagine: L'iconavetere di Foggia,' in Adembri, B. (ed.), *Scritti in ricordo di Giovanni Previtali*, vol. 1 (Florence), 90–6.

  1995. 'L'icona nella cattedrale tra XI e XII secolo: Ipotesi a confronto nel contesto pugliese' in Bux, N. (ed.), *L'Odegitria della cattedrale: Storia, arte, culto* (Bari), 11–22.

Belting, H. 1996. (trans. Jephcott, E.) *Likeness and Presence: A History of the Image before the Era of Art*, 2nd edn. (Chicago).

Bianco, R. 2000. 'La Madonna celata di Foggia: Culto e diffusione dell'iconografia della Madonna dei Sette Veli,' in Gravina, A. (ed.), *Atti del XX Convegno nazionale sulla preistoria – protostoria – storia della Daunia* (San Severo), 27–40.

Bloch, H. 1986. *Monte Cassino in the Middle Ages*, vol. 1 (Rome).

Bowes, K. and Mitchell, J. 2009. 'The main chapel of the Durres amphitheater: Decoration and chronology', *Mélanges de l'École française de Rome. Antiquité* 121/2 (Rome), 571–97.

Budak, N. 1985. 'Servi ranog srednjeg vijeka u Hrvatskoj i Dalmaciji', *Starohrvatska prosvjeta*, 3rd series, 15, 255–68.

Bux, N. 1995. 'La liturgia dell'Odegitria nel "proprio" barese tra culto locale e teologia bizantina', in Bux, N. (ed.), *L'Odegitria della cattedrale: Storia, arte, culto* (Bari), 133–9.

Calò Mariani, M.S. 1997. 'Foggia e l'arte della Capitanata dai Normanni agli Angioini', in Calò Mariani, M.S. (ed.), *Foggia medievale* (Foggia), 73–131.

Carile, M.C. 2016. 'Production, promotion and reception: The visual culture of Ravenna between Late Antiquity and the Middle Ages', in Herrin, J. and Nelson, J. (eds.), *Ravenna: Its Role in Earlier Medieval Change and Exchange* (London), 53–85.

Cioffari, G. 1995. 'La Vergine sui sigilli di piombo degli arcivescovi di Bari nel Medioevo', in Bux, N. (ed.), *L'Odegitria della cattedrale: Storia, arte, culto* (Bari), 115–31.

Coniglio, G. (ed.) 1975. *Codice diplomatico pugliese*, vol. 20, *Le pergamene di Conversano*, vol. 1, *901–1265* (Bari).

Constantine Porphyrogennetos. *De cerimoniis aulae Byzantinae*, ed. Reiske, J.J. (Bonn, 1929).

Cormack, R. 2007. *Icons* (Cambridge, Mass.).

— 2015. 'Review of *The Sensual Icon: Space, Ritual, and the Senses in Byzantium* by Bissera V. Pentcheva', *The Catholic Historical Review* 101/3, 601–2.

Cosentino, S. 2008. *Storia dell'Italia bizantina (VI–XI secolo): Da Giustiniano ai Normanni* (Bologna).

Cotsonis, J. 1995. *Byzantine Figural Processional Crosses* (Washington, DC).

Dante. 2000. *Paradise*, trans. Finn Cotter, J. (Stony Brook).

Davis, C. 2006. *Byzantine Relief Icons in Venice and along the Adriatic Coast: Orants and Other Images of the Mother of God* (Munich).

Davis, R. (ed. and trans.) 1995. *The Lives of the Eighth-Century Popes (Liber pontificalis): The Ancient Biographies of Ten Popes from* AD *817–891* (Liverpool).

— (ed. and trans.) 2007. *The Lives of the Eighth-Century Popes (Liber pontificalis): The Ancient Biographies of Nine Popes from* AD *715 to* AD *817* (Liverpool).

Demori Staničić, Z. 2017. *Javni kultovi ikona u Dalmaciji* (Split).

Dobschütz, E. 1903. 'Maria Romaia: Zwei unbekannte Texte', *Byzantinische Zeitschrift* 12, 173–214.

Donati, A. and Gentili, G. (eds.) 2001. *Deomene: L'immagine dell'orante fra Oriente e Occidente* (Milan).

Effenberger, A. 2006. 'Die Reliefikonen der Theotokos und des Erzengels Michael im Museum für byzantinische Kunst, Berlin', *Jahrbuch der Berliner Museen* 48, 9–36.

Esbroeck, M. van 1988. 'Le culte de la Vierge de Jérusalem à Constantinople aux 6e–7e siècles', *Revue des études byzantines* 46, 181–90.

Evans, H.C. and Wixom, W. (eds.) 1997. *The Glory of Byzantium: Art and Culture of the Middle Byzantine Era AD 843–1261* (New York).

Fabri, G. 1664. *Le sagre memorie di Ravenna antica* (Venice).

1675. *Efemeride sagra ed istorica di Ravenna antica* (Ravenna).

Falkenhausen, V. von 1978. *La dominazione bizantina nell'Italia meridionale dal IX all'XI secolo* (Bari).

1984. 'A provincial aristocracy: The Byzantine provinces in southern Italy (9th–11th century)', in Angold, M. (ed.), *The Byzantine Aristocracy IX to XIII Centuries*, BAR International Series 221 (Oxford), 211–35.

Fantuzzi, M. 1802. *Monumenti ravennati de' secoli di mezzo*, vol. 2 (Venice).

Gay, J. 1904. *L'Italie méridionale et l'Empire byzantine depuis l'avènement de Basile Ier jusqu'à la prise de Bari par les Normandes (867–1071)* (Paris).

Garruba, M. 1834. *Eoniade della translazione della miracolosa immagine di Maria SS. di Costantinopoli nella città di Bari* (Naples).

Gelao, C. 1995. 'L'icona della Madonna di Costantinopoli nella Cattedrale di Bari tra storia e leggenda', in Bux, N. (ed.), *L'Odegitria della cattedrale: Storia, arte, culto* (Bari), 25–35.

Grabar, A. 1968. 'Découverte à Rome d'une icône de la Vierge à l'encaustique', in *L'art de la fin de l'Antiquité et du Moyen Âge*, vol. 1 (Paris), 529–34.

Guillou, A. 1996. *Recueil des inscriptions grecques médiévales d'Italie*, Collection de l'École française de Rome 222 (Rome).

Guillou, A. and Burgarella, F. 1988. *L'Italia bizantina: Dall'esarcato di Ravenna al tema di Sicilia* (Turin).

Holt, E.G. 1957. *A Documentary History of Art*, vol. 1, *The Middle Ages and the Renaissance*, 2nd edn. (New York).

Jenkins, R.J.H. and Mango, C. 1956. 'The date and significance of the tenth homily of Photius', *Dumbarton Oaks Papers* 9–10, 123–40.

Kazhdan, A.P. (ed.) 1991. *The Oxford Dictionary of Byzantium*, 3 vols. (New York and Oxford).

Kehr, P.F. and Holtzmann, W. (eds.) 1986. *Regesta pontificum Romanorum: Italia pontificia*, vol. 9, *Samnium – Apulia – Luciania* (Berlin).

Križman, M. 2000. *Translatio corporis beatae Euphemiae / Prijenos tijela blažene Eufemije* (Pula).

Lange, R. 1964. *Die byzantinische Reliefikone* (Recklinghausen).

Leo of Ostia. *Chronica monasterii Cassinensis*, in Hoffmann, H. (ed.), *MGH Scriptores*, vol. 34 (Hanover, 1980).

Liber pontificalis, in Duchesne, L. (ed.), *Le Liber pontificalis: Texte, introduction et commentaire*, vol. 2 (Paris, 1892).

Lidov, A. 2004. 'The flying Hodegetria: The miraculous icon as bearer of sacred space', in Thunø, E. and Wolf, G. (eds.), *The Miraculous Image in the Late Middle Ages and Renaissance* (Rome), 291–321.

Loud, G.A. 2007. *The Latin Church in Norman Italy* (Cambridge).
Loverdou-Tsigarida, K. 2000. 'The Mother of God in sculpture', in Vassilaki, M. (ed.), *Mother of God: Representations of the Virgin in Byzantine Art* (Milan), 237–49.
Mango, C. 1958. *The Homilies of Photius, Patriarch of Constantinople* (Cambridge, Mass.).
Martin, J.-M. 1993. *La Pouille du VIe au XIIe siècle*, Collection de l'École française de Rome 179 (Rome).
— 1994. 'Quelques remarques sur le culte des images en Italie méridionale pendant le haut Moyen Âge', in Alzati C. (ed.), *Cristianità ed Europa: Miscellanea di studi in onore di Luigi Prosdocimi*, vol. 1 (Rome), 223–36.
Maruli, S. 1613. *Historia sagra intitolata Mare Oceano di tutte le religioni di mondo*, vol. 1 (Messina).
Mason, M. 2012. 'Venezia o Costantinopoli? Sulla scultura bizantina a Venezia e nell'entroterra veneto e ancora sulla Beata Vergine dell Cintura di Costantinopoli', *Saggi e memorie di storia dell'arte* 36, 7–56.
Mazzotti, M. 1991. *La chiesa di S. Maria in Porto Fuori: Scritti editi ed inediti*, edited by E. Russo (Ravenna).
Ménager, L.-R. (ed.) 1981. *Recueil des actes des ducs normands d'Italie (1046–1127)*, vol. 1, *Les premiers ducs (1046–1087)* (Bari).
Montfaucon, B. de 1725. (trans. Henley, J.) *The Antiquities of Italy: Being the Travels of the Learned and Reverend Bernard de Montfaucon from Paris through Italy in the Years 1698 and 1699*, 2nd edn. (London).
Munitiz, J.A., Chrysostomides J., Harvalia-Crook, E. and Dendrinos C. (eds.) 1997. *The Letter of the Three Patriarchs to Emperor Theophilos and Related Texts* (Camberley and Athens).
Musca, G. 1992. *L'emirato di Bari, 847–871*, 4th edn. (Bari).
Nesbitt, J. and Oikonomides, N. 1991. *Catalogue of Byzantine Seals at Dumbarton Oaks and in the Fogg Museum of Art*, vol. 1, *Italy, North of the Balkans, North of the Black Sea* (Washington, DC).
Nitti de Vito, F. (ed.) 1903. *Codice diplomatico barese*, vol. 5, *Le pergamene di S. Nicola di Bari 2: Periodo normanno (1075–1194)* (Bari).
Nitto de Rossi, G.B. and Nitti de Vito, F. (eds.) 1897. *Codice diplomatico barese*, vol. 1, *Le pergamene del duomo di Bari 1 (952–1264)* (Bari).
Osborne, J. 2003, 'Images of the Mother of God in Early Medieval Rome', in Eastmond, A. and James, L. (eds.), *Icon and Word: The Power of Images in Byzantium. Studies Presented to Robin Cormack* (Aldershot), 135–56.
Parani, M. 2003. *Reconstructing the Reality of Images: Byzantine Material Culture and Religious Iconography (11th–15th Centuries)* (Leiden).
Patterson Ševčenko, N. 1991. 'Icons in the liturgy', *Dumbarton Oaks Papers* 45, 45–57.
Pentcheva, B.V. 2010. *The Sensual Icon: Space, Ritual, and the Senses in Byzantium* (Pennsylvania State University Park).

2014. *Icons and Power: The Mother of God in Byzantium*, 2nd edn. (Pennsylvania State University Park).
Petrucci, A. (ed.) 1960. *Codice diplomatico del monastero benedettino di S. Maria di Tremiti (1005-1237)*, vol. 2 (Rome).
Pinto, G. 1995. 'La *traslationis historia* del prete Gregorio', in Bux, N. (ed.), *L'Odegitria della cattedrale: Storia, arte, culto* (Bari), 69-90.
Pitarakis, B. 2006. *Les croix-reliquaires pectorales byzantines en bronze* (Paris).
Rizzardi, C. 1985. *Mosaici altoadriatici: Il rapporto artistico Venezia, Bisanzio, Ravenna in età medievale* (Ravenna).
   2001. 'La "Madonna greca" di Ravenna nella cultura artistica, nella leggenda e nella memoria storica della città', in Donati and Gentili (eds.) 2001, 44-7.
Ruotolo, G. and Cioffari, G. 2002. *I sigilli della basilica di San Nicola di Bari: Periodo bizantino, normanno e svevo* (Vicenza).
Serricchio, C. 1986. 'La cattedrale di S. Maria Maggiore di Siponto e la sua icona', *Archivio storico pugliese* 39, 69-100.
Sheppard, J.M. 1982. 'The eleventh-century choir-screen at Monte Cassino: A reconstruction', *Byzantine Studies / Études byzantines* 9/2, 233-42.
Skoblar, M. 2012. 'Marble relief of enthroned Christ from Rab', *Starohrvatska prosvjeta*, 3rd series, 39, 171-82.
   2014. 'The Hodegetria icon of tourmarches Delterios at Trani', *Medioevo adriatico* 5, 165-208.
   2017. *Figural Sculpture in Eleventh-Century Dalmatia and Croatia: Patronage, Architectural Context, History* (London and New York).
Stipišić, J. and Šamšalović, M. (eds.) 1967. *Codex diplomaticus regni Croatiae, Dalmatiae et Slavoniae*, vol. 1, *Diplomata annorum 743.-1100. continens* (Zagreb).
Sulfrini, P. 1887. *Storia della Madonna greca* (Ravenna).
Tosti, M. 2003. *Santuari cristiani d'Italia* (Rome).
Vinaccia, A. 1981. *I monumenti medioevali di terra di Bari*, vol. 1. (Bari, 1915, repr. Rome, 1981).
Vita S. Nicolai in Græcia, in *Acta sanctorum, Iunii*, vol. 1 (Antwerp, 1695; repr. Brussels, 1969), 231-7.
Walter, C. 1997. 'Iconographic considerations', in Munitiz *et al.* (eds.) 1997, li-lxxviii.
Wassiliewsky, V. and Jernstedt, V. (eds.) 1965. *Cecaumeni Strategicon et incerti scriptoris De officiis regiis libellus* (St Petersburg, 1896; repr. Amsterdam, 1965).
Weinryb, I. 2011. 'The inscribed image: Negotiating sculpture on the coast of the Adriatic Sea', *Word & Image* 27/3, 322-33.
Wixom, W.D. 1997. 'Byzantine art and the Latin west', in Evans and Wixom (eds.) 1997, 435-49.

11 | The Rise of the Adriatic in the Age of the Crusades

PETER FRANKOPAN

Writing in the middle of the fourteenth century, the Italian writer Boccaccio set out a story in the *Decameron* that he expected would appeal to readers of his famous work. The tale tells of Alatiel, the daughter of the sultan of Babylon and 'according to everyone who saw her, the most beautiful woman in the world'. The story sets out her struggles to reach her promised husband, the king of Algarve in faraway Portugal. Her adventures and travails saw her being shuttled between the nobles of Majorca to merchants from Genoa; Alatiel comes across a succession of heroes and villains who include the duke of Athens, princes of Achaea and Constantinople, and walk-on roles for the emir of Smyrna in western Asia Minor and the ruler of Cyprus (Boccaccio, *Decameron*, 134–56).

While the narrative about Alatiel poses questions about gender and the objectification of women, it is also a story that links the Mediterranean into a single connected body of water that ties the Atlantic with the Aegean and Adriatic, and ties Europe and north Africa with the heart of the Middle East. It speaks of a deeply interconnected world where people, goods and information (and misinformation) travelled over long distances and where perspectives spanned regions and even continents (Di Sisto 1994; Ferrante 1993, 165–74).

This marks a striking change from the long centuries of decline that characterised the Mediterranean and the Adriatic in the years following the collapse of Rome's western provinces. Although the period following the seventh century saw new connectivities emerge between the Islamic world that was established in the decades following the death of the Prophet Muḥammad, other parts of the Mediterranean, Adriatic and Aegean became economic and cultural backwaters – as indeed did much of northern Europe. The scale of collapse was so great, notes one leading scholar, that 'the ancient trading centres of the western Mediterranean vanished off the commercial map' (Abulafia 2014, 256).

They were replaced by a series of regional emporia in Italy like Comacchio and Torcello that were in due course mirrored by similar markets in northern Europe in places like Verdun or Birka in Scandinavia. However, these were characterised by the fact that they were set in peripheral, ecologically marginal locations. No less important, however, was the fact that for all the intensive, low-level exchange that is testified by the literary and non-literary sources, these were trade centres where the velocities and modalities of commercial enterprise were highly internalised. There were no networks that linked individual locations with each other; rather, trade took place between producers and consumers within each location (McCormick 2013).

It would be hard, in other words, to conceive of a world that was less like that inhabited by the fictional Alatiel and her fellow *dramatis personae*. Boccaccio's evocation of free and wide-ranging movement of people, goods and ideas between towns and cities that were distant from, and where seas and bodies of water facilitated exchange and connections bore no resemblance to the realities of large swathes of the Mediterranean in Late Antiquity and the Early Middle Ages.

Despite this disjointed picture, it is clear that the imperial authorities in Constantinople did what they could to track what was going on in city states on the western shin of Italy in places like Naples, Capua, Amalfi, Gaeta and Salerno, with accounts like the *De administrando imperio* (27.3–14) recording almost mournfully how the Romans used to hold sway in these cities and how the practical administration of empire used to take place. However, a combination of factors ranging from weak elite authority, the limited stimuli, incentives and capability to expand networks, the dislocation caused by piracy and the limitations of Constantinople's engagement and interest in Italy and in the Mediterranean meant that connections that were not local in nature remained tenuous and superficial.

Things began slowly to change from the early ninth century. After describing the constellation of towns lying south of Rome, the *De administrando imperio* goes on to report on the rise of another location that seemed to have the same characteristics of a small city that could serve as a central point of contact for its own hinterland – but little beyond. According to the text, people known as Venetians (Ενετικοί and subsequently Βενέτικοι) had sought sanctuary from dislocation and anarchy on the mainland by fleeing to a series of islands in the very north of Adriatic. They built a fortified citadel (κάστρον ὀχυρόν) to provide security from their neighbours and unwanted attention from further afield – who included the Huns of Attila the Great, at least according to the *De administrando imperio* (27.75–78; 28.6–11).

It was an unlikely and unpromising spot to choose – one that even today defies logic. Venice was located in a position that was desolate, devoid of inhabitants and given over to marshland: 'of old, Venice was a desert place, uninhabited and swampy' ('Ιστέον, ὅτι ἡ Βενετία τὸ μὲν παλαιὸν ἦν τόπος ἔρημός τις ἀοίκητος καὶ βαλτώδης, *De administrando imperio* 28.3–4). This meant there were natural barriers for the city's future expansion, but also presented problems of accessibility for those wishing to reach Venice both by land and by sea, as well as presenting challenges for Venetians looking to explore opportunities further afield.

Venice's rise into an economic, political and cultural powerhouse of the Middle Ages was sparked by two factors, one of which was contextual and the other linked to the wider reconfiguration of the Adriatic and the eastern Mediterranean. The transformation of Byzantium began to gather pace in the second half of the ninth century, as military achievements on the eastern frontier were mirrored by a new determination to reorganise its Balkan provinces – evidenced by the creation of the theme of Dalmatia around 870. This was the prelude to a century of stunning military success that cleared the eastern Mediterranean of pirate nests, restored Crete and Cyprus to imperial control, and rolled the frontier in Asia Minor back several hundred miles as major cities like Edessa and Antioch were recovered (Whittow 1996, 307).

To judge from the tax records of the tenth century, the numismatic material and a wide range of primary sources, an economic and demographic boom went hand in hand with the expansion of the state. A lengthy period of major investments into the infrastructure of empire saw the creation of a new series of themes and concomitant administrative reforms that widened the military and civilian elites and expanded the wealth and position of provincial landowners. Government revenues rose steadily as a result of the competence of the army, the removal of enemies and the stability that followed – as well as thanks to the addition of lucrative towns and provinces to the fisc (Harvey 1989; Neville 2004).

These developments naturally had a knock-on effect for towns and regions that were the edges of Constantinople's political and diplomatic orbit, but which stood to gain from what was happening in Byzantium. While it was not simply change in the empire that drove sharply rising exchange within, between and beyond clusters of towns in Italy, not many sparks were needed to galvanise urban networks that in Chris Wickham's (2009, 584) words were 'poised on the edge of an economic lift-off'.

Along the Dalmatian coast, the stimulus of stability and greater levels of connectivity explain the dispatch in the early ninth century of the relics of St Anastasia from Constantinople to Zadar and of St Tryphon to Kotor and the subsequent construction of a church in his honour (*De administrando imperio* 29.268–9; Rački 1877, 306–9). This was just one of a series of new religious foundations that sprang up on the eastern side of the Adriatic in the course of the later ninth and tenth centuries, with new Benedictine monasteries in Zadar, Biograd, Selo, Trogir and elsewhere signs of rising prosperity and the dissemination of religious ideas and cultural forms (Supičić 1999, 192–3).

The expansion of civic centres in the Adriatic was not unique to this region and finds natural and obvious parallels elsewhere – most notably in Campania in Italy, where the trajectories of towns like Naples, Gaeta, Amalfi and Salerno in this period followed a similar arc of urban growth, the endowment of religious foundations and the rise of local elites whose fortunes and authority grew as the towns blossomed (Wickham 2009, 547–8).

The expansion of Byzantium's horizons was an important catalyst, especially in the case of the Adriatic and southern Italy where increasing resources and attention began to be paid to developments in Dalmatia and the western Balkans as well as to those in Apulia and Calabria. This included the granting of titles to individual rulers that while effectively recognising the reality on the ground also served as a sign of increasing levels of engagement with regions on the periphery. In the first half of the tenth century, for example, a certain Ljutovid was recorded as holding the rank of *strategos* of Serbia and Zahumlje (von Falkenhausen 1970; Stephenson 2000, 129).

Constantinople did not simply recognise the status quo, however, and occasionally could and did intervene more directly either on an ad hominem basis to get rid of individuals who were troublemakers, or to cement the imperial position in a more concrete fashion in locations that were strategically or commercially important (or both). In the first half of the eleventh century, for example, we learn that Dobrinja who held power in Zadar was forcibly detained along with his wife and son while in the imperial capital – where they remained until they died. While the fact that the Slav potentate was in Constantinople in the first place tells its own story, the point is that influence on and control over key points in the Adriatic was becoming an important part of the widening Byzantine views of its priorities concerning what had long been peripheral regions that had little impact or significance on the capital or indeed on the empire (Litavrin 1972, 302; Stephenson 2000, 129).

In the case of the Adriatic, there were supplementary causes that focused the mind in Constantinople. In 971, the Emperor John I Tzimiskes sent a delegation to Venice to complain about the fact that merchants from the city were selling weapons and ship timbers to Muslims that not only represented a threat to Byzantine shipping but also a military threat to Byzantium. The Venetians recognised that it was a sin to sell goods to pagan people and undertook not to sell breastplates, shields, swords and other weapons – as well as lumber – to Muslims in the future (Jacoby 2001, 105–11; Romanin 1853, 373–5).

The fact that a treaty was required (presumably following pressure from Constantinople) at a time when Venice was still at least nominally under Byzantine authority demonstrates the practical difficulties of maintaining and asserting control over places far removed from the centre, but also the extent to which trading networks were starting to expand. This can also be seen from a grant issued by Basil II and his brother Constantine (later Constantine VIII) in 992 that set out taxes payable by Venetian merchant ships arriving at Abydos – the entry and exit point for the Hellespont. At the very least, this testifies to the growing geographic reach of traffic originating in the north of the Adriatic and the importance of growing trade along maritime routes (Pertusi 1990, 88–94).

Venice's own capabilities were also growing as is clear from the procession led by Duke Pietro II Orseolo in 1000 along the coast where he was acclaimed by inhabitants of one town after another who were keen to celebrate their gratitude to Venetian military might for pushing the Slavs into the hinterland. That, at least, is what we learn from accounts written in Venice (Andrea Dandolo, *Chronica* 4.1; John the Deacon, *Istoria Veneticorum* 4.46–54).

Ironically, the city's location at the very north of the Adriatic meant that it was less exposed to instability caused by Slavic raids than other locations along the coast – and therefore subject to less economic dislocation. This meant in turn that it neither had to compromise by coming to terms with local rulers, nor was it forced to undertake the high levels of expenditure that went hand in hand with fortifying and maintaining walled cites – and protecting the agricultural hinterland beyond. In fact the opposite was true: while there were obvious challenges to Venice's physical setting, the difficulties of assaulting the city by land or by sea, combined with the lack of need to build walls that might offer protection – but also limit urban expansion – meant that it had few of the problems that rival locations suffered from further south and furthermore, could take advantage of their weaknesses to become ever stronger itself.

A good case in point comes from Arab attacks on Bari, on the heel of southern Italy, at the very start of the eleventh century, which offered the Venetians the opportunity to intervene in support of Constantinople – thereby generating further goodwill and rising status within the Byzantine empire (Lilie 1984, 1–6). This was one reason why well-connected families in the empire began to consider leading Venetians as suitable marriage material for their sons and daughters, such as the Argyropouloi, one of whose members married the son of Duke Pietro II Orseolo and moved to Venice. Not all were enamoured with the airs and graces of Maria Argyropoula – whose high status is clear from the fact that her brother Romanos later became emperor – with one writer complaining that she brought with her eunuch servants and the habit of taking perfumed baths (Ciggaar 1996, 226).

Such indications of petty jealousies mask that fact that the economic expansion of the city was a catalyst for social change. Study of ducal documents in Venice from the second half of the tenth century reveals a widening of the number of families in positions of prominence in the city. The numbers of those endorsing ducal decisions rose sharply in this period; what is more, some 60 per cent of those signing these documents belonged to families that were unknown from previous sources relating to the city. While it is hard to know how far to use such material to talk about rising levels of elite wealth or inequality, it presumably shows how more people had a stake in Venice's growing success and represents a widening of the share of the economic gains through civic society (Puga and Trefler 2014, 761).

The growing range of Venice's field of vision was facilitated by the series of troubles that afflicted Byzantium in the second half of the eleventh century. Turkish raids in Asia Minor became increasingly common and severe, to the point that even major towns deep in the interior of Anatolia were not safe – as is clear from the sack of Caesarea in 1070. At the same time, turbulence on the steppes north of the Black Sea led to pressure rising on the Danube frontier and to attacks into the Balkans by Pecheneg nomads, which were dealt with poorly and ineffectively. This was aggravated by competition around the person of the emperor and by intense internal disruption that brought the empire to its knees by the 1070s (Frankopan 2012a, 26–41).

These pressures led to Constantinople turning a blind eye to what was happening both in the Adriatic and in southern Italy, where the Normans under the leadership of Robert Guiscard and his brother, Roger of Sicily, were able to pick off cities one by one and to prise Apulia and Calabria away from centuries of imperial control. Although there was local resistance in some cases, in large part, these cities passed over to the Normans without even token resistance from Constantinople (Hoffmann 1969; Loud 2000). So irrelevant were affairs in the West in the wider struggles facing successive leaders that the fall of southern Italy receives a handful of sentences in one of the leading Byzantine accounts of the period (Bekker 1839, 720–4) – and none at all in several others.

The disengagement had consequences in the Adriatic, where Zvonimir took the opportunity not only to claim a royal title for himself but also to look to Rome for recognition and confirmation. The fact that Pope Gregory VII acquiesced itself reveals the opportunities on offer in an arena where disengaged leadership from afar allowed the brave and the bold to take matters into their own hands (Cowdrey 1998, 440–4). So too does the fact that the pope can be found soon after his award of the crown to Zvonimir not only protecting his new ally (and his own interests) but threatening the king's neighbours with the 'sword of St Peter'. In other words, new spaces were opening up for those alert to the possibilities of extending their own authority, patrimony and influence (Košćak 1991, 263; Stipišić and Šamšalović 1967, 171).

The accession of Alexios I Komnenos led to change, not only in the system of government in Byzantium but also in a refocusing on the western provinces. This was itself spurred by the growing efforts of the Normans to use their successes in Italy to build a bridgehead across the Adriatic and Ionian Seas. We know from records from the Dalmatian coast that some towns in the region were already fending off the attention of the Normans as early as the 1070s (Stipišić and Šamšalović 1967, 136). The stakes rose dramatically, however, at the start of the 1080s when Robert Guiscard launched a major attack on Byzantium's western flank.

While some commentators argue that the ultimate aim of the assault was nothing less than Constantinople itself, the targets, routes and priorities identified by the Normans in 1081–3 and again during a second invasion in 1084–5 suggest that aims were more local and were primarily aimed at taking control of the eastern sides of the Adriatic and Ionian Seas – both as part of a concerted effort to strangle pinch points allowing access to the eastern Mediterranean and also as a pre-emptive strike to prevent future Byzantine attempts to restore control of or even gain influence over its former, recently lost provinces in southern Italy (Theotokis 2014, 137–84).

The early 1080s saw an important reconfiguration of strategic priorities, instigated by Alexios I who set about pacifying problems caused by the Turks in Asia Minor in order to free himself to pay full attention to the Normans and the threat they posed. A deal was reached with the leading Turkish emir, Süleyman, that was evidently so favourable for the latter that he agreed to provide military support against Robert Guiscard – at least according to the author of the *Alexias* (Anna Komnene, *Alexias* 5.5.2), the most important source for this period.

The defeat of the Normans was in part facilitated through close co-operation with Venice which had much to lose from the expansion of Norman authority to the eastern side of the Adriatic and Ionian Seas: not only did this threaten to undermine ties that the Venetians had forged with many of the coastal cities of Dalmatia, but it also raised the prospect of Venice being strangled from access to markets beyond the pinch point between Italy and the coast of Epiros – not least with Constantinople itself.

Scholars have long argued that Byzantium's desperation to deal with Robert Guiscard was so acute that the emperor was forced to make a sweeping series of concessions to incentivise Venice to co-operate against the Normans and send naval forces to block supply lines and to help repulse the invasion. This is based on a serious two-stage error that involves not only changing the date provided in the trade treaty in a way that has no orthographic or palaeographic justification, but also discarding the report of the account of the concession from where it appears in the *Alexias* and arbitrarily moving it to a date that seems to fit circumstances that are deemed more appropriate. Neither of these two steps is ideal, let alone a combination of the two. In fact, there were indeed rewards given to Venice in 1082 for the help provided in dealing with a common enemy: however, these related to the award of the high title of *protosebastos* to its duke and the grant of property in Constantinople – but not to sweeping commercial privileges that were only granted a decade later (Frankopan 2004a).

Although Robert Guiscard's attacks of the 1080s were eventually dealt with, the likelihood of renewed Norman focus on Epiros led to the emperor in Constantinople paying considerably more attention to Byzantium's western flank. The fact that appointment to the command over Dyrrachion (modern Durrës) – the gateway to the interior but also the most important listening post to gather intelligence from southern Italy – was placed in the hands of the immediate family of Alexios I provides one example of how high the Adriatic and Ionian Seas ranked in strategic thinking in the late eleventh and early twelfth centuries (Frankopan 2002). The attention paid by the imperial army, under the command of the emperor in person, to the Serbs and the Balkans in the same period provides another (Frankopan 2012b). It is striking too that there are also grounds to think that Alexios I made a specific appeal to King Zvonimir for military support, perhaps in connection with the problems posed by major

Pecheneg invasions of the Balkans in the late 1080s and early 1090s (Frankopan 2004b).

Change in the West was being actively monitored and managed – to the best of Byzantium's abilities at a time when pressure in Asia Minor and the east were reaching the point where Alexios' options became increasingly limited and his position on the throne precarious (Frankopan 2012a, 71–86). As we learn from a series of documents relating to St Christodoulos, the late 1080s and early 1090s saw major disruption both to shipping in the Aegean that was so acute that simple travel between islands was not so much compromised as curtailed (Miklosich and Müller 1890, 19–21, 34–8, 42–4, 57–8). Things were so bad that governors on Crete and Cyprus detached from Constantinople and effectively became independent during this period (Frankopan 2004c).

The strains of multiple pressures on the economy resulted in a major recoinage in 1092 – the first by a Byzantine emperor since the reforms of Anastasios at the end of the fifth century (Metcalf 1979, 104–7). They also led to a further grant of concessions to Venice, including a new title for the patriarch, but also the extensions to the authority of the duke to include the Dalmatian littoral (Frankopan 2004a, 158–60). While it could be argued that this latter was simply a recognition of a reality where Constantinople was struggling to deal with simultaneous problems that threatened not only the overthrow of the emperor by his closest intimates but potentially the viability of the empire as a whole, the fact that Venice's ruler was able to secure concessions tells its own story as to how the Venetians were increasingly able to expand their field of vision – and indeed their commercial and political footprint – southwards.

In this sense, almost as important as the titles awarded to Venice in the early 1090s were the extensive trade concessions that incentivised Venetian merchants and shipping to trade with Byzantium. We know that there several Italian city states had communes living not only in Constantinople but also in other parts of the empire by the end of the eleventh century as did many other nationalities (Lemerle *et al.* 1970, 233–5, 258–9; Ciggaar 1995, 117–40). However, the award of quays in the harbour of the imperial capital, plus the dramatic reduction in taxes that would henceforth be charged on cargoes gave Venice a substantial discount on those paid by their commercial rivals – and therefore a significant competitive advantage as well.

While the connection between the trade privileges and its direct (and indirect) impact on the Byzantine economy are difficult to assess, what is striking about the award of 1092 is that the advantages offered to the

Venetians were not restricted to Constantinople alone. As the grant notes, traders from Venice were offered similar terms in a swathe of cities across the Byzantine empire. The twenty-three cities named in the grant included locations like Dyrrachion, Corinth and Thebes, but also towns like Attaleia, Tarsus and Mamistra that were either precariously hanging on in the face of substantial Turkish pressure or had surrendered or reached accommodations with them (Pozza and Ravegnani 1993, 40). Evidently, concessions to trading rights in such places were offered as bait to encourage an expansion of business if (and when) they were restored to the empire (Frankopan 2004a, 146–9).

As such, the commercial privileges of 1092 offered Venice a blueprint to expand the networks it had been able to build in the Adriatic and extend them deep into the Aegean and the eastern Mediterranean. The terms, granted at a time of profound Byzantine weakness, laid the basis for the later dramatic growth of Venice. Ultimately, they helped underpin the city's transformation from a regional power that had managed to dominate local rivals in the Adriatic, into one with a much broader geographic reach and one that was well placed to benefit from the pressures that Byzantium was under.

It is, therefore, neither a coincidence nor a surprise to learn that the 1090s saw another surge in the number of new families whose names are found on ducal documents: the rise in the number of newly rich merchants seeking to be active participants in the life of the city is testimony to the fact that as Constantinople reeled, Venice boomed. It was not so much that Byzantium's loss was the Venetians' gain, but that the empire's difficulties opened up new possibilities for the city to look beyond the Adriatic (Castagnetti 1992, 625–6, 636–7).

From Venice's point of view, serendipity of timing proved crucial. When Alexios I turned to Pope Urban II for massive military support and sparked what became the First Crusade in 1095, it soon became apparent that Venice could take advantage of the needs of the Westerners who fought their way to Jerusalem and captured it in 1099. Although a major Venetian fleet – listed by some accounts as numbering as many as 200 vessels – was not in position to offer support for the assault on the Holy City itself, it was able to play a role in the fall of Haifa not long after (Queller and Katele 1986, 21–5).

The establishment of Latin states in what became known as Outremer meant that there was both the demand and the need for supplies to keep the newly arrived Westerners provisioned and able to resist the attention of the multiple threats that surrounded them. Venice found itself in an enviable position to do well both spiritually and commercially. While early Venetian accounts of the First Crusade talk of angels rejoicing at the success of the expedition, it is not hard to see more clear-headed approaches to how the city could dovetail support for fellow Christians with rewards of a more immediate kind.

As the Crusade got underway, we learn from Dandolo (*Chronica* 4.40; Queller and Katele 1986, 16–7; Stipišić and Šamšalović 1967, 207–8) that the duke, Vitale I Michiel, sought to raise men from the towns of Dalmatian coast. Not only that, but as the fleet sailed south through the Adriatic, the Venetians were careful to use their military presence to ensure the loyalty of the towns along the coast – which were encouraged to pledge further men but also allegiance to Venice (Queller and Katele 1986, 20).

This was a pattern that was repeated regularly, as Venetians used their muscular presence to settle scores – and gain position against their rivals. In 1099, for example, a Venetian fleet took on squadron from Pisa that was also at large in the eastern Mediterranean, ostensibly to provide support for the Crusaders. It was clear from the agreement forced from the Pisans after they were worsted that it was business – not God – that was at stake. According to the Monk of the Lido (*Historia de translatione magni Nicolai* 7), Pisan sailors were forced to give binding undertakings that Pisan fleets should 'never again enter Romania [the Byzantine empire] for commercial purposes'.

Venice's wariness was compounded by the fact that their Italian rivals were quick off the mark to leverage the precarious position in the Crusader states to strike valuable deals for themselves. In 1101, for example, the Genoese managed to be awarded lucrative terms in Caesarea both as a reward and as an incentive to bring goods to the Holy Land (Barber 2012, 67–9).

These rewards were soon replicated and mirrored by Venice, which demanded and obtained extensive concessions and privileges from the kingdom of Jerusalem from Tyre, one of the most important ports and trade emporia of the region, which was captured in 1123 (Barber 2012, 140–2). The Venetians proved able and adept at flexing their muscles to maintain their position as and when they needed to.

They did so emphatically in early twelfth century after Split, Zadar and other towns on the Dalmatian coast were occupied by the Hungarians who had already succeeded in establishing control over large parts of the Croatian hinterland. A strong and quick response was needed and duly organised, with a powerful fleet dispatched to restore order and make an emphatic statement that the towns of the eastern Adriatic should look to the duke (doge) of Venice – and not to King Coloman of Hungary – for leadership (Andrea Dandolo, *Chronica* 4.41; *Historia ducum Veneticorum* 1).

This was repeated on several occasions. In 1112, for example, soon after concessions were awarded to Pisa by Alexios I Komnenos – presumably as a way of balancing the growing power of Venice – messages were sent to the emperor to protest at the 'forgotten promises' that had been made not long beforehand to the doge. At stake was position in markets in the Byzantine empire but also influence in the Adriatic where renewed encroachment by the Hungarians again threatened to destabilise Venice's regional position (Andrea Dandolo, *Chronica* 4.41). Once more, the Venetians were not just alert to the danger, but moved decisively, using force against Zadar and Šibenik to protect their dominance on the coastal towns (Smičiklas 1904, 393; Stephenson 2000, 203).

In the 1120s, Venice's confidence and capabilities were so extensive that the city's leaders were even prepared to take matters into their own hands against Constantinople, equipping and dispatching a military expedition that successfully forced John II Komnenos to reconfirm the terms of the grant made by his father Alexios I three decades earlier (Lilie 1993, 97–100). By the 1130s and 1140s, Venetian merchants were starting to bypass Constantinople altogether. Trading with local cities and towns like Thessaloniki, Thebes and above all Alexandria clearly offered higher margins and better financial returns. By this time, warehouses (*funduqs*) had been founded along the north African coast not only by Venice, but by Genoa and Pisa too. But Venice in particular did well thanks to the adoption of financial instruments that enabled the pooling of money and the spreading of risk (Christie 2014; Jacoby 1995).

Concepts like the *commenda* and the *collegeanza* drew heavily similar ideas from the Muslim world such as the *mudaraba* and the *qarid* which were effectively partnership models that allowed a wide body of investors to benefit from successful trade missions (González de Lara 2008). In the case of Venice, this meant that a broad cross section of society was able to participate in the city's commercial expansion which in turn gave non-elites who did invest – such as nuns, craftsmen and the less wealthy – a stake in its success.

Venice's growth, spurred by long-range access to markets, reshaped the Adriatic. On the one hand, rising levels of prosperity spurred the demand for social stratification which in turn drove the demand for luxury goods like spices, silks and textiles. On the other, it provoked demand for manpower and staple commodities, such as wheat, wine, oil and olives.

In this context, coastal towns in the Adriatic – like Ancona, Trogir and Split – looked more like rivals than potential sources of wealth in themselves. None was a producer, beyond what its immediate hinterlands could provide, and while some were vibrant, successful and rising in prosperity themselves in the twelfth century as a result of widening long-distance trade networks, Venetian anxiety about access to supplies led to increasingly strong-arm methods to control the Adriatic.

Of particular concern was the ability to gain steady access to foodstuffs, with the result that Venice not only looked to the Adriatic as a source of manpower but as a space that was able to 'fulfil many of the conventional functions of an agricultural hinterland' (Dorin 2012, 241). This made for tense relations on both sides of the sea, with Ancona the recipient of a withering warning not to compromise or affect Venetian trade with markets like Fano and Pesaro (Abulafia 1984).

Efforts such as these represented efforts to ensure that Venice protected resources that the city authorities considered important. But the use of the carrot could be equally effective as the use of the stick, as Ancona found when first its own citizens were granted privileges in Venice and Venetian territories in 1152. The fact that these were swiftly rescinded in 1154 provided a reminder that antagonisms could appear and sharpen at speed. That Venice was so quick to respond to challenges and threats speaks volumes about its vulnerability – perceived or otherwise – in its own backyard (Dorin 2012, 245).

Part of the reason for this was that cities in the Adriatic were developing into vibrant commercial centres in their own right. Al-Idrīsī, for example, talked of Otranto as being home to 'flourishing markets where much commerce is done', while noting that Trani was also a 'very well-known market', comments that are echoed by other sources from the twelfth century such as Benjamin of Tudela (Dorin 2012, 266).

Perhaps inevitably, the rise of locations such as these – as well as of Venice itself – led to animosities in Constantinople, where the reality of the situation started to dawn on the emperor. Once, the Venetians had been part of Byzantium's methods of control of the Adriatic but it was starting to become clear that they were now also part of the problem – and a serious challenger in their own right. According to John Kinnamos (*Epitomē* 4.14; Abulafia 1984), putting Venice in its place was the primary reason why Manuel I Komnenos launched a major offensive in Italy in 1157, targeting Ancona as a specific and direct means of weakening the Venetians' hold on the Adriatic.

Things were soon to deteriorate even further. In 1171, the emperor gave the order to arrest thousands of Venetians living in Constantinople. One hostile source states that the reason for the sudden and mass rounding-up of Venetian citizens was that they had grown too rich – and had done so at the expense of the Byzantine population (Madden 1993). While there may have been some truth in such claims, it is no coincidence that life was becoming harder in the imperial capital and in the empire as a whole as it came under increasing pressure both in Asia Minor and in the Balkans (Magdalino 1993, 140–71).

While the context for the mass arrests is not entirely clear, the fact that markets in Egypt had suddenly been placed under much closer supervision by the Muslim authorities and in some cases even closed altogether, meant that there was a sharp contraction that evidently had a major impact not only on Venice but on Byzantium too.

The sense of panic that ensued in the former led to the doge of Venice himself setting sail for Constantinople to try to negotiate terms with the emperor, Manuel I Komnenos. His failure to do so had dramatic consequences. When he arrived back in Venice without good news to report, the doge was pursued through the streets of the city and lynched on his way to the convent of San Zaccaria (*Historia ducum Veneticorum* 7; Madden 1993, 166–70).

By this time, the structure of the Adriatic was changing, with new connections weaving the towns and regions of the coast together. By 1195, for example, the see of Kotor was formally under the metropolitan of Bari – that is to say, administered by a cleric based across the water. We know too of intensifying cultural and commercial exchange between Dubrovnik (*Ragusa*) and Molfetta, Ravenna and even Rovinj, several hundred kilometres away. What is more, new entrants were evidently trying to participate in this web of interchanges, with Pisa seeking to establish and build ties with Split, Zadar and Dubrovnik in this period (Dorin 2012, 169).

Venice responded aggressively. A failed punitive assault on Zadar in 1180 that was designed to teach the city a lesson was followed up by an all-out assault in 1202 by the knights of the Fourth Crusade operating under Venetian direction – and in direct contravention of orders by Pope Innocent III to leave the city unharmed. Two years later, Venice was at the forefront of the dismemberment of Constantinople and of the Byzantine empire, again taking advantage of the manpower of the crusaders to force a settlement that sought to protect and enhance the long-term future of the city (Gál 2014; Philipps 2004).

While it is certainly true that what happened in Zadar, Constantinople and Byzantium owed something to chance, it is also clear that a deliberate strategy was in place to ensure that Venice not only retained access to long-distance trade, but also prevented rivals and potential rivals from doing the same. Monopolistic and protective measures were put in place, for example, to prevent ships unloading their cargoes north of Lefkada – to force trade to pass through Venice itself (Cessi 1931, 94). On occasion, this involved engaging with their rivals, as witnessed by the heavy defeat of the Pisans off Modon in 1195 and a pre-emptive strike on Brindisi to drive Pisan settlers away soon afterwards (Buenger Robbert 1985, 410–2).

Shipments of salt and of wheat were not only carefully monitored but also bought by the Venetian state authorities directly in order to keep prices down. Wheat grown south of the lateral between Ancona and Zadar, meanwhile, was subsidised in order to ensure security of supply – and to ensure Venetians were not caught out by inflationary pressure. The extent of such problems is not to be overestimated: in the 1220s, a poor harvest that followed a severe winter led to the price of wheat rising by rising by nearly 50 per cent, putting strain on the wider economy (Buenger Robbert 1994, 381).

Steps were even taken with regard to how Venetians invested or spent their own money, with capital controls being introduced to control the flow of money and direct how that was used too after the closing of the nobility in the late thirteenth century. This was a move that was designed to protect the interests of the richest members of society first by guaranteeing them (and their heirs) a say in the governance of the city but also, no less importantly, by denying that same right to newcomers (Puga and Trefler 2014, 757–9, 787–93).

This was not to say that Venice's success deprived other cities in the Adriatic of economic or cultural oxygen. On the contrary, the plentiful evidence relating to the development of civic society on the eastern coast bears witness to how towns in Dalmatia and the Kvarner (Quarnero) Gulf developed their own identities and even their own laws in the early Middle Ages.

Different views were taken, for example, about gambling which was forbidden in Split but allowed in Šibenik (Fabijanec 2012). Each town developed clearly defined rules regarding acceptable standards of street hygiene and of latrines (Ažman et al. 2006, 166–7). The way in which local markets were supervised, monitored and taxed differed too, as did ideas about animal husbandry. Dubrovnik passed laws prohibiting the shipping of imported wine, with transgressors forced to watch as their illegal cargoes were tipped over the side of their boats if they were caught with contraband (Ravančić 2014).

Despite Venice's determination to control long-distance trade, it is clear that towns in the Adriatic benefitted from the uplift in connectivity in the twelfth and thirteenth centuries. The foundation of hospices and hospitals in Zadar in the 1250s provide one example of the increasing levels of disposable wealth in the town in this period, while expanding elite and non-elite networks and rising literacy levels too indicate a time of accelerated socio-economic change (Petaros *et al.* 2013).

Nevertheless, the towns of the Adriatic were unable to keep up with the city that had risen in the lagoons of the north. Venice had managed to dominate partly because it was able to concentrate its resources and to look beyond into the Aegean and the eastern Mediterranean as part of a long-term strategy that paid off handsomely in the long run. Cities that might once have been considered rivals suffered from the fact that while they did well from local, interregional trade, the limitations to their economic firepower ultimately meant that they could not keep up as Venice took off.

Venice's investments also paid off as the city became the pre-eminent entry point for goods that were in demand across Europe. Towns like Dubrovnik, Split and Trogir were less convenient gateways to Asia and Africa, while Venice's proximity to royal courts that were both increasingly wealthy and whose horizons were themselves expanding were much in its favour.

While Venice rose to pre-eminence in the Adriatic, it was also striking that the east and west sides of the sea were on fundamentally different trajectories. Those on the west were part of a system of production that was not just important but crucial for Venice – especially in terms of agricultural production. In 1226, for example, Ravenna agreed to sell all its surplus food to the Venetians, as part of an agreement that offered the former plentiful rewards in exchange for their co-operation.

Those on the eastern side of the Adriatic had less to offer and its rhythms of exchange and interaction became to diverge accordingly. Petrarch was one who noted this. While 'we have the sea in common', he remarked, 'the shores are opposite, the souls are diverse, the teachings are different and the language and customs completely dissimilar' (Petrarch, *Letters on Familiar Matters*, 33).

For Petrarch, the sea was means of linking peoples, ideas and goods together, but rather as an all but impassable body that prevented connections being made. 'As the Alps separate us from the Germans and the French, and the stormy Mediterranean keeps us from the Africans', he wrote, 'so too does the Adriatic set us apart from the Dalmatians and the Pannonians' (Petrarch, *Letters on Familiar Matters*, 33).

Venice's rise had eclipsed towns that were older, more established and had once been more powerful. The change in Venice's fortunes was a cipher for the wider transformation of Europe in the Early Middle Ages and the greater focus on the Holy Land and the east. The Adriatic had been transformed from a peripheral body of water into one of the most important arteries linking Europe and a series of new worlds beyond.

References

Abulafia, D. 1984. 'Ancona, Byzantium and the Adriatic, 1155–1173,' *Papers of the British School at Rome* 52, 195–216.
  2014. *The Great Sea: A Human History of the Mediterranean* (London).
Anna Komnene. *Alexias*, in Reinsch, D. and Kambylis, A. (eds.), *Annae Comnenae Alexias*. Corpus fontium historiae Byzantinae – Series Berolinensis 40 (Berlin, 2001).
Andrea Dandolo. *Chronica*, in Pastorello, E. (ed.), *Andreae Danduli ducis Venetiarum Chronica per extensum descripta aa. 46-1280 d.C.*, Rerum Italicarum scriptores 12/1 (Bologna, 1938–58).
Ažman, J., Muzur, A., Frković, V., Pavletić, H., Prunk, A., and Škrobonja, A. 2006. 'Public health problems in the medieval statutes of Vinodol, Vrbnik and Senj (West Croatia)', *Journal of Public Health* 28/2, 166-7.
Barber, M. 2012. *The Crusader States* (New Haven).
Bekker, I. (ed.), *Georgius Cedrenus, Synopsis historion Ioannis Scylitzae ope*, vol. 2, Corpus scriptorum historiae Bizantinae (Bonn, 1839).
Boccaccio, G. *The Decameron*, ed. Rebhorn, W. (New York, 2013).
Buenger Robbert, L. 1985. 'Venice and the Crusades', in Zacour, N.P. and Hazard, H.W. (eds.), *The Impact of the Crusades on the Near East*, vol. 5 of Setton, K.M. (ed.), *A History of the Crusades* (Madison), 379–451.
  1994. 'Money and prices in thirteenth century Venice', *Journal of Medieval History* 20, 373–90.
Castagnetti, A. 1992. 'Famiglie e affermazione politica', in Cracco Ruggini, L. (ed.), *Storia di Venezia: Dalle origini alla caduta della Serenissima*, vol. 1, *Origini: Età ducale* (Rome), 613–44.
Cessi, R. (ed.) 1931. 'Precepta, iuramenta, interdicta', in *Deliberazioni del maggior consiglio di Venezia*, vol. 1 (Bologna), 17–111.
Christie, N. 2014. 'Cosmopolitan trade centre or bone of contention? Alexandria and the Crusades 487–857/1095–1453', *Al-Masāq* 26/1, 49–61.
Ciggaar, K. 1995. 'Une description de Constantinople dans le Tarragonensis 55', *Revue des études byzantines* 53, 117–40.
  1996. *Western Travellers to Constantinople: The West and Byzantium, 962-1204, Cultural and Political Relations* (Leiden).
Constantine Porphyrogennetos. *De administrando imperio*, in Moravcsik, G. and Jenkins, R.J.H. (eds.), *Constantine Porphyrogenitus. De administrando imperio* (Washington, DC, 1967).

Cowdrey, H.E.J. 1998. *Pope Gregory VII, 1073–1085* (Oxford).

Di Sisto, L. 1994. 'Boccaccio, friend or foe? An examination of the role of women in the *Decameron*', *Spunti e ricerche* 10, 63–75.

Dorin, R.W. 2012. 'Adriatic trade networks in the twelfth and early thirteenth centuries', in Morrisson, C. (ed.), *Trade and Markets in Byzantium* (Washington, DC), 235–79.

Fabijanec, S. 2012. '*Ludus zardorum*: Moral and legal frameworks of gambling along the Adriatic in the Middle Ages', in Miljan, S. and Jaritz, G. (eds.), *At the Edge of the Law: Socially Unacceptable and Illegal Behaviour in the Middle Ages and the Early Modern Period* (Krems), 31–49.

Falkenhausen, V. von 1970. 'Eine byzantinische Beamtenurkunde aus Dubrovnik', *Byzantinische Zeitschrift* 63/1, 10–23.

Ferrante, J.M. 1993. 'Politics, finance and feminism in *Decameron*, II, 7', *Studi sul Boccaccio* 21, 151–74.

Frankopan, P. 2002. 'The imperial governors of Dyrrakhion in the reign of Alexios I Komnenos', *Byzantine and Modern Greek Studies* 26/1, 65–103.

  2004a. 'Byzantine trade privileges to Venice in the eleventh century: The chrysobull of 1092', *Journal of Medieval History* 30/2, 135–60.

  2004b. 'Co-operation between Constantinople and Rome before the First Crusade: A study of the convergence of interests in Croatia in the late eleventh century', *Crusades* 3, 1–13.

  2004c. 'Challenges to imperial authority in Byzantium: Revolts on Crete and Cyprus at the end of the 11th century,' *Byzantion* 74/2, 382–402.

  2012a. *The First Crusade: The Call from the East* (London).

  2012b. 'Expeditions against the Serbs in the 1090s: The Alexiad and Byzantium's north-west frontier on the eve of the First Crusade', *Bulgaria medievalis* 3/1, 385–98.

Gál, J. 2014. 'The roles and loyalties of the bishops and archbishops of Dalmatia (1102–1301)', *The Hungarian Historical Review* 3/3, 471–93.

González de Lara, Y. 2008. 'The secret of Venetian success: A public-order, reputation-based institution', *European Review of Economic History* 12, 247–85.

Harvey, A. 1989. *Economic Expansion in the Byzantine Empire, 900–1200* (Cambridge).

Hoffmann, H. 1969. 'Die Anfänge der Normannen in Süditalien', *Quellen und Forschungen aus italienischen Archiven und Bibiliotheken* 49, 95–144.

Jacoby, D. 1995. 'Les Italiens en Égypte aux XIe et XIIe siècle: Du comptoir à la colonie', in Balard, M. and Ducellier, A. (eds.), *Coloniser au Moyen Âge: Méthodes d'expansion et techniques de domination en Méditerranée du 11e au 16e siècle* (Paris), 76–88.

  2001. 'The supply of war materials to Egypt in the crusader period', *Jerusalem Studies in Arabic and Islam* 25, 102–32.

John the Deacon. *Istoria Veneticorum*, in Berto, L.A. (ed.), *Giovanni Diacono. Istoria Veneticorum* (Bologna, 1999).

John Kinnamos. *Epitomē*, in Meineke, A. (ed.), *Ioannis Cinnami Epitome rerum ab Ioanne et Alexio Comnenis gestarum* (Bonn, 1836).

Košćak, V. 1991. 'Gregorio VII e la Croazia: Presupposti politico-sociali', *Studi Gregoriani* 14 = Stickler, A.M., Capitani, O., Fuhrmann, H., Maccarrone, M., Schieffer, R. and Volpini, R. (eds.), *La riforma gregoriana e l'Europa, Congresso internazionale Salerno, 20–25 maggio 1985*, vol. 2, *Comunicazioni* (Rome), 253–64.

Lemerle, P., Guillou, A., Svoronos, N. and Papachryssanthou, D. (eds.) 1970. *Actes de Lavra I: Des origines à 1204*, Archives de l'Athos V (Paris).

Lilie, R.-J. 1984. *Handel und Politik zwischen dem byzantinischen Reich und den italienischen Kommunen Venedig, Pisa und Genua in der Epoche der Komnenen und der Angeloi (1081–1204)* (Amsterdam).

1993. (trans. Morris, J.C. and Ridings, J.E.) *Byzantium and the Crusader States, 1096–1204* (Oxford).

Litavrin, G. (ed.) 1972. Советы и рассказы Кекавмена. Сочинение византийского полководца IX века (Moscow).

Loud, G.A. 2000. *The Age of Robert Guiscard: Southern Italy and the Norman Conquest* (Harlow).

Madden, T.F. 1993. 'Venice and Constantinople in 1171 and 1172: Enrico Dandolo's attitudes towards Byzantium', *Mediterranean Historical Review* 8/2, 166–85.

Magdalino, P. 1993. *The Empire of Manuel I Komnenos, 1143–1180* (Cambridge).

McCormick, M. 2013. 'Comparing and connecting: Comacchio and the Early Medieval trading towns', in Gelichi, S. and Hodges, R. (eds.), *From One Sea to Another: Trading Places in the European and Mediterranean Early Middle Ages. Proceedings of the International Conference, Comacchio, 27th–29th March 2009* (Turnhout), 477–502.

Metcalf, D. 1979. *Coinage in South-Eastern Europe, 820–1396* (Oxford).

Miklosich, F. and Müller, I. (eds.) 1890. *Acta et diplomata Graeca medii aevi sacra et profana*, vol. 6, *Acta et diplomata monasteriorum et ecclesiarum Orientis* 3 (Vienna).

Monk of the Lido. *Historia de translatione magni Nicolai*, in *Recueil des historiens des croisades. Historiens occidentaux*, vol. 5 (Paris, 1895), 253–92.

Neville, L. 2004. *Authority in Byzantine Provincial Society, 950–1100* (Cambridge).

Pertusi, A. 1990. 'Venezia e Bisanzio nel secolo XI', in Parente, G.B. (ed.), *Agostino Pertusi: Saggi veneto-bizantini* (Florence), 67–107.

Petaros, A., Škrobonja, A., Čulina, T., Bosnar, A., Frković, V. and Ažman, J. 2013. 'Public health problems in the Medieval statutes of Croatian Adriatic coastal towns: From public morality to public health', *Journal of Religion and Health* 52/2, 531–7.

Petrarch. (trans. Bernardo, A.) *Letters on Familiar Matters: Books IX–XVI* (New York, 2005).

Philipps, J. 2004. *The Fourth Crusade and the Sack of Constantinople* (London).

Pozza, M. and Ravegnani, G. (eds.) 1993. *I trattati con Bisanzio, 992–1198*, Pacta Veneta 4 (Venice).

Puga, D. and Trefler, D. 2014 'International trade and institutional change: Medieval Venice's response to globalization', *The Quarterly Journal of Economics* 129/2, 753–821.

Queller, D. and Katele, I.B. 1986. 'Venice and the conquest of the Latin kingdom of Jerusalem', *Studi veneziani* n.s. 12, 15–43.

Rački, F. (ed.) 1877. *Documenta historiae Chroaticae periodum antiquam illustrantia* (Zagreb).

Ravančić, G. 2014. "Wine-contamination of the Adriatic': Examples of punishing wine smugglers from medieval Dubrovnik', *Acta Histriae* 22, 839–42.

Romanin, S. 1853. *Storia documentata di Venezia*, vol. 1 (Venice).

Historia ducum Veneticorum, in Simonsfeld, H. (ed.), *MGH Scriptores*, vol. 14 (Hanover, 1883), 72–97.

Smičiklas, T. (ed.) 1904. *Codex diplomaticus regni Croatiae, Dalmatiae et Slavoniae*, vol. 1, *Diplomata saeculi XII continens* (Zagreb).

Stephenson, P. 2000. *Byzantium's Balkan Frontier: A Political Study of the Northern Balkans, 900–1204* (Cambridge).

Stipišić, J. and Šamšalović, M. (eds.) 1967. *Codex diplomaticus regni Croatiae, Dalmatiae et Slavoniae*, vol. 1, *Diplomata annorum 743.–1100. continens* (Zagreb).

Supičić, I. 1999. *Croatia in the Early Middle Ages: A Cultural Survey* (London).

Theotokis, G. 2014. *The Norman Campaigns in the Balkans, 1081–1118* (Woodbridge).

Whittow, M. 1996. *The Making of Orthodox Byzantium, 600–1025* (London).

Wickham, C. 2009. *The Inheritance of Rome: A History of Europe from 400 to 1000* (London).

12 | Venice in the Twelfth Century

Between the Adriatic and the Aegean

MICHAEL ANGOLD

At the battle of Cape Matapan in 1718 a Venetian fleet of twenty-six ships fought a superior Ottoman fleet of thirty-six ships to a standstill.[*] These were many more ships than the French and English committed to the battle of Aboukir Bay eighty years later (Lane 1973, 410). This may seem to be a slightly odd starting point for a note on Venetian history in the twelfth century, but it brings home that in the early eighteenth century Venice continued to battle prodigiously – and suffer heavy casualties – as it had done for centuries, in order to maintain its foothold in Greece. It makes one wonder why an Adriatic power, such as Venice, persisted over so many centuries in linking its destiny to Greece and the eastern Mediterranean. Was Venice's involvement with the East built into its development as a polity from its earliest history as an outpost of the Byzantine empire? Why was it that Venice was unable to escape the Byzantine embrace, which continued, if in a rather different form, after the Venetians had helped the crusaders to conquer Constantinople in 1204? The argument of this paper is that in the twelfth century Venice had the opportunity and good reason to break its close ties with Byzantium, but chose not to. Economic and political self-interest and commercial rivalry with Genoa and Pisa were obvious factors. Less obvious was sentiment. It manifested itself as loyalty to the Byzantine empire, however self-serving it may have been in practice.

The Byzantine emperor was after all the guarantor of Venetian privileges within the Byzantine empire. The mutual benefits, which co-operation in the shape of naval assistance offered Byzantium and Venice, were first formalised in the imperial chrysobull of 992 (Lilie 1984, 1–8; Pertusi 1965, 155–60; Tůma 1984). Only one of its provisions need detain us. It treated the Venetians as outsiders (*extranei*, Maltezou 1995, 235; Pozza and Ravegnani 1993, 22.4; Tafel and Thomas 1856, 37.3). This is in contrast to the chrysobull issued by Alexios I Komnenos, traditionally dated to 1082 but doubt remains as to its exact date (Borsari 1969–70, 111–31; Frankopan 2004), where the Venetians were now upstanding subjects

---

[*] On Venice and the Byzantine empire in the twelfth century in general, see Angold 2007; Borsari 1988; Lilie 1984; Nicol 1988, 50–124; Ravegnani 2006, 47–102; Thiriet 1959, 29–62.

(*recti duli*) of the Byzantine empire (Pozza and Ravegnani 1993, 42.4, 44.8; Tafel and Thomas 1856, 54.15). However one chooses to understand the word 'outsider', becoming subjects of the Byzantine empire represented a radical change of status, which tied the Venetians ever closer to Byzantium. The main concession made to the Venetians by Alexios I Komnenos was exemption from merchandise tax (*kommerkia*) and other dues, which ostensibly applied to 'all parts of Romania'. However, this was then qualified by a list of a restricted number of ports and cities. The places included cluster around Dyrrachion (modern Durrës), the Peloponnese and mainland Greece and around the Sea of Marmora. This makes sense in that they were along the route from Venice to Constantinople, while the ports along the southern coast of Anatolia, which are also included, were along the route to the ports of Syria, which are singled out as a final destination.

The list is notable, however, for omitting within the regions covered many important commercial centres. Of the Aegean islands only Chios appears in the list and the absence of Rhodes is striking. In the Peloponnese Monemvasia is missing, as is Patras, and on the opposite coast Naupaktos, and further inland Arta. It is more than likely that the imperial government was trying to channel Venetian activity along specific routes without offending local interests. It may also be, to judge by the example of Dyrrachion, which was already a Venetian trading counter or *embulo* before 1082 (Anna Komnene, *Alexias* 5.1.1) that the Byzantine government had earmarked places already frequented by the Venetians. The documentation we have to go on is of course skimpy. In the collection of commercial documents edited by Raimondo Morozzo della Rocca and Antonino Lombardo (1940) there are barely twenty-five which date to before 1100 and only eight of these deal with trade in the Byzantine empire. Is it pure coincidence that, of these, two concern Venetian business ventures to Thebes which was one of the very few inland towns included in the list? They date to 1072 and 1073 and point to a long Venetian association with the city, which in the twelfth century allowed Venetian traders to put down roots (Morozzo della Rocca and Lombardo 1940, vol. 1, nos. 12–13).

It was a time of experimentation. For the first and only time an anchor, or shares in an anchor, represented important capital (Morozzo della Rocca and Lombardo 1940, vol. 1, no. 20; for a voyage to Antioch see no. 24), which was clearly in short supply and limited the amount of business that the Venetians could do. They had to import coin or bullion with all the attendant difficulties of exchange rates. The disadvantages can be inferred from the way that, before long, Venetians operating in Constantinople started to make exclusive use of Byzantine currency whether in their transactions or when forming companies and business associations, which are attested from the early 1120s (Morozzo della Rocca and Lombardo 1940, vol. 1, nos. 46, 54). The obvious conclusion is that Venetians were generating capital for trade in the Byzantine empire on the spot. This was an important milestone. It gave those Venetians operating in the Byzantine empire under Alexios I Komnenos a distinct advantage over others. They soon became a powerful voice in Venetian politics. It was involvement with Byzantium that allowed some of the greatest of Venetian families to build their fortunes, including all those that supplied doges in the twelfth and thirteenth centuries. They invested the profits made from trade with Byzantium in property back home (Fees 1988).

They saw the advantages of Venetians becoming upstanding subjects of the Byzantine emperor, but not all did. The advantages of the Byzantine connection were called into question by the serious defeat suffered by the Venetians in 1084 at the hands of the Normans. Such was the popular fury that the Duke Domenico Silvo abdicated. However, his successors remained true to the Byzantine alliance, which received material form in the shape of the altarpiece known as the *Pala d'Oro*, given to Doge Ordelafo Falier (1101-18) by the Emperor Alexios I Komnenos. However reconstructed, the altarpiece was originally a statement of Byzantine supremacy and reflected the acceptance by the doge of the part assigned to him: that of an upstanding subject of the Byzantine empire (Hahnloser and Polacco 1994).

Twelfth-century Byzantine emperors did not always reciprocate this display of Venetian loyalty. In 1119 Alexios' son and successor John II Komnenos refused to renew the Venetian privileges (Nicol 1988, 77-8). The explanation of the Byzantine historian John Kinnamos is that the Venetians were insufficiently upstanding subjects. The emperor apparently took exception to their insolence, which was directed not so much against the general population as against the powerful, including members of the imperial family (John Kinnamos, *Epitomē* 6.10; *The Deeds of John and Manuel Comnennos* 210). It was almost certainly a question of jurisdiction, which the 1082 chrysobull did little to clarify, beyond exempting the Venetians from the authority of a whole series of officials from the prefect of the city downwards. Included in this list were local officials and members of the imperial family (Pozza and Ravegnani 1993, 41.11-20; Tafel and Thomas 1856, 53.11-16). It would seem that the Venetians interpreted this exemption as permission to manage their own affairs, when resident in the Byzantine empire. This is borne out by a document of March 1112 drawn up at the Thessalian port of Halmyros (Morozzo della

Rocca and Lombardo 1940, vol. 1, no. 35). Though only a matter of winding up a company, it was done under the supervision of the doge's legate and without regard to the Byzantine authorities. Another point of contention was the payment of *kommerkion* on deals concluded between Venetians and Byzantines. The former insisted that under the terms of the chrysobull nobody was liable for payment, whereas the Byzantine authorities refused to accept that such transactions were exempted (Pozza and Ravegnani 1993, 55.5–17; Tafel and Thomas 1856, 97–8). There was a further difficulty with trading in Crete and Cyprus, which the Byzantines tried to prevent on the grounds that these islands were not included in the list of ports given in the 1082 chrysobull (Pozza and Ravegnani 1993, 63–4; Tafel and Thomas 1856, 124.1–22).

The expansion of Venetian interests in the Byzantine empire necessarily created friction. Whether this was enough to justify the drastic action that John II Komnenos took against them is another matter. It may just have been that the Norman threat, which prompted the grant of such extensive privileges to Venetians, was in abeyance – temporarily as it turned out – with the result that Venetian naval assistance was less necessary. It was a risky thing to do, because Byzantine naval forces had been allowed to run down (Niketas Choniates, *Historia*, 54–6). Using the cover of an expedition going to the rescue of the kingdom of Jerusalem, the Venetians attacked the fortress of Corfu before proceeding to the Holy Land. On the return journey in 1124 the Venetians raided Rhodes and then established a base on the island of Chios. Having terrorised the islands of the Aegean they made their way back to Venice, but this was not the end of it. In 1126 the Venetians raided the island of Kephalenia (Lilie 1984, 367–75; Riley-Smith 1986). This concerted naval campaign brought John II to the negotiating table, where he confirmed the chrysobull of 1082 and added the necessary clarifications (Pozza and Ravegnani 1993, 51–6; Tafel and Thomas 1856, 96–8). The single-mindedness with which Doge Domenico Michiel (1118–29) pursued the recovery of Venetian privileges indicates how much was at stake, particularly for families, such as the Michiel, which invested in Byzantine trade. But it was not entirely a matter of trade. Status was important. John II Komnenos made one slight but significant adjustment: the Venetians were not just the most beloved subjects; they were now also friends or allies of the Byzantine empire (Pozza and Ravegnani 1993, 54–5; Tafel and Thomas 1856, 97.28). It gave due recognition to their exemption from the surveillance of government officials. Supervision of the affairs of the Venetian communities scattered around the Byzantine empire was in the hands of legates sent out at irregular intervals by the doge (Morozzo della Rocca and Lombardo 1940, vol. 1, no. 95).

The continuing importance of the Byzantine connection to the Venetian patriciate was underlined in 1129, when Doge Domenico Michiel arranged for the succession to go to his son-in-law Pietro Polani who came from another of those families with a vested interest in Byzantium. His father Domenico Polani enjoyed the prestigious Byzantine court title of *protonobellisimos*, as we learn from the document recording the establishment of a confraternity of St Stephen, whose relics were brought back to Venice from Constantinople by a group of Venetians (Lanfranchi 1968, no. 144). Their names are, in fact, a roll call of the families who dominated trade with Byzantium from the turn of the eleventh century: Badoer, Contarini, Corner, Dandolo, Giustiniani, Gradenico, Mastropietro, Michiel, Morosini and Sanudo (Borsari 1988, 65–8). Although the choice of doge was still nominally by popular acclamation, there seems to have been no opposition to Pietro Polani's accession. In some ways, it looks like a takeover by families with Byzantine interests. Polani appointed to the position of judge members of just such families, for example, the Dandolo. It was while Polani was doge that the council of the *Sapientes* or *Savi* is first attested. There is no need to assume that its purpose was to limit the power of the doge. It is far more likely to have already come into existence informally as a way of easing the burden of the doge's growing responsibilities. Its formalisation under Pietro Polani may have been the result of the challenges he had to face from abroad: the Hungarians were threatening Venice's hold along the Dalmatian coast, while there were pressures on the *Terraferma* from Padua and Ancona. This council was at the heart of the Venetian commune – the word makes its first appearance in a Venetian context at this time (Castagnetti 1995, 81–8; Fasoli 1965, 71–102). However, it was an instrument of oligarchic, not popular power. It was an oligarchy, whose members favoured the Byzantine connection because of the resources it supplied both communally and individually to support ambitions closer to home. The appearance of the council of the *Sapientes* did not mean a reduction in the power of the doge – to judge by the way Polani was able to exile members of the Dandolo and Badoer families, who were traditionally supposed to have opposed his election as doge and his support for Byzantium. If this were indeed the reason for their enmity with the doge, it would put a completely different complexion on the politics of the time. However, Thomas Madden has demonstrated that the quarrel between Doge Pietro Polani and the Dandolo and Badoer families was over ecclesiastical matters. It was a conflict of jurisdiction between Enrico

Dandolo the Elder, who was patriarch of Grado, and Giovanni Polani, the doge's brother, who was bishop of Castello (Madden 2003, 25–36).

Those families that grew rich through their involvement with Byzantium invested their profits in property back in Venice. It is clear that along with this went control of ecclesiastical appointments, which could be a cause of great friction (Rando 1992). It did not mean that there was any inclination on the part of leading families to jettison the advantages that came from the Byzantine connection. Enrico Dandolo the Elder was at the heart of opposition to Doge Pietro Polani, but as patriarch of Grado he was perhaps the largest Venetian property owner in Constantinople where in October 1169 he leased out on very favourable terms to the famous Venetian entrepreneur Romano Mairano his personal property together with the holdings of the patriarchate of Grado (Morozzo della Rocca and Lombardo 1940, vol. 1, no. 245)

The structure of the Venetian presence in the Byzantine empire becomes clearer from the mid-twelfth century, because the documentation is that much fuller. This in turn reflected a greater awareness of the vital importance of Venice's privileged position in the Byzantine empire, defence of which was to become a leitmotif of Venetian history. It forms a thread binding Venice to Byzantium, which might seem to be at odds with an almost total neglect of the original texts: whether in Greek or in Latin translation. The text of the 992 chrysobull was not kept in the state archives and survives quite by accident, while the original of the famous chrysobull of Alexios I Komnenos disappeared in the twelfth century and we only have a copy embedded in a later privilege. However, from the middle of the twelfth century the Venetians insisted that the texts of old privileges should be included word for word in the new diplomas issued by the Byzantine emperors. At a time when Venetian institutions were beginning to take shape, it is indicative of a greater appreciation of official documents. It was paralleled by a greater concern for the preservation of private documents with the consequence that our information becomes far more systematic from the mid-twelfth century (Bartoli Langeli 1992).

We find that members of patrician families with a tradition of involvement with Byzantium are the major investors and their younger members participate in Byzantine trade. Around them there were the smaller fry responsible for finding new openings and doing the heavy work. The best documented are the Mairano brothers who were sea captains and traders (Borsari 1988, 116–28; Heynen 1905, 86–120). It was therefore not only a few patrician families which had a stake in the trade of the Byzantine empire, but whole networks of traders and seafarers who represented a cross section of Venetian society.

In a famous article Peter Schreiner (1979) argued that the permanent Venetian presence in the Byzantine empire before 1204 was negligible. He demonstrated that the figures given by chroniclers for Latin settlers in the Byzantine empire were inflated several times over. On that, he is certainly correct, but it does not mean that the Venetian presence was negligible. His assertion that it was only in Constantinople that the Venetians had a quarter is correct in the sense that it was officially handed over and its boundaries established, but unofficially there were Venetian quarters in several Greek provincial cities. For example, at Halmyros – much frequented by the Venetians in the twelfth century – there was a complex of Venetian property around the Venetian church of St George (Tafel and Thomas 1856, 126.9–13, 128.12–16, 130.25–9). This is likely to have been the pattern followed in other Byzantine ports and towns where a Venetian church or monastery is attested in the twelfth century. Leaving aside Constantinople these are found at Halmyros, Corinth, Sparta, Thebes, Abydos, Rodosto – where there were two – and on the island of Lemnos (Borsari 1988, 40–1).

The churches formed the core of Venetian settlements. They performed invaluable services in the Byzantine empire. They kept the weights and measures for the Venetian community. Their importance transpires from a privilege issued by the doge in 1145 to the church of St George at Rodosto, granting it exclusive control over the weights and measures used by Venetians in their transactions (Tafel and Thomas 1856, 104.15–26). Two years later legates of the doge were holding a hearing at Rodosto, because the local Venetians were unwilling to abide by the privileges granted to the church of St George. The legates forced them to respect the privileged position over weights and measures enjoyed by the church and established a tariff of how much they paid for the privilege. Anybody ignoring this ruling was to be held as 'somebody who diminishes and holds in contempt the honour of his *patria*' and would be subject to a fine from the doge's court (Lombardo and Morozzo della Rocca 1953, no. 8). It is interesting that any Greek using the weights and measures had to pay double the Venetian rate (Tafel and Thomas 1856, 108.4–5).

Control of weights and measures was clearly a source of considerable revenues to Venetian churches which performed a service akin to banks. It was quite usual for Venetians to put any spare capital they had on deposit with their local church for safekeeping (Borsari 1988, 56–7; Lombardo and Morozzo della Rocca 1953, no. 23; Morozzo della Rocca and Lombardo

1940, vol. 1, nos. 88, 94, 108, 110, 363). These churches also invested in property. There is the example of the church of St Mark's in the Venetian quarter at Constantinople advancing a very large sum of over 800 gold coins (*hyperpyra*) against the surety of a plot of land in the Venetian quarter in the Thessalian port of Halmyros, which the borrower then surrendered to the church in exchange for the loan (Tafel and Thomas 1856, 125–33). Attached to these churches there was very frequently a priest who doubled as a notary capable of dealing with the business activities of the local Venetian community.

These included transactions with local people, such as those between Venetian merchants working at Sparta (or Lakedaimonia) with the local *archontes* for the export of olive oil to Constantinople (Lombardo and Morozzo della Rocca 1953, nos. 9, 11). The Venetians active in the Greek lands were mainly interested in the export of agricultural goods to Constantinople, though this was not the exclusive destination. For example, Venetians trading in olive oil from Sparta are first attested in 1135 (Morozzo della Rocca and Lombardo 1940, vol. 1, no. 65). It was a trade that required extensive travelling and contracts sometimes specified the itinerary to be followed. One drawn up in 1155 in Constantinople directed the merchant to Corinth and Thebes and then to return overland to Constantinople (Morozzo della Rocca and Lombardo 1940, vol. 1, no. 110). Several from Thebes required a sweep of the Peloponnese and the Greek lands and could be followed by the overland route to Thessaloniki (Morozzo della Rocca and Lombardo 1940, vol. 1, nos. 137, 235, 239).

A miracle of a Byzantine saint suggests that these Venetian establishments in the provinces were not as transitory as Schreiner would like. It concerns two brothers from Aquileia, by which the Byzantine author is likely to have meant *Equilo*, which was a mainland settlement within the Venetian orbit. It supplied a number of traders specialising in commerce with Byzantium (Lombardo and Morozzo della Rocca 1953, nos. 9, 11; Morozzo della Rocca and Lombardo 1940, vol. 1, nos. 27, 46, 67, 144, 146–7, 173, 182, 217, 233–4, 288, 418, 426). The brothers settled in Sparta for reasons of trade. Once there, one went mad and became violent. Neighbours advised the other brother, whose name was Vitale, to take him to the sanctuary of the local saint, Nikon *ho Metanoeite* (d. c.1000). There he had the saint's chain put around his neck, which was a normal part of the healing process, but this time it failed. The monks were reluctant to take responsibility for the sick man – there were problems because he was a foreigner – and sent him back to his brother. All, however, turned out for the best because St Nikon appeared to him in a dream and he was healed (*The Life of St Nikon*, 250–7; Armstrong 2009a; 2009b). We may be able to tie this incident a little more closely to the activities of Venetian merchants operating in Sparta. In October 1151 two inhabitants of *Equilo*, Vitale Urso and Vitale Senatori, testified that they were witnesses to a transaction at Sparta over the export of olive oil, which involved one party handing over documents in Greek to the other (Lombardo and Morozzo della Rocca 1953, no. 11). It is hard not to believe that one of these inhabitants of *Equilo* was not the Vitale in question. There was also a Frugerio Senatori from *Equilo*, who in October 1170 testified at Thebes that he had previously been at Sparta (Morozzo della Rocca and Lombardo 1940, vol. 1, no. 233). Although relations between the people of Sparta and the Venetian settlers were not free of tension, the brothers were sufficiently part of the community to seek the intervention of the local saint. That the Venetians put down roots in the Byzantine provinces is evident, if we look ahead several years to 1171 and the internment of Venetian merchants at the orders of Manuel I Komnenos. Venetian activity in the Byzantine empire was supposed to be at an end, but at Thebes we find that Venetian merchants with a history of trading in Greece were still doing deals as late as 1176 (Morozzo della Rocca and Lombardo 1940, vol. 1, nos. 272–5). The only conclusion is that the Byzantine authorities allowed them to continue their activities, which suggests not only their long-standing connection with the place, but also their indispensability.

At the heart of Venetian commerce in the Byzantine empire was of course its factory, referred to as its *embulo*, at Constantinople. It was here rather than on the Rialto that the bulk of the capital for trade in the Byzantine empire and Syria was raised. It was here that the mass of Venetians participating in Byzantine trade congregated. From Constantinople Venetians would organise voyages not only throughout the Byzantine empire and back to Venice, but also to Syria and Egypt. The use of the word *mudua* for the seasonal fleets linking Venice to Constantinople (Morozzo della Rocca and Lombardo 1940, vol. 1, nos. 69, 183, 235, 353) and points in between suggests some sort of organisation though less developed than it was to become in the fourteenth and fifteenth centuries.

The Byzantine authorities were never comfortable with communities that aspired to a degree of autonomy. The Venetians encountered hostility. 'Against the violence of the governor and people' (*contra violentiam senioris et populi*) seems to have become a mantra in a set of Venetian documents from Halmyros of 1151 (Tafel and Thomas 1856, 129.3–4, 132.7–8, 132.15). The hostility of the local governor suggests something different from the routine xenophobia that the brothers from *Equilo* encountered at Sparta, which took the form of prowlers and burglars targeting their property (*The Life of St Nikon*, 252.35-7). It was a reflection of a tense phase of Venetian relations with Byzantium, which began with the reluctance shown by Manuel I Komnenos (1143–80) at the beginning of his reign to renew Venetian privileges. Their renewal was forced upon him by the naval campaign that King Roger II of Sicily launched in 1147 against the Aegean and the Greek lands (Lilie 1984, 404–6; Nicol 1988, 84–6). Famously, Corinth and Thebes were sacked during this campaign; this was hardly in the Venetian interest, because both places were vital for Venetian trade in Greece and the Peloponnese. In fact, we know that olive oil dispatched by Venetian merchants from the Peloponnese to Constantinople was seized by Roger's fleet (Lombardo and Morozzo della Rocca 1953, no. 11).

Once their privileges were renewed in 1148 the Venetians were willing to put their sea power at the service of the Byzantine emperor, but relations did not noticeably improve. The most urgent task was to drive the Normans from Corfu. It proved to be anything but straightforward. A major assault failed and in their disappointment the Byzantine and Venetian forces came to blows. The Venetians got the worse of it and sailed away. From a base on the mainland they started attacking Byzantine ships (Lilie 1984, 407–12; Nicol 1988, 86–8). It was on this occasion that they seized the imperial flagship and enacted that famous charade with a black dwarf standing in for Manuel Komnenos. It was an incident that only the historian Niketas Choniates records. He included it as part of an explanation for Manuel Komnenos' otherwise irrational hatred for the Venetians, which, the historian contended, exploded twenty-two years later with the emperor's coup against them (Niketas Choniates, *Historia*, 86.77–86). It was not an explanation that another contemporary historian John Kinnamos was willing to entertain, but being that much closer to official thinking at Manuel Komnenos' court than Niketas Choniates he was unlikely to include an episode that cast the emperor in a slightly discreditable light.

As it was, the Norman garrison at Corfu duly surrendered and entered Byzantine service. With Venetian help Manuel Komnenos thus secured the empire's western flank against the Sicilian threat, but relations between the two powers remained tense because building on the victory over the Normans, Manuel Komnenos sought to strengthen the Byzantine hold on the southern Adriatic, which was to trespass on the Venetian sphere of influence. The forward policy adopted by Manuel Komnenos in the late

1160s along the Dalmatian coast strained relations with Venice as did his support for Ancona (Abulafia 1977, 141–53; 1984; Nicol 1988, 95–6; Stephenson 2000, 261–6). However, there are no clear indications in the narrative sources, whether Byzantine or Venetian, that this was a factor in the emperor's decision taken in March 1171 to have all the Venetians in the Byzantine empire arrested and their property sequestered.

Do the relatively abundant Venetian commercial documents provide any pointers? If we take documents drawn up at Constantinople by Venetians we find brisk business throughout the 1160s – between February and August 1168 there were no less than fifteen surviving contracts drawn up between Venetians at Constantinople – until suddenly there is a gap between August 1169 and October 1170. The lack of activity at Constantinople was compensated at Halmyros where eight contracts between Venetians are attested from October 1169 to March 1170 (Morozzo della Rocca and Lombardo 1940, vol. 1, nos. 214–17, 219, 221–3). This pattern suggests a retreat by Venetian merchants from Constantinople in 1169. This is quite unprecedented and suggests that for a whole year Venetians avoided Constantinople. It gives some support to the version of events provided by the *History of the Doges of Venice* which has Manuel Komnenos sending two ambassadors to Venice and apparently offering the Venetians, as an inducement to return to Byzantium, a monopoly of its trade: exactly what was meant by this is not explained. Despite reservations about Manuel Komnenos, Doge Domenico Michiel eventually relented and gave the Venetians permission to return to Byzantium, which they did to the tune of some 20,000. The doge also sent two leading patricians to Manuel to obtain personal guarantees of the Venetians' safety, which he gave, but this was not quite enough because Venetian sympathisers among leading Constantinopolitans informed the ambassadors that Manuel was intending something against the Venetians. The ambassadors were able to elicit from the emperor a public declaration of his good intentions (*Historia ducum Veneticorum* 6; Nicol 1988, 96–7).

Forget about the disproportionately large figure of 20,000 Venetians returning to the Byzantine empire and this narrative is perfectly credible, except that there is no explanation for the apparent embargo by the Venetians on trade with Byzantium in 1169. In other cases where a doge imposed an embargo against foreign trade it was done to protect Venetian interests close to home: for example, in 1158 when at war with Hungary (Morozzo della Rocca and Lombardo 1940, vol. 1, no. 143). In 1169 the only apparent threat was from Pisa which was meddling in the

Adriatic (Abulafia 1984, 206). There may be a connection between the Pisan threat and the supposed offer of a monopoly of trade to the Venetians. In 1169 the Pisans and the Genoese too were negotiating with Manuel Komnenos over their trading privileges, an initiative that the Venetians were bound to be aware of (Lilie 1984, 478–84). Manuel may only have been reassuring the Venetians that these negotiations would in no way affect their existing trade privileges, including their complete exemption from customs duties which continued to distinguish them from their Italian competitors.

That Manuel Komnenos was attempting a blanket solution to existing difficulties caused by the presence of Italian merchants at Constantinople emerges from a detail preserved by the Byzantine chronicler John Kinnamos (*Epitomē* 6.10; *The Deeds of John and Manuel Comnennos*, 210–11). Part of the problem was that there were Venetians who had settled permanently in Constantinople, had married local women and had taken up residence outside the confines of their *embulo*. Niketas Choniates even says that they became indistinguishable from Byzantines (Niketas Choniates, *Historia*, 1741.47–55). Manuel Komnenos therefore proposed that they should be given special status as *Bourgesioi* or burgesses, which would entail pledging direct obedience to the Byzantine empire (John Kinnamos, *Epitomē* 6.10; *The Deeds of John and Manuel Comnennos*, 211). It was a solution not unlike that of the imperial *lizios* or liegeman, which seems to have received more general application under Manuel Komnenos as a way of binding Western clients, mercenaries and other experts to imperial service (Ferluga 1961; Magdalino 2000, 106–7, 223, 226). There is a difference. One can be fairly sure that the status of *lizios* was fairly widespread and strong enough to survive the upheavals of 1204. *Bourgesios* is a term that is rarely found.

It therefore seems safe to infer that Manuel Komnenos' proposal hardly got off the ground and is likely to have intensified Venetian suspicions which had in any case been aroused by the emperor's grant of an extension to the Genoese quarter. The Venetians took matters into their own hands and attacked the Genoese quarter inflicting considerable damage. This was not an incident that an emperor could overlook. He insisted that the Venetians make good the damage and imposed reparations. Their ambassadors not only refused to pay, but also threatened a punitive expedition, like that mounted against John II Komnenos. It was this threat that will have triggered Manuel Komnenos' drastic action against them. But the latter are unlikely to have made any such threat unless there was something serious at stake, such as a threat by the Byzantine emperor to rescind their privileges should they refuse to carry out his orders over the damage done to the Genoese quarter (Lilie 1984, 489–94; Nicol 1988, 97–8).

The Venetians were outraged. They did not send ambassadors to protest, but prepared an armada with the intention of bringing the Byzantine emperor to the negotiating table, in a way reminiscent of the actions of Doge Domenico Michiel nearly half a century before. But the present doge, Vitale II Michiel, was less fortunate. Like his predecessor he established his base at Chios, but the Byzantine emperor refused to negotiate. The Venetians were forced to abandon their base because of plague and harried by Byzantine flotillas returned to Venice. It was an utter failure. The returning doge was assassinated, the victim of popular fury (Niketas Choniates, *Historia*, 171–4; *Historia ducum Veneticorum* 7; John Kinnamos, *Epitomē* 6.10; *The Deeds of John and Manuel Comnennos*, 212–14; Lilie 1984, 494–6; Nicol 1988, 98–100). Denied access to the Byzantine empire the Venetians were forced back on the Adriatic where a combination of Byzantine intrigue and Hungarian ambition left them on the defensive. Adding to their discomfiture was the interest that the Pisans were still taking in the Adriatic, using Ancona as an outport (Guarnieri 1967; Heyd 1959, vol. 1, 237). The Venetians responded by engineering a realignment of forces, which produced the peace of Venice in 1177. It was one of the great events of the twelfth century. Venice hosted a summit which brought together the Emperor Frederick Barbarossa, Pope Alexander III and King William II of Sicily (Madden 2003, 69–76). It should have spelt the end of Venice's attachment to Byzantium. It should have been an act of emancipation, but it turned out not to be.

One explanation for this is that the same families continued to dominate the political life of Venice. The assassination of the doge in 1172 reinforced the hold of the council of the *Sapientes* on the political process (Gasparri 1992, 817–21). It made sure that Vitale Michiel was succeeded as doge by one of his closest associates, Sebastiano Ziani (Madden 2003, 57–8). It is not immediately clear why the political elite insisted on pursuing the Byzantine connection; why, having positioned Venice advantageously in its immediate geographical setting (Lane 1973, 57–8) it should at once begin negotiations for a return to Byzantium and why it should have persisted with them for ten years until they were brought to a successful conclusion (Madden 1999). It reflected the hold exercised over the political process at Venice by patrician families with a stake in Byzantium, who could ill afford to ignore the losses they had suffered in 1171, but this equally applied to those of more modest fortunes (Morozzo della Rocca and Lombardo 1940, vol. 1, nos. 313, 316, 336, 338, 358, 360–1, 365).

They wanted compensation for Venetian wealth and property seized in 1171. It represented many things: capital and a trading network that Venice could ill afford to lose, but most of all reparations would be concrete proof that the Byzantine emperor had been in the wrong.

Return to Byzantium on Venetian terms would constitute a moral victory and this was something that counted at Venice. Reparations were finally fixed at 35 *kentenaria* or 252,000 *hyperpyra*. Even if an underestimate of the value of Venetian wealth seized, this figure – roughly eighteen times the sum demanded as a ransom a few years later for a Byzantine general (Niketas Choniates, *Historia*, 533.49–50) – suggests the importance of trade with Byzantium to the Venetian economy. But this leaves out of account the access Byzantium provided to an international market and currency, which became an ever more important consideration as commercial rivalry with Genoa and Pisa intensified. It also leaves out of account not only the interests of the ruling elite, but also sentiment, not a word one usually associates with the Venetians. But they took pride in their loyal service – at a price admittedly – to the Byzantine empire or *Romania*, as they called it. Defenders of Byzantium – *semper defensores Romanie* – became a Venetian watchword in the course of the twelfth century (*Historia ducum Veneticorum* 2 and 4). It would continue to be so at least until 1453, though what was understood by *Romania* would change. It would no longer be the Byzantine empire, so much as the interests that the Venetians had in what was once the Byzantine empire.

The importance of Venice's role as the defender of *Romania* comes out in the 1187 peace treaty with the Emperor Isaac II Angelos. It begins with the emperor grudgingly admitting that the Byzantines were mostly to blame for the break and that the Venetians had rendered earlier emperors exemplary service in the defence of the empire (Pozza and Ravegnani, 85.5–12, 91.6–10; Tafel and Thomas 1856, 179–80, 195–6). The emperor hailed the grafting onto the body of the empire the severed limb that was Venice, as a restoration of his empire's integrity (Pozza and Ravegnani 1993, 85.10–12; Tafel and Thomas 1856, 180.12–14). It was a moral victory for the Venetians, which was nearly as important as the compensation itself. However, in the sixteen years since the coup of 1171 much had changed. *Romania* was no longer what it had been under the Emperor Manuel I Komnenos. It could no longer guarantee security at sea with the result that Venice's position both in the Adriatic and the Aegean was far from secure (Brand 1968, 14–30).

The swift withdrawal of Byzantine forces from Dalmatia after Manuel Komnenos' death produced growing levels of disorder, as Hungarians moved in and began to infiltrate northern Dalmatia which was a Venetian sphere of influence (Stephenson 2000, 262-3). The flashpoint was Zadar, which had passed under Hungarian control. Venice sought to retrieve the situation by mounting expeditions against it in 1187 and 1190, but these were notable failures (Madden 2003, 111-13). Worryingly, Zadar made a pact with Pisa in 1188 (Guarnieri 1967, 361-2). It was part of Pisa's search for a secure base in the Adriatic from which to challenge Venice. Pisan privateers ensured that piracy along the Dalmatian coast, which was always a problem, became worse. Piracy also became a problem in the Aegean with Pisans, Genoese and Sicilians to the fore, for example a Venetian ship delayed departure out of fear of Pisan privateers in May 1193 (Morozzo della Rocca and Lombardo 1940, vol. 1, no. 417). Among the attractions of the 1187 treaty with Isaac Angelos were the provisions for naval co-operation and the recovery of Venice's role as *defensor Romanie*. It gave hope that with Venetian support the Byzantine imperial regime might recover the stability lost in the turmoil which followed the death of Manuel Komnenos. That at least is suggested by the quite unprecedented investment in property in and around the Venetian quarter at Constantinople, which started as soon as negotiations for a normalisation of relations with Byzantium began. First off the mark was Giovanni Dandolo, the brother of the future doge, Enrico Dandolo. In February 1184 he leased out a workshop attached to a wharf on the Golden Horn for one year (Morozzo della Rocca and Lombardo 1940, vol. 1, no. 344; Tafel and Thomas 1856, 177-8). Although we are only dealing in a handful of documents their number and frequency are quite unprecedented when compared to what was happening before 1171 (Angold 2007, 76-7; Magdalino 2000, 222-6). Despite the objections of, for example, David Jacoby (2001; 2007), I think they should be taken at face value and seen as evidence not only of the Venetians' determination to recover and develop their quarter, but also of their relative success.

This was in contrast to failures in the Adriatic, which made the maintenance of good relations with Isaac Angelos all the more important. The situation changed, however, in 1195 when Isaac's brother Alexios seized the throne. He refused to honour the payments for reparations agreed by the Venetians with Isaac. There were other actions harmful to Venetian interests. In contravention of Venetian privileges he imposed trade tariffs and encouraged the Pisans to attack the Venetian quarter in Constantinople (Brand 1968, 200-21). At the same time, the Pisans sent a fleet into the Adriatic using Zadar as a base. The new doge, Enrico Dandolo got together a fleet which chased the Pisans out of the Adriatic

(Madden 2003, 112–13). He followed this up by dispatching another fleet to Byzantine waters, which in March 1196 was at anchor off Abydos at the mouth of the Hellespont. The intention was to keep the fleet at sea because the members of the expedition raised the sums necessary there and then. As they said, 'it is incumbent on each one of us, when we happen to be outside our homeland either on an expedition or for any other reason to exert ourselves for the honour of our homeland, going so far as to pawn our goods should it seem to be the honourable thing to do' (Tafel and Thomas 1856, 217.19–23). The urgency of the matter was such that they did not wait for the doge's approval (Maltezou 1995, 238; Tafel and Thomas 1856, 217.19–23). If the original goal of the expedition, as seems likely, was to attack Pisan shipping, its continuing presence in the Hellespont within striking distance of Constantinople can only have been to overawe the Byzantine emperor. It seems to have worked because after long negotiations an agreement was finally struck with Alexios III Angelos in November 1198 (Pozza and Ravegnani 1993, 119–37; Tafel and Thomas 1856, 248–78).

Like all previous agreements it took the form of an imperial chrysobull, but it marked a new stage in Venice's relations with Byzantium, because it was not just a matter of reconfirming earlier commercial privileges, but more about regulating the legal status of Venetians within the Byzantine empire. It was agreed that in pecuniary matters if a Greek brought an action against a Venetian, it should be heard before the legate sent by the doge to Constantinople, and if vice versa it should be heard before the *logothete of the drome* who had responsibility for foreign affairs. The Byzantine emperor explicitly recognised that this implied a degree of extraterritoriality (Pozza and Ravegnani 1993, 133–4; Tafel and Thomas 1856, 273–4). This was reinforced by the care given to the protocol for the reception of the ducal legate and his assessors on arrival in Constantinople, which was tantamount to recognition that the representative of an outside power could exercise legal authority within the empire, for although the Venetians are described as most loyal to the empire, there is no longer any suggestion that they are somehow subject to it. The emperor was content to acknowledge 'the loyalty and good will' that the Venetians had in respect to *Romania* (Pozza and Ravegnani 1993, 127.21–5; Tafel and Thomas 1856, 255.24–7).

With the 1198 treaty a line was crossed. Venice's claims on the Byzantine empire were no longer a matter of exemption from customs duties, but extended to the exercise of legal authority. The good order of the Byzantine empire was very much a Venetian concern. If circumstances conspired it might be incumbent on Venice to intervene to ensure the sound health of *Romania*'s body politic. Though convinced as ever I was of the accidental nature of the Venetian involvement in the overthrow of the Byzantine empire in 1204, by 1198 Venetian devotion to *Romania* was such – I mean by this that it was there to serve Venice's best interests – that some kind of an accident, such as 1204, was bound to happen. The surprise is that it happened as soon as it did. It was paradoxically the consequence of the conscious decision on the part of the Venetian patriciate to remain loyal to an alliance with the Byzantine empire. While the fortunes of some of the most influential Venetian families – certainly those that were *dogabile* – were founded on involvement with the Byzantine empire, this does not mean that it was simply a matter of naked self-interest. There was a moral dimension implied in the slogan *semper defensores Romanie*, which justified Venice in its self-appointed role of saving Byzantium from itself.

References

Abulafia, D. 1977. *The Two Italies: Economic Relations between the Norman Kingdom of Sicily and the Northern Communes* (Cambridge).

1984. 'Ancona, Byzantium and the Adriatic, 1155–1173', *Papers of the British School at Rome* 52, 195–216.

Anna Komnene. *Alexias*, in Reinsch, D. and Kambylis, A. (eds.), *Annae Comnenae Alexias*. Corpus fontium historiae Byzantinae – Series Berolinensis 40 (Berlin, 2001).

Angold, M. 2007. 'The Venetian chronicles and archives as sources for the history of Byzantium and the crusades (992–1204)', in Whitby, M. (ed.), *Byzantines and Crusaders in Non-Greek Sources, 1025–1204*, Proceedings of the British Academy 132 (Oxford), 59–94.

Armstrong, P. 2009a. 'Merchants of Venice at Sparta in the twelfth century', in Cavanagh, W.G., Gallou, C. and Georgiadis, M. (eds.), *Sparta and Laconia: From Prehistory to Pre-Modern* = British School at Athens Studies 16 (London), 313–21.

2009b. 'The monasteries of St Nikon: The Amyklaion, Sparta and Lakonia', in Gallou, C., Georgiadis, M. and Muskett, G.M. (eds.) *Dioskouroi: Studies Presented to W.G. Cavanagh and C.B. Mee on the Anniversary of Their 30-Year Joint Contribution to Aegean Archaeology*, BAR International Series 1889 (Oxford), 352–69.

Bartoli Langeli, A. 1992. 'Documentazione e notariato', in Cracco Ruggini, L., Pavan, M., Cracco, G. and Ortalli, G. (eds.), *Storia di Venezia: Dalle origini alla caduta della Serenissima*, vol. 1, *Origini: Età ducale* (Rome), 847–64.

Borsari, S. 1969–70. 'Il crisobullo di Alessio I per Venezia', *Annali dell'Istituto italiano per gli studi storici* 2, 111–31.

1988. *Venezia e Bisanzio nel XII secolo: I rapporti economici*, Miscellanea di studi e memorie 26 (Venice).
Brand, C.M. 1968. *Byzantium Confronts the West, 1180–1204* (Cambridge, Mass.).
Castagnetti, A. 1995. 'Il primo comune', in Cracco, G. and Ortalli, G. (eds.), *Storia di Venezia: Dalle origini alla caduta della Serenissima*, vol. 2, *L'età del comune* (Rome), 81–130.
Fasoli, G. 1965. 'Comune Veneciarum', in *Venezia dalla prima crociata all conquista di Costantinopoli del 1204* (Florence), 71–102.
Fees, I. 1988. *Reichtum und Macht im mittelalterlichen Venedig: Die Familie Ziani*, Bibliothek des Deutschen historischen Instituts in Rom 68 (Tübingen).
Ferluga, J. 1961. 'La ligesse dans l'Empire byzantin', *Zbornik radova Vizantološkog instituta* 7, 97–123.
Frankopan, P. 2004. 'Byzantine trade privileges to Venice in the eleventh century: The chrysobull of 1092', *Journal of Medieval History* 30/2, 135–60.
Gasparri, S. 1992. 'Dagli Orseolo al comune', in Cracco Ruggini, L., Pavan, M., Cracco, G. and Ortalli, G. (eds.), *Storia di Venezia: Dalle origini alla caduta della Serenissima*, vol. 1, *Origini: Età ducale* (Rome), 791–826.
Guarnieri, G. 1967. 'Intorno alle relazioni commerciali marittime nel Medioevo fra la Toscana e gli scali adriatici Dalmati', *Archivio storico italiano* 125, 352–64.
Hahnloser, H.R. and Polacco, R. 1994. *Il tesoro di San Marco: La pala d'oro*, 2nd edn. (Venice).
Heyd, W. 1885. *Histoire du commerce du Levant au Moyen Âge*, vol. 1 (Leipzig, repr. Amsterdam, 1959).
Heynen, R. 1905. *Zur Entstehung des Kapitalismus in Venedig* (Stuttgart).
Historia ducum Veneticorum, in Simonsfeld, H. (ed.), *MGH Scriptores*, vol. 14 (Hanover, 1883), 72–97.
Jacoby, D. 2001. 'The Venetian quarter of Constantinople from 1082 to 1261: Topographical considerations', in Sode, C. and Takács, S. (eds.), *Novum Millennium: Studies on History and Culture Dedicated to Paul Speck* (Aldershot and Burlington), 153–70.
  2007. 'Houses and urban layout in the Venetian quarter of Constantinople: Twelfth and thirteenth centuries', in Belke, K., Kislinger, E., Külzer, A. and Stassinopoulou, M.A. (eds.), *Byzantina Mediterranea. Festschrift für Johannes Koder zum 65. Geburtstag* (Vienna), 269–82.
John Kinnamos. (trans. Brand, C.M.) *The Deeds of John and Manuel Comnennos*, Records of Civilization 41 (New York, 1976).
  Epitomē, in Meineke, A. (ed.), *Ioannis Cinnami Epitome rerum ab Ioanne et Alexio Comnenis gestarum* (Bonn, 1836).
Lane, F.C. 1973. *Venice: A Maritime Republic* (Baltimore).
Lanfranchi, L. (ed.) 1968. *San Giorgio Maggiore*, vol. 2, *Documenti 982–1159* (Venice).
The Life of St Nikon, trans. and commentary Sullivan, D.F. (Brookline, Mass., 1987).

Lilie, R.-J. 1984. *Handel und Politik zwischen dem byzantinischen Reich und den italienischen Kommunen Venedig, Pisa und Genua in der Epoche der Komnenen und der Angeloi (1081–1204)* (Amsterdam).

Lombardo, A. and Morozzo della Rocca, R. (eds.) 1953. *Nuovi documenti del commercio veneto dei secoli XI–XIII*, Monumenti storici n.s. VII (Venice).

Madden, T.F. 1999. 'Venice's hostage crisis: Diplomatic efforts to secure peace with Byzantium between 1171 and 1184', in Kittell, E.E. and Madden, T.F. (eds.), *Medieval and Renaissance Venice* (Urbana and Chicago), 96–108.

2003. *Enrico Dandolo and the Rise of Venice* (Baltimore).

Magdalino, P. 1993. *The Empire of Manuel I Komnenos, 1143–1180* (Cambridge).

2000. 'The maritime neighbourhoods of Constantinople: Commercial and residential functions, sixth to twelfth centuries', *Dumbarton Oaks Papers* 54, 209–26.

Maltezou, C.A. 1995. 'Venetian 'habitatores', 'burgenses' and merchants in Constantinople and its hinterland', in Dagron, G. and Mango, C. (eds.), *Constantinople and Its Hinterland*. Society for the Promotion of Byzantine Studies Publications 3 (Aldershot).

Morozzo della Rocca, R. and Lombardo, A. (eds.) 1940. *Documenti del commercio veneziano nei secoli XI–XIII*, 2 vols., Regesta chartarum Italiae 28–29 (Rome).

Nicol, D.M. 1988. *Byzantium and Venice: A Study in Diplomatic and Cultural Relations* (Cambridge).

Niketas Choniates. *Historia*, in Dieten, J.A. van (ed.), *Nicetae Choniatae Historia*. Corpus fontium historiae Byzantinae – Series Berolinensis 11, vol. 1 (Berlin and New York, 1975).

Pertusi, A. 1965. 'Venezia e Bisanzio nel secolo XI', *La Venezia del Mille*, Storia della civiltà veneziana 10 (Florence), 117–60 = repr. Parente, G.B. (ed.) 1990. *Agostino Pertusi: Saggi veneto-bizantini* (Florence), 67–107.

Pozza, M. and Ravegnani, G. (eds.) 1993. *I trattati con Bisanzio, 992–1198*. Pacta Veneta 4 (Venice).

Rando, D. 1992. 'Le strutture della Chiesa locale', in Cracco Ruggini, L., Pavan, M., Cracco, G. and Ortalli, G. (eds.), *Storia di Venezia: Dalle origini alla caduta della Serenissima*, vol. 1, Origini: Età ducale (Rome), 645–75.

Ravegnani, G. 2006. *Bisanzio e Venezia* (Bologna).

Riley-Smith, J. 1986. 'The Venetian crusade of 1122–1124', in Airaldi, G. and Kedar, B.Z. (eds.), *I comuni italiani nel regno crociato di Gerusalemme*, Atti del Colloquio 'The Italian Communes in the Crusading Kingdom of Jerusalem' (Jerusalem, May 24–28, 1984) (Genoa), 337–50.

Schreiner, P. 1979. 'Untersuchungen zu den Niederlassungen westlicher Kaufleute im byzantinischen Reich des 11. und 12. Jahrhunderts', *Byzantinische Forschungen* 7, 175–91.

Stephenson, P. 2000. *Byzantium's Balkan Frontier: A Political Study of the Northern Balkans, 900–1204* (Cambridge).

Tafel, G.L.F. and Thomas, G.M. (eds.) 1856. *Urkunden zur älteren Handels- und Staatsgeschichte der Republik Venedig mit besonderer Beziehung auf Byzanz und die Levante vom neunten bis zum Ausgang des fünfzehnten Jahrhunderts* (Vienna; repr. Amsterdam, 1964).

Thiriet, F. 1959. *La Romanie vénitienne au Moyen Âge: Le développement et l'exploitation du domaine colonial vénitien (XIIe-XVe siècles)* (Paris).

Tůma, O. 1984. 'Some notes on the significance of the imperial chrysobull to the Venetians of 992', *Byzantion* 54/1, 358–66.

13 | Venice, the Ionian Sea and the Southern Adriatic after the Fourth Crusade

GUILLAUME SAINT-GUILLAIN

To explain the origins of a conflict opposing the Venetians to the commune of Bologna, the Venetian chronicler Martino da Canale, who wrote his *Estoires de Venise* in French between 1267 and 1275, starts from a precept which for him is almost a truism: 'It is a fact that the Adriatic Sea is part of the duchy of Venice' (*Voirs est que la Mer Arians est de le ducat de Venise*, see *Estoires de Venise* 161). This is actually one of only two passages of his text where he uses the expression 'Adriatic Sea' (*Mer Arians*): he speaks otherwise simply of 'the Gulf' (*le coulf*) and later Medieval Venetian sources generally do the same. It is of course part of a wider imperial vision of Venice's maritime destiny which is conveyed in the *Estoires*, from their first pages and the description of the mythical origins of the city arising from the azure main. This, however, is a reconstruction of the past. Venetian domination in the Adriatic was not a juridical precondition but a process and this expansion had its roots not just in its internal evolutions, or in a maritime destiny planned by God or by Nature, but also in the very fact that the city was part of the Byzantine empire. The turning point of the year 1000, when a fleet commanded by the Duke Pietro II Orseolo (991–1009) imposed a still shaky and symbolic Venetian authority on the Dalmatian coast, is traditionally taken as the starting point of the Adriatic expansion, but it must be understood also as a part of the wider restoration of imperial order in the Balkans under Emperor Basil II (Ferluga 1978, 194–204; Ortalli 2002). Even the purely symbolic assumption of the title of 'duke of Dalmatia' by Pietro II Orseolo must be considered in the Byzantine administrative frame (Lazzarini 1903; Ferluga 1978, 218, 226). Paradoxically, it is only when Venetians became much more involved in the economic machinery of the empire that Venetian expansion began to conflict with imperial authority.

If in Martino's times it would already have been difficult to refute his affirmation that Venice was ruling the Adriatic waves, some three-quarters of a century earlier, at the turn of the thirteenth century, this economic and political control was far from being undisputed. Then the city of St Mark was still confronted by the challenging competition of various Italian and Dalmatian ports (Ducellier 2001). Moreover, for obvious geographical reasons, turning the Adriatic into a Venetian lake always made strategic and economic sense only if it was expanding into the control of the Straits of Otranto and of the waters north and south of it. This strategic passage situated between Italy and the Albanian coast is the only access toward the rest of the Mediterranean (Sivignon 2001, 13–14). Even the expedition of Orseolo to Dalmatia in 1000 had already been connected two years later in 1002 by a sister expedition to assist the Byzantine port of Bari in southern Italy and prevent the threat of Muslim control or disruption of the strait (Ortalli 2002).

It is true, however, that the economic limitations imposed by the geography of the Adriatic as an almost enclosed sea must not be overestimated, because there were also the outlets of important commercial land roads on both the western and the eastern Adriatic coasts. Nevertheless, the ports connected to the roads leading in the eastern direction were situated toward the southern Adriatic where direct access by sea to the Mediterranean and, more importantly, the eastern Mediterranean had become absolutely critical for the Venetian economic system, as it had developed so dramatically since the eleventh century. For the commercial and later political expansion of Venice in the East, the pacification of the southern Adriatic and of the northern Ionian Sea was an absolute *sine qua non*.

What I intend to consider here briefly are the political and diplomatic tools through which the Venetians tried to manage their relations with this true threshold of the Adriatic in the unexpectedly auspicious, but at the same time tumultuous and dangerous, situation created in the region by the fall of Constantinople at the hands of the men of the Fourth Crusade. This will be limited to a short period – the decade following the capture of the Queen of Cities – and to an examination of the available corpus of documents.

Until 1204, although with varying degrees of obedience, the south Adriatic and the north Ionian Seas had been part of the Byzantine empire which had provided the institutional and administrative framework within which Venetian merchants had operated (Borsari 1988). Despite some occasional difficulties – the most stinging had been the almost complete exclusion of the Venetians from the Byzantine markets on imperial orders from 1171 to the mid-1180s – this framework proved helpful and brought prosperity to the Venetians, whose commercial expansion in other parts of the East and the Balkans was built mainly on the firm base of their success story in Byzantium.

On paper, the replacement of the Byzantine empire by a political structure jointly managed by the Venetians and the Frankish lords they had conveyed to Constantinople might look like a bright opportunity for the Venetian takeover of the threshold of the Adriatic. Indeed, an analysis of the *Partitio terrarum imperii Romanie*, the document listing the Byzantine territories assigned to the new Latin emperor, the crusaders and the Venetians respectively in September 1204 (Carile 1965), shows that the bulk of the Venetian share of the spoils consisted of the regions bordering the Adriatic and Ionian Seas. This was, however, purely theoretical and the Venetian central authorities were not even informed of it until the following year.

To understand how the Venetians reacted to this completely unforeseen situation, we have at our disposal some archival documents, to which we will return later, and the Venetian chronicles which were all written much later. Among these historiographical sources, the one least remote from the events, the anonymous *Historia ducum Venetorum* (41) jumps directly from the events of the crusade to the conquest of the island of Crete and completely ignores the Adriatic episode of the Venetian expansion in the Byzantine empire. Later chronicles, starting from the *Estoires* of Martino da Canale, display narratives, sometimes contradictory, which single out one, two and sometimes even three successive expeditions sent from Venice toward the region between Dyrrachion (modern Durrës) in the north to the region of Messenia in the south-west Peloponnese. From what can be understood from these sources, a first fleet that brought the newly elected Latin patriarch, Tommaso Morosini, to Constantinople would have occupied Dyrrachion *en passant*, as early as the summer of 1205. One or perhaps two other expeditions in 1206–7 would have permitted the occupation of Corfu, where the pirate Leon Vetrano would have been eliminated, and then of the Messenian ports of Coron (*Korone*) and Modon (*Methone*).

That is all that can be extracted from the historiographical sources. To learn how the story ends, one has to turn to the documentary sources. They show that despite the occupation of Dyrrachion (Ducellier 1981, 121–59) and of the two strategic places of Coron and Modon, the Venetians did not try – or were not able – to conquer that share of the Peloponnese along the coast of the Ionian Sea, which had been attributed to them by the *Partitio* of 1204. The same is true for the territories situated further north along the Adriatic coast. Instead, what they tried to establish through a process of diplomatic negotiation was the acceptance by the de facto lords of a loose form of Venetian suzerainty, implying collaboration, friendly relations and economic advantages. Clearly, in this phase of their post-1204 expansion the Venetians tried to use the *savoir faire* accumulated in the relations they had struck notably with their Adriatic neighbours and competitors: a diplomatic culture of reciprocal obligations and negotiated, documented submission, which they had already settled in their dealings with their fellow Frankish crusaders during the Fourth Crusade (Madden 1993; Queller and Madden 1997).

Eight documents have come down to us recording the stages and the methods of this process. In the Venetian archival tradition they are all called 'pacts', even if it uses a more specific typology to define each individual document, to which we will come back later. One must understand, however, that each of these documents was only part of a larger set of agreements which could involve negotiations, exchanges of embassies and a large range of other documents which have not been preserved. The first of these eight documents is of course the *Partitio* of September 1204 (Carile 1965), which, in dividing the empire, awarded the south Adriatic and northern Ionian Seas to Venice, and on which later Venetian claims and 'pacts' were based. There was a form of ambiguity about the holder of the rights conferred by the *Partitio*: they were granted to 'the lord doge and the commune of Venice', but after the death of Doge Enrico Dandolo in June 1205 the question was left open as to whether the successor to his rights in *Romania* was the new doge, who would be elected in Venice, or the *podestà* (magistrate) of Constantinople whom the Venetian army remaining in the empire selected on its own.

This explains the existence of the second document of our dossier. One year after the *Partitio* had been written down, in October 1205, Marino Zeno, the Venetian *podestà* of Constantinople, relinquished to Doge Pietro Ziani and to the Venetian commune his rights to the territories bordering the Adriatic Sea, though not to all the other territories awarded by the *Partitio* (Tafel and Thomas 1856–7, vol. 1, 569–71). The central authority in Rialto was not just asserting its authority over the *podestà* and the Venetians of Constantinople: this document, characterised as a *refutatio* in the registers where it was copied, was actually partitioning the lands allocated to Venice and it leaves no doubt that this had been one of the preconditions of the recognition of the *podestà* by the central government. While the Aegean territories were supposed to remain under the power of the *podestà* of Constantinople and his successors, the Adriatic and Ionian territories were transferred to the direct suzerainty of the doge and the commune itself. The latter were not just some strategic places along the coasts, but entire Byzantine provinces.

Of course, all this was purely theoretical, since what these first two documents have in common is that they concerned lands which still had to be conquered. Moreover, they took their place in a series of other pact-like agreements, several of which are lost, which framed or modulated the relations between Latins (and sometimes also between Latins and Greeks) within the new political context. They do not concern us here because they did not deal with the western coastline of Byzantium. This is not the case for the next documents, much less theoretical and much more practical, which occurred two years later (in 1207), after the naval expeditions sent from Venice and briefly discussed above, resulting in the effective occupation of Dyrrachion, Corfu, Coron and Modon.

The first of these six documents (*Concessio castri Corphuensis* of July 1207) concerns the investiture of the island of Corfu to Venetian feudatories and specifies their rights and their obligations toward the commune (Tafel and Thomas 1856–7, vol. 2, 54–9). The two contracting parties are thus Venetian. The second of these documents (the act of Geoffrey I of Villehardouin of June 1209), in contrast, seals the agreement reached between the commune and a crusader lord, the Champenois Geoffrey of Villehardouin, nephew of the French historian of the same name (Nanetti 2009, 55–8). At that time, Geoffrey the nephew had still not taken the title of prince of Morea, which he would assume some months later. The title given to the document by the Venetian archivists (*Pactum principis Goffredi*, Tafel and Thomas 1856–7, vol. 2, 96–100) is thus slightly anachronistic. The purpose of this document is simultaneously to sanction the direct possession of Coron and Modon by Venice, but also her suzerainty over the Peloponnese or, more exactly, those parts of the Peloponnese which had been promised to her five years earlier by the *Partitio* and primarily the part bordering on the Ionian Sea.

Finally, the last four documents work in pairs. The first two, both dated June 1210, are similar to the one relating to the agreement with Villehardouin reached one year earlier. Here also the aim was to negotiate a compromise with a local lord who had de facto occupied some of the territories granted to Venice by the *Partitio*, the only difference being that in the present case this lord was a Greek and not a Frank: his name was Michael Angelos Komnenos and, even if of illegitimate birth, he belonged to the former Byzantine imperial family. In the first document, *Privilegium Michaelis Comneni*, Michael testifies to the oath which he has taken toward Venice (Tafel and Thomas 1856–7, vol. 2, 119–20) and in the second, *Promissio Michaelis Comneni*, he commits himself toward the commune (Tafel and Thomas 1856–7, vol. 2, 120–3). The last two documents in the dossier under consideration were made three months later, in September 1210, and they regulated the future relations of the Latin archbishop of

Dyrrachion, Manfred, and his successors with the Venetian state (Tafel and Thomas 1856–7, vol. 2, 123–6).

At first sight, these documents might look just like additional pieces in a long and slightly boring collection of 'treaties' between Venice and various foreign powers; they are isolated here from the bulk of those documents only because they relate to the southern Adriatic and the Ionian Sea. At the same period and also in the following decades, Venetians used the same kind of documents and the same strategies of preservation to keep track of the covenants of alliance or domination concluded with other local powers, in the Aegean as well as in Italy or Dalmatia. However, this small southern Adriatic ensemble forms a block which is both chronologically and strategically coherent: after this specific moment around 1210, the region never appears in the following sequence of the collection of thirteenth century 'treaties', to which we will return.

Nonetheless, this south-Adriatic dossier is not typologically homogeneous. The *Partitio Romanie* (Carile 1965) is essentially no more than a list of territories and the segments of this list regarding the Ionian and Adriatic regions have been attentively scrutinised by specialists of the geographical history of the Byzantine empire. This document is indeed the main source for imperial administrative geography at the end of the Komnenian era, but from that point of view there is a lot to learn from its confrontation with the other documents of the dossier, despite their much narrower scope, as well as with documents preceding the Fourth Crusade, most particularly the 1198 chrysobull granted by Emperor Alexios III to the Venetians. Indeed the *Partitio* lists the territories in an order which is not necessarily always geographic and sometimes puts side by side places which can be situated far from each other. On the contrary, our documents relate to well-identified zones. Nevertheless, it is obvious that in both cases the Byzantine administrative divisions are used as a basic canvas.

This suffices to show the importance of considering these documents in relation to each other and I will not elaborate more on that. I would rather come back now to the question of the typological diversity of the south-Adriatic dossier. The reader has probably noted that, once the peculiar case of the *Partitio* is put aside, none of these documents has the Venetian commune or the Venetian doge as its author or co-author in the diplomatic sense. These are not documents from the Venetian state – and in most cases not even 'Venetian documents' – any more than treaties or pacts in the sense of synallagmatic contracts, despite the broad designation to which the archival tradition has assigned them, and contrary to other deeds written more or less during the same period. They most surely preserve traces of prior diplomatic negotiations. For example, the 1209 act of Geoffrey I of Villehardouin mentions the agreement of the Venetian negotiator of the arrangement, but only in the past tense and the third person (Tafel and Thomas 1856–7, vol. 2, 99). Effectively, all those documents present themselves as acts of recognition, renunciation or submission from the other party toward the Venetian party in reaction to a prior concession by the doge, the commune or their representatives. It is clear that what we have are only fragments of the negotiation and communication mechanisms between the contracting parties, which were composed of many more pieces.

Moreover, the surviving documents have notable differences between them. The Corfiot so-called *concessio*, for example – actually an act of *promissio* from the new feudatories and not the *concessio* from the doge – has several authors, namely the eleven feudatories (Tafel and Thomas 1856–7, vol. 2, 55). This document strikingly announces, four years in advance, the much more famous – and much more perennial – concession of the island of Crete to Venetian feudatories in 1211 (Jacoby 1998), as well as similar later documents that coincide with the stages in the Venetian appropriation of the island. If the Corfiot *promissio* is purely Venetian in its diplomatic form, the document from Geoffrey I of Villehardouin is more hybrid, retaining some traits of a French seigneurial act, although it is written down by an Italian notary (Tafel and Thomas 1856–7, vol. 2, 96–100).

But it is the Epirote part of the dossier – relating to negotiations with Michael Komnenos and with the bishop of Dyrrachion – which stands apart, since in both cases the two documents are preserved rather than just one. In the first case, the difference between the two documents is rather clear: the longer one (the *promissio*) is similar in its form to the Villehardouin and Corfiot documents, although it has some striking diplomatic peculiarities (Tafel and Thomas 1856–7, vol. 2, 120–3). The other document (the *privilegium*) delivered by Michael is much briefer (Tafel and Thomas 1856–7, vol. 2, 119–20). Even if it was written or at least preserved in Latin, the *formula* of the document belongs more closely to the Byzantine documentary tradition, as we will see later.

The same relationship exists between the two documents relating to the archbishop of Dyrrachion, although in that case Byzantine tradition has nothing to do with it. As with the previous case, the first document (the *privilegium*) recalls the concession and investiture of a money fief made in Venice by the doge himself to the representatives of Archbishop Manfred and the obligations of the beneficiary who, among other things, has to make sure that 'the community and inhabitants of the city of Dyrrachion and that city itself, with all its dependencies, remain faithful to us, to our successors and to Venice' (*comunitas hominum civitatis Durachii et ipsa civitatis cum omnibus suis pertinentiis debeat stare ad fidelitatem vestram et successorum vestrorum et Venecie*, Tafel and Thomas 1856–7, vol. 2, 124).

Similarities of redaction between these documents or pairs of documents explain the similarities of the rules they establish and the obligations they impose, despite the variety of positions of Venice's new partners. Safety and security for the Venetians in the territories involved is obviously a recurring clause: it also implies freedom of circulation and tax exemption for their trade commodities. In the two cases of Epiros and the Peloponnese, this is supplemented by another clause concerning the freedom to establish a *fondaco* and a church, so as to found a permanent Venetian settlement (Tafel and Thomas, 1856–7, vol. 2, 97 and 121). Only the Epirote case also includes a clause concerning lost shipwrecks and their recovery (Tafel and Thomas, 1856–7, vol. 2, 122). More generally, all those clauses are not fundamentally different from the various advantages obtained by the Venetians from the Byzantine sovereigns during previous centuries. The needs had remained the same but the political conditions had dramatically changed and a different diplomatic idiom was needed, in which Venice assumed the higher symbolic position in the dialogue, and the documentary models for this were found in her previous relations with her Adriatic environment. The authors of the documents also promised to align themselves with Venice's foreign policy, since they proclaimed in advance that her friends and enemies would be theirs. Last but not least, the acceptance of Venetian overlordship was to take the form of ceremonial gestures and recognised rents.

All the obligations do not appear in the same order in every document. Although the clauses are sometimes very close in their purpose, the wording is too different to assume a textual transmission from one document to another, or even the partial use of a similar *formula*. It seems probable that none of the redactors of these documents was looking at one of the other documents – except, of course, in the two cases in which we have paired documents – and this is important in understanding their channels of transmission.

Indeed, they only tell part of the story and themselves testify that they are just pieces of a complex mechanism of negotiation that produced other documents which have subsequently been lost. The two documents of Michael Komnenos, for example, are the result of a diplomatic initiative of the Venetian duke of Dyrrachion, followed by an embassy of Michael to the doge and the granting of the privilege by the latter, but all the related documentation (including the ducal privilege) is lost and only Michael's two acts survive (Tafel and Thomas, 1856–7, vol. 2, 119–23). No doubt in other cases, it is the whole dossier which is lost and its existence can only be postulated. In the available documentation the absence of the Ionian islands (except Corfu) is striking, but scholars have proposed that a process of accommodation similar to the ones described above must have existed with Maio, the count who governed much of the Ionian archipelago at that time; however, if it ever existed, nothing of it remains in the *Libri pactorum* of the Venetian archives (Kiesewetter 2006, 345–6).

What is surprising, of course, is not that many documents may have been lost, but rather that some of them survive. One must ask, firstly, why those have survived rather than others and, secondly, how their preservation can have oriented later interpretations of Venetian policy immediately after the Fourth Crusade. Indeed, none of the documents discussed above has been preserved in its original form: all are known exclusively through copies and the preservation of those copies is the result of the Italian documentary revolution of the twelfth and thirteenth centuries (Cammarosano 1991) in which, however, Venice was far from playing the leading role (Saint-Guillain 2015, 68–9). At the very end of the twelfth century, in 1197–8 more precisely, so just a few years before the crusade, the commune began to take careful measures, probably for the first time, for keeping track of the privileges it received and the agreements it concluded by copying them into a parchment register (Pozza 2002).

Until the end of the twentieth century, many scholars believed that this register, identified as the first *Liber pactorum*, was made much later, in the second half of the thirteenth century. Indeed, during the thirteenth century, additional squires and folios were inserted in the *Liber*. On these squires and folios new documents were copied, a number of them relating to the Fourth Crusade and its consequences. This campaign of registration began around 1210, precisely at the time of the redaction of the originals of our documents and it was pursued in the following decades, that is, at a time when those documents were losing any practical value, due to the political failure of negotiated domination in the region of the southern Adriatic and Ionian Sea. This means that their inclusion in the *Liber pactorum* is not testimony to their actual initial function in Venice's management of relations with local powers in the region at the time. Rather, it is evidence of their posthumous life in an international diplomatic context, which had profoundly changed in a few years, but in which they could nevertheless reveal themselves to be useful as diplomatic pressure tools.

What makes this obvious is that not all these documents were deemed worthy of registration in the *Liber pactorum*. The act of Geoffrey of Villehardouin was not selected; one would have thought that this document, which contains the recognition of the Venetian occupation of Coron and Modon, would have had some significance for the compilers of the ducal chancery. One explanation could be that by the second decade of the thirteenth century the reality of what was now the principality of Morea and of its relations with Venice had become much too far removed from the constitutional order planned in the document to make it more than a diplomatic curiosity.

So in the second half of the thirteenth century, the documents relating to the failed attempt to establish Venice's negotiated overlordship over the southern Adriatic and Ionian coasts still continued, with many others, their subterranean secret life enclosed within the walls of the Venetian chancery: the main proof of this life is that they continued to be copied and recopied. By that mechanism, they were becoming part of the memorial patrimony of the *Serenissima*. In 1291 the Great Council of Venice decided to make a second *Liber pactorum*, which would be a fresh copy of the first one, and in the middle of the fourteenth century all those texts were reunited, but this time they followed a logical order in a new compilation commanded by Doge Andrea Dandolo. This was the *Liber albus*, which collected all the main diplomatic documents relating to the relations of Venice with the East (a parallel *Liber blancus* gathered those relating to relations with the West). The act of Geoffrey of Villehardouin was exhumed and duly registered in the *Liber albus*, even if it was absent from the two *Libri pactorum*.

Of course, despite the care and professionalism of Venetian chancery notaries, with each successive copy the texts were subjected to small alterations. Given that, unfortunately, the nineteenth-century editors worked mostly from the latest copies, this is why the place names that appeared in print were sometimes in badly mutilated forms. But, more importantly, the people working in the chancery – some of whom were actually historians – were looking at the documents with an increasingly historical eye. This does not mean that their approach was in any sense becoming apolitical – the copying of those texts implied that they were still seen as potentially useful in political terms and history itself was highly political – but in the sense that their understanding and appropriation increasingly needed an effort of interpretation and even reinvention.

In any case, with their registration in the *Liber albus*, those documents, like so many others, entered the memorial patrimony of Venice once and for ever. In fact, when Doge Andrea Dandolo and the team working with him compiled the famous chronicle known by his name, which was a decisive turning point in the evolution of Venetian historiography, they used a sequence of events borrowed from a previous Venetian chronicle interwoven with another, taken from the mendicant tradition of universal chronicles, but they stuffed this composite frame, more or less aptly, with summaries of documents, for the most part those copied in the *Liber albus* and the *Liber blancus*. The few documents we have considered here were then transformed into episodes of a more or less official narrative of the history of Venice, some of which retained that function until the present time. However, one must keep in mind that this is the result of a process both of conservation and selection of the documentation, which must also be analysed for itself.

Note

I would like to thank Professor Judith Herrin for reading this chapter and suggesting stylistic improvements to this paper, which records the text as presented during the conference. A fuller version of this paper, with exhaustive references to the sources and bibliography, will be published elsewhere.

References

Borsari, S. 1988. *Venezia e Bisanzio nel XII secolo: I rapporti economici,* Miscellanea di studi e memorie 26 (Venice).

Cammarosano, P. 1991. *Italia medievale: Struttura e geografia delle fonti scritte* (Rome).

Canale, Martino da. *Les estoires de Venise*, in Limentani, A. (ed.), *Les estoires de Venise: Cronaca veneziana in lingua francese dalle origini al 1275,* Fondazione Giorgio Cini – Civiltà veneziana. Fonti e testi, serie 3, vol. 3 (Florence, 1973).

Carile, A. 1965. 'Partitio terrarum imperii Romanie', *Studi veneziani,* 1st series, 7, 125–305.

Ducellier, A. 1981. *La façade maritime de l'Albanie au Moyen Âge: Durazzo et Valona du XIe au XVe siècle,* Documents et recherches sur l'économie des pays byzantines, islamiques et slaves et leurs relations commerciales au Moyen Âge 13 (Thessaloniki).

2001. 'L'Adriatique du IVe au XIIIe siècle', in Cabanes, P. (ed.), *Histoire de l'Adriatique* (Paris), 109–99.

Ferluga, J. 1978. *L'amministrazione bizantina in Dalmazia* (Venice).

Historia ducum Venetorum, in Berto, L.A. (ed.), *Testi storici veneziani (XI–XIII secolo)* (Padua, 2000), 1–83.

Jacoby, D. 1998. 'La colonisation militaire vénitienne de la Crète au XIIIe siècle: Une nouvelle approche', in Balard, M. and Ducellier, A. (eds.), *Le partage du monde: Échanges et colonisation dans la Méditerranée médiévale* (Paris), 297–313.

Kiesewetter, A. 2006. 'Preludio alla Quarta Crociata? Megareites di Brindisi, Maio di Cefalonia e la signoria sulle isole Ionie (1185–1250)', in Ortalli, G., Ravegnani, R. and Schreiner, P. (eds.), *Quarta Crociata: Venezia, Bisanzio, Impero Latino* (Venice), 317–58.

Lazzarini, V. 1903. 'I titoli dei dogi di Venezia', *Nuovo archivio veneto* n.s. 5, 271–313.

Madden, T.F. 1993. 'Vows and contracts in the Fourth Crusade: The treaty of Zara and the attack on Constantinople in 1204', *The International History Review* 15/3, 441–68.

Nanetti, A. (ed.) 2009. *Il patto con Geoffroy de Villehardouin per il Peloponneso, 1209* (Rome).

Ortalli, G. 2002. 'Pietro II Orseolo *dux Veneticorum et Dalmaticorum*', in Fiorentin, N. (ed.), *Venezia e la Dalmazia anno Mille: Secoli di vicende comuni. Atti del Convegno di studio, Venezia, 6 ottobre 2000* (Treviso), 13–27.

Pozza, M. 2002. 'I Libri pactorum del comune di Venezia', in *Comuni e memoria storica: Alle origini del comune di Genova. Atti del Convegno di studi, Genova, 24–26 settembre 2001 = Atti della Società ligure di storia patria* n. s. 42/1 (Genoa), 195–212.

Queller, D.E. and Madden, T.F. 1997. *The Fourth Crusade: The Conquest of Constantinople* (Philadelphia).

Saint-Guillain, G. 2015. 'Venetian archival documents and the prosopography of the thirteenth-century Byzantine world: Tracing individuals through the archives of a diaspora', in Christ, G., Morche, F.-J., Zaugg, R., Kaiser, W., Burkhardt, S. and Beihammer, A.D. (eds.), *Union in Separation: Diasporic Groups and Identities in the Eastern Mediterranean (1100–1800)* (Rome), 37–79.

Sivignon, M. 2001. 'Le cadre naturel', in Cabanes, P. (ed.), *Histoire de l'Adriatique* (Paris), 13–22.

Tafel, G.L.F. and Thomas, G.M. (eds.) 1856-7. *Urkunden zur älteren Handels- und Staatsgeschichte der Republik Venedig, mit besonderer Beziehung auf Byzanz und die Levante vom neunten bis zum Ausgang des fünfzehnten Jahrhunderts*, 3 vols. (Vienna; repr. Amsterdam, 1964).

14 | Sea Power and the Evolution of Venetian Crusading

CHRISTOPHER WRIGHT

One of the more distinctive qualities of crusading was the degree to which its ideological power drew its participants outside their normal geographical context. This is most emphatically true of the original and pre-eminent strand of the movement directed to the eastern Mediterranean, which was most directly underpinned by Latin Europe's pilgrimage tradition in its most ambitious, far-flung form. For the maritime mercantile communities of the Mediterranean, this did not hold as true as it did for others. For many sailors and merchants, long journeys, sometimes to the regions sought by pilgrims and crusaders or to those through which these groups passed, were part of normal experience. This closer correspondence with other aspects of life applied also to the role of crusading in the affairs of whole societies and their rulers. The maritime communities occupied an intermediate position between the circumstances of their western European neighbours and those of the Latins who settled in the East, having their centres far from the theatres of action but maintaining important material interests there and often also along the routes of crusading expeditions.

This reflects the wider patterns of mercantile communities' relationship with their geographical context. To derive one's wealth from long-distance trade, especially by sea, was to be in some part freed from the constraints of local geography, able to make direct links with faraway places and find sources of wealth not limited by the productive resources available locally. It was also to become dependent on a much larger geographical context of interlocking land and sea routes, obstructions and choke points. For crusaders from such a background, the space separating their place of origin from their destination was not merely an arduous obstacle for the military pilgrim to overcome but an environment with which their native society was or became persistently engaged. In consequence, their participation in crusading was bound to be entwined with other activities and concerns in ways that set them apart from other Westerners. These entanglements, with their tendency to blur lines between the business of the Cross and business as usual, contributed to the traditional reputation of the Italian sea powers and the Venetians in particular, for approaching crusading with more than the average degree of cynical self-interest (Marshall 2003, 60–79; Schein 1986, 679–89).

Of all the maritime communities of the Mediterranean, Venice was the one whose fortunes were most profoundly shaped by its geographical situation and the one whose interests were mostly inextricably linked to the East. Its interaction with this context bore upon its crusading activity in ways whose significance shifted over time as the areas of conflict and the role of sea power in the crusade changed. From the beginning of the crusades, its geographical context differentiated its experience from those of its peers, in ways that moderated the impact of crusading upon Venice while intensifying the impact of more continuous and more worldly concerns on Venetian crusading. For the western Mediterranean cities of Genoa and Pisa the First Crusade was a transformative experience that drew them into the East in an unprecedented fashion and thus profoundly altered their economic development. For Venice, with the eastward alignment and long-standing connections arising from its location and its Byzantine ties, reaching the Holy Land meant traversing the regions already central to its commercial activities. While the First Crusade resulted in a marked increase in its trade with the south-eastern Mediterranean, this effect was more moderate than in the case of Pisa or Genoa, as Byzantium long remained Venice's foremost eastern market (Buenger Robbert 1985, 389–402; France 2000, 271–3). With areas of vital interest arrayed all along the space through which crusades passed, there was a heightened inclination to draw subsidiary benefits from such an enterprise not only at the destination but along the way. Venetian crusading expeditions repeatedly intervened both in Dalmatia and in the city's relations with Byzantium as they passed, but in the early decades of crusading their interventions in these two areas remained firmly distinct from one another. This was due both to the obvious political distinctions and to the different roles of the two zones from Venice's perspective, as respectively a strategic corridor which it could and did aspire to dominate politically and a vital market where it sought a privileged commercial position. In this respect, it was only the fact that both areas were vital parts of Venice's eastward network of interests and that both flanked the routes of the city's crusading fleets that connected them.

The tendency to intervention along the way was already on display in Venice's contribution to the First Crusade, launched in 1099 (Andrea Dandolo, *Chronica* 9.10; Bellomo 2009, 420–43; 2010, 64–74; France 1997, 392–5; Monk of Lido, *Historia de translatione magni Nicolai*; Pryor 2008, 98–101; Queller and Katele 1986, 15–26). On its way through the

Adriatic the fleet cemented Venice's rights in Zadar and elsewhere in Dalmatia (Andrea Dandolo, *Chronica* 9.10; Monk of the Lido, *Historia de translatione magni Nicolai* 3). A clash with the Pisan fleet at Rhodes may have been related to the wish to check Pisan ambitions in the Byzantine world; according to the Monk of the Lido (*Historia de translatione magni Nicolai* 6, 22), the defeated Pisans had to swear not to enter *Romania* to trade in future (Andrea Dandolo, *Chronica* 9.10; Bellomo 2009, 426–7, 437, 443).

The entwining of crusading purposes in the Levant with the vigorous pursuit of Venetian interests along the way was most fully exemplified by Doge Domenico Michiel's expedition of 1122–5, which again asserted both Venice's overlordship in Dalmatia and its special commercial position in Byzantium. Unlike other Italian naval campaigns of the early twelfth century in support of the crusader states, including Ordelafo Falier's Venetian expedition of 1110, which assisted in the capture of Sidon, this may fairly be classed as a crusade (Andrea Dandolo, *Chronica* 9.11; Tafel and Thomas 1964, vol. 1, 91). The result of appeals for help to Venice from King Baldwin II of Jerusalem and Pope Calixtus II, its participants took the Cross and were promised an indulgence and Venice was awarded a papal banner. The Venetians were joined by volunteers setting out from other parts of Europe, with scattered evidence of participation from Bohemia, Germany, France and England. However, the expedition's progress was delayed by its use to put pressure on the Emperor John II to reinstate Venice's commercial privileges in Byzantium, beginning with an attempt to seize Corfu. Following an appeal for haste from Jerusalem, the fleet then proceeded directly to the Holy Land where it defeated a Fatimid fleet near Ascalon, helped capture Tyre and secured a far-reaching grant of commercial privileges. On the return voyage it carried out widespread raiding against Byzantine islands in the Aegean, before subduing by force Split, Trogir and Biograd, which had rejected Venetian authority and gone over to Hungary during the expedition (Andrea Dandolo, *Chronica* 9.12; *Annales Venetici breves*, 92; Bellomo 2010, 74–6; Cerbani, *Translatio mirifici martyris Isidori*; Devaney 2010, 132–40; Fulcher of Chartres, *Historia Hierosolymitana* 3.14, 3.20, 3.27, 3.32, 3.36, 3.41; *Historia ducum Venetorum* 3–5; Queller and Katele 1986, 29–39; Riley-Smith 1986, 337–50; Tafel and Thomas 1964, vol. 1, 79–94; William of Tyre, *Chronicon* 12.22–5).

The geographical disposition of their interests broadened the potential usefulness of crusading expeditions for the Venetians and thus increased the inclination to use them to advance their own interests by means other than fighting the designated targets of the crusade. Such mundane temptations would have been especially strong during the first century or so of crusading, precisely because of the early fervour of the movement and the exceptional exertions this enthusiasm called forth. The crusading fleets launched by Venice in 1099, 1110, 1122, 1189 and 1202 were all apparently on an unusually grand scale and led in person by the doge, or in the first case by Duke Vitale I Michiel's son Giovanni and the bishop of Castello.

Numbers reported for the early fleets are mostly round figures, probably inflated but suggestive of grand efforts. The fleet of 1099 is numbered at about 200 vessels by the Monk of the Lido (*Historia de translatione magni Nicolai* 27), a figure repeated by Andrea Dandolo (*Chronica* 9.10–11) who puts that of 1110 at about 100 vessels. That of 1122 is numbered at 200 ships and galleys by the *Historia ducum Venetorum* (3) and Dandolo (*Chronica* 9.12) and at 120 substantial ships and galleys, besides small craft, by Fulcher of Chartres (*Historia Hierosolymitana* 3.14.2), while William of Tyre (*Chronicon* 12.22) gives a more precise and probable breakdown of forty galleys, twenty-eight beaked ships (*gatti*) and four very large transports. Different sources give a range of figures for the fleet of 1202, but broadly concur around 200–300 ships, including fifty to sixty-two galleys (Venice having pledged to provide fifty at its own expense), about 100 oared horse transports (*huissiers*) and forty to 100 large ships (Andrea Dandolo, *Chronica* 10.3; *Devastatio Consantinopolitana,* 87; Geoffrey of Villehardouin, *La Conquête de Constantinople* 23; Niketas Choniates, *Historia,* 539; Pryor 2003, 115, n. 61; Robert of Clari, *La Conquête de Constantinople* 6, 28; Tafel and Thomas 1964, vol. 1, 306, 371).

The crusades of 1122, 1189 and 1202 at least were boosted by special decrees summoning all Venetians home from their business overseas to assist in the enterprise (Andrea Dandolo, *Chronica* 10.2; Lanfranchi 1955, 25–7; Queller and Madden 1997, 17, n. 60; Robert of Clari, *La Conquête de Constantinople* 7, 11; Tafel and Thomas 1964, vol. 1, 204–6). Those of 1099 and 1122 are known to have enlisted Dalmatian contributions as well (Andrea Dandolo, *Chronica* 9.12; Ljubić 1868–91, vol. 1, 3–4). Such great and unusual concentrations of naval power represented exceptional opportunities for power projection. The degree to which these opportunities were exploited, however, depended on the circumstances. Their expedition during the Third Crusade, setting out in 1189, followed closely on the failure of a major Venetian offensive against Hungarian-held Zadar. In this discouraging context, the Venetians opted to capitalise on the crusade's imperative for peace between Christians, reinforced by a direct injunction from the pope, to conclude a truce, rather than to resume the conflict using a crusading fleet as on other occasions. They brought some relief to the besieged in Tyre before helping to besiege Acre and returning home in 1190 (Andrea Dandolo, *Chronica* 10.2). The particular urgency of the situation in the Holy Land provided an intensified impulse to proceed there without delay, but the wish to get back as soon as possible to reassert Venice's position in the Adriatic after the recent setback may help explain the apparent brevity and obscurity of Venetian participation in the Third Crusade, little noticed by non-Venetian sources. Fresh offensives against Zadar followed in 1190 and 1192, again without success (Andrea Dandolo, *Chronica* 10.3; Praga 1925, 47–54). In 1125, by contrast, they were incited to act by the recent occurrence of the latest Hungarian encroachment, while in 1202 the infusion of Frankish muscle provided by the Fourth Crusade and the scale of their own mobilisation seems to have offered the Venetians renewed hope of subduing Zadar after their previous repeated failures.

Though the clashes with Byzantium were denounced by Fulcher of Chartres (*Historia Hierosolymitana* 3.41), the detours of the 1120s do not seem to have generated the kind of severe controversy that would arise from the Fourth Crusade's digressions, though the largely Venetian sources give no indication of the attitude of the non-Venetian crusaders on the expedition. Most of the fighting occurred on the way home, after the fulfilment of the Venetians' vows, while the attacks in Dalmatia could reasonably be construed as a response to Hungarian aggression undertaken while the Venetians were absent fighting for Christendom. This inverted the situation of the Fourth Crusade, where the Franco-Venetian attack on Zadar violated the protection accorded to King Emeric by the fact that he had taken the Cross, albeit that he showed little sign of fulfilling his vow and was accused by the Venetians of undertaking his crusading vow as a pretext to guard against such attacks (Queller and Madden 1992, 447–50; 1997, 61–2, 65–6, 78–80). The non-Venetian participants in the 1120s may also have been fairly small in number relative to the Venetians, which would naturally have reduced the practical impact of any dissent as to the expedition's course of action. Fulcher of Chartres (*Historia Hierosolymitana* 3.15.2) states that the fleet transported a total of 3,000 men-at-arms, made up of both Venetians and others (*tam de Veneticis quam peregrinis sibi adiunctis*). This campaign pioneered the transport of crusading land forces by sea in ways that foreshadowed later developments, but probably did not represent a drastic break with the more usual patterns of early crusading, in which the major armies travelled by land and crusading fleets therefore remained independent forces at the disposal of the societies from which they came.

During the early years of the movement, naval forces contributed to crusading through combat against Muslim fleets, logistical support and help in the capturing of ports by blockade and amphibious assault. The significance of these functions in the eastern Mediterranean dwindled as the ports of Syria and Palestine were captured by the Christians and Egyptian naval power receded (Hamblin 1986, 77–83; Lev 1991, 107–21). The reduced relevance of sea power to crusading in the Holy Land by the mid-twelfth century may help account for the lack of any notable Venetian contribution to the Second Crusade, while Genoa, which did take part on a grand scale, sent its fleet to Spain rather than to the East (Phillips 2007, 50–66). The collapse of the kingdom of Jerusalem in 1187, reducing it to a handful of coastal enclaves, combined with a short-lived revival of Egyptian naval power, brought littoral combat back to the fore during the Third Crusade (Painter 1955, 46–7, 52–3, 67–8, 84; Rose 1999, 567–9). Even after the return of much of the coast to Christian control, the prominent role of amphibious campaigns against Egypt in thirteenth-century crusading sustained the importance of this sort of contribution, on the coast and in the channels of the Nile delta (Strayer 1969, 494–502; Van Cleve 1969a, 397–418, 424–6).

However, by the thirteenth century the transportation of crusading armies to the East by sea had become universal. The fleets of the Mediterranean maritime communities largely ceased to crusade as independent operators and became inextricably entwined with the movement of land forces. Not only did armies cease to travel to the East without the aid of transport fleets, major fleets also largely ceased to set out without the impetus of an army requiring transport, with the Third Crusade marking the moment of transition on both sides. Fleets retained their traditional functions of combat against Muslim ships, provisioning, communications and help in capturing ports, but their involvement was now usually instigated by their enlistment for transport. Their role thus moved closer to that of the northern European fleets, whose involvement in the crusades had always been driven in large part by the demands of transport. The disappearance of autonomous fleets was not as complete as that of armies following the land route. For instance, in 1220 a Venetian fleet appeared off Egypt in support of the Fifth Crusade, with no mention of any land forces aboard, although at a mere fourteen galleys it presents a marked contrast with the Venetian armadas of earlier campaigns (Buenger Robbert 1995, 28–9; Oliver of Paderborn, *Historia Damiatina* 49). Nonetheless, the integration of land and sea forces transformed the dynamics of crusading for the maritime powers.

The increased importance of sea transport made their landward geographical context a major force shaping the crusading activities of the maritime cities, whereas earlier enterprises had impinged almost exclusively on the seaward side of their networks. By tying together land and sea movements into a single route system, it brought their crusading role into closer alignment with their role in commerce and in pilgrimage, as the focal point of the connections linking their western European hinterland with the eastern Mediterranean. In the case of Venice, the land power whose geographical position most forcefully pushed its crusaders towards the use of Venetian shipping was Hungary, for which the Adriatic was the most convenient maritime outlet. Of course, owing to that same position it was also the land power with which Venice was most persistently in conflict. King Andrew II of Hungary's departure on the Fifth Crusade in 1217 shows how the shift to sea routes offered new means for maritime powers to draw material advantage from crusading through co-operation. From the outset, a perennial preoccupation of the Italian maritime communities on expeditions to the Holy Land had been to secure their share of the material gains of the crusade in the form of urban quarters and privileges, granted in exchange for their naval assistance by their landbound allies in the main theatre of action (Balard 1993, 43–64; Favreau-Lilie 1989, 327–496; Jacoby 1997, 155–75).

The assertion of their interests along the route had been extraneous to the intended purpose of the crusade and achieved by force or threat. The requirement for sea transport now created openings for advantageous reciprocal deals born of crusading co-operation at the homeward end of crusading journeys as well as at their destination. In return for providing King Andrew with shipping, Venice received not only financial payment but the renunciation of Hungarian territorial claims over Zadar and a new commercial treaty (Buenger Robbert 1995, 19–20; Ljubić 1868–91, vol. 1, 29–31). Perhaps seeking to limit his dependence on the Venetians, the king contracted for only a portion of his expected shipping needs from Venice, hiring ships from Ancona, Zadar and other Adriatic ports as well, though despite this the ships procured were insufficient for the number of crusaders who gathered to embark with him from Split (Archdeacon Thomas, *Historia Salonitana* 25).

Venice played a rather limited part in the carriage of crusading armies from other regions. Geography, often reinforced by political considerations, normally led French and English crusaders using Mediterranean shipping to set out through the western Mediterranean rather than the Adriatic, typically using ships from Genoa and Marseilles and embarking from these ports or from Aigues-Mortes. During the Third Crusade, Richard I sailed with a contingent from Marseilles, joining his main fleet from England, while Philip Augustus' French army sailed from Genoa. Others did sail from Venice, as well as from the southern Italian ports of Barletta, Brindisi and Messina. Genoa was employed again by French elements of the Fifth Crusade. The bulk of Thibaut of Champagne's and Richard of Cornwall's expeditions used Marseilles. Both of Louis IX's crusades sailed from his own port of Aigues-Mortes, on ships hired from both Genoa and Marseilles, although on the second occasion he had also negotiated with Venice (Ailes and Barber 2003, vol. 1, 6–9; vol. 2, 34–7; Donovan 1950, 44–5; Painter 1955, 50, 55–8, 61–2, 64–5; Strayer 1969, 492–3, 511–2, 514–5; Van Cleve 1969a, 402–3, 415).

Venice had greater natural prospects as a port for crusaders from inland parts of northern Italy, especially the Po basin, and during the Third and Fifth Crusades it is known to have shipped Italian contingents, including in the latter case some Milanese, though of course northern Italians had no shortage of other convenient ports (Andrea Dandolo, *Chronica* 10.2; Morozzo della Rocca and Lombardo 1940, vol. 2, 125–6). Besides those of Hungary, the crusaders who would seem most naturally inclined to seek passage from the head of the Adriatic would have been those from elsewhere in central Europe and from Germany, on the grounds of both convenience and the background of commercial ties with Venice. Bohemians may have sought passage on the Venetian fleet of 1122 (Cosmas of Prague, *Chronica Boemorum* 3.50; Riley-Smith 1986, 343). Duke Leopold V of Austria sailed from Venice on the Third Crusade, while his successor Leopold VI led a considerable German contingent accompanying Andrew of Hungary's force on the Fifth (Ansbert, *Historia de expeditione Friderici imperatoris*, 96–8; Archdeacon Thomas, *Historia Salonitana* 25; Oliver of Paderborn, *Historia Damiatina* 1). For the most part, however, Germans made little use of Venice. On the Third Crusade they largely stuck to the land route and used their own northern shipping (Johnson 1969, 90–4, 115; Painter 1955, 50). On subsequent expeditions, besides northern fleets, they relied mostly on the ports of southern Italy. These had obvious advantages for any crusaders who wished to minimise the length of their sea voyage and played a subsidiary role even on expeditions which embarked largely at other ports, such as the Third Crusade or the ventures of Thibaut of Champagne and Richard of Cornwall in 1239–40 (Ailes and Barber 2003, vol. 1, 9; vol. 2, 37; Painter 1969, 468,

471–2, 482–3). In the case of the Germans, the possession of the kingdom of Sicily by successive German emperors led to an overwhelming preference for using its ports and shipping. Henry VI's expedition in 1197 sailed from various southern ports, chiefly Messina (Johnson 1969, 119–21).

On launching the Fifth Crusade, Pope Innocent III specified that all those travelling by sea should sail from Messina or Brindisi, although he subsequently relaxed this to accommodate Andrew of Hungary's departure from Split. Many, particularly Germans and Italians, are known to have used the southern ports, while others sailed directly from northern Europe (Donovan 1950, 27, 30–2, 36–7, 44–6, 48; Oliver of Paderborn, *Historia Damiatina* 8, 10, 16, 44, 54; Van Cleve 1969a, 382, 395–6, 423). Frederick II launched his own belated expedition in 1227–8 from Brindisi (Van Cleve 1969b, 439–40, 444–7, 451). In no case other than the Fourth Crusade, in which German participation was quite modest, does Venice seem to have been the main conduit for a German crusading enterprise. Thus, in this case political geography overrode physical geography and the most important crusading group from its apparent catchment area largely bypassed Venice, markedly diminishing its importance during the era when maritime crusading was most dominated by the provision of transport.

The Fourth Crusade was of course the great exception to this, and one that went against geographical inclinations in a different way. In opting for Venice over the western Mediterranean ports its leaders diverged from the pattern followed by other predominantly French expeditions of the period. This choice, apparently envisaged at an early stage by Pope Innocent III, seems to have been prompted by the preoccupation of Genoa and Pisa by war with one another, and by the sheer scale of Venice's shipping capacity (Geoffrey of Villehardouin, *La Conquête de Constantinople* 14, 32; Queller and Madden 1997, 6–8; Robert of Clari, *La Conquête de Constantinople* 6). The latter point would have been especially significant for leaders wishing to concentrate as many crusaders as possible into a single force carried from one port by one fleet, owing to their intention to attack Egypt, a destination liable to go against the preferences of many participants. This imperative had all the more force given that the leaders lacked the advantages offered by royal or imperial authority in achieving such a concentration (Geoffrey of Villehardouin, *La Conquête de Constantinople* 30; Queller and Madden 1997, 14–16).

Of course, the potential for disagreement over targeting Egypt was mild compared to the controversy aroused by the actual diversions of the crusade. The financial embarrassment of the non-Venetian participants had the effect of blurring the contrast arising from the shift from land to sea routes for crusading armies, enabling Doge Enrico Dandolo to turn the expedition to Venetian purposes in seizing Zadar, as though this had been one of the largely or exclusively Venetian fleets of earlier decades (Queller and Madden 1992, 444–50; 1997, 55–63). Given sufficiently credulous partners, crusades could be turned to such purposes even in the absence of such constraints. The Franco-Genoese expedition of 1390 sacked Catalan-controlled ports and extracted concessions from Pisa while returning from its unsuccessful attack on Hafsid Mahdia, the Genoese convincing their French cohorts to assist on the pretext that these places sold provisions to the Hafsids (Setton 1976–84, vol. 1, 338).

Before the attack on Zadar, the Venetians had been able to detach a portion of the fleet to impose renewed submission and tribute on Trieste and Muggia at the head of the Adriatic (Andrea Dandolo, *Chronica* 10.3; Queller and Madden 1997, 71–2; Tafel and Thomas 1964, vol. 1, 387–8). Regarding the much-debated question of the second diversion of the crusade, if we may suppose, in line with the consensus of most recent scholarship, that the capture of Constantinople was not the product of a Venetian plot, the outcome here tends rather to highlight the contrast between the old pattern of freely operating fleets and the new one in which their destiny was bound up with the armies they carried (Balard 2005; Koumanoudi 2009; Madden 2012; Queller and Madden 1992). The enlistment of Mediterranean fleets as paid subsidiaries of other crusading groups harnessed them together, constraining both parties' freedom of action, and the scale of the debt that arose in this case turned debtors and creditors into one another's hostages.

The volcanic consequences of the Fourth Crusade triggered a profound transformation in the context of Venetian crusading, changes that were intensified by the events of the following centuries. By definitively shattering the Byzantine-dominated Aegean basin into a zone of violent insecurity, it created an environment where Venice would have to assert itself more directly and persistently to defend its interests, while by giving the Venetian zone of activity in Greece and the Aegean a firm territorial footing it gave those interests a more fixed character, pushing Venice towards clashes with expansionist powers in the region. This reduced the distinction between the nature of Venetian activity in the Adriatic and that further east, entrenching its efforts to dominate maritime space further along its eastern routes. It also helped turn the erstwhile Byzantine world into a destination for crusading.

This was manifested first through the temporary transformation of Byzantium into a target for crusading, which arose from the repercussions of the Fourth Crusade, the Byzantine counteroffensives that destroyed the Latin empire of Constantinople and the subsequent schemes for its reestablishment (Chrissis 2012; Setton 1976-84, vol. 1, 63-5, 134-9, 162-9). It continued more forcefully and enduringly through the advance of the Anatolian Turks into the Aegean and the Balkans, at the expense of the weakened empire and the other small polities that had emerged from its fragmentation (Housley 1986, 25-49, 199-259; 1992, 56-95; Setton 1976-84, vol. 1, 177-238, 285-329, 341-404; vol. 2, 1-107; Zachariadou 1983, 21-81; 1989, 212-25). This meant an increasing overlap between zones Venice sought to dominate and the crusading front line, not only in regional terms, but also through the renewed extension of crusading combat into the maritime sphere, since both Michael VIII's Byzantium and the Turks from the fourteenth century onwards possessed significant naval power and were strongly associated with corsair or pirate activity. These developments generated recurrent conflict outside the ambit of crusading between Venice and the same groups that were now most often targeted by crusades (Gullino 1996, 26-38, 51-82; Nicol 1988, 179-80, 201-7; Zachariadou 1983, 6-7, 13-33, 41-5, 49-60, 64-81). This contrasts with the preceding period, when the naval weakness of Muslim powers had restricted their capacity to threaten Venice at sea, while the remoteness of Muslim territories from the Adriatic and Venice's lack of a territorial footprint outside it, except in its possession of quarters in the ports of the Crusader States, had reduced the scope for conflict over land. Consequently, non-crusading clashes with Muslim powers had been much less common. Thus the distinction between crusading and normal activity was now further reduced.

However, the effect of this was far from redoubling Venetian commitment to the crusade. Rather, Venice became increasingly subject to the contradictory impulses that had always affected regimes on the front line of crusading, which had most to fear from the unchecked power of their Muslim neighbours, but also most to fear from provoking them. This complicated further the inclination to keep the peace with trading partners which always necessarily influenced the policy of the mercantile communities, redoubled in the fourteenth and fifteenth centuries as Muslim markets, once secondary to the Byzantine connection, became increasingly vital to Venetian trade (Ashtor 1983, 114-26).

The geographical realignment of crusading to the Aegean and the Balkans, which over the decades after the extinction of the crusader states in 1291 emerged as the main focus of Mediterranean crusading, also complicated Venetian policy by creating a new direct overlap between

Venice's crusading activity and its relations with its neighbours in the Adriatic. Given the proximity of this new crusading zone, it was natural that the other major Latin powers of the Adriatic, whose geographical situation tended to make them natural rivals of Venice, became shared upholders of Latin Christian interests and the crusading cause in the adjacent regions to the east, making them and the Venetians natural crusading partners. The contradictions of this first arose through Charles of Anjou's crusading projects against Byzantium, whose success would probably have enabled the ruler of southern Italy to control both sides of the Straits of Otranto, a prospect to which Venice was normally inclined to be violently opposed. Only after long hesitation did the temptation of restoring its old position in the Latin empire of Constantinople and aggravation at the actions of Michael VIII's piratical allies induce Venice to agree in 1281 to provide an escort fleet for Charles' planned, but never launched, expedition against Byzantium (Chrissis 2012, 204, 214–5, 241; Nicol 1988, 201–9; Nicolini 1935, 261–6; Setton 1976–84, vol. 1, 134–5; Tafel and Thomas 1964, vol. 3, 287–308).

The increased confrontation faced by the Latins in the naval sphere was naturally accompanied by a further shift in the role of sea power in crusading. Sea transportation of land forces continued in the mid-fourteenth century, but these were now usually small, while in the face of Turkish seaborne raiding there was a renewed emphasis on naval combat and coastal assault and on the goal of hamstringing the sea power of Muslim states. The need for a continuing defensive effort at sea, a sphere in which fixed positions were of less use than on land, contributed to the innovation of the Christian maritime league (Housley 1986, 25–7, 32–9, 117–22, 250–8). Venice was a key participant in the league fleets that operated against the Turks in the Aegean in 1332–7, 1344–50 and 1357–62, whose chief exploit was the capture of the harbour of Smyrna in 1344. It contributed two to five galleys at a time, generally amounting to between a quarter and three-eighths of the total forces of these leagues, whose other habitual participants were the knights of St John, the kingdom of Cyprus and sometimes the papacy (Housley 1986, 25–49; Setton 1976–84, vol. 1, 179–223, 231; Zachariadou 1983, 21–81; 1989, 212–25). Genoa notably refrained from participating on its own account, though it did outfit galleys paid for by the papacy, as well as doing likewise for Amadeo of Savoy. It contributed three galleys to the expedition of Peter I of Cyprus against Egypt, while Genoese dependencies in the East took part in a local league and negotiations for other such arrangements in the late fourteenth century (Belgrano 1877–84, 953–67).

Though the fleets of the fourteenth century were composed of small contingents drawn from multiple ports, the leaders of land forces carried on them now showed a striking preference for making their own embarkation from Venice even when, as in the case of Humbert of Viennois in 1345, Peter I of Cyprus in 1365 or Amadeo of Savoy in 1366, they faced Venetian reluctance and sometimes suspicion. King Peter shipped his European recruits from Venice and the Venetian government pledged to provide transport at its own expense, but it was ultimately able to escape this commitment and avoided supplying any vessels to his fleet on its own account. As it became clear that his target was Mamluk Egypt, Venice became increasingly reluctant to help, at one point banning its ships from carrying troops to Cyprus, but Venetians suffered along with other Christian merchants from the repercussions of Peter's sack of Alexandria (Ashtor 1983, 88–102; Setton 1976–84, vol. 1, 249–83). Amadeo, who launched his own expedition having been too late to join Peter's, had to overcome Venetian reluctance to outfit vessels due to fears that he might further provoke the Mamluks, despite his declared intention of assisting Byzantium against the Turks (Setton 1976–84, vol. 1, 291–2).

Amadeo and Humbert before him were both based in the natural hinterland of Genoa and Marseilles and procured the majority of their shipping there, but they too opted to set out from Venice. Humbert hired his galleys from Marseilles and, having set out from Avignon, sailed from that port, but then sent his squadron on separately while he himself crossed by land from Porto Pisano to Venice and was shipped as far as Glarentza, where he presumably made the rendezvous with his own vessels. He also sought to engage Venetian ships to carry horses from Brindisi to Smyrna. Amadeo appears to have hired at least eleven galleys from Genoa and three from Marseilles, besides eight from Venice, while vessels from Nice are also mentioned, but he opted to sail from Venice rather than a port closer to his starting point in Piedmont. He made it the gathering point for the other contingents who joined him from France, Burgundy and the Low Countries, making his rendezvous at Coron with the rest of his fleet, sailing from Genoa, Marseilles and Aigues-Mortes (Faure 1907, 516–26; Girardi 2004, 124–6; Ljubić 1868–91, vol. 2, 286; *Cronique de Ame V^e*, 126–30; Setton 1976–84, vol. 1, 195–201, 291–7).

In Humbert's case, Venice was a major participant in the crusading league he was going to join, and attempts to discourage him from passing through the Adriatic were presumably aimed at avoiding the interference of this first cousin of the king of Hungary in the latest struggle over Zadar. In the event, such fears were to some extent realised, since as he passed

Humbert convinced the Venetian commanders to negotiate under a truce with the besieged citizens of Zadar, to the great displeasure of the Venetian government, which saw this as an encouragement to continued resistance (Faure 1907, 519–20; Ljubić 1868–91, vol. 2, 292–3). The persistent preference for Venice as a point of departure may be related to its status as the chief hub for communications between East and West, making it an advantageous point for commanders to make final plans and preparations with access to the latest information.

By the end of the fourteenth century, as the Ottomans became the main preoccupation of crusading, the pattern shifted again. Turkish expansion into Europe removed the rationale for transporting armies by sea, so that as in the early days of crusading armies and fleets proceeded to their destinations separately. Indeed, the separation was now greater than it had been then, since land and sea elements of the early crusades had usually acted together in the main theatre of war. Now they were in practice generally engaged in widely separated areas, with armies attacking from the Danube while fleets operated around the Bosphorus and Dardanelles, typically with the aim of blocking Ottoman troop movements across the straits, though also intending to link up with the armies once these had fought their way to Constantinople, something that was never actually achieved. However, this separation did not revive the independent operation of fleets, since in contrast to the grand expeditions and enthusiasm of earlier times, Venice now made much smaller and more cautious contributions to coalition fleets, themselves small in total, in which many of the vessels put to sea by maritime powers were provided at the expense of other rulers, who sometimes supplied their commanders or whole crews.

The Ottoman advance into the Balkans also extended the zone in which Venetian interests were under pressure into the lower Adriatic, where indeed this pressure was largely responsible for the establishment of Venetian territorial control, as local rulers submitted to Venice to secure its protection against the Turks (Fine 1987, 418–22; Gullino 1996, 14–18). Although Venetian territories were exposed to Ottoman attack here and elsewhere, they were also comparatively defensible, many being islands and even the continental possessions mostly being a long way from the centres of Ottoman power, increasing the feasibility of armed resistance. The resulting fine balance between the respective benefits of confrontation and of appeasement contributed to the array of contradictory pressures influencing Venice's ambivalent approach to anti-Ottoman crusading. The reluctant but persistent participation in crusading coalitions that resulted contrasts with the less combative attitude of the Genoese, whose concentration of interests in the Black Sea and north-eastern Aegean made them more vulnerable to Ottoman hostility, and with the minimal involvement before the 1450s of the Catalans, who now lacked territorial interests in the area. It contrasts also with Venice's own consistent antipathy to conflict with the Mamluks, who posed no threat to Venetian territories and controlled what were now indispensable markets for Venice's trade (Ashtor 1983).

Venice's particular reluctance to provoke the Mamluks was thrown into sharp relief during the Crusade of Varna, when the commanders of the Venetian contingent in the fleet sent to fight the Turks in 1444 were forbidden to help defend Rhodes, where a major Mamluk attack was impending, or Cyprus, while assurances were sought from the fleet's other leaders that they would act only against the Turks. In the event of Mamluk vessels coming to the straits to join forces with the Ottomans, the Venetians were, as far as possible, to disclaim responsibility for any ensuing conflict (Valentini 1967-79, vol. 18, 195-9, 224-6, 251-4, 256-9). The following year, the Venetian government excused itself from transporting soldiers to Rhodes as requested by the pope, explicitly on the grounds that this might provoke the Mamluks and thus threaten Venetian commercial interests (Valentini 1967-79, vol. 19, 57-60).

Hungary similarly combined exposure to Ottoman attack with a degree of remoteness that afforded some protection and sufficient military power to make armed confrontation a credible option. Its position was nonetheless more exposed, while it lacked Venice's commercial interests in and around Turkish territory. Whereas Venice's participation in anti-Ottoman crusading tended to be hesitant and parsimonious, Hungary was the principal driving force behind the movement, both as the leading participant and, along with Byzantium, as the state in whose defence expeditions were generally launched (Bak 2004, 116-27; Housley 1992, 73-69, 83-8, 100-4; Kintzinger 1997, 23-33; Setton 1976-84, vol. 1, 341-55; vol. 2, 74-92, 171-84). In a strategic context where crusading on land and on sea had become largely separate endeavours, but where it was believed that naval action was of key importance in supporting an effort on land, they formed a complementary pair at the heart of any projected effort against the Turks. However, as in the case of Charles of Anjou, this logic was obviously complicated by their continuing rivalry in the Adriatic. It is hard to gauge how far this really obstructed co-operation against the Ottomans, but it certainly concerned contemporaries. During the early fifteenth century Byzantium and the papacy put sustained effort into mediating peace between Venice and Hungary in the interests of collective action against the Turks (Nicol 1988, 353, 356, 364). Similar complications would appear later in Venice's dealings with Alfonso V of Aragon, who emerged after his conquest of the kingdom of Naples as both a would-be champion of Christendom and an ambitious force in the Adriatic and Ionian Seas in a manner echoing the career of Charles of Anjou. In his efforts to extend his power into the Balkans and check the Ottomans, Alfonso supported Skanderbeg in his revolt against the Turks and his clashes with Venice in Albania in the 1440s, eventually going to war with Venice in 1449–50 after it tried to take control of the Ionian Islands, traditionally a dependency of Naples (Gullino 1996, 47–51).

The weight placed on Venice's naval contribution as a critical adjunct to Hungarian efforts might have offered opportunities for trading off action in support of Hungarian crusading for concessions in the Adriatic, as at the time of the Fifth Crusade. This would seem particularly likely in the case of the Crusade of Nikopolis of 1396, since at that time Venice had a great deal to gain. Hungary was still in possession of Dalmatia, which it had seized from Venice in the 1350s, while Venice had been obliged to pay an annual tribute of 7,000 ducats since the end of the War of Chioggia in 1381 (Krekić 1997, 59–66; Ljubić 1868–91, vol. 4, 124–7). The Venetians were striving to maintain a neutral posture in the succession struggle between the crusade's main protagonist King Sigismund and Ladislas of Naples, but vigorous support for the crusade might have been a useful means of capitalising on Sigismund's needy position without actually having to take sides (Krekić 1997, 66–77). In fact there seems to have been no exploitation of these opportunities to advance Venice's position in the Adriatic. The Venetian government committed only four galleys to support the expedition and that merely by extending the period of service of part of a squadron already in the vicinity of Constantinople. It also, after some deliberation, turned down Sigismund's request for a loan to help pay for his expedition (Ljubić 1868–91, vol. 4, 363–5, 374–6). Even this was represented by Venice as something of a concession, since it had pledged to participate (supplying a quarter of any fleet to a maximum contribution of five or six galleys) only on condition that the dukes of Burgundy, Orleans and Lancaster fulfilled their declared intention of joining the crusade, or were substituted by other leaders of comparable heft, which had not occurred (Ljubić 1868–91, vol. 4, 340–3).

While the king undertook to pay for ten galleys of his own, they were to be outfitted not by Venice but, a little improbably, by Byzantium (Ljubić

1868–91, vol. 4, 360). Venice did however make use of the debacle of the crusade and Sigismund's return home on the galley of the Venetian commander Tommaso Mocenigo to relaunch its persistent diplomatic efforts to reoccupy the island of Tenedos near the Dardanelles, which it had been obliged to demilitarise and evacuate after the War of Chioggia (Ljubić 1868–91, vol. 4, 130–1, 393–400; Thiriet 1953, 228–45). Sigismund, other crusade leaders and the Emperor Manuel II were reported to have expressed the view that the desertion of Tenedos was responsible for the growth of Ottoman power around the straits, an opinion they had no doubt reached after some prompting (Senato Secreta, reg. E, fols. 138v–139, 140, 142, 145). With regard to the tribute obligation, the only concession was Sigismund's transfer of 1,000 ducats per year to Mocenigo as a personal reward for his services (Commemoriali, reg. 9, fols. 91v–92, 107). The repercussions of the crusade did in fact lead to the termination of the tribute, but that was an incidental consequence of Sigismund's transfer of the remaining income to the duke of Burgundy as his contribution to ransoming the crusade leaders, giving Venice the opportunity to refuse further payments (Commemoriali, reg. 9, fols. 91v–92; Delaville 1886, vol. 1, 327–34; vol. 2, 36–7, 41–2).

The diffidence of Venice's response fits into the wider tendency to parsimonious restraint that marked Venetian policy in the period following the costly War of Chioggia (Lane 1973, 196–200). By the time of the Crusade of Varna, although now much stronger and more expansionist, Venice initially hesitated to join the war against the Ottomans, but was emboldened by the early successes of the enterprise in 1443, enabling a crusading fleet to be deployed the following year (Gullino 1996, 53–4; Setton 1976–84, vol. 2, 66–8, 77–8, 84–90). At eight galleys, Venice's self-funded contribution was not vastly greater than in 1396, but it also provided another ten galleys paid for by the pope and eight for the duke of Burgundy, amounting to the vast majority of the crusading fleet, which was commanded by the Venetian Alvise Loredan. The republic also now took a more ambitious approach to the opportunities seemingly promised by the offensive against the Ottomans. Before the 1444 campaign the Venetians sought their allies' consent to their retention of Gallipoli, Thessaloniki and Maroneia on the north coast of the Aegean and Panidos on the Sea of Marmora, if these were taken from the Turks (Valentini 1967–79, vol. 18, 218–22). At the same time, they laid plans to exploit the pressure the Ottomans were under to negotiate the peaceful cession of Valona, Kanina, Argyrokastron and Ioannina on the Balkan side of the Straits of Otranto and the Ionian Sea, in an ironic inversion of the manner of Venice's earlier acquisitions in the region from rulers threatened by the Ottomans (Valentini 1967–79, vol. 18, 226–9, 261–2, 265–6).

This simultaneous exploitation of the opportunities raised by the same crusading enterprise to advance Venetian interests both in the Adriatic and in the former heart of the Byzantine world echoes the pattern of Venetian conduct since the very beginning of the crusading movement. The methods envisaged for making gains on these two fronts differed, reflecting both the area of operations of the land army and the as yet limited and precarious Ottoman presence on the western shores of the Balkans. However, the similarly territorial nature of the goals in both areas and the fact that both sets of putative acquisitions would have been made from the intended target of the crusade highlights the degree to which the context of Venetian crusading action had changed, as the zone through and past which earlier expeditions had passed on the way to their goal had become the main theatre of operations. The lapsing of the need for sea transport for crusading armies had severed the harnessing of the land as well as the sea connections of the maritime communities into their crusading practice, but on the seaward side the collapse of Byzantine power, which Venice's crusading actions had done so much to bring on, and the converging advance of Muslim powers and Venice's own expansion, were well on the way to binding the seas and coasts extending from the head of the Adriatic to the Bosphorus into a single strategic space.

In so far as a crusade retained the character of a pilgrimage, the journey was a fundamental part of its spiritual significance, and it was in any event central to its practical demands. For the maritime communities, the journey was the most ordinary part of the undertaking, whereas for others it was perhaps the most exceptional, but it was also at the heart of their participation and the part of the endeavour where their role was most distinctive. In the early stages of crusading, the Venetians' own journey and the opportunities of traversing the broad space that separated them from their main objectives but was a critical part of their own world formed a major element of their crusading activity. Later, their role in facilitating the journeys of others became a dominant influence, in ways that both undercut their role in crusading and made it the catalyst for the most dramatic turning point in the republic's history. That transformation helped usher in the final permutations of their involvement, as the extension of Venice's geographical footprint and the closer approach of the enemy elided the distinction between the journey and the destination.

References

Unpublished Sources

Senato Secreta, reg. E, fols. 138v–139, 140, 142, 145, Archivio di Stato di Venezia.
Commemoriali, reg. 9, fols. 91v–92, 107, Archivio di Stato di Venezia.

Published Sources

Ailes, M. and Barber, M. (eds. and trans.) 2003. *The History of the Holy War: Ambroise's Estoire de la Guerre Sainte*, 2 vols. (Woodbridge).

Andrea Dandolo. *Chronica*, in Pastorello, E. (ed.), *Andreae Danduli ducis Venetiarum Chronica per extensum descripta aa. 46-1280 d.C.*, Rerum Italicarum scriptores 12/1 (Bologna, 1938–58).

Annales Venetici breves, in Berto, L.A. (ed.), *Testi storici veneziani (XI–XIII secolo)* (Padua, 2000), 85–99.

Ansbert. *Historia de expeditione Friderici imperatoris*, in Chroust, A. (ed.), *MGH Scriptores rerum Germanicarum* n.s., vol. 5, *Quellen zur Geschichte des Kreuzzuges Kaiser Friedrichs I* (Berlin, 1928), 1–115.

Archdeacon Thomas of Split. *Historia Salonitana*, in Perić, O., Karbić, D., Matijević Sokol, M. and Sweeney, J.R. (eds.), *Thomae archdiaconi Historia Salonitanorum atque Spalatinorum pontificum / Archdeacon Thomas of Split. History of the Bishops of Salona and Split* (Budapest, 2006).

Ashtor, E. 1983. *Levant Trade in the Later Middle Ages* (Princeton).

Bak, J.M. 2004. 'Hungary and crusading in the fifteenth century', in Housley, N. (ed.), *Crusading in the Fifteenth Century* (London and New York), 116–27.

Balard, M. 1993. 'Communes italiennes, pouvoir et habitants des états francs de Syrie-Palestine au XIIe siècle', in Shatzmiller, M. (ed.), *Crusaders and Muslims in Twelfth-Century Syria* (Leiden), 43–64.

2005. 'L'historiographie occidentale de la quatrième croisade', in Laiou, A.E. (ed.), *Urbs Capta: The Fourth Crusade and Its Consequences / La IVe croisade et ses conséquences* (Paris), 161–74.

Belgrano, L.T. 1877–84. 'Seconda serie di documenti riguardanti la Colonia di Pera', *Atti della Società ligure di storia patria* 13, 931–1003.

Bellomo, E. 2009. 'The First Crusade and Latin East seen from Venice: The account of the *Translatio sancti Nicolai*', *Early Medieval Europe* 17/4, 420–43.

2010. 'Gerusalemme, Terrasanta e crociata nelle memorie agiografiche veneziane (1116–c.1135). Note circa le *translationes* dei santi Nicola ed Isidoro', *Luoghi del desiderio: Gerusalemme medievale*, Quaderni di storia religiosa 17 (Verona), 63–85.

Buenger Robbert, L. 1985. 'Venice and the Crusades', in Zacour, N.P. and Hazard, H.W. (eds.), *The Impact of the Crusades on the Near East*, vol. 5 of Setton, K.M. (ed.), *A History of the Crusades* (Madison), 379–451.

1995. 'Venetian participation in the Crusade of Damietta', *Studi veneziani* n.s. 30, 15–33.

Cerbani, C. *Translatio mirifici martyris Isidori a Chio insula in civitatem Venetam (Jun. 1125)*, in *Recueil des historiens des croisades, Historiens occidentaux*, vol. 5 (Paris, 1895), 321–34.

Chrissis, N.G. 2012. *Crusading in Frankish Greece: A Study of Byzantine-Western Relations and Attitudes, 1204-1282*, Medieval Church Studies 22 (Turnhout).

Cleve, T.C. Van 1969a. 'The Fifth Crusade', in Wolff, R.L. and Hazard, H.W. (eds.), *The Later Crusades, 1189-1311*, vol. 2 of Setton, K.M. (ed.), *A History of the Crusades* (Madison), 377–428.

1969b. 'The Crusade of Frederick II', in Wolff, R.L. and Hazard, H.W. (eds.), *The Later Crusades, 1189-1311*, vol. 2 of Setton, K.M. (ed.), *A History of the Crusades* (Madison), 429–62.

Cosmas of Prague. *Chronica Boemorum*, in Bretholz, B. (ed.), *Die Chronik der Böhmen des Cosmas von Prag, MGH Scriptores rerum Germanicum* n.s., vol. 2 (Berlin, 1955).

Cronique de Ame V^e et XIIIIe conte, appelle Vert, in Servion, J. (ed.), *Gestez et croniques de la mayson de Savoye*, vol. 2 (Turin, 1879), 67–267.

Delaville le Roulx, J. 1886. *La France en Orient au XIVe siecle: Expéditions de maréchal Boucicaut*, 2 vols. (Paris).

Devaney, T. 2010. "'Like an ember buried in ashes': The Byzantine-Venetian conflict of 1119-1126', in Madden, T.F., Naus, J.L. and Ryan, V. (eds.), *Crusades: Medieval Worlds in Conflict* (Farnham), 127–47.

Devastatio Consantinopolitana, in Hopf, C. (ed.), *Chroniques gréco-romanes inédites ou peu connues* (Berlin, 1873), 86–92.

Donovan, J.P. 1950. *Pelagius and the Fifth Crusade* (Philadelphia).

Faral, E. (ed.) 1938. *Geoffrey of Villehardouin. La conquête de Constantinople*, vol. 1, *1199-1203* (Paris).

Faure, C. 1907. 'Le Dauphin Humbert II à Venise et en Orient (1345-1347)', *Mélanges d'archéologie et d'histoire* 27, 509–62.

Favreau-Lilie, M.-L. 1989. *Die Italiener im Heiligen Land vom ersten Kreuzzug bis zum Tode Heinrichs von Champagne (1098-1197)* (Amsterdam).

Fine, J.V.A. 1987. *The Late Medieval Balkans: A Critical Survey from the Late Twelfth Century to the Ottoman Conquest* (Ann Arbor).

France, J. 1997. 'The First Crusade as a naval enterprise', *The Mariner's Mirror* 83/4, 389–97.

2000. 'The western Mediterranean powers and the First Crusade', *Journal of Mediterranean Studies* 10/1-2, 265–74.

Fulcher of Chartres. *Historia Hierosolymitana*, in Hagenmeyer, H. (ed.), *Fulcheri Carnotensis Historia Hierosolymitana (1095-1127)* (Heidelberg, 1913).

Girardi, F. (ed.) 2004. *Venezia – Senato: Deliberazioni miste, Registro XXIII (1345-1347)*, Venezia Senato 10 (Venice).

Gullino, G. 1996. 'Le frontiere navali', in Tenenti, A. and Tucci, U. (eds.), *Storia di Venezia: Dalle origini alla caduta della Serenissima*, vol. 4, *Il Rinascimento: Politica e cultura* (Rome), 13–111.

Hamblin, W.J. 1986. 'The Fatimid navy during the early crusades, 1099-1124', *The American Neptune* 46, 77–83.

Historia ducum Venetorum, in Berto, L.A. (ed.), *Testi storici veneziani (XI-XIII secolo)* (Padua, 2000), 1–83.

Housley, N. 1986. *The Avignon Papacy and the Crusades, 1305-1378* (Oxford).

1992. *The Later Crusades: From Lyons to Alcazar, 1274-1580* (Oxford).

Jacoby, D. 1997. 'The Venetian privileges in the Latin kingdom of Jerusalem: Twelfth and thirteenth century interpretations and implementation', in Kedar, B.Z., Riley-Smith, J. and Hiestand, R. (eds.), *Montjoie: Studies in Crusade History in Honour of Hans Eberhard Mayer* (London), 155–75.

Johnson, E.N. 1969. 'The Crusades of Frederick Barbarossa and Henry VI', in Wolff, R.L. and Hazard, H.W. (eds.), *The Later Crusades, 1189-1311*, vol. 2 of Setton, K.M. (ed.), *A History of the Crusades* (Madison), 87–122.

Kintzinger, M. 1997. 'Sigismond, roi de Hongrie, et la croisade', in Paviot, J. and Chauney-Bouillot, M. (eds.), *Nicopolis 1396-1996: Actes du Colloque international organisé par l'Académie des sciences, arts et belles-lettres de Dijon et le Centre national de la recherche scientifique réuni à Dijon, au Conseil régional de Bourgogne, le 18 octobre 1996*, Annales de Bourgogne 68/3 (Dijon), 23–33.

Krekić, B. 1997. 'Venezia e l'Adriatico', in Arnaldi, G., Cracco, G., and Tenenti, A. (eds.), *Storia di Venezia: Dalle origini alla caduta della Serenissima*, vol. 3, *La formazione dello stato patrizio* (Rome), 51–85.

Koumanoudi, M. 2009. 'Βιβλιογραφία', in Moschonas, N.G. (ed.), Η Τέταρτη Σταυροφορία και ο ελληνικός κόσμος (Athens), 417–33.

Lane, F.C. 1973. *Venice: A Maritime Republic* (Baltimore).

Lanfranchi, L. (ed.) 1955. *Famiglia Zusto, 1083-1199*, Fonti per la storia di Venezia, sez. 4, Archivi privati (Venice).

Lev, Y. 1991. *State and Society in Fatimid Egypt* (Leiden).

Ljubić, S. (ed.) 1868-91. *Listine o odnošajih izmedju južnoga Slavenstva i mletačke republike*, 10 vols. (Zagreb).

Madden, T.F. 2012. 'The Venetian version of the Fourth Crusade: Memory and the conquest of Constantinople in Medieval Venice', *Speculum* 87/2, 311–44.

Marshall, C. 2003. 'The crusading motivation of the Italian city republics in the Latin East, c.1096–1104', in Bull, M. and Housley, N. (eds.), *The Experience of Crusading*, vol. 1, *Western Approaches* (Cambridge), 60–79.

Monk of the Lido. *Historia de translatione magni Nicolai*, in *Recueil des historiens des croisades. Historiens occidentaux*, vol. 5 (Paris, 1895), 253–92.

Morozzo della Rocca, R. and Lombardo, A. (eds.) 1940. *Documenti del commercio veneziano nei secoli XI-XIII*, 2 vols., Regesta chartarum Italiae 28-29 (Rome).

Nicol, D.M. 1988. *Byzantium and Venice: A Study in Diplomatic and Cultural Relations* (Cambridge).

Nicolini, N. 1935. 'Sui rapporti diplomatici veneto-napoletani durante i regni di Carlo I e Carlo II d'Angio', *Archivio storico per le province napoletane* 60 (n.s. 21), 264–5.

Niketas Choniates. *Historia*, in Dieten, J.A. van (ed.), *Nicetae Choniatae Historia*. Corpus fontium historiae Byzantinae – Series Berolinensis 11, vol. 1 (Berlin and New York, 1975).

Oliver of Paderborn. *Historia Damiatina*, in Hoogeweg, H. (ed.), *Die Schriften des Kölner Domscholasters, späteren Bischofs von Paderborn und Kardinal-Bischofs von S. Sabina Oliverus* (Tübingen, 1894), 161–282.

Painter, S. 1955. 'The Third Crusade: Richard the Lionhearted and Philip Augustus', in Baldwin, M.W. (ed.), *The First Hundred Years*, vol. 1 of Setton, K.M. (ed.), *A History of the Crusades* (Madison), 45–85.

——— 1969. 'The crusades of Theobald of Champagne and Richard of Cornwall, 1239–1241', in Wolff, R.L. and Hazard, H.W. (eds.), *The Later Crusades, 1189–1311*, vol. 2 of Setton, K.M. (ed.), *A History of the Crusades* (Madison), 463–85.

Phillips, J. 2007. *The Second Crusade: Extending the Frontiers of Christendom* (New Haven and London).

Praga, G. 1925. 'Zaratini e veneziani nel 1190: La battaglia di Treni', *La rivista dalmatica* 8, 47–54.

Pryor, J. 2003. 'The Venetian fleet for the Fourth Crusade and the diversion of the crusade to Constantinople', in Bull, M. and Housley, N. (eds.), *The Experience of Crusading*, vol. 1, *Western Approaches* (Cambridge), 103–23.

——— 2008. 'A view from the masthead: The First Crusade from the sea', *Crusades* 7, 87–151.

Queller, D.E. and Katele, I.B. 1986. 'Venice and the conquest of the Latin kingdom of Jerusalem', *Studi veneziani* n.s. 12, 15–43.

Queller, D.E. and Madden, T.F. 1992. 'Some further arguments in defense of the Venetians on the Fourth Crusade', *Byzantion* 62, 433–73.

——— 1997. *The Fourth Crusade: The Conquest of Constantinople* (Philadelphia).

Riley-Smith, J. 1986. 'The Venetian Crusade of 1122–1124', in Airaldi, G. and Kedar, B.Z. (eds.), *I comuni italiani nel regno crociato di Gerusalemme, Atti del Colloquio The Italian Communes in the Crusading Kingdom of Jerusalem (Jerusalem, May 24–28, 1984)* (Genoa), 337–50.

Robert of Clari, *La Conquête de Constantinople*, ed. and trans. Dufournet, J. (Paris, 2004).

Rose, S. 1999. 'Islam versus Christendom: The naval dimension, 1000–1600', *The Journal of Military History* 63/3, 561–78.

Schein, S. 1986. 'From 'Milites Christi' to 'Mali Christiani'. The Italian communes in Western historical literature', in Airaldi, G. and Kedar, B.Z. (eds.), *I comuni italiani nel regno crociato di Gerusalemme, Atti del Colloquio*

'The Italian Communes in the Crusading Kingdom of Jerusalem' (Jerusalem, May 24–28, 1984) (Genoa), 679–89.

Setton, K.M. 1976–84. *The Papacy and the Levant (1204–1571)*, 4 vols. (Philadelphia).

Strayer, J.R. 1969. 'The Crusades of Louis IX', in Wolff, R.L. and Hazard, H.W. (eds.), *The Later Crusades, 1189–1311*, vol. 2 of Setton, K.M. (ed.), *A History of the Crusades*, (Madison), 487–518.

Tafel, G.L.F. and Thomas, G.M. (eds.) 1964. *Urkunden zur älteren Handels- und Staatsgeschichte der Republik Venedig mit besonderer Beziehung auf Byzanz und die Levante vom neunten bis zum Ausgang des fünfzehnten Jahrhunderts*, 3 vols. (Amsterdam, repr. Vienna, 1856–7).

Thiriet, F. 1953. 'Venise et l'occupation de Tenedos au XIVe siècle', *Mélanges d'archéologie et d'histoire publiés par l'Ecole française de Rome* 65, 219–45.

Valentini, J. (ed.) 1967–79. *Acta Albaniae Veneta: Saeculorum XIV et XV*, 25 vols. (Rome).

William of Tyre. *Chronicon*, in Mayer, H.E and Rösch G. (eds.), *Willelmi Tyrensis archiepiscopi Chronicon*, Corpus Christianorum continuatio medievalis 63–63A (Turnhout, 1986).

Zachariadou, E.A. 1983. *Trade and Crusade: Venetian Crete and the Emirates of Menteshe and Aydin, 1300–1415* (Venice).

1989. 'Holy War in the Aegean during the fourteenth century', in Arbel, B., Hamilton B. and Jacoby, D. (eds.), *Latins and Greeks in the Eastern Mediterranean after 1204* (London), 212–25.

15 | Reassessing the Venetian Presence in the Late Medieval Eastern Adriatic

OLIVER JENS SCHMITT

Venice succeeded in securing undisputed hegemony in the Adriatic in a period of steady expansion between 1392 and 1420, thus revising the peace treaties of Zadar (Zara) and Turin in 1358 and 1381 respectively. This process of Venetian reaffirmation in an area of vital importance for the *Serenissima* began in the south with the incorporation of Corfu (1384–7) and ended with the conquest or acquisition of all major Dalmatian towns and Friuli in 1420. In 1420, Venice almost completely controlled the eastern shore of the Adriatic Sea, with the exception of Habsburg (Trieste) and Hungarian possessions (Rijeka [Fiume], Bakar [Baccari] and Senj [Segna, Zengg]), the republic of Dubrovnik, officially part of the Crown of St Stephen, and parts of the south Albanian coast. The year 1420 marks the apogee of Medieval Venetian expansionism in the eastern Adriatic in terms of hegemonic power – although it is true that as Benjamin Arbel (2013; 2015) has recently remarked, in terms of territory it was the sixteenth-century *Serenissima* and not the fifteenth-century *Dominium* that reached its maximal extension. Venice controlled major ports such as Durrës (Durazzo) (1392), the starting point of the trans-Balkan highway – the Via Egnatia, Kotor (Cattaro) (1420), Split (Spalato) (1420), Šibenik (Sebenico) (1420) and the Dalmatian metropolis of Zadar (1409), while its most important bulwark in the hinterland was Shkodër (Scutari) (1396) (Israel and Schmitt 2013; Ivetic 2014; Raukar 2013).

Since the nineteenth century, the major steps of Venetian conquest and incorporation have been the object of scholarly interest and political passion on both sides of the Adriatic Sea. Given that both were all too often intermingled, politicised research distorted interpretations until the 1990s. Almost everything, perhaps with the exception of chronology, became a matter of dispute: the motives of Venetian expansionism, the nature of its rule in the eastern Adriatic, the consequences of its economic strategy, the terms for describing this process (expansion, conquest, occupation) and the categories used for describing groups and communities. The Second World War witnessed the nadir of the political and historiographical dispute between Italian and Croatian elites over Dalmatia and when the war ended there was virtually no room for national or ideological otherness in Dalmatia. Mainstream post-war historiography in Italy reacted with silence to the instrumentalisation of Dalmatia's Venetian past by Fascist ideology, while Yugoslav historiography legitimised Yugoslav claims on the region by establishing a parallel between Venetian and Fascist rule.

After the end of the Cold War, research was virtually unfrozen and twenty-five years later, historians on both sides of the Adriatic present perspectives of Venetian rule in the Late Medieval Adriatic that differ radically from what most non-specialists still deduce from major history manuals. The present chapter aims at retracing important milestones of this reinterpretation and at offering insight into recent approaches to assessing the nature of the Venetian presence in the Late Medieval eastern Adriatic.

The *Società dalmata di storia patria* has recently published the volume *Giuseppe Praga storico dalmata da Zara a Venezia* (2013) which analyses the scholarly work of Giuseppe Praga, the leading Italian specialist in the field in the first half of the twentieth century. Praga is the author of a short and dense *Storia di Dalmazia*, first printed in 1944, republished several times until the early 1980s and widely cited by historians not acquainted with the Croatian language and, consequently, Croatian historiography. This volume of the *Società dalmata* marks an important step for Italian studies on Dalmatia: historicising Praga means a paradigm shift. It is no coincidence that around the same time Egidio Ivetic published *Un confine nel Mediterraneo* (2014), a history of the eastern Adriatic as a multiple border zone, a book which summarises Italian, Croatian and international scholarship of the last twenty-five years and aims, successfully, at writing a common history of South Slavs and Italophones, avoiding traps such as projecting modern national identity onto a distant past. At the same time, he does not replace a narrative of national confrontation with an irenic model of cultural hybridity and fluent identities and thus circumvents ideological convictions of the last twenty-five years that are slowly becoming outdated. There are good reasons to believe that Ivetic, who published extensively on Praga, will replace the old classic. This would be particularly important (Ivetic 2019), because Praga's rather one-sided interpretation of Dalmatian history had an extremely strong impact on international Mediterranean studies. Ivetic is also one of the first Italian scholars to make full use of relevant works written in Croatian, Slovenian and German, which are usually passed over by specialists in Venetian and Medieval Adriatic studies.

Slavica non leguntur is an observation which is valid for most scholarship in the field of Venetian overseas history, where historians with a classical education made full use of Modern Greek publications while Croatian Medieval studies remained literally in the shadows with the exception of Dubrovnik, of course, which was not part of, but the counterpart to, the Venetian commercial and economic presence in the area. As noted, after 1945, Italian research on Medieval Dalmatia almost completely ceased and the field was left to Croatian historians. The reasons are self-evident: in the period of Fascism, the interpretation of Venice as an Italian hegemonic state in the eastern Mediterranean, legitimising the expansionism of the Italian nation state, reached its apogee and the Lion of St Mark was hailed as proof carved in stone of Italian historical claims to the eastern shore of the Adriatic. As in other ethnically contested areas, nationalising history dated back to the nineteenth century. Extreme violence in the Second World War virtually put an end to the almost millenarian bilingual (or trilingual) culture of Dalmatia. The Venetian lions were taken down in many places and Communist monuments celebrating the liberation of Fascist rule replaced them. Only a few years after Praga's monograph, Grga Novak (1888–1978), his main counterpart on the Croatian side, issued his *Prošlost Dalmacije* (*The Past of Dalmatia*) in 1944. Novak was a historian of all seasons who had begun his career in interwar Yugoslavia, written his major monograph in the time of the Ustaša dictatorship and died as a leading historian of Communist Croatia. While in Praga's book the Slavs almost completely disappeared from Dalmatian history – or, to be more precise, were divided into Italianised and therefore civilised Slavs on the coast and *štokav* 'barbarians' in the hinterland – Novak applied the same strategy and minimised or eliminated the Romance/Italian element from his narrative.

The less well-known Albanian case developed differently: there was no Italo-Albanian national competition in the nineteenth and the early twentieth century. Albania was perceived by Italian elites as an object of colonial politics and not as a part of the historical Italian lands like Dalmatia. Categories of classification and perception were clearly Orientalist and closer to Italian strategies in Africa than to Italian expansionist politics in Mediterranean Europe. Italian scholars and politicians did not have an intellectual counterpart in Albania. On the contrary, after the end of the Austro-Hungarian monarchy, the cradle of Albanian studies before 1918, it was predominantly due to Italian efforts that research institutions were established in Albania, especially in the short period of the Italo-Albanian Double Monarchy (1939–43). After 1944, Venice and Mussolini's Italy were just two sides of the same coin for what quickly developed into one of the most ideologised historiographies in the world. The Albanian interpretation did not differ substantially from the Croatian: Venice was described as the Medieval predecessor or even the model of Fascist occupation in the twentieth century – a nationalist or even racist colonial oppressor and economic exploiter backed by a fifth column of traitors and collaborators from within. However, Albanian historians had to cope with Italian scholarship in the field at least implicitly – it was forbidden to cite foreign historians with the exception of a few specialists who wholeheartedly supported the regime, such as the French scholar Alain Ducellier (Božić 1979; Ducellier 1981; Malltezi 1988; Schmitt 2001; Šufflay 1924). Italy's traditional Albanian Uniate minority, the Arbëresh, political refugees and Italo-Albanian clergymen who had served in the interwar Albanian school system maintained and even enhanced a high level of consistent research. While Italian scholars hardly ventured into debate with Croatian medievalists, researchers such as Giuseppe Valentini (1900–79) or Arshi Pipa (1920–97) openly criticised or condemned the nationalist, and even increasingly racist, official interpretations of Tirana historians (Pipa 1990; Schmitt 2009a).

When trying to compare historiography on Venetian Dalmatia and Venetian Albania, one has to bear in mind considerable structural differences in Adriatic connections between Italians and Croats and between Italians and Albanians. These structural discrepancies also help explain the different paths of Adriatic historiographies after the breakdown of Communist rule: in Albania, the state and considerable parts of society collapsed. Italy became a major destination of a chaotic emigration but, at the same time, especially in the 1990s, it re-established an almost hegemonic position in Albania. It seemed as if Albania had once again become a political, economic and, via the mass media, cultural annexe of Italy. Under the circumstances of dramatic change, the Albanian scholarly elite almost collapsed and there was virtually no audience for Italian initiatives to open a new chapter in historiographical discussions. When Albania regained internal stability, nationalism served as an important tool for mobilising voters and Medieval history, Skanderbeg and the interpretation of Ottoman conquest were widely and emotionally discussed in politics and mass media and on the Internet. Venice and its rule in northern Albania were rehabilitated by those circles which had already welcomed Italian influence in Albania in the interwar period: the cultural elite of north Albanian Catholics, while medievalist research was seriously hampered by the lack of specialists and ongoing (self-)isolation of scholars (Schmitt 2009a).

The transition from Communist rule was even more difficult in Croatia: years of warfare, mass expulsion and occupation of one-third of the national territory. Nationalism did not spare historiography but a steady archive-based process of reassessing the Venetian presence in Dalmatia was not stopped by these circumstances. Leading medievalists such as Tomislav Raukar (1977; 1997; 2007) and Josip Kolanović (1995) had already started to rewrite central chapters of Late Medieval Dalmatian history in the 1970s but since they did not noisily proclaim a 'turn' or a 'paradigm shift' as Western historians like to do, the significant changing of the guards of major representatives of Croatian historiography passed almost unnoticed. A closer reading of their key articles, however, reveals an almost complete reversal of central elements of the traditional narrative. One of those elements, the idea of a colonial economic system, also cherished by Albanian historians, was particularly prominent: Venice had indeed interfered drastically in Dalmatian salt production and limited regional shipbuilding; it redirected the flow of commercial goods to Venice by establishing the metropolis as a compulsory staple market of all Venetian subjects conducting trade in the Adriatic. Historians such as Grga Novak (1928) popularised the idea of an economic decline of Dalmatia, which had flourished under the liberal rule of the Croato-Hungarian kings in the fourteenth century. Raukar (2000) and Kolanović (1979) were able to demonstrate on the basis of export registers that Venice did not interrupt trans-Adriatic trade and that many ships which left Šibenik and Split obtained export licences which in principle contradicted the centralistic commercial strategy of the Venetian state. They, furthermore, illustrated the rapid integration of Dalmatian shipowners and mariners into the Venetian Mediterranean commercial system.

The ruin of Dalmatian trade turned out to be a historiographical myth to be explained with undue concentration on normative sources and salt production. Indeed, salt was of particular importance for the Venetian economy, but scholarly focus on this single product obscured the fact that cheese, salted fish, figs, wine and labour were actually Dalmatia's most important export goods. Dalmatian entrepreneurs exported salted fish even to the Ionian Islands and Crete and their ships called at all major ports of the Venetian overseas possessions (Schmitt 2009b, 86–7). Several Dalmatian ports flourished because of Venetian protection from Dubrovnik: one way Venice tried to shut Dubrovnik merchants out of Mediterranean trade was by protecting its own Dalmatian subjects. The *Serenissima* was also unable to suppress smuggling of salt and arms between Dalmatia and Apulia, Dalmatia and Herzegovina and Dalmatia and the Greek shores of the Ionian Sea, not at least because on Korčula, for instance, where the leaders of the smugglers' gang belonged to leading patrician families on whose support Venetian control of the island had to rely. These patricians simply maintained traditional trade routes that Venice unsuccessfully tried to cut after 1420 (Schmitt 2008). In recent years, local monographs have been published by Croatian and Slovenian scholars investigating public spaces and social networks. These studies contribute significantly to our understanding of local dynamics vis-à-vis the Venetian presence on the Dalmatian shores (Benyovsky Latin 2009; Dokoza 2009; Nazor 2015; Mlacović 2008).

Almost at the same time, major changes occurred in Italian Venetian studies, culminating in a conference in 2013 at which the very essence of Venetian statehood was reconsidered. For the last two decades, *statualità* has been a major topic of Italian Medieval studies and much of the discussion in Venetian studies has also been inspired by general debates on the Early Modern European state (Ortalli *et al.* 2015). In recent years scholars such as Gherardo Ortalli, Ermanno Orlando and Egidio Ivetic have underlined the composite character of the Venetian state, analysed the strategies of its actors and emphasised treaties, contracts and negotiations as major tools of exercising power. International Venetian studies actively discusses concepts such as 'colonialism' in assessing the nature of Venetian rule in its overseas possessions (for recent contributions to this debate see Ortalli *et al.* 2015). It is evident that key publications in the field were published under the impact of decolonisation in the 1950s and 1960s and the impression of colonial exploitation was reinforced by the focus on the Greek part of Venice's overseas possessions in the Early Modern period (Thiriet 1959).

Crete was indeed a settler colony, although the number of colonists remained very modest. However, the emergence of a Veneto-Cretan elite that articulated its own economic and political interests reveals colonial patterns (McKee 2000). Benjamin Arbel (2015, 155–6) has recently put forward convincing arguments for the colonial character of Early Modern Venetian rule on Cyprus and Crete. Dalmatia, however, was a different case: the city communes at the eastern shore of the Adriatic shared with Venice a confession, in Latin a sacred language, a constitution and political organisation and a common space of trade and migration. There was never a colonisation of Dalmatian towns by Venetians and Venice insisted on preserving local law and constitutional traditions. Although the treaties concluded between Venice and Dalmatian communes did not fully conceal the inequality of power between the contracting partners, they nevertheless constituted the legal cornerstone of Venetian rule in most of Venice's eastern Adriatic possessions. The linguistic difference – which also existed in the Greek part of the *Stato da Mar* – mattered much less than the confessional gap which enduringly divided Catholics and Orthodox on Crete and Cyprus, while the common Catholic faith contributed very much to an alliance based on mutual interests in the face of Ottoman expansion.

For two decades, Dalmatia and to a much lesser degree Albania have been slowly emerging from the shadow of Veneto-Greek studies and this renewed interest is gradually changing Venetian overseas studies. There are still only a few historians who construct a new analytical framework combining the Adriatic and the Greek part of the *Stato da Mar*. But focusing on the Venetian Adriatic possessions quickly transcends a revival of regional history. One of the milestones in this context is the detailed analysis of contractual bounds between Venice and east Adriatic urban communities or an Adriatic model of expansion that operated quite differently from Venetian strategies applied in the Orthodox part of the overseas possessions. Indeed, most Catholic communities entered the Venetian state on the basis of a contract (Orlando 2013). There were admittedly different models of integration: cession by the formal sovereign as in the case of Zadar, voluntary alignment of an urban community in the case of Kotor, negotiations under the circumstances of war in the region in the case of Korčula, Split and Šibenik, military pressure in Trogir and negotiations with local princes in northern and central Albania. Everywhere there were opponents to Venetian rule, in Dalmatia mostly patricians who remained loyal to the Hungarian crown and noble dynasties in the hinterland kingdom of Croatia such as the houses of Nelipić or Frankopan (Birin 2006). In Albania, several noblemen repented having handed over their port towns to the *Serenissima* in moments of imminent Ottoman threat. Venice succeeded, however, in swiftly eliminating these forces from local political life and usually did so with the support of local pro-Venetian forces. Contracts not only guaranteed local urban constitutions, legal systems and property rights but also defined the place of Dalmatians in Venetian economy and society. They obliged Venice to maintain peace and social order in its overseas possessions and, particularly importantly, to mediate the frequent strife within local communities

It is no exaggeration to state that one of the main pillars of Venetian rule was equilibrating sociopolitical tensions between patricians and non-patricians in Dalmatia and northern Albania. Venice's self-image was that of a conservative, law-abiding power according to its state idea of *honor et proficuum* and *pax et iustitia*. Control over its Dalmatian possessions was exercised not so much by military power and a huge administrative apparatus – on the contrary, the administrative personnel was more than modest and in many smaller ports there were no Venetian mercenaries at all – Venice secured control rather by negotiation and communication. It offered communication channels open to all social strata which had the right to send delegations to Venice presenting their claims (*capitula*) to the senate and the doge. These petitions were a formal part of Venetian rule and they constituted a key element of stability in what evolved into a quadrangular power system composed of Venetian central authorities, Venetian representatives in the overseas possessions, local patrician elites and local non-patrician elites (Schmitt 2009b, 93–100). Research on Dalmatia demonstrates that colonialism is hardly an appropriate term with which to assess sociopolitical structures in the Late Medieval eastern Adriatic and that Venetian studies should operate with a clear conceptual differentiation between the Adriatic and the Aegean part of Venice's overseas empire and an equally clear distinction between the Late Medieval and the Early Modern period.

New approaches focusing on actors and agencies have revealed that categories such as 'dominators' and the 'dominated', 'Venice' and its 'subjects' were far too monolithic and distorted much more complex political and social realities (Dursteler 2011; Mueller 1996; O'Connell 2009; Rothman 2012). Venice imposed neither a common compulsory currency nor a homogenised and centralised legal system. It did not create major administrative units for the sake of premeditated centralisation, but merely reacted both to claims from its overseas possessions and the Ottoman threat when creating regional courts (as in Shkodër or Zadar) and military commands. Local city statutes remained in use and Venetian law was applied only in cases where local law was lacking.

An extremely important step forward was a new vision of Venice's ethnic and cultural structure. It constituted not only a Medieval and Early Modern composite state, but a multi-ethnic one too. There was never the slightest attempt on the part of Venice to Italianise its overseas societies. Indeed, research has made it quite clear that Italianisation of Dalmatia started slowly during French rule and was then accelerated by the Austrian administration (1806–1918). During the long centuries of Venetian rule, Latin, Venetian and eventually Italian were used in justice and administration, but these languages, especially Latin and the vernacular, had been traditional languages of administration before while Croatian continued to serve as the language of the Catholic religious brotherhoods and poetry, which flourished in the fifteenth and especially the sixteenth century (Graciotti 2009; Metzeltin 2009). Dalmatia was described as a trilingual region and Croatian even used three alphabets – Latin,

Glagolithic and Cyrillic. Not only did Venice not suppress the Croatian language, but, on the contrary, the metropolis became the media capital of its overseas possessions, with printing houses publishing in Croatian and Greek.

Recent research has paid much attention to migration, especially Venice's role as the immigration metropolis of its overseas possessions (Čoralić 2001; 2006; Ducellier *et al.* 1992; Imhaus 1997; Malcolm 2015; Nadin 2008; Orlando 2014; Petta 1996; 2000). Following Dalmatia's demographic collapse due to constant Ottoman raids from the late 1460s onwards, the metropolis counted more inhabitants than the narrow coastal strip that remained under Venetian rule. But even before, a steady stream of Dalmatian and Albanian labour was almost magically attracted by the possibilities of the market in Venice. Far less well known are migration movements within the *Stato da Mar* which did not touch the capital: Dalmatian mariners and soldiers in the Orthodox part of the *Stato da Mar* and Greek mercenaries, mariners and merchants in Dalmatian port towns. Together with the intensive trade between the Venetian provinces in the Adriatic and the Aegean, migration was a cohesive element of the Venetian state and society.

This reinterpretation was possible due to fresh evidence and new methodological and theoretical approaches. For decades, non-Croatian historians overlooked the fact that Dalmatian archives provide abundant primary source material that often surpasses archives in major towns of the Veneto and has remained in many cases almost untouched. For eight years I have been working with the most complete island archive of Venetian Dalmatia, the archive of Korčula, which has never been systematically studied in the context of the fifteenth-century Venetian presence (Schmitt 2011a; 2011b; 2011c; 2013). For major towns such as Split, there has been until recently no up-to-date monograph despite an enormous wealth of archive material (Andrić 2011; 2014; Orlando 2019). The Korčula archive has preserved text genres which had disappeared in other collections, such as daily reports of field guardians which allow us to penetrate deep into the capillary veins of daily life in village communities (Schmitt 2011a; the mainland is less documented, see Nazor 2015). This extraordinary evidence, mainly almost complete series of penal law suits, virtually open the doors for microhistorical case studies. Microhistory as established by Italian and French scholars since the 1970s has been taken up by specialists of Dubrovnik's history such as Zdenka Janeković Römer (2008).

In the case of Venetian Dalmatian, studies on Korčula provide thorough archive-based evidence for much of what has been depicted as major changes in recent historiography. I would like to emphasise only the quadrangular system of power briefly outlined above: the biographies of local political actors in village communities can be retraced over several decades. The life of the peasant leader Zuanin Dragačić from the village of Čara is currently the best-known case (Schmitt 2013; 2016): the son of a modest peasant, he became, in the late 1430s and early 1440s, a vociferous and violent spokesman of peasants' interests against the urban patriciate, already at this early stage leading protest delegations to Venice where he negotiated directly with Doge Francesco Foscari. While Korčulan patricians formed coalitions with local Venetian governors against the non-patricians, the latter obtained the support of Venetian central authorities – when the Venetian governor condemned Dragačić in a false trial, Francesco Foscari sent him home to Korčula with a solemn Ducale. Venice, however, did not offer unconditional support to the non-patricians and declined their claim for separate peasant and villages councils; on the other hand, it successfully reminded those patricians who showed sympathies for Hungary or Naples that the *Serenissima* could unchain peasant resentment against the upper class at any moment. Dragačić's political success was accompanied by a steady economic advancement as an export trader, landowner and leaseholder of taxes. His case demonstrates that despite strong political tensions, peasant leaders maintained personal relations to some of the patricians and did business with them. Of particular importance are many speech acts by political protagonists, especially elaborated pleas at the local court which reflect the degree to which local actors had internalised key elements of official Venetian state rhetoric and used it to push their own political interest. The analysis of internal mechanisms of village communities also helps us understand mechanisms of indirect rule: indeed, in most villages Venice was present just in name and the pre-Venetian administration continued unchanged. The extremely high degree of literacy in the administration even in rural areas was not a Venetian invention; the *Serenissima* simply benefitted from existing structures.

In summary, studies on the Venetian possessions in the eastern Adriatic are currently undergoing a process of almost complete reinterpretation, replacing outdated models of colonial rule with the model of a composite state based on continuous negotiation of power in a structurally and culturally rather homogenous region. Despite linguistic differences in the world of daily oral practice, Dalmatia and Venice belong to a shared Adriatic world, they shared a common tradition of organising urban life, religious life and education, economy and trade. From the second half of the fifteenth century, they also shared the same enemy, the Ottoman

Empire, and the constant Ottoman threat and the political decline of Hungary and Naples eventually cemented unwavering Dalmatian and north Albanian loyalty to Venice. The fresh wind in east Adriatic studies is also a gentle breeze for research on the *Stato da Mar* in general, which is slowly overcoming its fragmentation in national historiographical schools. Exploring huge swathes of fresh primary evidence combined with methodological approaches such as microhistory will see this field develop into one of the most exciting subjects of Late Medieval Mediterranean studies in the coming years.

Acknowledgements

This contribution is based on a project sponsored by the Austrian Science Foundation (FWF) SFB F 42 Visions of Community (VISCOM).

References

Andrić, T. 2011. 'Položaj obrtničkih naučnika i pomoćne radne snage u Splitu sredinom 15. stoljeća', *Zbornik Odsjeka za povijesne znanosti Zavoda za povijesne i društvene znanosti Hrvatske akademije znanosti i umjetnosti* 29, 127–47.

—— 2014. 'Oprema stambenih i radnih prostora splitskih obrtnika u kasnom srednjem vijeku', in Basić I. and Rimac, M. (eds.), *Spalatumque dedit ortum: Collected Papers on the Occasion of the 10th Anniversary of the Department of History, Faculty of Humanities and Social Sciences in Split* (Split), 240–71.

Arbel, B. 2013. 'Venice's maritime empire in the early modern period', in Dursteler, E. (ed.), *A Companion to Venetian History, 1400–1797* (Leiden), 125–253.

—— 2015. 'Una chiave di lettura dello Stato da Mar veneziano nell'età moderna: La situazione coloniale', in Ortalli, Schmitt and Orlando (eds.), 2015, 155–79.

Birin, A. 2006. 'Knez Nelipac i hrvatski velikaški rod Nelipčića' (PhD thesis, University of Zagreb).

Benyovsky Latin, I. 2009. *Srednjovjekovni Trogir. Prostor i društvo* (Zagreb).

Božić, I. 1979. Немирно поморје XV века (Belgrade).

Čoralić, L. 2001. *U gradu svetoga Marka: Povijest hrvatske zajednice u Mlecima* (Zagreb).

—— 2006. *Barani u Mlecima: Povijest jedne hrvatske iseljeničke zajednice* (Zagreb).

Dokoza, S. 2009. *Dinamika otočnog prostora. Društvena i gospodarska povijest Korčule u razvijenom srednjem vijeku* (Split).

Ducellier, A. 1981. *La façade maritime de l'Albanie au Moyen Âge: Durazzo et Valona du XIe au XVe siècle*, Documents et recherches sur l'économie des pays byzantines, islamiques et slaves et leurs relations commerciales au Moyen Âge 13 (Thessaloniki).

Ducellier, A., Doumerc, B., Imhaus, B. and De Miceli J. (eds.) 1992. *Les chemins de l'exil: Bouleversements de l'Est européen et migrations vers l'Ouest à la fin du Moyen Âge* (Paris).

Durstelen, E.R. 2011. *Renegade Women: Gender, Identity and Boundaries in the Early Modern Mediterranean* (Baltimore).

Giuseppe Praga storico dalmata, da Zara a Venezia 2013 = Atti e memorie della Società dalmata di storia patria 2, 3rd series, 35 (Rome).

Graciotti, S. 2009. 'Das Wechselverhältnis zwischen Literatursprachen und Kulturen auf dem westlichen Balkan zwischen dem 16. und dem 18. Jahrhundert', in Ortalli and Schmitt (eds.) 2009, 179–98.

Imhaus, B. 1997. *Le minoranze orientali a Venezia, 1305–1510* (Rome).

Israel, U. and Schmitt, O.J. (eds.) 2013. *Venezia e Dalmazia* (Rome).

Ivetic, E. 2014. *Un confine nel Mediterraneo: L'Adriatico orientale tra Italia e Slavia, 1300-1900* (Rome).

2019. *Storia dell'Adriatico: Un mare e la sua civiltà* (Bologna).

Janeković Römer, Z. 2008. *Maruša ili suđenje ljubavi: bračno-ljubavna priča iz srednjovjekovnog Dubrovnika* (Zagreb).

Kolanović, J. 1979. 'Izvori za povijest trgovine i pomorstva srednjevjekovnih dalmatinskih gradova s osobitim osvrtom na Šibenik', *Adriatica maritima* 3, 63–150.

1995. *Šibenik u kasnome srednjem vijeku* (Zagreb).

Malcolm, N. 2015. *Agents of Empire: Knights, Corsairs, Jesuits and Spies in the Sixteenth-Century Mediterranean World* (London).

Malltezi, L. 1988. *Qytetet e bregdetit shqiptar gjatë sundimit venedikas, 1392-1478: aspekte të jetës së tyre* (Tirana).

McKee, S. 2000. *Uncommon Dominion: Venetian Crete and the Myth of Ethnic Purity* (Philadelphia).

Metzeltin, M. 2009. 'Le varietà italiane sulle coste dell'Adriatico orientale', in Ortalli and Schmitt (eds.) 2009, 199–237.

Mlacović, D. 2008. *Građani plemići: Pad i uspon rapkoga plemstva* (Zagreb).

Mueller, R.C. 1996. 'Aspects of Venetian sovereignty in Medieval and Renaissance Dalmatia', in Dempsey, C. (ed.), *Quattrocento Adriatico: Fifteenth-Century Art of the Adriatic Rim* (Bologna), 29–56.

Nadin, L. 2008. *Migrazioni e integrazione: Il caso degli Albanesi a Venezia (1479–1552)* (Rome).

Nazor, A. 2015. *Splitsko-poljički odnosi u XIV. i XV. stoljeću* (Split).

Novak, G. 1928. 'Quaternus izvoza iz Splita 1475-1476. godine', *Starohrvatska prosvjeta* n.s. 2, 1–2, 92–102.

1944. *Prošlost Dalmacije*, 2 vols. (Zagreb).

O'Connell, M. 2009. *Men of Empire: Power and Negotiation in Venice's Maritime State* (Baltimore).

Orlando, E. 2013. 'Politica del diritto, amministrazione, giustizia: Venezia e la Dalmazia nel basso Medioevo', in Israel and Schmitt (eds.) 2013, 9–61.

   2014. *Migrazioni mediterranee: Migranti, minoranze e matrimoni a Venezia nel basso Medioevo* (Bologna).

   2019. *Strutture e pratiche di una comunità urbana: Spalato, 1420–1479*, Schriften zur Balkanforschung 2 (Venice and Vienna).

Ortalli, G. and Schmitt, O.J. (eds.) 2009. *Balcani occidentali: Adriatico e Venezia fra XIII e XVIII secolo / Der westliche Balkan: Der Adriaraum und Venedig, 13.–18. Jahrhundert* (Vienna).

Ortalli, G., Schmitt, O.J. and Orlando, E. (eds.) 2015. *Il commonwealth Veneziano tra 1204 e la fine della repubblica: Identità e peculiarità* (Venice).

   2018. *Comunità e società nel Commonwealth veneziano* (Venice).

Petta, P. 1996. *Soldati albanesi in Italia (sec. XV–XIX)* (Lecce).

   2000. *Despoti d'Epiro e principi di Macedonia: Esuli albanesi nell'Italia del Rinascimento* (Lecce).

Pipa, A. 1990. *Albanian Stalinism: Ideo-Political Aspects* (Boulder).

Praga, G. 1981. *Storia di Dalmazia* (Verona).

Raukar, T. 1977. *Zadar u 15. stoljeću: Ekonomski razvoj i društveni odnosi* (Zagreb).

   1997. *Hrvatsko srednjovjekovlje: Prostor, ljudi, ideje* (Zagreb).

   2000. 'Jadranski gospodarski sustavi: Split 1475–1500', *Rad Hrvatske akademije znanosti i umjetnosti* 480/38, 49–125.

   2007. *Studije o Dalmaciji u srednjem vijeku: Odabrane studije* (Split).

   2013, 'La Dalmazia e Venezia nel basso Medioevo', in Israel and Schmitt (eds.) 2013, 63–87.

Rothman, N.E. 2012. *Brokering Empire: Trans-Imperial Subjects between Venice and Istanbul* (London).

Schmitt, O.J. 2001. *Das venezianische Albanien 1392–1479* (Munich).

   2008. "Contrabannum': Der adriatisch-balkanische Schmuggel im ausgehenden Mittelalter', *Südost-Forschungen* 67, 1–26.

   2009a. "Die Monade des Balkans' – die Albaner im Mittelalter', in Schmitt O.J and Frantz, E.A. (eds.), *Albanische Geschichte: Stand und Perspektiven der Forschung* (Munich), 61–80.

   2009b. 'Das venezianische Südosteuropa als Kommunikationsraum (ca. 1400–ca. 1600)', in Ortalli and Schmitt (eds.) 2009, 77–101.

   2011a. *Korčula sous la domination de Venise au XVe siècle: Pouvoir, économie et vie quotidienne dans une île dalmate au Moyen Âge tardif* (Paris), available online at books.openedition.org/cdf/1511 (last accessed 1 May 2020); printed edition 2019.

   2011b. 'L'apport des archives de Zadar à l'histoire de la Méditerranée orientale au XVe siècle', in Franchini S., Ortalli G. and Toscano G. (eds.), *Venise et la Méditerranée* (Venice), 45–54.

   2011c. 'Micro-history and *Lebenswelten* as approaches to late medieval Dalmatian history: A case study of Korčula', in Rudić, S. (ed.),

Споменица академика Симе Ћирковића: *Homage to Academician Sima Ćirković* (Belgrade), 137–58.

2013. 'Storie d'amore, storie di potere: La tormentata integrazione dell'isola di Curzola nello Stato da Mar in una prospettiva microstorica', in Israel and Schmitt (eds.) 2013, 89–109.

2016. 'Addressing community in Late Medieval Dalmatia', in Hovden, E., Luttner, C. and Pohl, W. (eds.), *Meanings of Community Across Medieval Eurasia* (Leiden).

Šufflay, M. 1924. *Städte und Burgen Albaniens hauptsächlich während des Mittelalters* (Vienna).

Thiriet, F. 1959. *La Romanie vénitienne au Moyen Âge: Le développement et l'exploitation du domaine colonial vénitien, XIIe-XVe siècles* (Paris).

16 | 'Strangers in the City?'

The Paradoxes of Communitarianism in Fifteenth-Century Venice

ÉLISABETH CROUZET-PAVAN

Venice in the fifteenth century was undoubtedly a cosmopolitan city. Indeed, cosmopolitanism is considered by some historians (Hansen 2000) to be one of the characteristics of the transhistorical model of the city state and, among paradigmatic city states, Venice ranks high. But there is no need to resort to categories constructed by later and modern-day historians given that we have the observations of late fifteenth-century visitors to document contemporary representations and tell us how Venice was then seen. They include the ambassador Philippe des Commynes, who emphasises the number of foreigners in the Venetian metropolis. Statements of this kind abound and together reveal that this cosmopolitanism was part of the fascination exercised by Venice, which was described in many travellers' accounts as a world city. Migrants flowed into Venice. Some came from nearby countries and the Venetian hinterland, which was penetrated at an early date by Venetian economic enterprises, while others arrived from much further afield. Without them, how would the city have been able to surmount the demographic crises it suffered in the first decades of the fourteenth century, that is, even before it experienced the far more serious shocks of the great plagues (Crouzet-Pavan 1990, vol. 1, 116–18; Mueller 1979a; 1979b)?

As is well known, many of these strangers were from a Balkan world that was hit hard by war and poverty in the fifteenth century and they arrived in a capital that was in need of men for its armies as well as manpower for its galleys and industries. Prominent among these immigrants were the Dalmatians and Albanians from the other shore of the Adriatic who are the subject of this article. It is difficult to establish the size of these populations although estimates have been proposed that we may use. We should not forget that the privileges which granted Venetian citizenship, though meticulously listed for the last centuries of the Middle Ages, are of little help here. First, these privileges concerned only the elite among the immigrants. Of the 4,000 persons who sought a privilege of 'veneta' citizenship at the end of the Middle Ages only 130, according to Mueller (1998; Mola and Mueller 1994; 1996), were natives of Istria, Dalmatia or Albania. These figures are enough to show that most of the new arrivals would never become *Veneti facti privilegio*. In addition, we need to remember another factor which renders this documentation even less useful for our purposes. When Venice once again imposed its sovereignty on Dalmatia at the beginning of the fifteenth century, all the citizens of the subject cities – of Zadar (Zara) and northern Dalmatia in 1409–12, followed by those of Šibenik (Sebenico) – became Venetians *de intus*, that is, half-citizens like those in the towns on the *Terraferma*.

Nevertheless, 'Schiavoni' and 'Albanesi' were numerous and I will look first at the ways in which they were integrated into Venetian urban space. These immigrants clustered together in micro-communities, documented in the fiscal sources and through toponyms, but they also dispersed throughout the Venetian *contrade* so we can see how, for at least some of them, their establishment proceeded in stages. Not all of them were poor, as the social careers of a few individuals within certain occupations reveal. But I also want to look beyond these personal itineraries illustrating the successes of integration and show how these communities collectively embarked on the road to recognition in the second half of the fifteenth century. The creation of confraternities associated with these segments of the Venetian population, the increasing importance of the cult of certain saints and the translations of their relics enabled Albanians and Dalmatians to compensate for their lack of belonging. Furthermore, they played a part in the construction of the image of a warlike Venice which, at least in the deafening discourse of its political communications, was mobilised for the defence of Christendom against the Turk.

What, then, do we know about the migrants who in the fifteenth century bombarded the captains of barques, more or less untrustworthy smugglers, with requests for a passage to what they believed to be rich and welcoming lands on the other side of the Adriatic, on the Italian coast from Apulia to the Marches and from the Marches to Venice?

In the Venetian metropolis, the fiscal sources are our first guide. East of the Piazza San Marco, in the courts and the *calli* of the *contrade* of San Provolo or Sant'Antonin, the housing deteriorated. This was, above all, the port quarter. The tax declarations of the first decades of the sixteenth century, for example those for the parish of San Giovanni in Bragora, reveal large numbers of immigrants from the east who lived crowded together in poor-quality houses, a whole poverty-stricken and cosmopolitan community of both men and women. The buildings, each of only a single room, are said to be 'old' and 'in poor condition', descriptions which should not be dismissed as the mere exaggerations of owners seeking to reduce their taxes. Prohibitions notwithstanding, sailors, oarsmen, porters, dockers and prostitutes lived cheek by jowl in cramped conditions, eight or ten to a room. Though they paid by the month and not annually as elsewhere in Venice, these often penniless tenants made frequent moonlight flits, taking the wooden beds, the locks and even the doors along with them (Crouzet-Pavan 2004, 202–4). The structural crisis affecting the shipping industry of that time had social consequences. Shipping routes were abandoned, the merchant galleys were laid up, wages decreased and the bottom fell out of the job market. It was the end of full employment for people who lived by the sea and the *estimo* of property of 1514, together with its revisions, throws vivid light on the living conditions of this 'proletariat of the sea'.

So, foreigners, at least those who came from the *Stato da Mar* and the Mediterranean region in general, were present in large numbers in the fifteenth century in the parishes of the *sestiere* of Castello, between the port and the vast shipyard of the Arsenal, and especially in the parishes of San Giovanni in Bragora and San Pietro di Castello (Imhaus 1997). These migrants had often first reached the ports of Dalmatia, Albania and western Greece before leaving for Venice. A first great wave of migration dates to the 1430s. After that, the Turkish advance in the 1460s caused other groups to migrate: they landed on the Adriatic coast and in Venice (Ducellier *et al.* 1992, 150–69) where many of these foreigners provided cheap labour and the crews needed for a rapidly expanding fleet. It was in this same quarter, dominated by activities associated with shipbuilding, maritime trade and all the business of a port, in the *contrada* of Santa Trinità, that a confraternity dedicated to the Holy Trinity and St Anastasius (Dieci, Miste, reg. 5, fol. 88r; Scuole Piccole, B. 704) had been founded in 1360. The parishioners who sought permission to establish this *scuola* included many of Dalmatian origin and the small bequests the *scuola* received during the first half of the fifteenth century were often made by testators whose surnames reveal their Dalmatian origin, most of them from Split (Spalato). So, a strong polarising dynamic encouraged if not a regrouping, at least the settlement of a majority of these new arrivals in the port quarter.

This picture, however, needs qualification. If we look at another periphery of Venice, behind Canareggio, we find everywhere 'courts of small houses', 'little houses', 'old buildings rotted by the humidity', 'little buildings in a piteous state', that is, many wooden buildings, housing that was decaying and badly maintained, rented out in tiny units. The rents were low, estimated at between three and five ducats a year, and the lodgings were home to workers, the poor and unskilled immigrants. The lists of tenants in the tax declarations throw further light on this world. Certain trades were over-represented: alongside workers employed in the dyeing industry, soap manufacture and shipbuilding, we also find a proletariat of *barcharol* and *fachin*, of those who rowed and who carried, a population probably in and out of work and always on the edge of poverty. Among them, revealed by their recurring patronyms (Vexentin, Veronese, Trivisan, Padoan), were also immigrants from the Venetian hinterland as well as other new arrivals, for example Dalmatian men and women, the latter often employed as maidservants (Romano 1996). They settled in this periphery where prices were low and where lodgings, if of poor quality, were easy to find. It is as if these outsiders were fated to remain on the margins, in peripheral spaces, and as if Venice, the city without walls, had recreated on its borders suburbs which had absorbed a substantial proportion of the new immigrants (Crouzet-Pavan 1990, vol. 2, 751–8).

If we stand back a little, we get a different angle on this spatial distribution. In the towns of the past, as in those of today, migrants settled wherever they could, in areas of cheap housing and where they could find work. They probably clustered together to ease their arrival and provide mutual support, especially when coming from the same town such as Dubrovnik (Ragusa), Zadar, Split or Kotor (Cattaro) for the Dalmatians; Durrës (Durazzo), Shkodër (Scutari) and Bar (Antivari) for the Albanians. Here we should evoke not only the mobilisation of familial and professional networks but also the presence of intermediaries able to offer advice to the new arrivals and thus influence the way they settled within the city. This did not stop some of the immigrants from dispersing throughout Venice as their integration gradually proceeded, that is, as outsiders became locals. In short, the obvious polarising logic did not exclude intra-urban movement and a degree of dispersal throughout Venice as one generation of migrants succeeded another and as some achieved success. The new arrivals tended to settle en masse in certain parishes and both the dynamics of proximity and the socio-economic character of these areas encouraged them to stay put, which is why the cartography of their settlement appears to change very little over time. But this relative permanence, the result of Venice shunting its immigrants into its peripheral spaces, should not obscure the reality of individual movements. In fact it is difficult to imagine that things could have happened differently, which would be to ignore the phenomena of social mobility and the mechanisms of integration. Let us now turn to the social levels of these populations, beginning with the Albanians.

Recorded Population Size of Albanian and Dalmatian Migrants

Between 1300 and 1510 there were 637 Albanians recorded in Venice, from 1300 to 1454 there were 398, while between 1454 and 1509 the recorded number was 239 (Ducellier *et al.* 1992, 40). It hardly needs saying that their real number was almost certainly significantly higher than these figures suggest. Furthermore, we should not forget that a part of this population was mobile and did not, therefore, settle permanently in the city. Many of these immigrants were rowers or wool carders and shearers. Some Albanians lived in a state of servitude. Those who had been unable to pay the cost of their sea passage from the eastern shore of the Adriatic were effectively forced to commit themselves to serving a Venetian master without payment for a period of years. Such contracts, entered into by men and women alike, were tantamount to forced labour. When, between 1388 and 1393, Venice imposed its rule on Corfu, Durrës (Durazzo), Lezhë (Alessio) and Shkodër (Scutari) these practices, responsible for what came close to a slave trade in the direction of the metropolis, seem to have become less common. However, they did not disappear and continued to supplement the Albanian population of Venice until the late fifteenth century (Ducellier *et al.* 1992, 146–8). Nevertheless, some sailors succeeded in acquiring a small boat fit for coastal navigation and so acceded to the status of shipmaster (*patronus navis*). Other Albanians, though not in such large numbers as the Dalmatians, were active in the trade in animals for slaughter, and in cheese and wine, which extended from one shore of the Adriatic to the other and helped feed Venetian bellies.

There is similar uncertainty regarding the number of Dalmatians: a total of 662 are known for the period between 1300 and 1454, and for the years from 1454 to 1509 the number was 548. What we can be sure of is that the flow of migrants increased in the second half of the fifteenth century before slacking off early in the next. The pattern is almost identical in the case of both Albanians and Slavs. Once again, in order to characterise these migrants from Kotor or Zadar we need to stress the importance of employment in the maritime sector – the occupation of a proletariat – before we turn to some individual histories. We need to pay proper attention to some of these trajectories, because, far from fragmenting the history of the migrations into many individual biographies, they show how integration was achieved in the last decades of the fifteenth century. Let us look first at some Albanian glassmakers.

Success Stories: Albanian Glassmakers and Dalmatian Printers

The measures that prevented or, on the contrary, facilitated the employment of foreigners in the glass industry of Murano changed according to the demographic situation (Crouzet-Pavan 2005). At the end of the fifteenth century, in spite of the desire to protect manufacturing secrets, the needs of the glass industry made flexibility essential and the master glassmakers employed foreigners. Not all of the latter were confined to the worst jobs and some of them prospered. We may cite the example of a family, documented until the first decades of the sixteenth century, the first known member of which was Andrea di Giorgio, an Albanian. His sons became business owners and chose for their furnace and their glass shop the sign 'alla Pigna', a name they would also take as their surname (Zecchin 1990). Their case was not exceptional; in 1501 the master 'Nicolaus de Drivasto, quondam Blasii' was elected guild master (*gastaldo*) of the glassmakers' guild (Moretti 1998).

Another dynamic sector of Venetian industry was printing and at least three Dalmatian printers are known before 1500: Giorgio Dalmatino (active in 1483 when he was associated with another printer), Andrea de Paltasichis (attested between 1476 and 1492) and Bonino de Boninis. The second of these, Paltasichis, was a native of Kotor. He was associated with his compatriot Bonino and two other printers but also with booksellers, and seems to have been well integrated into this professional community. Bonino, a citizen of Dubrovnik, was also a spy in the service of Venice, for which he was rewarded with ecclesiastical benefices (Cioni 1971; Donati 1927a). He probably died in 1529, in debt to the printer Andrea Torresani (Avogaria di Comun, reg. 3889, fasc. C 23). Like Andrea de Paltasichis, he also printed books in Glagolitic. It is known that Glagolitic books, initially breviaries but soon followed by alphabet primers, manuals of grammar and historical and geographical texts, were produced in Venice. The aim of the Venetian printers was to dominate the market in printed versions of liturgical and religious texts destined for the Catholic communities of Croatia, Dalmatia and Istria. This phase of Venetian printing ended in 1561 with Gian Francesco Torresani (Donati 1927b; Pelusi 1989). We may presume that Dalmatian correctors and typographers also worked for Italian printers.

It is clear that, at least for some, social mobility and integration were realities. Dalmatians and Albanians did not only provide cheap labour for the ships and the workshops of the metropolis. At the end of the fifteenth century, when some industrial sectors in Venice experienced a real upturn, a replenished labour force was essential in order to meet market demand. The protectionism of the crafts and of the tutelary administrative authorities was far from being an immutable fact of the labour market. The foreigners who were active in these sectors might even accede to a mastership or join the ranks of the entrepreneurial class, proof that they had escaped their status as strangers lacking local roots or local resources – here I use the definitions of Simona Cerutti (2012) – and that they had mastered the culture of the Venetian economic and social scene.

The Role of Confraternities

There was another way in which change came about within the communities from the other shore of the Adriatic in the decades under examination. The road to integration could also be collective and here I turn to the foundation of the Albanian and Slavonic confraternities. We should first note that in 1442 a group of Albanians began to meet in the Church of San Severo close to the monastery of San Gallo: most of the Albanians in Venice, who came from the north of the country, were Catholics. They founded a confraternity under the protection of the Madonna del Buon Consiglio – also known as Our Lady of Scutari (Shkodër) (Mladjan 2003, 39–40) – which was based, like many other *scuole piccole* lacking their own home, in a parish or monastic church. In this case, it was the former and we are back in the *sestiere* of Castello. The brethren had drawn up their statutes and chosen their rector and the fraternity was established on 22 October 1442 (*Matricola della Scuola di S. Maria, di S. Gallo e S. Maurizio*, cap. III; an almost identical copy is in Proveditori di Comun. reg. U, fols. 60–75). Despite the text in the *mariegola*, some authors give an incorrect foundation date, for example Vio (2004, 302; for background, see Ortalli 2001). However, for a confraternity to be founded, it was necessary to have the authorisation of the Council of Ten and the confraternity obtained it from the *capi* of the magistracy in 1443. But, it seems that because the obligatory procedure preceding the vote had not been followed, the decision was annulled the following year, on 10 September 1444. On the same occasion, it was discovered that the number of Albanians registered in the *scuola* under the authority of their *gastaldi* had already reached 200. The confraternity was prohibited from organising further meetings until the statutes and the register in which the names of the brethren were recorded had been submitted to the Ten. Let no one think that this was merely a procedural matter – such fraternities, said the Ten, were reserved for Venetians alone: *Quod congregationes huiusmodi scolarum non conceduntur nisi Venetis* (Dieci, Miste, reg. 12, fol. 160r). However, this claim was false. To give just one example, the Florentines of Venice obtained permission to found a fraternity 'because other nations, settled in Venice, had benefited from a similar authorisation' (Ceriana and Mueller 2014). They met under the dedication to the Virgin and St John Baptist, initially in the Dominican convent of Santi Giovanni e Paolo. Then, in 1436, they made an agreement with the Franciscan convent of Santa Maria Gloriosa dei Frari where their chapel was completed in 1443 (Corporazioni religiose soppresse, Santa Maria Gloriosa dei Frari, reg. 2, fol. 24r; Crouzet-Pavan 1990, vol. 2, 944–6). We may reasonably conclude that the Albanian community, largely made up of people who were poor and not as well integrated into the local society as the Florentines, was held in some suspicion.

The prohibition imposed on their confraternity did not prevent the Albanians from continuing to meet until they obtained the right to transfer their *scuola* to the Church of San Maurizio in the *sestiere* of San Marco in 1447. The fraternity was finally recognised on 21 February 1448 (Dieci, Miste, reg. 13, fol. 91). At first it had only a simple altar in the church but in 1489 it acquired land close by on which they could build their seat: work seems to have begun in 1497 or 1498 and been completed in 1502. Citing the example of the Armenian community who had a hospice, the brethren had one constructed at the same time as their meeting place. The Albanian community in Venice had been swollen by a large number of refugees, particularly after the loss of Shkodër in 1479 at the end of the first Venetian-Ottoman war (1463–79), resulting in the need for a new building and new burial sites and so an agreement was reached with the convent of Santi Giovanni e Paolo. Also needed was housing for the poor (*casette degli poveri*) as one of the typical functions of the fraternity was the provision of assistance to its poorest members.

The Dalmatians, meanwhile, obtained the right to found their confraternity – the *scuola* of Santi Giorgio e Trifone – on 19 May 1451 (Dieci, Miste, reg. 14, fol. 47v.; Vallery 2000). In support of the request which the sailors of this nation presented to the Council of Ten, a terrible picture was painted of the wretched state of these immigrants. It was a community that included many poor, often wounded while serving in the armies of the Republic, and many sick, none of whom, as foreigners, received either aid or support. In addition to this, many were in such dire straits that they were unable to pay for their own burial and were forced to beg under the porticos of the Doge's Palace (Cancogni and Perocco 1967; Vio 2004, 132–3). Nearly 200 Dalmatians met for the first time in their confraternity on 23 May 1451. An agreement was made with the prior of the Church of San Giovanni in Tempio, situated in the parish of Sant'Antonin in the *sestiere* of Castello. The new confraternity had an altar in this church and a meeting place in the hospice adjoining Santa Caterina, which they shared with the confraternity of San Giovanni Battista (Vio 2004, 132).

So, two confraternities of foreigners had been created within the space of a few years to promote the interests of the members of their respective nations, to organise assistance, encourage mutual aid and solidarity, express devotion and preserve their culture and language. Let us look more closely at the patron saints under whose aegis the Albanians and the Dalmatians met. For the former, the Virgin, patron saint of Shkodër, took pride of place. However, the Albanian fraternity was also under the patronage of St Gall because the brethren first met in the monastic church dedicated to this saint and the fraternity also honoured St Maurice after its seat was transferred to the aforementioned church of San Maurizio; these two saints surrounded the Virgin on the bas-relief over the entrance to the *scuola* when the façade was completed in 1532. The Virgin was, nevertheless, the chief protector of the nation of the Albanians and the Life of the Virgin was represented in the cycle of paintings they commissioned from Carpaccio (Borean 1994; Ludwig and Molmenti 1906; Mason 2000), which were probably painted between 1502 and 1504 (Fortini Brown 1989, 290–1). The confraternity's *mariegola* was in no doubt: the *scuola* was that of Santa Maria e San Gallo degli Albanesi in San Maurizio, that is, of Santa Maria, San Gallo and San Maurizio.

The fraternity of the Dalmatians was perhaps even more single-minded in putting itself under the protection of three saints who had a special meaning for the brethren from 'over there': St George, patron saint of various cities on the western shore of the Adriatic and, in particular, Bar, from where many of the Dalmatians in Venice came, St Tryphon, patron saint of Kotor, where his relics were preserved and also birthplace of quite a few of the brethren, and St Jerome who was born in Roman Dalmatia and particularly revered in a number of towns on the Dalmatian coast, including Trogir (Traù), Vis (Lissa) and Hvar (Lesina). Dalmatian fraternities in Udine and Rome were also dedicated to St Jerome (Mladjan 2003, 86; for the Albanians see Esposito 2014). In Venice, the confraternity of the Dalmatians initially met under the patronage of St George and St Tryphon: the *mariegola* of the *scuola* states it was that of *missier san Zorzi e missier san Trifon* but St Jerome is always named in the sources documenting the early years of the existence of this pious association (Vallery 1995). The new fraternity attracted the members who belonged to the aforementioned confraternity dedicated to St Anastasius. It is not clear what had caused the Dalmatians to join the latter in the first place unless it was the result of a confusion with another St Anastasius, patron saint of Split, who was martyred under Emperor Diocletian. When an overtly national *scuola* was opened up to the Dalmatians, this old devotion fell into decline and the number of its members decreased. The *scuola di Sant'Anastasio* was placed under the responsibility of the silk spinners' guild on 9 August 1488 (Scuole Piccole, B. 704).

Several factors seem to have accentuated the communitarian nature of these fraternities. For example, the Dalmatians took on the obligation of arranging for members of their nation living in Venice to be buried in the same place (Ball 1975). This meant they were able to assume responsibility for those who died alone, far from home and the metropolis. From the beginning, these pious associations were careful to preserve their own specific features. Hardly had the *scuola* of the Dalmatians been founded before it was laid down that no Albanians were allowed in. In the *scuola* of the Albanians, only members of their nation could hold office, a measure voted in 1455 and confirmed in 1502 (Vio 2004, 302–3). At the very end of the sixteenth century, when Dalmatian immigration had decreased, the confraternity probably opened up to others who were not members of this Slavonic nation, but only Dalmatians could hold senior positions. From the creation of the Dalmatian fraternity, the mass on Sundays and holy days could be said in *Latino sermone aut Dalmata* and it seems that the *sermone Dalmata* was done more often, so much so that in 1505 the prior of the Church of San Giovanni protested to the patriarch of Venice against this usage which, nonetheless, continued undiminished (Vio 2004, 132–3). There was also competition between the different nations in Venice and this must have exacerbated the reciprocal identities and feelings of belonging. It is enough to observe that the Greeks obtained the right to form a *scuola* in 1498. Under the patronage of San Nicolò, it met in the church of San Biagio where they had been able to worship *more Greco* since 1410. Central to the request they submitted to the Council of Ten was their desire to benefit from a right already enjoyed by *Schiavoni, Albanesi et altre nazioni* (Ball 1975, 109; Fedalto 1967, 25–6; 1977; 1980; Geanakoplos 1966, 189–91; Porfyriou 1998).

It is striking that the confraternities of the Dalmatians and the Albanians embarked on a decorative programme probably in the same year (Fortini

Brown 1989, 70-1; Mladjan 2003, 41) and that they called on the same painter, Carpaccio. In these early years of the sixteenth century, this artist was at the height of his fame (Fortini Brown 1989, 71). In 1501 he was commissioned to produce a painting for the Senate Hall in the Doge's Palace and in 1507 he joined the ranks of the painters working on the great decorative cycles of the Hall of the Great Council (Crouzet-Pavan 2004, 76–8). Patricia Fortini Brown (1989, 71) notes that Carpaccio was the only member of the team of artists working here who was paid at the same rate as Giovanni Bellini. It was to Carpaccio that the Albanians and the Dalmatians turned in 1502 and the decorative programme continued until 1507 in the first *scuola* while the one in the Dalmatian *scuola* was certainly completed the following year (Mladjan 2003, 41; Palluchini 1961; Perocco 1955; 1964; Pignatti 1969). Moretti (1998, 14–15) believes that the confraternity of the Albanians issued the commission in 1504. All art historians have emphasised that the cycle for the Albanians, depicting the Life of the Virgin, pales in comparison with that of San Giorgio degli Schiavoni (Fortini Brown 1989); the Albanian brethren, many of them artisans and sailors, were a good deal less well off than the Dalmatian ones! What matters for us here are the commissions to Carpaccio, that is, the painter who is said to have oriented Venetian painting of this period towards the East, and the rivalry in the service, as has often been claimed, of an assertion of identity on the part of the two nations. According to some recent interpretations, the prime aim of the cycle in San Giorgio degli Schiavoni and particularly the portrayal of the saints of their native land was to enable the Slavonic diaspora on the other side of the Adriatic to remember the absent Dalmatia and make it live on in its distinctive culture in the very heart of the *La Dominante* (Mladjan 2003).

I have no wish to add another layer to the dense strata of readings which have, for more than a century, been devoted to the *istorie* painted by Carpaccio in San Giorgio degli Schiavoni. Nine of his canvases survive and it is not known whether they originally formed a single cycle. Two have as their subject the life of Christ while the others are devoted to the lives of Dalmatian patron saints: St Jerome (three), St George (three) and St Tryphon (one). But to me it seems that the communitarian interpretation does not take full account of the complexity of the story of the migrations as the particular historical sequence in which these confraternities emerged, grew and beautified themselves in Venice.

Concluding Remarks

This brings me to some concluding observations. First, if we are to deepen our understanding of these national confraternities, we need to put the realities of the competition between them into perspective. All studies devoted to the communities of eastern European origin tend to emphasise the importance of these rivalries, in support of the thesis of a particularly strong national identity. I do not deny the existence of these rivalries, but they were probably no fiercer than those between the other Venetian fraternities. Notwithstanding a whole series of regulations intended to fix the order of precedence in processions, the brethren still occasionally came to blows in the Piazza San Marco over who was to occupy the best positions. We should also remember the competition raging between the *scuole grandi*, the great confraternities of flagellants. A solid financial base underpinned their role of assistance but also made possible other investments (Pullan 1971; 1994). They rebuilt and enlarged their buildings from the first decades of the fifteenth century onwards and marked the monumental landscape of different *sestieri* (Paoletti 1893). These *scuole* also commissioned great decorative programmes, many of which have survived and are amongst the most famous achievements of Venetian painting (Crouzet-Pavan 2007, 364–7; Fortini Brown 1987). None wished to be outdone. As for the measures reserving the leading offices of the *scuole* to members of their respective nations, they prove only that it was not just Albanians and Dalmatians who belonged to these associations. Their customary functions of providing mutual aid in life and in death are enough in themselves to explain their attraction for the inhabitants of Venice. Albanians and Slavs, once they had acquired citizenship, were free to participate in sea trade. They then put to good use the funds that the other brethren had deposited with the chapter of the *scuola*, which consequently functioned, as with other religious institutions, as a bank and an investment company.

But we need to delve more deeply and ask what the true meaning of these fraternities was. What do we know about the state of 'foreignness' of these immigrants? Are we not presupposing that these population groups, many of whom had had dealings with Venice over a long period, must have inevitably been strangers in the city? Should we not ask if, without prior discussion, we are using analytical categories that derive from a period when clear and extensive juridical definitions of nationality existed? Not everyone within the Venetian population, we should remember, had the same juridical status and the rules distinguished between the nobles, the citizens who constituted the elite of the non-nobles and the rest (Bellavitis 2001; 2008). I do not claim that this mobility always turned out well. The criminal archives and the fiscal sources demonstrate the realities of exclusion and the poverty of Dalmatians and Albanians. But relegation to the urban and social periphery of Venice was not confined to the strangers who had arrived from the other shore of the Adriatic. It applied also to other marginal elements of the population, such as men and women from Friuli or the valleys above Brescia or men and women born in the city of Venice. The Venetians who lived in the centre and the dominant economic and social spaces probably felt a similar feeling of distance, even suspicion, with regard to all those who lived in what they called 'the distant and incommodious parts' of Venice, whatever their origin.

By obtaining the right to form congregations, the men and women from Shkodër and Bar and from Zadar and Dubrovnik also obtained the right to integrate more fully into Venetian society and gain access to its resources. To understand the singular form of the ways in which Venice operated politically and socially, it is necessary to emphasise the number of structures and associations that constituted so many social spaces and created cohesion at a time when the world of work was fragmented between a very large number of crafts and all forms of concentration were shunned. Our Dalmatians and our Albanians adopted one of the routes to integration, even more so in that they were not members of their own national confraternities alone. I do not speak here of the most recent arrivals or of the very poorest who were doomed to beggary. For the others, and we need only remember the various individual trajectories I discussed above, integration was a possibility and one of the expressions of social integration in Venice was membership of two, three or even four confraternities, for example devotional confraternities, confraternities of foreign communities, male-only confraternities, mixed confraternities, flagellant confraternities, socially mixed confraternities, craft confraternities and occupationally diversified confraternities. Multiple membership was one way of rooting oneself in the social tissue of Venice.

The history of emigration has shown that the exiled usually locate themselves somewhere between a willed or suffered rupture and the continuity they tend to maintain with their country of origin. This produces what Abdelmalek Sayad (1997; 2014) has described as a daily negotiation of exile. His approach seems to me to be particularly relevant in the case of our communities from the other side of the Adriatic. The use of the Slavonic language in worship, the shared devotion to the saints of their town of origin represented on the paintings, gonfalons (pennants) and walls of the confraternities' halls, together with the simple pleasure of being amongst their fellows, were all ways of 'living here without forgetting there', that is, of living a multifaceted identity. In my view, it is another flaw in the analyses that I have called communitarian to believe and have us believe that identity is monolithic.

Furthermore, the social transactions were not a one-way process. The centre of Venice had a strong integrative power in the second half of the fifteenth century, as at other periods in its demographic history. But, the people from elsewhere were not only useful to it because they contributed to its demographic recovery and economic vitality. The foreign confraternities whose members provided sailors and soldiers for the Republic at war were also integral to the image the Republic wished to construct of itself, that of the metropolis defending its empire and that of the bulwark of Christianity against the Infidel.

According to a long historiographical tradition, the Venetians did not so much seek to combat an increasingly aggressive Turkish power as to establish the means for a *modus vivendi* with it. Though the first warlike episodes between the two powers took place in the Mediterranean, it is well known that *La Serenissima* went on the offensive in close alliance with the Hungarians and the rebellious Albanians only in 1463. It should be added that the war of 1463–79 brought home to the Republic the reality of the Ottoman military threat. One need only read the Venetian chroniclers, such as Girolamo Friuli, to realise that at the end of the fifteenth century Venetians began to reflect on the succession of empires. Those who had believed that they, unlike all the empires before them, could escape decadence, wrote the chronicler Malipiero, saw their pride humbled. They were dependent on the Turks even for their corn supplies. I have no wish to deny the complexity of the relations between Venice and the Turks any more than the existence of long periods of peace between the two powers, characterised by active commercial exchanges. Nevertheless, to me it seems a little reductive to analyse Venetian politics only in terms of a realpolitik.

In the last years of the fifteenth century and first years of the next, Venice was suffused with a culture of anxiety and religious engagement and, among the elements which crystallised it, fear of the Turk was a decisive factor although not the only driver. In phases of active fighting against the Ottomans, this culture became even more fraught and it was within this culture that the Dalmatian and Albanian confraternities operated. Here, we should remember that the Dalmatian fraternity was established in premises belonging to the priory of the Knights of St John of Jerusalem and that the first indulgence granted to it, by Cardinal Bessarion in 1464, has been attributed to the role played by the brethren in the organisation of the crusade which was to leave from Ancona in response to the appeal of Pope Pius II. Another indulgence, in 1481, rewarded the fraternity for the part it played in the collection of funds destined for the defence of Rhodes which was besieged by the Turks. The decorative cycle portraying St George slaying the dragon and the great conversion scene of St George baptising the Selenites were commissioned from Carpaccio in 1502; this almost certainly occurred after Polo Vallaresso, unfortunate commander at Modon and Coron during the second Venetian-Ottoman war, gave the relics of St George he had received from the patriarch of Jerusalem to the fraternity, which installed them with great solemnity on 24 April 1502 (Vio 2004, 133). Vallaresso was a member of the *scuola* and his family had links with Dalmatia. Nor should we forget that, with the continuation of the Venetian retreat in the eastern Mediterranean, the chroniclers could at least rejoice that the relics were saved and transported to Venice where, along with all the others that had been transferred in successive waves, they assured, as Marino Sanudo claimed, the serene preservation of the city.

This is not to claim, of course, that the *Signoria* determined the iconographical choices in the paintings any more than it dictated the decision to decorate the façade of the confraternity of the Albanians with a relief carving commemorating the two sieges of Shkodër (in 1474 and 1479) and honouring the Venetian heroes of these two battles – Antonio Loredan and Antonio da Lezze (Fortini Brown 1989, 71–2) – by the inclusion of their coats of arms. But, in moments of heightened collective religious feeling, Venice benefitted from the presence of groups that fought with it against the Infidel on the frontiers of Christendom and that portrayed that resistance on the walls and gonfalons of their confraternities. We should also not forget that as early as between 1444 and 1450, Michele Giambono completed a painting of St Chrysogonus, the patron saint of Zadar, in the church of San Trovaso which housed a relic of this saint, and that it depicted St Chrysogonus on horseback, in line with the iconographical model then prevailing in Zadar (Willis 2012). This was not so much a way of asserting rivalry with Zadar, by capturing the cult and the protection of the saint who had suffered martyrdom at Aquileia, as argued by some art historians, but an indication that Venice sheltered and protected all the sacred things of the 'dominion' to the benefit of *Il Dominio* and the whole of Christendom.

It is difficult to write the history of the Dalmatians and Albanians who emigrated to Venice in the fifteenth century. The sources do not always allow us to trace them and when they do, they do not always make it possible to determine when the migrants arrived in Venice. Yet, how can length of stay not be taken into account as a parameter of possible social mobility? How can migrants who had been settled in Venice for a few months or a few years and migrants who had become immigrants (Sayad 2014) be lumped together as if they constituted a homogenous group? Not to speak of the fact that any study is inevitably partial and Veneto-centric since it only dips into these lives and itineraries and looks at these 'strangers' only when they were already established in the city. In addition, we have to be aware that our vocabulary tends to project onto this society categories as inadequate as they are anachronistic and to fix a history made out of multiple mobilities and individualised trajectories in a static image or succession of static images. None of which is to suggest that the group was not also capable of functioning as a group and, on particular occasions, the community could indulge in its preferences and mirages, offering its members the possibility of living here 'without forgetting there' – a possibility each individual might, according to their situation, adhere to with greater or lesser conviction or even not at all. Furthermore, the last decades of the fifteenth century marked a particular period in the processes of negotiation between these migrants and the host society, a period in which apparent communitarianism promoted integration. Though the Albanians and the Slavs were for the most part poor, they were loyal to the Republic, fighting for it on the other shores of the Adriatic, and it was this loyalty and these battles that were depicted on the walls of their confraternities. Their patron saints were added to the cohort of saints under whose protection Venice placed itself. Their relics were added to the treasury of relics which continued to grow and to which, as the chronicler Marino Sanudo (Fulin et al. 1879–1903, vol. 20, col. 99) declared, the city without walls owed its serene preservation. Exchange was always implicit and necessarily unequal and through it we catch a glimpse of the cosmopolitan and the Adriatic aspect of Venice.

Translated by Jean Birrell

Acknowledgements

I would like to thank C. Kikuchi and P. Vuillemin for sharing with me their knowledge about about Bonino of Dubrovnik and the details about the transfer of the Albanian *scuola* to the Church of San Maurizio respectively.

References

Unpublished sources

Avogaria di Comun, reg. 3889, fasc. C 23, Archivio di Stato di Venezia.

Corporazioni religiose soppresse, Santa Maria Gloriosa dei Frari, reg. 2, fol. 24r, Archivio di Stato di Venezia.

Dieci, Miste, reg. 5, fol. 88r; reg. 12, fol. 160r; reg. 13, fol. 91; reg. 14, fol. 47v, Archivio di Stato di Venezia.

Matricola della Scuola di S. Maria, di S. Gallo e S. Maurizio, cap. III, Ms It. VII, 737 (= 8666), Biblioteca Nazionale Marciana, Venice.

Proveditori di Comun, reg. U, fols. 60–75, Archivio di Stato di Venezia.

Scuole Piccole, B. 704, Archivio di Stato di Venezia.

Published Sources

Ball, J. 1975. 'The Greek community of Venice: 1470–1620' (PhD thesis, University of London).

Bellavitis, A. 2001. *Identité, mariage, mobilité sociale: Citoyennes et citoyens à Venise au XVIe siècle*, Collection de l'École française de Rome 282 (Rome).

2008. *Famille, genre, transmission à Venise au XVIe siècle*, Collection de l'École française de Rome 408 (Rome).

Borean, L. 1994. 'Nuove proposte e interpretazioni per le storie della Vergine di Carpaccio nella Scuola degli Albanesi', *Saggi e memorie di storia dell'arte* 19, 21–72.

Cancogni, M. and Perocco, G. 1967. *L'opera completa del Carpaccio* (Milan).

Ceriana, M. and Mueller, R.C. 2014. '*Radicamento delle communità straniere a Venezia nel Medioevo: 'Scuole' di devozione nella storia e nell'arte*', in Del Bo (ed.) 2014, 299–332.

Cerutti, S. 2012. *Etrangers: Étude d'une condition d'incertitude dans une société d'Ancien Régime* (Paris).

Cioni, A. 1971. 'Bonino de Boninis', in *Dizionario biografico degli Italiani*, vol. 12 (Rome).

Crouzet-Pavan, É. 1990. *Sopra le acque salse: Espaces, pouvoir et sociéte à Venise à la fin du Moyen Age*, 2 vols. (Rome); 2nd edn. = *Le Moyen Age de Venise. Des eaux salées au miracle de pierres* (Paris, 2015).

2004. *Venise triomphante: Les horizons d'un mythe*, 2nd edn. (Paris); trans. Cochrane, L., *Venice Triumphant: The Horizon of a Myth* (Baltimore and London, 2002).

2005. 'Le verre vénitien: Les savoirs au travail', in *La trasmissione dei saperi nel Medioevo (secoli XII-XV)*, Atti del XIX Convegno internazionale di studi, Pistoia, 16–19 maggio 2003 (Pistoia), 289–320.

2007. *Renaissances italiennes, 1380–1500* (Paris).

Del Bo, B. (ed.) 2014. *Cittadinanza e mestieri: Radicamento urbano e integrazione nelle città bassomedievali (secc. XIII-XVI)* (Rome).

Donati, L. 1927a. 'Bonino de Boninis', *Archivio storico per la Dalmazia* 3, 54-64.

1927b. 'Alcune note su stampatori dalmati', *Archivio storico per la Dalmazia* 4, 54-63.

Ducellier, A., Doumerc, B., Imhaus, B. and de Miceli, J. (eds.) 1992. *Les chemins de l'exil: Bouleversements de l'Est européen et migrations vers l'Ouest à la fin du Moyen Age* (Paris).

Esposito, A. 2014. 'Le minoranze indesiderate (corsi, slavi e albanesi) e il processo di integrazione nella società romana nel corso del Quattrocento', in Del Bo (ed.) 2014, 283-97.

Fedalto, G. 1967. *Ricerche sulla posizione giuridica ed ecclesiastica dei Greci a Venezia nei secoli XV e XVI*, Fondazione Giorgio Cini - Civiltà veneziana. Saggi 17 (Florence).

1977. 'Le minoranze straniere a Venezia tra politica e legislazione', in Beck, H.G., Manoussacas, M. and Pertusi, A. (eds.), *Venezia centro di mediazione tra Oriente e Occidente (secoli XV-XVI): Aspetti e problemi*, Atti del II Convegno internazionale di storia della civiltà veneziana (Venezia, 3-6 ottobre 1963), vol. 1. Fondazione Giorgio Cini- Civiltà veneziana. Studi 32 (Florence), 143-63.

1980. 'Stranieri a Venezia e Padova', in Arnaldi, G. and Pastore Stocchi, M. (eds.), *Storia della cultura veneta: Dal primo Quattrocento al concilio di Trento*, vol. 3/1 (Vicenza), 499-535.

Fortini Brown, P. 1987. 'Honor and necessity: The dynamics of patronage in the confraternities of Renaissance Venice', *Studi veneziani* n.s. 14, 179-212.

1989. *Venetian Narrative Painting in the Age of Carpaccio*, 2nd edn (New Haven and London).

Fulin, R., Stefani, N., Barozzi, F. and Allegri, M. (eds.) 1879-1903. *I diarii di Marino Sanudo*, 58 vols. (Venice).

Geanakoplos, D. 1966. 'La colonia greca di Venezia e il suo significato per il Rinascimento', in Pertusi, A. (ed.), *Venezia e l'Oriente fra tardo Medioevo e Rinascimento* (Florence), 183-204.

Hansen, M.H. (ed.) 2000. *A Comparative Study of Thirty City-State Cultures* (Copenhagen).

Imhaus, B. 1997. *Le minoranze orientali a Venezia, 1305-1510* (Rome).

Ludwig, G. and Molmenti, V. 1906. *Vittore Carpaccio: La vita e le opere* (Milan).

Mason, S. 2000. *Carpaccio: I grandi cicli pittorici* (Milan); trans. Ellis, A., *Carpaccio: The Major Pictorial Cycles* (London, 2000).

Mladjan, M. 2003. '"Soldiers of Christ" in the Schiavoni confraternity: Towards a visualization of the Dalmatian diaspora in Renaissance Venice' (MA thesis, Queens University, Ontario).

Mola, L. and Mueller, R.C. 1994. 'Essere straniero a Venezia nel tardo Medioevo: Accoglienza e rifiuto nei privilegi di cittadinanza e nelle sentenze criminali', in Cavaciocchi, S. (ed.), *Le migrazioni in Europa, secc. XIII–XVIII*, Atti delle Settimane di studi dell'Istituto internazionale di storia economica 'F. Datini' 25 (Florence), 839–51.

1996. 'Aspects of Venetian sovereignty in Medieval and Renaissance Dalmatia', in Dempsey, C. (ed.), *Quattrocento Adriatico: Fifteenth-Century Art of the Adriatic Rim, Papers from a colloquium held at the Villa Spelman, Florence, 1994* (Bologna), 29–56.

Moretti, S. 1998. 'Gli Albanesi a Venezia tra XIV e XVI secolo', in Calabi, D. and Lanaro, P. (eds.), *La città italiana e i luoghi degli stranieri. XIV–XVIII secolo* (Bari), 5–20.

Mueller, R.C. 1979a. 'Aspetti sociali ed economici della peste a Venezia nel Medioevo', in *Venezia e la peste 1348/1797* (Venice), 71–6.

1979b. 'Peste e demografia. Medioevo e Rinascimento', in *Venezia e la peste 1348/1797* (Venice), 93–6.

1998. "Veneti facti privilegio': Stranieri naturalizzati a Venezia tra XIV e XV secolo', in Calabi, D. and Lanaro, P. (eds.), *La città italiana e i luoghi degli stranieri. XIV–XVIII secolo* (Bari), 41–51.

Ortalli, F. 2001. *'Per salute delle anime e delli corpi': Scuole piccole a Venezia nel tardo Medioevo* (Venice).

Palluchini, R. 1961. *I teleri del Carpaccio in San Giorgio degli Schiavoni* (Milan).

Paoletti, P. 1893. *L'architettura e la scultura del Rinascimento in Venezia* (Venice).

Pelusi, S. 1989. 'La stampa in caratteri glagolitici e cirillici', in Abbiati, S. (ed.) *Armeni, Ebrei, Greci stampatori a Venezia* (Venice), 101–14.

Perocco, G. 1955. 'La Scuola di San Giorgio degli Schiavoni', in *Venezia e l'Europa. Atti del XVIII Congresso internazionale di storia dell'arte, Venezia, 12-18 settembre 1955* (Venice), 221–4.

1964. *Carpaccio nella Scuola di S. Giorgio degli Schiavoni* (Venice).

Pignatti, T. 1969. *Carpaccio: San Giorgio degli Schiavoni*, 2nd edn (Milan).

Porfyriou, H. 1998. 'La presenza greca: Roma e Venezia tra XV e XVI secolo', in Calabi, D. and Lanaro, P. (eds.), *La città italiana e i luoghi degli stranieri. XIV–XVIII secolo* (Bari), 21–38.

Pullan, B. 1971. *Rich and Poor in Renaissance Venice: The Social Institutions of a Catholic State, to 1620* (Oxford).

1994. *Poverty and Charity: Europe, Italy, Venice, 1400–1700* (Aldershot and Brookfield).

Romano, D. 1996. *Housecraft and Statecraft: Domestic Servants in Renaissance Venice, 1400–1600* (Baltimore and London).

Sayad, A. 1997. *L'immigration ou les paradoxes de l'altérité*, 2nd edn (Brussels and Paris).

2014. *La double absence: Des illusions de l'émigré aux souffrances de l'immigré*, 2nd edn (Paris).

Vallery, T. 1995. 'I santi della Dalmazia', *Scuola dalmata dei SS Giorgio e Trifone* 28/1, 5–14.

2000. 'La scuola dalmata dei SS Giorgio e Trifone', *Scuola dalmata dei SS Giorgio e Trifone* 39/2, 14–22.

Vio, G. 2004. *Le scuole piccole nella Venezia dei dogi: Note d'archivio per la storia delle confraternite veneziane* (Vicenza).

Willis, Z.F. 2012. 'Saint cults and the politics of power in the Dalmatian commune of Zadar (1000–1468)' (PhD thesis, University of Warwick).

Zecchin, L. 1990. 'La fornace muranese dei Dalla Pigna, oriundi albanese', in Zecchin, L. (ed.), *Vetro e vetrai di Murano: Studi sulla storia del vetro*, vol. 3 (Venice), 55–9.

Conclusion

CHRIS WICKHAM

Venice, and then the Adriatic, was the main route to Byzantium for the whole Medieval period, for anyone coming to the former eastern Roman empire from or through northern Italy. The geographical position of the sea makes that inevitable. The west–east sea route via Sicily worked for some Europeans, but only on a large scale after the Normans conquered the island from the Arabs in the late eleventh century and even then less prominently than the Adriatic did; the land route through Hungary, which had a border with Byzantium in the eleventh and twelfth centuries, suited some armies, but it was never an easy passage; and the Danube was underused as a route for a long time. So the Adriatic had a major role as a path to the Byzantine empire in every Medieval century, and this book amply shows what sorts of roles it took, in the sometimes dramatically changing economic and political environments of nine centuries.

For most people, however, for a long time, the Adriatic was only a route; that was so even under the Roman empire, the only power in history to have ruled it all and to have imposed a single language, Latin, on it. The coasts for the most part turn their back on the sea. Much of the Dalmatian coast is a mountain slope; the lowlands around Zadar, from Nin to Šibenik, and the lowlands around Durrës, from Shkodër to Vlorë, are most of the good land there is. Small wonder that the former was both the location of Byzantium's main political centre on the central coast and also the core of the early kingdom of Croatia (Trpimir Vedriš), with the latter the major outlet onto the Adriatic of the main land route from the Byzantine heartland; but neither is large all the same. The strip of lowland stretching on the Italian side from Rimini right down to Termoli is not much wider and has never been a major political focus; in the south, only Apulia was a serious Adriatic player (Jean-Marie Martin). Which leaves the Po plain in the north, with Venice as its major port since 800 at the latest, as by far the most substantial economic region which looks onto the Adriatic. If at first sight in this book one notes the absence of much discussion of the long central section of the Adriatic – only Vedriš and Oliver Schmitt treat the eastern side directly and no one discusses the west – then this geography is certainly a large part of the explanation. Which means that our eyes here turn to Venice and its predecessors in the north and to the Otranto-Vlorë straits in the south, the latter acting as a proxy for the Ionian Sea beyond and the way into Byzantium itself – even if on the eastern side more attention is actually paid here, and rightly, to Butrint, a less important Byzantine town than Vlorë probably and Durrës certainly, but far and away the best-excavated site on the eastern side of the sea in our period (Richard Hodges, Joanita Vroom). Here, then, to conclude this stimulating book, I will look at these two ends of the Adriatic in turn, beginning with the latter.

The Otranto-Vlorë straits mark the entry to Byzantium, but can also block it. An ambitious power might well seek to control both sides of the sea and thereby potentially cut the northern Adriatic from the Ionian Sea and the lands southwards and eastwards of that. This was not so much of a problem when that power was the Byzantine empire itself (as in the seventh century and later, above all in the tenth and early eleventh centuries: Martin, Pagona Papadopoulou), for this was where Adriatic boats were trying to get to most of all, as long as the empire existed as a powerful focus; but other powers were much more dangerous. Small wonder that the Venetians were very happy from the 1080s onwards to help Alexios I and his successors prevent the Normans of southern Italy from gaining a stable foothold in the western Balkans; small wonder that they also worked hard to keep the straits open by establishing treaties in the decade after 1204 (Guillaume Saint-Guillain). But the tightness of the straits all the same held more economic advantage than political danger. Southern Apulia and Albania/northern Epiros (extending after 1300 or so north to Ragusa, modern Dubrovnik) were often in Medieval history, as also in late Antiquity, virtually a single economic unit, each of them often rather better linked to the other than either were to the lands beyond, and to an extent a cultural one too (Magdalena Skoblar). That meant that anyone coming from the north met a coherent exchange network at the southern end of the Adriatic, probably always the strongest east–west exchange network across the sea as a whole, which could be a goal in itself and which acted as a sort of recharging point for ships seeking access to the major regions of the eastern Mediterranean.

It is in this context that we can understand the ceramic networks discussed by Vroom. It is striking how far we find the same pottery types in Apulia and in Albania/Epiros, in every century. Eighth- and ninth-century globular amphorae, tenth- to twelfth-century Otranto 1 and 2 amphorae, twelfth-century Fine Sgraffito ware, thirteenth-century Proto-Maiolica and RMR: the interconnections at different times favoured productions from one side, or the other, or both, but they were constant. Hodges proposes that this was only real commerce after 830 or so and that the quite wide range of imports to Butrint attested around 800 were directed exchange, attached to single officials; this seems an unnecessary distinction, especially given the availability of Aegean wares in Comacchio in the same period (see here Francesco Borri, but Comacchio has been extensively studied and published in recent years, see Gelichi 2007 and Gelichi *et al.* 2012). I do think it is the case that the globular amphora network, now ever more clearly seen as the type fossil for excavations in the Byzantine lands in the eighth and ninth centuries, as an important conference published in *Archeologia medievale* 45 (2018) in particular shows, had something to do with the state throughout; these amphorae are found so rarely outside the Byzantine lands that it is fair to see them as linked in part, probably, to army supply. But even then there must have been some commercial spin-offs, given their distributions, as there were for sure for all later ceramic types. Anyway, their distributions mark connectivity, whether of merchants or armies/navies, which linked the Aegean heartland to the western lands – probably richer at the time – around the Ionian Sea, from Sicily to the western Peloponnese, and which in particular connected Apulia to Epiros and then, as a secondary consequence, to Comacchio and increasingly Venice at the top of the Adriatic. So for much of the Early Middle Ages the Ionian Sea, including the Adriatic outlet, was not just the entry to Byzantium, but actually Byzantium itself. Early Venetian commercial vessels may not have greatly cared whether they got to Constantinople, or to Corinth, or just to the Epirote towns; they could have got much the same goods from all of them.

Seen from Byzantium, Venice was a minor urban centre of the empire, hardly even a city, for a long time; culturally primitive (see Skoblar's introduction), with a strange absence of back history (Sauro Gelichi), Latin-speaking and hard to control (Stefano Gasparri), but an outpost of empire all the same. As it expanded, it was increasingly also a source for quite entrepreneurial shipping, but that shipping was still part of Byzantine exchange very largely and Venice developed economically as the Aegean heartland did. Even in the twelfth century the Byzantines could see Venice as part of their world, and not wrongly, as Michael Angold stresses here. This may not have actually changed until 1204 (Angold, see also Peter Frankopan); but even if it was earlier, it hardly predated 1171, when Manuel I confiscated Venetian property and ships throughout the Aegean and a set of easy interconnections thus rapidly became less easy. This is itself an important corrective to the old heroic story of the maritime city par excellence, independent from everyone, steadily establishing political power and then commercial routes in the Adriatic, as a preparation for commercial routes throughout the eastern Mediterranean and then political power in the Byzantine heartland itself. But, as three-quarters of the papers here concern Venice above all, it is right to invert the perspective too and look at Byzantium from the Venetian standpoint, as it changed across time.

It is now increasingly accepted that Venice developed slowly and plurifocally, with an urbanisation hardly visible until the tenth century (Gelichi), although the Rialto islands already by then had a bishopric, a ducal palace and soon after 829 a church purpose-built to house the stolen relics of St Mark. It was at the start a town based on salt production, particularly but not only in the great set of salt pans at Chioggia, and that was its initial role in the eyes of the north Italian towns. It was one which it took over from Comacchio, in the realignment of politics, demography and exchange after Ravenna's old centrality as a major Byzantine provincial centre slowly weakened (Borri, Tom Brown). How important its longer-distance commerce initially was remains unclear; Michael McCormick is convincing that it was a focus of slave-trading from the start, but that was a luxury or semi-luxury trade, not so very large in scale; it was enough to bring Byzantine ceramics – as well as luxuries such as silk – back into the lagoon area, but not enough to transform a wider economy (McCormick 2001, 244–54, 526–31, 625–30, 637–8, 733–77; contrast, for example, Rio 2017, 19–41). Timber was added to that by the 970s (Cessi 1942, vol. 2, no. 49, a. 971), by when the Venetians were certainly trading with Arab Sicily, Tunisia and Egypt, from where they also bought spices for the north Italian market; but again we cannot trace a large scale for this (Venetians are rarely mentioned in the Cairo *geniza*, see Goldberg 2012, 19–21, 306–9, 334–5) and it did not transform the general picture we have of Venice as very much in the Byzantine orbit. Venetian commercial credit documents are often for the loan of anchors up to 1100 (Luzzatto 1954, 94–5) and the relative lack of resources of shipmen who needed to borrow anchors indicates that the scale of Venetian trade with anywhere was not so very large before that date.

Things changed in the twelfth century, certainly. This was not as a result of the crusades, which, as Christopher Wright clearly shows, were less transformative for Venice than for Pisa and Genoa until, of course, the war of 1202–4. The twelfth century was the first in which Venice seems to have sought dominance in the Adriatic, partly indeed in the context of crusading (Frankopan, Wright) – though this was a generalised political-economic hegemony and by no means direct rule; and it was also, for separate reasons, the first century in which Venetians penetrated the Byzantine Aegean as merchants on any scale (Angold). Frankopan and Angold indeed stress that Venetian power in the Adriatic was by no means to be taken for granted and that Ancona and Zadar, plus the Apulian cities, were potentially rival powers, interesting to Byzantines, Hungarians and Pisans alike as alternatives to Venice. Venetian history is full of might-have-beens.

All the same, because of the Fourth Crusade, there were no more might-have-beens in the Byzantine lands and things changed for the island city even more substantially thereafter. We here enter into the great centuries of Venetian political control of much of the eastern Adriatic coast and much of the Aegean and a Venetian-led hegemony over all the trade routes of the eastern Mediterranean. That tale has been told many times and, precisely because of the Adriatic and Byzantine focus of this book, did not need to be told here. But the two papers which focus on the Late Middle Ages, Schmitt and Élisabeth Crouzet-Pavan, show that there is a different story in these centuries too, one with a greater continuity with before 1200: the cosmopolitan and composite nature of Venetian dominance in the Adriatic. Schmitt strongly contests an older narrative of Venetian colonial power over Dalmatia and reinstates instead an image of negotiation and communication between the *Serenissima* and the small communities of the coast and the islands, along the lines of his remarkable earlier work on this theme (Schmitt, 2011): this is much more like the pre-thirteenth-century situation than it is like the standard historiography of the *Stato da Mar*. As a mirror image of that, Crouzet-Pavan sets out the way Dalmatian Slavs and Albanians immigrated into fifteenth-century Venice (in particular into the area east of the great basilica and palace) and established themselves, mostly as poor half-citizens, but some as more successful entrepreneurs, in ways that made them not much different from the Veronesi and the immigrants from other *Terraferma* towns. Venice was by now very large by Medieval standards and far more powerful than it had ever been, but its relationship with the rest of the Adriatic remained reciprocal and less coercive than was the case for most Late Medieval powers. This is a more interesting way of looking at the relationship between the Late Medieval city and the world to its south than are the standard tales of argosies from Alexandria. It is also one which the rest of the articles in this book, multifaceted as they are, properly prepare us for. The Adriatic becomes here not only a route to the east and the entry point to Byzantium – by now, former Byzantium – but also what it had not been so fully before, a location in which local communities on all the coasts of the sea were interlocking, with power and economic relations that by no means privileged one end of the sea or the other. That is an exciting direction for us to continue to move along.

References

Cessi, R. (ed.) 1942. *Documenti relativi alla storia di Venezia anteriori al Mille*, vol. 2 (Padua).

Gelichi, S. (ed.) 2007. *Comacchio e il suo territorio tra la tarda Antichità e l'alto Medioevo* (Ferrara) = extracted from Berti, F., Bollini, M., Gelichi, S. and Ortalli, G. (eds.), *Genti nel Delta da Spina a Comacchio: Uomini, territorio e culto dall'Antichità all'alto Medioevo, Catalogo della mostra 16 dicembre-14 ottobre 2006* (Ferrara), 365–689.

Gelichi, S., Calaon, D., Grandi, E. and Negrelli, C. 2012. 'The history of a forgotten town: Comacchio and its archaeology', in Gelichi, S. and Hodges, R. (eds.), *From One Sea to Another: Trading Places in the European and Mediterranean Early Middle Ages. Proceedings of the International Conference, Comacchio, 27th–29th March 2009* (Turnhout), 169–205.

Goldberg, J. 2012. *Trade and Institutions in the Medieval Mediterranean: The Geniza Merchants and Their Business World* (Cambridge).

Luzzatto, G. 1954. *Studi di storia economica veneziana* (Padua).

McCormick, M. 2001. *Origins of the European Economy: Communications and Commerce AD 300–900* (Cambridge).

Rio, A. 2017. *Slavery after Rome 500–1000* (Oxford).

Schmitt, O. J. 2011. *Korčula sous la domination de Venise au XVe siècle: Pouvoir, économie et vie quotidienne dans une île dalmate au Moyen Âge tardif* (Paris), available online at books.openedition.org/cdf/1511 (last accessed 1 May 2020).

Index

Page numbers in italics are figures; with 't' are tables. A number after 't' shows the number of the lead seal in the table.

Aachen, treaty of 105, 107, 135, 161
abandonment, Roman cities 111–12, *112*
abbeys
   Lokrum 268
   Monte Cassino 192, 196–7
   St Chrysogonus at Zadar 163, 266
   San Vincenzo al Volturno 192
   Santa Sofia at Benevento 192, 196–7
   Tremiti 254–7
Abulafia, David, *The Great Sea* 18
Adelfreda, Bishop of Nin 160
Adelheid, Queen and Empress (wife of Holy Roman Emperor Otto I) 178
Adria *113–14*, 113–14
Adriatic 1–3, 385–6
   after the Fourth Crusade 316–26
   sigillographic evidence of trade (800–1100) 203–4
   trade and movement 600–800 83–92
   see also Venetian lagoon area
Aenona see Nin
Aethicus Ister, *Cosmography* 88
Agathias of Myrina 84
Agilulf, King of the Lombards 99
Agnellus of Ravenna, *Liber pontificalis ecclesiae Ravennatis* 85–7, 174, 180
Aistulf, King of the Lombards 91
Albania
   Butrint 18–40, *19*, 21–2, *22*, 24–5, *25*, 25–6, 28–31, *46*
      pottery 45–8, *47*, 48–52, *49–50*, 49–50, *49*, *51*, *62*, 70–1, *71–2*
      seals 203–4
   historiography 353–4, 357
Albanians, immigration to Venice 369–70, 374–5, 379–80
Alexander, Emperor 189
Alexander II, Pope 256
Alexander III, Pope 308
Alexios I Komnenos, Emperor 282–5, 287
   and the altarpiece *Pala d'Oro* 298

chrysobulls 232, 296–8, 301
gold seals 214–15t1, 220–4, 237
Alexios III Angelos, Emperor 310–11
Alexios Komnenos, *sebastos* and *doux* of Dyrrachion 225–6t9, 232
Alfonso V, King of Aragon 343
Altinum 111–12, *112*, 115–16, *116*, 119–21
Amadeo of Savoy 339–40
Amalarius of Metz 137, 144, 153–5
amphorae
   from Butrint 25–6, 28–9, 32, 48–52, *49–50*, *49*, *51*, *62*
   from shipwrecks 52–6, *53*, *54–5*
   Günsenin 1/Saraçhane 52–3, 57–62, *59–60*, *62*
   Günsenin 3/Saraçhane 62–4
Anastasia, St, relics of 143–4, 150–2, 155, 278
Anastasius Bibliothecarius 138
Anastasius, St, confraternities 367, 374
Ancona 287–8
Andrew II, King of Hungary 334–6
Andrew, *prior* of Zadar 146
Anna Komnene 232
   Alexias 283
Annales Barenses 219
Annales regni Francorum 91–2
Apulia 188–99, 386–7
   icons 245–6
      Bari 251–3, 269
      Foggia 257–8, *258–9*, 269
      Otranto 253–4
      Trani 247–51, *248–9*, 269
      Tremiti 254–7
   katepanate of Italy 190–3
   new cities 193–6
   society 196–9
   theme of Longobardia 188–90
   use of seals 212

391

Apulia et Calabria 188–90
Aquileia
  Council of 149
  and Grado 101, 111
  and Nin 160
  patriarch of 156, 175, 181
  and Pope John VIII 159
  and St Chrysogonus 379
archon/archontes 88–9, 141–3
  Diokleia 88, 143
  letter to the Western *archons* 139
  seals 225–6 t11, 13, 27, 235, 238
  see also dukes; Zadar
Argyros (son of Melus), Duke of Apulia 193, 198
Armenia/Armenians 372
arrest of Venetians in Constantinople 288–9
Arsenios of Corfu 20
Arta 69, 214–15 t29a/b, 223, 297
Atenolf II, Prince of Benevento 189
Ateste see Este
Athens
  metropolitan see 154
  Metropolitan Niketas 214–15 t28, 219–20, 223–4

Bagenetia see *Vagenetia*
Baiunetai 19
Baldwin II, King of Jerusalem 330
Bardanes Tourkos 140
Bari
  Arab attacks 280–1
  Cathedral 251–3, 269
  Emir of 188
  icon of *hodegetria* 251–3, 269
  St Nicholas (church) 257–8, 266
Basić, Ivan 140, 147, 153–4
Basil II, Emperor 280, 316
basilicas see churches/basilicas
Basilicata 189–90, 194–5
Beatus, Duke of Venice 105
Benevento 189, 194, 196, 254
Bessarion, Cardinal 378–9
Bisantius, Archbishop of Bari 196, 251
Blachernai monastery 254
Bloch, Herbert. 256
Boccaccio, *Decameron* 276
Bochomakes, Christopher, *spatharokandidatos* 197
Boioannes, Basil, *katepano* of Italy 194
Boninis, Bonino de 370
Bono, Bishop of Adria 113–14
Borna, Duke of the Guduscani 156, 158

Bozburun (shipwreck) 52–3, *53*, 56
Branas, John, *sebastos* 214–15 t29a/b, 222–4
Branimir, Duke of Croatia 160
Braudel, Fernand 15–16, 36
  Mediterranean and the Mediterranean World in the Age of Philip II 15
Bryennios, *strategos* of Dalmatia, seal of 142–3
Butrint (*Buthrotum*) (Albania) 18–40, *19*, *21–2*, *22*, *23–6*, *24–5*, *25*, *25–6*, *28–31*, 46
  pottery 45–8, *47*, 48–52, *49–50*, *49–50*, *49*, *51*, 62, 70–1, *71–2*
  seals 203–4
Byzantios, judge in Bari 197
Byzantios, Archbishop of Bari 214–19, 214–15 t4

Calabria 89, 188–91
  use of seals 212
Calixtus II, Pope 330
Candiano, Pietro I, Duke of Venice 138
Cape Matapan, battle 296
Capitanata 192, 194–5, 197–8
Carolingians 149–50, 156
  missionaries 156, 159
  and Ravenna 178
  Treaty of Aachen 105, 107, 135
  and Venice 103–5
Carpaccio, Vittore 375–6, 379
Cassiodorus 119–20
Chalkoprateia Church (Constantinople) 254, 259
Charlemagne, Emperor 104–5
  and the Danube council 156
  letter from Hadrian I 144
Charles of Anjou 71, 339, 342–3
Choniates, Niketas 305, 307
Chronicle of Monemvasia, on the Slavic attack on Patras 23
Chronographia 89
chrysobulls
  of Alexios I Komnenos 232, 296–8, 301
  of Alexios III Angelos (1198) 311–12, 321
  of Basil II and Constantine (992) 280, 296, 301
  of Leo VI and Alexander 189
Chrysogonus, St 133, 379
Church 357
  Ravenna 178
  schism (1054) 250
  in Venice 101

in Zadar 145, 147–55, 158–61
see also *individual popes*
churches/basilicas
    Butrint 23–5
    see also Great Basilica (Butrint)
    Chalkoprateia Church (Constantinople) 254, 259
    Church of St Sophia (Thessaloniki) 60
    Great Basilica (Butrint) 26, 30, *30*
    Holy Trinity (Zadar) 150–3, 155
    Our Lady of the Assumption (Adria) *113–14*, 113–14
    St Nicholas (Bari) 257–8, 266
    St Peter (Rome) 259
    San Basilio (church at Rovigo)114
    San Francesco del Deserto (Venice) 119
    San Marco (Venice) 102
    San Nicola (Bari) 205–6, 213
    San Prisco *in loco Sao* (Triggiano) 252
    Santa Maria Assunta (Torcello) 83–4, 100–1
    Santa Maria in Porto (Ravenna) 259–64
    Shën Jan (Albania) 38, *39*
    Siponto 254, 257
    and Venetian settlements 302–3
    see also abbeys; Church; confraternities; icons
ciborium 177
Cittanova (Istria) *see* Novigrad
Cittanova (Veneto) 90, 111, *112*, 121
climate
    and Ravenna 176
    Venetian lagoon 118–20
Codex Bavarus 175
Codex Carolinus 89–90
coins
    in Apulia 198–9
    in Butrint/Vrina Plain 20, 24–9, 31–2, 203
    in Dalmatia 139–40
    gold 178–9
    Rovigo, San Basilio 114–15
colonialism 134, 353–61
Comacchio 83, 90–1, 105–8, 175, 177–9
Concessio castri Corphuensis 320
confraternities 366, 371–80
    Albanian 371–5, 377
    Dalmatian 372–5, 377–9
    Florentine 372
    Holy Trinity and St Anastasius 367
    St Stephen 300
Conon (Pope) 86
Constans II, Emperor 86
Constantine I, Emperor 2

Constantine IV, Emperor 86
Constantine IX Monomachos, Emperor 221, 259
Constantine, Pope 87–8
Constantine V, Emperor 89–90, 180
Constantine VI, Emperor 139
Constantine VII Porphyrogennetos, Emperor
    De administrando imperio 89, 140–1, 189, 277–8
    De cerimoniis 221, 261
    De thematibus 141
Constantine VIII, Emperor 280
Constantinople
    arrest of Venetians 288–9
    attack on the Genoese by the Venetians 307–8
    Chalkoprateia Church (Constantinople) 254, 259
    Mangana Palace 60, 259–60
    podestà of 319
    Venetian *embulo* 304, 306–9
    see also Yenikapı
consul (*hypatos*) 104
Corfu 5
    concessio 320, 322
    and the Crusades 223, 299, 330
    and the Normans 305–6
    Straits of *19*, 23, 28, 45
Corinth
    pottery 63, 66–7, 69
    sacking 305
    seals 209, 211, 214–15 t29b, 223, 225–6 t11, 12, 233, 236
    Venetian churches 302
Council of Ten 371–4
covers for icons 252
Crete 5, 278, 284, 318, 322, 356–7
    trade 299
Croatia 3–4
    icons 247, 264–8, *265*
    seals 214–15t24, 238
    see also Dalmatia; Zadar
Croats 136–8
    and Zadar 146, 156–7
Crusade of Nikopolis (1396) 343
Crusades 328–46, 388–9
    1099 (First Crusade) 285–6, 329–31
    1110 (Doge Ordelafo Falier's expedition) 331
    1122 (Doge Domenico Michiel's expedition) 331
    1189 (Third Crusade) 331–3, 335–6
    1202 (Fourth Crusade) 289, 331–2, 336–7
    Fifth 333–6
    Second 333

Cyprus 278, 284, 299, 356–7
   and the Crusades 339–40
   pottery 57, 63–4, 235

Dalmatia 83–92, 133–44
   scholarship of Venetian rule 351–61
   seals 225–6t11, 235, 237–8
   see also Zadar
Dalmatians, immigrants in Venice 369–75, 378–80
Dalmatino, Giorgio 370
Dandolo, Andrea, Doge of Venice 286, 326, 331
Dandolo, Enrico, Doge of Venice 310–11, 319, 337
Dandolo, Enrico, Patriarch of Grado 300–1
Dandolo family 300
Dante, *Paradise* 264
Delterios (*tourmarches*) 250–1
Desiderius, Abbot of Monte Cassino 255–7
Desiderius, King of the Lombards 92
Diocletian, Emperor 2
Diokleia (Montenegro) 88, 143
Dobrinja 279
doges
   Dandolo, Andrea 286, 326, 331
   Dandolo, Enrico 310–11, 319, 337
   Falier, Ordelafo 298, 330
   Foscari, Francesco 360
   Michiel, Domenico 299–300, 306, 330
   Michiel, Vitale II 286, 308
   Orseolo, Pietro II 3, 123–5, 138, 280–1, 316–17
   Polani, Pietro 300–1
   Ziani, Pietro 319
   Ziani, Sebastiano 308
Domagoj, Duke of Croatia 137–8
Donatus, St, Bishop of Zadar 105, 136, 148–50, 153, 176
Donus, Pope 86
Dragačić, Zuanin 360
Drivasto, Nicolaus de 370
Dubrovnik, seals 214–15t19, 224
dukes (*duces*) 107, 136
   Venetian 101, 103
   see also Beatus; Candiano; Galbaio; Orseolo; Orso; Particiaco; Silvo; Tradonico; Ursus
   see also doges
Durrës (Dyrrachion) 38, 143, 297
   amphitheatre chapel 39, 246–7
   seals 212–13, 214–15 t7, 8, 222, 224, 225–6 t9, 227–8, 231–2
Dyrrachion *see* Durrës

Edict of Rothari 190
Egypt 289, 333, 336, 339–40, 342
ekthesis ('edict of union') 100
Elias, Archbishop of Bari 251–2
Elias the Younger, St 19–20
embassy of the Venetians and Dalmatians to Aachen 105
Emeric, King of Hungary 332
environment *123–4*
   Venetian lagoon 121–2, *122*
Ephesus, pottery 57–62, *57–9, 59–60, 62*
epi ton oikeiakon (title) 207–8
epigraph, *Petrus peccans* 262
Epiros 20, *32–3*, 386–7
   and negotiations between Michael Komnenos and the Archbishop of Dyrrachion 322
   and the Normans 283
   see also Albania; Butrint
Equilo see Jesolo
Escorial Taktikon 142
Este (*Ateste*) 115
Eudokia (daughter of Emperor Alexios III) 223
Euphemia, St 261
Eustathios, *strategos* of Dalmatia, seal of 142
Euthymios, *spatharokandidatos* and *doux* of Dalmatia seal of 142
Eutychius, Exarch of Ravenna 91, 101

Falier, Ordelafo, Doge of Venice 298, 330
Felix, Bishop of Zadar 149
Ferluga, Jadran 143
Florentines, confraternity 372
Foggia, icon in cathedral 257–8, *258–9*, 269
Fortunatus, Patriarch of Grado 103, 149, 176
Foscari, Francesco, Doge of Venice 360
Franks
   in the Adriatic 87
   and Ravenna 181
   and Zadar 136 *see also* Carolingians
Frederick Barbarossa, Emperor 308
Frederick II, Emperor 336
Friuli, Girolamo 378
Fulcher of Chartres 331–3

Galbaio, Maurizio, Duke of Venice 101
Gall, St 373
Ganos (Ephesus), amphorae 57–62, *59–60, 62*
gastalds 190–1, 196
Gell, Alfred 36

Genoa/Genoese
    attack by Venetians in Constantinople 307–8
    and the Crusades 329, 333, 335, 339–40
    war with Pisa 336
Geoffrey I of Villehardouin, act of 320, 322, 325
George, *spatharios* and *archon* of Dalmatia 142
George, St 373–4, 379
George, *strategos* of Longobardia 197
Gerardus, Archbishop of Siponto 254–7, 267–8
Giambono, Michele 379
Giorgio, Andrea di 370
Glagolitic books 370
glassmakers, Albanians in Venice 370
glazed white wares *see* pottery, glazed table wares
globular amphorae 28–9, 32, 50–1, *51*, 52–6, 54–5, *55–6*, 83, 386–7
Gottschalk of Orbais 137
    De praedestinatione 140
    on the Greeks in Dalmatia 144
    Responsa de diversis 140
Grado 101, 111, *112*, 156
    Enrico Dandolo the Elder, Patriarch of Grado 300–1
    Fortunatus, Patriarch of Grado 103
    see of 149
    taxes 92
Great Basilica (Butrint) 26, 30, *30*
Greeks
    bishoprics in Apulia 195–6
    confraternities in Venice 374
    in Zadar 144
Gregory, Bishop of Nin 160
Gregory the Great, Pope 83–5
    and Sabinianus 149
Gregory II, Pope 101, 259
Gregory IV, Pope 252
Gregory (patrician) 99–100
Gregory, *protospatharios* at Zadar 267
Gregory VII, Pope 267–8, 282
Grimoald, King of the Lombards 100
Guaimar I, Prince of Salerno 189
Guiscard, Robert, Duke of Apulia 252, 257–8, 281–3
Guisenolf, Abbot of Tremiti 255
Günsenin 1/Saraçhane 54 amphorae *53*, 57–62, *59–60*, *62*
Günsenin 3/Saraçhane 61 amphorae 62–4, *63*
Günsenin, Nergis 58

Hadrian I, Pope 149
    letter to Charlemagne 144
Hadrian II, Pope 138
Halmyros 298–9, 302, 306

Henry VI, Emperor 336
Heraclius, Emperor 100
Hilduin, Abbot (of St Denis) 153–4
Historia ducum Venetorum 306, 318, 331
hodegetria icons
    Bari 251–3
    Trani 247–51, *248–9*, 269
Holy Trinity (church at Zadar) 150–3, 155
Hrodgaud, Duke of Friuli 90
Humbert of Viennois 340–1
Hungary/Hungarians 309–10, 342–3
    and Croatia 286–7, 331–2, 334
hypatos (consul) 104

Iader *see* Zadar
Icona vetere (Foggia Cathedral) 257–8, *258–9*, 269
iconoclasm 101
icons 245–7, 268–70
    Apulia 254–7
    Bari Cathedral 251–3, 269
    Christ at Rab (Dalmatia) 247, 264–8, *265*
    covers 252
    definition of 246–7
    Foggia Cathedral (*icona vetere*) 257–8, 269
    Mangana 259–60
    Monte Cassino 255–7
    Otranto 253–4
    Ravenna (*Madonna greca*) 247, 259–64, *260–1*
    Trani (*Hodegetria*) *248–9*, 248–51
    Tremiti 254–7
al-Idrīsī, Muhammad 288
    Book of Roger 5
Illyricum 84–5, 87
Innocent III, Pope 289, 336
Ionian Sea, and Venice after the Fourth Crusade 316–26
Isaac II Angelos, Emperor 309–10
Isacius, Exarch of Ravenna 100
Islam 37, 338
Istria 103–4

Jerome, St 373–4
Jerusalem 286, 330
    collapse of 333
Jesolo (*Equilo*) 111, *112*, 121, 123–5, *125–6*, 126–9
John the Almsgiver 83
John of Biclaro 84
John the Deacon
    Istoria Veneticorum 112, 116–17, 128

John the Deacon (cont.)
    ducal elections 102
    Duke Pietro II Orseolo 123–5
    Duke Ursus 137
    government 103
    Maria Argyropoula 3
    the Narentines 137
    the rebellion of Bardanes Tourkos 140
John, Duke of Istria 104
John, Exarch of Ravenna 87
John I Tzimiskes, Emperor 279–80
John II, Archbishop of Trani 250
John II Komnenos 287, 298–300, 330
John IX, Archbishop of Ravenna 180
John, Patriarch of Grado 91–2
John, *patrikios, protospatharios* and *strategos* of Sicily 203–4, 214–15t25
John, *protospatharios* and *tourmarches* of Spartaron 210
John, *spatharokandidatos* at Zadar 267
John VIII, Archbishop of Ravenna 180
John VIII, Pope 137–8, 159
Joseph (*vestitor*) 209
judicial assemblies (*placita*)
    Risano 103–5
    Venice 107
Julian the Apostate, Emperor 2
Justinian I, Emperor 2
Justinian II, Emperor 86–8, 92

Kallonas, *protospatharios* and *epi ton oikeiakon*, seal of 207
Karabisianoi 87
kastra 22–3, 29–30, 141, 194
    and Apulia 190, 194
katepanate of Italy 190–3
    seals 225–6t2, 3, 19, 231
Kephalenia (theme) 139–41, 143, 154
    and *kommerkiarioi* 209
    seals 214–15t30, 225–6t10, 17, 20, 232–4
Kibyrrhaiotai (theme) 143
Kinnamos, John 288, 298, 305, 307
Kletorologion of Philotheos 142, 207
kommerkiarioi 208–10, 225–6t14, 18, 24, 26, 233–4
Korčula, archive 359–60
kouratores 234
Kyparissiotes, N., *spatharios* and *megas kourator* of Italy 225–6t32, 234–5

Ladislas, King of Naples 343
Lantolf I, Prince of Benevento 189

Laskaris, Theodore 23, 35
law, Lombard 190
Le Goff, Jacques 2
lead seals
    Butrint/Vrina Plain 24, *25–6*, 203–4
    of Exarch Paul of Ravenna 139
    found outside the Adriatic 225–6t, *225–6*, 225–38
    found within the Adriatic *213–15*, 213–24, *214–15*, 214–15t
    seal of Niketas 249, *249–50*
    types of evidence 205–13
    Zadar 142–3
Leo, Bishop of Ohrid 250
Leo III, Emperor 88–9, 92, 139
Leo III, Pope 252
Leo, *kommerkiarios* of Hellas, the Peloponnese and Kephalenia 211, 225–6t12, 233–4
Leo of Ostia 255–7
Leo, *protospatharios* and *katepano* of Dalmatia 267
Leo, *spatharokandidatos* from Croatia 267
Leo, *strategos* of Kephalenia, seal 143
Leo VI, Emperor 189, 264
Leopold V, Duke of Austria 335
Leopold VI, Duke of Austria 335
Letter of the Three Patriarchs 259
Lezze, Antonio da 379
Liber albus/blancus 325–6
Liber pactorum 324–5
Liber pontificalis 85–6, 88–9, 252
Liutprand, King of the Lombards 90, 101
    Novels of 190
lizios 307
Lombards
    and Apulia 188–90, 198
    and Comacchio 106
    conquest of Ravenna 91
    pact with Cittanova 90
    and Padua 115
    and Venice 98–100
Longobardia (theme) *see* Apulia
Loredan, Alvise 344
Loredan, Antonio 379
Louis IX, St, King of France 335
Louis the Pious, King of the Franks 135
Luke, St 250, 269
Lydda (Palestine), image of the Virgin 249, 259

Madonna greca icon (Ravenna) 247, 259–64, *260–1*
magistri militum see masters of soldiers
Mairano brothers 301

Mairano, Romano 301
Malipiero, Domenico 378
Manfred, Archbishop of Dyrrachion 321–3
Mangana Palace (Constantinople) 60
　icon 259–60
Manuel I Komnenos, Emperor 2, 182, 288–9, 304–8
Manuel II Palaiologos, Emperor 344
Marcellinus, *scholasticus* 84
Maria Argyropoula 3, 281
Martino da Canale, *Estoires de Venise* 316
masters of soldiers (*magistri militum*) 84, 91, 100, 103, 107, 176
Maurex, Michael, *vestarches* and *katepano* of Dyrrachion 211, 225–6t23
Maurice, Emperor, seal of 143
Mauricius (*magister militum*) 100
Mauritius, Bishop 144–5
Maurus, Archbishop of Ravenna 86
Maximian, Archbishop of Ravenna 174
mayors (*priores*), Zadar 143, 146–7
Mazzotti, Mario 262
Mediterranean 16–18, 40
Menander Protector 84
Mesardonites, Basil, *katepano* of Italy 192, 196
Metamauco *112*, 112, 121
Mezezius 86
Michael Angelos Komnenos, Despot of Epiros 320–3
Michael, *anthypatos, patrikios, katepano* of Italy 225–6 t2, 231
Michael I Keroularios 250
Michael II, Emperor 137
Michael III, Emperor 264
Michael (*protospatharios* and *katepano*) 207, 213, 214–15t2
Michiel, Domenico, Doge of Venice 299–300, 306, 330
Michiel, Vitale II, Doge of Venice 308
migration 359
　of Albanians and Dalmatians to Venice 365–80
Miracula s. Demetrii 85
Mislav, Duke of Croatia 137
missionaries, Carolingian 156, 159
Mocenigo, Tommaso 344
Monk of the Lido 286, 330
Morosini, Tommaso, Latin Patriarch of Constantinople 318
mouseholes 23, 35–6

Narentines (*Narentani/Arentanoi*) see Croats
Nicaea, Council of 150, 155

Nicholas, Archbishop of Bari 214–15t5, 6, 219, 252
Nicholas I, Pope 159
Nicholas II, Pope 250
Nicholas of Myra, St 251–2
Nicholas the Pilgrim, St 253–4, 269–70
Nicholas (*spatharios* and *archon* of Dalmatia), seal of 143
Niketas (metropolitan of Athens) 214–15 t28, 219–20, 223–4
Nikon, St 303–4
Nikopolis (theme) 20, 205
　Crusade of 343
　seals 214–15t30, 225–6t17, 2831, 232–3
Nin (*Aenona*) *145*, 155, 157–8
Normans
　and Corfu 305
　and Dalmatia 267, 386
　invasion of Apulia 193, 197–9
　and Sicily 385
　siege of Trani 250
　and Venice 281–3, 298
Notitia episcopatuum 3, 154
noumera of Dyrrachion 214–15 t8, 222
Novak, Grga 355
　Prošlost Dalmacije (*The Past of Dalmatia*) 353
Novigrad 177

Obelerius, Duke of *Venetia* 105
Obertenghi 115
Oderzo see Cittanova
Odoacer 173
'of the West' 208–10, 233–4
oikos, Butrint 23–7, *24–5*, *25*, *25–6*, 203
Olivolo 101, 121–2, *122*
Onesto (son of Petrus de Onesto) 262
orans, Virgin Mary 247, 252, 254, *263–4*, 264, 269
Orseolo, Pietro II, Duke of Venice 3, 123–5, 138, 280–1, 316–17
Orso, Duke of Venice 101–2
Ostrogothic kingdom 120
Otranto
　700s 88
　icon and Tuesday processions 253–4
Otranto-Vlorë straits 386
Otto I 178
Ottomans see Turks
Our Lady of the Assumption (church) (Adria) *113–14*, 113–14
Outremer 285

P. or B. (*spatharokandidatos* and *strategos*) of Dyrrachion 204, 214–15t7
Pact of Comacchio 83
'pacts', definition 319
Pactum Hlotharii 137
Pactum principis Goffredi 320
Padua *112*, 112, 115
Pala d'Oro (altarpiece) 298
Palatinos, Eustathios (*protospatharios* and *katepano*) 213, 214–15t3
palatium, Venice 121–3
Paltasichis, Andrea de 370
Pankrates, *kommerkiarios* of the West 225–6 t24, 234
Pardos, Peter, *exkoubitos* of Longobardia 211–12, 214–15 t27, 223–4
Particiaci family 122–3
Particiaco, Giustiniano, Duke of Venice 102
Partitio terrarum imperii Romaniae 19, 318–21
Patras, Slavic attack on 23
Paul the Deacon
    area of Venice 99
    on death of Friulian dukes 99
    on the destruction of Padua 115
    on the journey of Rodoald 86
    Slav expedition in the Adriatic 87
Paul, Duke of Zadar 105, 136, 141, 148
Paul, Exarch of Ravenna 139
Paul, patrician and *strategos* of Sicily 89, 139
Paul, Pope 89–90
Peloponnese 318, 320, 323
    and Kephalenia 233–4
    pottery 65–70, *66–7*, *68–9*, *69–70*
    tax exemptions by Alexios I Komnenos 297
    trade 305
    see also Corinth; Sparta
Perenos, *doux* of Dyrrachion and *katepano* of Italy 193
Petar Krešimir IV, King of Croatia 266
Peter Damian, St 3
Peter I, King of Cyprus and Jerusalem 339–40
Petrarch 291
Petrus, prior of Santa Maria in Porto at Ravenna 262
Philip Augustus, King of France 335
Photius, Patriarch of Constantinople, letter to John VIII, Archbishop of Ravenna 180
Pietro degli Onesti 261–4
Pippin III, King of the Franks 102, 180
piracy 138, 277, 310, 318
Pirenne, Henri 15
    Mohammed and Charlemagne 15

Pisa/Pisans 286, 289, 306–8, 310–11, 330
    pact with Zadar 310
    war with Genoa 336
placita see judicial assemblies
Plea of Rižana (Risano) 91, 144, 147, 175
Po Valley 85, 106–7, 177–8, 385
podestà
    of Constantinople 319
    of Split 182
Polani, Pietro, Doge of Venice 300–1
Polignano, icons 270
pottery 386–7
    amphorae
        Butrint 25–6, 28–9, 32, 48–52, *49–50*, *49*, *51*, 62
        from shipwrecks 52–6, *53*
        Günsenin 1/Saraçhane 54 amphorae *53*, 57–62, *59–60*, *62*
        Günsenin 3/Saraçhane 61 amphorae 62–4, *63*
    Butrint 25–6, 45–8, *47*, 48–52, *49–50*, 49–50, *49*, *51*, *51*, 62, 70–1, *71–2*
    glazed white wares 56–9, *57–8*, *57–9*
    from shipwrecks 52–6, *53*, 60–1, 63–4, *63*, 64–70, *65–7*, *68–9*, *69–70*
    glazed (table wares) *49*, 49
        distribution 64–70, *65–7*, *68–9*, *69–70*
        glazed white wares 56–9, *57–8*, *57–9*
        Proto-Maiolica wares 67–70, *69–70*, 386–7
        RMR Ware 67–70, *69–70*, 386–7
Praga, Giuseppe 352–3
printing, Venetian 370–1
priores
    Santa Maria in Porto at Ravenna 262
    of Zadar 143, 146–7
Privilegium Michaelis Comneni 320
processions, and icons 250–4, 269–70
Procopius 2
Promissio Michaelis Comneni 320
Proto-Maiolica wares 67–70, *69–70*, 386–7
provincia Iadrensis see Zadar

Rab (Dalmatia) *134*, 141
    icon of Christ 247, 264–8, *265*
Ravenna 100–3
    and Dalmatia 139
    decline 36, 103
    exarchate established 2
    exarchs
        Eutychius 91, 101
        Isacius 100
        John 87
        Paul 139
        icons 259–64, *260–1*, *263–4*, 269

and the Lombards 91, 99
as rival to Venice 173–83
taxes 86–7
Ravni Kotari 136
refutatio 319
relics, gifts of 143–4
Rialto 121–4, *122*
Richard, Earl of Cornwall 335
Richard I, King of England 335
riots, and Emperor Leo III 89
Rižana (Risano) 103
RMR Ware 67, 69–70, *69–70*, 386–7
Rodoald, Duke of Friuli 86
Roger Borsa, Duke of Apulia 257–8
Roger II, King of Sicily 305
Rogoi (Epiros) *32–3, 32*
Roman empire 2, 40
Butrint 19
Romania, Venice as defenders of 309–11
Romanos IV, Emperor 255–7
Rome *see* Church
Romualdo, *protospatharios* and Archbishop of Bari 219
Rothari, King of the Lombards 100, 190

Sabinianus, Bishop of Zadar 149
Sabinus, St 251
St Nicholas (church at Bari) 257–8, 266
saints 177
see also *individual saints*
Salento 32, 193, 195
pottery 26, 28–9, 49, 52, *57–8, 57*, 69
processional icon 253–4
Salona (Split) 84, 133, 139, 148–9, 155–6, 161, 182
and the Church 148, 155
salt production 119, 355–6, 388
San Basilio (church at Rovigo) *114*, 114–15
San Francesco del Deserto (Venice) 119
Santa Maria Assunta (church at Torcello) 83–4, 100–1
Santa Maria in Porto (church at Ravenna) 259–64
Sanudo, Marino 379–80
Sapientes (*Savi*), council of 300–1, 308
schism, of 1054, 250
Schlumberger, Gustav 88
scuole see confraternities
seals
gold 214–15t1, 220–2, 237
and *hodegetria* 249–50, *249*, 251–2
of Peter 88 *see also* lead seals
Second World War 351–3

sekreton 207–8
Senatori, Frugerio 304
Senatori, Vitale 304
Serblias, Stephen, *protospartharios* and *kommerkiarios* of Longobardia 225–6 t26, 234
Serge, rebel 89
Sergius II, Pope 252
settlements *see* Butrint; Venetian lagoon area
Sgouros, Leo 214–15t29b, 223
Shën Jan (Albania), church 38, *39*
shipwrecks 85
and pottery 52–6, *53*, 60–1, *63*
Sicily 37, 89, 177, 188, 192, 205, 336, 385
and Mezezius 86
pottery 52, 54
seals 203–4, 214–15t25, 224–5, 233, 236
Sigismund, King of Hungary and Holy Roman Emperor 343–4
Silvo, Domenico, Duke of Venice 102, 267, 298
Siponto 188, 254, 257
Skanderbeg 343, 354
skaramangion 254–5
Skylitzes, John 204
slaves/slavery 88–9, 388
Slavs
in the Adriatic 87, 137–9
attack on Patras 23
Baiunetai 19
expedition in the Adriatic 87
Sparta (Lakedaimonia) 210, 303–5
Split *see Salona*/Split
Statualità 356
Stephen, *banus* of Croatia 265–6
Stephen I, King of Croatia 266
Stephen V, Pope 160
strategos/strategoi 141–4
Süleyman (Turkish emir) 282–3
Symbatikios, *strategos* of Longobardia 196–7

Taktikon Beneševič 142
Taktikon Uspensky 141–2
Taranto 194, 196
Tarchaneiotes, Gregory, *protospatharios* and *katepano* of Italy 194, 225–6t3, 231
taxes 91–2, 208
Apulia 192–3
and the chrysobull of Alexios I Komnenos 297
Grado 92
Ravenna 86
themes *see* Apulia; Dalmatia; Kephalenia; Kibyrrhaiotai; Longobardia; Nikopolis; Thessaloniki
Theoderic 173–4

Theodora, Empress 252
Theodore, army commander of Longobardia 190
Theodore, St, relics of 143–4
Theodosius, Bishop of Nin 159–60
Theodosius I, Emperor 2
Theophanes, *Chronographia* 89
Theophylaktos, *episkeptites* of Longobardia 211, 234
Theophylaktos, *protospatharios* and *strategos* of Nikopolis 225–6 t28–29, 233
Thessaloniki (theme) 208, 344
    Church of St Sophia 60
    icons 259–60
    trade 287, 303
Thibaut of Champagne 335
Thomas, Archdeacon 160
    Historia Salonitana 182
Thomas, *tourmarches* of Kephalenia 225–6 t20, 233
Torcello 111–12, *112*, 121
    Santa Maria Assunta (church) 83–4, 100–1
Torresani, Andrea 370
Torresani, Gian Francesco 370
tourmarches 190–1, 196, 233
towers
    Butrint *21–2*, 21–3, *22*, 47–8, *48*
    pottery 48–52, *49–50*, 49–50, *49*, 51, *51*
trade 388
    Adriatic (600–800) 83–92
    Alexios I Komnenos and Venetian 284–5
    Butrint 27, 34–7
    influence of Venice on Dalmatian 355–6
    and lead seals 203–5
    with Muslims 279–80
    Ravenna 177–82
Tradonico, Pietro, Duke of Venice 138
Trani, *Hodegetria* icon 247–51, *248–9*, 269
    siege of 250
Translatio beati Grisogoni martiris 133, 135–6, 145–6
Translatio S. Anastasiae 150, 153
Tremiti abbey 254–7
tribunes (*tribuni*) 102, 104, 146–7, 176
Triconch Palace (Butrint) 28–9, *29*, 31, 46, 57
Triggiano, San Prisco *in loco Sao* icon 252
Trpimir, Duke of Croatia 137
Tryphon, St 143–4, 278, 373–4
Turks 281–3, 338–45, 357–61, 378–9

Urban II, Pope 285
Urso, Vitale 304
Ursus, Abbot of Tremiti 254
Ursus, Archbishop of Bari 153–5, 251–2
Ursus, Duke of Venice 137

Vagenetia (*Bagenetia*) 19, 225–6t11, 13, 27, 235
Varna, Crusade of 342, 344–5
Venantius, *scholasticus* 85
Venetia et Histria 98–102
Venetian lagoon area 111, *112*, 113–14, *114*, *116*, *117–18*, 119–20, *122*, 123–4, *125–6*, *125–8*, *126–9*, *127–8*
Vetrano, Leon 318
Via Egnatia 39, 212–13, 351
Virgin Mary
    patron saint of Albanians in Venice 373
    see also icons; Our Lady of the Assumption; Santa Maria Assunta; Santa Maria in Porto (Ravenna)
Vitalis, Archbishop of Dubrovnik 267–8
Vrina Plain *see* Butrint

Walpert, Patriarch of Aquileia 159
weights and measures 302
William II, King of Sicily 308
William of Tyre 331

Yenikapı (Istanbul) 53, *53*, 56, 60–1

Zadar 90, 133–47, 160–3, 289–91
    and the Church 145–55, 158–62
    abbey of St Chrysogonus 163, 266
    and Dobrinja 279
    hinterland of 155–8
    location 135–6
    pact with Pisa 310
    priores of 143, 146–7
    seals 238
    Venetian attack on 331–2
Zeno, Marino 319
Ziani, Pietro, Doge of Venice 319
Ziani, Sebastiano, Doge of Venice 308
Zoetos, *protospatharios* and *epi ton oikeiakon* of Thessaloniki 208
Zuckermann, Constantin 189
Zvonimir, King of Croatia 282
Živković, Tibor 89, 133, 141–2

CPSIA information can be obtained
at www.ICGtesting.com
Printed in the USA
LVHW050055290721
693947LV00005B/538